W9-CBW-543

Studies in Media Management

A. WILLIAM BLUEM, General Editor 1968–1974

BROADCAST MANAGEMENT

RADIO · TELEVISION

Studies in Media Management

BROADCAST MANAGEMENT
Radio-Television,
First Edition by Ward L. Quaal and Leo A. Martin
Second Edition, Revised and Enlarged
by Ward L. Quaal and James A. Brown

CLASSROOM TELEVISION
New Frontiers in ITV
by George N. Gordon

CASE STUDIES IN BROADCAST MANAGEMENT
by Howard W. Coleman

THE MOVIE BUSINESS
American Film Industry Practice
Edited by A. William Bluem and Jason E. Squire

THE CHANGING MAGAZINE
Trends in Readership and Management
by Roland E. Wolseley

FILM LIBRARY TECHNIQUES
Principles of Administration
by Helen P. Harrison

THE FILM INDUSTRIES
Practical Business/Legal Problems
in Production, Distribution and Exhibition
by Michael F. Mayer

AMERICAN NEWSPAPERS IN THE 1970s
by Ernest C. Hynds

BROADCAST

Radio · Television

SECOND EDITION
REVISED AND ENLARGED

by

Ward L. Quaal

and

James A. Brown

MANAGEMENT

Communication Arts Books

HASTINGS HOUSE · PUBLISHERS
NEW YORK 10016

First published, May 1968
Second printing, February 1969
Third printing, October 1969
Fourth printing, August 1970
Fifth printing, April 1971
Sixth printing, September 1972
Seventh printing, September 1973
Eighth printing, July 1974

Second Edition, Revised and Enlarged, January, 1976
Reprinted, September, 1976

LIBRARY OF CONGRESS CATALOGING IN PUBLICATION DATA

Quaal, Ward L   Broadcast management.

  (Studies in media management) (Communication arts books)
  Bibliography: p.
  Includes index.
  1. Radio broadcasting—United States—Management.
2. Television broadcasting—United States—Management.
I. Brown, James Anthony, 1932–   joint author.
II. Title.
HE8689.8.Q38   1976   658'.91'38454   75-16179
ISBN 0-8038-0763-5
ISBN 0-8038-0764-3 pbk.

Published Simultaneously in Canada
by Saunders of Toronto Ltd., Don Mills, Ontario

Designed by Al Lichtenberg
Printed in the United States of America

Contents *

* Notes are at the end of each chapter.

B. *Regulatory Practices and Issues:* License Renewals—Need for Legal Counsel—Program Report Forms—Program Issues—The Right to Equal Access.

C. *Appraising the Role of Regulation:* The Larger Issues of Regulating Programming and Advertising—The Manager's Relationships with Federal, State and Local Government—The Status of the Communications Act—Reorganization of the FCC—Industry Self-Regulation

LIST OF TABLES

ACKNOWLEDGMENTS

We gratefully acknowledge the professional support and practical assistance of many colleagues in broadcasting and education, especially Terrance Sweeney, S.J. (theory of management), Marcus Cohn (regulation), Hugh Paul (engineering), E. Boyd Seghers, Jr. (sales and promotion), and W. Thomas Delaney, S.J., Alan Labovitz, and Dan Calibraro (editorial aid). We thank many old and new-found friends at broadcast stations, networks, agencies, and research companies, and on the staffs of WGN Continental Broadcasting Co. and the University of Southern California. We thank Russell F. Neale of Hastings House for his patience, confidence, and gracious effort at all stages of this revision. And we acknowledge the contribution made to media and education by the late A. William Bluem; as general editor of the Studies in Media Management series, he also brought us together in felicitous collaboration.

W.L.Q.
J.A.B.

Preface

IN AN ERA OF social change, often unprecedented in nature, an institution as dynamic as broadcasting cannot afford complacency. It must face a future which will require many changes and it must come to accept greater commitments to social leadership.

The time has passed when broadcasters can boast that commercials have effects on people and then claim that most programs do not have effects. So is the time gone when broadcasting was almost exclusively an entertainment medium; although its show-business aspects still predominate, it can no longer disregard the fact that progressively greater proportions of its time are being devoted to news, public affairs and other informational services. New methods of sales and advertising must be designed if broadcasting is to remain competitive in a changing communications climate.

The industry must continue to reappraise and modify employment practices and its system of personnel relations if it intends to attract competent and creative people. Pressures on broadcasters from outside sources need to be eased by positive approaches instead of the usual defensive maneuvers. Above all, broadcasters need to realize that, whether they like it or not, the public expects them to behave responsibly as members of a profession.

The commercial station exists to offer community service while making a profit for its shareholders. It is, however, an overemphasis on profit return that causes some commercial managers to lose sight of the many other rewards to be achieved through radio and television broadcasting operations. When everything is subordinated to the dollar, standards of good broadcasting are sacrificed. Managing a radio or television station then holds no more meaning or challenge than operating a lemonade stand. To be penny-wise is in many instances to be socially foolish. Neither men nor institutions grow in stature through huckster interests in a narrow field.

Lee DeForest, pioneer in radio broadcasting, lamented towards the end of his life:

> As I look back today over the entire history of radio broadcasting since [1907] . . . I . . . am filled with a heartsickness. Throughout my long career I have lost no opportunity to cry out in earnest against the crass commercialism, the etheric vandalism of the vulgar hucksters, agencies, advertisers, station owners—all who, lacking awareness of their grand opportunities and moral responsibilities to make of radio an uplifting influence, continue to enslave and sell for quick cash the grandest medium which has yet been given to man to help upward his struggling spirit.[1]

While that may be a harsh evaluation by an inventor who met ill success as an entrepreneur of radio, echoes of his criticism are voiced today by broadcasters as well as critics.[2] The late Edward R. Murrow, in his last speech (October of 1964), noted the need for proper human harnessing of these man-made media:

> The speed of communications is wondrous to behold. It is also true that speed can multiply the distribution of information that we know to be untrue. The most sophisticated satellite has no conscience. The newest computer can merely compound, at speed, the oldest problem in the relations between human beings, and in the end the communicator will be confronted with the old problem, of what to say and how to say it.[3]

Perhaps DeForest himself provided appropriately balanced commentary on the shared responsibility inherent in any kind of communication between sender and receiver who together made the process happen: "To me the quality of radio broadcasting is the index of the mental or moral qualities of the people who formulate its policies, or who continue faithfully to listen to its output." [4]

This book is directed to those who formulate those policies and to those who aspire to that role, the station managers and administrators of broadcast companies, as well as students taking courses in telecommunications management.

Intelligent and responsible management cannot be realized by uncreative and imitative methods. There must be a considerable evaluation of the potential that generally has not been put to use in broadcasting. Few station managers have achieved the genuine stature their calling makes possible. Such accomplishment depends upon the manner in which the true executive approaches his task and the results that he produces. Collectively, the various instances of achievement can change the image of broadcasting.

On the other hand, we believe that the broadcast industry has been unnecessarily hampered in the accomplishment of some of its greatest achievements by too much governmental regulation and the threat of still more regulation, by discriminatory practices that are not experienced by other mass media, and by overly idealistic and sometimes naive expectations on the part of observers and groups with little but superficial knowledge of the realities of broadcast operations. Throughout this book, we will note the need for more and greater freedoms for broadcasters in general and station managers in particular. Yet we realize that with every new freedom gained an equivalent responsibility must also be expected. Freedom and responsibility are parallel expectations of any mature individual or social institution. The mature station manager will know what those responsibilities are because he will have planned for them within the framework of the freedoms which he desires.

We may seem at times to be overly critical of present managerial practices. We believe there are better ways to get better results. We criticize out of a background of devotion to the broadcasting industry. Our professional and academic lives have thus far been bound up in it. We have seen considerable progress since those early days when the mere sound of a human voice coming into the home by wireless was a thrilling and almost unbelievable phenomenon. We are not, however, wholly satisfied with broadcasting's accomplishments, as varied and as marvelous as they have been. We believe that continuing improvement is always possible and generally we have been gratified to find that this is true. To paraphrase Winston Churchill, we have seen not the beginning of the end, but the end of our broadcast beginnings.

Therefore, while this book offers representative patterns of practical management procedures, it does not attempt merely to set down minutely detailed and standardized practices for managing radio or television stations. Such a volume would be obsolete before publication and useless to those managers who want their stations to have distinct images or personalities that make them stand out because they are importantly different. Thus, we believe it appropriate to suggest *areas* for improved managerial leadership, to point out the values of change in those areas, and to inspire individual managers to action on the basis of their particular present and future local resources.

In this revision of the original text, we have attempted to provide considerable statistical documentation as well as excerpts from and references to other commentators about media management. Hopefully these data, together with the authors' syntheses and conclusions, will challenge the reader to analyze more fully the facts and principles involved, before accepting or rejecting either the status quo or alternate options in broadcast administrative practices. Regularly cited in footnotes and end-of-chapter references are related publications about specialized aspects of management; secondary sources are sometimes cited when they are more readily available than the original publications or reports. Our intent has been to offer to broadcasters, teachers, and students of broadcast management a range of generally available sources that provide fuller detail and differing viewpoints. We urge readers not to overlook those further discussions of controverted issues which are in the end-chapter notes.

Because the authors bring to this revision their respective training, experiences, and perspectives, they have chosen to de-emphasize personal assessments in the body of the text, in order to devote a new final chapter to their own professional and academic judgments about the management of broadcasting in America. We trust that not only the concluding chapter but the entire revision will reflect the discerning appraisals of the late Leo A. Martin, who collaborated on the original work.

Chicago and Los Angeles   WARD L. QUAAL
January 1976   JAMES A. BROWN

NOTES

Preface

1. Lee DeForest, *Father of Radio* (Chicago: Wilcox & Follett, 1950), pp. 442–443.

2. See the appraisals by CBS alumni Fred W. Friendly, *Due to Circumstances Beyond Our Control . . .* (N.Y.: Random House, 1967) and Alexander Kendrick, *Prime Time: the Life of Edward R. Murrow* (N.Y.: Little, Brown, & Co., 1970).

3. Quoted by Kendrick, pp. 13–14.

4. *Father of Radio,* p. 446.

A NOTE ON SOURCES

FOOTNOTE REFERENCES in the notes at the end of each chapter provide extended discussion of significant issues as well as documentation of sources. Permission to quote material from published works was provided generously by the holders of copyright, usually the publishers or authors cited in the notes. To those references the following credits should be added:

BROADCAST MANAGEMENT

RADIO · TELEVISION

1

Broadcast Management in Perspective

Perfection of means and confusion of goals seem in my opinion to characterize our age.

—ALBERT EINSTEIN

THE STATUS OF BROADCAST MANAGEMENT

THE FLAT STATEMENT is all but incredible: electronic communication has progressed from Marconi to Telstar well within the biblical life span of three score years and ten. Only some 40 years lie between the beginnings of mass radio broadcasting and the first international television by satellite. In that short time-span the major technological developments of radio and television were introduced, refined and expanded. From the crystal set grew the marvels of high-powered transmitters, FM radio, stereo, videotape, transistorized receivers, color television, videocassettes and cartridges, computerized station operation, laser and holograph and satellite transmission.

Superimposed on these achievements were the arts and skills of production and programming as well as the techniques of sales and advertising. The producers, programmers, salesmen and advertisers came to be more closely associated with broadcasting in the public mind than were the scientists and engineers who made it all possible.[1]

Engineering, of course, remains a vital part of the broadcasting service. Without the contributions of electronic engineers, producers and salesmen could not keep radio and television stations on the air. But the relative importance of the technical contributions to broadcasting made by the engineering fraternity often is overlooked in favor of the social, cultural and commercial applications made of their creations.

Broadcast management, given the incentive, freedom of enterprise, inspiration and some sense of direction, can achieve results in programming and in sales that will parallel, if not exceed, the technical accomplishments of the industry.

3

Growth of Management Opportunities

The growth of management opportunity peaked in the years following World War II. At war's end, there were about 900 radio stations on the air, most being managed by men who had been in radio since its infancy. Yet, the desire of many returning veterans to go into business "for themselves," the financial resources available to them, the "glamour" of broadcasting and the thousands of authorized but unused frequency assignments made local radio an attractive (if unusual) form of investment.

Those stations that were on the air were, for the most part, substantially financed operations with network affiliations. The real growth of local radio began at this time. From 1946 through 1950, some 1,800 new radio stations came into existence. In 1948 alone, 533 stations began operations. This was the largest number of new station authorizations in any single year since broadcasting had its birth. By the mid-1960s, the number of radio stations had more than quadrupled. The rush to seek station licenses was so great that the FCC, in 1962, established a temporary "freeze" on new authorizations. Yet, despite the freeze, 14,000 license applications were filed the following year, and a decade later (despite another five-year freeze on AM licenses) there were more than 7,000 commercial radio stations authorized by the FCC.[2]

By 1973 there were 2,001 radio stations on the air competing among one another in 262 major metropolitan markets. Another 266 stations broadcast in non-metropolitan areas where three or more stations vied for audience and advertising. In 542 other regions of the country 1,084 stations operated in two-station competition towns. And in each of 1,484 other areas there were single stations serving the local population.[3]

The sale of radios, the number of people listening, and station profits have kept pace with the general population growth and the increase in the number of stations. While these developments will be treated in succeeding chapters, it is worth noting here that with 99 per cent of all U.S. homes having radio sets, the average number of sets was 5.4 per home, more than one radio for each individual family member.

Among factors that influenced radio's growth have been the development of the transistor, printed circuits and miniaturization. The high degree of mobility associated with radio has become increasingly true also of television; not only receivers but color cameras and transmitting units have become lightweight, compact and highly portable. Radios installed as factory equipment in cars, and bulky but carryable portable radios brought out-of-home listening to millions; miniaturization made possible pocket radios—and a geometric increase in out-of-home listening. The proliferation of radio was demonstrated dramatically on November 9, 1965, when a massive power failure plunged the northeast portion of the nation into darkness. Radio, its studio and transmitting equipment powered by emergency generators and its miniature receivers powered by batteries, kept millions informed, averting the panic of non-information, until electric power was restored and the lights came on again. No other event, no educational campaign, could have convinced so many people, so quickly, of the importance of having a transistorized, battery-powered radio handy, and of the reliability of free-enterprise radio in a major emergency.

The radio which kept a quarter of the nation's population informed of the power "blackout" in November of 1965 was similar to the radio of the 1920s, at least in basic technology. While there had been improvements such as miniaturization, those who turned to their battery-operated sources of information and security were turning to AM radio.

Just before World War II, there was the promise of television. Picture and sound had been transmitted simultaneously in 1931 and people visiting the 1939 New York World's Fair were fascinated by the novel "toy." Being developed at the same time was another form of radio called frequency modulation or FM.

The development of FM, like the development of television, was put aside for the duration of the war while those with the technological skills needed to develop these media, including many broadcast engineers, went to work in behalf of the nation's defense effort. They developed the most elaborate communications system yet devised, and applied electronics to highly sophisticated weaponry. When they returned to civilian life, they addressed themselves to such developments as FM, bringing with them new technology to speed progress.

There are 100 FM channels available (providing 1,098 specific FCC assignments by state and city); this compares with the 107 AM channels available on standard broadcast frequencies (in 1975 totaling 4,483 stations, including 24 unduplicated Class I clear channel stations). Investors for many years found little success with FM due to various factors, including a general public disinterest in the system—partly prompted by modifications in the FM band spectrum location and by introduction of high-fidelity sound reproducing systems and of television. The technological development of stereocasting, followed by quadraphonic capability, added new public appeal to FM and the channels became more appealing to applicants. The sharpest increase in applications for radio station licenses since 1964 has been for FM licenses. By 1972, more than one-third of all commercial radio stations in the U.S. were FM, and more than one-third of all portable radios had FM turners (up from only 2 per cent in 1961). Four out of five homes had sets capable of receiving FM.[4]

For those aspirants to the more than 1,000 available FM assignments, the following advice from Byron G. Wells may be useful:

> . . . You're going to need many things before you even get close to going on the air—things like aspirin, money, aspirin, patience, aspirin, money . . .
>
> After a while, if your programming is good, if the advertising comes in, and if you get a few lucky breaks, the station may start to pay. . . . In fact, you might even start drawing a bit of salary for yourself. . . .[5]

Due to the larger investments necessary for the installation and operation of television stations, their locations have been generally restricted to metropolitan areas. As compared with the 4,483 commercial AM and the 2,819 commercial FM stations which had been authorized by the end of March, 1975, there were only 759 commercial television stations.

Nonetheless, television was found in approximately 97 per cent of U.S. homes by 1975; and 45 per cent of all homes had two or more sets, while 70 per cent of all homes had color TV.[6] Most homes could choose from three or more stations, including the offerings of the three national commercial television networks and the Public Broadcasting Service.[7]

Television's initial development was in the very high frequency (VHF) range, channels 2 through 13, bisected by the 88–108 megacycle FM band. Not enough channels to meet the demands of would-be licensees and the desires of the general public led to the development of another band of the spectrum for television use, ultra-high frequency (UHF).

The portion of the spectrum allocated to UHF provided for 70 channels. While this spectrum band is not contiguous to the VHF band, the UHF channels were designated 14 to 83 (reduced two decades later by 14 channels to provide additional spectrum space for land-mobile radio). Presently, the two frequency bands, channels 2–13 and 14–69, require separate tuners. UHF station operators have led efforts to develop an acceptable continuous tuner for all channels now in use. (Channel 1 frequencies were redesignated many years ago for non-broadcast services.)

UHF stations were slow to develop due to the small number of sets capable of receiving UHF transmission. It was not uncommon for operators of UHF stations, after attempts to provide competitive broadcast service, to suspend operations and return their licenses to the FCC. Federal legislation required that all television receiving sets manufactured after May 1, 1964 must include both VHF and UHF channels; this led to a steady increase in applications for UHF station licenses. And FCC authorization for low-power UHF stations opened the way for the construction and operation of television stations in small towns and rural areas.

Such growth could somewhat parallel the expansion of radio following World War II if it were not for the questions raised by the developments in cable television. As community antenna television (CATV), this system was originally designed to bring the services of television stations to outlying areas where TV reception was limited or non-existent. Entrepreneurs, including many broadcasters, began to dream of vast profits from investments in such systems whereby monthly subscription fees are collected from users. Consequently, areas which were considered likely prospects for new UHF stations suddenly became high risks due to either the installation, or the threat of installation, of CATV systems. In April, 1965, the FCC asserted jurisdiction over some 400 CATV systems that used microwaves for transmission, and in March of 1966 some 1,200 systems that delivered service by means of telephone lines were brought under its control. By 1975, some 3,240 CATV systems in 6,980 communities served some 8 million subscribers.[8] The FCC actions for the first time brought all CATV under government regulation and imposed certain conditions for their operation. The systems were required to give nonduplication protection in the carrying of programs which are broadcast by any local commercial or educational station. Any CATV system which proposes to bring programs from distant stations into the prime service or grade-A area of any station in the top 100 markets of the country must first secure FCC approval. Information concerning all officers and subscribers to each CATV system must be submitted to the FCC.

However the CATV controversy is ultimately resolved, the ability of U.S. homes to receive UHF signals has steadily increased. A U.S. Census Bureau study in August of 1965 showed that almost 23 per cent of the households of the country had sets which were equipped to receive UHF broadcasts; at the end of 1971, the figure had risen to about 81 per cent of homes in the top 100 markets (those markets include 86 per cent of all TV households). By 1973 almost 86 per cent of all TV households in the U.S. had sets capable of UHF reception.

The growth of color television hinged on a factor of added expense for colorcasting equipment. In 1965 color TV sets suddenly began to be purchased in quantity, brought about partly by a healthy economy and partly by the greater availability of color programming together with other factors such as reduced costs for sets. Most, if not all, prime-time programming by each of the three television networks for the 1966–67 season was in color. The local station could hardly afford to offer only black-and-white programs and commercials so, except for older feature films and reruns of earlier monochrome TV series, locally-originated broadcasts were converted to color at most television stations. By 1975, over 47 million households (68% of all homes in the U.S.) owned color television receivers.

A Confusion of Problems

With the increase in the sheer number of TV and radio stations during the 1950s and 1960s, competition became a major factor for many managers for the first time. Stations that had enjoyed a virtual monopoly of the local broadcast audience found new and aggressive competitors attracting their listeners and viewers. Where innovation, change, and hard work may not have been particularly necessary in a static situation, they were suddenly essential. Nevertheless, small-market broadcasters had to be aggressive even if theirs was the sole TV station in town. They were excluded from the advertising budgets of many of the giant national advertisers whose spot dollars were allocated to the largest 50 or 100 markets. And they had to compete for the small local business advertising with the hometown newspaper and radio station.[9]

While enormous profits can be earned by large and successfully managed broadcast stations in major markets, the majority of AM and FM radio and UHF television stations profit modestly, if at all. The industry is considered a small-business field because of the proliferation of FM and low-wattage AM stations with staffs of less than a dozen, and UHF stations with minimum staffs and budgets. The FCC reported that radio stations in 20 per cent of 227 metropolitan areas lost money in 1971; and one out of four smaller non-metro areas reported combined losses for their three or more radio stations.[9a] Almost one-third of 564 daytime-only radio stations lost money in 1971. The average profit, before tax, of the other two-thirds was $7,000—about 6 per cent profit margin (the relation of profits before federal taxes to revenues).[9b] Meanwhile, although major television stations in the largest markets profited greatly in 1971, one out of five VHF stations and two out of three UHF stations lost money that year. Those losses ran strongly into six figures for most of the 189 stations whose expenses outstripped their revenues.[9c] Similar profit-loss margins were reported for 1973 (see Chapter 7).

As the broadcasting industry grew, problems began to multiply. Some were so universal and complicated that associations of broadcasters were formed to deal with them. Criticism continued to come from the FCC, intellectual critics and other opinion makers, political leaders, and consumer organizations.[10]

The term "vast wasteland," coined in 1961 by then-FCC chairman Newton Minow to describe broadcasting's schedule of programs, has since haunted station managers and network executives.[11] Critics seized upon the phrase and proceeded to blast away at broadcasting in general, often with charges not always justified. Broadcasters soon became supersensitive to criticism and devoted far too much time to defensive reactions instead of making positive adjustments in more significant problem areas.

An observer of, and a prominent force in, broadcasting throughout its history, Sol Taishoff, Chairman and Editor of *Broadcasting* magazine, received the 1966 annual Distinguished Service Award of the National Association of Broadcasters. On that occasion, he challenged the broadcasters of the nation to establish "a proper heritage of imagination and boldness" for those people of the new generation who would some day be in charge of stations. "The current climate of the broadcasting business," said Mr. Taishoff, "is not especially conducive to imaginative ventures and risky progress." [12] Rather, he said, the prevailing attitude is "conservative," with suggestions not to "rock the boat." Later, and with justification, he lamented: "Everybody has become an expert." [13]

Men in administrative positions usually know more about the problems of their own organizations than the critics think they know. It is not unusual for these executives to receive ill-tempered and inaccurate critical comments. A common reaction is to suspect all criticism, even that which might have some validity. Broadcasters need to respond constructively to complaints and comments by non-broadcasters. Over-sensitivity can lead to a tendency to condemn unfavorable comment and to note only the observations which are favorable. Too soon, the general public comes to doubt the objectivity of the broadcaster and to resent his defenses. It would be more profitable in the long run to show a little less persistence in promoting the medium's virtues and publicly to recognize and work toward the elimination of some communication shortcomings. The broadcast manager has usually risen to his position because he understands the complexity of his industry and has proved that he can guide station personnel and procedures properly (and profitably). But unlike many businesses, no matter how effective his effort is on the basis of business, his decisions affect program service which reaches out day and night into the community of non-broadcast citizens. Their reactions, and the appraisal of critics, *often* are valid on grounds other than business and economics. He cannot ignore this "social reach" of his medium.

Some administrators have been reluctant to take positions on issues of public importance, concerned that such stands might limit future business from advertisers who view these issues differently. But strong stands on vital issues can gain as much business as they lose, while increasing the stature of the broadcast manager who "states his mind," earning new respect for him and his station. The late Edgar Kobak, former executive of ABC, NBC, and the Mutual Broadcasting System, claimed that in his professional lifetime he had lost significant business only twice for refusing to compromise his standards in operating those broadcast chains. One such instance involved the late Henry Ford personally, who eventually returned his advertising to the network because he respected Kobak's firmness and integrity. Broadcasters have a special obligation to assume such leadership since their industry by its very nature generates interest in, and is itself a part of, the social environment. Yet, nothing is so unproductive as to take a strong editorial position on the air and to initiate no follow-up activities of leadership on important issues. Nevertheless, some stations continually exhort the people to "do something" and then leave the implementation of the projects to a disorganized public; often no constructive activity follows.

A predominant tendency among managers of radio and television stations is to imitate the successful program formats and business practices of other stations. Evidences of originality or true creativity are rare. Whenever significant issues arise within the industry, a few leaders devote great amounts of time toward their solution; the individual station manager's voice is seldom heard.[14]

The ratings services, which we shall treat in a later chapter, are accorded a disproportionate amount of respect by station management at the expense of other measures of impact perhaps more significant for the long-range future.

There are danger signs, as well. One danger is that people who are given too much of the same kind of programming may grow bored and turn to other forms of recreation for their gratifications. Broadcasting's greatest asset has always been its popularity with the people. If the people acquire a blasé attitude toward radio and television, the industry will indeed fall on hard times. Such a possibility cannot be ruled out as unrealistic by any manager who is concerned about the future and who has the ability to inspire originality in his station staff.

Too often, broadcasters have separated themselves from their listener-viewers by what advertising executive Gene Accas has called "an idea-tight, communications-proof wall constructed of ego, misplaced self-importance and misunderstandings."[15] The time is long past when the broadcaster can afford such luxury. Today, an empathy with the audience can reveal much-needed information that rating services cannot provide. Yale Roe has proposed that, at least out of *noblesse oblige,* successful corporation leaders (including broadcast executives) in a city should collaborate with one another in an effort to share resources and ideas for local broadcast programming. He cites John D. Rockefeller's view that the true justification for economic power lies in service to the public.[16]

Playing it safe is seldom really "playing it safe." Imitating other stations' practices and clinging to conservative trends already established by competing applicants for licenses are hardly challenges at renewal time. With a growing availability of personnel both trained and experienced in broadcasting, as well as a significant body of professional consultants, it may well be that alternative proposals submitted by competitors may find a considerable amount of favor in the offices of the FCC. In 1971 there were 11 cases of AM, FM and TV renewal applicants contending with challengers to their licenses—sometimes multiple challengers; in mid-1972 approximately 100 petitions to deny license renewals were filed with the FCC against stations. Even if the operating station were to assume that it could hold its license, it still would have to face the possibility of a costly and time-consuming comparative hearing. It would be more efficient operational procedure to make sure of prevention than to have to prescribe and effect a cure.

A constant preoccupation with merely defensive strategy has plagued broadcasters throughout the history of radio and television. The time is long overdue for a new positive approach. The station manager must exercise initiative and leadership.

Each manager needs to supplement the work of state, regional, and national groups with a considerable amount of thinking in terms of his own station, his own market, and his own audience. He should determine where he wants the station to be at the end of another decade and then concentrate a share of his physical and mental powers on achieving that goal. He might include in his goal greater professional practice, a wide public acceptance, expanded services by the station, and consequent profit increases. He cannot run only a "holding" operation, sandbagged and dug in, and expect to succeed.

Perhaps a fundamental problem lies in differing philosophies of "what it's all about" as reflected in the perennial question of who owns the airwaves. Often enough the licensee who has invested risk capital in an uncertain venture in a highly competitive market is impatient with the question. He is acutely conscious of the enormous amount of money that he has already put into legal and technical fees, equipment, personnel and "software" supplies; he knows that the potential listeners or viewers will pay nothing more or less whether his station transmits or not. So the broadcast investor-owner finds the question of ownership academic at best, and a point of law at worst. But that point of law is also a point of fact. As for the law, the Communications Act of 1934 (section §301) clearly states that no licensee possesses property rights over channels or frequencies. The Act provides "for the use of such channels, but not the ownership thereof, by persons for limited periods of time, under licenses granted by

Federal authority, and no such license shall be construed to create any right beyond the terms, conditions, and periods of the license.'' The Communications Act further reaffirms that any license is granted conditionally by the FCC, because it ''shall not vest in the licensee any right to operate the station nor any right in the use of the frequencies designated in the license beyond the term thereof nor in any other manner than authorized therein.'' [17] Apart from the legal technicalities, there is the question of capital investment in facilities as a criterion of who really owns ''the airwaves.'' The billions of dollars invested by the owners of receiving sets balance off against the billions of dollars invested by owners of station facilities and property. The dollar figures do not clearly imply ''ownership'' of the electronic medium, which depends as much on continued reception by an audience as it does on continued transmission by stations in order to exist at all.[18] And so these considerations throw the resolution of the issue back into the not insignificant area of philosophy. To whom does the phenomenon of the ''natural resource'' of the electromagnetic spectrum rightly belong—to the individual broadcast licensee or to the public at large? [18a] Thus the viewpoint about this single pivotal question affects the professional and pragmatic, as well as philosophical, policies of the broadcast manager and his staff.

In the final analysis, nothing is ''owned'' until it is used. The airways were always there. It took dedicated men, with courage, with money, and with faith in themselves and the potential of radio and television to develop the present system of American broadcasting.

The Management Potential

Long before personnel could be formally trained in broadcast management, early stations were necessarily administered by people who had been successful in enterprises other than broadcasting, such as newspapers, accounting, or even raising livestock. Few were acquainted with business administration although their records as profit producers in many fields had been impressive. None had previous experience in the curious amalgam of engineering, sales, and programming that was to become broadcasting.

It might even be possible to discern some trends in the backgrounds of broadcast managers, especially in higher administration of networks and group owners of stations. Whereas top management in the 1930s and 1940s included former entertainers from show business and on-air broadcasting, in the 1950s and 1960s successful sales personnel assumed increasingly greater roles. And in the 1960s and 1970s personnel with legal backgrounds began to emerge into the administrative ranks. The next pattern may well reflect still other forces affecting broadcasting in today's world, where social-oriented researchers and behavioral scientists have increasingly collaborated with broadcasters in assessing and planning broadcasting's role in contemporary society.

Over the years, much effective management has been achieved in broadcasting. Most of it was learned by trial and error and often with great expense and frustration. Errors made in the management of stations usually have been errors of omission rather than of commission. As a general rule, those people who have accepted management responsibilities in broadcasting have worked hard for their success. In some cases, it is true, there has been a lack of realization of the true power of the station's programs to inform, to entertain, and to influence. In some other cases, there has been an inadequate understanding of the methods whereby the station might be made a true element of community life. There have been instances of shoddy business practices and the broadcasting of questionable materials on the air. But these cases have been very much in the minority. Examples of downright incompetence have been rare.

Most managers in broadcasting are socially responsible people. The screening of license applications and station transfers by the FCC acts as a safeguard for the public against the possibility that stations might be operated by people of questionable character (granted that owners, as licensees, are scrutinized—not their hired managements and staffs). Consequently, the man or woman who is in charge of a radio or television station is usually a very good and responsible citizen of the larger community.

Today, station owners are in a position to select managers with considerable amounts of experience in broadcasting. In some cases, personnel are available who have successfully managed other radio and television properties. Graduate students in a few colleges and universities, often people with years of experience in broadcasting, are now able to study station management as well as other aspects of broadcasting. Continuing seminars in station management are arranged for those who are actively engaged in the administration of radio and television stations. Here, management transcends narrow concepts and routine tasks.

The preparation of tomorrow's managers in broadcasting and the services provided for those who are in management today seem to presuppose that there is a common set of principles and methods which can be used to advantage in any station. Is this true? Can the manager of a 250-watt, daytime-only radio station serving a rural small-town community use the same procedures which are in effect in the 50,000-watt, clear-channel metropolitan radio station? Are the decisions which must be made in the independent television station similar to those in the station with network affiliation? And are there significant differences in the management of any broadcast property which makes demands that are not present in the management of other enterprises? Obviously there are differences in all managerial situations, but successful methods should apply universally if ingenuity is used in their adaptations.

After some 50 years of radio and some 25 years of television, the time has arrived when broadcasters generally have come to realize that two broad areas of need exist. First, the special nature of radio and television as commercial enterprises seems to make an organization of the principles of station management not only advisable but imperative. The increasing complexity of the managerial assignment and the probability of significant developments in the future call for a definition of the basic areas of duties and responsibilities as well as the challenges which confront the manager in broadcasting. First principles can have immeasurable value when used as a yardstick by which the manager can evaluate his own accomplishments (or lack of them) against others who are engaged in a similar activity.

A second area of need is for a genuine philosophy concerning broadcasting. The public nature of the electronic media and their overall supervision by a government commission have brought an almost constant set of crises to an industry operating under the spur of risks and rewards of private and free enterprise. The station manager in broadcasting has been anything but "free" to conduct his affairs as other businessmen have been able to do. As an individual, he is virtually powerless to effect any changes in the overall system. As a group, broadcasters have seldom been able to mobilize anything approaching unanimity of opinion on any issues except those which would penalize them individually, as as well as collectively. As a result, they have become easy targets for negative criticism, some of it valid and needed, some of it vitriolic and wholly without foundation.

A positive philosophy is that which defines the purposes of broadcasting, its place in contemporary society, and the ethics to which broadcasters subscribe. The preoccupation of station managers with governmental pressures and with a constant assault by critics and opinion leaders requires far too much of their time and energies. From the viewpoint of efficient management, surprising advances might be accomplished were these defensive maneuvers supplanted by more constructive attention to station and community needs. A few leaders in the industry are kept busy defending the actions of a majority of their fellow broadcasters and arguing for conditions under which all broadcasters might benefit. All too often, however, a hard-won right is not used by enough broadcasters after it has been granted. Such has been the case with the right to editorialize and the right of access to report electronically from state legislatures. The broadcast executive should not be a faceless proprietor of a peepshow, but a man responsible and responsive to the urgencies of his time.

In the final analysis, the broadcaster will not be given a place in the community unless he earns it. That place is not one of an obsequious servant of surveys and profit statements, but of a powerful participant in the free society of the future.

Toward a Theory of Broadcast Managing

After defining the terms "broadcasting" and "management" (including the etymology of the latter), we will analyze the phenomenon of management and formulate principles for a coherent theory. Such a theory helps clarify the essential characteristics of the management process. Following chapters will then explore implications of that theory for broadcast management. Frederick W. Taylor, often referred to as the father of scientific management, was strongly committed to the belief that "scientific management was not a collection of techniques to increase efficiency, but a philosophy of management and a way of thinking." [18b]

Terminology

"Broadcasting" includes transmission of electromagnetic energy that is intended to be received by the public.[19] This book concentrates on local commercial radio and television stations. Network administration is discussed only insofar as local station management is affected by network decisions about programming and sales. Public (non-commercial or educational) broadcasting is noted only in passing. Similarly, cable television (and pay-TV or subscription TV) is considered only as a competitive consideration for local station managers rather than as part of management's planning for expansion or collaboration.

"Management" means many different things, partly because the roots of the word are ambiguous and its range of meanings has grown over the years. The academic and professional field of management itself recognizes no standard terminology or universally accepted semantic content to the term "management."[20] Here lies the problem of developing a theory of management with clear structural and functional elements. The validity of a theory has its initial basis in the integrity of its terms; but with the word "manage" there is considerable etymological ambiguity.[21]

Most authors agree that management is an art. And business management is the art of accomplishing desired results through and with the members of the organization. Management is defined by Filley-House as "a process, mental and physical, whereby subordinates are brought to execute prescribed formal duties and to accomplish certain given objectives."[22] Terry defines management as "a distinct process consisting of planning, organizing, actuating, and controlling, performed to determine and accomplish the objectives."[22a] Major constitutive factors in management include leadership, planning, staffing, and controlling.[23] Koontz classifies schools of management according to the principles that each theory emphasizes. The "management process" school emphasizes managers' functions in getting things done by people who act in groups. The "empirical" school stresses case study to derive experience and principles from the success and failures of others. The "human behavioral" school focuses on interpersonal relations and on understanding what people expect from work situations and how they perform in groups. The "social system" school views management as a cooperative, social system of cultural relationships; it emphasizes communication and personal behavior.[24] Koontz somewhat anticipates our own effort to formulate a theory when he notes that, being a logical process (which can thus be applied in similar situations), management can be expressed in terms of mathematical symbols and relationships; this highly scientific study can be considered the "mathematics" school of management.[25] To these categories, Terry adds schools of decision theory and of economic analysis and accounting.[25a]

A further clue to the fuller meaning of the term "management" is derived from what people have meant by it when they used it. That is how words get their operative meaning, and those meanings change and can even evolve over decades and centuries until they vary widely from their original denotations. This is useful to keep in mind when considering Douglas Mc-Gregor's assertion that conventional, classical principles of theories of organization and management are derived from the military and the Catholic Church.[26] He cautions that ''new theory, changed assumptions, and more understanding of the nature of human behavior in organizational settings'' are needed before applying to contemporary business the models drawn from far different political, social and economic contexts. Yet, by reflecting back through the centuries of mankind's social groupings together, we realize that without sophisticated weaponry or transportation or communication even the military as well as the Church depended on face-to-face transactions (and hand-to-hand battle!). In our own present era, military or ecclesiastical management includes material resources of administrative paperwork and files, buildings, vehicles, equipment and elaborately complicated procedures—as well as personnel. But the root of the word ''manage'' came from the more directly personal phenomenon of influencing and directing individual persons—in their consciousness and conscience as decision-makers and doers and even in contact body against body.[27] Indeed, the major modes of transportation and communication were animals and human-propelled boats (by oars or by wind-assisted hand-hauled sails); and early vocabulary such as *manège* bespoke the personal handling and directing of animals to collaborate with men in achieving some physical goal. Management thus has everything to do with people and actions, and only by default of historical accretion with mere physical resources of things. These reflections, drawn from an analysis of the etymology of ''management,'' lead to a distinctive theory of management, after related terms have been clarified.

A common contemporary meaning of ''management'' is the spectrum of all those who have any authority or jurisdiction over other workers or who participate in executive decision making and planning, thus distinguishing them from all members of the labor force. In this book we do not necessarily refer to that class of ''management'' as differentiated from union-organized ''labor'' because some levels of broadcast management may well be members of unions (e.g., engineers, announcers).

The rungs of the management ladder might be divided roughly into executives at the higher end, through middle managers, to supervisors at the lower end. The distinctions might derive from the fact that the executive charts the course or initiates entrepreneurial risks and sets creative directions for an enterprise, but he does not directly work with the people doing specific tasks. At the other end of the spectrum, the supervisor oversees detailed procedures and activities (for example, in a shop, office or assembly line) and appraises and reports back or merely applies predetermined sanctions; but he does not creatively rearrange or strategically ''manipulate'' the movement of material or the relationships of people. That would be the role of the manager. In the middle, the manager does not establish major policy (as does the executive); nor does he merely oversee the procedures involving things (appraising them and reporting back, as does the supervisor); he "handles" or "directs" or "manipulates" (in the good sense) *people*.[28]

Finally, a distinction may be made about persons identified as "professionals." While not among management as such, they are still quite different from the regular laboring workforce. Professionals are hired as consultants and experts; they may be part of the staff as resource-input people; they may be on the staff or line, and may come from special fields such as education.[28a]

Throughout this book, we use "management" as a composite term sometimes including several of the categories above, at other times specifying a particular management position or role (e.g., station manager, program director, broadcast company executive).

Background: Theories X and Y

Douglas McGregor, in his watershed book *The Human Side of Enterprise,* cut across decades of management studies by positing his "Theory Y" that focuses not on physical resources but on human ones, especially on the collaborative interaction among people engaged in an enterprise.

He cautioned that every practical action by management grows out of at least implied theory—in the form of assumptions, generalizations and hypotheses—and that acting without explicitly examining those theoretical bases results in widely inconsistent managerial behavior. McGregor emphasized that

> . . . the theoretical assumptions management holds about controlling its human resources determine the whole character of the enterprise. They determine also the quality of its successive generations of management.[29]

He typified previous literature on organization and management practice as supporting an absolute concept of authority in which authoritarian structures and procedures effect the goals of an enterprise. Labeling that conventional analysis as "Theory X," he described it as attempting to manage people by motivating them in earlier times through physical force and power and more recently by moral authority coupled with monetary compensation. In opposition, he posits "Theory Y" whose assumptions are dynamic rather than static because they emphasize the need for selective adaptation and flexibility in forms of control, based on the essential possibility of continued human growth and development. Thus his Theory Y offers to improve management's ability to control through influencing others, not by the amount of authority they can exert but by appropriate selection of different means of influence according to given circumstances.[30] And those "means of influence" are drawn from the underlying assumptions of Theory Y which look upon human persons as having wants and needs; it is precisely by responding to those needs that management most positively influences or controls and dynamically motivates his subordinates.[31] McGregor outlines the hierarchy of importance of those human wants as: physiological needs; safety and security needs (protection against danger, threat, deprivation, and "for the fairest possible break"); social needs (for belonging, for association, for acceptance by one's fellows, for giving and receiving friendship and love); and finally two kind of egoistic needs, which are most significant to the man himself and thus to management in attempting to motivate him:

1. Those that relate to one's self-esteem: needs for self-respect and self-confidence, for autonomy, for achievement, for competence, for knowledge
2. Those that relate to one's reputation: needs for status, for recognition, for appreciation, for the deserved respect of one's fellows.[32]

McGregor claims that the success of any effort towards social influence and control by management thus depends fundamentally on affecting other persons' ability to achieve their personal goals or satisfy their human needs. He stresses *integration* as the central principle derived from Theory Y: "the creation of conditions such that the members of the organization can achieve their own goals *best* by directing their efforts toward the success of the enterprise." [33] His theory necessarily looks to the manager's role as a complex one that must be flexible in the superior-subordinate relationship. The manager must sometimes be a leader of his group, but in other circumstances he must be more a member of a peer group; he must variously deal with other departmental managers, with an immediate superior, or with administrators and executives at various higher levels in the company.

Thus Theory Y emphasizes the nature of relationships among people in the organization. Guided by the Theory Y assumptions as his theoretical base, the manager seeks to create "an environment which will provide opportunities for the maximum exercise of initiative, ingenuity, and self-direction in achieving them." [34] So McGregor looks to the limits of human collaboration in the changing circumstances of the organizational setting as dependent not on human nature or a static assessment of line-and-staff people's past record of productivity but rather on management's ingenuity in discovering ways to tap the potential commitment and achievement (and thus personal fulfillment) of those employees, who constitute the organization's human resources. At the same time he notes that management which is creative, flexible, and socially responsible to employees is not the same as merely permissive management.

Translating those principles into more concrete terms, by following Theory Y assumptions, managers try to motivate a person to find within the enterprise a way to live his life as fully free a human being as possible in the specific context of an organization and job. That employee is prompted to look to the job as an integral part of his personal daily living. The place of employment and the job should contribute to what an employee is becoming as a person; it should not just be a place where the employee makes money in order to go home or on vacation in order to really "be" and grow. Management's role is to find the right people for whom working in that specific enterprise with its given goals and procedures will be attractive and rewarding. And precisely by joining the enterprise to help achieve the goals of that organization, the individual at the same time contributes to his own growth and fulfilment as a person.

This brief background provides the context for a new theoretical formulation drawn from McGregor's Theory Y assumptions, offering more precise emphasis on the dynamics of those managerial relationships in action.

The "V Theory" of Management

"Management," as commonly used today, may refer either to (1) that complex of actions that constitute the process of managing, or to (2) that complex of persons who possess the managing authority. What these two common uses of "management" lack is not a general sense of what management involves (indeed, the generalness is so expansive that confusing and widely divergent definitions are employed to describe this phenomenon) but a structurally specific and comprehensive explanation of what managing must entail if it is to be management at all.

> MANAGING IS THIS BI-RELATIONAL PROCESS: THE
> INTENTION OF THE MANAGER IS DIRECTED TO AND
> EXECUTED IN THE ACTION OF THE MANAGEE.[35]

The managing process is bi-relational in that it is absolutely dependent on both the manager and the managee; without one there is not the other. If a manager gives directives that are not carried out by the managee, then properly speaking he is not managing (just as when he does not initiate directives or oversee in some way their carrying out, he is not managing); if the managee acts on matters unrelated to or different from the directives of the manager, then properly speaking he is not acting as a managee. Thus "managing" is a process involving persons relating to one another through directives. It is this dynamic interrelation of person to person through directives and their being actualized through execution which constitutes the essence of management.

Management is thus triadic and may be investigated according to any one of, or any combination of, its three components: manager, managing, managee. The comprehensiveness or universality, and therefore validity, of any science of management will be in proportion to its thoroughness in describing the nature and functions of these three components. Summing up: the dynamism of management (V) is a function of the manager as subject (M) directing (D) the managee as object (m) to actualize (a) the manager's intention; or

$$V = (M \rightarrow D)\,(a \leftarrow m)$$

Furthermore, the dynamism of the manager's purposeful intention in his directives may be considered as either micro-intention or macro-intention. The micro-intention is that activity (consisting of specific directives) which establishes, maintains or furthers the relationship between the manager and the managee. The macro-intention is that activity (consisting of the stated purposes and policies of the total enterprise) which establishes, maintains or furthers the relationship between one unit or level of management and another unit or level of management.

The formulation attempts to express the dynamics of management as tri-valent (thus the "V Theory"), with three interacting vectors consisting of "the one who" (M), "the one whom" (m), and "the how-what" or the actualizing (a) of directives (D). Strictly speaking, without the central dynamism of those directives being actualized (D, a), there is no relationship operative, and to that extent neither the manager (M) nor the managee (m) is acting in his respective role within the enterprise. The operative intentionality occurs precisely in the process of directing/actualizing.[36]

Therefore the "V Theory" focuses on the *act* of managing as the heart of all management theory and practice. The V Theory underscores the dynamic relation of the manager as person to the managee as person, which relation is constituted by the managee's actualizing the manager's directives. This empha-sis has immediate implications for establishing criteria and for appraising the success of given management situations.

Intentionality. Although it is not explicated in the formula, the central el-ement of intentionality (the intention or purposefulness of the enterprise) is fused into every part of the V Theory. As such it is the primary *content* with which the entire bi-relational *process* of managing can be evaluated. To ask what is the primary and abiding intentionality of management is to address one-self, properly speaking, to the philosophy of management. (Needless to say, a critical and well-timed examination of an enterprise's management philosophy can be enormously beneficial.)

Intentionality includes both "micro-intention" and "macro-intention." The micro-intention refers to the specific intent of the manager in directing a managee to execute some action in his area of the organization. The macro-in-tention refers to the total enterprise as dictated by owners, stockholders, gov-ernment, and the public (as actual or potential customers, as consumers in the public market generally, as critics, as voting citizens), and even by employees. The macro-intention can refer to all those elements of public, governmental and economic factors that go into shaping the whole enterprise—its product or ser-vice, its policies, and its procedures.[37]

The key managerial function of planning involves selecting organizational objectives and policies, programs, and procedures, together with methods for achieving them. Intentionality expressed in planning is essentially the providing of a framework for integrated decision-making which is vital to all collabo-rative activities involving men and machines.[38]

The macro-intention gives the criteria against which to appraise the man-ager's success as manager, in one sense as himself interpreting and forming directives, in another sense as motivating the managees to respond to his in-terpretative directives. Insofar as these central vectors in the management process—directives (D) and actualization (a)—manifest disparity or imbalance or are at cross-purposes, there is inefficient and ineffective organization pro-cess; managerial actions are to that extent not fulfilling their purpose or macro-intentionality; this means chaos and failure in the enterprise.

The Manager (M). While the manager's knowledge of intended product and of processes is important in order to determine directives, it is not the detailed factual knowledge that this theory looks to so much as the ability of the manager to communicate effectively those directives (''micro-intention'') in a way that motivates the managee(s) to actualize them. And communicating refers not merely to adroit interaction, verbally or by gesture, between the manager and his managee(s); it embraces the entire complex dynamic discussed by McGregor in his Theory Y and further embodied in our formula of $V = (M \rightarrow D)$ $(a \leftarrow m)$. The very relationship between the manager and those whom he manages is undercut without at least some knowledge and even experience of the processes and product with which the managee is engaged. The more the manager knows, the better he can make judgments about the managees and their quality of work, precisely in the context of the organzation's goals (''macro-intention''). But a person who knows only factual details and minute procedures may not be an effective manager if he cannot also motivate his subordinates; another person who does not fully know detailed processes and product but who understands people and knows how to motivate and direct them may yet be an effective manager.[39]

Therefore the manager must know primarily the structures and relationships involved in the company's activity and in the activity of the personnel who put forth a product. If the manager has solid knowledge of these relationships and knows how to ''power'' them, he can then call upon resource people who are able to contribute more particularized expertise about details of those structural areas which the manager can appraise as necessary to achieve the organization's goal.

This makes logically supportable and consistent, then, the practice of advancing a person good in managing one area to a new and broader sphere of responsibility where he may well be just as effective. And this in spite of his less detailed knowledge and experience of the expanded area of responsibility. He can be truly effective as a manager if, while he endeavors to learn what he reasonably can about the larger activities which he oversees, he continues to apply his previous ability to manage *per se*. Certainly one cannot know personally all that can be learned about an enterprise—especially when a person rises to top management involving several corporations or clusters of companies in distantly related fields, as happens in mergers. For example, a successful program director at a station who has background in performance and producing may well have learned a good bit along the way about sales; then he is made station manager with responsibilities over not only programming and sales but also engineering; eventually he may become an executive of a group of broadcast stations in charge of several radio and television stations and even of cable and more distantly-related subsidiaries; finally he may become an executive administrator within a conglomerate. The point is that a successful manager knows how to get the right people to do the job well; and he has ability to select subordinates who themselves also know how to get yet other apt people to do the job well. Thus the manager—despite changing work procedures and factual data—is continually dealing with the same context: collaborating with people and motivating those who are competent while accurately assessing them and their work.[40] This is the manager's essential role in the enterprise.

Directives. The manager's role in the bi-relational process is to communicate the micro-intentionality directly, and indirectly the undergirding macro-intentionality of the enterprise, through directives. The operative note here is *communicated* intent that has been selected from among the cluster of intentions that constitute the policy and planning process of management and which are not communicated similarly to all managees. The power of this bi-relational process (as expressed by the V Theory of management) lies in the directives' being actualized. Therefore the closer the manager gets to expressing his intention perfectly in his directives, the greater the probability of its being actualized. If a managee knows the directive in such a way that it is translucent of the manager's full intention—including the "why" of the directive—then the managee is thereby more capable of understanding and of fully actualizing that directive.

Actualizing. The word chosen for the V Theory formula is not "execute" but "actualize" because the former suggests a literal, one-for-one carrying out of what is directed, where the direction (D) comes and the execution is precise.[41] (That might be desirable in some instances, but it reflects the X Theory authoritarian emphasis of mere subservience to management.) But the Y Theory would support the term "actualize" because that connotes more flexibility for the managee to interpret and apply at the point of action not merely the literal directive but even the micro-intentionality of the manager (and even the fuller aspects of the macro-intentionality of the enterprise), thus allowing the managee to participate in the total purposefulness of the manager's directives. Of course it is the further role of the manager to determine means to assess actualizing of his directives, to ensure (by correction or variant motivation or further guiding directives) a growing equation between his directives (D) and managees' actualizing (a).

Managee. Whereas the manager's role in the dynamic relationship is the directive one, on the correlative side of actualizing those directives is the managee. To the extent that he does put them into action, he is then acting precisely as managee of this given manager in a dynamic management relationship. To the extent that he is unable to actualize the directives because of competence, attitude or the like, he is less a managee—whether in the specific management phenomenon of a given directive, or in the cluster of directives through time which constitute a continuing relationship in the manager-managee roles. To the extent that $D = a$, we have an ideally efficient management process and perfectly correlative roles of manager and managee. To the extent that there is some discrepancy between D and a (directives and actualization), there is less efficient or even less proper a relationship between the two.

It is that dynamic relationship between his directives and the managee's actualizing (so that $D = a$) about which the manager is primarily concerned—not the details of that actualizing so much, but the relationship of the actualizing to the directives and thus to the overall "why?" of the micro- and macro-intentionality in the management process. The manager's role is to select the managees who can best bring about this equation. And the manager's further responsibility is to plan, control and discern through feedback, testing and other techniques to what extent there is a favorable equation between D and $a,$ and then to modify or correct elements (D, a, m) in the management process, including replacing the managees with others who will better actualize management's directives. This is the essential role of management.

A theory of management must include, regardless of the particular content or concrete circumstances to which applied, the dynamic relationship (the vectors of the V Theory) among people (M, m) and the directed collaborative activity (D, a) of those people to produce the product or service (the micro- and macro-intentionality of the enterprise). Thus the formulation of the V Theory of management: $V = (M \rightarrow D) (a \leftarrow m)$.

We have here attempted to provide a definition of managing which includes the essential structural elements of that dynamic social phenomenon. And we have suggested various sources by which a person can verify the major propositions of the V Theory of management: linguistic analysis, etymology, and semantics; McGregor's "X" and "Y" theories of managing; other specialists' writings; commonsense meanings of executive-manager-supervisor; as well as people's own experience of what motivates them regarding their job and the place of the job in their life.

The present book emphasizes this relationship of persons in action within the common enterprise of a broadcasting company (Chapters 2 and 3), and then explores more detailed applications of management knowledge and decision-making to specific areas of broadcasting (Chapters 4 to 10). The book approaches the broad area of radio and television broadcasting from the viewpoint of the manager rather than from the viewpoint of an expert in each of the areas of programming, sales, engineering, regulation. The burden of comprehensive knowledge of each of these specialized areas is placed neither on the authors of this book nor on the managers about whom they are writing. In later chapters, therefore, the primary emphasis will be on the broader, structural kinds of knowledge that a manager should have in order to address the problems that will arise in those areas, rather than focusing on the subordinate kind of detailed knowledge that no manager with even a very fine memory could possibly have at his recall in his daily duties even if he were competent in many of the areas. Other books describe and analyze specific data and procedures involved in operating broadcast stations. We emphasize management's effective collaboration with middle-managers or supervisors and their staffs. Management's proper concern is how to get that total staff producing creatively while fulfilling themselves as persons and professionals, and thereby achieving the purposes of the enterprise. Thus the distinctions between network and station management, or between local and group management, or independent and affiliate and owned-&-operated management, or even radio and television management, are not that critical. To those areas of broadcasting can be applied the broader theoretical analysis embodied in the V Theory of management.

NOTES

Chapter I

1. For a definitive history of broadcasting's beginnings and historical development, see Sydney W. Head, *Broadcasting in America,* 2nd ed. (Boston: Houghton Mifflin Co., 1972), Chapters 5–11. For a readable and judgmental account, see the three volumes by Erik Barnouw, published by the Oxford University Press in 1966, 1968, and 1970 respectively: *The Tower of Babel, The Golden Web,* and *The Image Empire.* See also Lawrence W. Lichty and Malachi C. Topping, *American Broadcasting: A Source Book on the History of Radio and Television* (N.Y.: Hastings House, 1975).

The authors highly recommend that readers of this book on management familiarize themselves with Dr. Head's outstanding survey of broadcasting in the United States. His lucid and precise style, supported by painstaking documentation—including 53 figures and 35 tables—offers the single best analysis of major patterns and structures in radio and television in America.

2. "Summary of Broadcasting: According to the FCC, as of Oct. 31, 1973," *Broadcasting,* Dec. 10, 1973; p. 57; see also "Interpreting the FCC Rules & Regulations," *BM/E (Broadcast Management/Engineering),* April 1973, p. 12.

3. Source: FCC data reported for 1972, tabulated in "Buyer's Guide" section, *Broadcasting Yearbook 1974* (Washington: Broadcasting Publications, Inc., 1974), pp. 19–23.

4. Unless noted otherwise, source of these statistical data was Ogilvy & Mather Inc., *O & M Pocket Guide to Media,* 5th ed. (N.Y.: Ogilvy & Mather, Inc., 1973), which compiled statistics from reputable sources in the broadcast industry and government.

5. Byron G. Wells, "How to Start Your Own FM Station," *Hi-Fi/Stereo Review,* September, 1965.

6. American Research Bureau, *Television U.S.A.:* February/March 1975. An Arbitron Report.

7. Among the 230 U.S. markets, 140 with the largest populations had three or more local TV stations; one-third of the 90 remaining smaller markets had two local channels; some areas may also have received distant signals from adjoining markets (in addition to supplementary service by cable systems relaying TV programming from remote stations). *"O & M Pocket Guide to Media,"* 5th ed. (N.Y.: Ogilvy & Mather, Inc., 1973), p. 13.

8. *Broadcasting,* April 14, 1975, p. 56.

9. See Yale Roe, *The Television Dilemma: Search for a Solution* (N.Y.: Hastings House, 1962), pp. 28–29.

9a. In those 44 metro areas, 331 reporting stations lost a total of $6,420,074 "before federal taxes"; although various-sized successful and unsuccessful stations competed in those markets, the average total loss per market was $145,911, and the average loss per station was thus $19,396. In 26 non-metro areas with three or more stations, 90 stations reported total losses of $1,062,806, or an average of $11,809 per station; some other stations that earned profits (before taxes) were still not very lucrative: three stations in one market reported a total profit of $393; another three stations elsewhere profited $174 among them; and yet three other stations reported a yearly combined profit of $130. Where two stations competed in each of 296 non-metro areas, they averaged profits of $8,536 each. Stations with no competitor in 1,608 towns averaged $7,873 profit before Federal taxes in 1971. Source: FCC data tabulated in *Broadcasting Yearbook 1973,* "Buyers' Guide" section, pp. 20–24.

9b. "Daytimers Show Gains," *Broadcasting,* Aug. 21, 1972; p. 26, reporting a financial study by the NAB.

9c. While the average profit (before federal taxes) of the 15 network-owned ("O&O") TV stations was over $6 million each, and another 98 VHF stations profited more than $1 million each, yet 94 TV stations in the U.S. profited less than $100,000 that year. And, of those 189 TV stations that reported losses, 72 lost between $100,000 and $400,000 while another 36 stations lost more than $400,000 each. Fourteen markets with three or more stations reported combined losses for their stations totaling $4,084,000, or an average of more than a quarter of a million dollars in each market; that means an average loss of almost $87,000 for each TV station. Source: data reported by FCC and tabulated in *Broadcasting*, Aug. 21, 1972; pp. 14–20.

10. Among many representative samples of criticism which note the positive service of broadcasting coupled with its weaknesses are: Harry J. Skornia and Jack William Kitson (eds.), *Problems and Controversies in Television and Radio* (Palo Alto, Calif.: Pacific Books, 1968); John Pennybacker and Waldo W. Braden (eds.), *Broadcasting and the Public Interest* (New York: Random House, 1969)—especially Part Two on Programming, for former Commissioners Kenneth A. Cox and Lee Loevinger, W. H. Ferry, vice president of the Fund for the Republic and the Center for the Study of Democratic Institutions, and David M. Blank, executive of the Columbia Broadcasting System, Inc.; and Les Brown, *Televi$ion: the Business Behind the Box* (New York: Harcourt Brace Jovanovich, Inc., 1971), especially pp. 174–182.

11. Minow's speech to the NAB convention (his first as FCC Chairman, appointed by President John F. Kennedy) might well be reread today, to compare with the criticism of more than a decade later. Newton N. Minow, *Equal Time: The Private Broadcaster and the Public Interest,* ed. by Lawrence Laurent (N.Y.: Atheneum, 1964), pp. 48–64.

12. For example, see Alexander Kendrick, *Prime Time* (pp. 25–29) for aspects of affiliates' program interests vis-a-vis the networks and the issue of "public interest"; Les Brown, *Televi$ion: the Business Behind the Box* (pp. 199–203), notes the problems encountered in producing the documentary "Harvest of Shame," showing the dangers and pressures to station management in presenting controversial topics.

13. Sol Taishoff, "Penalty of Success," *Broadcasting,* June 6, 1966, p. 102.

14. See Yale Roe, *The Television Dilemma,* pp. 146–148, for his proposed "Television Manifesto," which itemizes the broadcasters' various responsibilities to the government, the public, and the owners and stockholders.

15. Gene Accas (Vice President, Leo Burnett Co.), "An Open Letter to the NAB's Future President," *Broadcasting,* December 21, 1964, p. 18.

16. Roe, *Television Dilemma,* pp. 130–136. A former Federal Communications Commissioner recounted various recommendations through ten years for some sort of national citizens' committee to appraise the general performance of broadcast media; he listed ten activities for such a commission to analyze, to evaluate and to make public their findings. This kind of solution attempts to avoid the twin problem of industry favoritism and of governmental intrusion into free enterprise broadcasting. Of course there are strong objections to such efforts as unwarranted meddling; thus even these recommendations constituted part of the problem or "dilemma" of broadcasting. See Nicholas Johnson, *How to Talk Back to Your Television Set* (N.Y.: Little, Brown, 1970); paperback edition (N.Y.: Bantam, 1970), pp. 175–183.

17. Communications Act of 1934, Section §309 (n, 2), Public Law 416, 73rd Congress, June 19, 1934.

18. In 1963 an estimate was reported to the Federal Government that the public's share of capital investment in broadcasting was 96 per cent, the radio-TV industry's was 4 per cent—a ratio of more than 20 to 1 (source: Head, pp. 250–251, and n. 6, quoting testimony in government hearings). A study of two decades (1946–1966) by the Rand Corporation showed that, for each dollar spent on physical facilities by the television industry to send out programming, forty dollars were spent by consumers for the equipment needed to receive those programs. Americans are estimated to have spent $35 billion for TV sets. (WBAT-FM and The Network Project, "Feedback 2: The Television Industry," *Performance* No. 3 [July/August 1972], pp. 42–43). Not included in these estimates was the percentage of each consumer dollar spent on retail purchases which a company devotes to advertising those products through television—a further "hidden tax" paid by the broadcast audience for commercially sponsored programming, according to some critics.

While the total investment in tangible broadcast property for television in 1969–70 was slightly more than $1 billion, with the number of new stations and consequent newly-invested money fairly stabilized among UHF and VHF licenses, the costly television receiving sets increased from about 65 million sets in 1965 to almost 80 million in 1968. Even averaging only $150 per set (with color sets far more expensive), that totals $12 billion in receiver sales alone, not counting maintenance of sets or antenna mounts or electricity. If "who owns the airwaves" is determined by dollar investments, then the public clearly has major proprietary rights in those airwaves.

Of course risk investment of costs to operate stations and provide program service must also be taken into account; TV networks and stations profited $494 million on a depreciated investment of $706 million in 1968 (source: Head, pp. 319–320, citing FCC data). Cash flow for 3 networks and 690 stations in 1972: revenues amounted to $3,179,400,000 while expenses totaled $2,627,300,000; total income before Federal income tax was $552,200,000 (source: FCC, *39th Annual Report* [Washington: Government Printing Office, 1973], p. 223).

Yet, it must be noted that many individual stations do not make a profit. In fiscal 1972, more than 14 per cent of VHF stations and 56 per cent of UHF stations reported losses; 14 VHFs and 20 UHFs averaged $150,000 losses, 13 VHFs and 18 UHFs averaged $300,000 losses, and 7 VHFs and 22 UHFs each lost more than $400,000 (FCC, *39th Annual Report,* p. 234). In 1972, almost one out of five metropolitan radio markets reported "total broadcast income" for all stations as a loss; and 15 per cent of non-metro markets with three or more radio stations reported overall "loss" in their operations. The metro-market radio losses totaled $4,989,741, and the non-metro-market losses totaled another $431,767. Those figures did not include non-metro areas of only one or two stations whose losses, if any, were not made public. (Data derived from FCC, *39th Annual Report,* pp. 260–266.)

See Chapter 7, "Managing for Profit."

18a. Former secretary of state Dean Rusk told the Georgia Radio-TV Institute at the University of Georgia in 1975 that "the people do not own the airwaves any more than they own the North Star or gravity"; *Broadcasting,* Jan. 27, 1975, p. 30.

18b. William J. McLarney and William M. Berliner, *Management Training,* 5th ed. (Homewood, Ill.: Richard D. Irwin, Inc., 1970), p. 391.

19. The operative word, "intended," is used by the *Communications Act of 1934,* Section §3(o), to distinguish signal radiation of AM, FM and TV from other services such as citizens' band, amateur, maritime, mobile, etc.

20. See George R. Terry, *Principles of Management,* 4th ed. (Homewood, Ill.: Richard D. Irwin, Inc., 1964), p. 14.

21. For an interesting etymological odyssey, the reader may wish to trace the development of the word *manage,* especially in its Low Latin root *manidiare.* An attempt to discover an explanation consistent with the evolution of this unattested form, though it clearly derives from the Latin word *manus* (meaning *hand*), leads to a semantic sea only slightly less tortuous than that between Scylla and Charybdis. Of the plethora of meanings for the word *manage,* the following selections appear to be the more indicative: to handle, direct, govern, or control in action or use (a horse); to succeed in accomplishing; to handle, wield, make use of (a weapon, tool, implement, etc.); to control and direct the affairs of (a household, institution, state, etc.); to operate upon, manipulate for a purpose; to bring (a person) to consent to one's wishes by artifice, flattery, or judicious suggestion of motives. Cf.: *Random House Dictionary of the English Language* (Unabridged ed., 1967); *A New English Dictionary on Historical Principles,* edited by Sir James Murray, Vol. VI, Part II M - N (Oxford: Clarendon Press, 1908), pp. 104–5; A. Ernout and A. Maillet, *Dictionaire Etymologique de la Langue Latinae, Histoire des Mots* (Paris: Librarie C. Klincksieck, 1949), pp. 590–91; Alfred Hoare, *An Italian Dictionary,* 2nd ed. (Cambridge: University Press, 1925), p. 363; R. E. Latham, *Revised Medieval Latin Word List* (London: Oxford University Press, 1965), pp. 287–88; Charles Grandgent, *From Latin to Italian* (Cambridge: Harvard University Press, 1940), p. 110.

22. Alan C. Filley and Robert J. House, *Managerial Process and Organizational Behavior* (Glenview, Ill.: Scott, Foresman & Co., 1969), p. 391. See Chapter 2 below, for analysis of principles of management.

22a. Terry, p. 56.

23. J. W. Haynes and J. Massie, *Management: Analysis, Concepts and Cases* (Englewood Cliffs, N.J.: Prentice-Hall Inc., 1961), p. 3.

24. See Harold Koontz, *Principles of Management* (N.Y.: McGraw-Hill Book Co., Inc., 1959), pp. 89–98.

25. Koontz, p. 99.

25a. Terry, pp. 18–23.

26. Douglas McGregor, *The Human Side of Enterprise* (N.Y.: McGraw-Hill Book Co., 1960), p. 18.

27. The early Christian community of people had nothing to do with institutionalized money and buildings; it had everything to do with an authority structure that grew out of a people united together under a God believed to be personal (in traditional Catholic belief, a God of triune personhood).

28. Note that to the extent that top administrators are such, they are not managers (of people). They may spend only a small percentage of their time guiding people (a management function), but almost all their time administering fiscal affairs, data research, planning, etc. Similarly, at the lower end of the spectrum—while it is hard to delimit supervisory or foreman-type activities from purely management ones—insofar as a person is merely carrying out assigned duties, prescribed tasks, policy guidebooks, assessing, and passing the word back up for directives about further actions, he is then only supervising and not managing.

28a. Cf. McLarney and Berliner, pp. 672–677.

29. Douglas McGregor, *The Human Side of Enterprise* (N.Y.: McGraw-Hill Book Co., 1960), p. vii; cf. pp. 6–7.

30. See McGregor, pp. 11, 31.

31. McGregor itemizes his six key assumptions in Theory Y, pp. 47–48: (1.) The expenditure of physical and mental effort in work is as natural as play or rest. . . . (2.) External control and the threat of punishment are not the only means for bringing about effort toward organizational objectives. Man will exercise self-direction and self-control in the service of objectives to which he is committed. (3.) Commitment to objectives is a function of the rewards associated with their achievement. . . . (4.) The average human being learns, under proper conditions, not only to accept but to seek responsibility. . . . (5.) The capacity to exercise a relatively high degree of imagination, ingenuity and creativity in the solution of organizational problems is widely, not narrowly, distributed in the population. (6.) Under the conditions of modern industrial life, the intellectual potentialities of the average human being are only partially utilized.

32. McGregor, p. 38.

33. McGregor, p. 49.

34. McGregor, p. 132.

35. As the word "employee" relates to the word "employer," so the word "managee" relates to the word "manager."

36. The centrality of the dynamic verbal element, which gives content to the nouns precisely as subject of that verbal action or as object, is clear in the literary paradigm. This formula and definition of "managing" was derived from the SVO Theory of communication of Terrance A. Sweeney, S.J., first presented in May 1973, as part of his doctoral presentation for the Graduate Theological Union, Berkeley, California. The SVO Theory is a detailed language paradigm that investigates philosophically the structure of cinema and kerygma as communication events. The theory—so named because the foundations of its paradigm are Subject (S), Verb (V), Object (O)—has wider implications and applications than filmic and kerygmatic communication events: it presents an explanation of the structure of all human communication. (It should be noted that the prefixes "micro" and "macro" applied to the V Theory of management do not have the same structural referents as do "micro" and "macro" found in the SVO Theory of communication.)

37. George R. Terry, *Principles of Management*, 4th ed. (Homewood, Ill.: Richard D. Irwin, Inc., 1964), p. 174, diagrams the tripartite clusters of "wants" which management must attempt to unify. (1) *Owners* want: the enterprise kept solvent and efficiently operated; a fair return on their invested capital; current information about the status and prospects of the enterprise; greatest possible efficient utilization of facilities; and long-range planning for stability and growth. (2) *Employees*

want: protection and security from accidents, sickness, old age; steady employment; fair wages; "completeness of daily living—satisfaction from their jobs, a feeling that they are making a contribution"; information about what is going on. (3) The *public* wants: goods and services available at fair prices; greater usefulness by improvements in goods and services; "harmonious relations among owners, employees, and managers"; and more fulfilling lifestyle provided by these goods and services. All of these "wants" are intentions, unified by management.

38. See Richard A. Johnson, Fremont E. Kast, and James E. Rosenzweig, *The Theory and Management of Systems* (New York: McGraw-Hill Book Co., Inc., 1967), p. 4.

39. Malcolm P. McNair cautioned against over-emphasis of human relations by business and industry, resulting in executives' losing perspective about their primary responsibilities in achieving results, especially if such emphasis was merely intended to develop skills in manipulating people to achieve pragmatic goals. "Thinking Ahead: What Price Human Relations?" *Harvard Business Review,* XXXV:2 (March–April 1957), pp. 15–23; cited by McLarney and Berliner, *Management Training: Cases and Principles,* 5th ed. (Homewood, Ill.: Richard D. Irwin, Inc., 1970), p. 405. The latter authors themselves also note on pp. 529–530 that a lower-management supervisor can make good decisions about work and lead his people to successful performance if he has adequate knowledge of details of that work; his own competence generates confidence which communicates to his people and engenders respect. On the other hand, George R. Terry, *Principles of Management,* 4th ed. (Homewood, Ill.: Richard D. Irwin, 1964), p. 15, emphasizes that "Management, by its very nature, implies social and ethical considerations. In the final anaysis, the whole being for most management exists for the betterment of human beings."

40. Administration of a university reflects these necessary qualities of management: vice presidents and deans do not themselves possess knowledge about the details of every course of study in the institution, nor even about the precise manner of teaching by each faculty member. Yet those administrators must oversee, appraise, plan and activate policies that affect the students and faculty as well as the curricular structures and daily operation of the total enterprise. To the extent that administrators themselves analyze and revise curriculum content and classroom methodology without collaborating with the persons involved first-hand, those administrators are no longer managing but actually mismanaging by assuming lesser (or at least different) non-administrative roles. The same may be said for family-owned and operated factory, office, or broadcast company.

41. We do not use this term (actualize) in the same sense as Terry uses the term "actuating"—where he refers to the methods by which the manager puts a group into action (such as by leadership, communication, instruction and discipline); Terry, p. 51, and Part V, "Actuating," pp. 463–587.

2

Principles
of Management and
the Station Manager

There is no business that so thoroughly punishes the amateur. In a business such as ours, where boys and girls become men and women rapidly, you have to have a lot more than heart. You have to have that—plus responsibility, sensitivity, judgment and understanding.

—CHARLES BROWER, Chairman of the Board,
Batten, Barton, Durstine and Osborne, Inc.

THE V THEORY of managing outlined in Chapter 1 can be applied to management generally, in the form of principles, and to broadcast management specifically by exemplifying those principles in the role of the station manager.

In mid-1972 a European Broadcasting Union conference analyzed "the possibility of applying modern management techniques to cultural organizations like radio and television." [1] Their 41 reports studied personnel matters in broadcasting, budgets, computers as a management tool, and the internal organization of broadcasting. They cited the increasingly complex structure of many advanced management matters to equal the importance of engineering, programming and legal problems.

Management responsibilities and skills are exercised throughout an organization. But executive or "top management" (e.g., heads of networks and group-owned clusters of stations as well as licensee-owners of single stations, and even vice-presidents and general managers) are concerned with the broadest goals of the total organization, the overall planning to achieve those goals, and relationships of the organization with outside agencies in society (the community, industry and government). "Middle managers" report to those execu-

28

tive superiors and are responsible for the detailed productivity and efficiency of the people who make up the station staff and of the material and facilities with which they work.[2]

In attempting to define the manager's role, various criteria might well be used.

> Who is a manager can be defined only by a man's function and the contribution he is expected to make. And the function which distinguishes the manager above all others is his *educational* one. The one contribution he is uniquely expected to make is to give others vision and ability to perform. It is vision and moral responsibility that, in the last analysis, define the manager.[3]

Some commentators on management, equating it with leadership, describe it as getting the job done through other people. But managers at various levels of most organizations are also occupied with tasks that they do themselves rather than delegate to others who report to them. Those kinds of activity, however, are non-managerial and are engaged in by default of available and competent personnel or perhaps by the manager's personal choice for the satisfaction he derives from them.[3a]

The manager is responsible for accomplishing the objectives planned by company strategy (the "intentionality" of the enterprise and its upper or top management) by effectively directing the people and their equipment and materials, as well as by guiding the efficient use of time and procedures. All of this relates back to the manager's responsibility for the capital invested in the enterprise and for the further cash flow involved in the daily business of that company. The middle manager spends time planning, organizing, and coordinating the work by other department heads who report to him and of those persons who report directly to him. But he leaves to departmental heads the details of accomplishing the plans that he has formulated and communicated to them. He must watch over costs and plan policies for his areas. And he must compile these data, appraise them, and forward them to the top management either periodically as reports or at least on occasion when unusual developments warrant.

Those descriptions of management's role reflect somewhat the classic theory of administration outlined by Henri Fayol.[4] His 14 principles emphasize the structural components of an authoritarian-centered system of management: division of work; authority and responsibility; disciplines; unity of command; unity of direction; subordination of individual interests to the general interests; remuneration of personnel; centralization; line authority; order equity; stability of personnel tenure; initiative; esprit de corps.[5] In contrast, McGregor's Theory Y and our own V Theory of management look not to static structures imposed on a laboring force but rather to dynamic collaborative relationships among all personnel—executives, middle managers, staff and line workers.

While primary aspects of management include planning, staffing and controlling, the V Theory emphasizes the central role of leadership in effective management.[6] Management is an art more than a science precisely because "much of the manager's work is solving problems among people." These kinds of problems demand that the manager acquire not merely detailed knowledge and experience of an enterprise's operation but more especially skills of social interaction. Those skills include supervisory methods in leadership, communication, counseling, brainstorming and group dynamics, and use of staff and delegation.[7] The manager's role is to motivate people so they can work for the company's and management's objectives. They can do this effectively only if the manager understands their abilities and needs. And understanding them, he must be skillful in communicating with them.

Management becomes even more of an art in the context of radio and television because, beyond distinctive executive skills and ability in business administration, the broadcast manager must be proficient in a field that is "a unique blending of public utility, private business, and showmanship." [8]

Few who listen to radio and view television programs know the station managers. It is natural for people to identify stations by call letters, positions on the dial or channel numbers, air personalities and programs. Few people not engaged in broadcasting are aware that a station "image" is developed on the basis of carefully planned policies that are determined and implemented by management. The degree of public response to a station's services is largely determined by the ability, beliefs, attitudes, character, personality and philosophy of the station manager.

A position which carries such power and responsibility should require certain qualifications. Its range of duties should be well defined. The motivations and gratifications of the assignment should be known. We should be able to understand the position better by an analysis of the people who are managers of stations.

QUALIFICATIONS OF STATION MANAGERS

Extensive experience in broadcasting seems to be accepted as one prerequisite to executive status in the industry. Other factors, though, are not so clear. Once, we might have said that station administration is for men, but today there are many examples of highly successful women managers of stations. And minority persons are beginning to move into management-related positions.

Because the manager's role is to motivate others to work for management objectives, his ability to deal with people is critical to his success in managing. His attitude towards those other persons on the staff is the key to giving them purpose and guiding them in carrying out their duties. He must therefore have some understanding of their abilities, their wants and feelings, and their behavior patterns (including the causes behind various kinds of actions). And he must be able to communicate with them effectively.[9] In order to accomplish their managerial responsibilities, supervisors must possess (or grow into) qualities that they must convey to those who report to them; Haimann lists "direction, enthusiasm, friendliness, affection, integrity, technical mastery, decisiveness, intelligence, teaching skill, and faith." [10]

From among many possible criteria, we isolated seven specific personal characteristics and attitudes we feel vital to success in station management. Even though these are subjective evaluations, we have checked our colleagues who are successful managers in radio and television and find that they possess the seven characteristics of leadership, intelligence, knowledge, judgment, personal integrity, sense of responsibility, attitude toward work, and showmanship.

Leadership

Although there should be little argument over the premise that an effective manager should be a leader, there might be wide differences of opinion about what human factors tend to produce station managers who provide leadership. Leadership may be defined as a process by which a person exerts social influence over members of a group in order to influence their behavior.[11] Consonant with the V Theory of management, Filley and House caution against looking merely to the personal characteristics of the leader himself for a high level of group effectiveness, because that effectiveness is a function of interaction between the leader and the group and also between individual members of the group. McGregor insists that leadership is a relationship among at least four major variables that have been identified as constitutive of the phenomenon: (1) the characteristics of the leader himself (as discussed below); (2) the attitudes and needs and other personal characteristics of the followers (below, and in Chapter 3 on personnel); (3) the characteristics of the organization, including its purpose, structure, process and kinds of tasks (subsequent chapters); and (4) the wider social, economic, and political milieu. Thus, McGregor concludes that depending upon those several other factors, the personal characteristics needed by a leader for effective performance may vary. *"It means that leadership is not a property of the individual, but a complex relationship among these variables."* [12] That relationship between the leader and the rest of his context or situation is "essentially circular."

Because this circular phenomenon is a process, it is subject to adjustment, application and interpretation.[13] Therefore, a characteristic of supervisory leadership is flexibility—undergirded by the macro-intention of the enterprise which provides overall direction and coherence. A manager must retain flexibility and creative decisiveness in the context of his understanding of the larger purposes and policies of the organization, in order to achieve the overriding intention of the enterprise. Intermediate intentionality may have to be modified by the manager, at times by passing along some duties or not passing them along to subordinates. There will be some decisions that the manager presents to his associates (or "managees") for their reactions and advice. But there will be other decisions that the manager makes without even consulting his subordinates—depending upon his discernment of the balanced operation of the enterprise, taken as a totality. This suggests that there cannot be excessive participation in decision-making by "managees," who must know that proper flexibility may demand that their manager on occasion either override their recommendations or anticipate by prior decision some deliberations that he might otherwise have them share. The manager-"manageee" relationship can be kept clear and effective as long as "managees" know the implications of flexibility in management decision-making, and as long as the manager communicates such actions after the fact so that they may know when something has been done and as much of the reason for it as possible.[14] Providing seemingly "managee"-centered type of participatory planning and decision-making, but then usurping it occasionally without any anticipation or explanation, will destroy credibility and even the authenticity of this shared role in the enterprise. There must be appropriate flexibility in management; but this flexibility must be known and accounted for when it is exercised.

Leadership is successful when it is able to accomplish the company's planned objectives and at the same time allow employees to enjoy and fulfill themselves. Sometimes the superior-subordinate relationship might be one of social collaboration instead of command-over-people.[15] Leadership functions primarily through personality and administrative techniques. Personality-oriented techniques emphasize social contexts and the attitudes and responses of the individual person as person in order to achieve corporate work goals. These techniques are effective in organizations of fewer than 50 people; beyond that number the interrelationships are too many and complex for leadership to be exercised adequately without administrative techniques.[16] Those latter seek to instill high morale by setting goals and then by assisting employees to achieve those goals. This is particularly apt for the inner-directed person who is goal-oriented and who derives satisfaction and value directly from his work and from achieving those work-oriented goals. "His grasp of the job enables him to initiate self-correction and to grow with his accomplishments." [17]

Psychological factors are operative in a person's effectively assuming the role of management leadership. A person will strive to lead if at the same time he can fulfill himself (just as a person will follow that leadership if it leads him to self-fulfillment).[18] Although a manager's self-fulfillment within an organization probably depends essentially on a "people-centered" approach to leadership,[19] it derives also from freedom in the job, status, and directing subordinates.[20] Leadership may be desirable for a manager because it offers power, or opportunity for growth in wisdom, or even respect and affection,[21] or because the person has a different approach or a "unique way of thinking about administration," [22] or because he experiences something of the role of a teacher to his subordinates [23] by which he tries to communicate to others something that he finds rewarding and in which he believes.[24] In terms of problem solving, the manager must be able to motivate the group of people for whom he is responsible so that he can gain their "emotional participation" not only in the total enterprise but in his specific directives.

The leadership role demands a high degree of confidence on the part of the manager. Normally, his training and experience qualify him to meet many unexpected problems. Essentially a realist and aware that some problems have to be settled without benefit of precedent, he is willing to stake his future on his ability to face issues squarely. He develops the ability to thrive under pressure.

Motivation. The station manager should be sincerely interested in the welfare of the people who work at his station and people who live in his community. If he has a genuine regard for people plus an understanding of human motivations and aspirations, he can be influential in leading them toward positive growth. The extent of his concern for personal development of staff employees will characterize his success or failure as a leader. While the successful manager develops skill in correcting the mistakes of others, he is equally adept at showing his appreciation for good work. Employees appreciate his interest in their personal growth and development.

People expect certain advantages or satisfactions from their work in an organization. McLarney and Berliner note that surveys of what people want from those jobs can be translated into what they expect their supervisors to be concerned with on their behalf:

> Respect for their personal dignity and worth. Concern for their success on the job, their safety and health. Acceptance of their limitations and appreciation of their abilities. Understanding of their needs for security, fair play, approval, belonging, importance and recognition. Willingness to listen to them, to try to understand them, to spare them from unnecessary unpleasantness and worry.[25]

The manager's attitude affects the employees' self-image and ability to be pleased with their work; the manager, to foster this unpressured yet productive relationship, might deemphasize his role as commanding or directing subordinates and should promote a relationship of social collaboration among people.[26] This he should do in spite of the fact that the manager will sometimes have to communicate with and motivate individual persons who may be simply bored or frustrated, anxious, dissatisfied or even maladjusted.[27] This is particularly true for broadcasters, many of whom can be designated "professionals" by virtue of their awareness of, and ability to contribute to, the social and legal and economic sectors of society. For example, newsmen are concerned with such issues as journalistic privilege and applications of the First Amendment to press freedoms; and their associations promote professional standards for reporting news events. Similarly, salesmen and on-air talent such as announcers and disc jockeys participate in national and regional organizations that establish guidelines for proper and effective activity in their respective fields. Publications report their activities; and schools of broadcasting and college departments offer formal courses of study in these areas. Thus, to the extent that these characteristics of the "professional" apply to members of a station staff, the manager will have a somewhat different relationship with them from the one that he has with more ordinary staff-line or rank-and-file personnel drawing paychecks for five-day work-weeks. Because the professional-oriented staff members often follow schedules suited to the station's larger needs (rather than 9-to-5 routine) and because they tend to exercise socially responsible roles in addition to their salary-producing job with the station, the manager may find it appropriate to treat them as "semi-peers." Further, a manager who really knows his "managees'" qualities and expertise and responsiveness to motivation will, in the instance of professional persons, delegate to them responsibilities (and accountability) proportioned to their knowledge. To repeat in this context: the manager must exercise leadership by finding ways to motivate "managees," so that they can fulfill themselves while also fulfilling the macro-intention of the whole enterprise. This merely restates that there is no average man and that the individual tends to rise to the level that challenges his full capabilities.[28]

The manager needs to have either a high degree of creativity or a fine sensitivity to creative efforts. Otherwise, it would be difficult for him to furnish the interest and inspiration which are needed by the many creative people who work in radio and television. Regular challenges should be made to these people if they are to do their best work. In short, the manager must stress building and maintaining excellent staff morale. Somehow, he causes each person on his staff to feel that his work is vitally important to the success of the station. He is pleased when this feeling exists even among custodial employees.

Delegation. Closely linked to motivation, as central factors in effective management, are delegating and communicating among "managees." Although the subheadings below of intelligence and judgment (and the later section on management structures) involve the role of delegating, this characteristic is central to leadership because it affects the level of creativity in a staff that includes professionally-oriented persons. This is particularly apparent when we consider McLarney and Berliner's enumeration of what the manager wants his leadership of "managees" to achieve.

1. Willing, sustained, and high-level job performance.
2. Readiness to accept change.
3. Acceptance of responsibility.
4. Involvement of people so they will use their brains, abilities, initiative and ideas.
5. Improvement in problem solving, in cooperation, and morale.
6. Development of people to be self-starting and self-controlling.
7. Reduction of turnover, absences, grievances, tardiness and waste.[29]

It is in this area of delegation, or decentralization, that the V Theory of management offers descriptive criteria. The more a manager deals exclusively with other people ("managees," or at least peer-level colleagues in his own company or in other companies), rather than with informational data and specific procedures, the better he is managing. The less he is dealing with people and instead is dealing with material things and procedures, the less he is acting as a manager and the more he is performing functions of a staff member.

The obvious conflict arises, which Dr. Laurence J. Peter identifies as "the Peter Principle," when a person who is competent and effective in an area is promoted to greater responsibilities.[29a] His competence in the higher position warrants a further promotion. The moves continue until he reaches a position where he does not function effectively; then he is no more promoted, but left to malfunction in this area of his incompetence. But even along the way—optimistically assuming that he never reaches that plateau of ineffectiveness—he successively learns each job well and adds that experience to his previous competence. Thus he gains considerable ability in the several areas over which he manages. Yet if he reverts to his earlier positions and gets involved in those details himself, he is forsaking his larger role as manager and is doing other people's jobs. This underscores the repeated theme: managing is not doing the job itself, but it is guiding, motivating and directing other people to do those jobs.

This is particularly clear in broadcasting. Often a sales manager subsequently becomes broadcast station manager where he oversees not only sales (in which he is experienced) but also programming (where he may have some lateral knowledge) and administration (where he may have some related experience) and engineering (where he may have no background whatever).

In terms of the V Theory of management (and the underlying SVO Theory of communication), the manager's key role is to interpret the enterprise's intentionality (its purpose, policies, procedures) through directives to the "managees," who can then exercise appropriately creative responsibility in actualizing those directives, in the light of the understood macro-intentionality of the company. This means that the manager does not want subordinates to come to him *for* decisions, but rather with decisions which they have already made. Thus the "managees," who were "objects" (O) in the SVO paradigm become themselves "subjects" (S) in initiating activity. As long as they understand the larger "why" (micro-intentionality of directives by managers), they can exercise responsible initiative and provide creative input, by participating in the rationale and philosophy of the company. Often, too, they are in a better position to exercise concrete judgment about true efficiency in carrying out specific directives. Because delegated responsibility includes accountability in actualizing and even interpreting decisions of management, that delegation involves true risk. And *true risk* permits *true creativity!* (Risk means that there is a genuine chance of mistake, error, or failure—which affect both the manager and the "managee.") The manager must accept this context of real risk; if there is no possibility of mistake then he has overly routinized things, and no genuine creativity can be exercised.[30]

We must note that this discussion opens the door to considerable latitude of interpretation in "managees' " actualizing directives from managers. But this is precisely the genius of Theory Y (McGregor) and of the V Theory of management: human beings collaborate in a common enterprise. There is not a "dictatorship of meaning"—assigning actions that must be performed in one exclusive and unique way—which is imposed univocally on all actions and directives by management. Personal initiative, in the context of informed commitment to the company's purposes, is supported and encouraged. McGregor again and again stresses the need for this higher "unity of *purpose*" (macro- and micro-intentionality) instead of that older factor ascribed to management

organization dynamics, the "unity of command," where each person is responsible to one and only one boss for his action.

> The inadequacy of the conventional principles of unity of command and of
> equality of authority and responsibility . . . must be recognized. Not only are
> these principles unrealistic in the modern industrial corporation, they are the
> source of many of the difficulties we are trying to correct. They are logically nec-
> essary within the context of Theory X, but flatly contradictory to Theory Y.[31]

This effective and perhaps bold, but reasonable, form of delegating is essential
for a creative, productive, person-fulfilling enterprise. Theodore Roosevelt appraised proper management leadership in delegating when he noted that "the
best executive is the one who has enough sense to pick good men to do what he
wants done, and self-restraint enough to keep from meddling with them while
they do it." [32]

Communication. Closely tied in with delegation of responsibility, because
it depends on a shared vision or commitment to the enterprise's intentionality,
is communication. Managers must clearly communicate the degree of freedom
and its boundaries in implementing or adapting directives. A wide scope for
freedom and interpretation, yet with clearly stated boundaries, will yield the
highest quality of creative, productive collaboration by "managees." [33] Results become increasingly unsatisfactory as the area of freedom is lessened and
the boundaries are defined vaguely. A "managee" can be responsive to a manager's directives:

(1) when he understands the communication;
(2) when he believes it to be consistent with the purposes of the organization;
(3) when it is compatible with his interests as an employee; and
(4) when he is mentally and physically able to to comply with it.[34]

Various forms of communication in a company are described in Chapter
3. Here it might be useful to note merely that meetings and conferences provide
few benefits to management if the "managee" participants perceive that the
manager's motive is primarily to win over the group to his position or to manipulate their attitudes, even if he does not indicate specifically what they
should think or decide. "Managees" will be aware of whether the sessions are
for open discussion of ideas or merely to confirm the manager's judgments and
to communicate them orally to the staff.[35]

While effective communication is an important element of leadership, it
includes more than being highly articulate in both written and spoken communication, having the ability to say "yes" or "no with firmness, and knowing
how to ask the right questions at the right times. It also includes the skill (and
virtue) of being able to listen and to attempt to understand the other person's
statements, meanings, and implied attitudes. Effective listening by both manager and "managee" is critical for creative collaboration, because mutual communication is the instrument by which motivation is generated.[36] Guidelines for

better communicating, and for making possible new ideas and insights shared between management and staff, include: avoid making value judgments, listen to the full story, recognize feelings and emotions, restate the other's position to clarify your understanding of it, and question with care.[37] Effective listening includes attending to the main thought or idea, noting verbal and also non-verbal communication, and summarizing what you think the speaker has just said.[38] Rapid and honest communication through conversation, through meetings and through formalized procedures such as memos, bulletin boards or house organ, will dispel haphazard informal communicating through the "grapevine" of gossip and rumor which undermines "managees' " confidence in management.

Finally, as a leader, the manager does not confine his activities to his station. He seeks out further responsibilities in his community and in various professional associations. Not content to assume a passive role, he volunteers for active service on committees, runs for office, and makes speeches at local, regional and national meetings. His fellow broadcasters recognize him as a leader in his industry and he has a similar image as a leader in his community. Winick discovered a much higher participation in community activities by television managers than by other business leaders.[39] The evidence suggests that their high degree of activity in civic and charitable organizations is motivated, at least in part, by strong inclinations for contacts with a wide variety of people.

Leadership is the keystone of effective management. Other characteristics reflect this quality or are constitutive of it.

Intelligence and Knowledge

It should be obvious that the intelligence of the manager should be well above average. Whether a superior I.Q. would be of any particular advantage to the manager is another question. Apparently, on the basis of the opinions of various authorities in the field of management, success may be achieved in the managerial position with an intelligence which is less than superior but considerably above the norm. (In the mid-1960s, Winick found that three-fourths of television station managers had been to college and one-sixth had done postgraduate work.)

The manager of a radio or television station is expected to have a considerable amount of knowledge concerning the specialized nature of the broadcasting industry, of his own station, its market and its people. To the degree that his intelligence enables him to acquire knowledge faster, retain it longer and apply it effectively to the various new and continuing problems of broadcasting, we may safely conclude that his intellectual endowments are vital to his success as a manager in broadcasting.

In order to keep abreast of all the changes which occur regularly in the broadcasting industry, the manager must read extensively. He needs to read the important trade publications, as well as many periodicals and books in the field of business and other more general magazines and newspapers. Time might be saved if digests of important publications were prepared for him by some knowledgeable member of his staff; this *is* feasible in large stations. But digests of information have been poor substitutes for the reading of original sources by the executive himself. Analyses of the materials are as important as the reading; this is a time-consuming activity but it is essential. Winick's survey reported that 88 per cent of TV station managers read magazines about current events; only one-third read business magazines; and one-third read "intellectual" magazines such as *Scientific American*. Bernard Gallagher reported in 1971 that almost nine out of ten radio station managers read *Broadcasting* magazine weekly, one-third read *Wall Street Journal* regularly; one in five read *Business Week* (*Time, Newsweek* and *U.S. News & World Report* were not listed). Of several major trade magazines, in media and sales, *Television/Radio Age* ranked a distant second after *Broadcasting;* 8 per cent read *Variety* regularly.[40] Among small-market radio managers, Bohn and Clark cited *Broadcasting* as the most read magazine, the *Wall Street Journal* as the "top newspaper choice."

Not only are there *changes* in the business world, in entertainment forms, in governmental regulation, and in radio and television broadcasting; there is continued acceleration in the *rate* of change which the manager must keep abreast of to remain competitive and to be truly a leader within his company and among his colleagues. The publisher of *Television/Radio Age* reflected on this enormous challenge to the manager, noting that "we can safely say that there will be more changes in every facet of this business in the next five years than there have been in the past two decades." The manager must increasingly become expert in a broad range of duties and responsibilities:

> The scope of the station manager's responsibilities has been greatly widened in the past few years. In addition to knowing first-hand operations, sales and programming, he is more involved with community action groups and in dealing with organized minorities and consumer interests. He is also walking the delicate line between these groups and "Big Brother," in the form of the Federal Communications Commission. It becomes pretty apparent that the pioneer-type who really built this business has been "out-flanked." On the other hand, the accountant-type who watches only the bottom line has a too-narrow perspective to do the complete job. Profitability is the most important aspect of the station manager's job. However, if he does not concern himself with other facets of station operations, he will find himself knee-deep in some monumental problems. There is an old adage that the station that serves best sells best. Some cynics in this business—and there are far too many—may challenge this premise, but the fact remains a station's image is an important asset. A well managed station with a manager who is concerned with all aspects of his responsibilities can be both highly respected and extremely profitable.
>
> But what about the future? What direct effect will cable have on the broadcast business? What will satellite reception mean to broadcasters? Will domestic satellites mean the entry of one, possibly two additional television networks? Will the network structure change with the networks eventually selling programming to affiliates? What about the future of the rep business? [41]

While the constant study of changes within the broadcasting industry is in itself a giant assignment, the manager is also compelled to expand his knowledge of his own station. Most station managers are well acquainted with either sales or programming or engineering. Few, if any, are personally experienced in more than one of those operations. Yet, the manager must be prepared to discuss each department intelligently, analyze the operations and practices of each, and provide them with continuing challenges. It is he who must establish effective working relationships among the three departments.

Aspirants to management positions would be well advised to acquire considerable knowledge about all aspects of station operations early in their careers when they are primarily involved with only one station activity.

The manager is further obligated to acquire a wealth of knowledge about his market and to use his intellectual capacities to make shrewd analyses of the business potential of the market and of the interests and the needs of the people in the station's coverage area. It is obvious that a complete knowledge of retailing strategies and problems is necessary, as is a specialized understanding of the role of advertising in the business economy.

When a man becomes manager of a station, he enters a new working world with a new set of requirements and demands. He finds much to learn about the whole field of broadcasting which he did not find necessary in his previous communications positions. He develops new curiosity about the audience that his station serves and he becomes aware of research methods and research organizations. Laws and Federal regulations become highly important in his new environment. The many allied fields of the advertising agencies, station representatives, trade associations, unions, film and transcription companies, music-licensing companies, and wire services take on new meanings. He reads the trade publications with greater purpose. He comes to realize the need for more complete knowledge concerning new broadcasting equipment and he develops a greater understanding of and respect for the show-business atmosphere of programming and of talent.

The alert manager notices the pronouncements of the critics of broadcasting more than he did formerly. He finds himself examining the broadcasting Codes and the merits of Code membership for his station. He becomes public-relations conscious and he reassesses his own station's facilities for publicity, promotion and merchandising. He becomes well versed in the problems and the achievements of all mass media and of all forms of show business. He becomes active in efforts to improve his community. He studies ways to achieve greater efficiencies in budgeting and he learns to be fascinated by the financial affairs of the station.[42] His mind, stretched by all of this new knowledge and experience, can never return to what it once was.

The manager who has a liberal education or background and who maintains a true intellectual curiosity should be able to converse intelligently on almost any subject. His wide range of interests should make him a popular and a stimulating guest at those social events which are important to his professional career.

Judgment

Every executive is required to make decisions regularly. In broadcasting, countless problems arise which have few, if any, precedents. Often, they must be solved in a matter of minutes. In this industry, much is regulated by the clock, and the chief commodity for sale is time itself.

Mature judgment is needed to make decisions in broadcasting. Such maturity usually is a product of wide experience and comprehensive knowledge. Some people are capable of intuitive reasoning but the decision must be right most of the time. In this game, a ".500 batting average" is not good enough!

It would be easy to manage a radio or a television station by imitating the policies and practices of successful managers of other stations. This sort of management hardly appeals, however, to the man who places a high premium on his ability to think for himself. Take away the need for the use of wisdom and the management position loses all of its attractiveness for the man who regards decision-making as a personal challenge.

When decisions need to be made on long-range problems, the most effective managers know how to define those problems, how to gather all of the important facts, how to determine all possible solutions, how to arrive at decisions, and how to implement those decisions in a manner which gets employee support. Good managers will not settle for insufficient evidence nor will they be influenced by unimportant or trivial data.[43]

The effectiveness of long-range thinking may depend upon how much time the executive has available for uninterrupted reflection. Any manager would be wise if he were to block out periods of time when he could think about major issues.

A useful summary of judgmental skills needed for management includes:

Having the ability to develop goals and objectives.
Being able to build a plan to implement these goals interrelating them with others.
Capable of effective communications, especially with people but also written and formal presentations.
Able to resolve or balance conflicts between work, interests and people.
Good at problem-solving in all its phases, with work processes and people problems.
Balanced decision-making, carefully weighing the important elements and generally using good judgment.
Able to determine priorities with flexibility, to change as needed, and stick with them when necessary.[44]

Personal Integrity

The station manager must be a man of strong character. His position is in the "spotlight" and he can influence his station personnel and the people who live in the community. He is obligated, by the nature of his position, to command respect.

The manager should be a person whose sensitivity to deeper values reflects depth of character and humility. People should be able to look to him for strength; and they should be able to experience that the longer they know him, the stronger they find him to be.

An even temper and the ability to control extremes of emotion are distinct assets for the manager. When successes come his way or when he suffers reverses, he needs to be able to react with an outward appearance of stability. A sense of humor can provide a necessary balance for many problems encountered. Often, tensions can be relieved in other people if humor is used advantageously. Successful executives seem to be able to develop a remarkable facility for laughing at themselves and for being amused at their own mistakes. Amused, but not too self-forgiving, either.

"Integrity" means "wholeness"—a balanced composite of sensitivities and values based on insight and experience, which supports principled convictions about oneself and about one's fellow human beings. This sense of ethics or morality may derive from institutional religious commitment or from a self-understanding of man's respect for and responsibility to fellow men under God, in order to help others in society develop fully as individual persons. Such integrity goes far beyond mere personal piety or scattered efforts at "good works"; it is the fabric of a man's life.[45]

The keynote of an ethical sense and a healthy morality is freedom—freedom to innovate, freedom to select from among real alternatives, freedom to counter the prevailing climate of value-structures; Haselden concludes that this freedom "is the habitat of authentic morality." [46] Otherwise, these alternatives may eventually be provided by other sources. For example, alternative concepts in content, form and scheduling could come to be supplied by default by cable TV and pay television and by videocassette distribution, if the commercial broadcasters (owners-licensees, stockholders, managers, staffs) and the advertising agencies and their clients restrictively stereotype programming patterns for a broad level of mass audiences.

William Lynch appeals for synergistic collaboration among what he refers to as sources of "intelligence and imagination . . . maturity, competence and common sense." [47] These sources he identifies as the authentic artist and writer, creative theologians and the creative mind in general, critics, and educators—all of whom are "concerned with the life and the images of the people," plus the full reality of human nature itself which "can respond to the presence of beauty and style if only given a chance." [48] Just as Rivers and Schramm excoriate the preponderance of merely "kitsch" or mass culture as the popular standard of American media,[49] Lynch notes four major areas of problems in media, especially in the sector of artistic creativity. These problem-areas challenge the broadcast manager of substantive integrity who must ultimately answer to society for the role that his station plays in his human community's daily living.

   1. The failure, on a large scale, of these media to differentiate between fantasy and reality; the result is a weakening, throughout the nation's audiences, of the power to differentiate between these two things.

2. The weakening and flattening out of the area of feeling and sensibility in the public consciousness.

3. The extent to which freedom of imagination is being restricted, not by the moralist or the censor, but by the purveyors of all the techniques for the fixation of the imagination.

4. The "magnificent imagination": the spectacular projection of the dream on the screens of the movies and TV, in which all the true lines of our human reality are lost.[50]

Every person of integrity, including the broadcast manager, should be concerned with the problem of preserving and helping to create (rather than protesting against) freedom of imagination in mass media.[51] Integrity raises a challenge against imitating repeated presentations of merely one or other partial aspect of the human condition (violence, physical relations, war, unfairness, glib banter, superficial sense pleasure, etc.). Integrity supports the attempt to portray more of the fullness of reality all around us: in entertainment programs and also in the range of cultural and informational programs, incuding news, documentaries and public affairs. What Lynch calls the "mass media diseases" of fantasy, flatness, fixation, and empty pretentious magnificence affect "the condition of human sensibility in our civilization."[52] Against this mediocrity of craftsmanship with routinely-fixed technique and stereotypical image-and-sound clichés, broadcast leaders of integrity must continue to strive to support media creativity that "knows how to move us from insight to insight."[53]

Although no single broadcast manager can hope by himself to correct all media weaknesses or to change major aspects of media content and practices, each manager might well exercise personal integrity of judgment by reflecting on the potential of mass media in today's world. International churches, as well as secular professional organizations, have noted what has been referred to as "the centrality of the communications vocation in modern society":

> The newsman, the broadcaster, the playwright, the film maker cannot be considered—or consider themselves—merely as entertainers or technicians. As much as anyone in contemporary society, they form the world-view of modern man. They convey information and ideas that are essential to the functioning of society; even more important, they help to shape the very ethos of the world in which we live. Theirs is, then, a calling of high honor—of heavy responsibility.
>
> Communicators in our country have generally met this responsibility with a conscientiousness and dedication which does them deep credit. In some areas, however, there are problems.[54]

Although any change in mass communication involves a long process, change must come about in people before it can affect the larger system.[55] Professionalism, individual as well as institutional, contributes to the ethical integrity of media through its managers.

> In the practical terms of day-to-day operations, the private conscience and sense of responsibility of the individual worker—writer, salesman, air personal-

ity, control operator, editor—govern what goes out over the air. The multitude of their small decisions determines the actual quality of the broadcast service. Legal regulation and institutionalized self-regulation can govern only a small proportion of these decisions; most remain personal.[56]

While Rivers and Schramm note that "except in a few cases, the practitioners of mass communication are employees, and thus the ultimate responsibility for their work and the quality of their service rests on their employers," they stress the individual sense of responsibility instead of the corporate sense, looking to the communicator's responsibility "as a public servant and as a professional, quite apart from his obligations to the business that employs him." [57] Professionalism is founded on each broadcaster's sense of personal ethic. In Head's phrasing, professionalism implies "the voluntary adoption of high standards of ethical personal conduct in the pursuit of an occupation fraught with social responsibility." [58]

Sense of Responsibility

Closely linked with the manager's personal integrity is his attitude toward his various responsibilities. He cannot avoid an awareness of his many obligations to the owners of the station, to the station employees and to the public. There are almost constant reminders that he, and he alone, is accountable for the many decisions which have to be made in their interests.

The most effective managers do not permit material considerations to dominate their existence. While they are fully aware of the importance of profits, they also recognize values which are as important to their success as the accumulation of dollars. This is one reason why they become active in groups which work for the improvement of conditions in their communities. They are aware that such activity usually results in material benefits for the station, but only if they are sincere and effective in their interest and participation.

"Responsibility" suggests a broadcast manager's ability to respond to the enormous social challenge and ethical burden of overseeing these media of mass communication. This responsibility was appraised by a world-wide church:

> The channels of social communication, even though they are addressed to individuals, reach and affect the whole of society. They inform a vast public about what goes on in the world and about contemporary attitudes and they do it swiftly. That is why they are indispensable to the smooth functioning of modern society, with its complex and ever changing needs, and the continual and often close consultation that it involves. This exactly coincides with the Christian conception of how men should live together.
>
> These technical advances have the higher purpose of bringing men into closer contact with one another. By passing on knowledge of their common fears and hopes they help men to resolve them.
>
> . . . .
>
> These means, in fact, serve to build new relationships and to fashion a new language which permits men to know themselves better and to understand one

another more easily. By this, men are led to a mutual understanding and shared ambition. And this, in turn, inclines them to justice and peace, to good will and active charity, to mutual help, to love and, in the end, to communication. The tools of communication, then, provide some of the most effective means for the cultivation of that charity among men which is at once the cause and the expression of fellowship.

All men of good will, then, are impelled to work together to ensure that the media of communication do in fact contribute to that pursuit of truth and the speeding up of progress. . . .which is the brotherhood of man under the fatherhood of God.[59]

Rivers and Schramm describe the multiple role of mass communications in contemporary society as helping us: to anticipate and be forwarned about approaching events and their patterns (in the arts as well as public affairs); to correlate our responses to coming challenges and opportunities; to reach consensus on social action; to transmit our culture; to entertain us; and to sell goods and services.[60] Thus the responsibility of the broadcaster involves him in value-judgments about people, about society at large and events within it, and about the content of media presentations. Beyond the specifically legal guidelines (described in Chapter 9), the ethical sense of the broadcast manager can help assure that radio and television programming reflects the community's pluralistic population (including minorities) and views (thus the need for impartiality and fairness, for accuracy and reliability in presenting news and other local programming).[61] Internal station guidelines can be coupled with professional associations' self-regulatory codes (as the NAB's), as means by which to exercise responsibility in the many matters that involve hard and patient management decision-making—including problems of access, fair and unfair criticism, pressure groups, and less direct pressures by large businesses and government (all of which touch upon program decisions, staff, news coverage, editorials, and business practices generally, including sales).[62] A manager's sense of the tastes, cultural level, needs and aspirations of his community contributes to his appraisal of his station's proper balance of service.[63] These kinds of concerns, expressed in responsible supervision of his station's policies and practices for programming, at the same time will serve well the manager's legal obligations on behalf of the owner-licensee for the "public interest, convenience and necessity."

Attitude Toward Work

Some people—including, unfortunately, some station employees—visualize the manager's assignment as an easy one. They seldom see him when he is at the station, and he arrives and leaves at irregular hours. Usually, his office is carpeted and well furnished, sometimes luxuriously. He enjoys personal and social amenities. His secretary often seems to be in command of the station while he plays golf or goes out of town. Daily on-the-air operations do not require his direct involvement. On the surface, it would appear that he devotes a minimal amount of time to his work and a maximum amount of time to something like leisure.

Most station managers *do* have "fun," but a large share of their enjoyment comes from problem-solving and decision-making. They work longer hours than their employees and they carry work with them when they go home at night or leave on business trips. The high degree of informality which exists in radio and television stations can be deceiving. A television monitor or a radio receiving set in the manager's office means work rather than recreation. Pressures from stockholders, owners, station personnel, the audience, government and the critics are so constant and the changes in the industry are so regular that the manager becomes preoccupied with thoughts of his station and its problems during most of his waking hours.

Former Federal Communications Commissioner Robert Wells asked broadcast educators to put these questions to their college students majoring in radio and television:

> Do you like to work peculiar hours? Do you enjoy being in the public eye and being criticized with some regularity—not just by your boss or fellow workers, but by every citizen in town? Do you enjoy holding a position which brings with it great responsibility? Can you wonder on some days whether anybody appreciates anything you do without getting upset? [64]

Because of the social, economic, and political importance of broadcast media, he noted that those who go into broadcasting forsake the comfortable category of "ordinary citizen" and assume responsibilities far greater than in most careers. He cautioned:

> If they don't feel some sort of dedication, they probably are in the wrong business. The job will become more and more demanding. That is the history of broadcasting in the 50 years since its inception. But the very fact that broadcasters have continued to accept these responsibilities and to improve their techniques and service has made them vulnerable to criticism, because people expect more and more and the pressures mount. There is no indication that this will change.

To manage a broadcasting station is a privilege which is afforded few men and, as we have noted, there are many responsibilities which go with that privilege. The "strong" manager not only accepts these duties, but he expects them and goes out of his way to create them when they are not present. He knows that his success is dependent upon constant progress. He knows, too, that the *easy* assignment can be assumed by any number of people.

A general public impression of broadcasting is that it is a "glamour" business. Yet, any description of the manager's position could hardly include the term "glamorous." His job is basically hard work. It is, in effect, a way of life that has to be lived most of the time. That is the way he wants it!

Showmanship

Coupled with creativity (described above with "integrity"), the element of showmanship is perhaps more important to a manager of a radio or a television station than it is to managers of most other kinds of business. It is not demonstrated, however, by flamboyance in actions, speech or dress, but rather in an innate sense of timing and in an intuitive sense of dramatic values, which seem to be basic qualifications of all good showmen.

A large measure of the attractiveness of the station-management assignment is undoubtedly based on the opportunity to work with show people. Their talents add much excitement to a business which might be fairly routine without them. They constitute the station's most valuable contacts with the public. The task of finding the most effective methods to reach that public using the best show techniques that are known to man is a truly challenging kind of work. In broadcasting, the show or program is the product. Any good manager must fully understand and appreciate his company's product.

DUTIES OF THE MANAGER

The varied duties and activities of the radio and television manager will be discussed throughout the succeeding chapters of this book. Yet the essential managerial task is the planning of goals, objectives, and operational procedures of the station. This precedes and accompanies all other duties.

Policy Planning

Well defined plans of both a short-term and a long-range nature are needed by all broadcasting stations [65] Because these immediate and ultimate targets affect and apply to every phase of the station's operation, the manager is the person who is in a position to evaluate them in true perspective. Key station staff people can supply him with some important data. Certainly, their opinions should be important in his considerations. But all final decisions regarding policy have to be made by management.

Effective planning involves forecasting. Most of the employees of a station work in a "here and now" atmosphere. Their assignments for the most part involve today's deadlines or those of tomorrow or of next week. It is imperative that someone take the long view and make accurate predictions about the station's future. As the person who is most directly responsible to the station owners, the manager is expected to provide answers concerning long-range business prospects and their probable effect on the station's future. He must be aware of trends and signs in program popularity, in advertiser expectations, in new developments in technical equipment. He is expected to analyze and project this knowledge into future plans so that the station can lead, rather than follow, its competition.

Wise planning takes all possible future eventualities into account. Without such planning, unexpected or unforeseen events may occur which could cause temporary chaos. Valuable time can be saved through prior consideration of the measures which could be followed in any possible major emergencies in the future. Such crises might stem from anything from the loss of a tower in a tornado to the possible loss of a valued employee in an accident. Pre-planned actions, while never entirely adequate in emergencies, are preferable to spontaneous decisions which have to be made while in a state of shock or when under heavy emotional stress. (The best ad-libs are almost always well rehearsed.)

Managerial plans should be clear to the employees of the station. The team nature of the broadcasting activity makes such understanding particularly necessary. A station should be composed of people who believe in the objectives of the manager and who are keenly interested in working toward their achievement. Well conceived planning can reduce tendencies toward employee ideas of indispensability, chances of personality conflicts, displays of temperament, and the evils of internal politics in the organization.

The principal objective of the planning function is to achieve greater efficiency and thus produce maximal returns on the investment in the station, while serving the community that is the station's audience. Achievement of this goal is dependent upon a clear policy, a well organized plan of attack and a dedicated staff.

It is as essential to have adequate planning in small radio and television stations as in large stations or networks. All stations of comparable size have basically the same type of facilities and equipment. The important differences between those stations are due to the *people* who work in the stations and the manner in which their activities are coordinated, guided and challenged. Consonant with the V Theory of managing, the manager must plan carefully how to select the persons on his staff and motivate them for effective activity. The general manager or station manager must select the key people who are competent in their specialities as well as able administrators.[66]

Furthermore, the manager must be able to plan, direct, and control his own use of time. He must be sure to emphasize supervision of personnel, not personally looking after things and procedures. He should plan the use of his time so that he spends most of it in creative work and a minimum of time on merely routine work, leaving a cushion of unallocated time for emergency work.[67] A good manager is able to manage his own affairs and himself. "The difference between good planning and poor planning is the difference between order and confusion, between things done on time and not being done on time, between cooperation and conflict, and between pleasant working conditions and a workday full of discord."[68]

Owners of stations need to give managers the authority to make whatever changes are necessary whenever they are needed. In a business that changes as fast as broadcasting, the manager should not be throttled by a need to obtain the approval of his superiors in all matters requiring decision. He should be regarded as the person fully-in-charge and he should be authorized to act in the owners' behalf with only courtesy consultations or advisements.

When a change of managers is made, the new executive should expect to draw his own plans for the future of the station (within the context of what we have called the macro-intention of the station and its owners). This same privilege is accorded every new President of the United States, every new Governor of a State or every new manager of a baseball team.

It should be clear that the planning function calls for the most realistic thinking and projection that is possible. In consideration of the responsibility for service and profit which the manager assumes with his appointment, anything short of realistic planning is inexcusable. Some radio and television stations, unfortunately, operate with highly unreal goals, and there are a few which can produce no clearly defined objectives. These stations properly deserve the various kinds of negative results they get.

Improvements in or replacements of facilities or equipment, the responses to and actions upon new regulations from the FCC, variations in either individual or overall programming formats, changes in rate structure or in selling methods, revised office procedures—these are examples of variables that require new decisions and consequent alterations in policy. Most of them are made under the pressures of time.

The first important obligation of the manager, then, is to determine the goals and objectives, the policies and the procedures of his particular radio or television station in his market. Some operational practices which have become standard throughout the broadcasting industry may be borrowed from other stations. But the good manager will want all of the important station decisions, the goals, objectives, policies and procedures to be custom-made for his particular station.

The Station Policy Book

Once station policy has been formulated, it needs to be put in writing and copies need to be given to each employee and to the owners of the station. Some stations have found it advisable to circulate some sections of their policy statements to various community groups which might be interested and affected.

Some of the advantages of having station policies in writing are: (1) the achievement of greater efficiency; (2) a reduction of the chances for misunderstandings; (3) less need for continual routine decisions of a repetitive nature; (4) a provision for additional managerial time for concentration on other station problems; (5) a standard and equitable treatment for all employees; and (6) a guide that sometimes may be incidental to the total station operation but that may be of prime importance to the employees as individuals.[69]

Without a clear station policy in writing, a manager can find himself devoting a disproportionate amount of his time to decision making on relatively minor issues. With a clearly defined policy, many of these cases need never arise. If they do occur, they can be settled quickly by a referral to the station policy.

In the absence of a policy on "moonlighting," plans for rotating announcer's shifts may be upset due to a second job that an announcer is holding away from the station. An employee may be reprimanded for taking excessive sick leave if it has never been made clear just how much sick leave is "excessive." There can be a problem of staffing the station on holidays unless employees know which people are expected to work and why. Station clients may complain about improper treatment on the telephone by station employees if no rules of telephone etiquette have been formulated. Cleanliness can be a continual problem in the various station offices or washrooms or in the reception room if no rules exist. The manager may note that the coffee breaks for office personnel tend to get longer, that the conversations around the water cooler tend to increase, that smoking continues in restricted areas, that more and more attention has to be given to requests for the use of station properties by employees, that official stationery of the company is used for personal correspondence, that the only satisfactory way to deal with letters of reply to people in the audience is to read them before they are mailed, that some people on the staff engage in long telephone conversations of a personal nature during working hours. In such cases, a manager can discover that he spends far too much time issuing memoranda which have been circulated before; the same problems may seem to re-occur involving different people. Most employees, aware of operating policies, accept and follow established rules and practices.

Policy statements can cover a wide range of employee interests, including wages and salaries and the bases for salary increases and advancements, rules concerning vacations and other fringe benefits, and job descriptions.[70]

Complete job descriptions are particularly important in defining the limitations and responsibilities of each staff member and in giving him an understanding of the relationship of his work to that of other people on the staff as well as to the other station functions. Job specifications need to be clearly framed. It is more efficient to define functions and then find people who match them and who will be good members of a team than it is to find people and then attempt to adapt the jobs to them. Station positions should be so well defined that each replacement of an individual will find the basic assignment unchanged.

Written policy is particularly valuable for *new* personnel. In far too many cases, new employees at radio and television stations learn their job routines and absorb the station's philosophy in a most inefficient manner—by talking with other employees, by making mistakes and having to be corrected, or by asking questions. Broadcasters have been notoriously negligent of indoctrination procedures for new people. Minimally, a statement of station policy, including the various job descriptions as well as the station rules, should be given to each candidate for a position before he is hired. This policy statement can be regarded as a part of the employee's contract. Any prospective addition to the station's staff has every right to know all the conditions of his employment before accepting a position.

It is next to impossible to compose a complete station policy book in the first writing. New situations will constantly arise and conditions will frequently change. Provision should be made for regular revisions. The most carefully defined rules should cover most cases but there will always be exceptions which are sufficiently different to require separate decisions. It is advisable to create policies that permit a limited amount of flexibility. Then, if exceptions have to be made, explanations can be given without fear of embarrassment. Extreme care should, of course, be exercised in exceptional cases in order to insure fair treatment.

The preparation of a satisfactory policy statement is a time consuming process. It should, however, make for greater management efficiency and it should improve station morale.

Policy Implementation

In the implementation of policy, the human qualities of the manager are extremely important. His skill in administration and his clarity in the communication of his ideas will determine the degree of their acceptance by the employees, the public, the advertisers and the owners. Ineffective communication of the true intent and meaning of the plans or a reliance on an authoritarian approach to enforce their acceptance can result in compliance by the employees out of a sense of duty rather than with enthusiasm. There can be negative defensive or antagonistic reactions. To achieve positive results, the communicative and leadership abilities of the manager are truly put to the test. He must be a good salesman and a good listener.

In the communication of new plans to the staff, it is important for explanations to be given as to why the changes are being made. There should also be clear instructions concerning the benefits to be gained by the station from the changes.

Implementation should never be exclusively a downward process whereby all of the impetus for action is instigated by the manager. If such practice were followed, many good ideas would be lost to the station. All of the station's personnel should be encouraged to contribute suggestions for station improvement. Whenever any employee makes a workable suggestion, he should be given full credit for the contribution which he makes.

Sometimes, the station employees may be aware of changes that might be necessary but the manager may not know of them. Some employees may feel reluctant to report irregularities; others may be inclined to give only a partial accounting of the facts. It is important for the manager to have the confidence of his staff. Often, he may need to convey to them his desire to be kept informed of any irregularities which might affect the station adversely.

The conference approach, whereby an administrator gathers together his junior executives for the discussion of problems and issues, has produced many benefits to organizations.[71] Consideration of possible alternatives is usually more effective when several minds concentrate. But while groups can make effective policy, only individuals can implement and administer that policy. The station manager must provide the insight which brings the problems to the conference table, guide an objective appraisal of the problems, and then be prepared for the administration of the policy measures which are adopted.

When duties are delegated to others, there needs to be an explicit understanding concerning the limits of authority. The expectations of all administrative and supervisory roles as well as their relationships to the duties and responsibilities of other station executives should be clearly stated in station policy. General managers and station managers need to make special efforts to keep department heads supplied with all information which has any application to the areas of their jurisdiction.

Delegation of authority is a requirement, of course, for executive efficiency. Station managers need to be freed from detail work in order to be able to concentrate on major policy and on the variety of duties which are combined in the managerial position. Those managerial duties constitute the remaining portions of this book: (1) regular attention to the motivation, rewards and working conditions of the station's *personnel;* (2) supervision of the office *staff* of the station; (3) continuing study of the *audience* which is served by the station; close working relationships with (4) the *program* manager, (5) the *sales* manager, and (6) the *chief engineer;* (7) preparation of the overall budget and maintenance of controls over income and expenses in order to earn *profits;* (8) continued acquisition of information about *government* concerning the proposals, rules and regulations of the Federal Communications Commission (and maintaining proper relationships with the FCC and other officials at the Federal, state and local levels); and (9) active participation in national, regional, and local *professional* activities.

There is continual interaction among these areas in the station. By way of concrete example, the seven steps of problem-solving technique might be applied to a typical broadcast context.[72] First, *clearly define the problem;* the sales manager may note difficulty in finding clients (through their agencies) to buy spot commercial time available in the local schedule in the early evening of a given night of the week. The next step is to *gather the information,* perhaps by having the research staff or program manager get the demographic data on the audience in that market, coupled with comparative statistical data on competitive stations' ratings for that time period; further, the program manager may have his people provide information about feasibility of scheduling local program production in their own studios if that is a possible option. Third, the manager and his staff must *interpret the information,* in the light of the sales manager's initial definition of the problem, the program manager's appraisal of production scheduling (if that is part of a possible solution), and the chief engineer's assessing the capabilities of studio facilities and crews for feasibility in mounting more programming or commercial production in the studios (again, if that is a recommendation by programming). Fourth, specific *solutions must be developed,* providing alternate ways to meet the sales problem. The manager collaborates with other personnel to outline all possible solutions. Fifth, *the best practical solution is selected* by the station manager, in the context of all the ''input'' from his staff. The actual exercise of that decision, to *put the solution into operation,* is the responsibility of the several people and departments affected by the decision. For example, if the solution chosen is to buy filmed programming for the schedule, there is little problem for the chief engineer; but if the choice is to produce some local programming, in addition to traffic and programming, the engineering department must determine how best to supply staff, crews, and facilities. Finally, the seventh step is to *evaluate the effectiveness of the solution;* again, the manager is provided with data from his staff so that he can appraise the results with them. In some instances, it may be noted, the data coming back to the manager from his competent staff may be almost self-determining, so that the decision to be made is apparent. Or else the decision might be only one of several reasonable alternatives, and he may choose to let the staff determine among themselves for him what is their composite recommendation. Thus the manager's primary role is to support his staff so they may work creatively and effectively; his role in actually appraising the informational data and selecting the preferred option among possible solutions may well be secondary.

Although television demands some different specific duties, the following job description for radio management outlines major responsibilities of the typical broadcast station manager.

Job Description—Radio Station Manager [73]

A. Planning, development and administration to ensure the profitable operation of the station within the policies and procedures of the Company, FCC, and NAB.
  1. Ensures that requirements and program standards are upheld within the established station format as outlined through Company policies and procedures, FCC rules and regulations, and the NAB Code for commercial broadcasting facilities.
  2. Directs station resources and facilities toward generating the maximum possible revenue.
  3. Creates public awareness of the station, its programs and policies.
  4. Ensures the availability and proper operation of technical facilities necessary to produce high quality radio broadcasts.
  5. Supervises proper administration of station accounts and records in accordance with Division Finance policies and procedures.
  6. Develops station editorial positions.
B. Continuous review and evaluation of station broadcasts; application of appropriate measures to improve program content, attract listeners and increase sales.
  1. Monitors broadcasts frequently to ensure a high degree of quality and consistency.
  2. Studies audience rating results to determine what areas of programming could be improved.
  3. Appraises constantly the effectiveness of sales techniques and seeks ways to improve total sales.
  4. Meets regularly with Director, News and Programs and General Sales Manager to discuss methods of improving programming to increase sales.

5. Confers with owners (or radio division head) with regard to recommended major alterations in programming and sales policies and practices.
6. Monitors and evaluates competitive stations.

C. Maintenance of personal and station contact with the community in order to develop ways to effectively service community needs through radio broadcasting.

1. Maintains memberships in appropriate community organizations and makes guest appearances, as necessary, to represent the station.
2. Encourages station directors and managers to join community organizations in behalf of the station.
3. Conducts seminars, meetings, etc., for the various community organizations to get to know the station and provide first-hand information on their programs and objectives.
4. Keeps informed of trends, events and developments within the industry through the various media.
5. Attends industry conferences, conventions, etc.
6. Maintains a continuing dialogue with community and civic leaders to determine community problems.

D. Development of a staff of competent personnel to maintain management continuity.

1. Selects or ensures adequate selection of station personnel.
2. Evaluates and recommends staff personnel for salary increases and advancement.
3. Provides for optimum utilization and development of station personnel.
4. Counsels frequently with staff to keep them informed of all happenings relevant to station operations and policies.

The Administrative Structure

A manager's duties are reflected in the administrative structure, which consists of both his managerial colleagues and the clusters of personnel for whom he is responsible to the company. All of these managers and "managees," in their directives and their actualizing, are constitutive of the process which is what the organization is all about in its macro-intentionality. Therefore, process is more important than structure; process gets the job done and achieves the goals of the enterprise, especially in such a flexible and people-oriented business as broadcasting. But structure is important to stabilize the organization and to clarify efficient relationships among personnel with various responsibilities for that process.[74]

The management structure of relationships can be schematically portrayed by organization charts, as long as two points are kept in mind: (a) probably no two broadcast companies will operate effectively with precisely the same organizational structure, and (b) within any single company's organizational relationships there must be room for flexibility in order to emphasize efficient process carried out by human beings under conditions that are not static.[75] On the following pages are samples of organization charts for small and large radio and television stations in markets of different populations; they demonstrate

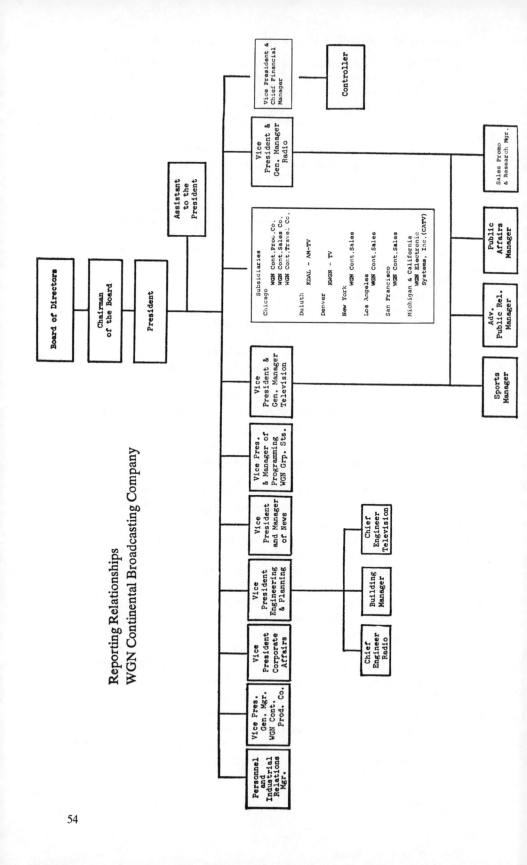

Reporting Relationships
WGN Continental Broadcasting Company

Board of Directors

Chairman
of the Board

President

Assistant
to the
President

Vice President &
Chief Financial
Manager

Controller

Vice
President &
Gen. Manager
Radio

Subsidiaries

Chicago   WGN Cont.Prod.Co.
           WGN Cont.Sales Co.
           WGN Cont.Travel Co.

Duluth   KDAL - AM-TV

Denver   KWGN - TV

New York   WGN Cont.Sales

Los Angeles WGN Cont.Sales

San Francisco WGN Cont.Sales

Michigan & California
           WGN Electronic
           Systems, Inc.(CATV)

Sales Promo
& Research Mgr.

Public
Affairs
Manager

Adv.
Public Rel.
Manager

Sports
Manager

Vice
President &
Gen. Manager
Television

Vice Pres.
& Manager of
Programming
WGN Grp. Sts.

Vice
President
and Manager
of News

Vice
President
Engineering
& Planning

Chief
Engineer
Television

Building
Manager

Chief
Engineer
Radio

Vice
President
Corporate
Affairs

Vice Pres.
Gen. Mgr.
WGN Cont.
Prod. Co.

Personnel
and
Industrial
Relations
Mgr.

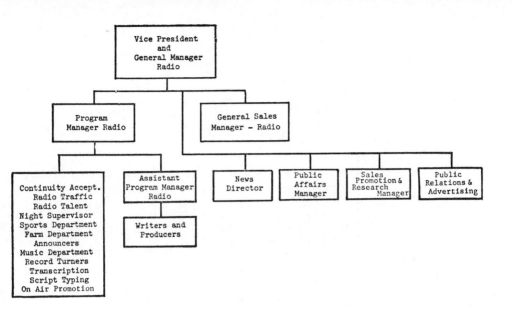

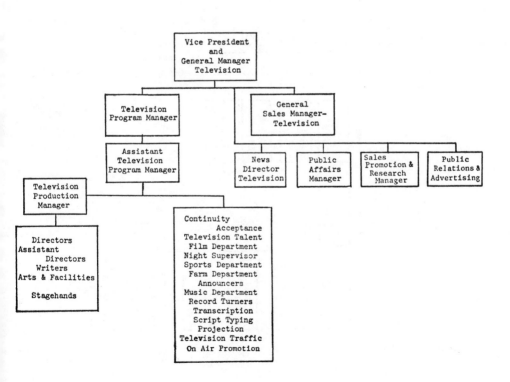

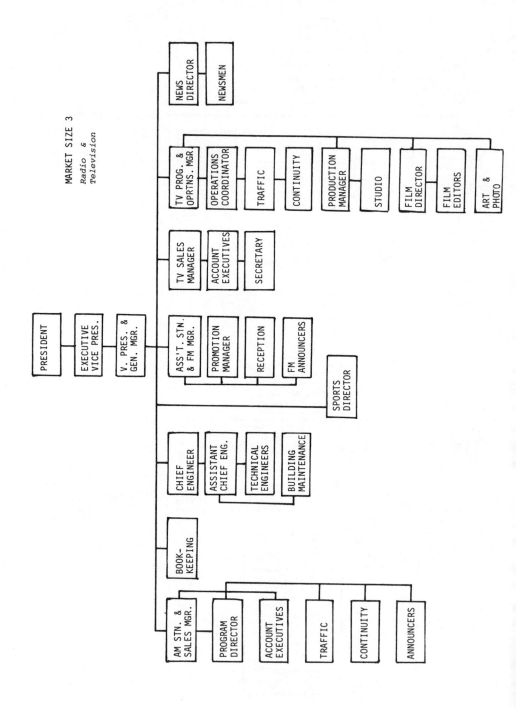

MARKET SIZE 3
Radio &
Television

56

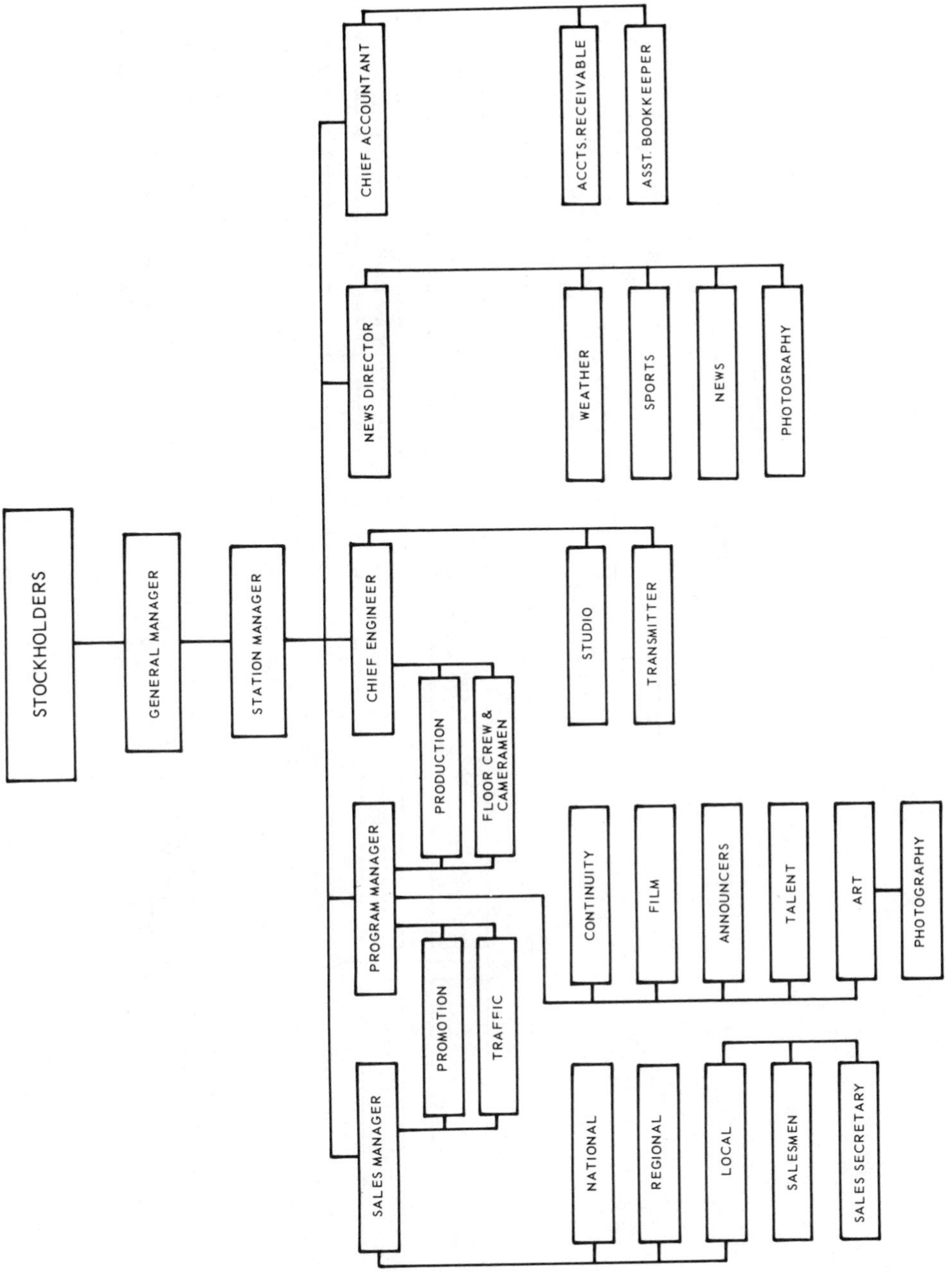
STOCKHOLDERS
GENERAL MANAGER
STATION MANAGER
SALES MANAGER
NATIONAL
REGIONAL
LOCAL
SALESMEN
SALES SECRETARY
PROMOTION
TRAFFIC
PROGRAM MANAGER
CONTINUITY
FILM
ANNOUNCERS
TALENT
ART
PHOTOGRAPHY
PRODUCTION
FLOOR CREW & CAMERAMEN
CHIEF ENGINEER
STUDIO
TRANSMITTER
NEWS DIRECTOR
WEATHER
SPORTS
NEWS
PHOTOGRAPHY
CHIEF ACCOUNTANT
ACCTS. RECEIVABLE
ASST. BOOKKEEPER

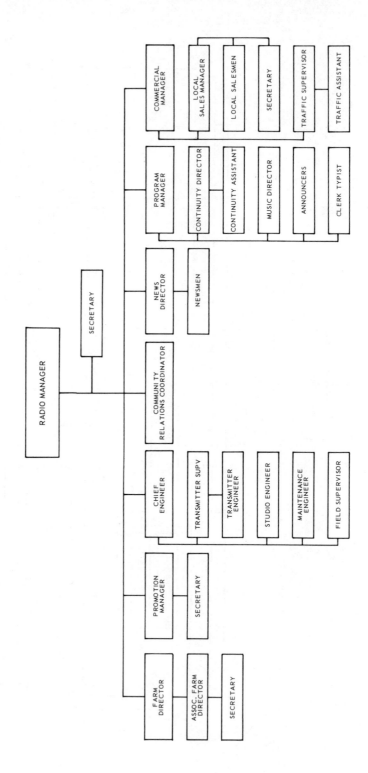

GENERAL MANAGER

- SECRETARY
- RECEPTIONIST

SALES MANAGER
- SALESMEN
- SALES PROMOTION
- TRAFFIC CONTINUITY

ACCOUNTING

CHIEF ENGINEER
- ENGINEERS
- MAINTENANCE DEPARTMENT

PROGRAM DIRECTOR
- ANNOUNCERS
- MUSIC LIBRARIAN
- STAFF TALENT
- TRAFFIC
  - CONTINUITY

NEWS DIRECTOR
- NEWS REPORTERS

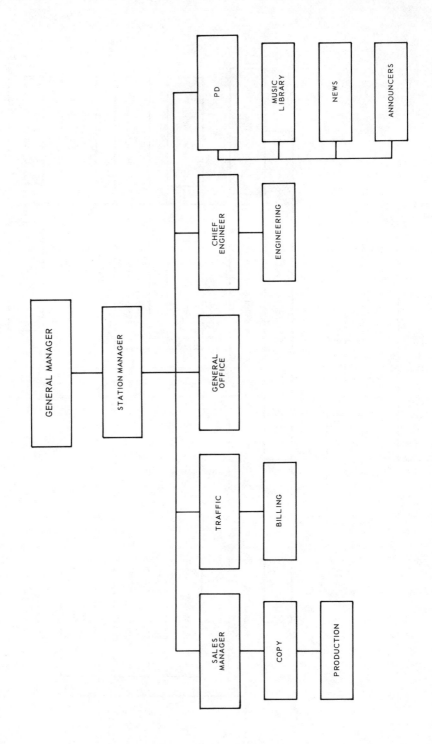

that beyond the very basic design of departmental and personnel relationships, each station must develop its own line and staff structures.[76]

The basic administrative arrangement in broadcasting consists of three executives who are in charge of engineering, programming, and sales; they report directly to the station manager.[77]

In some small radio stations, the manager doubles as sales manager or as program manager or both; in a few cases, he is the station's chief engineer. He may also take a regular shift as an announcer and he may write some of the commercial copy. The total staff of some small radio stations may be no more than five or six people. Such stations are ideal training grounds for the young person who is starting a career in management, for he is forced by the circumstances to become engaged directly in all aspects of station operation.

The opposite extreme of size is represented by a radio and a television station which are under joint ownership and are located in a metropolitan market. In such operations, it is not unusual to find a *general* manager of both stations in addition to a station manager for radio and a station manager for television. In stations with large numbers of personnel, assistant managers may be added for radio and for television.

Many group-owned stations, in addition to their local administrative structures, have central headquarters offices. Common operating policies for all of the stations owned by the company may be framed in the central office, or the company may prefer a more flexible arrangement whereby each station may decide its own procedures. Usually, the central office coordinates financial data from the various stations and often adopts personnel standards and practices that the stations follow. Often, it represents all owned stations which may be involved in union negotiations. In a few cases, the central office maintains a program and production unit which plans and even produces programming for all of the stations.

The sizes of broadcast station staffs reflect the size of the markets which those stations serve. The National Association of Broadcasters surveyed the numbers of persons employed by TV and radio stations in 1974.[78] The average television staffs by market size were:

TV AVG. NO. EMPLOYEES		ARB Marketsize
Full-time	*Part-time*	*Ranking*
90	8	1–10
103	7	11–25
88	6	26–50
70	3	51–75
55	5	76–100
42	5	101–125
37	6	126–150
30	4	150+
(60)	(5)	(Nationwide Avg.)

Obviously, the network-owned stations might employ staffs of 125 or more, but the UHF independents in the same markets lower the average with their small staffs. Similarly, in the nation's markets are both large and small radio stations; the largest stations in major markets might have staffs of 50 while low-power stations in the same cities might employ only a dozen people. The *average* radio staffs by market size in 1974 were:

RADIO AVG. NO. EMPLOYEES		Marketsize by
Full-time	*Part-time*	*Population*
17	4	Over 2.5 million
13	3	1–2.5 million
17	3	500,000–1 million
13	4	250,000–500,000
12	3	100,000–250,000
12	3	50,000–100,000
11	3	25,000–50,000
9	3	10,000–25,000
6	3	Less than 10,000
(10)	(3)	(Nationwide Avg.)

Another graphic way to conceptualize the size and variety of staffs necessary for an operational broadcast station is to study representative building floorplans that depict the working areas for station personnel. (Non-broadcasters tend to assume that even a major television station building consists mostly of studio space; but a local TV station is primarily a business and only secondarily a production site—with about one-tenth of its space devoted to studios and the rest devoted to offices and support areas in the building.) Sample floorplans follow.[79]

The organization charts and the floorplans suggest the size and composition of station staffs for which management is responsible in the administrative structure. An apt caution by McLarney and Berliner might be paraphrased: whenever the number of employees in an organization is increasing (or the size and complexity of physical plant is growing) at a faster rate than business, then top management should suspect that some of these people and facilities are there just to keep the "system" going and that the "system" and mere structure are becoming more important than the business.[80]

CHARACTERISTICS OF MANAGERS

The detailed analysis of staff personnel which constitutes Chapter 3 can be here introduced by a brief look at the characteristics of broadcast managers. Several surveys over the past decade indicate that the management of radio or television station requires certain characteristics differing from those usually considered typical of managers of other business enterprises.

At KRON-TV (San Francisco) the architect and station engineers worked out floorplans after considering countless alternatives. Some of the features of those plans (reproduced in the accompanying diagrams) were described in RCA's *Broadcast News:*

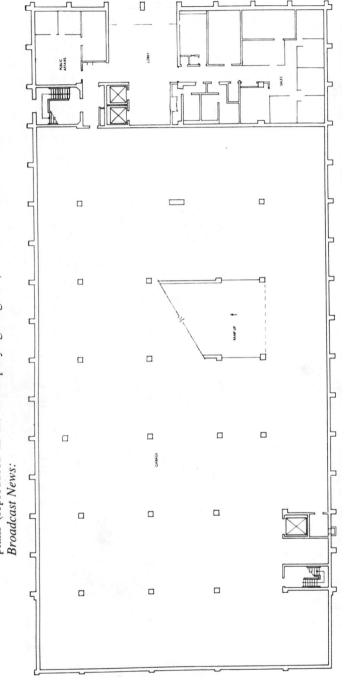

FIRST FLOOR The main entrance—into an impressive two-story lobby area—is at the front of the first floor (street level on Van Ness Street). The Sales Department is located in a group of offices just to the left of the lobby—the Public Affairs office at the right. These are the two groups having the most local business contacts and hence are logically placed in the most accessible location. Together with the elevators these offices occupy about one-fourth of the first-floor area. The garage—down a ramp from an entrance halfway back on the alleyway—occupies the other three-fourths of the floor. Space is provided for 48 cars.

63

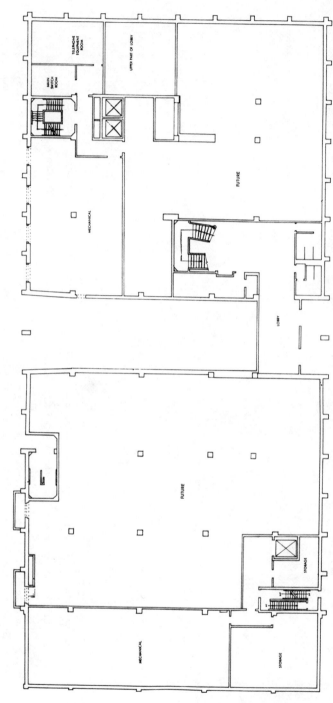

SECOND FLOOR The entrance lobby for public attending studio shows is halfway back along the building on O'Farrell Street. From this public lobby stairs lead to the third-floor studio lobby—and to the studio seating area. This arrangement keeps the public away from business operations (and VIP's). Also on this floor are business operations, a large, consolidated "library" and file room, and space for telephone and other equipment. These take about one-fourth of the floor space. The remainder is for future expansion.

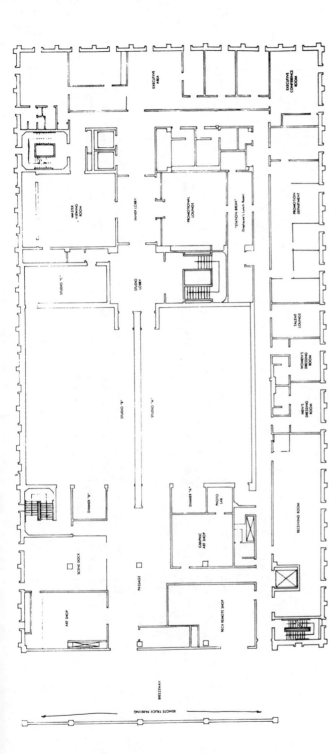

THIRD FLOOR   This is the executive and studio floor. At the front of the building are the executive offices (President at the right front, General Manager next), the program department and an executive conference room. Note that a private passageway isolates VIP traffic from other station business. Off the center lobby—reached by elevator from the main entrance on the first floor, or stairs from the public entrance on the second floor, are the following: (a) a small theater (viewing room) for the public, (b) a conference "viewing room" for station promotional business, (c) entrances to the two large (45 feet by 60 feet) studios and (d) the small 18 by 31 studio (announcements, VIP's, etc.). Along the left side of the building (and isolating the studios from the street noise) is a corridor off of which are the promotion department offices, the talent lounges and dressing rooms, and the "receiving" department. At the rear of the big studios is the art shop and the art storage area. At the very back is an area into which trucks can be driven from the street level (alley entrance). There is a large elevator which could be used to move props to a (future) second-floor storage area. Note that "receiving" is directly adjacent to this truck drive-in area. Also that "talent" and "prop" areas have their own corridors to separate them from the public at the front of the building.

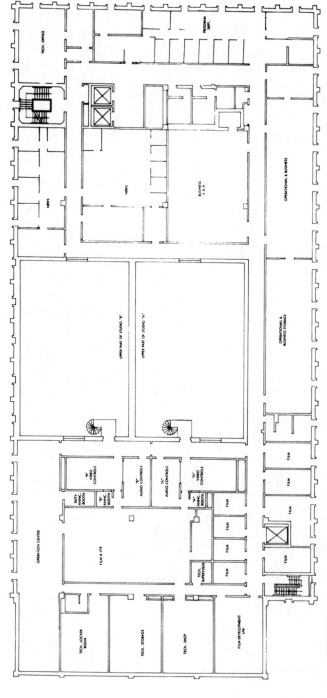

FOURTH FLOOR Is the "operating" floor. Here are the business, programming, news, documentary, operations and engineering areas. At the left of the studios is a corridor off of which open news, film and tape editing rooms; tape and film storage. Programming offices are in front—also engineering offices. In the center there is an electronic data processing room. The "technical block" is directly behind the studios but separated by a corridor.

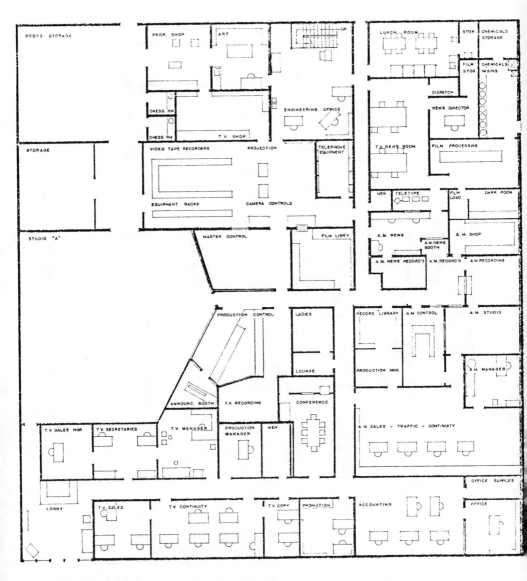

KOB AM-FM-TV, Albuquerque, N. Mex.

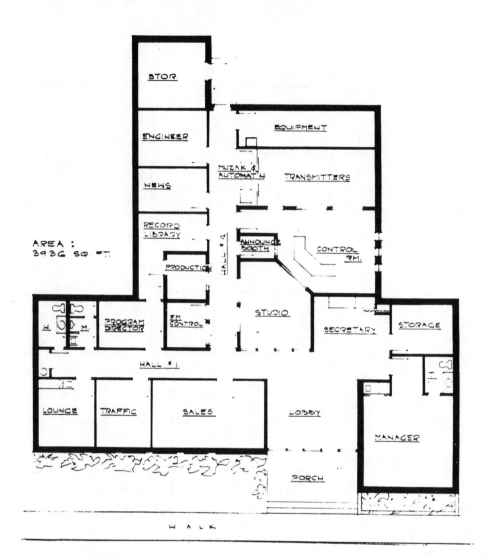

KDMS/KRIL, Eldorado, Ark.

Multipurpose station includes AM, FM and Muzak services in well laid out plant. Separate heating and cooling systems operate for control and studio areas when rest of station is closed at night. Transmitter heat is used for general building heating in the winter, needing no extra heating until the mercury dips below 20°. Equipment includes low-power standby AM xmtr.

Source:
"Idea Portfolio: Station Floor Plans that Work," *BM/E*, August 1968, p. 36.

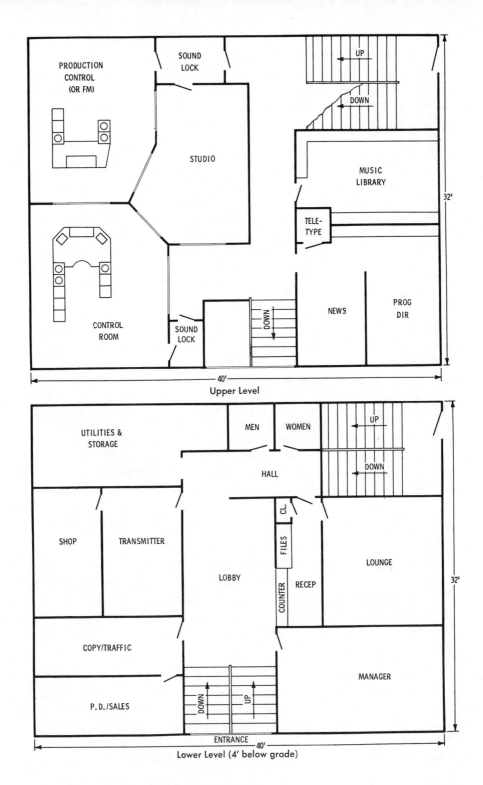

PRODUCTION
CONTROL
(OR FM)

SOUND
LOCK

UP

DOWN

STUDIO

MUSIC
LIBRARY

TELE-
TYPE

32'

CONTROL
ROOM

SOUND
LOCK

DOWN

NEWS

PROG
DIR

40'

Upper Level

UTILITIES &
STORAGE

MEN

WOMEN

UP

HALL

DOWN

SHOP

TRANSMITTER

CL.

FILES

LOUNGE

LOBBY

COUNTER

RECEP

32'

COPY/TRAFFIC

MANAGER

P. D. /SALES

DOWN

UP

ENTRANCE

40'

Lower Level (4' below grade)

A joint research project of the Association for Professional Broadcast Education (renamed the Broadcast Education Association since 1973) and the National Association of Broadcasters collected information in 1962 from 201 radio station managers and 167 television station managers.[81] Those data are corroborated, supplemented, and updated in subsequent surveys.[82]

The studies found that broadcast managers, with an average age in the early forties, are generally younger than other American business managers. The APBE-NAB study reported the average age of television managers as 44 and of radio managers as 41; a decade later 457 managers averaged 44.2 years, but 112 radio managers in small market averaged 42 years (while newspaper editors in those same small markets averaged 47 years). The APBE-NAB study reported many cases of young men in their early thirties who assumed the responsibilities of radio management in small-market stations, but few such examples in television where larger markets and greater financial investments were involved. Many current television managers were previously managers of radio stations.

The management studies disclosed that few managers of broadcast properties came to the positions from fields other than broadcasting. Most managers were employed in another position by the station which they now managed, usually radio or television sales—far in excess of the percentage who follow that route to executive status in business generally. Many broadcast managers came from backgrounds in programming and a few from station engineering; almost half of the respondents to the Gallagher survey of radio managers reported that their first broadcast jobs were in announcing, one-third in time-sales, and one-tenth in engineering.

Winick found that most television station managers came from small-town backgrounds (under 100,000 population)—as contrasted with the city backgrounds of most business leaders. He also found military service in the experience of most TV station managers, as did Bohn and Clark of most radio station managers. Winick's study found that most of the television station managers made their decisions to enter the field of broadcasting while they were enrolled in a college or university.

Those several studies through the decade reflected the role of higher education for a managerial position in broadcasting. Winick discovered that three-fourths of all television managers had been to college and one-sixth had taken postgraduate study. The APBE-NAB study had found that about half of the managers of radio and TV stations were college graduates. Bohn and Clark found that 85 per cent of small-market radio managers had attended or graduated from college.[83]

Broadcast respondents to the APBE-NAB study, published in 1962, reported that they majored in the areas of liberal arts (40%), business administration (24%), engineering (10%), radio-TV (8%), and journalism (7.5%), among others. The Bohn and Clark study reported a decade later that small-market radio managers predominately majored in business-related areas (20%), with 6 per cent majoring in journalism and 2 per cent in radio-televison.

The kind of experience which all broadcast respondents to the APBE-NAB study recommended most often for people interested in broadcasting management careers was sales or promotion work. The kind of education which the managers recommended as most valuable for executive careers in broadcasting was training in business, including the study of sales, marketing, and accounting.

It is interesting to note that, in another section of the same APBE-NAB study which dealt with responses from employees other than managers in broadcasting, the most highly recommended type of education was a professional curriculum in broadcasting. Significant in this response is the fact that the average age of the employees is somewhat younger than managers' and more of them were able to study broadcasting in the colleges and universities. The managerial group, for the most part, did not find such courses available at the time they attended college; hence, the probable tendency not to equate the value of such training for careers in broadcasting.[84]

The study by Winick in 1965 found the income of television managers "competitive with that of executives at a similar level of responsibility in other industries." Bohn and Clark's data (gathered in 1968 but reported in 1972) reported for small-market radio managers a general salary range of $10,000 to $15,000 (compared with a peak of less than $10,000 for newspaper editors in the same-sized markets). The Gallagher survey reported that almost half of 467 radio station managers earned between $10,000 and $20,000 in 1970; another quarter earned between $20,000 and $30,000; about one out of ten (12.9%) earned less than $10,000, and a smaller number (8.4%) earned between $30,000 and $40,000 a year.[85]

Among small-market radio stations, more than two-thirds of the managers participated in ownership, with 29 per cent owning more than half of their company. Among all sizes of radio stations surveyed by Gallagher, one-third of the managers reported that they were principal owners of their stations.

Predictably, all surveys reported heavy involvement of station managers with local community activities and organizations, including holding public office.

It might be appropriate to conclude this analysis of the duties and characteristics of the broadcast station manager with the sobering yet obliquely encouraging results of Louis Harris surveys in 1972 and 1973 about the public's level of confidence in people running various private and public institutions.[86] In those two years respondents selected the highest rating of "a great deal of confidence" (rather than "some confidence" or "hardly any confidence") for leaders in various major sectors of society (see tabulation on next page). While only leadership in medicine received a vote of "great confidence" from almost half of the survey respondents, television leadership was judged clustered with related and unrelated public sectors. But a single year later, the same Harris public-opinion survey reported greatly increased confidence in broadcast media (specifically television news). This first opinion poll ever commissioned by the U.S. Congress (the Senate Subcommittee on Interstate and Foreign Af-

	1972	*1973*
Medicine	48%	58%
Military	34	39
Higher Education	32	43
Organized Religion	29	35
U.S. Supreme Court	27	32
Federal Executive Branch	27	19
Major Companies	26	28
U.S. Senate	21	29
Press	18	30
Television News	17	41

fairs) surveyed 1,596 Americans in September, 1973, who expressed greater confidence in every category offered the previous year except for the executive branch of Federal government (down from 27% to 19% by late 1973). The greatest gains in public confidence over a seven-year period of three Harris polls (1966, 1972 and 1973) were by television news, which rated 25, 17 and 41 per cent respectively, and by the press, which rated 29, 18 and 30 per cent. Yet, both media categories received lesser votes of confidence from state and local leaders in 1973 than they did from the general public; only 17 per cent claimed a great deal of confidence in leaders in television news, and 19 per cent expressed confidence in press leadership.

Broadcast managers might reflect on this continuing challenge to them as they exercise leadership within their stations and among the people of their local and national communities.

NOTES

Chapter 2

1. Robert Wangermee, "Towards Modern Management in Broadcasting," *EBU Review: Programmes, Administration, Law,* XXIII:6 (Nov. 1972), pp. 30–38. See his summation in *Towards Modern Management in Radio & Television: International Colloquy,* Brussels, May 1972 (Brussels: European Broadcasting Union, [1974]), pp. 459–471.

2. William J. McLarney and William M. Berliner, *Management Training: Cases and Principles,* 5th ed. (Homewood, Ill.: Richard D. Irwin, Inc., 1970). In outlining principles of effective management that apply to broadcasting, we will draw heavily on McLarney and Berliner's *Management Training: Cases and Principles;* it is a synthesis of good sense and research findings drawn from a wide range of reliable sources in the field of scientific management.

3. Peter Drucker, *The Practice of Management* (N.Y.: Harper & Row, 1954), p. 350. See also: Peter F. Drucker, *Management: Tasks, Responsibilities, Practices* (N.Y.: Harper & Row, 1973, 1974).

3a. McLarney and Berliner, p. 5.

4. Henri Fayol, *General and Industrial Management,* trans. Constance Storrs (New York: Pitman Publishing, 1949); McLarney and Berliner, pp. 13–14, cite the five-fold division of management activities by Fayol: planning, organizing, directing, coordinating, and controlling. See J. Thomas Cannon, *Business Strategy and Policy* (N.Y.: Harcourt, Brace and World, Inc., 1968), p. 347, who notes that twentieth century management began with Fayol who first developed and practiced management principles from the perspective of the chief executive.

5. Listed by Howard F. Merrill, *Classics in Management* (N.Y.: American Management Assoc., 1960), pp. 217–223.

6. Cf. W. Warren Haynes and Joseph L. Massie, *Management: Analysis, Concepts, and Cases* (Englewood Cliffs, N.J.: Prentice-Hall Inc., 1961), p. 9.

7. See Douglas McGregor, *The Human Side of Enterprise* (N.Y.: McGraw-Hill, 1960), pp. 216–221.

8. J. Leonard Reinsch and E. I. Ellis, *Radio Station Management*, 2nd rev. ed., (N.Y.: Harper & Row, 1960), p. 9; cf. Gene F. Seehafer and Jack W. Laemmar, *Successful Television and Radio Advertising* (N.Y.: McGraw-Hill, 1959), p. 542.

9. See Chapter 3, on "The Management of Personnel."

10. Theo Haimann, *Professional Management* (Boston: Houghton Mifflin, 1962).

11. Alan C. Filley and Robert J. House, *Managerial Process and Organizational Behavior* (Glenview, Ill.: Scott, Foresman & Co., 1969); pp. 391 ff. provide extended treatment of theories of leadership.

12. McGregor, p. 182. Italics in the original.

13. McLarney and Berliner, pp. 526–7.

14. See McLarney and Berliner, p. 526, for a listing of seven levels of leadership patterns, based on a study by Tannenbaum and Schmidt. McLarney and Berliner note: "It is important that the manager be honest in letting the group know how much authority he is keeping for himself and how much he is giving to the subordinates. If the boss intends to make the decision himself, he should not try to fool the subordinates into thinking it was their idea in the first place. Using participation as a technique to manipulate employees is a shortsighted policy that is apt to backfire."

15. See Elizabeth Marting and Dorothy MacDonald (eds.), *Management and Its People* (New York: American Management Association, 1965), pp. 236–7.

16. See Burleigh Gardner, *Human Relations in Industry*, (Homewood, Ill.: Richard D. Irwin Inc., 1955), p. 379.

17. William B. Eddy, *Behavioral Science and the Manager's Role*, (NTL Institute for Applied Behavioral Science, 1969), p. 114.

18. See Harold Koontz and Cyril O'Donnell, *Principles of Management: An Analysis of Managerial Functions*, 4th ed., (New York: McGraw-Hill, 1968), p. 615.

19. Henry L. Sisk, *Principles of Management* (New York: South-Western Publishing, 1969), p. 393.

20. Haimann, p. 446.

21. Sisk, p. 404.

22. David Ewing, *The Managerial Mind* (London: Collier-MacMillan, 1964), p. 31.

23. Ewing, p. 156.

24. Robert Dubin, *Human Relations in Administration* (New York: Prentice-Hall, 1951), p. 101.

25. McLarney and Berliner, p. 12.

26. See Elizabeth Marting and Dorothy MacDonald (eds.), *Management and its People* (New York: American Management Assoc., 1965), pp. 236–237.

27. Cf. Henry Clay Smith, *Psychology of Industrial Behavior* (New York: McGraw-Hill, 1955), pp. 420–422.

Efficiency in work correlates with level of motivation: "When motivation is low, fatigue effects become apparent very early, but, when motivation is high, the evidence of fatigue may not be apparent until considerable physical exhaustion is manifest": Norman Maier, *Creative Management* (New York: John Wiley & Sons, 1962), pp. 302–303. In terms of expenditure of energy, the level or amount of motivation generated by work (and by management's support) will equal the amount of energy available for that work.

28. Cf. Reinsch and Ellis, pp. 247–252; and see Chapter 3 below on personnel.

29. McLarney and Berliner, pp. 519–520.

29a. Laurence J. Peter, *The Peter Principle* (New York: William Morrow, 1969; Bantam ed., 1970).

30. McLarney and Berliner, pp. 69, 74, 82, 103–105.

31. McGregor, p. 172. Cf. McLarney and Berliner, p. 82: "There should be more emphasis on the purpose or *why* of routines, more dependence upon people and less upon the system. The trend in better management today is to build meaning into jobs—to design jobs in such a way as to promote individual responsibility. If a man feels that responsibility rests upon him rather than upon a system, he will exercise initiative and judgment. But if he feels that he has to buck the routine in order to protect the company's interests, he may choose to follow routine. As a result he will be of less value to the company and he will have less satisfaction in his job. Procedures can't operate without people, and the performance of people hinges upon their knowledge, ability, and attitude, the design of their jobs, and the quality of the supervision."

32. Quoted by Filley and House, p. 239.

33. Cf. Norman Maier, *Creative Management* (New York: John Wiley & Sons, 1962), pp. 41–42.

34. Milton L. Blum, *Industrial Psychology and its Social Foundations* (New York: Harper and Brothers, 1949), p. 306.

35. Cf. Maier, *Creative Management,* pp. 43–64; also Harold Leavitt, *Managerial Psychology* (Chicago: Univ. of Chicago Press, 1964), pp. 249–250.

36. See Marting and MacDonald, p. 246.

37. Sisk, pp. 440–441; cf. Ewing, p. 36.

38. William B. Eddy, *Behavioral Science and the Manager's Role* (NTL Institute for Applied Behavioral Science, 1969), p. 75.

39. Charles E. Winick, "The Television Station Manager," *Advanced Management Journal,* XXXI:1 (Jan. 1966), pp. 53–60. Winick's survey reported the average TV station manager as "actively involved" with more than 40 community social and welfare groups; one manager was cited as serving on the board of no fewer than 17 different civic organizations. Cf. "The Gallagher Report," Dec. 7, 1971 (second section), pp. 3–4, where job description of radio station managers included a list of six kinds of community activity "to develop ways to effectively service community needs through radio broadcasting"—including memberships, guest speeches, conducting seminars and meetings, attending conferences, and maintaining continuing dialogue with community and civic leaders.

40. "The Gallagher Report," Dec. 7, 1971 (second section), p. 2, listed the following responses:

WHICH OF THE FOLLOWING PUBLICATIONS DO YOU READ?

	Regularly	Occasionally	Never
Advertising Age	7.1%	31.4%	61.5%
Broadcasting	88.7	10.2	1.1
Business Week	20.1	38.7	41.2
Dun's Review & Modern Industry	1.1	5.3	93.6
Forbes	4.6	13.5	81.9
Fortune	9.1	21.7	69.2
Harvard Business Review	1.3	7.7	91.0
Journal of Commerce	0.9	4.4	94.7
Media Decisions	5.1	15.3	79.6
Marketing/Communications	6.9	19.7	73.4
Nation's Business	11.5	30.8	57.7
Sales Management	11.1	23.7	65.2
Television/Radio Age	11.5	24.1	64.4
Variety	8.4	22.8	68.8
Wall Street Journal	31.4	34.3	34.3

41. S. J. Paul, "Publisher's Letter," *Television/Radio Age,* September 3, 1973; p. 10. Bernard Gallagher, in his candid and sometimes unflattering "The Gallagher Report," noted in his February 23, 1972, issue that television needed more imaginative executives who did not rely on network formulae for "prime-time access" programming but who responded to each market's dif-

ferent needs with local news and community shows; who increased production departments in order to serve local advertisers better, to expand into syndication (in spite of Westinghouse's long-term marginal efforts), and to prepare for the time when stations might become local programming centers for cable TV. Five months later (issue of July 31, 1972), he lamented the state of newspaper editorial management by headlining an item "Dry Rot Sets in at New York *Times*"; Gallagher criticized that print medium's management for letting a large number of young reporters use the newspaper as a ladder rung to better jobs elsewhere, while a smaller group of veteran *Times*men comfortably enjoyed the status quo, and a third group meanwhile was a "small power clique concerned more with internal politics than with editorial product." That caution, however justified or not in appraising the *Times*' staff, might be kept in mind by major broadcast companies where, according to *Television/Radio Age* publisher Paul, "with station management—many of the stalwarts in the business, the familiar names and faces and leaders of the past 20 years are nearing retirement age. In some cases, there is a second or even a third generation to take over. In a few instances, an orderly transition has been planned."

42. Among overlooked areas of budgeting is the matter of efficient communication and bookkeeping. The cost of paperwork alone contributes to office expenses and clerical salaries. Day-Timers, Inc. cites studies documenting how paperwork chokes business efficiency. A one-page, 250-word business letter dictated to a secretary increased 67 per cent from 1960 ($1.83) to 1972 ($3.05). A middle-manager earning $250 a week averages seven minutes dictating a letter, or about 72 cents, while higher-paid managers and executives invest up to $25 or more per letter dictated. An invoice is estimated to cost from $10 to $15, a purchase order $10, and a multi-part sales order with production and shipping papers costs $20. More significantly, for every dollar spent on a paper form, approximately $25 must be spent on clerical and administrative costs! The volume of paperwork is estimated to double by early 1980s. Further, people can waste up to 20 or 30 per cent of their time merely looking for filed information—not analyzing or using it, just trying to find it. Management engineers estimate the expense of a misfiled item as $61.23. Extra paperwork that demands hiring of an extra clerk at only $80 a week salary forces the company to do $80,000 additional business at 5 per cent profit to pay that salary. (Sources cited: National Records Management Council, Stanford Research Institute, Dartnell Corporation of Chicago, consultant Robert A. Shiff.) "The Gallagher Report" (July 24, 1972) estimates paperwork for $1 million of ad billings costs an agency $30,000 (compared with less than $10,000 a decade earlier). Management must be alert to these cumulative costs from the administrative paperwork involved in broadcasting, and must attempt to cut those costs by greater efficiency in communicating.

43. See William J. McLarney and William M. Berliner, *Management Training: Cases and Principles,* 5th ed. (Homewood, Ill.: Richard D. Irwin, Inc., 1970). pp. 20–26, and Alan C. Filley and Robert J. House, *Managerial Process and Organizational Behavior* (Glenview, Ill.: Scott, Foresman & Co., 1969); pp. 101–130 for detailed theoretical and practical analysis of the process of decision making by management.

44. Rosalind Loring and Theodora Wells, *Breakthrough: Women into Management* (N.Y.: Van Nostrand Reinhold Co., 1972), p. 61.

45. Cf. Kyle Haselden, *Morality and the Mass Media* (Nashville, Tenn.: Broadman Press, 1968), Chapter 10, esp. p. 185: "Authentic morality has its focus in people, its objective in the transforming of people into persons, its habitat in freedom, its criterion and energy in love, and its source in God."

46. Haselden, p. 138.

47. William F. Lynch, S.J., *The Image Industries* (New York: Sheed and Ward, 1959), p. 6.

48. Lynch, p. 8.

49. William L. Rivers and Wilbur Schramm, *Responsibility in Mass Communication,* rev. ed. (N.Y.: Harper & Row, 1969), Chapter 7, pp. 190–233.

50. Lynch, p. 20.

51. Cf. Lynch, pp. 68–69: "In all the works of the human imagination, but especially in the mass media, the two great enemies of freedom are what I shall call fixation and seduction."

52. Lynch, pp. 113, 145.

53. Lynch, p. 150. That this pertains not only to national television *production* centers but also to small-market radio stations is attested to by Robert H. Coddington, *Modern Radio Broadcasting: Management & Operation in Small-to-Medium Markets* (Blue Ridge Summit, Pa.: Tab Books, 1969) pp. 10–14.

54. Most Rev. John L. May, Bishop of Mobile, Ala., chairman of Communications Committee, U.S. Catholic Conference, "Commentary on the Pastoral Instruction on Social Communication," June 3, 1971; *Communications: A Pastoral Instruction on the Media, Public Opinion, and Human Progress* (Washington, D.C.: U.S. Catholic Conference, 1971) p. ix. This title appeared on the booklet cover, in which was reprinted the document cited below by the Pontifical Commission for the Media of Social Communications.

55. Cf. Rivers and Schramm, p. 240.

56. Sydney W. Head, *Broadcasting in America* (Boston: Houghton Mifflin, 1972), p. 471.

57. Rivers and Schramm, pp. 241, 242; cf. further comments, pp. 240–248.

58. Head, p. 472. Cf. McLarney and Berliner, pp. 672–676, 682–684.

Although broadcast stations, especially in radio, are usually small business, many stations are parts of larger companies. It is possibly illuminating to apply to broadcast media management some of the data and appraisals available from larger corporate enterprises, since broadcasting does share to a great extent in American business' impact on the general social scene.

Joseph C. Wilson, president of Xerox Corporation, has held firmly that the corporation is an integral part of society and has concomitant social responsibilities. He has noted that "inevitably the corporation is involved in economic, social, and political dynamics whether it wills it or not." (L. L. L. Golden, "Public Relations: the Why of Xerox," *Saturday Review,* Aug. 14, 1971; p. 53). He claimed that "it seems beyond belief that anyone could contest the view that the businessman, who wields a vast amount of economic, and therefore social power, must expand his vision beyond the limits of making maximum profit, the traditional definition of his primary function, to encompass many of society's harassing problems that wash the edges of his island." Wilson and Xerox have been notable sponsors of major television dramas and documentaries on commercial networks and of award-winning cultural/educational series through the Public Broadcasting Service.

Perhaps there has been a tendency for profit cycles to lead to dehumanization, so that a business system whose original function was to serve society by helping the people has reversed priorities and has made people a function of the system; John Sack in *The Man-Eating Machine* (N.Y.: Farrar, Straus, & Giroux, 1973) criticizes business administration which rises beyond technology to a level of technocracy.

Certainly younger people perceive the role of business in a less than flattering light. A nationwide sample of teenagers by the U.S. Chamber of Commerce (reported in the editorial section of the Cleveland *Plain Dealer,* Section B, p. 1; Mon. Sept. 4, 1972) reported that 61 per cent did not believe in making a profit, and 82 per cent judged that competition was unnecessary! Two-thirds of those teenagers judged that the government should own banks, railroads and steel companies; and the same proportion believed that jobs should be provided by government. Those are chilling appraisals of the role of free enterprise in the competitive business world.

Further illustrating the discrepancy between what younger people think of business and what businessmen themselves think, are comparable data from a national study and from samplings of college students in the midwest and far west: 97 students in three classes at the University of Detroit in 1968 and 1969, responded similarly to 85 students in three courses at the University of Southern California (Los Angeles) in 1972 and 1973. Those 182 college students at private universities were given a list of phrases from which they could choose "what ethical means" for them, and also *what they would presume "ethical" means for businessmen.* A total of 45 students judged that, for businessmen, "ethical" would mean "customary behavior in society"; 42 said businessmen would consider ethical whatever was "about the same as 'legal' "; and 33 presumed that businessmen's ethical norm would be "what does the most good for the most people." As for their own personal choices about the meaning of "ethical," 72 students listed "what does the most good for the most people"; 63 responded "what my feelings tell me is right"; only 7 students listed "customary behavior in society," and only 1 student put "about the same as 'legal'." But top-level businessmen who were surveyed by a management and business administration scholar from

Harvard reported in the late 1960s that "what my feelings tell me is right" determines what is "ethical" for half of those executives (50), while one-quarter (25) judged as ethical what was "in accord with my religious beliefs" and one-fifth (18) what "conforms to the 'Golden Rule'." Not a single executive used as a criterion of ethics what was "about the same as legal" and only 3 responded "customary behavior in society"—yet college students sampled through half a decade presumed those two categories to be the major criteria for businessmen's ethics today! These discrepant judgments suggest that college students' perceptions of business criteria for integrity are far off the mark, whereas their own judgments about what constitutes ethical norms are somewhat more similar to the business executives' actual judgments about themselves. (The surveyed businessmen also reflected greater ethical concern over personnel problems than about questions directly pertaining to the profit-making aspects of business.)

Comparative tabulations from the original study (Raymond Baumhart, S.J., *An Honest Profit* (N.Y.: Holt, Rinehart & Winston: 1968)—cited in "Book Reviews," *America*, Sept. 14, 1968, p. 190) and from the seven college class surveys of predominantly broadcast majors follow:

Businessmen's actual choices in survey		List of choices about what "ethical" means (listed choice by U.S. businessmen)	Students' personal choices		Students' presumption of what businessmen would choose	
1st	2nd		1st	2nd	1st	2nd
50	8	What my feelings tell me is right	63	31	12	12
25	14	In accord with my religious beliefs	4	4	1	0
18	15	Conforms to the "Golden Rule"	13	13	3	7
3	7	What does the most good for the most people	72	44	33	36
3	6	Customary behavior in society	7	26	45	45
1	1	Corresponds to my self-interest	1	1	10	9
0	1	About the same as legal	1	14	42	39
0	1	Contributes most to personal liberty	18	20	0	4
0	1	What I want in that particular situation	2	6	12	7

59. Pontifical Commission for the Means of Social Communication, "Pastoral Instruction for the Application of the Decree of the Second Vatican Ecumenical Council on the Means of Social Communication" (Washington, D.C.: U. S. Catholic Conference, 1971), pp. 1, 3–4.

60. Rivers and Schramm, p. 15.

61. Cf. Rivers and Schramm, Chapter 5, "Truth and Fairness," pp. 130–174.

62. Cf. Rivers and Schramm, Chapter 3, "Freedom and Government," and Chapter 4, "Freedom and Society," pp. 53–129.

63. Cf. Rivers and Schramm, Chapter 8, "Responsibilities: the Government, the Media, the Public," pp. 234–252; and the Pontifical Commission for the Means of Social Communication's "Pastoral Instruction . . . ," *passim,* especially pp. 22–25.

64. Excerpts of Commissioner Wells' speech to the Assoc. for Professional Broadcasting Education, March 27, 1971, were quoted by John Pennybacker (ed.), "Feedback," (APBE newsletter), May 1971, p. 17.

65. General concepts of managerial planning are well provided by McLarney and Berliner, pp. 14–21, 199–228; Filley and House, pp. 191–210. The latter authors emphasize that planning consists of searching for alternatives, and finally of selecting the optimum alternative (pp. 194–196).

66. Cf. Milton D. Friedland, "The Network-Affiliated Station," pp. 61–62, and Richard B. Rawls, "The Independent Station," pp. 77–78; both in Yale Roe (ed.), *Television Station Management—the Business of Broadcasting* (N.Y.: Hastings House, 1962).

67. McLarney and Berliner, p. 203. They suggest indicators that a manager should study the way he is misusing his time: "If he is just keeping up with his work—that is, taking care of one emergency after another—or if he is just getting or not quite getting his essential job done, if he needs to be in three places at the same time, if he has to put in excessive overtime, if he has not time for self-improvement, if he has to do everything himself, or, finally, if he dare not take a day off when he is ill: when it behooves him to make an evaluation of how he is spending his time" (p. 204). By redistributing his time he can reduce strain and excessive fatigue at his work, thus remaining fresh for the creative responsibilities that are unique to him as manager.

See also some helpful cautionary advice from Clarence B. Randall, "The Myth of the Overworked Executive," *The Folklore of Management* (N.Y.: Mentor ed., 1962), pp. 80–85.

68. McLarney and Berliner, p. 216.

69. McLarney and Berliner outline the role of policies and procedures on pp. 68–89, listing the characteristics by which to evaluate policies: stable, flexible, compatible, understandable, sincere, realistic, and written (p. 71). On the other hand, Robert Townsend, *Up the Organization* (Greenwich, Conn.: Fawcett ed., 1970), p. 129, is unalterably opposed to written policy manuals; he claims "don't bother. If they're general, they're useless. If they're specific, they're how-to manuals—expensive to prepare and revise." He cautions that company manipulators on the staff can misuse such manuals "to confine, frustrate, punish, and eventually drive out of the organization every imaginative, creative, adventuresome woman and man."

70. See next chapter on Personnel.

71. See Yale Roe (ed.), *Television Station Management*, pp. 61–62, 77–78. For views of the questionable value of meetings, see Robert Townsend, *Up the Organization*, pp. 89–91, but also p. 171, where he advocates that "some meetings should be long and leisurely. Some should be mercifully brief. A good way to handle the latter is to hold the meeting with everybody standing up. The meetees won't believe you at first. Then they get very uncomfortable and can hardly wait to get the meeting over with."

72. McLarney and Berliner, p. 22.

73. Bernard Gallagher, "The Gallagher Report," Dec. 7, 1971 (second section), pp. 3–4. See also Reinsch and Ellis, *Radio Station Management*, pp. 329–330, for 36 points listed as "Appendix II-Management Check List."

74. Excellent descriptive analyses of structures and organizations in management can be found in McLarney and Berliner, pp. 38–56 and 100–119, including discussion of "span of supervision," "chain of command," and "unity of command," as well as functions of line and staff personnel. See also Filley and House, Chapters 4, "Management Process and Organizational Design" (pp. 69–100), 9, "Division of Labor" (pp. 212–238), and 11, "Line and Staff Relationships" (pp. 257–280). Cf. George R. Terry, *Principles of Management*, 4th ed., (Homewood, Ill.: Richard D. Irwin, Inc., 1964), Chapters 15, "Modern Organizational Concepts and Departmentalization" (pp. 303–331), 18, "Authority Relationships" (pp. 388–418), and 20, "Organization Charts and Manuals" (pp. 443–462).

75. Cf. Reinsch and Ellis, pp. 38–39: "Guiding an organization is not an exact science. . . . Most people think of organization planning in terms of an organization chart—a picture of the relationships among departments and, to some extent, among people working in these departments. But no chart can reveal all the complexities of the human relationships in an organization and there is no such thing as a perfect plan for any organization. The best plan reconciles the theoretical ideal with the human resources available to do the job." Similar cautions are noted by Robert Townsend, *Up the Organization*, p. 187, who urges managers to assume that every man and woman is a human being, not a rectangle. In *The Folklore of Management*, Clarence B. Randall distinguishes between the usefulness of preparing an organization chart and the mindlessness of abusing the chart by letting it replace team play among persons and causing it to inhibit flexibility and responsible enterprise on the company's behalf.

76. Except where noted, the charts were submitted to and anonymously published by the NAB in *Television Station Organization Charts* (1968) and *Radio Station Organization Charts* (1969). Sources of other charts were WGN-AM-TV, Chicago (the original edition of *Broadcast Management*, pp. 32–33), and WSJV(TV)-WTRC/WFIM(FM) South Bend-Elkhart, Indiana.

77. For brief comments on specifically broadcast station organization relationships, see Edd Routt, *The Business of Radio Broadcasting* (Blue Ridge Summit, Pa.: Tab Books, 1972), pp. 167 ff. and 186–188 (itemized lists of on-air personnel needed for various kinds of radio formats); Johnson and Jones, *Modern Radio Station Practices* (Belmont, Calif.: Wadsworth, 1972), pp. 20–23; Robert H. Coddington, *Modern Radio Broadcasting: Management and Operation in Small-to-Medium Markets,* Chapter 9, "The Staff," pp. 143–158; and Sol Robinson, *Broadcast Station Operating Guide* (Blue Ridge Summit, Pa.: Tab Books, 1969), Chapter 5, "Staffing a Station," especially pp. 103–104, 109–112, and 136–138.

78. NAB Dept. of Broadcast Management, "Television 1974/Employee Wage & Salary Report," and "Radio 1974/Employee Wage & Salary Report," (Washington, D.C.: National Assoc. of Broadcasters, 1974). These figures are similar to those reported by Lawrence W. Lichty and Joseph M. Ripley, "Size and Composition of Broadcasting Stations' Staffs," *Journal of Broadcasting,* XI:2 (Spring 1967), pp. 139–151. See also similar data in annual editions of *Broadcasting Yearbook* (Washington, D.C.: Broadcasting Publications, Inc.)

79. Floorplan: KOB, Albuquerque, N. Mex., *Broadcast News* (RCA), July 1968, p. 11. Complete description and floorplans of KRON-TV, San Francisco in "How KRON-TV Planned a $5 Million All-Color 'New Look' Station," *Broadcast News* (RCA), December, 1966, pp. 10–27. Floorplan: KDMS/KRIL, Eldorado. Ark., "Idea Portfolio: Station Floor Plans that Work," *BM/E,* Aug. 1968, pp. 34–37. Floorplan: "Plan C," in "Radio-Station Floor Plans," *Broadcast Engineering,* Mar. 1966, pp. 21–25. For photographs, floorplans, and descriptive texts about well-designed, efficiently laid out AM, FM, and TV stations, see "Best Station Award Contest," *BM/E,* December 1974, pp. 26–57.

80. McLarney and Berliner, p. 50. The EBU management conference in Brussels in 1972 recognized that many broadcast organizations reach a growth threshold beyond which it is no longer possible to direct and control them adequately without extensive decentralization of powers and responsibilities. They also pointed out that joint management of both radio and television operations may be feasible only with an employed staff of up to 100 people; "above this threshold, management becomes so complex that the [two] media must be separated if their specificity is to be respected," Robert Wangermee, "Towards Modern Management in Broadcasting," *EBU* (European Broadcasting Union) *Review,* XXIII:6 (Nov. 1972), p. 34.

81. "People in Broadcasting," National Assoc. of Broadcasters, Washington, D.C., 1962. Among several articles based on those data which were published separately, see "Broadcasting Management," *Journal of Broadcasting,* VI:3 (Summer 1962), pp. 255–264.

82. Charles E. Winick, "The Television Station Manager," *Advanced Management Journal,* XXXI:1 (Jan. 1966), pp. 53–60, reported data from 287 managers of television stations. Bernard Gallagher summarized replies from 457 radio station managers in "The Gallagher Report," Dec. 7, 1971, (second section), pp. 1–2. Thomas W. Bohn and Robert K. Clark, under a grant from the NAB, studied survey responses from 112 radio station managers in communities of 10,000 population or less: "Small Market Media Managers: A Profile," *Journal of Broadcasting,* XVI:2 (Spring 1972), pp. 205–215.

83. *Sic* Bohn and Clark, p. 213; but figures cited in their table on p. 207 indicated that only 38 per cent of radio station managers had attended or completed college and 6 per cent had done graduate studies.

84. Until recent years, college courses related to broadcasting tended to be speech-oriented for public performance and on-air announcing. Except for electrical engineering, only speech or journalism (for news) or business (economics) offered curriculum listings for prospective broadcasters. Within the last 20 years or less, major universities and even smaller colleges introduced academic courses such as history and criticism of radio and television, writing for the media (copy and continuity as well as dramatic scripting), advertising, regulation and law, management, analysis of social effects of media, in addition to radio and television studio production.

By 1975 the NAB reported in its 14th survey of American institutions of higher learning that 205 schools offered the bachelor's degree with a major in broadcast studies, 99 schools offered a master's degree, and 27 schools offered a doctorate with an emphasis in broadcasting. A total of 228 four-year colleges responded to the survey that they offered a major or at least course work in radio-television; 62 junior or community colleges also offered programs of study in broadcasting or at least radio-TV courses. Harold Niven, *Fourteenth Report: Broadcast Programs in American Colleges and Universities, 1974–1975* (Washington, D.C.: National Association of Broadcasters, 1975).

85. Complete figures can be compared with the 1962 APBE-NAB study, which tabulated the average earnings of radio station managers at $12,500 per year and the average annual earnings of television station managers at $20,000. Gallagher's question #10 provided multiple categories, and were reported according to 1970 station income levels listed in the first column. (Percentages of the 457 responding stations were, respectively: 29.5% under $100,000; 34.4%, 24.1%, 7.4% and 4.6%.)

APPROXIMATE 1970 INCOME AS RADIO STATION MANAGER

Station Income	Under $10,000	$10,000– 19,999	$20,000– 29,999	$30,000– 39,999	$40,000– 69,999	$70,000 or more
Under $100,000	38.9%	54.8%	6.3%	0 %	0 %	0 %
$100,000 to $199,999	3.3	61.8	31.6	2.0	1.3	0
$200,000 to $499,999	2.8	33.9	40.3	16.5	6.5	0
$500,000 to $999,999	0	8.8	44.2	32.4	11.7	2.9
$1,000,000 or more	0	0	15.0	25.0	50.0	10.0
All	12.9	46.0	26.8	8.4	5.3	0.6

86. Cited in "Editorials: the Confidence Gap," *Broadcasting*, Nov. 29, 1972, p. 100; and in "What America Thinks of Itself," *Newsweek*, Dec. 10, 1973, pp. 40, 45, 48. See the final pages of Chapter 10 below.

3

The Management of Personnel

It is important to realize that conformity must be taught, whereas truth and principle are ultimately learned.
—ALDEN DOW, Architect [1]

THE NUMBER OF PEOPLE who are employed in American broadcasting is relatively small, compared with other major industries. Some 141,700 persons were employed full- and part-time in commercial and noncommercial radio and television when the FCC surveyed the industry in 1974.[2] General Electric in Schenectady, New York, and Boeing aircraft in Seattle, Washington, each employ almost that many full-time persons. For 1972, the FCC reported 61,858 full-time and 18,344 part-time employees in radio, and 52,858 full-time and 6,528 part-time employees in television (one out of five TV employees worked at networks).[3] Detailed figures are in Table I.

Men outnumber women in broadcasting by a ratio of four to one; 35,765 or 25.2 per cent of employees were women in 1974. Those women hold responsible positions in all phases of broadcasting. More than 3,000 women were either salaried managers or owners of stations.[4] In 1974 more than one in ten broadcast employees was a member of a major minority group: 11,188 Blacks (7.8%), 4,745 Spanish-surnamed (3.3%), 1,018 Orientals (.7%), and 611 American Indians (.4%).

When we speak of managing personnel at broadcast stations, about how many people are we talking? Approximately three times as many persons are employed by television stations, as are employed by radio stations. One out of five TV stations employed fewer than 25 people in 1974, while another one-fourth in the largest markets employed from 80 to over 100 people. Half of all the TV stations in the United States employed approximately 50 persons. One-half of all AM and FM stations employed fewer than 11 full-time persons; only one-tenth of the radio stations had more than 25 staff members.[5] (Staff numbers vary with the sizes of the station and of the markets, as described in Chapter 2.)

TABLE I

Broadcast Employment, 1972

	FULL-TIME	PART-TIME
RADIO		
AM & AM-FM		
4 Networks *	876	25
20 O&O Stations †	1,476	106
4,229 other stations	49,708	15,289
FM Only		
832 stations ‡	5,798	2,924
TOTAL, *Radio:*	61,858	18,344
TELEVISION		
3 Networks	10,465	1,945
15 O&O Stations	4,543	249
648 other stations: 475 VHF	31,905	3,453
173 UHF	5,945	881
TOTAL, *Television:*	52,858	6,528
GRAND TOTALS, *Radio & Television:*	114,716	24,872

* CBS, Mutual, NBC, and ABC's 3 AM and 1 FM networks.
† 14 AM, 6 AM-FM combination stations.
‡ Includes 14 network O&O FM stations.
Source: FCC, *39th Annual Report, Fiscal Year 1973* (Washington, D.C.: U.S. Government Printing Office, [1974]), pp. 238, 249, 253.

No other element of the broadcasting enterprise is capable of delivering as great a return on investment as its human resources. Superior physical plants and technical facilities depreciate in net worth over a period of years. But the values of people to a station should increase as their period of employment lengthens.

The station manager should realize that his ultimate successes are dependent upon the interests and the abilities of his station employees. He needs to give top priority to the maintenance of good human relations. If he regards the management of people as one of his major responsibilities and gives adequate attention to this aspect of administration, he may discover that the efficiency of his employees increases proportionately.

Whenever those employees have excellent morale plus a high degree of station loyalty, creativity and productivity may be expected to expand. Continual vigilance, then, is necessary in employee relations. Regular managerial attention needs to be directed to matters of paramount importance to the working staff. Equitable wages and salaries, proper recognition for work achievement, and opportunities for advancement in the organization are vital. Most employees want assurance that, if their assignments are accomplished satisfactorily, they need not be concerned about their job security.

Because it is identified as a form of show business, broadcasting attracts many creative people. If such talented persons find that their work assignments are merely routine, the odds are that the most creative will seek positions elsewhere. Creative people must have opportunity to use their talents.

It is one achievement to hire the best qualified people available. It is another to keep them. To sustain their top performance is an all-important duty of successful management.

SELECTION OF PERSONNEL

Broadcasters in many companies follow the standard of two weeks' notice for resignation or for dismissal. The notice gives the station only the two-week period to locate replacements. This is hardly adequate for looking over the field of available personnel and for making a satisfactory selection. Sometimes, as the time period for securing a replacement nears an end without likely prospects, the first available person is hired.

Where do stations find short-notice replacement personnel? Sometimes, desperate telephone calls are made to commercial and educational placement bureaus. A few positions are filled by "drifters" who just happen by when there is a vacancy. Contacts with other broadcasters may unearth a few prospects. Many stations advertise for help.

Small stations often have to settle for people currently unemployed in broadcasting. Seldom can they make offers lucrative enough to interest employees of other stations. In some cases, they turn to people who are employed in other lines of work in the community. Larger stations usually can find people in smaller operations who have worked long enough to prove their abilities. Some stations keep people on their payrolls who are not as able as they should be rather than face the task of giving notice of termination and then searching for replacements.

What about hiring personnel from other stations? Walter Lowen of the Walter Lowen Placement Agency has listed four factors that motivate people to change positions: greater security in the new position, more opportunity for advancement; promise of greater happiness in the new environment; and more money. While money is an important consideration, usually it does not constitute sufficient motivation to change positions unless the other three factors are also favorable.[6] And, of course, larger stations can seek replacements by advancing personnel already within the company, selecting by seniority, ability, competition or other basis. Then outside recruitment centers mostly on the lower-level job replacement (as reflected in the CBS policy statement on internal promotion, described below).

Neither recruitment nor replacement is an easy task. Both involve a greater amount of searching than is usually done at present by many broadcasters. A station committed to a rational long-range employment policy will enjoy notable advantages over the station that merely fills vacancies with the first chance applicants available.

Whatever the source of new people, someone on the staff should be designated as personnel director. In the smaller stations, this may be the responsibility of the station manager or of the program manager. At the opposite extreme, some metropolitan stations that operate radio and television properties have found it desirable to employ a full-time personnel director, who is assigned the leadership function for all non-union employees plus, frequently, a director of industrial relations responsible for relations with union personnel. Sometimes it is a combined executive position.

In addition to the authority to choose new or replacement staff people, the director of personnel (and/or industrial relations) should be in charge of employee development. He should also be the official representative to confer with all staff personnel in matters concerning individual and corporate welfare, complaints and benefits.

College and University Recruitment

It is, perhaps, an insufficient concern with the long-term future of stations that as much as anything else accounts for the general apathetic attitude of broadcast management toward planned recruitment. Yet, there is enormous waste in a system that does not provide an adequate screening of employees to select the very best. Also, it hardly seems efficient for large stations to pirate people from the smaller stations as a general policy and not develop at least a few new people on their own. Somehow, it is basically wrong to expect small stations to accept all the gambles of experimentation with inexperienced people, thereby absorbing the high costs of frequent "turnovers." No one doubts the advantages of an informal "farm system," but an essential factor even in a baseball farm club system is a carefully conceived and executed recruitment plan.

It would seem profitable even for small stations to conduct annual interviewing sessions at the colleges and universities nearest them whether vacancies are anticipated or not. Most colleges maintain facilities for the interviewing of graduating seniors; those facilities are usually used to capacity throughout the academic year. But seniors interested in careers in broadcasting seldom have opportunities to talk with recruiters from broadcasting stations. Consequently, many outstanding young prospects for the radio and television industry are lost to other businesses and industries. This has been particularly true of those young people who are interested in careers in sales. It seems wasteful to disregard almost completely this resource of the college campus, as the majority of station managers have done.

Usually, college graduates are available at two, three or four times each year, with most availabilities coming in May or June. Other times when the talent pool is replenished to some extent by the colleges are usually August, December, January and March. Correspondence with college authorities will pave the way toward interviews and selections. A college degree in itself is no automatic guarantee of excellence. Interviews with the recommended students should be combined with a follow-up check with the faculty in the students' major areas of study.

Minority persons can be recruited from colleges and from local minority organizations which can identify apt prospects for broadcast training and employment, including minority people who have demonstrated leadership and a sense of organization among their own groups and who might be very capable in management-related responsibilities in a radio or television station in their community.

Problems in Finding Qualified Employees

Even a decade ago, before the delicate issue of minority employment in broadcasting crested, broadcasters noted the difficulties in finding fully qualified personnel.[7] Most station managers in radio and television reported their greatest difficulty lay in attracting competent salesmen. But they had little difficulty in finding persons interested in being announcers and disc jockeys, although too many of those interested were not adequately qualified. Newsmen and continuity writers of competence were also difficult to find. Recurring reasons for "under-qualified" for all categories of jobs included: applicants lacked knowledge of the industry, they desired to advance rapidly without commensurate expertise, and they were overly impressed by the "glamour" of broadcasting.

Obviously radio stations in small markets must particularly concern themselves with adaptability of new employees who can perform various kinds of jobs and who can work comfortably in a small physical area and close to the rest of the small staff.[8] This need for versatility and compatability is often coupled with the limited experience of a new employee who is hired for relatively low wages. Further, the small station in a small market repeatedly experiences the turnover of personnel who have achieved moderate success in that station and, having perfected their skills, are then attracted away to larger operations. Hoffer encourages the local station manager whose talent continually moves on to larger markets by noting that the local broadcaster

> . . . obviously must possess the ability to develop talent—to find it, nuture it, and stand back as it blossoms. . . . The point is not to set up goals that cannot be attained realistically, yet still provide sufficient challenges to the newcomer. Make it exciting, not boring. Make it fruitful, not deprecating. Once such a favorable reputation can be established for an operator, chances are that people will want to come to you.[9]

Coddington recommends that small-market stations seek employees who prefer the less hectic pace and wide local recognition and respect of small towns where they can participate in civic activities as leaders. In this way small stations can attract professionally qualified staff members whose turnover will be minimal.

What motivates people to enter the broadcasting industry, in the first place? In the NAB's national survey of almost two thousand broadcast employees, one-fifth cited "professional suitability"; another one-fifth looked to "opportunity for self expression"; and another fifth of the respondents noted a "general liking for the industry." [10] More than one-tenth chose broadcasting

for career advancement. Another tenth attributed their entrance into broadcasting to "chance or expediency." About one in twenty said they were influenced
by others already in the field. The largest disparity of purpose between radio
(only 2.9%) and television (11.3%) employees was "challenge of new media
for advertising purposes." Having entered the field and experienced it first-
hand, those same respondents offered recommendations for work experience
prior to broadcasting employment.[11] The largest single category (recommended
by 16%) was technical education and/or experience in fields related to broadcasting such as photography, radio-TV repair and amateur radio. Almost as
many (14%) recommended broadcast training—in high school, college, vocational school and on-the-job in stations. About one-tenth of the respondents
suggested general liberal arts education in high school and college, emphasizing English, grammar, dramatics. Another tenth recommended sales and/or
promotional training and experience. Slightly fewer (8%) urged show business
experience in professional or amateur theatrical work, music and motion pictures. About 6 per cent commended business education and experience (marketing, accounting, law). That these recommendations probably reflected their
own interests, talents and current jobs in production or management or sales
was indicated in the disparity of support for "public contact experience" (public speaking, lecturing, politics, or other activities where personality must be
projected), recommended by only 3.9 percent of television respondents and by
11.5 per cent of radio respondents.

     While most of those employees had attended high school, half of those in
radio and one-third in television had also attended vocational or training
schools, the greatest number emphasizing radio-TV engineering (42%) and
radio-TV production and announcing (22%). Of the 72 per cent of TV employees and 60 per cent of radio employees who went to college (one-half of
them through to graduation), about one-third majored in liberal arts, one-fifth
majored in radio-television, one-seventh majored in business administration,
and another seventh in engineering; about one in 14 majored in journalism. Finally, about a tenth of all employees in television and 6 per cent of those in
radio had taken graduate courses (one-third of both groups completing their
degree work). Emphasis in graduate school was about 30 per cent in liberal arts
and 30 per cent in radio-television courses. About 13.5 per cent took graduate
work in fine arts; 10 per cent studied law, and 7.5 per cent studied business.
One in 20 employees had done graduate study in government, and the same
proportion had studied science. Although no radio employees did graduate
work in public relations, almost one-twentieth of TV employees studied that
area.

     From those 2,000 employees, averaging about 35 years of age, with 10
years in broadcasting at the time, it seemed that liberal arts and broadcasting
studies as well as vocational training served as background to their positions in
radio and television. But by the early 1970s, the development of television
news at local stations threw greater emphasis on background knowledge and
skills more specifically related to that phase of broadcasting. In 1971 Fang and

Gerval reported that news directors at 425 commercial VHF and UHF stations in the U.S. checked the following first choice responses to the question, "Given the following choices, who would you hire as a reporter?":

176–Reporter with 2 years' experience, no college education
165–College graduate in broadcast journalism, no experience
 50–College graduate with another major, no experience
 24–Local youth, junior college graduate, no experience
 10–Broadcasting trade school graduate, no experience [12]

Those news directors who preferred to hire as reporters college graduates with majors other than broadcast journalism listed the following: political science, 14; English, 11; liberal arts, 9; history, 6; print journalism, 4; telecommunications, 3; speech, social science, humanities, 1 each. In addition to formal educational background, those news directors mentioned the following skills which they sought in reporters whom they hired: writing ability (160 mentions), on-air characteristics (90), knowledge of photography (60), knowledge of film editing (22), reporting skill (12), ability to type (12), knowledge of how to use sound equipment (10). Finally, kinds of descriptive adjectives or nouns used by respondents about applicants' personal qualities were categorized:

90 times: energy, desire, eagerness, self-starter, enthusiasm.
53 times: positive attitudes, good manners, maturity, stable personality.
22 times: hard worker, not afraid to work long hours, a real work horse.
20 times: imagination, creativity, ingenuity, expressiveness.
17 times: good habits, clean and neat, clean-cut, no personal hangups.
16 times: ability to work with others, congenial, cooperative.
14 times: objective, open-minded, clear-headed.
13 times: dependable, reliable, dedicated.

EMPLOYMENT OF MINORITIES, INCLUDING WOMEN

Larger broadcast companies may have, in addition to personnel directors, "affirmative action officers" who are responsible for attracting, and recommending for hiring and promotion, members of minority groups. Loring and Wells urge that, if at all possible, hiring and advancement of minority persons should not be internally competitive, whereby one minority (such as male Blacks or Chicanos) will be given advantageous treatment over another minority (such as women or Puerto Ricans).

To pit one group against the other is to undermine the objectives of both. One way to avoid such problems is to select an aware woman who can work with the minority man who is now in affirmative action work. Equal status between them eliminates possible conflicts of interest and makes visible management's equal commitment to both groups. This delicate balance in black/white, male/female advancement must be weighed in the final selection and placement of affirmative action officers as well as in implementing the program.[13]

Such affirmative action officers (or personnel director or manager at smaller stations) should report directly to top management and, among other duties, should be responsible for reviewing the provisions and goals of minority hiring practices, including job availability announcements and advertising, listing of job descriptions and qualifications, application forms and testing, training and subsequent development programs for further job progress, and the handling of personnel records—including files on appraisals, promotion, discipline, and terminations— which document data about minority persons, including women, on the staff.[14]

Logic, as well as good business sense aware of a station's role in its total community, can be coupled with humanity and a sense of ethics to support broadcast companies' efforts to attract minority persons. Of course the Federal law and agencies, including the FCC, strengthen such resolve.[15] Among the 204 million U.S. citizens in the early 1970s, 22 million were Black, 10 million Spanish-surnamed, 2 million Asian-Oriental, and almost 1 million American Indians.[16] Thus almost one-sixth of the U.S. population are minorities. Further, of all U.S. citizens, 51 per cent are female. Women make up 39 per cent of the work force (and that proportion is expected to remain stable) but women constitute only 2 per cent of the supervisory, professional, managerial, and executive personnel.[17] Nationally, of all the jobs that paid over $15,000 a year (approximately 5,050,000 positions), 96 per cent were held by white males. Women held 3 per cent of such jobs, and minorities held 1 per cent.[18]

Special attention will have to be given for many years to the complex problem of assimilating into management roles persons who are not male "Anglo-Europeans." Sources of guidelines and recommendations multiply annually.[19] When imbalances have eventually come to be righted, then the commentary throughout this book about broadcast station personnel will apply equally to all persons. In the meantime they *should* apply equally, and present executive management must take positive, affirmative steps to ensure aggressive recruitment, training and promotion of all persons capable of productive employment in broadcasting and of advancing to broadcast management.[20]

Initial misunderstandings can arise among personnel at generally white-staffed stations when incoming minority persons are hired, often because for both sides it involves effort to communicate effectively beyond cross-cultural lines. A three-year doctoral study of young black persons active in daily educational broadcast management responsibilities reported that most problems able to be anticipated and stereotyped as "black" were actually common to people raised in a culture of poverty, whatever the race or ethnic background.[21] Such problems included poor orientation towards delayed goals and future time planning, lack of teamwork, suspicion of one another, preference for concrete and immediate experiences over abstract ones, dislike of reading and writing, "fatalistic responses." More specifically identifiable as black-related problems, which initially hampered the advancement of talented blacks but were eventually minimized, included a fear of failure in a white person's estimation, reservations in complying with sources of authority, loyalty to a "brother" even if he were wrong, disagreement about sources and directions of black awareness, and semantic misunderstandings of words that blacks considered derogatory or demeaning. Emotional and nonverbal communication by facial expression and tone of voice were often observed to be more significant to black persons than the cognitive content of the messages. Finally, the data implied that black young persons, especially males, initially learned more rapidly under the guidance of another black person, but such a need lessened as they gained knowledge and confidence.

Statistics and descriptions can both lend perspective to the issue of minority employment; but in a continually changing national scene these data can only reflect representative points in time.

An average of 10 per cent full-time minority employment at commercial TV stations in the U.S. in 1972 was reported from FCC records by the United Church of Christ's Office of Communications (Table II).[22] But stations in the top-ten TV markets, with 34 per cent minority populations, employed an average of 14.5 per cent of minority representatives. One-third of the 609 TV stations employed no minority persons in four key job categories: managerial, professional, technical, and sales; almost one-fifth of the stations employed no women in those four categories. In those four classifications, the number of minorities increased from 7 per cent of the total employment in 1971 to 8 per cent in 1972 (1,816 up to 2,143), and the number of women increased from 6 per cent to 7 per cent (1,672 to 1,865). The study reported full-time and part-time minority employment in all levels of jobs at 4,781 in 1972 (up from 4,081 the previous year, an increase from 10% to 11% of stations' total employment), and women's employment at 9,647 in 1972 (up from 9,396 the previous year, remaining 22% of total employment). A total of 136 stations in 41 states (in regions that did have some measure of minority-group populations) were claimed by the church group to be "pure white."

As of July 31, 1969, 104 black persons were employed by the four major VHF television stations in Washington, D.C., or 11 per cent of the total labor force of 937, including professional, technical, sales, clerical, and custodial workers.[23]

In the Los Angeles television market in 1972, of 1,419 fulltime employees at stations studied, 184 were minorities (121 male, 63 female) or 12 per cent of the total fulltime labor force at commercial and public broadcast stations tabulated (See Table III)—up from the national average of 10 per cent (according to the FCC data in 1972), but less than the average for the top-ten markets (14.5%). And Los Angeles TV stations' overall average of 22 per cent full-time female employees was exactly the national average as reported in the FCC data.

Citing a final major metropolitan center, women are gradually moving into more major roles in Chicago's broadcasting, advertising and film companies. Their roles included, in mid-1972, advertising and sales promotion manager of WIND Radio, public relations and promotion departments at WGN (AM-TV), WCFL, WSNS (TV) and WDAI; publicity manager, publicity represen-

TABLE II

NATIONWIDE COMPARATIVE EMPLOYMENT REPORT FOR TV

As compiled by Office of Communication, United Church of Christ (Source: *Broadcasting Magazine*, Nov. 27, 1972, p. 31)

	Total	All Employees Male	Female	Black Male	Female	Oriental Male	Fe-male	American Indian Male	Fe-male	Spanish-American Male	Female	All Minorities
Full-time officials & managers												
Current year	5515	4985 90%	530 10%	77 1%	23 —	14	12	9	3	112	15	265 5%
Prior year	5290	4832 91%	439 8%	56 1%	14 —	15	9	9	2	98	7	210 4%
Change	225+	153— 1%—	91+ 2%+	21+ %	9+ —	1—	3+		1+	14+	8+	55+ 1%+ .
Full-time professionals												
Current year	7925	6915 87%	1010 13%	386 5%	119 2%	35	8	16	5	172	35	776 10%
Prior year	7637	6648 87%	929 12%	339 4%	96 1%	24	6	8	4	137	22	636 8%
Change	288+	267+ %	81+ 1%+	47+ 1%+	23+ 1%+	11+	2+	8+	1+	35+	13+	140+ 2%+
Full-time technicians												
Current year	11057	10989 99%	118 1%	486 4%	12 —	84	2	24		358	5	971 9%
Prior year	11146	11008 99%	110 1%	419 4%	11 —	71		26		333	5	865 8%
Change	89—	19— %	8+ %	67+ 1%+	1+ —	13+	2+	2—		25+		106+ 1%+
Full-time sales workers												
Current year	2634	2442 93%	207 8%	62 2%	10 —	4	3	4	1	38	10	131 5%
Prior year	2546	2350 92%	195 8%	48 2%	5 —	3	3	6	1	32	7	105 4%
Change	88+	92+ 1%+	12+ %	14+ %	5+ —	1+		2—	1—	6+	3+	26+ 1%+
Full-time office & clerical												
Current year	7347	841 11%	6491 88%	166 2%	515 7%	6	70	2	35	59	219	1072 15%
Prior year	7492	915 12%	6551 87%	166 2%	427 6%	11	48	4	24	50	183	913 12%
Change	145—	74— 1%—	60— 1%+	7+ %	88+ 1%+	5—	22+	2—	11+	9+	36+	159+ 3%+
Full-time craftsmen												
Current year	2474	2329 94%	145 6%	206 8%	13 1%	9	3	10	1	96	5	340 14%
Prior year	2441	2298 94%	119 5%	185 8%	11 —	15		8	1	82	3	306 13%
Change	33+	31+ %	26+ 1%+	21+ %	2+ 1%+	6—	1—	2+		14+	2+	34+ 1%+
Full-time operatives												
Current year	1337	1267 95%	69 5%	162 12%	9 1%	8		4		73	3	259 19%
Prior year	1427	1347 94%	79 6%	155 11%	9 1%	5	1	4		68	5	246 17%
Change	90—	80— 1%+	10— 1%—	7+ 1%+		3+	1—			5+	2—	13+ 2%+
Full-time laborers												
Current year	146	139 95%	7 5%	42 29%	4 3%	2		2		21	3	71 49%
Prior year	184	179 97%	4 2%	47 26%	2 1%	2		1		27	5	81 44%
Change	38—	40— 2%—	3+ 3%+	5— 3%+	2+ 2%+			1+		6—	2—	10— 5%+
Full-time service workers												
Current year	684	590 86%	94 14%	279 41%	37 5%	1				51	6	374 55%
Prior year	736	643 87%	90 12%	316 43%	43 6%	1		4		45	3	412 56%
Change	52—	53— 1%—	4+ 2%+	37— 2%—	6— 1%—			4—		6+	3+	38— 1%—
Full-time total												
Current year	39071	30390 78%	8682 22%	1851 5%	793 2%	162	95	72	43	771	277	4064 10%
Prior year	38619	30125 78%	8487 22%	1664 4%	616 2%	145	67	70	33	662	196	3453 9%

90

TABLE III

Minority Fulltime Employment at Los Angeles Television Stations, 1972

(Public Inspection File Data, F.C.C. Employment Report, Form 395)

Ch. #	Call Letters	Sex	Total Empl.	Black	Oriental	Amer. Ind.	Spa. Amer.	ALL MINORITIES by Sex	Total %
2	KNXT	Male	255	17	2	0	12	31 (12%)	13%
	(CBS-Owned)	Female	62	4	2	0	5	11 (17)	
5	KTLA	Male	204	5	1	0	5	11 (5)	9
	(Ind.-Golden West)	Female	49	7	2	1	3	13 (27)	
7	KABC	Male	116	9	1	0	12	22 (18)	18
	(ABC-owned)	Female	27	2	0	0	2	4 (14)	
9	KHJ	Male	130	3	3	1	7	14 (10)	10
	(Ind.-RKO Gen.)	Female	44	1	1	1	2	5 (11)	
11	KTTV	Male	168	7	2	0	12	21 (12)	16
	(Ind.-Metromedia)	Female	52	9	2	0	5	16 (30)	
13	KCOP	Male	120	4	3	0	3	10 (8)	9
	(Ind.-Chris-Craft)	Female	36	2	2	0	1	5 (13)	
28	KCET	Male	105	6	0	1	5	12 (11)	13
	(Non-comm.-PBS)	Female	51	6	2	1	0	9 (17)	
TOTALS:	78%	MALE	1,098					121 (11)	
	22%	FEMALE	321					63 (19)	
	100%		1,419					184	12%

[No data on other stations, including KNBC/4 (NBC-Owned)]
Data gathered by Lynda Redman, project at Univ. of Southern California, Dept. of Telecommunications; spring 1972.

tative, and advertising manager at WBBM-TV; publicist at WBBM Radio; on-air reporters at most stations, especially television; saleswomen at WBBM-FM and WMAQ; women program producers and on-air hosts at several stations.[24] At WGN (AM-TV) by 1974 women had risen to key positions in administration, community affairs, news and film departments.

Meanwhile, at the national network level, Columbia Broadcasting System, Inc. (including a dozen and a half divisions, among them the CBS radio and television networks, television stations and news divisions) reported that minority employment had risen from 4.8 per cent in 1965 to 12.2 per cent in 1969 and further to 14.3 per cent by the end of 1971.[25] The president of CBS, Inc., cited a dramatic increase of minority employees as officials, managers, professionals and technicians in all divisions of the corporation. Ms. Grace Johnsen has headed continuity acceptance for the ABC networks for many years, as did Dorothy Brown on the west coast from the 1940s until her recent retirement. NBC-TV has a firm record of advancing women in program production and on-air positions: in the news division alone, Pauline Frederick for years headed the United Nations bureau, Aline Saarinen became the first woman to head an overseas bureau for television news when she was appointed chief of the NBC News Paris bureau in 1971 (she died in mid-1972). Ms. Saarinen and Liz Trotta both reported for NBC from Vietnam. Barbara Walters has co-anchored the "Today Show" for years on NBC-TV. And Sally Quinn became co-anchorperson on the CBS-TV morning news late in 1973.

Progress continues to be made in hiring and salary practices. It is worth noting that during the first years in which the FCC studied employment figures (1972–1974), total full- and part-time broadcast employees increased by 11,044 persons (from 130,656 to 141,700). Of those new employees, 5,701—slightly over half—were women (from 30,064 in 1972, to 35,765 in 1974). And fully one-third, 3,589, were minorities of both sexes (up from 13,973 to 17,562).[26]

The challenge ahead lies in assisting apt minority persons to move into decision-making positions so that they may compete with and contribute to others on a basis of actual equality. Black leaders have noted the meager development of capable minority persons to serve eventually in managerial capacities; they identify these practices (or lack of them) as based on the traditional white-oriented structure and thus constituting "institutional racism," unintentional or otherwise. Lionel J. Monagas, Director of the Office of Minority Affairs for the National Association of Educational Broadcasters, discussed the issue with public broadcasting representatives. His lament reflects similar problems in commercial radio and television, in spite of the accelerated rate of progress in minority employment in broadcasting in the last half decade.

> There have been blacks in public broadcasting for some time. Very few of us, but some for quite a few years. And look where we are. We have not risen to any levels of responsibility at all, until very recently, and you can count on the fingers of one hand, and maybe only part of those fingers, the number of blacks within this whole industry that are at any level of authority. And we are not in decision-making levels. I am not a decision-maker. I'm in management, at a corporate level now, but I am not a decision-maker. And I would assume that at this point in time, as far as I have been able to ascertain, I am the only black who is working on any kind of corporate level within this industry.[27]

Concurrent with efforts by minority persons, including women, to move up in the ranks of established broadcast companies (and to participate in on-air programming, as discussed in later chapters), is the growth in minority ownership of broadcast stations. Radio stations in the U.S. owned by blacks and other minority persons in 1972 numbered 15 (of a national total of approximately 7,000 stations). WSOK-AM, after four months of black ownership, moved into first place in the Savannah, Georgia, radio market according to ARB reports ending May 10, 1972. Black Communications Corporation bought the station from previous owners who programmed a black-oriented format and expanded the range of music and public affairs community-involving programs. This resulted in increased audience and growth in number of local advertisers.[28] And in mid-1972 the FCC granted a construction permit for a new UHF station in Detroit, Channel 62, to WGPR, Inc., a subsidiary of the International Free and Accepted Modern Masons, Inc., a black fraternal organization centered in Detroit and already licensee of WGPR-FM. This was to be the country's first black-owned television station, and marked the entry of a major minority group into becoming fully a part of the establishment of broadcast ownership.[29] These companies in the future will share the burden of existing stations of finding apt employees, training them and advancing them to management positions. Hopefully, stations may eventually vie against one another in open and equal competition for the most skilled and successful broadcast personnel—minority or otherwise.

On the other hand, some black broadcasters suggest that to own and operate an exclusively black or other minority-oriented station may tend to disenfranchise parts of the total community who might otherwise be part of their audience and thus attract greater advertising for the station. Instead, minority persons might consider entering into ownership and management with colleagues who are white. "Integrated stations," by serving the entire service area, might better attract greater portions of mixed metropolitan audiences and thus more sales support.[30]

THE EMPLOYMENT INTERVIEW

A word of caution about audition tapes: they can be poor substitutes for live performance tests because they often are not a true indication of the applicant's abilities. Tapes can be carefully planned, edited and polished by the applicant before they are submitted. The employer has no opportunity to observe how the applicant would react under pressure or how he would perform with unfamiliar announcer or news copy. Furthermore, it is always better to have an opportunity to judge the poise, personality and appearance of the applicant in addition to his submitted sample of performing ability.

In short, there is no real substitute for the personal interview as a method of judging the potential of the applicant. There is no substitute, either, for a skilled and experienced interviewer. Personality, manners, appearance, sincerity, emotional stability, intelligence, the abilities to articulate and listen, and the applicant's opinions and attitudes about broadcasting can be judged through the interview. The kind of questions asked by the candidate and the directness of his response to questions asked of him should be noted. Evidence of his energy, enthusiasm and drive should be sought.[31]

Some broadcasters recommend that, in addition to application forms and references, two separate interviews should be held with prospective applicants for employment. Reinsch and Ellis suggest that the personnel director interview first, and then the department head under whom the employee would work. Beyond these techniques of ascertaining the abilities and character of prospective employees, aptitude tests can be devised by the station staff in order to determine more precisely and with objectivity a person's qualifications for specific duties.[32]

Even though there may be no openings at the moment and even though many who are interviewed cannot be hired, the fact that the station provides the opportunity for interviews can reflect nothing but favor on its public image. Interviewing is a time-consuming task, but it can bring rich dividends to the station in terms of favorable impressions.

In case an immediate job is available, specifications should be clearly explained, including duties, hours and working conditions, compensation, the fringe benefits and any other pertinent information. The actual hiring process, in most instances, should not be a part of the interview even though the interviewer may feel that he has discovered the person he is seeking. The interviewer, too, may profit by a second thought. Usually, it is the better policy to let the candidate wait a day or so before extending a formal proffer of employment.

It is a wise policy to have a credit check made on any applicants who seem desirable for possible employment as cashiers, payroll clerks, mailroom personnel and those who are responsible for valuable equipment.

The one area where the director of personnel should be given less than a free hand is in the selection of key executives. In these cases, the personnel director may do some preliminary screening and referral of prospects to the chief engineer, the program manager, the sales manager or the station manager for further interviewing. Much valuable administrative time can be saved and much order can be given to the general employment process if preliminary screening takes place before the department heads see the outstanding candidates. For that matter, it is better to choose top executives by invitation rather than through formal application.

JOB INDOCTRINATION

In too many instances a new employee reports for his first day of work to find that no one has been assigned to give him any introduction to station policy or operations. Station practices and routines taken for granted by the employer can be complicated and strange to a new person. New duties can be downright frightening, especially when exercised among strangers and in unfamiliar surroundings.

The NAB and the Association for Professional Broadcasting Education surveyed broadcast station personnel a decade ago, and found that over one-third of the employees of both radio and television stations reported no on-the-job training for their first position with their current employer. Almost another one-tenth of the respondents appraised their initial training as "inadequate," while about one-half reported such training to have been "adequate" (31% for TV, 33% for radio) or "excellent" (20% for TV, 21% for radio).[33] When asked to note areas of management that needed improvement, 21 per cent of the respondents from TV stations and 16 per cent from radio stations urged "better on-the-job training." [34]

A brief printed or mimeographed booklet should be prepared which contains detailed information about the station and its operating policies which affect all employees.[35] This booklet could be given to new employees after they are hired and before they report for work. The Department of Broadcast Management of the NAB has prepared an excellent sample of such a manual for new employees. It includes representative contents for a typical manual: [36]

Welcome
The Growth of Broadcasting
Your Station—A Thumbnail Sketch
Coverage and Service Area
The Management—Who's Who
Get Started Right—Don't Be Afraid To Ask
Pay Day and Your Check
Fringe Benefits
Basic Work Policies and Practices
Leave of Absence
Conclusion
Personnel Directory

Even with the booklet as an aid, proper indoctrination of new employees also requires personal attention once they report for duty. On the first day, a tour of the facilities and introductions to all employees of the station are minimal expectations. This is the time to discuss the employee's responsibilities to other employees, the station's administrative structure, its lines of authority, its functions and philosophy.[37] Reinsch and Ellis also recommend that a new employee spend "at least a half-day in each department of the station" to become familiar generally with how each operates and relates to other departments. Without being overly rigid, an organization chart of the station's executives and other personnel can graphically clarify relationships as well as titles and numbers of people employed at the station—with whom a new employee will be working and to some of whom he will report directly.[38]

Radio and television stations are not normally geared for extensive training periods. Many stations, however, could profitably devote three to six months on a part-time basis for the thorough indoctrination of a few promising recruits. Even the small station could arrange for a few hours each week when new personnel could learn about those activities of the station which are not a part of their regular assignments.

Caution should be expressed to station management, present and potential, regarding a special ability which should be expected of any station's key personnel. Those individuals who occupy assignments as heads of the leading departments in the station need to have the capacity to understand, direct and guide employees for whom they have direct responsibility. The most creative-minded department head in the world is of questionable value to a station unless he also has skill in the direction of people, as discussed in the first part of this chapter.[39]

SALARIES AND WAGES

Major expenses for stations include studios, transmitter, and complementary equipment. But, once the capital has been invested and then amortized, the single greatest operating expense is salaries. This is particularly true of broadcasting, because people are the greatest resource of the station; and to the audience personnel "are" the station, especially in radio.

Thus station management can destroy its operation by either excess: underpaying staff and losing key members or at least undercutting their strong, enthusiastic support of the company; overpaying some staff members enormous amounts annually and unnecessarily dissipating potential profits.

The obvious guideline is that salaries should be equitable to each person's ability, creativity, length of service and overall value to the total operation. This must be assessed partly on an individual basis; but payment can be grounded on some kinds of representative averages. Clearly pertinent are the size and kind of station, the market size, the volume of advertising carried on the air and the size of the station staff.

The National Association of Broadcasters has made public average fulltime salary levels for ranges of markets and stations.[40] While the cited figures are for 1969, 1970 and 1974, they nevertheless demonstrate relative pay scales for various kinds of positions in radio and television and can therefore be compared internally (weighted to adjust to contemporary price and wage indexes). Gross weekly compensation figures include the following: for nonsupervisory employees, the basic weekly wage plus premium pay for overtime; for announcers and producer-directors, the basic weekly wage, plus overtime pay and fees; for sales managers and salesmen, their average weekly income whether paid by straight salary, straight commission, salary plus commission, or any other method.

For television stations (320, or 47%, of U.S. commercial TV stations responded to the survey in 1969, and 200 or 28.4% responded in 1974) the average gross weekly compensation for 22 positions placed the producer-director midway in the listing (see Table IV). Newsmen, salesmen and departmental managers typically earned more than producer-directors, while announcers, studio production crews and technicians earned less than the producer-directors' average weekly compensation. To indicate the range of comparative salary levels for selected positions according to market size, Table V was derived from the NAB survey data.

For all commercial AM radio stations (1,463, or 34% of U.S. stations, responded to the survey in 1970 and 1,035 or 15% responded in 1974) the average gross weekly compensation for 17 positions placed the radio newsman midway in the listing (see Table VI). Salesmen and supervisors (managers of departments) as well as fulltime technicians earned more than newsmen, while announcers and combination men (announcer-salesmen and announcer-technicians) and other office personnel earned less than newsmen's average weekly compensation of $183 in 1970. Table VII documents the range of comparative

TABLE IV

AVERAGE GROSS WEEKLY COMPENSATION, NATIONWIDE: TELEVISION

	1969	1974		1969	1974
Sales Manager	$452	$572	Staff Announcer	$174	$229
National Sales Manager	409	467	News Cameraman	166	184
Local Sales Manager	377	484	Film Department Head	162	194
Head of TV Engineering	270	319	Art Director	160	217
Head of TV Programming	267	321	Staff Photographer	147	—
Salesman	262	270	Filmman	136	155
Head of TV News Operation	254	325	Studio Cameraman	133	129
Promotion Manager	207	234	Productionman	129	146
Newsman	184	196	Traffic Manager	124	188
Technician	179	213	Floorman, Unskilled	119	126
Producer/Director	176	189	Continuity Writer	112	128

Source: "Wages, Hours and Employment / Television 1969," National Assoc. of Broadcasters, Washington, D.C., 1969, p. 4; "Television 1974 / Employee Wage & Salary Report," National Assoc. of Broadcasters, Washington, D.C., 1974, p. 3.

TABLE V

GROSS WEEKLY COMPENSATION, SELECTED TV EMPLOYMENT FULLTIME POSITIONS, BY MARKET SIZE *

Market Size & Region † (ARB Rankings)		Studio Cameraman 1969	Studio Cameraman 1974	Producer-Director 1969	Producer-Director 1974	Head of TV Programming 1969	Head of TV Programming 1974
1–10	North and South	$220	‡	$228	$262	$419	$497
11–25	North and South	185	‡	203	214	329	364
26–50	North	138	‡	176	195	295	372
	South	97		168		296	
51–75	North	154	‡	177	188	265	291
	South	101		153		249	
76–100	North	114	‡	186	162	229	294
	South	93		163		221	
101–125	North	138	118	167	166	234	—
	South	97		142		227	
126–150	North and South	126	‡	159	173	210	244
151 & Over	North and South	80	‡	151	151	197	228
(NATIONAL AVG. [Table IV])		($133)	(‡)	($176)	($189)	($267)	($321)

* Source: Dept. of Broadcast Management, "Wages, Hours and Employment / Television 1969," NAB, 1969, pp. 4–17; "Television 1974 / Employee Wage & Salary Report," NAB, 1974, pp. 3–11.
† Included in the South were 18 States and the District of Columbia: Alabama, Arizona, Arkansas, Delaware, District of Columbia, Florida, Georgia, Kentucky, Louisiana, Maryland, Mississippi, New Mexico, North Carolina, Oklahoma, South Carolina, Tennessee, Texas, Virginia, West Virginia.
‡ Insufficient data reported. For current union scales for minimum compensation, consult the NAB's Dept. of Broadcast Management's "Labor Contract Summary" for announcers and talent (AFTRA) and for technicians (IBEW and NABET).

TABLE VI

Average Gross Weekly Compensation, Nationwide: Radio

	1970	1974		1970	1974
Sales Manager	$299	$353	News Director	$182	$234
Salesman	225	207	Announcer-Salesman	167	181
Promotion Manager	217	216	Staff Announcer	154	150
Chief Engineer	215	247	Announcer-Technician	147	150
Editorial Director	213	—	Music Librarian	126	137
Program Director	191	218	Traffic Manager	112	115
Technician	190	174	Continuity Writer	104	120
Public Affairs Director	186	185	Traffic/Sales Clerk	96	112
Newsman	183	160			

Source: "Wages, Hours and Employment / Radio 1970," NAB, 1970, p. 3; "Radio 1974 / Employee Wage & Salary Report," NAB, 1974, p. 3.

salary levels for selected positions at AM radio stations, according to market size and size of station.

In 1962, radio and most TV employees reported to the NAB that they regarded their compensation in their current jobs as "satisfactory" or "very satisfactory"; only one-fifth appraised their pay as "unsatisfactory." [41] Further responses to that survey indicated that not the wages themselves but rather the handling of wage increases was a source of problem at their stations. More than one-third of all radio and TV employees appraised their stations' procedures for handling wage increases as "unsatisfactory (one in seven judged procedures as "very satisfactory," while another one-third judged them to be "satisfactory"). Reasons given most often were representative of what employees felt were deficiencies in both radio and television stations' procedures:

> Personality was favored over job experience.
> Seniority was favored over ability.
> Absence of policy governing regular review of wages.
> Management did not keep promises or showed partiality toward certain groups (cited several times were special pay arrangements for sales personnel).
> Unions prevented recognition of ability and forced everyone into the same mold.
> Increases did not keep up with increases in the cost of living.

Almost one-third of all full- and part-time staff employees in radio and television stations have duties in the area of news.[42] News directors for 350 VHF and UHF television stations (slightly more than 50% of total) responded to a survey late in 1970.[43] The average weekly starting salary in the fall of 1970 was $139, with stations in the East paying more ($152) and in the South paying less ($122). After five years of news work, employees were paid an average of $194 nationally; by region, weekly salaries after five years in news

TABLE VII

GROSS WEEKLY COMPENSATION, SELECTED AM RADIO EMPLOYMENT FULLTIME POSITIONS, BY MARKET SIZE AND STATION SIZE *

Market Size	Station Size †	Traffic Mgr.		Newsman		Salesman	
		1970	1974	1970	1974	1970	1974
2,500,000 or More	Large	$158	‡	$282	$213	$346	$217
	Small	114		152		227	
1,000,000 to 2,500,000	Large	148	‡	205	207	322	246
	Small	112		142		183	
500,000 to 1,000,000	Large	119	‡	181	178	259	227
	Small	98		155		181	
250,000 to 500,000	Large	112	‡	153	163	231	217
	Small	99		142		193	
100,000 to 250,000	Large	120	‡	169	155	246	204
	Small	97		138		177	
50,000 to 100,000	Large	‡	‡	150	136	217	196
	Small	106		136		175	
25,000 to 50,000	All Stations	108	‡	129	150	185	209
10,000 to 25,000	All Stations	96	‡	137	142	173	195
Less Than 10,000	All Stations	93	‡	121	136	175	180
(NATIONAL AVG. [Table VI])		($112)	($152)	($183)	($160)	($225)	($207)

*Source: Dept. of Broadcast Management, "Wages, Hours and Employment / Radio 1970," NAB, 1971, pp. 3–18, "Radio 1974 / Employee Wage & Salary Report," NAB, 1974, pp. 3–12.
† Large stations = 16 or more fulltime employees; small stations = 16 or less fulltime employees [sic NAB explanation, with 16 as "the best breaking point"]. Markets with populations less than 50,000 tended to be served only by stations with staffs of fewer than 16 persons. (Where only one figure is reported, that is the average for all stations, both large and small.)
‡ Insufficient data reported.
Note that these data are averages for 1970 and 1974. For current union scales for minimum compensation, consult the NAB's Dept. of Broadcast Management's "Labor Contract Summary" for announcers and talent (AFTRA) and for technicians (IBEW and NABET).

were: East, $218; West, $205; Midwest, $196; and South, $169. In 1972, responses from 752 radio and TV news operations indicated a median weekly salary for radio news directors was $150, compared to $253 for TV, and $256 for combined radio-TV news direction.[43a]

Wages & Hours: the Fair Labor Standards Act

Guidelines from the U.S. Department of Labor pertain to minimum wage, equal pay, record keeping, maximum hours, overtime pay, and child labor.[44] Managers should be familiar with the major considerations here; they ought to have competent bookkeepers and consult with CPA or other auditors as well as with legal counsel on the details of these federal requirements.[45]

Minimum wages are set for all employees in communications and other industries if the business enterprise grosses an annual sales volume of $250,000 or more. In radio and television stations, news-gatherers, reporters and clerical employees, as well as office, maintenance and custodial employees are guaranteed minimum wages by federal law. But executive, administrative and professional employees or outside salesmen are exempt from minimum wage and overtime pay standards. Also exempt are announcers, news editors or chief engineers of broadcast stations whose major studio is located: (a) in a city or town of 100,000 population or less unless it is part of a standard metropolitan statistical area (as defined and designated by the Office of Management and Budget) having a total population in excess of 100,000; or (b) in a city or town of 25,000 population or less which is part of such an area but at least 40 airline miles from the principal city in that area.[46] "Stringers" or similar intermittently paid persons are considered by the law to be free-lance personnel and not employees.

Wage differentials may be based on seniority, merit, quantity or quality of production, but not on sex.[47] Unless specifically exempt, all employees receive at least one and one-half times their regular rate of pay for all hours worked more than 40 during a seven-day workweek. Employees' "regular rate" (on which overtime is based) includes all remuneration for employment except several specifically listed kinds such as discretionary bonuses, premium payments for overtime work, gifts, and—significantly—talent fees to announcers in addition to their fixed salaries (e.g., for special on-air services, spot commercial announcements). Specifically included by law are other payments such as production bonuses and commission. The Federal act prohibits arbitrary discrimination in employing older workers, who are to be judged on ability rather than age regarding hiring, discharge, compensation and other terms of employment.

Child labor provisions of the law set 16 years as the minimum age for nonagricultural, nonhazardous occupations. But children 14 to 16 years of age are permitted to do clerical and other office work up to 3 hours on school days, 18 hours in a school week, 8 hours on a nonschool day, and 40 hours a week when school is not in session. Working hours cannot begin before 7:00 AM nor extend beyond 7:00 PM (except between June 1 and Labor Day when they may work up to 9:00 PM). The law specifically permits minors from 14 to 16 years old to perform such duties as "announcing, reading advertisements and spinning records on radio and TV." [48] The Federal laws about "child labor" do not apply to children employees as actors or performers in broadcast productions. Employers should keep in their files certification of the age of all young workers to document meeting the required minimum age.

Federal regulations, Part 516, demand such specific information to be kept on file as the following:

Full name of employee
Home address, including zip code

Date of birth, if under 19
Sex and occupation
Time of day and day of week when employee's workweek begins
Regular hourly rate of pay in which overtime premium is due; basis of wage
   payment (such as $2.00/hour; $16.00/day; $80.00/week; plus 5% commission)
Daily and weekly hours of work
Total daily or weekly straight time earnings
Total overtime compensation for the workweek
Total additions to or deductions from wages paid each pay period
Total wages paid each pay period
Date of payment and the pay period covered by payment

Wage-Hour Inspections

The Wage-Hour Division of the U.S. Department of Labor staffs ten regional offices and approximately 90 field offices which annually check a large percentage of broadcast stations, usually without advance notice. Inspections are either randomly determined, or else they result from employee complaints. Managers should not attempt to learn the names of any persons who may have filed complaints. Inspectors must notify the manager or an authorized representative whenever he is present at the station; management may wish at the initial meeting to confirm the investigator's credentials. Obvious courtesies are mutually helpful: provide the inspector with adequate work space where possible (otherwise the Wage-Hour Division can subpoena station records and remove them physically for proper examination); give access to documents pertinent to payrolls ("wage records and other pertinent data" included are listed on pp. 31–32 of the NAB's *The Broadcaster's Wage-Hour Guide*) or check with local counsel about access to doubtful documentation beyond the obvious such as monthly financial statements; assist the inspector to meet with any employees for interview, without participating in such confidential sessions. The investigator may copy whatever he needs of the documents, but the station is not expected to provide employees to do the copying. Nor may the investigator request any reworking of documentation; no single form is required for keeping records, as long as the station keeps complete records.

The NAB notes that, because of the investigator's familiarity with the employee and earning records of many kinds of stations, he may be able to comment on more efficient ways to keep necessary records with less clerical effort; the manager should keep alert to this possibility.

If the final report by the inspector claims that money is owed to present or past employees, and the Regional Office supports this finding (and if the governmental Division has written authorization from the employees to press a court claim for payment), the manager usually pursues one of four responses, according to the NAB: immediate payment of all money claimed, immediate refusal to pay, "wait and see" to negotiate at a later date, or immediate negotiation of some settlement.

Hours and Working Conditions

Certainly, the 40-hour week should be regarded as standard at any broadcasting station. With the higher cost of every phase of broadcasting, it would work to the financial disadvantage of the station, and in the long run to the detriment of the employee, if these hours for staff personnel were shortened. Problematic for employees are split-shifts of two periods a day, or a continuous shift but at hours that a person finds personally difficult to accommodate to or even disruptive. But there should be little employee discontent over a 40-hour week if excellent working conditions are maintained.

At the time of the NAB's national study, 38 per cent of TV employees and 42 per cent of radio employees regarded their physical working conditions (including space, lighting, heat, etc.) as "very satisfactory"; another one-fourth reported "satisfactory," with about one in ten commenting "satisfactory with reservations." Less than one-fifth in TV and radio responded "unsatisfactory," citing such reasons as technical equipment outmoded or in poor condition, station located too remotely, air conditioning and heating inadequate, poor lighting, not enough room and too noisy.[49]

It goes without saying that office facilities should be comfortably arranged, clean, well lighted, warm in the winter months and comfortably cool in the summer. A few large stations have installed their own cafeterias or food services. Service is provided throughout the periods of maximum working activity at out-of-pocket cost. This convenience can be a morale builder. Furthermore, it can save, over the period of a year, thousands of hours of time otherwise lost for coffee breaks across the street or somewhere else in the building. Stations not large enough to sustain this kind of service may make arrangements either for vending by caterers or for the installation of coin-operated machines, thus making wholesome food and beverages available on the premises during working hours.

In large cities, free company parking facilities are important. Many stations in large markets buy real estate adjacent to their studio buildings for this purpose. Parking lot land is thus available for future building expansion. It should be well lighted and safe for parked automobiles and for employees at night.

In recent years, many television stations have relocated in outlying areas. Offsetting some loss of glamour, business convenience, and central urban transit facilities in leaving the downtown area, benefits can accrue to the employee as well as the company in a shift to locations permitting horizontal rather than high-rise building development. Television operations always need more space; and employees appreciate less obtrusive security precautions, relatively uncongested highway access to their place of work, and even landscaped grounds.

Fringe Benefits and Incentive Plans

No standard pattern exists throughout the broadcasting industry in regard to fringe benefits and incentive plans for employees. Most workers now share in health and welfare plans at least partially supported by their employers. It is not unusual for companies to pay up to half of the costs of life insurance, hospitalization and medical care. Paid sick leave and vacations are provided by most, if not all, stations. Some companies provide such additional benefits as moving allowances, layoff benefits, severance pay, pensions, paid holidays and company-financed college scholarships for dependents of employees.

Many employees take fringe benefits for granted. Often they are not aware of the extent of those contributions. It should be in the interest of the organization to see that all people on the payroll are well informed of substantial company contributions. Some stations have found it advantageous to itemize the costs of the various benefits and give this information to their employees along with their W-2 forms. In general, vacation periods, as well as other fringe benefits, tend to be more liberal in the larger markets.

Most employees who responded to the NAB national study appraised very favorably their stations' policies for such matters as vacations, holidays, leaves of absence. Only 7 per cent of TV employees judged their stations' policies as "unsatisfactory," while 15 per cent of radio employees so responded.[50]

Biennial NAB surveys of employment in broadcasting do not include data for office workers. However, NAB recommends that station managers review the regular studies of office personnel conducted by: (1) the telephone companies, (2) The Bureau of Labor Statistics and (3) The National Office Management Association. The report of the latter organizations showed that the predominant pattern for office employees was a one-week paid vacation after the completion of six months of employment and two weeks of paid vacation after one year of work. The trend appears to be to grant eight paid holidays each year for office workers.[51]

Stations providing sick leave to workers can qualify for tax advantages of up to $100 per week of an employee's sick benefits, but only if there is an organized plan and if it is communicated to the employees.

Employees drafted or enlisting for military service are entitled to regular pay up until the time they stop work. If an employee resigns and then is not accepted for military duty, or if he is released after he has been accepted, he is entitled to re-employment if he applies for such reinstatement within 30 days. (He also retains his full seniority rights, in accordance with provisions of Section 9 of the Universal Military Training and Service Act.) The personnel manager must keep abreast of governmental regulations and industrial developments. Matters of military leave, adjusted compensation for men in service, and so on, become vexatious problems only if solutions are improvised out of ignorance or neglect.

Few radio and television stations have started retirement plans for their employees. After a pioneering survey of 64 broadcasting organizations with retirement plans, the NAB prepared a general guide for broadcasters who contemplated instituting such benefits. Forty-four of the companies surveyed had fixed benefit pension plans, seventeen had deferred profit sharing plans, and three companies had both.[52]

Unions and Labor Relations

Radio and television stations in major markets have occasion to deal with most of the labor unions active in broadcasting. The programming department, especially the announcers and other talent, comes under the jurisdiction of the American Federation of Television and Radio Artists (AFTRA) and, in the case of television, the Screen Actors Guild (SAG) as well. The International Alliance of Theatrical Stage Employees (IATSE) and the American Federation of Musicians (AFM) are active in programming aspects of broadcasting. In the engineering and technical fields, the National Association of Broadcast Employees and Technicians (NABET) and the International Brotherhood of Electrical Workers (IBEW) are the most active unions.[52a]

Smaller-market stations may be involved with only one union or with none at all. By 1973, about one-third of the television stations in the U.S. dealt with one or more unions, but only some 8 per cent of the radio stations were unionized.[53] Broadcast employees have joined unions for many reasons, including inaction or unfair action by management, supervisors who are arbitrary or insensitive, and unfair or inequitable wages. In recent years job security and protection have caused concern to employees because of increasing changes in ownership of stations and in format. The NAB advises managers of non-union stations to spend more time on their greatest assets, their employees, who may not be getting the attention, consideration, and rewards that they ought. For the mid-1970s, the NAB anticipated even wider efforts to organize non-union stations, with station-wide labor units instead of unions for single departments or for related job classifications. Also anticipated was unionization of clerical workers who constitute the only large group of station employees yet unorganized in otherwise union shops.

Two other developments will complicate union negotiations with station management. One is the continued growth of automation in program operations, where quality control (immediacy, flexibility, creativity) and especially personnel considerations (size of staff, jurisdiction over procedures, impersonal working conditions "with machines") can be greatly affected.[54] The other is equal pay and opportunity for minority persons, including women, as directed by Federal legislation.[55] The Civil Rights Act legislates equal opportunity in matters such as hiring, firing, promotion, seniority, benefits, conditions and terms of employment; it bans discrimination (based on sex, race, color, religion or national origin) by private employers of 25 or more persons; in 1972 the law was extended to cover managers and professionals among others.

Commentators on broadcasting and unions have briefly described general guidelines for management attitudes and overall procedures in dealing with employees and their labor representatives.[56] They emphasize the essential relationship that should exist between persons who in their own right are individual human beings, some of whom are supervisory managers and others of whom are employees. In a climate of mutual collaboration in the business and creativity of a broadcast station operation, they should communicate freely with one another lest initially ignored minor difficulties grow into areas of grievance and eventually become issues of contention. In unionized stations, the contract should be honored exactly by both parties as a set of agreements mutually entered into, and not as a tool to take advantage of the other side. Nor is the time of negotiating a contract the only important period in these relationships; those negotiations will have grown out of the year-around context in the daily station operation either of harmonious collaboration or of tenseness marked with altercations and misunderstandings.

CBS, Inc., outlines in its manual for office employees in New York, "The Company You Keep" (1974 edition, pp. 26–27), recommended procedures for handling problems or grievances of non-unionized personnel.

1. Salary grade employees who have grievances are encouraged to discuss them with their supervisors and department heads.
2. If problems cannot be resolved in this manner, they are brought to the attention of the employee's representatives on the Employee-Management Committee. The employee representatives are elected annually and listed in TIE-LINE.
3. In an effort to settle grievances on a department level, representatives may discuss the problems with the department heads involved.
4. If a satisfactory settlement is not reached, representatives present the grievances to a designated member of Personnel.
5. If problems still remain, meetings are set up including:
    (a) the employee
    (b) the representative and one other member of the Employee Group
    (c) a representative of the Personnel Department
    (d) the supervisor and/or department head of the employee involved.
6. If still not resolved, problems are turned over to a sub-committee composed of two members of the Employee Group and two members of the Management Group. The sub-committee may invite other persons to confer with them.
7. As a last resort, grievances are turned over to the full Employee-Management Committee.

The National Labor Relations Board notes the accepted fact and even desirability of unionism:

> Employees shall have the right to self organization, to form, join, or assist labor organizations, to bargain collectively through representatives of their own choosing, and to engage in other concerted activities for the purpose of collective bargaining or other mutual aid protection.[57]

At the same time the NLRB notes the correlative rights of all parties involved in collective bargaining through union representation, and supports management's defense of its own policies and responsibilities:

> It is an unfair labor practice for either party to refuse to bargain collectively with the other. The obligation does not, however, compel either party to agree to a proposal by the other nor does it require either party to make a concession to the other.

Reinsch and Ellis note that "signing of the union contract does not mean that you must or should be expected to give up your fundamental authority in the determination of company policy and in exercising management control and direction of the radio station." [58]

The basic responsibility imposed by the Labor Management Relations Act on the employer as well as the labor organization is to bargain in "good faith" about rates of pay, hours, and terms and conditions of employment. This pertains to the actual negotiation of a contract and also to conferring about questions that arise during the period covered by contract. Such bargaining does not include acceptance of any particular demand by the opposite party, nor does it require compromise on any issue regarded as truly basic (unless such refusal clearly indicates "bad faith"). [59]

Usually, the station manager and the station attorney are directly responsible for dealings with unions. In some hard pressed properties, one poor union contract can mean the difference between profit and loss. A poorly written agreement can deny a company the necessary flexibility it needs in the development of its operation. Companies of large size, with more than one union contract, frequently have a director of industrial relations, who devotes most, if not all, of his time to the labor relations area. This individual must know every function of every union employee in the company. He must be thoroughly knowledgeable in each of the agreement clauses under existing contracts and he must be aware of what can be accomplished in future negotiations in the interest of better relationships between the union and the company. Effective collective bargaining includes careful preparation, including precise knowledge of NLRB and Labor Department requirements, and thorough knowledge and as much experience as possible of the techniques and procedures used at the bargaining table in the critical process of "give and take" toward mutually acceptable compromise. The NAB recommends (along with competent legal counsel for advice) such steps as these in management's planning for labor negotiations: determine management's position on labor issues, whether economic or "non-economic" (money demands, and demands involving either operational practices or matters of principle); study current contract and how it affects operational procedures, then get supervisors' judgments about contract improvements; list proposals according to priority (those desired but optional, those very important, and those "strike-worthy"); review salaries of employees compared with comparable stations elsewhere and with all stations in local market; gather factual documentation (e.g., the NAB labor contract summaries from elsewhere); estimate probable demands by the union, and determine management's position on each; and, finally, draft the management proposal as the basic working document for bargaining (although some employers at this point wait for the union to present its demands first).

The negotiator for management, or the negotiating team, must be selected for detailed knowledge of the station's policies, operations, labor laws, as well as for authority and ability to be firm yet flexible where appropriate. The management's goals upon entering into negotiations should be realistic and reasonably attainable; and the initial proposals should be continually evaluated during the counter-proposals by the union so that modification can be made when necessary.[60] The NAB notes that "the best negotiations are those in which there is no winner and no loser. If management did achieve that which it set out to secure, it is wise to be discreet."

There have been costly strikes in the broadcasting industry because either labor or management or both did not approach negotiations in a mature manner. There has been a degree of irresponsibility on both sides. Hopefully, there can be more intelligent handling of labor-management problems in the future. Nothing is more essential in union and labor relations than careful explanations of the rationale of company policies accompanied by thorough factual documentation. When people know the reasons for doing something in a particular manner, they can be expected to have more understanding of the task. In cases where complete explanations are given, difficulties usually can be precluded. The bargaining table is, or should be, a meeting place of reasonable men.

INTERNAL COMMUNICATIONS

A weekly or monthly house organ reporting the activities of the company and its people can be very valuable regardless of station size. The house organ provides an exchange of information between employees. It is an informal channel of communication between personnel and management. Employee suggestions for station improvement can be incorporated in such a publication. Any specific changes in working conditions or hours can be announced and adequately explained. General industry news of importance can be reviewed. The physical appearance and style of the house organ are not as important as the content and the very fact that it is available. In small stations, a mimeographed publication can accomplish the function.

Beyond recounting "chatty bits" of news about employees' travels, families and hobbies, a newsletter should provide the specific information that employees want: explanations of the general organization and operation of the company; corporate and station policies directly affecting them; progress in achieving stated objectives of the operation; company planning related to business environment, advances in technology, and political developments which might affect jobs or wages; how their own jobs relate to company strategy, including opportunity for advancement; reasons for any personnel reductions and how such will affect remaining employees.[61] Through a candid newsletter with accurate and pertinent information, management can preclude unwarranted speculation and assumptions about any number of rumors, always seeming to abound, about matters that might loom as threats to employees and distract them from the work at hand. The fact that people tend to communicate far more freely to members of their own subgroups than to other persons, and only to those higher in status when they are not supervisors, accelerates the spread of speculation based on partial data or misinformation.[62] This occurs particularly when salaries, promotions, or other important personnel matters are at stake. Rumors erupt when personnel are confused and unclear about what is happening and when they feel unable to affect matters touching their careers; gossip and guessing become a means for employees to express and thus alleviate anxiety about the results of pending or fancied changes.[63]

The survey by CBS, Inc. in 1971 revealed that over half its employees (53% of respondents) judged internal communications as so inadequate that they "learn more through the grapevine" than any other way.[64] While it is best to communicate as often and fully with as many personnel as possible—through meetings, posted notices, circulated memoranda or a newsletter—sometimes word-of-mouth carries information more swiftly and widely and with greater credibility than the more formalized means. The obvious shortcoming in the grapevine is the possibility of distortion or misinformation. But management does have some control over the work environment in which the grapevine operates, and can even use feedback from this informal source as a cue to what information must yet be relayed to personnel, or where public clarification about misinformation is appropriate.[65] No one can control the "grapevine" as a channel of communication, but it is possible to influence it properly; above all, it must not be discounted as a significant factor in employees' understanding and support of management plans and goals.

While management would agree that people should have information about those things that directly affect them, it should also realize that employees should be told what they want to know rather than simply what management wants them to know, and as early and often as possible. This is particularly important in such matters as change of ownership where jobs, assignments, formats, station schedules, and even some company policies may be subject to major changes.

> Personnel losses, transfers, promotions and replacements are occurring. Decisions about new policies and procedures are being made, and often modify people's relationships. Some people are informed about changed relationships before others; some are not informed at all. Although it is common practice to communicate decisions to all the persons who are affected by them, the problem is often to determine who are the relevant persons. Unless we are extremely sensitive to the social structure of our organization, it is likely that we shall restrict communication too narrowly. The restrictive communication of decisions about change, however, can be extremely disruptive to any consensus people have about their relationships to one another.[66]

The relationships between management and employees should reflect and support mutual esteem and self-respect. And a person's self-respect is based on true ability, recognized achievement, and respect from others.[67] Such collaboration, assisted by two-way communication among staff and management, breeds satisfied, productive employees as well as more efficient and creative work. And this is essential to a well-managed broadcast station.

Employee Suggestion Systems

Beyond contributing to productivity by supporting morale, the suggestion box or other procedure for employees to propose their ideas to management can seriously advance the pooling of skill and vision. Department managers should encourage creative suggestions by making everyone on the staff feel free to discuss ideas. Such casual conversation can be partly structured by holding brain-storming sessions where all participants openly contribute whatever comes to mind about a project proposal or specific problem, so that the good ideas can be identified and evaluated.

A possible way to foster employees' sense of participation in the company, as well as to profit from their creative recommendations and opinions, is to organize an employee-management committee. If set up according to departments, representatives can be selected by their colleagues to forward to management constructive ideas or reactions or inquiries concerning policies or points of factual information.

Some of the best program concepts and some of the greatest cost-control ideas at WGN Radio and Television in recent years have stemmed from suggestions made by station personnel. In an operation the size of WGN-AM-TV (some 600 employees in the Chicago offices), suggestions are generally confined to the areas of office procedures, engineering, or production techniques. Occasionally, though, a splendid idea is submitted in general programming or community affairs. The fact that every person on the staff thinks about station improvement is, for management, ample reward in itself. Reinsch and Ellis emphasize this point:

> Creative thinking develops only in a permissive atmosphere, where every employee knows about his job, respects his company, and understands what they both represent to the public. You cultivate creative thinking by real two-way communication, and by running a station where anybody on the staff feels free to walk through your open door, sit down, and give out his ideas.
>
> More sound programming ideas have been hatched over a casual bull session than have come out of a dozen formal conferences.
>
> If the atmosphere in a station is truly permissive, each employee knows he can drop in to talk whenever the inspiration strikes him and that his superior will listen to him. This requires listening carefully, attentively, sympathetically. It is vitally important to continue listening with courtesy and interest until the entire idea has been presented.
>
> Remember, too, that, no matter how far-fetched or impractical a proposal may sound, it is not ridiculous. It has dignity and it demands a respectful hearing,

because somebody on your staff thought enough of it, and enough of you, to express it to you.[68]

Apparently most stations already operate on this principle. Over 85 per cent of those responding to the NAB's employee survey were satisfied with the opportunity their stations gave to make suggestions and contribute ideas; again, about 85 per cent responded that the consideration given their suggestions was satisfactory, half of them stating "very satisfactory." Obviously, management's positive reaction to their interest supported further efforts to contribute to the company's success as well as to their own self-esteem.

ACTIVITIES OF PERSONNEL IN THE COMMUNITY

The station manager must set the example for employee involvement in community affairs. He must show his interest in the well-being of his city, his state and the general coverage area. He should encourage all of his employees to do likewise, whether in support of a particular program of the mayor or the city government, or of the governor, or in church or school projects or any other areas of community public service that the employee may prefer. If the employees who are active in community affairs conduct themselves properly, they will bring much credit to the station. In a business that depends so much upon public support, this is vital.

One of the benefits from the outside activities of employees is the gaining of confidence and additional self-respect. Such development can add to their prospects for promotions in radio or television. More immediately, they can become acquainted through first-hand experience with the kinds of people who make up the station's audience, and whose interests, activities and needs should be reflected in the local news broadcast daily by the station and in other areas of local programming and scheduling. It may even reflect favorably upon the sales staff's efforts to win advertising support from that same community.

At all times, while working in the offices and studios and when participating in or merely attending civic affairs, staff members must be instinctively aware that they *are* the station to the people with whom they speak by telephone, whom they meet personally, and with whom they collaborate on community projects. Especially in small markets, the staff members' dress, attitude, vocabulary and tone of voice represent the station itself; obviously his other personal characteristics of strength or weakness (courtesy, carelessness, unconcern, or attraction to alcohol) all may be perceived as direct manifestations of the station.[69] Management should make sure that all employees are aware of this unique, personal responsibility to themselves, their station and their community.

OPPORTUNITIES FOR EMPLOYEE GROWTH

The station manager really doesn't develop anyone on the staff. Rather, he can provide an environment in which responsible and ambitious people can develop themselves. To this end, he should carefully plan a long-range program of continuing employee education with opportunities to learn about the obligations of the licensee, the provisions of the Communications Act, program responsibilities and, in general, the basic realities confronting management in a broadcasting station.

Few station employees know very much about revenues and expenses, nor are they highly cognizant of the problems of depreciation and obsolescence of broadcast equipment. Yet, they should be interested in information of this nature if given an opportunity to learn about it. Management should explain its areas of primary concern to the company employees and, in open discussion, join with them in considerations of mutual problems of a professional concern. The resources of a college or university may be employed to organize and assist with an employee-development program.

Top executives in broadcasting have many opportunities to attend professional meetings. They sometimes lose sight of the need of their employees for a wider perspective than they usually get within the limitations of their work assignments. An employee development program should pay dividends in employee appreciation and in an expansion of professional interests.

Reinsch and Ellis describe many useful kinds of staff meetings for internal communication of information and training as well as shared decision-making.[70] These include sessions among the managers and key supervisors, meetings of department heads with their staffs, and general meetings of the entire organization several times a year. Trade papers and magazines should be made available to all staff members, to help them keep abreast of current factual data, trends and significant issues in the field. These might be kept in a station library, with most recent copies in the reception and employees' lounge areas. Beyond the studio building, further training can be made available through college courses, vocational seminars, participation in trade meetings and conventions, and attendance at events of media and social significance in the city. Employees should be encouraged to visit stations in other markets. Reports might be made to the home station staff at meetings mentioned earlier.

Almost one-half of those broadcast employees who told the NAB that they did not wish to make a career of radio or television intended to leave because of dissatisfaction with the field. The negative reasons for most of them included "full capabilities not recognized, lack of advancement, and scheduling irritations."[71] A decade later CBS, Inc. found that more than two out of every five of its employees claimed that they did not have all the opportunity needed to develop their skills; only 37 per cent judged their development opportunity to be adequate.[72]

CREATIVITY IN THE EMPLOYEE

In the early days of radio, it was exciting to work in broadcasting because it was all so new. Almost anything could be tried. It was easy to be different. Innovations in programming and in production were encouraged. In those days, there were real premiums on creativity; imitated formats were rare. The early days of television brought a renewed emphasis on experimental programming and production. People were challenged by the opportunity to try something new and they were generally given the freedom to do so. Outstanding advancements were made in programming, in the uses of the camera, in lighting and staging, and in performance techniques.

The opportunity to innovate has always been a prime motivating force for creative people. Standardized formats and routine assignments discourage men and women capable of new discoveries and new ideas. Stations that offer little or no opportunities for experimentation tend to attract a plodder type of employee satisfied by the performance of routine assignments. Highly creative people avoid this kind of broadcast operation. It is to a station's advantage to encourage the development of new program formats and new production methods, thereby attracting employees capable of producing new ideas for their own and the station's benefit.

The process of creativity and the personal characteristics of creative people were studied under three grants from the Carnegie Corporation.[73]

The Institute of Personality Assessment and Research of the University of California conducted a six-year study of the differences between highly creative people and those less creative. The study found that while intelligence and special aptitudes are important factors in creativity up to a point, they are not perhaps the crucial elements. A person with even average intelligence can be creative if his environment is conducive to creativity. The Institute isolated for study the *interests* of highly creative people and made some valuable discoveries. Persons who are highly creative are not likely to be interested in small details or in the practical or the concrete; they are more concerned with what things mean and what the implications of those meanings might have for new discoveries. All creative people in the study were consistent in choosing that which was complex over that which was simple. They were not bound by what was already known, but more frequently interested in what might *become known*. The creative person was usually a nonconformist in the field of ideas but not usually in the fields of behavior or social patterns. The creative person was generally independent, able to find satisfaction in those elements of challenge that other people might not even perceive.

Several characteristics of the creative person identified by the study should be particularly desirable in an employee of a radio or television station: easy adjustment to people and situations, an attraction to problems and their solutions, a high degree of sensitivity, and a wide range of interests. The creative person's preference for the new, the unknown and the complex over the traditional, the known and the simple should interest any station manager who wants his station to be different. The creative employee should be in demand in any station where conformity is desired in behavior and social patterns but is not wanted in the field of ideas.

A second study, undertaken by psychologist Morris I. Stein at the University of Chicago and at New York University, analyzed the environments of creative people to determine which kinds of working conditions were most conducive to creativity. Among other findings, Stein concluded that, in contrast to less creative workers who expect quick achievement, the creative person works more slowly at first on a problem, but then moves much more quickly toward a solution. The work of the creative person, in addition to being more original, is usually more efficient; far less time is spent by the creative individual in checking back over his work once he has completed it, whereas the uncreative person is prone to spend considerable time in checking and re-checking.

A third study, conducted by the Institute of Social Research at the University of Michigan, investigated the conditions that seem to lead to high scientific creativity: scientists are likely to be more creative when they are in a state of uncertainty and when they are somewhat uncomfortable about it. A feeling of basic security, however, must exist; anxiety about oneself or about the social environment or about the work itself can stifle creativity. Thus, to be creative, the scientist must have sufficient degrees of uncertainty to stimulate his interest, yet he must have enough sense of security in what he is doing to offset deep anxieties.

The three studies seem to suggest that the creative employee needs an atmosphere of unfettered accomplishment in order to produce his best ideas. Any time that any organization consciously or unconsciously deprives itself of the creative climate, it stands to lose important benefits—novel and challenging ideas, new and exciting program concepts, departures from established practices in sales and public relations, and (perhaps most important) the exhilarating atmosphere of the daring and the different in almost any phase of the station's activities.

Dominance and Creativity

The dominating person can inhibit staff creativity. Managers or supervisors who show concern for the employees as people, both on and off the job, normally achieve better productivity than those who like to show their authority. The creative, productive person needs a considerable amount of freedom and a minimum of supervision. He appreciates constructive criticism when sensibly made and helpfully voiced. Supervisors who exercise authority to criticize, while having no ability to make constructive comments, can cause obstinate problems. The creative person is generally quite sensitive to criticism and cannot easily be objective about negative reaction. But perhaps an innovative person's morale and creative power can be most destroyed by management's indifference or even cynicism, much less ridicule, about an original and imaginative idea.[74]

Creativity must be regulated by its own process of development. If it is forced by artificial deadlines or hectored by authority the results may be disappointing. Everyone knows how an idea may pop into the consciousness after he has struggled for days with a problem and then put it aside. The solution may appear all at once during a drive home from work or while taking a walk or even while dozing. Once facts have been gathered and after considerable study and meditation have taken place, it is not at all unusual for an inspiration to flash into the mind when least expected. The truly creative idea cannot be regulated by deadlines in the same manner as the routine assignment.

This raises the challenge of balancing creativity with the demands of standardization required by the realities of broadcast planning, scheduling and programming. Intelligent leadership by management must provide sound guidance and fulfill its own responsibilities in overseeing policies and procedures, while at the same time "clearing the air for action and establishing a climate in which a creative spirit can live and stay healthy." [75]

The Motivation of Creativity

What can management do to provide a favorable climate for creative people and to motivate them properly? Management cannot force employees to be motivated. But it can create a context that stimulates the employee to his best efforts. Reinsch and Ellis describe the process of motivation as "stimulating, listening, challenging, encouraging, inspiring, providing an atmosphere for self-expression and self-fulfillment," adding that the substantive motivation for staff members to throw their creative energy into the broadcast enterprise depends on the station itself and its program service—"if it is sensitive to the needs and wants of the community, if it has a conscience and lets it speak." [76]

Countless broadcasters have made original contributions in writing, directing and performance, usually because they received some encouragement from peers and, at the right moment, from superiors. There have been others who have weathered misunderstanding, rejection and even opposition, but who have developed their creativity in the broadcast and advertising fields—to their own fulfillment, but more importantly to the audience's satisfaction and to the advancement of their profession and their companies. Edward R. Murrow and Fred Friendly innovated in news and documentaries, largely encouraged and usually supported by CBS administration; Sylvester "Pat" Weaver's innovations when he was president of NBC outlived his stay with the network ("Today," "Tonight," "Monitor," the program spectaculars which later were dubbed the "specials"); Mary Wells and Stan Freberg took their creativity to their own newly-formed advertising agencies and succeeded beyond expectations; Joan Ganz Cooney developed for PBS the award-winning creative program series, Sesame Street, as well as other children's programming. Where creativity was not supported by station, network and advertising companies, some creative people (especially playwrights, directors and actors from network drama) fled to other media such as motion pictures and legitimate theater. Not only the companies that lost them, but broadcasting generally, suffered incalculable loss.

The really important developments in broadcasting may not have been made as yet. Whatever progress there may be in the future will depend upon the type of people who are chosen to work in the industry and upon how they are treated. Creative people are the most important part of any radio or television station.

PROMOTION POLICIES

It is difficult to set up standard guidelines for promotions. It is painful to acknowledge that some stations and some managers neglect to reward persons who make important contributions to the company. Often promotions cannot be implemented when deserved. But a token cash bonus can be used in lieu of an immediate promotion; reassignment is another possibility. Every encouragement should be given the apt employee in the hope that he will remain with the company and aspire to an improved position. Proverbs 13:12 cautions that "Hope deferred maketh the heart sick." Also it maketh the foot loose. Laggard promotions and grudging recognition can strip a station of its most promising people. And much time and money is lost while replacements learn the details of a job before they reach the level of first-hand experience and productivity of a departed employee.[77]

When in 1962 the NAB surveyed nearly 2,000 broadcast employees about station promotion policies of their employers, almost two-thirds of those in television and slightly more than half of those in radio indicated they were "satisfied" or "very satisfied." Almost one-third of all employees, however, judged that their stations' promotion policies were either "unsatisfactory" or "satisfactory with reservations." [78] Interestingly, they judged that stations other than their own tended to offer better promotion policies (three-quarters in TV and two-thirds in radio judged other stations' policies as "satisfactory" or "very satisfactory," while only about one-fifth of all employees judged other stations as "unsatisfactory").

In 1971 a management consultant firm studied all CBS employees in positions above those entitled to overtime—thus considered as part of management.[79] Slightly more than half the "executive"-related employees in all divisions of CBS, Inc. judged their promotion opportunities to be limited to the departments in which they worked, while about one-quarter (27%) disagreed with that view. One-third of the respondents agreed with, and another third did not dispute, the statement that success depends more on whom you know than on what you know. Again, over half (53½%) responded that they knew little about how performance was evaluated; slightly more (56%) claimed infrequent feedback on their performance and on how they might improve. Of those responding, one-third (34%) did not think that CBS used its manpower efficiently compared with other companies, almost half (48%) expressed neutral judgment, and only 18 per cent appraised CBS's manpower use as efficient.

CBS emphasizes internal promotion not only to reward effective employees but also to expedite the hiring of competent personnel for job openings. The CBS policy statement for its office employees in New York might prompt similar but simplified procedures for large broadcast stations and companies:

1. A job opening notice will be sent to the department head by the Placement Office. This is posted immediately in the department for two full working days so that eligible employees in the department may be given first consideration. . . .

2. Each Monday, the positions that were not filled within the department during the past 2½ working days are posted on five central bulletin boards. . . .

Employees who believe their background, length of service in their current job and job performance may qualify them for a posted position, may contact the Placement Office. . . .

[Most] employees are eligible and encouraged to participate in the Career Inventory System [which] is the computer-supported data bank of individual employees' backgrounds and interests used to search for and identify qualified candidates to fill executive (exempt) openings. . . .

Only when no qualified person is found through the above process will the Placement Office recruit from outside sources.[80]

CBS employees are urged to notify Personnel of special skills, education, or other background not noted before which might warrant consideration for transfer or promotion when openings occur in the company.[81]

In promotion as in hiring there is the knotty problem of adequate consideration for minorities, including women, who may have been systematically excluded from regular advancement in past years. Often this imbalance has developed because of the very structure of the organization. Managers who themselves might be willing to promote women and other minorities may find it very difficult within the prevailing climate, real or imagined, within the management level of the company (with authoritarian rather than egalitarian emphasis).[82] Although there are various "climates" within single organizations, each company tends to have a general characteristic climate. Loring and Wells suggest that the *exploitative* climate requires obedience, and all employees tend to be passive, dependent and subordinate (McGregor's Theory X; see previous chapter). The *paternalistic* climate requires deference; and patterns of advancement are traditional and sex-typed, although this benevolent authoritarian organization may occasionally advance women to positions in lower management. The *consultative* climate requires involvement; managers must perceive employees—including women and minority persons—less as stereotypes and more as individual persons (McGregor's Theory Y organization). Finally, the *egalitarian* climate invites participation, where women as well as men can contribute productively to the enterprise, with individual competence as the criterion rather than sex- or minority-role expectations (our own Theory V emphasis).[83]

All persons intended for promotion towards managerial positions need some appropriate training, at least by moving progressively through increasingly responsible positions where abilities can be demonstrated and where accountability for results grows. A special concern must be exercised by top management for properly preparing minority persons for such advancement. Loring and Wells express this concern on behalf of women, but their caution applies equally to all minorities, and indeed to all employees:

To knowingly select a person who is underqualified without giving the essential support for probable success is a waste of time and effort on the part of the organization and the woman [or other minority] trainee. It will be better to take more preparatory time and adjust the timetable for accomplishing an increase in the number of women [and minorities] in management training. However, it will be necessary to convince most compliance officers that any delay is not, in fact, lack of good faith. Objective evidence of the need to delay management training pending further preparatory training may be required. Surely some indication that such training is in process is essential. The pressures for promotion will undoubtedly increase as affirmative action programs are implemented.[84]

Reinsch and Ellis suggest that all employees should know their opportunity for promotion; but they also warn against overemphasizing long-range advancement possibilities at the risk of taking attention away from what is most important—the need to do each day's job as well as possible.[85] Robert D. Wood was sales manager of KNXT, the CBS-owned television station in Los Angeles, when he strongly advocated the philosophy of "Do the job you're in now the best way you know how, and you can't miss." He noted that one person in ten follows that policy and so stands out clearly above all other employees to managers who are seeking persons for promotion. (Wood subsequently became general manager of KNXT, then president of the CBS Television Stations Division, and finally president of the CBS Television Network; he excelled at each position, retained his personal concern for people, and CBS executives could not overlook his obvious record of success at each step.)

EXECUTIVE RECRUITMENT AND DEVELOPMENT

Many of the serious problems in the broadcasting industry in recent years stem from the lack of trained administrative personnel to manage all the new broadcast properties as they came on the air following World War II. To attain the true potential of broadcasting, the industry needs well-trained management personnel—men and women who, early in life, can begin the study of station administration, mindful of their very sober responsibilities and truly dedicated to broadcasting as a profession.[86]

It is hard to understand the attitudes of station managers who refuse to pay attention to the need for executive recruiting and training. Some managers, particularly in smaller markets, act as if their positions might be in jeopardy should they hire assistants with management potential. We know of actual cases of the firing of staff people suspected of executive abilities. Fortunately, this sort of selfish and stupid practice is on its way out. The able manager surrounds himself with the ablest talent he can find and afford. The fact is that people of real executive endowments and potential are in exceedingly short supply. The age group from 25 to 45, which is the source of most executive potential, constitutes a lessening segment of the population and it will continue to show a proportional decrease for several years. General expansions in business and industry, along with diversifications and acquisitions, have created unprecedented demands for executives.

Broadcast progress depends not upon systems and gadgets but upon brilliant minds. Ultimately, radio and television properties, much as major-league baseball organizations, develop their own executives. If top management takes the time to meet with and help develop young staff employees, there should be little need in many cases to have to go beyond the confines of the company in order to find potential talent. Where a need for future station leadership is anticipated, an orderly and effective course of executive training can be instituted for the development of young men and women for key posts in the organization. These courses of training can avoid being haphazard in structure and results if organizers study the methods and procedures of other stations and agencies experienced in similar projects.

WTOP-TV in Washington, D.C. has conducted since 1952 successful executive training in programming and production. The Corinthian Broadcasting Corporation has a summer executive training program for selected college students. The Avco Broadcasting Corporations and the Group W (Westinghouse) stations have similar programs for the development of news personnel. NBC, in conjunction with Northwestern University, has operated a summer training program for interns for 25 years. The Michigan Broadcasters Association sponsors a program in which various radio and television stations in the state accept interns from the state universities and pay their expenses for three-month periods so they may learn station operations and management procedures while in residence at the stations. The International Radio and Television Society annually conducts a summer-long internship for a half dozen advanced students of broadcasting from U.S. colleges, who are paid while they meet personnel and observe procedures at stations, networks, agencies, production companies, and research firms in New York City. WGN Continental Broadcasting Company maintains a year-around internship program for college and university students selected on the basis of their interests in either television production, or arts and facilities, news, public affairs and sales promotion; five internees are accepted each quarter for a total of 20 each year. In addition, 17 college students are employed during the school year on a part-time basis and 12 students are added to the payroll each summer as vacation replacements.

In all these and other equally successful programs, station executives have the opportunity to observe people at close range and on a daily basis. Those who have exceptional promise are available for future employment. At WGN Continental Broadcasting Company a considerable number of former interns have joined the regular payroll. This very capable and promising group was assembled with the cooperation of Northwestern University and a forward looking recruitment policy, but it now also includes other mid-America colleges and universities.

Broadcasters are realizing they must either participate in the growing continuing education movement or be left at the post in the race for acquisition of new knowledge. Notable steps have already been taken. The NAB has conducted executive development seminars at Harvard University, designed to develop the skills used in the analysis and solution of broadcast management problems. Seminars in sales management and in engineering have also been sponsored by the NAB. The Chicago Council of the American Association of

Advertising Agencies, in cooperation with Northwestern University, held a 30-week training school for young executives. Thirty-five ad agency employees, generally in the 25- to 35-year bracket, were given rigorous training in all aspects of the agency business. The cost of $500 per enrollee was paid by the advertising agencies.

The International Radio and Television Society annually conducts four-day intense seminars bringing together broadcasters and college teachers of radio-television, to explore current issues developing in the field.[86a]

These are but samples of the kinds of activity going on in broadcasting and in advertising to update knowledge and stimulate minds. Elsewhere, state associations, group-owned stations, network affiliate organizations, the wire services, music licensing organizations, and individual stations have arranged with colleges and universities to conduct program, engineering, sales and management seminars and workshops for radio and television employees. Instruction has been provided jointly by authorities in broadcasting and education.

In 1972 the Corporation for Public Broadcasting contributed a major grant to the National Association of Educational Broadcasters to help fund a series of professional training sessions across the country. The NAEB sought to include executive management development, because it judged that the national educational broadcasting service had siphoned off from local stations their most capable managers. At those stations replacement talent who demonstrated superior ability and durable leadership of local operations under stress was not being found. Complicating this problem was the questionable strength of conviction of such managers to pursue public television's goals while caught in the cross-pressures of local station boards and lower-level creative personnel seeking to initiate challenging program concepts.[87]

Local managers must have an intellectual understanding of issues, policies, patterns of possible actions, and the predictable consequences of given actions. This knowledge, sensitivity, and skill in decision-making can be strengthened by special study and collaborative exploration with specialists in training sessions—applying managerial concepts to innovative cultural and social-oriented programming, news and public affairs, minority topics and contemporary issues in a changing society. This demands the highest quality of leadership. Effective leadership does not just happen; it must be sought out and groomed.

The manager eager to enlighten and advance his junior executives will find academic opportunities ideal for his purpose. These people will discover new insights readily transferable to station advancements and their personal growth should be more than suitable repayment for the costs of their enrollment in the studies.

Unfortunately at too many broadcasting stations, opportunities for classes, seminars and conferences are denied everyone except the manager and, on occasion, the sales manager. This is one of the most shortsighted practices in the field of radio and television management.

The well-run radio or television operation sees to it that young executive talent is standing in the wings in each department. In those stations, the senior department executive works with those persons to encourage development in various areas of responsibility and to prepare them for possible future prime positions in the company.

Granted, the element of luck will be a factor. Many people with fine executive abilities have never had the opportunities to use outstanding talents because chance has not brought them to the right place at the right time. Still, the station must help. The station manager must be a student of human nature and a teacher of skills.

Many station managers find it desirable to keep retired employees on retainer as consultants, thus ensuring a continuity of wisdom and experience. This is an admirable idea. It may be suggested, however, that much consultative experience is, or should be, available before retirement. Too often management falls into stereotyped thinking, neglecting to make use of veteran employees who are sometimes relegated to routine tasks in corporate "backwaters." The point is that management may well find consultative resources within the organization before the retirement of men by the calendar. The practice of taking thought after a man's retirement is, sometimes, an admission that insufficient consideration was given to his potentials before retirement. This is a source of creativity too frequently overlooked.

SEPARATION POLICIES

The task of terminating an employee's employment is never easy. Authority to take such action must be vested in the heads of departments, and their decisions need to have the support of the station manager.

Broadcast stations typically reflect continuing turnover of personnel. Many employees leave of their own choice for presumably better job opportunities or for other personally-initiated reasons. But even a decade ago, one-third of the radio stations throughout the country had discharged almost 8 per cent of the persons employed in radio during a 12-month period. Less than one-half of the television stations had discharged 2.3 per cent of all TV employees that same year.[88] Those radio stations that had terminated employees on their staffs in 1961 discharged one out of every five of their personnel; small stations tended to discharge greater proportions of their staffs than did larger stations. That national survey listed the following reasons for discharge:

REASONS FOR DISCHARGE	RADIO	TELEVISION
A. Ability or training	33.0%	41.6%
B. "Employee's Behavior" (Total of:)	36.6	36.8
Application to job	(12.8%)	(28.7%)
Personal characteristics	(17.6)	(6.1)
Relationships with others	(6.1)	(2.0)
C. "Management" factors	30.3	21.5
	99.9%	99.9%

Respondents from radio and television stations indicated reasons pertaining to *"ability or training"* for discharging one-third of all fired employees: lack of ability, unsatisfactory work, incompetence, unfit, not qualified, replaced by more competent employees, work not up to standard (including "poor sales records"), lack of education, lack of technical know-how. The one-out-of-five employees dismissed for deficiencies in *"application to job"* were appraised as: inefficient, unreliable, irresponsible, unproductive, lack of interest, lazy, didn't improve, inattention to duty, lack of effort. *"Personal"* reasons for one-out-of-ten dismissals included the general references to simply "personal" and "conduct" as well as to drinking, personal indebtedness or not paying bills, dishonesty, emotional immaturity, maladjustments, conduct detrimental to station, and several single-instance reports (in 1961) of drug addiction, gambling, writing "hot checks," outside business interests, homosexuality, divulging sponsor information, moral irresponsibility, too many parties, bad credit, and "opium smoker." Characteristics catalogued under *"Relationships with other people"* (one-out-of-20 dismissals) included inability to get along with others, personality clashes, belligerent, insubordinate, non-cooperative, incompatible with team, breach of sales policy, did not take direction, failed to follow policy, quarrelsomeness, trouble-maker. *"Management factors,"* accounting for one-third of terminated employment, included factors over which employees seldom had any control, such as changes in operating procedure, economies in reducing size of staffs, job consolidation, combining AM and FM operations, automation, change in programming format and policies, change of station ownership.

Other authors and broadcasters have commented on the conditions that lead to eventual dismissal of an employee, such as failure to improve after repeated warnings, pressure on the supervisor from other supervisors, a culmination of a series of events, personality traits, and breaking of company rules.[89] Although discharging an employee is unpleasant and reflects an expensive process of hiring and training anew, as well as possible severance payments that can be high, management must not overlook or be indecisive about the failure of an employee to meet expectations. Close working relations in a company should not become involvement in the employee's personal life (unless embarrassing to the company), lest the warnings be extended beyond their proper limit. Reinsch and Ellis caution against two other mistakes: either ignoring a person's attitudes and actions because he is judged to be valuable to the station, or simply verbally criticizing and threatening, and even demoting, but never firing a person. One procedure undermines the confidence and morale of the rest of the station's staff; the other tactic can demean the person and merely force him into a passive, defensive, nonproductive posture for the future. After carefully investigating the problem situation, "talk with him calmly, seriously, sympathetically" to learn what cause lies at the base of the employee's difficulty in order to correct whatever may be legitimate in his dissatisfaction or lack of proper participation in the company's work.[90] At the same time, management cannot presume to be a special confidant with professional competence to deal with persons who have deeper problems of emotions, nerves, health in general, alcoholism, and the many personal situations that can affect all persons from time to time. The best advice seems to be to recommend that he seek adequate assistance from specialists.[91]

Separation payments should be given as settlement whenever an individual is removed because of a lack of need for his future services or for some other reason best known to the company. Such payments should not be made in the cases of individuals who are *dismissed for cause,* whether those individuals are union or non-union.

Should an employee be relieved of his duties for other than a violation of good conduct or irresponsible performance, the station is advised to make every effort to find employment for him elsewhere. Sufficient advance planning will usually make other employment possible. The good will that accrues from such gestures is of lasting benefit to the station. Usually it will not be necessary to look far afield. If displaced by automation or almost any other development, intelligent and dedicated people who have been with a sound broadcasting organization all their career lives can make a contribution—and, in some cases, a superior one—in another area at the same station.

The manager must also be prepared for possible reaction from clients if the severed employee is from the sales department, or from the public if the employee was a program personality. Honesty and brevity, with few or no details about the leave-taking, are appropriate for the client (according to Hoffer); and even less need be communicated to audience members who might telephone the station, with no comment appropriate or necessary from the air personality's successor.[92]

Finally, management must honestly respond to requests for references from a discharged person's prospective employers elsewhere. In fact, personnel who voluntarily leave a station are entitled to objective honesty in an appraisal by his former employers. It is appropriate to provide comment on their observable traits as persons in relation to other staff members and in performing their work assignments. Positive achievements as well as demonstrable, not merely suspected, shortcomings should be noted simply so that prospective employers can make a reasonable advance appraisal of this prospective addition to their staff.[93]

Many problems cannot be predicted until personnel have worked with a station staff. But perhaps many potential short-termed employees might be identified more carefully and eliminated at the time of application and job interview, to limit as much as possible the inefficiency and loss of morale that accompany frequent turnover of less-than-apt personnel. John M. Kittross of the *Journal of Broadcasting* editorialized that:

> No industry can hope to operate successfully for long when it must continually hire and train employees who do not individually have a professional attitude, enthusiasm, and a deserved feeling of mutual loyalty and cooperation with their employer. An employee who feels he has no real job stability, whether he is

a union member or on a so-called long term contract or not, will have few com-
punctions about quitting his job, often with little notice and great dislocation to
the station. A person who thinks he needs always to be alert to opportunities for a
new job is rarely giving his best effort to his present employer. It is probable that
the payola-plugola scandals developed in part from individual feeling that one had
to look out for himself; that nobody else would. Sponsors have expressed mistrust
of some salesmen who sell shoes today, station "A" tomorrow, and station "B"
the following day. Extreme job mobility in an industry that has a slowing growth
rate leads to ruthlessness, not the efficiency of a flexible operation. Although
many employees do their best when "running scared" or "hungry," some cannot
keep the pace. Those who have proven "track records" and enthusiasm need stability in their professional relationships for the sakes of their families if not for
themselves, and that stability must be encouraged by management. Stability need
not imply stagnation, and the manager does not lose his freedom of management
by paying more attention to the quality of his greatest resource, his employees.

Because broadcasting cannot afford to recruit indiscriminately, and then
delete "rejects," the solution seems to be not to let into the station in the first
place the man who is incompetent, irresponsible, dishonest, or incapable of responding in the same way to trust and loyalty. Better yet, don't let him into the
industry. The teachers of professional broadcasting already weed out misguided,
unmotivated and incompetent potential broadcasters in numbers that might surprise the station manager. On the other hand, the *normal* entrance into the industry is through a small job in a small station. If management of these stations
considered the eventual instead of the initial cost of people who are unable to
"cut the mustard," these people should never get to the point of deserving to be
fired. The possible consequent ill-will and loss of efficiency among both the
departed employees and the remaining ones could be avoided.

It is not easy to give the employee a feeling of stability without also stunt-
ing his motivation or drive. However, indiscriminate hiring and firing can lead to
tremendous waste of the ex-employee as an individual, of station morale, and of
the station's "image." [94]

A Final Word: Employees and Broadcast Companies

The broadcast company cannot be disassociated from its close bond with
its employees. If a station or network whittles away at its own creative and
social integrity in the quality of its program service, it will at the same time
erode the creative and ethical integrity of its personnel. When a broadcast company emphasizes economic strength to the detriment of its other capabilities and
responsibilities to its staff and society as a medium of mass communication it
will inevitably force its staff, especially its management, to compromise their
standards. The eventual result is the attrition of competent decision-makers and
creative artists who forsake the company and even the medium. Meanwhile, it
is continually necessary to retrain successors to those departed staff members
who as new executives must learn the corporate organizational structure and the
people on the job in whom they can have confidence and to whom they can delegate work and responsibilities. When this is coupled with severed employment

that calls for paying off the remaining portion of a contract, this is doubly expensive. This is waste and even economic suicide. It also erodes public confidence; and this engenders more vigilance—even restrictive and punitive action—by Federal agencies, sometimes resulting in exhaustive legal proceedings and possible loss of the broadcast license.

The late Edgar Kobak—top-ranking executive of ABC, NBC and Mutual, among other corporations during his long career—once noted that if the employee as well as his company always does what he knows or at least judges to be truly right, he or she will seldom lose business and will be able to sleep at night.

NOTES

Chapter 3

1. Alden Dow, in *Creativity and Its Cultivation,* Harold H. Anderson, ed. (N.Y.: Harper and Brothers, 1959).

2. FCC figures cited by *Broadcasting,* Mar. 10, 1975, p. 19. Cf. "FCC's Minority Breakdown," *Broadcasting,* July 2, 1973, pp. 32–33, reporting a 466-page report made public by the Commission, that agency's first report on employment practices in broadcasting.

3. Data derived from FCC, *39th Annual Report: Fiscal Year 1973* (Washington, D.C.: U.S. Government Printing Office, [1974]), pp. 238, 249, 253.

4. See Chapter 2 for profiles of characteristics of station managers. In 1962, of 368 radio and TV station managers responding to a survey, only three were women, who managed radio. "Broadcasting Management: A Report from the APBE-NAB Employment Study," *Journal of Broadcasting* VI:3 (Summer 1962), p. 255.

5. *Broadcasting Yearbook 1974* (Washington, D.C.: Broadcasting Publications, Inc., 1974), pp. 40–41.

6. *Sponsor,* May 25, 1957, p. 37.

7. Data from Glenn Starlin (ed.), "Problems in Finding Qualified Employees: A Report from the APBE-NAB Employment Study," *Journal of Broadcasting* VII:1 (Winter 1962–63), pp. 63–67. Survey responses from television station respondents were representative of all market sizes but responses from radio skewed heavily to the small markets. Managers responded from 167 television stations and 201 radio stations in the United States.

8. See Robert H. Coddington, *Modern Radio Broadcasting: Management and Operation in Small-to-Medium Markets* (Blue Ridge Summit, Pa.: Tab Books, 1969), pp. 16–18, 150–158; also Jay Hoffer, *Managing Today's Radio Station* (Blue Ridge Summit, Pa.: Tab Books, 1968), pp. 31–33.

9. Hoffer, p. 32. See Coddington, pp. 17–18.

10. Glenn Starlin (ed.), "The Broadcasting Employee," *Journal of Broadcasting,* VII:3 (Summer 1963), p. 236.

11. *Ibid.,* p. 241. 18 per cent did not respond to the question.

12. Irving E. Fang and Frank W. Gerval, "A Survey of Salaries and Hiring Preferences in Television News," *Journal of Broadcasting,* XV:4 (Fall 1971), p. 431.

13. Rosalind Loring and Theodora Wells, *Breakthrough: Women into Management* (N.Y.: Van Nostrand Reinhold Co., 1972), p. 45.

14. Loring & Wells, p. 43. These authors note sources of women to fill new positions and management-related jobs: colleges and universities, executive search and placement agencies, and from within the company itself; pp. 48–52; see also organization address list, "III. Possible Sources for Management and Professional Women," pp. 195–196.

15. Title VII of the Federal Civil Rights Act of 1964 and the Federal Equal Pay Act of 1963, plus enforcement powers given to the Equal Employment Opportunity Commission (EEOC)

in 1972, are discussed in detail—with particular reference to women's rights—in an excellently documented and reasoned analysis by Rosalind Loring and Theodora Wells, *Breakthrough: Women into Management* (N.Y.: Van Nostrand Reinhold Co., 1972). This is an excellent text for any manager wishing to understand better the evolving role of women in middle and executive management in the United States. See "Interpreting the FCC Rules and Regulations: Nondiscrimination in Employment Practices," *BM/E,* Sept. 1969, pp. 15–18, Cf. Docket No. 18244, RM-1·144, FCC 69–631.

16. 1970 Census, *Associated Press Almanac, 1973,* p. 142.

17. Loring and Wells, pp. 35, 171, for detailed discussion of the data demonstrating the stereotypical restriction of women and other minorities to non-managerial positions in business, government and education.

18. Loring and Wells, p. 27, citing *Fact Sheet on the Earnings Gap,* U.S. Dept. of Labor, Employment Standards Administration, Women's Bureau, 1971 (rev.), p. 16.

19. For example, just in the area of radio and television: the National Association of Broadcasters' Employment Clearing House, 1771 N St., N.W., Washington, D.C. 20036; Office of Minority Affairs, National Association of Educational Broadcasters, 1346 Connecticut Ave., N.W. Washington, D.C. 20036; Broadcast Education Association, Minority Education Committee, c/o 1771 N Street, N.W., Washington, D.C., 20036; Minorities Job/Scholarship Referral, Association for Education in Journalism, c/o Lionel C. Barrow, Dept. of Mass Communication, Univ. of Wisconsin, Milwaukee, Wis., 53201; as well as internship and scholarship projects organized and funded by group-owned stations such as Group W, Storer, Kaiser, Cox, and RKO General.

20. Commissioner Benjamin Hooks, the first Black appointed to the FCC, has noted in public comments—including a half-hour interview by Channel 13, KCOP, Los Angeles, Sunday, May 6, 1973—that while he is determined to assist minorities in their effort to enter broadcasting, he is equally insistent that these minority persons prepare themselves for such employment and that they continue to learn and to advance their skills and understanding in order to merit promotion within those broadcast companies.

21. Elizabeth S. Czech, "Interaction Between Black and Corporate Culture in Broadcast Management," unpublished doctoral dissertation, The Ohio State Univ., 1972.

22. "Parker Assails Hiring Practices at TV Stations," *Broadcasting,* Nov. 27, 1972, pp. 26, 31; citing the report by Ralph M. Jennings, "Television Station Employment Practices: the Status of Minorities and Women," United Church of Christ Office of Communication, November, 1972. The analysis was based on data from employment statements submitted to the FCC by 609 commercial TV stations: reports from another 76 commercial stations were unavailable or incomplete, according to the report.

23. Dorothy Gilliam, "When the Tube Goes Black," *The Washington Post* Sunday supplement *Potomac,* November 9, 1969, p. 56.

24. Ruth Ratny, "Gals Make Mark: Women's Lib Hits Chicago," *Back Stage* XIII:20 (May 19, 1972), pp. 1, 16, 30. By 1972 production assistants were increasing at advertising agencies; Leo Burnett employed two women as producers of a total of 16; Clinton Frank employed one woman out of four producers; Meyerhoff employed two producers, one a woman. Garfield-Linn had a Radio-TV director who was a woman; Earle Ludgin had a woman as vice president in charge of broadcast production. At film companies, women's occupations included positions of production manager, studio business manager (4 companies); two female directors; three freelance assistant directors. Three women were studio representatives. Three Hollywood-based film companies employed women as reps in Chicago. And women were executives, including managers and owners of several creative companies: a president, an executive vice president, a creative vice president, two different owner-partners, and midwest director of New York-based company.

25. "CBS Examines Its Ranks," *Broadcasting,* Nov. 26, 1972, p. 26, citing report by CBS, Inc. President, Arthur R. Taylor made public November 22, 1972.

26. FCC data cited by *Broadcasting,* Mar. 10, 1975, p. 19. And in mid-1975, Bernard Gallagher reported that women executives were advancing toward equal pay with men: "Study of 45 female respondents to GR's Annual Average Salary Survey (see May 5, 1975) indicates women move toward achieving pay parity with male executives. E.g., female executives v-ps employed by

advertisers post average $45,000 salary (+8.0%) vs. $48,471 (+9.1%) for men in same position. Female advertising v-ps report average $29,555 salary (+ 10.2%) vs. $29,996 (+ 12.8%) for male counterparts. Further gains still to be made. E.g., among advertiser respondents female chairmen/presidents make average $52,500 (vs. $76,216 for men); women v-p sales average $30,000 (vs. $43,541). Media companies pay female executive v-ps/general managers average $20,583 (vs. $48,937), women advertising v-ps $30,666 (vs. $35,555). Women average 8.6 years with present company (vs. 10.6 years for men). Have spent 4.7 years on present job (vs. 5.4 years for male executives). Major marketers continue search for top management female executives." "The Gallagher Report," May 12, 1975, p. 2.

27. "A Discussion of Institutional Racism in Public Broadcasting," National Association of Educational Broadcasters, Washington, D.C., pp. 8–9. His views were supported in that same discussion by the executive producer of *Black Journal* for the PBS network, Tony Brown: "We get to television, and Lionel says we don't have any black station managers. Well, that's the thing that the average white person who means well says, 'We are going to work on getting more.' But the very structure of television, commercial and public, is a racist structure. Not because anybody at this table sat down and figured it out. Something like 90 percent of the people in this country who have a job got a job because they heard about it from a friend. And if everybody in a given situation is white, because most whites have mostly white friends, only *they* are going to hear about the job and that's just on the social level. So you are going to have it perpetuated in that way, whites continually in control with no particular concern toward anybody else not white. . . .

"But in terms of blacks involved, there are no blacks making decisions because historically, as a vestige of overt racism which we know as slavery, the institutions that were structured were structured by whites, continually selected whites and institutionalized certain practices that perpetuate the same style of operating that has gone on for hundreds of years. So today, even in public television, it still operates although it is in a more subtle form. The same overt racist vestiges of slavery that we had during the 1600s, 1700s and the 1800s.

"So what I am saying is this: I think we must really understand *how* public television is being racist, unintended or intended. *Racism, simply, is when a structure or an individual subordinates another person or another group, culturally, socially, politically and economically. That's what racism is.* . . .

"I think that, until the individual whites who have the kind of power to make decisions change the institutional alignment in structure, then this industry will always remain a racist industry. If you are never in a situation where you have at least the counsel or participation of people other than yourselves, then all of your decisions will simply perpetuate and maintain what is now. And my way of looking at that is that no institution in this society can exist unless it becomes and remains very flexible. Particularly in terms of the very strong social, and now more important perhaps, psychological upheaval that this country is going through. And no institution is going to be able to keep itself structured in the 1970s or '80s the way it was structured in the 1920s and '30s. It won't work. It will simply lead to your own demise. And one of the things I would really hope is that particularly people like yourselves will understand that inclusions of people other than white people will only enhance and benefit your position and this industry. It will not destroy the industry and it will not threaten any position that you have. I mean, it will make the entire industry believable and viable; it will make it very productive. And I think that is one of the things you have to think about in terms of just what racism is. Without, you know, 'You're a racist and you are a no good nigger and you're this and that,' which to me is a waste of your time and a waste of my time and does nothing at all.

"When decisions are continually made, and I look at them, and when I bring them up to people, all of whom are white and they say, 'Oh, I really didn't think about that,' my answer is, 'Well, it's not your job to think about that. Your job is to have somebody who is not like you sit with you and say, 'Well, that's good, but have you thought of doing this?' Just think about it, you know, because it's another kind of answer."

28. Bob Knight, "Black Ownership: Case Study," *Variety*, May 31, 1972, pp. 31, 45.

29. "New Detroit U to Mark Blacks' Entry into Ranks of TV Ownership," *Broadcasting*, June 18, 1973, p. 38.

30. "Sparks Fly at Seminar on Minority Ownership," *Broadcasting,* Dec. 4, 1972, pp. 19–20.

31. Because there are predictable differences between interviews of business-oriented urbanites and less sophisticated minorities, the Broadcast Education Association (in the draft of a brief booklet "Minority Employment Guidelines for Broadcasters, Placement Offices, and Broadcast Educators," BEA, 1771 N St., N.W. Washington, D.C.) suggested the following guidelines to ease the initial interview of persons who are culturally or economically different from the interviewee: (1) Address the young man as "Mister" and young ladies as "Miss." Premature use of first names may be misunderstood as implication of inferior status. (2) Avoid being over-friendly and patronizing. (3) Know that black culture often discourages a firm handshake or direct eye contact, and do not read such responses as signs of uncertainty. (4) Avoid the terms "qualifications" or "competence"; use words like "skills," "knowledge," or "potential plus ambition." (5) Clarify that you offer a genuine job, not a token position. (6) Be explicit about job duties and promotion policies. (7) Review concepts of setting standards, station priorities and standard operating procedures, so the interviewee will know that all employees are expected to follow the same procedures and that no "bossism" is implied when orders are given. (8) Ascertain whether personal problems may inadvertently interfere with attendance or punctuality, such as serious transportation difficulty, illness at home, or existence of a second job elsewhere. Suggest ways to overcome such difficulties if they exist.

32. See J. Leonard Reinsch and E. I. Ellis, *Radio Station Management,* 2nd rev. ed., (N.Y.: Harper & Row, 1960), pp. 254–256, 259, and 48–49, for commentary on employee selection, placement testing, hiring and initial orientation.

33. Glenn Starlin (ed.), "Employee Attitudes Towards the Broadcasting Industry: A Report from the APBE-NAB Employment Study," *Journal of Broadcasting* VII:4 (Fall 1963), p. 360.

34. *Ibid.,* p. 367.

35. This should be distinguished from station manuals with details of policy for proper procedures required by Federal agencies, NAB, corporate policy, and local management's applications of those principles, such as Storer Broadcasting's lengthy printed loose-leaf binder.

36. NAB Department of Broadcast Management, "New Employee's Personnel Manual: Sample for Adaptation by Individual Stations" (Washington, D.C., NAB, 1964). For larger companies, including groups of broadcast stations that are linked with parent corporations, the 32-page mimeographed treatment "CBS: The Company You Keep," Clarence Hopper, vice president, Facilities and Personnel (N.Y.: CBS, Inc., October 1967), adds such categories as special company services (discounts on products, notary and optical service, etc.), stock purchase plan, legal advice, handling confidential information within the company, personal property and personal telephone calls. See November 1967 edition: "The Company You Keep."

37. See also Reinsch and Ellis, pp. 48–49, and 254–256.

38. See the preceding chapter for samples of such flow charts. For informally stated cautions about the questionable values and even misuse of such charts, see Robert Townsend, *Up the Organization: How to Stop the Corporation From Stifling People and Strangling Profit* (N.Y.: Alfred A. Knopf, 1970); Fawcett World Library ed., (Greenwich, Conn.: Fawcett Publications, Inc., 1970), pp. 35–36.

39. The Broadcast Education Association's Minority Education Committee prepared helpful guidelines in a brief booklet "Minority Employment Guidelines for Broadcasters, Placement Offices, and Broadcast Educators" (BEA, 1771 N St., N.W., Washington, D.C.). Interim text of draft included "Ways to Minimize Cross-Cultural Misunderstandings During Orientation of the Culturally Different": (1.) Appoint an orientation leader or "big brother" from the same cultural group, preferably one who already has earned a role in decision-making areas. (2.) Avoid grouping newcomers from disadvantaged backgrounds, to prevent reinforcement of negative behavior. (3.) Try to train individually rather than in groups. Provide reasons for all procedures, if necessary. (4.) Provide trainees with unhurried and explicit descriptions of assignments that can be completed in a short time before advancing to more complicated challenges. (5.) Ask him to demonstrate or to repeat instructions; do not assume he understands if he merely says he does. (6.) Oral instructions and demonstrations are more effective than written notes or guidelines. (7.) Communicate impor-

tant information either face-to-face or by phone, especially if the message is long. (8.) Avoid sending oral messages through a third person. (9.) Do not misread as lack of motivation what is really fear of failure. Help the candidate recognize his abilities and to build a strong self-concept. (10.) Admit to making mistakes when they occur; this frees the trainee to admit needs and errors, when necessary. (11.) Enable an applicant to save face and back out gracefully should he discover a new assignment is still too much for him to handle. Aspirations sometimes exceed ability. (12.) Be honest in expressing feelings as well as thoughts. (13.) Be aware that facial expressions and tone of voice often bear more weight than words. (14.) Listen more than you speak. (15.) Be willing and ready to talk things out on an emotional level when misunderstandings occur; and do it as soon as possible to prevent further emotional build-up. (16.) Encourage candidates to make notes, and to attend meetings, in order to learn how to express themselves in the business world. (17.) Provide practice in problem-solving based on actual station needs. (18.) Expose the trainee to standard business procedures. (19.) Clarify organizational goals and help him to see how his personal goals fit into organizational needs. (20.) Explain that promotion is based on ability, not on length of service. (21.) Reveal genuine interest in the minority employee's culture and ask his opinion when planning to air material relevant to his culture. (22.) Authoritarian methods work best initially, but participative managerial methods are more successful after the newcomer knows his job.

40. Department of Broadcast Management, "Wages, Hours and Employment / Television 1969" and "Wages, Hours and Employment / Radio 1970," National Association of Broadcasters, 1969 and 1971; "Radio 1974 / Employee Wage & Salary Report" and "Television 1974 / Employee Wage & Salary Report," National Association of Broadcasters, Washington, D.C., 1974.

41. Glenn Starlin (ed.), "Employee Attitudes Toward the Broadcasting Industry," *Journal of Broacasting,* VII:4 (Fall 1963), p. 360.

42. Radio-Television News Directors Association in collaboration with AP and UPI and Gale Adkins of the University of Kansas, in 1964 studied 2,028 commercial stations (45% of all TV stations, 37% of AM and 28% of FM radio stations) and estimated that 26,242 persons of the 80,000 in broadcasting at that time had news-related responsibilities. Reported in *"Feedback,"* Assoc. for Professional Broadcasting Education, December 1964, p. 4.

43. Irving E. Fang and Frank W. Gerval, "A Survey of Salaries and Hiring Preferences in Television News," *Journal of Broadcasting,* XV:4 (Fall, 1971), pp. 421–433.

43a. "Profile of a News Director," *Broadcasting* (Dec. 4, 1972), p. 47; citing unpublished report by Vernon A. Stone, "Radio and Television News Directors and Operations: An RTNDA Survey," for the Radio Television News Directors Association.

44. "The Communications Industry and News Media Under the Fair Labor Standards Act," Dept. of Labor, Employment Standards Administration, Wage and Hour Division; February 1972 (WH Publication #1355). A looseleaf subscription to published regulations and amendments pertaining to wages and hours, *Federal Labor Laws,* may be ordered by advance payment of $12.00 to the Superintendent of Documents, U.S. Government Printing Office, Washington, D.C. 20402.

45. See Coddington, p. 155; Yale Roe, *Television Station Management: the Business of Broadcasting* (N.Y.: Hastings House, 1964), pp. 94–100; Hoffer, *Managing Today's Radio Station,* pp. 30–31, cautions about confidentiality of bookkeeper's documentation and knowledge.

46. *Ibid.,* pp. 9–10.

47. That this can be a serious, practical matter for a station was demonstrated in December of 1971 when, for the first time, the women employees at WRC-AM-FM-TV in Washington, D.C. wrote to the FCC's Complaints and Compliance Division, asking it to require NBC (the owner) to reimburse those female employees for back pay deprived due to sex discrimination. In November the Washington office of the Equal Employment Opportunity Commission had presented findings implying such discrimination. The women also lodged a complaint against WRC and NBC with the Dept. of Labor. The 27-member WRC/NBC Women's Rights Committee recommended such financial compensation, plus setting up time tables and goals for hiring women in all job categories and for developing training programs. See: "WRC Women Win at EEOC, Now Come Back to FCC," *Broadcasting,* Dec. 20, 1971, p. 38. After two years, the U.S. Equal Employment Opportunity

Commission returned the first finding ever against a broadcaster, supportng most of the charges of discrimination against women and blacks at NBC's WRC-AM-FM-TV. See Chapter 9 below, "The Manager and Regulation"; cf. "EEOC Upholds Charges Against WRC Stations," *Broadcasting*, Feb. 5, 1973, p. 36; and "EEOC Also Upholds Blacks' Complaints Against NBC's Washington's Stations," *Broadcasting*, Feb. 19, 1973, p. 32.

48. *Ibid.*, p. 11.

49. Glenn Starlin (ed.), "Employee Attitudes toward the Broadcasting Industry," *Journal of Broadcasting*, VI:4 (Fall 1963), p. 366. The published summary of a southwestern U.S. station response offers encouragement, by contrast, to most other station personnel: "One [employee] stated that his station must be the only one in the country where one must be on a constant lookout for scorpions and rattlesnakes; the other volunteered the information that in order to make the technical equipment work, it was necessary to kick it. Both said their supervisor was a nice guy, but always looking for a new job."

50. Glenn Starlin (ed.), "Employee Attitudes Toward the Broadcasting Industry," *Journal of Broadcasting*, VII:4 (Fall 1963), pp. 361–362.

51. NAB, "Memo to Management," August, 1964. CBS, Inc. grants to its New York office employees three weeks of vacation after five years with the corporation, and four weeks vacation annually after fifteen years of employment.

52. NAB, "Retirement Plans in the Broadcasting Industry, 1963" (Booklet).

52a. For an excellent introductory study of labor unions (and guilds) in broadcasting, see the first book published on the subject: Allen E. Koenig (ed.), *Broadcasting and Bargaining: Labor Relations in Radio and Television* (Madison, Wis.: Univ. of Wisconsin Press, 1970). This collection of essays and analyses surveys factual data on the historical development of unionism in radio and television, the role of Federal mediation and arbitration, and selected problem areas (such as creative artists, minorities, and technical unions).

53. Ron Irion, NAB Director of Broadcast Management, in "Highlights," NAB, Washington, D.C., Nov. 30, 1972, p. 3.

54. Jay Hoffer, *Managing Today's Radio Station*, pp. 101–102.

55. The Federal Equal Pay Act of 1963, an amendment to the Fair Labor Standards Act, and Title VII of the Federal Civil Rights Act of 1964, as well as President Lyndon Johnson's Executive Order 11478, and Revised Order 4 issued by Secretary of Labor J. D. Hodgson in December 1971. The first equal pay cases were decided by the courts in 1970; enforcement powers were given to the Equal Employment Opportunity Commission in March of 1972. See Loring and Wells, *Breakthrough: Women into Management*, pp. 20–23, and 26–28 for "sex bias in pay and position."

56. Hoffer, *Managing Today's Station*, pp. 98–101, is cool to unions and suggests station policies that might preclude employees' choosing to organize. Reinsch and Ellis, *Radio Station Management*, pp. 259–267, offer practical recommendations for collaborating positively with union representatives. Coddington, *Modern Radio Broadcasting*, pp. 157–158, notes the bilateral responsibilities of management and employees toward each other, in consideration of each person's dignity, loyalty and professionalism, and adequate payment for work done. Specific procedures for contract negotiations between AFTRA and broadcast employer groups are described by Allen E. Koenig, "AFTRA and Contract Negotiations," *Journal of Broadcasting*, VII:1 (Winter 1962–63), pp. 11–22. The internal processes of AFTRA decision-making on behalf of its 16,000 members nationally are described by Allen E. Koenig, "AFTRA Decision Making," *Journal of Broadcasting*, IX:3 (Summer 1956), pp. 231–248; analyzed is the national convention procedure of AFTRA negotiators to determine what demands they plan to make for wage increases and better working conditions, and then how they decide to accept or not accept a particular three-year contract with national networks and advertising agencies.

57. National Labor Relations Board, *A Layman's Guide to Basic Law*, quoted by Dept. of Broadcast Management, *Negotiating the Broadcasting Labor Contract*, National Assoc. of Broadcasters, Washington, D.C., 1969 ed.; p. i, "Foreword."

58. Reinsch and Ellis, p. 265.

59. See the NAB's 26-page booklet cited in preceding note 57, pp. 2–3. Other NAB

publications about labor relations include: *The Right of Free Speech; Collective Bargaining Units in Broadcasting; Important Clauses in your Labor Contract;* and *The Eleventh Hour* (how to plan operations in the event of a strike). NAB's other services include reprints of union labor contract summaries, "Memo to Management" briefings about contracts, "Labor Relations Report" and "Arbitration Digest" which summarize current developments and sample cases.

60. See *ibid.,* pp. 11–24, for further procedures, such as when and where to meet, specific bargaining tactics, the problem of an impasse, use of mediators, drafting the contract, and follow-up details after the settlement.

61. See William Scholz, "How to Make Employee Publications Pay Off," *Personnel,* March, 1956.

62. Jay M. Jackson, "Analysis of Interpersonal Relations in a Formal Organization," Ph.D. thesis, U. of Michigan, 1953.

63. See Kurt Back and Leon Festinger, "The Methodology of Studying Rumor Transmission," *Human Relations,* 1950. Also Robert J. McMahon, "Some Principles of Communication Pertinent to Organization Mergers," term paper, Univ. of Southern California, Dept. of Telecommunications, July 1971.

64. "CBS Looks Hard at Its Manpower Policies," *Broadcasting,* Dec. 20, 1971, p. 38.

65. See Keith Davis, "Management Communication and the Grapevine," *Harvard Business Review,* Sept.–Oct. 1953.

66. Jay M. Jackson, "The Organization and Its Communications Problem," *Advanced Management Journal,* Feb. 1959. See also Hoffer, *Managing Today's Radio Station,* pp. 20–22; Reinsch and Ellis, p. 262.

67. Cf. Robert Sutermeister, *People and Productivity* (N.Y.: McGraw-Hill, 1963), p. 79.

68. Reinsch and Ellis, pp. 249–250; see also pp. 251–252, 258–259.

69. See Coddington, pp. 16–18, and 157–158; Reinsch and Ellis, pp. 49–50; also Hoffer, *Managing Today's Radio Station,* pp. 28–30 about problems of "the boozer" and p. 39 about careful attention to the role played by a telephone answering service for audience members and clients who phone the station at non-office hours.

70. Reinsch and Ellis, pp. 46–48.

71. Glenn Starlin (ed.), "The Broadcasting Employee," *Journal of Broadcasting,* VII:3 (Summer 1963), pp. 238–240.

72. "CBS Looks Hard at Its Manpower Policies," *Broadcasting,* Dec. 20, 1971, p. 38.

73. Carnegie Corporation, *Quarterly Report,* July, 1961, pp. 2–5.

74. See Reinsch and Ellis, pp. 258–259.

75. *Ibid.,* p. 33; see also 249–252.

76. *Ibid.,* p. 252.

77. See Hoffer, *Managing Today's Radio Station,* pp. 20–22.

78. Glenn Starlin (ed.), "Employee Attitudes towards the Broadcasting Industry: A Report from the APBE-NAB Employment Study," *Journal of Broadcasting,* VII:4 (Fall 1963), p. 262. Approximately 10% did *not* respond to the questions about promotion policies.

79. Highlights of the report by McKinsey & Co., were cited in "CBS Looks Hard at its Manpower Policies," *Broadcasting,* Dec. 20, 1971, p. 38. Although the questionnaire return for the entire company was 71%, the broadcast divisions' management personnel returned a higher percentage (undisclosed in article). Data were gathered from CBS, Inc.; the corporation includes not only the networks and stations of the radio and television divisions, but also recordings, publications, films, and a dozen and a half other divisions and subsidiaries of the total company.

80. "The Company You Keep" (N.Y.: CBS, Inc., 1974), pp. 21–23.

81. A cheerless commentary on hazards of promotions is offered seriously but in a light-hearted style by Dr. Laurence J. Peter and Raymond Hull in *The Peter Principle: Why Things Always Go Wrong* (N.Y. William Morrow & Co., 1969; Bantam ed. 1970), pp. 6–8, 19–21, and *passim.* Competent employees are identified and promoted progressively until they prove incompetent in a given position and there they then remain. Thus the Peter Principle that "in a hierarchy every employee tends to rise to his level of incompetence" (p. 7). The inexorable corollary states that "in time, every post tends to be occupied by an employee who is incompetent to carry out its

duties'' (p. 8). Nevertheless, another irreverent best-seller highly encourages internal promotion for efficiency as well as humane consideration of employed human beings: Robert Townsend, *Up the Organization: How to Stop the Corporation from Stifling People and Strangling Profits* (N.Y.: Alfred A. Knopf, Inc., 1970) Fawcett World Library ed., (Greenwich, Conn.; Fawcett Publications, Inc., 1970), pp. 138–139.

82. See Loring and Wells, pp. 62–63, 72–84.

83. A sample listing of successful female executives, with women's advice to other women about careers and administrative goals in broadcasting and advertising are recounted together with statistical data in "Special Report: Olivetti Girls Aren't Forever," *Broadcasting,* Aug. 7, 1972, pp. 39–43.

84. Loring and Wells, p. 62.

85. Reinsch and Ellis, p. 261.

86. See Loring and Wells, pp. 144–162, for detailed analysis of conventional mythology that stereotypes the capabilities of women in executive management roles.

86a. See Charles S. Steinberg (ed.), *Broadcasting: The Critical Challenges* (New York: Hastings House, Publishers, 1974) for a summary of the 1973 IRTS Faculty/Industry Seminar. This is the first volume of a continuing series to be published each year or so. See also Robert H. Stanley (ed.) *The Broadcast Industry: An Examination of Major Issues* (New York: Hastings House, Publishers, 1975).

87. Marcus Cohn, Washington communications attorney, noted that educational or public broadcasting's weakness "is not basically because of law, but because non-commercial broadcasting is controlled by conservative local elites, whom the station manager dare not affront" (quoted by A. Edward Foote, "The Crisis in PTV Station Management," *Educational Broadcasting,* Sept.–Oct. 1972, p. 14). A producer for National Educational Television in New York claimed that the managers of local public broadcasting stations were chosen to run the stations because they were acceptable to business and to "reactionary interests" in the communities. But this generalized appraisal was not true of public broadcast managers in other markets, including Chicago, according to their professional counterparts in local commercial broadcasting.

88. Data were drawn from responses by 696 radio stations with 10,724 employees in 16 selected states and by 276 TV stations with 15,653 employees in all states, for the year 1960; discharges were reported for 1961. Sherman P. Lawton, "Discharge of Broadcast Station Employees," *Journal of Broadcasting,* VI:3 (Summer 1962), pp. 191–196.

89. *Advanced Management Journal* (October 1965), p. 69; quoted with approval and detailed comments by Jay Hoffer, *Managing Today's Radio Station* (Blue Ridge Summit, Pa.; Tab Books, 1968), pp. 36–37.

90. Reinsch and Ellis, p. 258.

91. Cf. Hoffer, pp. 24–30.

92. *Ibid.,* p. 38.

93. *Ibid.,* pp. 32–33.

94. John M. Kittross (ed.), "Stability," *Journal of Broadcasting,* VI:3 (Summer 1962), pp. 189–190. See also Jay Hoffer, pp. 31–32, for his constructive reminders to small-market managers about their valuable role as the "Training Ground for Talent."

4

The Audience

Don't let anyone ever tell you that people don't change from one generation to the next. They change from one week to the next. People are better educated and more sophisticated, with more varied appetites, more cultivated tastes, longer weekends and wider interests. They are becoming harder to satisfy, harder to fool, easier to bore.

—Whit Hobbs, Vice President, BBDO [1]

PEOPLE WHO regularly tune in the radio or television station comprise its circulation. The advertisers who supply the station's operating revenue are interested in that circulation. Thus, the station's popularity, its income and its consequent profit are directly dependent upon audience receptivity to its services.

Actually, there is no one single homogenized station audience. Any station has different groupings of people who may be listening or viewing at different times throughout the broadcast day, week or month. At one time, for example, the audience may be composed mainly of children. At some times, a station may attract a large proportion of highly educated people; at other times, most of the people in the audience may have very little formal schooling. Some audiences are made up mostly of farmers; other audiences are composed mostly of high school students. There are any number of demographic differences in the makeup of the various audience groupings. But woven through all the compositions will be *some* people who have widely different backgrounds from those who predominate. What brings these people together to share common program experiences? What do these people, individually and collectively, really think about the radio and television programs which they see and hear? What causes them to prefer one station's programming over another? How can their loyalty to any specific station be assured? The station manager needs to be able to answer these questions.

Most of the knowledge broadcasters have about their audiences is *quanti-*

tative. That is, the approximate size of the audience at any particular time can be known. Various commercial research organizations are able to supply the manager with information concerning the numbers of homes where his programs are accepted.

Size of audience, while useful, if taken as the sole criterion for judging a station's value to the advertiser or its popularity with audiences, can lead to deceptive conclusions. The local manager needs additional *qualitative* information to supplement the findings of outside services. This information should reveal the interests, opinions and attitudes of the listeners or viewers. Such data are not found in program ratings. Because this qualitative information is not as readily available, the manager may regrettably conclude that too much money and effort are necessary in order to get it.

Managers in other forms of show business, such as the legitimate theater, the movies, the night clubs or the concert stage, are able to make a double check on the success of their offerings. They have the box office, which measures the quantitative audience for any performance. In addition, they are able to judge the responses of those audiences while the performance is in progress. The ultimate success or failure of a show has often been determined by these audience reactions after the people have assembled and have been counted. It is not unusual for major changes to be made in the show on the basis of the reactions. In radio and television, the argument is sometimes advanced that audience reaction is not so important for any single offering because the program is only broadcast once and then it is dead. The argument is hardly valid due to the heavy dependence on programs in series, on repeats and on syndication of programs.

In any communication system, feed-back from the receiver to the communicator is a necessary ingredient for maximum efficiency. It is the only true indicator of the effectiveness of the effort to reach people and it provides the only safe basis for alteration of any format.

In the mass media, communication is usually a one-way, almost authoritarian, process whereby a regular supply of messages is sent to the people. Direct feed-back, on the part of most of those people, is practically nonexistent. Viewers and listeners merely receive or consume without any communication of their reactions to the originator of the messages.

The broadcaster may hear from a small segment of his audience when they dislike something. Seldom does he receive praise from the people who appreciate what has been transmitted. Most of his audience appears to be apathetic or lethargic. The station manager cannot easily meet with members of his unseen audience to learn their opinions and attitudes about his station (although he attempts to do so in his continuing assertainment procedures). He cannot check his sales effectiveness with them directly as does the merchant with a customer in a store.

Most managers have resorted to either a reliance upon comparative numerical sizes of audiences or to reports of store traffic after commercials have been broadcast. Neither has been a very accurate barometer of public opinion.

Both, in the absence of more revealing information, have given some indication of a station's relative popularity in comparison with other stations.

Until recently, broadcasters were content to settle for quantitative information, which comes down to a kind of nose counting. The costs of securing qualitative data and the absence of pressures from advertisers or agencies for such information contributed to the almost total concentration on the quantitative figures. The time has come when the counting of noses will not provide the information that the broadcaster needs.

So long as most markets with broadcasting service had only one station, evidence of station popularity was easy to assess. Indications were the numbers of receiving sets purchased in the area, enthusiastic telephone calls and letters from those early audiences, and the regular references to broadcasting in most people's conversations. And, since local broadcasting meant only one station, there was little doubt concerning the existence of an audience for that station's programs.

As two or three or four or more stations came into those markets, the competitive nature of the broadcast service forced a burden of proof of audience on each station manager. He had to find out how many people preferred his station over his competitors in order to be able to sell his advertising at a respectable rate. Information relative to his audience could be purchased. Thus began the "battle of the ratings" from which the industry has never recovered. Decisions on the nature of programming began to be based not necessarily on whether a program was good but on whether it would be "popular," as determined by numbers of people tuned in to a station. Stations claimed dominance at various periods of the broadcast day often on the basis of a decimal point or two. With the widespread public that is attracted to radio and television, even a decimal point in the ratings can represent thousands of people.

DIMENSIONS OF THE BROADCASTING AUDIENCE

Both radio and television achieved almost universal public popularity within the relatively short period of a decade after their inception, then continued to expand with each subsequent year of their existence. The initial enthusiastic public reaction was shown by the purchase of receiving sets almost as fast as they could be produced and marketed. Brigadier General David Sarnoff predicted in 1920 that his "radio music box," which could be placed "on a table in the parlor or living room," would bring $75,000,000 in sales within three years. He was $8,500,000 short of his estimate.

Two years after the licensing of the first radio station in 1920, there were some 500,000 radio receiving sets in homes. At the end of the first decade of radio's history, there were 13,000,000 radio sets in use. The profile of growth has gone steadily upward each year. Now, the number of sets which are produced annually exceeds the total number that were in use at the end of radio's first decade. Radio sets (at least one in working order) are now in some 98.6 per cent of the homes of America, and it is estimated that the average household has 5.5 sets.[2] The total number of radio sets in working condition in the U.S. is 401,600,000. Two out of three radios sold at present are either self-powered portables or car radios. More than nine out of ten (91%) of new cars leave the factory equipped with radios; surveys have shown that the number-one accessory choice of most new-car buyers is a radio. Transistor sets are in use today wherever people can go; programs may be heard at the beach, in parks or picnic grounds, on hunting or fishing trips, in the cornfield, on excursions, in the retail store. While most listening takes place in the home, 16 per cent of the radio audience is in cars, and 15 per cent in places other than homes or cars.[3]

FM radio has started to become a profitable broadcasting service with sizeable and loyal special interest audiences. It has proved its ability to reach the quality audience on the local and the regional network levels. In several major metropolitan markets, some FM stations' audiences have been larger than most competing AM stations'. Nationally FM radio attracts one-third of the total radio audience, and even more than that in some major markets.[3a]

Some 32,000,000 American homes—almost half—are equipped with FM receiving sets, and the rate of increase has averaged about two million additional homes each year. Fifty-six per cent of the radio sets sold in recent years were equipped to receive FM. Studies have shown a higher proportion of people with high incomes, college education and professional status in FM homes than in non-FM homes.[4]

It appears that the economics of the FM audience will continue to support specialized program services, especially when the census figures reveal that professionals, executives, proprietors, and technical workers make up approximately 25 per cent of the civilian-male working population.

The manager of an AM radio station or a television station would do well to bear in mind that most of the FM homes are duplicated *homes* but not audiences. This is to say that most of these same homes could be reached through television or by AM radio if these stations were disposed to try to reach them.

The initial acceptance and expansion of television has been equally phenomenal. At the close of World War II in 1946, when television began its growth, only 8,000 homes had television sets. Twenty-eight years later, television could be seen in 68,500,000 homes; 45 per cent of those homes had two or more sets, and 70 per cent of all homes had color TV sets.[5] Television's national coverage, extending to 97 per cent of American homes, almost equals the 98 per cent of the homes that have radio sets, and it exceeds the 87 per cent of American homes with telephones or the 92 per cent with bathtubs and showers. The television antenna has become a familiar characteristic of the American landscape.

People have invested millions of dollars in radio and television sets and antennas and in their service and maintenance. In 1972 American consumers paid $4,700,000,000 on 17,100,000 new television receivers, half of them color.[6] It should be borne in mind that all the dollars people spend on radio and television receiving sets and on their repair and maintenance are purely voluntary expenditures. Here is true evidence of a high degree of public acceptance of broadcasting. Further, the average household has regularly increased daily hours of television set operation from 5 hours and 3 minutes in 1960 to 6 hours and 14 minutes in 1974.[7] It has become a cliché to say that the average American spends more time listening to the radio and viewing television than he spends on any other activity, with the exception of working and sleeping (3 hours 34 minutes with radio, and 3 hours 55 minutes with TV).[8]

Managers of stations can hardly afford to become complacent over the relatively high availability of audiences in comparison with other media. Broadcasters know that a figure of 50 per cent total *actual* audience (actually viewing or listening), representing one-half of the potential audience, is considered high most of the time (and 60–65% in prime time). The term "actual audience" is the same as another term used to describe the percentage of tune-in, namely, sets-in-use or households-using-television (HUT). It is in expanding actual audience or households-using-television that many broadcasters have been lax in their cooperative efforts with other broadcasters to increase the percentages (the ratings). Concentrated efforts by all broadcasters in an area to provide motivations for the listener-viewer to make greater use of the receiving set might result in a consistently larger actual audience in the area.

Competition between stations for the attention of the actual audience results in a "share" of that audience for each of the stations. That station which, at any particular moment, provides the programming which appeals to the largest segment of those people who have their sets in operation gets the largest share of the audience at that time. If it is consistent in achieving this result, it becomes the most popular station in the area on an overall basis but not necessarily during all of its hours of operation.

Broadcasters have had a tendency to devote most of their attention to increases or decreases in their share of audience. While this may be the logical focus of any individual station, it would be wise for all broadcasters in an area to give some of their attention to increasing not only their share of *actual* audiences but also of *potential* audiences that are *available*.[9]

GROWTH OF BROADCASTING STATIONS

In order to complete our look at the dimensions of broadcasting in the United States, we should note the growth of the radio and television stations serving the public.

The number of AM radio stations grew from a total of 30 at the end of 1921 to 955 by the middle of 1945. Fewer than a thousand radio stations provided service to the public through the period of the World War II years. In the five-year period from 1945 to 1950, more stations *began* broadcasting than had been on the air in all of the 25-year history of radio up to 1945. By the middle of 1950, there were 2,303 AM radio stations in the United States. Since that time, there has been a steady growth in the number of stations. Toward mid-1975, there were more than 4,436 commercial AM stations on the air.[10]

The growth pattern of FM stations was quite different, although present signs indicate a healthy growth of FM in the future. The first year of recorded totals of FM stations, 1945, showed a total of 53 stations in the United States. There were 732 stations in operation by July 1950. Then, for the next seven years, the number diminished year by year until there was a surviving total of but 541 by the middle of 1958. Since then, FM has had a rapid rate of growth in each subsequent year. There were 2,819 FCC-authorized commercial FM stations by mid-1975, plus an additional 830 educational stations.[11] It is difficult to equate the growth of FM stations with particular audience interests since there are different "kinds" of FM. In addition to the independently owned FM properties, there are those owned and operated by AM interests. Of the latter types, some duplicate many AM programs; others maintain a completely different program service on the FM outlet.[12]

The growth in the number of television stations was a post-World War II phenomenon. At the beginning of the year 1947, there were only six television stations in operation; there were only 17 by the end of that year. Enough applications for licenses were processed by the FCC prior to the 1948 "freeze" so that 33 stations were able to begin operation in 1948 and 47 more were added in 1949. Then the increase of stations slowed down considerably, with but 10 taking the air in 1950 and only one new station in 1951, bringing the total of stations on the air to 108 at the end of 1951. As soon as the "freeze" was lifted in the spring of 1952, there was a flood of applications. Twenty-one additional stations opened in that year. Then the industry really began its expansion, with an additional 227 new stations during 1953. Since that time, the total number of television stations on the air has increased each year. As of mid-1975, there were 759 FCC-authorized commercial television stations in the United States.[13] In addition, 253 non-commercial educational stations had been authorized by the FCC.[14]

RESEARCH IN BROADCASTING

The beginning of commercial research in broadcasting dates from 1935. In that year, the C. E. Hooper Company began supplying ratings of network radio programs, using the telephone coincidental method. For years, the Hooper rating was a powerful factor in the determination of the success or failure of many network programs. In 1950, the national services of the C. E. Hooper Company were purchased by the A. C. Nielsen Company; but Hooper continues to provide audience measurement services for local radio stations.

Cooperative Research Efforts

There have been two major attempts to establish cooperative research companies in broadcasting. Both were ill-fated.

Pre-dating Hooper as the first broadcasting-industry research organization was the Cooperative Analysis of Broadcasting (CAB), which was started in March of 1930 under the sponsorship of the Association of National Advertisers. By 1934 it had become a non-profit cooperative organization. The ANA

was joined by the American Association of Advertising Agencies and later by
the radio networks as financial contributors and joint managers. CAB used the
telephone-recall method as developed by Archibald Crossley for the measurement of comparatives sizes of network audiences. Later, a change was made to
the use of the telephone-coincidental method, which was already used by Hooper. In the summer of 1946, CAB announced that two ratings services using the
same methods were superfluous and therefore it would terminate its existence.

The idea behind the formation of the Broadcast Measurement Bureau in
1945 was to try to give broadcasters a kind of standard measurement service
similar to the Audit Bureau of Circulation in the publishing field. The governing board of BMB was made up equally of representatives from the National
Association of Broadcasters, the Association of National Advertisers and the
American Association of Advertising Agencies. Only two national studies were
undertaken, the first in 1946 and the other, after considerable difficulties in financing and administrative changes, in 1949. A mailed postcard survey, covering a million people, was conducted in each study. The advertising agencies
seemed to see great possibilities in the data collected but many radio station
managers believed that the information did not provide them with sufficient
sales ammunition. BMB was dependent upon station subscriptions for its financing. The indication of weak support from the broadcasters for any further
studies caused the failure of another cooperative venture into broadcasting
research. BMB came to an end in 1950.

The Big Three of Commercial Research [15]

Three commercial research companies entered the field of broadcasting in
the decade of the 1940s. All have remained leaders in broadcast measurement
ever since, although by the mid-1970s almost 60 companies were engaged in
research for broadcasting.

The A. C. Nielsen Company, an established marketing research firm,
began its work in broadcasting in the early 1940s. The company holds the pat-
ent on a mechanical recording device called the Audimeter. This device, when
attached to the receiving set, records which stations are tuned in and the
amount of time the set is tuned to each station. Since the Audimeter operates
continuously, it captures a profile of the complete activity or inactivity of each
set to which it is attached. In the mid-1970s the "instantaneous Nielsens" were
introduced by connecting approximately 1,200 U.S. homes by phone lines to a
central computer for overnight electronic tabulations.[16] These data are supplemented by "diary" surveys.

The Pulse, Incorporated entered broadcasting in the mid-1940s after notable success in the use of the personal-interview method in the field of public affairs. Adapting this method to broadcast measurements, Pulse began to supply
some qualitative as well as quantitative information about audiences.

A third company was organized in the late 1940s and opened its national
offices in 1952. The American Research Bureau selected the diary method,
using a different sample for each survey period. It added telephone coincidental

and recall surveys, to provide national and local ratings in radio and television—including overnight reports and customized studies. For years commonly referred to as the ARB, that broadcast rating service is now called Arbitron.

Other Commercial Research

Trendex, Incorporated was the first research organization in broadcasting to develop an instantaneous overnight rating service. The company, which was started in 1950, adopted the coincidental-telephone method of measurement. Through the middle of 1961, Trendex offered its clients the fastest national service in broadcasting by making 1,000 telephone calls every half-hour in 25 cities throughout the country. Only the evening programs of the networks were rated. Trendex national reports have not been prepared since June of 1961 but the company continues to make radio reports on special order from the networks and agencies.

Sindlinger and Company, using the telephone interview method, measures all of the mass media. Prior to its involvement in broadcasting, the company achieved success in its research on box-office reports from the motion picture industry. In the early 1960s, the company started a national radio and television measurement service which matches information about audience makeup with probable buying plans for specific products.

A research organization called Trace operates mainly in Hawaii, using an automobile coincidental system whereby motorists are checked during their stops at traffic lights.

A research company that stresses the qualitative approach is TV-Q, a division of Marketing Evaluation, Incorporated. This national service uses the mailed questionnaire method and contacts different families for each monthly survey. Attitudes and opinions about specific television programs are tabulated.

Three major research companies provide local area radio measurement. C. E. Hooper, Inc. offers telephone coincidental reports in some 150 markets. The Pulse, Inc. issues from one to six roster-recall reports per year in some 151 markets. Arbitron (diary method) issues from one to four reports in some 160 markets.

Changes in Kinds of Research Information

In the early days of program research, information supplied to the subscribers consisted of quantitative data including how many homes had receiving sets, the numbers of respondents who were listening to the sets, the stations and programs to which they were tuned, and the percentage who could identify the sponsors of the programs to which they were listening.

By the early 1960s, audience information was more detailed and included some demographic characteristics. Demography as here used expands the academic concept from a statistical study of populations with regard to birth, death, health, growth rates and so on, to include cultural, socio-economic and compositional data. In television terms, demography embraces a study of the audience as a potential viewing and buying group. Although demographic techniques are available, some station managers continue to rely upon guess, hunch and luncheon-table oracles. In general, communications executives are alert to the advances of engineering and technology, but they sometimes remain aloof from the resources of the social sciences.

Demographic disclosures have increasingly proved to be advantageous to the advertiser who wanted more understanding of the audiences for his commercials. Trendex, Nielsen, Arbitron and Pulse all began to publish additional data for their respective subscribers, including such information as the number of viewers per home for each program, the proportions and various age-ranges of men, women and children in the audience, and income, occupation and education stratifications.

PROBLEMS FOR COMMERCIAL RESEARCH

In spite of the present availability of additional audience data, various commercial research companies became the targets for a steadily increasing wave of negative criticism. It was the broadcasters who first raised doubts about the values of quantitative research findings.

The wide disparity of results from the various research companies bothered some broadcasters. The top-rated program or station in one research study might be considerably lower in the ratings of another organization. Performers, writers, directors, producers and others in programming became particularly sensitive to the variance in ratings. Often their careers, and sometimes their incomes, were dependent upon where they stood in comparative rankings.[17] When different audiences were measured by different methods, it was not too surprising that the results did not always agree. Nevertheless, the slavery to the decimal point decided the fate of many a program and it caused the renewal or termination of the advertising contracts of many sponsors. Casualties were common every season in the network schedules. A Wall Street analyst computed that a network's gain of a single rating point in prime-time throughout the eight-month season reflects increased national audience size to generate increased gross advertising revenues of almost $13.5 million a year.[18]

The trend in radio research on the national level seems to be toward *cumulative* studies. Rather than reports on the shares of audience during segmented parts of the broadcast day, the "cumes" show how many people listen to radio, or to a specified station, over a longer period, usually a week's time. This information is comparable to the circulation of a newspaper or magazine, where total numbers of sold copies of a particular issue are determined but not the readership of specific features. From a competitive standpoint with other media, the "cumes" may be sufficient. A certain amount of education in their use is needed by broadcasters. Hindsight now reveals that the early projects of BMB had considerable merit.

Writings on the nature, reliability and influence of the rating system are voluminous.[19] Probably the fairest evaluation—issued in 1966 by the Committee on Nationwide Television Audience Measurement (CONTAM), formed by the networks themselves—was simply that "ratings are an aid to decision-making, not goals in themselves." Unless and until the computer takes over human affairs completely, management will be well advised to rely upon courage and creativity. Broadcasting will otherwise abdicate the management of its own house.

Out of the welter of confusion over the ratings issue, several hard facts have emerged.

First, ratings are basically accurate in measuring what they claim to measure—audience size. In the absence of other means whereby audience response can be surveyed as rapidly and as comprehensively, ratings are essential to broadcasting. Stations and networks need to know how widely their programming is being received. The quandary of ratings seems to stem not so much from their existence as from their frequency and their interpretations and also from how they are applied in broadcast planning.

It is highly questionable whether surveys of audiences are needed every hour of every day. Some variation of the cumulative circulation tabulation would seem to be sufficient for competition with other media which are already established on that kind of long-term average basis. Yet audience ratings do reflect comparative audience sizes for competing programs on rival stations and networks.

The necessity for realistic interpretations of ratings should be obvious. Gross numbers of people, even when stratified by demographic characteristics, reveal comparative sizes and nothing more. Reading other meanings into the ratings can produce false conclusions that may be dangerous for management's decision-making.

Second, the industry must exercise control over the research which is conducted among its audiences. This must be a control based on complete objectivity and not, to any extent, on the profit motive. Scientific research must take precedence over the numbers game, and methodologies must be validated for their accuracy.

Third, the industry cannot bargain for cheap research; research that is meaningful is expensive and is worth supporting. Much experimentation is necessary in order to discover verifiable facts; such experimental projects demand patience.

Fourth, too many station managers either have not properly understood research or they have not had people on their station staffs who could interpret research realistically for them. Such understanding has become more and more of a necessity for every radio and television station.

Fifth, it should now be obvious to every broadcaster that there are other factors which are as important as, and perhaps even more important than, ratings in the determination of his success in reaching the people in his coverage area. Such factors as station image, creativity in programming, flexibility of station performance, the availability of the station to the community, and the costs of the station services to the advertiser in relation to the results the station is able to deliver—all should be related properly to any ratings used. The *composition* of the audiences should be of far greater import than the total size of those audiences. The race to be more popular—in sheer numbers—than the competition throughout the broadcast day has perhaps caused more distortion of the research effort in broadcasting than any other single factor.

Will audience measurement methods in use today be outmoded in tomorrow's broadcasting service? Unquestionably they will need modification. Advertisers and agencies are asking for more definitive information about stations and about the people they serve. More than measuring households, research must concentrate on individuals. The multi-set homes in both radio and television involve varied selections of programs. The increase of UHF and FM stations should mean an expanded competition resulting in greater audience selectivity. In the future, information concerning predefined *groupings* of people will be needed by advertisers. The coming fractionalization of the total mass audience by multi-sets and more stations may itself condemn a system which equated success with the largest audiences. Increasingly, the opinions and attitudes of the listener-viewer will be as important as the simple fact that he chooses a specific program or station at a specified time (psychographics distinguished from quantitative demographics).[20]

Changing Audience Characteristics

It would be easier for the broadcaster to understand his public if people's characteristics had not changed so radically in such a short time. These changes can be illustrated through an examination of three of the most basic categories of a society: age, education and income levels.

Age Categories

The U.S. Census reported that in 1973 almost half (44.9%) of the population in the United States was under the age of 25. One-fifth of all the people in this country were teenagers (ages 10–19).

At the other extreme of the age spectrum, another bulge continues to grow. In the decade between 1950 and 1960, the over-65 age group increased twice as fast as the expansion in the population as a whole (although in the next decade to 1970 the elderly's percentage increase more closely approximated the total population's). In the past 50 years, the over-65 populations increased almost three times as fast as the total population. A century ago, the proportion of people over the age of 65 was 1 in every 35; now, it is 1 in every 10.

As increases have occurred in the "under 25" and the "over 65" age groups, the percentages of people in the 25-to-65 age range and more particularly in the 25-to-50 range have decreased proportionately. This obvious conclusion reflects the ever-increasing mass media audience of youth and senior citizens.

Another general projection foresees a heavier burden on the working population to finance the increased needs of the young and the elderly, both of which groups are largely dependent.

Education Categories

In the 15-year period 1951–1966 the proportion of people between the ages of 18 and 21 who were enrolled in a college or university changed from 25 per cent to 40 per cent. Enrollments increased from a mid-1960 total of over 4 million to 7 million in 1970 and to 9 million by 1975. These figures pertain, of course, to just those students enrolled in colleges and universities at the respective times. It is perhaps even more revealing to add to those millions of people another 13 million who by 1972 were graduates of colleges or universities.

Elementary and secondary schools have shown proportionate bulges as a result of the population explosion following World War II. In 1940, some 10 million people in the United States had completed high school. By 1960, that total had increased to some 25 million, and in 1970 to 61 million; the projected total for 1980 is some 84 million.

Income Categories

Educators have long been aware of a direct correlation between education and income. A 1963 study made by R. H. Bruskin Associates concentrated on people in the 25-to-65 range. In this group, those who had completed high school had an average annual income of $6,102. The average annual income of the person with some college was $7,392; and for the individual with four or more years of college, it was $9,350.[21]

The number of American people who have moved into higher income categories has increased significantly in the past 20 years. It has been noted that in 1947 less than 3 per cent of U.S. families and individuals had incomes between $10,000 and $15,000; in 1972, 26 per cent were in that category, and another 23 per cent had incomes of $15,000 to $25,000 (granting the inflationary economy of the 1970s).[22]

The other end of the family-income range is an unpleasant picture. One out of four U.S. families in 1972 earned a gross income of less than $5,000 a year; and almost half of those low-income families had annual incomes of less than $3,000. More than 2 per cent of all American families subsisted on yearly gross incomes of less than $1,000 in 1972.[23]

Signs of Changing Interests

So the "average man" is somewhat different from his counterpart at the time of the beginning of broadcasting. His environment has changed, too, affecting his outlook, his interests, and his tastes. Radio and television, along with the other mass media, have been important factors in determining the directions of that change. Conversely, the new social climate has had its effect on the media and should continue to condition necessary changes in the nature of communication messages in the future.

There are signs, for example, of a growing public interest in the fine arts. Perhaps loosely referred to as a "culture explosion," this increase of interest in the fine arts should not be regarded lightly. Nor dare we disregard the increase in leisure time. The question as to what people will do with their increased participation in cultural interests and the growth of leisure time should concern every station manager. A search for the answer can hardly overlook some of the signs of a new appetite for cultural pursuit.

Some authorities are highly skeptical of the cultural trend. They believe that there is a lack of depth and meaningfulness in this search for culture. Other authorities maintain that the American society is in a period of change leading toward a time when there will be a general public appreciation for the fine arts. The station manager need not concern himself too greatly with the debate. He must appeal to the young, the elderly, the working population. Culture is not for him to invent, but to understand, to foster and to transmit.

THE CRITICS

It is in this confused area of public taste that broadcasting's critics and criticizers find their most fertile ground. (One should distinguish among public or private persons who criticize the media on subjective, sometimes irrelevant, and even invalid grounds, from professional or scholarly critics of media whose criteria are founded on socio-economic and aesthetic principles and data.) Regularly, critics denigrate the programming of radio and television, usually through the print media. Their highly vocal attacks have caused some people in the audience to question whether they should be as interested in broadcasting as they have been. Watching television is a personal indulgence and—likened to the afternoon cocktail, motorcycle riding or reading comic books—has been assailed as not "respectable" or called a "waste of time" by "authoritative" people and thus made suspect.

What troubles broadcasters is the amount of influence critics seem to possess, particularly when so many of them are poorly qualified commentators on broadcasting itself. Too often, broadcasting is indicted by the critics for not having enough of the kinds of programs the critics themselves would prefer; any wide appeal of such programs to the majority of the public would be purely coincidental. Les Brown, chronicler and critic for *Variety* and then the *New York Times,* noted the different emphases in assessments of television by critics and broadcasters:

> To the critic, television is about programs. To the broadcast practitioner, it is mainly about sales. This explains why most critics have nothing important to say to the industry and why, among all the critics in show business and the arts, the television reviewer is probably the least effective.[24]

The fact is that many ambitious broadcasters receive very little critical support. Brilliant and dedicated men have fought against odds to produce programs of dramatic value, information, and art appreciation. And, when, at last, some of their efforts are successful, the "intellectuals" rarely acknowledge or praise them. Nor does the public support those programs. For example, in the

1972–73 season, of the 197 network specials broadcast, Bob Hope scored 4 of the 13 top-rated shows (including 2nd and 5th places—with ratings of 38.1 and 34.1, and shares of 55 and 49 per cent of those evening's national viewing audiences); Bing Crosby and Jack Benny each rated among the top 10; others included a rerun of "Frosty the Snowman," and Academy Awards presentations, and two of the World Series games. At the other end of the rating scales among that season's special efforts were: Shakespeare's *Much Ado About Nothing* (174th, with a 9.5 rating and a share of 16); a three-hour version of *Long Day's Journey Into Night* with Laurence Olivier (193rd, 6.6 rating and 11 share); five *NBC Reports* (174th, 181st, 183rd, 196th, and—in absolutely last place—197th with a 4.0 rating and a 7 share of the national viewing audience that evening); and five *CBS Reports* (averaging about 8.0 ratings and about 13 per cent shares of audiences, placing 174th, 178th, 181st, 185th, and 188th).[25] Predictably (and unfortunately), the 20 specials least viewed or supported by the public were dominated by cultural, political and public affairs programs.

How many leading citizens of any given community who complain that broadcasting has nothing to offer watch the splendid documentaries and cultural programs on television, or listen to the news reviews or fine musical programs on radio? This does call for selective tuning, but there are enough of these programs to occupy hours of a person's time each week. Fine programs *are* available! [26] The critical minority exercises great care in the selection of the fine arts that they attend, and they buy tickets for these events weeks in advance. Yet those same people often seem perturbed because they have to make some effort to seek out what they want in broadcasting.

Millions of people have had the opportunity to experience performances of Shakespeare, Ibsen, Shaw, Conrad, Henry James, Stephen Vincent Benét, Dickens, Cervantes, Maugham, Hemingway, Maxwell Anderson, Wilder and many others. They have been given performances by Leonard Bernstein and the New York Philharmonic, the Moishiev Dancers, the NBC Opera Company, the Firestone Hour, the Bell Telephone Hour, the Boston Symphony, the Chicago Symphony with its *Great Music* series, and the best of the concert stage. They have had the chance to hear and see every important leader of the world. It is true that the majority of programs are not of this quality, but neither are the majority of plays and musicals produced or books written (consult any list of best sellers). There is a tendency on the part of certain critics to judge the traditional fine arts by only the best produced, but to condemn the mass media by the bulk of popular offerings.

Much of what concerns the critic today may well be taken care of in time. Once, there were those of the elite who looked with disfavor on the silent film; now it is exhibited as an art form. The same reaction has evolved with jazz. Who is to say that some time in the future a Red Skelton or a Bob Hope or the late Jack Benny may not be regarded as classic artists? It is even possible that some of the Westerns that the critics deplore may one day be exhibited as American classics.

The commercial message is a particular target for abuse. Yet, the printed media carry commercial messages similar to those carried on radio and television and in greater volume (although broadcast ads do tend to have greater salience because they interrupt the continuity of programs).[27]

It should be a source of pride to broadcasters that they have been instrumental in broadening public understanding. The majority of the achievements of broadcasting have been positive, but broadcasters have permitted a few deviant stations and biased criticism to distort their image. They need to take positive action against abuses while they still enjoy popular support.

Of all social institutions, broadcasting must be as modern as the people it serves. If it is true that people are becoming harder to satisfy and easier to bore, then there is a profound risk in operating a station by yesterday's standards. No one will detect out-of-date methods faster than the public, who can always tune to those other more advanced, responsive stations and make comparisons. People with significant shifts in age, income, interests and with greater amounts of formal education, with developing interests in culture, can hardly be expected to settle for the same values which they had formerly. It is vital to the future success of any radio or television station to find out in advance in what direction the people are moving.

All broadcasters have a long way to go. Given the opportunity to provide either popular entertainment or self-conscious cultural offerings, most station managers would not hesitate to give the audience what the majority prefers. The manager, charged with the responsibility for the making of profit for his owners, has small choice but to satisfy the majority. On occasion, when popular programs are canceled in order to carry special informational or cultural programs, the reactions from the audience are anything but conducive to repeated efforts. Networks and stations have been flooded with complaints, for example, when they have pre-empted regular offerings in order to carry the Republican and Democratic national conventions. Sizeable numbers of people have reacted negatively to stations when programs have been interrupted to carry news bulletins and "specials" of urgent timeliness. Educational television station WDNT (now WNET) in New York received a reported 350 complaints from its cultivated audience when it carried an important session of the United Nations instead of the scheduled ancient Charlie Chaplin film. In March, 1966, the three television networks pre-empted their regular programming one evening in order to provide coverage of the emergency splashdown of the "Gemini 8" spacecraft. The cost to the networks was reported as approximately $3 million. Even the cost was incidental to the service performed in providing instantaneous coverage of an important event. Nevertheless, there were thousands of angry telephone calls to the networks and their affiliated stations. Plenty of viewers resented the cancellation of *Batman*, *The Virginian*, and ironically, *Lost in Space*.[28] The first two days of network daytime coverage of the Senate Watergate hearings in 1973 lost one-quarter of the usual daytime audience (down from 13 million to 9.5 million viewers); the daily loss to the three commercial networks was about $900,000 in lost advertising billings (in the initial weeks no commercials were carried) plus shared production costs for the pooled live coverage.[29] It seems clear that whatever the signs may be for the long-range future, the present status of mass audience taste favors the popular arts.

Whether commercial broadcasters have an obligation to try to upgrade audience tastes continues to be a debatable issue. There is much to be said for knowing the audience well enough to be able to aim consistently a little higher than existing tastes and thus raise standards by degrees. But it would be financial suicide for most stations to move too fast too soon in that direction. There would seem to be an equal danger in playing down to an audience; condescension has a way of alienating people. The late Franklin Dunham (NBC and later chief of the Radio-TV division of the U.S. Office of Education) put it: "Give the people what they want most of the time, and a little of what they *would* want if they only knew about it."

It should be a sensible approach for any manager to make a sincere effort to learn the true interests of any specific audience. It would appear to be folly to make decisions on the basis of criticial diatribes, personal preferences and aesthetic guesswork.

STUDIES OF AUDIENCE ATTITUDES AND BEHAVIOR

There have been several comprehensive studies of the motivations and attitudes of viewers and listeners. Glick and Levy [30] discovered a certain degree of dissatisfaction among television viewers. The excitement and enthusiasm which existed in the first years of set ownership had somewhat subsided and had been replaced by a greater discrimination in program selection.

The late Gary A. Steiner [31] found that the factor of college attendance made the most significant difference in the amount of time devoted to television viewing. Those who had no more than a high school education were the most devoted fans. Steiner noted that people who had attended college were more selective viewers. They had a wider range of interests outside television and more sources of entertainment. Yet, they viewed few informational programs on either commercial or educational channels, even though they said they would like to have more of this type available.

A decade later Dr. Robert Bower replicated and updated Steiner's survey. He found that better-educated viewers held the television medium generally in lower esteem, were more inclined to prefer other media as dispensers of news, tended to be more selective in choosing programs to watch, and were less likely to enjoy what they viewed.[32] Yet the better-educated viewers in 1970 watched television about as much as other persons during evening and weekend hours; and they distributed their time among program types—comedy, movies, action, information, public affairs, etc.—in similar proportions as those with less education. Similarly, when the better-educated viewer had a specific choice between a program of information and one of regular entertainment, he tended to choose entertainment as much as other persons.

If those people who are the better educated and are in the highest income groups view television less than other people do, then an NBC study,[33] conducted by the American Association for Public Opinion Research in 1963, is particularly interesting. This study found that the "heavy" viewer watched the most informational programming; the "light" viewer usually chose entertainment programs. (All viewers sampled in 1974 estimated that they spent 3 hours 2 minutes daily with television; upper-income people spent 2 hours 47 minutes and college-educated spent 2 hours 23 minutes a day watching television.) [34]

Elmo Roper and Associates have conducted opinion studies at two-year intervals since 1959 for the Television Information Office.[35] In all these studies, favorable attitudes toward television have heavily outweighed unfavorable ones. Since 1963, most people have reported that they receive more of their news from television than they do from any other medium. Television also leads all other media in public believability of news reports, according to the Roper studies. Those surveys through 1974 reflect steadily increasing support for and dependence on television over other media. Between Steiner's 1960 survey and Bower's study in 1970, the percentage of respondents who perceived television as giving the most complete news increased from 19 per cent to 41 per cent. Similar advances in television's role as the people's major source of news were reported by other national studies.[36] The Roper study in 1974 reported that 51 per cent judged television to be the most believable medium, contrasted with 20 per cent selecting newspapers, 8 per cent radio, and 8 per cent magazines as most believable.

Media Statistics, Incorporated, studied New York City residents in March 1965 and found that the heaviest viewers of television were men and women over the age of 65 and the heaviest users of radio were people between 50 and 64. Heavy users of both radio and television included men over 65 and women in the 50 to 64 age group. The Mediastat study revealed a surprising finding about the teenage audience. Contrary to popular opinion, the teenage group in the New York Study was the lowest of all age groups in heavy radio listening. It was also surpassed by women in all age groups and by men 65 and older in amounts of television viewing. Average radio listening per day (6 A.M. to midnight) by adults 18 and older rose from 2 hours 23 minutes in 1967 to 3 hours 14 minutes in 1972—a 36 per cent increase in half a decade.[37] New York City has a multiplicity of radio stations offering a wide range of choice for the person who is disposed to listen. Yet, the Mediastat study found that the average radio listener rarely tuned to more than two stations. In 1972, Opinion Research Corp. reported that of all AM and FM listeners 60 per cent had a single favorite station for music and news, while 26 per cent had two favorite radio stations.[38]

Nielsen data for March–April 1973 showed that average television viewing time per home per day was greatest (7 hours 6 minutes) in homes where the lady of the house was between 36 and 49 years of age; lowest home averages (5 hours 47 minutes) came where the lady of the house was working.[39] Television homes' average viewing time per day was greatest (6 hours 48 minutes) where the head of the household had one to three years of high school education; average household viewing was least (5 hours 56 minutes) where the head of the house had one or more years of college. By the winter of 1974–75, greatest viewing (7 hours a day) was in households with incomes of $10,000 to $15,000, followed by households earning over $15,000 (6 hours 36 minutes). Homes with incomes of under $10,000 viewed an average of 6 hours 21 minutes daily; lowest average of viewing time (6 hours 6 minutes) was in homes with incomes of over $20,000.

PROFILE OF THE AUDIENCES

In general, what do broadcasters really know about the public? First of all, and of prime importance to broadcasters, they know that it is composed of many diversified publics. Each of these smaller units has its own particular interests and its members are apt to believe that their views are the correct ones.

Broadcasters know that most audiences for radio and television are far more interested in entertainment than they are in education or information. Whether a particular audience preference is for homemaking programs or baseball or music or dramatic fare, they *do* want to be entertained. Even those groups that prefer the fine arts find their own form of entertainment in that programming. A sure way to fail in any format is to neglect the element of showmanship that is an important ingredient of entertainment. Dr. Robert Bower reported in 1973 that 72 per cent of 1,900 respondents identified television as the most entertaining medium, 14 per cent cited radio, 9 per cent newspapers, and 5 per cent magazines.[40]

And yet, the public's attitude toward television changed through the 1960s, reflecting the events and changes in the world during that decade. In 1960 Steiner's survey found that people considered television primarily as an entertainment medium. But in 1970 Bower's national study discovered that people no longer thought of it as merely a source of entertainment: "much more, they were thinking of it as something that reflects what is going on in the world outside: in space, in Vietnam, in campus unrest, in politics." [41]

Most people tend to give perhaps too much credibility to radio and television sources. They tend to believe whatever Cronkite or Chancellor or the local newscaster or announcer tells them. In most cases, this faith is well placed but it is almost too much responsibility for the broadcaster to bear. Since that tendency does exist among people not accustomed to look very far beyond the headlines of a single newspaper, the trust of those people must never be ignored. Certainly, any exploitation of that trust must rank as one of the most serious forms of irresponsibility.

Bower's study confirmed other surveys showing that black Americans are among the most positive supporters of television, and that better-educated (including college graduates) and higher-income blacks view more than other blacks.[42]

Granted, it would be naive to expect the audience to appreciate all the efforts of the broadcaster. The moods of an audience are often fickle and difficult to estimate. This unpredictability factor, as much as anything else, is sufficient

reason for broadcasters to extend themselves to acquire a sounder understanding of the people they serve.

> In 1970 an oddly altered picture emerges. Now, ten years later, television
> is chosen ahead of the three other media on *all ten* of the positive items. Not only
> is it still the most entertaining, educational, interest-creating, politically informa-
> tive medium, and the one that is improving all the time; it also, says a plurality,
> brings information quicker, more completely, more intelligently and with less
> bias, and it does the most for the public.
>
> But while this positive evaluation of TV in its identifiable functions—to
> entertain, to educate, to inform—is advancing, there also seems to be an increase
> in *negative* evaluations on less specific items. As the medium that "is getting
> worse all the time," television *increases* from 24 to 41 per cent; as the medium
> which is "getting better" its vote *decreases* from 49 to 38 per cent. More people
> now think that television is getting worse than think that it is improving. Pre-
> viously the balance was tilted on the side of improvement. This is a marked nega-
> tive shift from the 1960 views, a shift that is taking place at the same time that an
> increasing number of people are giving television a high performance rating on
> other dimensions.[43]

The audience has been conditioned to expect regular *changes* in station
offerings. The wide variety of programs which they have come to expect from
broadcasting may have spoiled them somewhat, but a "mix" must be continued as the spice of quite ordinary lives. Broadcasters may be grateful for the
general *optimism* which the public has concerning changes. Next year's programs will be better, they hope. The resultant interest in new offerings is in the
station's favor.

Certainly these are *important* people. They have been given so much by
the media. They have seen most of the forms of show business and all of the
established story plots and they have been eyewitness to the great news stories.
Their expectation level for new and for novel programs is insatiable. At any
particular time, given too much repetition, they could turn to alternative forms
of entertainment and recreation as they once turned to broadcasting over their
former interests.

STATION RESPONSIBILITY

If broadcasters are both leaders and servants of the public, then a question
of proportion must be raised. When, how often and under what conditions
should the leadership function be exercised? How much of the broadcast schedule should be what the public wants and how much should be devoted to what
the public needs? It must, of course, be assumed that the broadcaster is aware
of the specific needs and wants of his audience, especially with the increased
emphasis on community ascertainment demanded of licensees by the FCC. It
must also be assumed that he knows some of the needs and wants of the people

which they themselves may not realize. The problem is further complicated by the changing nature of the public's desires.

Two problems arise from attempts to give the audience what it wants. First, it is doubtful whether most people *know* what they want at any particular time. Tuning usually involves two kinds of choices: whether to turn the set on or leave it off, and which station to select from the several that are available. The latter choice may not supply what the consumer wants at that moment. Rather, he makes his selection from whatever is being broadcast. In this sense, the listener adjusts to the media rather than vice versa. Paul Klein, former research executive with NBC, coined this exercise of options as the "least objectionable program" theory, which critic Les Brown agreed was a weakness of the program service.

A second problem is posed when ratings are used by the broadcaster as a basis for giving the audience what it seems to want. The fallacy of this reasoning is that the ratings show what may have been wanted *yesterday* or last week or last month. Ratings represent measurement of *past* choices. There is no assurance that the listener wants more of the same *today*.

It is no easy task to determine the best methods for satisfying most of the people most of the time. Certainly, the ideal combinations have not yet been discovered. The FCC asserts that broadcasters must serve the public interest, convenience and necessity. No one disagrees. This is something like discussing the weather; we'd like it improved but how to improve it escapes us.

A balance must be sought to reconcile complete responsibility toward the public welfare with complete responsibility toward commercial obligations. Perhaps the problem should not be expressed in terms of *giving* but rather *selling* the station's programs to the public since commercial broadcasting operates in a sales atmosphere. If so, then the test of effectiveness, as in sales endeavors, should be the mutual satisfaction of both parties.

A strange dichotomy exists in the area of alleged effects of programs on people. Some critics claim that some broadcast materials make radio or television addicts of some people, or that they may delay or prevent normal maturation or make some people select unrealistic goals or become generally apathetic. Other critics maintain that the very same materials may provide healthy relaxation for other people, to aid them in their normal maturation and to serve as an escape valve for channeling off certain aggressive impulses.

Broadcasters must admit that these powerful media do have effects on people. Such an admission is pure realism. Certainly, sales departments assert this fact whenever they try to sell air time to ad agencies' clients.

The effects of media, particularly the depiction of violence—whether fictional (drama, comedy) or nonfictional (news, documentaries)—have been studied over the decades. Research reports by scientific, academic, and governmental sources have provided supporting data for both or several sides of the debate about media's influence and effects on the audience.[44] The general appraisal that media mostly reinforce preexisting attitudes and behavior—with major formation of ideas and actions coming from family, peer group, school and church—has in recent years been modified to note that a small percentage (but a large number nationally) of children whose behavior or thought patterns are marginally normal may be triggered or even inspired to emulate what they see and hear in media presentations. There has been increasing scientific support for the probability of media's negative social effects on a large fringe group of the nation's children. The Surgeon General's commissioned studies and final five-volume report in 1972 interpreted evidence available that televised violence and depicted aggression increase aggression in the real world. Yet, even the senior research coordinator and science adviser to the Scientific Advisory Committee on Television and Social Behavior noted that those implications were subject to further research for corroboration, modification, or even reversal.[45] For example, Dr. Floyd Cornelison, Jr., head of the Department of Psychiatry and Human Behavior at Jefferson Medical College in Philadelphia asserted in 1973 that children ought to be allowed to watch all the aggressive TV programming they want: "Kids who grow up aware that life is full of violence and horror are apt to be normal because they're prepared to deal with reality." [46]

People with unstable characteristics who watch considerable television quite possibly could get destructive ideas and miss the constructive elements completely. True, they may get the same ideas in other places but perhaps not as graphically or as attractively demonstrated. Programming which might seem quite innocent to a normal person can be interpreted in an altogether different manner by an abnormal person.

When a President of the United States or a U. S. Senator or a civil rights leader is slain by an assassin's bullet, when eight student nurses are murdered, when 45 people are hit by the bullets of an unbalanced person on a major university campus, it is time to ask, "What and who will be next?" It is also time to ask whether the pleasurable rewards of depicted violence in broadcast programs for some people are worth the consequences. There still remains the question as to the amount of influence which broadcasting has, if any, on these and other acts of crime. If there is any chance at all that the media may be contributory factors, then broadcasters have a serious challenge to which to respond.

Certainly, the opposite extreme of naive, pollyanna types of programming would be just as questionable in its effect on people. There is evidence that some people would prefer a saccharine-treated news program instead of a display of battlefield corpses.

One of the broadcaster's greatest tasks is to discover a balance which neither narcotizes the public nor places individuals in danger.

Zsa Zsa Gabor's opinions can be more important than the opinions of a college professor to many people because she is more physically attractive, she is seen more often and she more closely represents the social aspirations of many admirers. Whether those desires are in the people's best interest is moot. They do exist and the public reacts accordingly. Broadcasters may not determine social standards, but celebrities and the roles they play do influence the public through the status which broadcasting confers upon them.

So long as broadcasting is so all-pervasive and can get into those homes where parental guidance is weak or non-existent, it should take advantage of its opportunities. It should not shift its responsibilities to sources which are not inclined to accept them.

Broadcasters *can* help make and shape the values people live by. People can, through radio and television, come to feel a sense of participation in current history. They can learn life's deeper satisfaction and, as a result, become active in helping to reduce the many injustices of modern society. They can come to believe in the values of man's compassion for his fellow man.

What is wrong with stimulating the *thinking* of members of the audience? One of the major accomplishments of the electronic media could be the raising of significant questions rather than the providing of neat answers. One can be accomplished as easily as the other without any discernible difference in the size of the audience. Either can be achieved within entertainment programs as well as within informational or educational formats.

The job broadcasters can do to protect and explain the true democratic ideal is practically unlimited. Here is a way that the industry can partially repay the public for the use of its airways.

The individual station must take the initiative in establishing rapport with its audience. Involvement in community affairs can be followed by on-the-air reports of those activities. The station's facilities can be used regularly to tell the people in the audience what the various staff personnel are doing for community improvement. The station's interest in the people in the audience and its efforts to serve them better should be told on the air.

If the broadcaster expects public support on important issues, he must begin to encourage a more vocal response from the people in relatively minor matters. He cannot anticipate sympathy when he needs it if he cultivates a one-way communication system. It is time for broadcasters to realize that an absence of audience response is a reflection on the management of stations. Oversensitivity to opinions that do not happen to coincide with those of management is not a healthy trait. It is through the conflict of ideas that any democratic institution is able to achieve greatness.

Apathetic audiences are of little practical value to the broadcaster in the selection of his program schedules. Yet, those same audience members can be highly critical of those offerings once they have been aired. The situation is somewhat comparable to the person who does not vote on election day, and then months later stands on the street corner to condemn the administration.

Manufacturers have discovered that their products are successful when they are "people-centered." They regularly conduct studies and marketing research to determine that their perception of the "people" is accurate, to ensure continued favorable response from consumers.

The station manager needs to maintain his own personal involvement with the "people" in his area. He won't necessarily find representatives of the majority at country clubs or among his associates. Lest he become isolated from the mass audience he serves, it is essential for him to keep in touch with them. He should ride a bus and talk with the people who are on it. He should converse with garage attendants, laborers on construction projects, taxicab or truck drivers, radio-repair men and the myriad of people who live outside his ordinary world. One of the most enlightening and profitable experiences he could undertake would be participation for a day or two in one of his station's personal interview surveys in the homes of his audience.

LOCAL STATION RESEARCH

The studies of national audiences which have been cited in this chapter do not provide information about particular station audiences. Qualitative information about local audiences must still be discovered through local effort. The station manager may choose to remain unenlightened concerning the real image of his station in the community. If, however, he wants to provide the best possible service to the local public and to local advertisers, he will want to learn the people's true attitudes and reactions.

Local audience research needs to be undertaken as a supplement to the other research services which the station buys. Its usefulness lies in disclosing how well the station is presently communicating and how it may improve its communication in the future. The results of local station research should be considered by management as an important aid toward achieving more efficient operations.

The NAB has suggested the areas where research can help a station: management planning for expanded operation, providing basic marketing data, determining competing stations' and other media's audiences and revenues, developing sales, evaluating programming, and measuring changes—the pattern of progress or erosion in audience, market, advertisers, and programming and sales service.[47]

Local audience research may reveal some shortcomings in the station service and it may confirm some station achievements. It is this kind of revelation, positive or negative, that the station needs to know. The true public attitude toward his station is of far greater value to a good administrator than distorted impressions based on guesswork or on comments from a closed circle of friends and colleagues. Local audience research, then, should be conducted primarily for the values which it will bring to station administration. Dr. Sydney Roslow of The Pulse, Incorporated, has said:

> There will be a lot less mis-use [sic] and abuse of research as more of us discover that research is not the action. It is not the judgment. It is only an aid to judgment. . . . It is a tool to complement all the other tools management needs for its cerebral decisions.

The NAB has similarly emphasized research as an information-gathering tool, for management and decision-making, and never as a substitute for judgment:

1. It can resolve differences of opinion among equally competent members of management as to what the facts really are.
2. It can help management assign a weight or an order of importance to a set of known factors.
3. It can disclose relationships among what were hitherto thought to be unrelated facts.
4. On occasion it can uncover things that no one had thought of before.[48]

Who should be in charge of local research? In order to answer that question adequately, the *purposes* of the research should be kept in mind. Those purposes should be to confirm or deny the effectiveness of past operational patterns and to provide guidelines for the future. Since any use of data for general circulation outside the station would defeat the diagnostic purpose and could also alert competitors to possible future station action, it is advisable that the research be conducted by a member of the station staff. Then, whether favorable or unfavorable reactions are received, the information can be used only by the station administration and in ways that can be determined internally.

In some of the larger stations, a director of research has been designated. In most of these instances, he has been assigned to coordinate various existing research efforts. Seldom have these men been given the opportunity to initiate and supervise significant independent local station research. Yet, with minimal rearrangement of job functions, the way could be cleared for them to begin to feed important information to management. It is imperative that when local research studies are undertaken, they should be completely divorced from the activities of the sales and promotion departments.

But many stations are not in a position to add a research director to the staff. In those cases, the manager may well employ someone qualified to perform regular staff duties who is also qualified to conduct qualitative research. Many young graduates from colleges and universities who have majored in radio and television have received research training as a part of that education.

If a station finds it impossible to support any staff-conducted research, it might seek to initiate studies either with colleges and universities or with state broadcasters' associations. The advantage of confidentiality of station-conducted studies may be impossible to achieve in these "farmed-out" or cooperative efforts because their results will be known by the sources which do the research. However, the information discovered can be useful and such studies certainly would be better than none at all. Often, a radio or television station is located near a college or university. In too many cases, the research facilities and resources of the academic institutions have not been adequately utilized by the broadcaster. Educational researchers are particularly suited for the kinds of studies which the local station needs to make of its audience. They generally have little or no interest in the quantitative "ratings" type of research but they can become interested in projects which propose to study audience opinions and attitudes.[49]

How often should local research be conducted? It would seem that over-researching a local audience could be as wasteful for a station as no research at all. A good, thorough, continuing study of the local audience once each year should provide a realistic venture for any station. The returns to management should far outweigh the investment.

The possibility of cooperative studies with leading merchants in the community should not be overlooked. Some stations have had outstanding success with return-postcard mailings in monthly statements of banks, public utilities or savings and loan associations. Information can be gathered about station or program popularity. In the ordinary arrangement, the station pays for the mailings and the financial institutions contribute the time for the tabulation of the results. Local businessmen accept the findings of such surveys because of the position of trust that those major business institutions hold in the community. The element of respect is also an advantage in terms of the reliability of the public response to the mailings.

OTHER STATION-AUDIENCE RELATIONSHIPS

A station manager dare not stop at the acquisition of knowledge about his audience. He needs to use all of the methods at his command to maintain cordial relationships between the station and the people. His attitude toward the audience will be reflected in the attitudes of his employees and in the nature of his service to the people.

Those stations with the best records of successful audience relationships usually are managed by men who are truly concerned about, and who work to maintain, a feeling of mutual understanding and respect between the station and the people served by the station.

The not-so-simple matter of ensuring the proper handling of telephone calls and mail from the audience can reflect to the advantage of the station. The cordial telephone voice and manner can win people and influence them favorably. A lack of courtesy and consideration can destroy goodwill that has taken years to establish. Some stations use recorded answers to telephone calls during nighttime or week-end operations; such a practice can provoke people so much that the loss in favorable image can be far more than the station can afford. The "personal touch" is essential for close relationships.

Unanswered mail is inexcusable. The use of form letters should be avoided except in cases where mass mailings are necessary for contests or promotional efforts. Even letters which might come to the station from "crackpots" deserve the courtesy of a reply, although they may be difficult to answer.

Stations can achieve tangible benefits from organizing a working advisory council made up of responsible men and women from the coverage area of the station. Such a council might be composed of active men and women prominent in general civic affairs and in club work throughout the station signal area. For example, the WGN Continental Broadcast Advisory Council has members representing persons from Illinois, Indiana, Iowa, Wisconsin and Michigan.

Full membership meetings of two to four hours' duration are conducted at least semi-annually; frequent additional meetings are held with subgroups of that membership. The members of the Council have an opportunity to talk with key department heads and other station and corporation executives. They make suggestions for changes in programming. Many of the ideas have been excellent; some, while well meant, have been thoroughly impractical. Members of the Council are fully aware that theirs is an advisory capacity and that the station officials must make all final decisions. These dedicated men and women have contributed to the benefit of everyone in the audience reached by the station's broadcast signal.

In a smaller community, such a council can have an immediate and highly personal impact. It can be extremely beneficial in aiding those broadcasting operations that are limited in their program resources. It can direct people's attention to the station and, through the various organizations represented by the members of the council, advise the general public of what the broadcaster has done and is doing to contribute to the good of the home community.

When the broadcaster, his audience and the critics pool their resources, self-interest can change to mutual cooperation. Then, all of the true benefits of broadcast communications can be realized.

NOTES

Chapter 4

1. Whit Hobbs, VP and Copy Director, Batten, Barton, Durstine and Osborn, Inc.

2. These and following data were provided by the Radio Advertising Bureau, March 1973, Set Sales Revisions, and RAB "Radio Facts" Pocket Piece 1975.

3. *Variety,* June 21, 1972, p. 1, citing Statistical Research Inc., for RADAR (Radio's All Dimension Audience Research).

3a. Rufus Crater, "Special Report: The Upbeat Tempo of FM 1974," *Broadcasting,* Oct. 7, 1974, pp. 41–48.

4. CBS Radio Network Affiliate Research/Promotion Reference Guide, September 1972.

5. Data in these paragraphs were derived from American Research Bureau, "Estimate of United States Television Households: 1973–74"; National Association of Broadcasters, "Dimensions of Television," November 1973; *Broadcasting Yearbook 1974;* Radio Advertising Bureau, "Radio Facts" Pocket Piece 1973; American Research Bureau, *Television U.S.A.:* February / March 1975; A. C. Nielsen Co., *Nielsen Television '75.*

6. Television Bureau of Advertising, quoted in *Variety,* July 25, 1973, p. 1.

7. In 1961, hours per home per day were 5:00; in subsequent years the average rose progressively: 5:06 (1962), 5:12 (1963), 5:24 (1964), 5:30 (1965), 5:30 (1966), 5:42 (1967), 5:48 (1968), 5:48 (1969), 5:54 (1970), 6:00 (1971), 6:12 (1972), 6:15 (1973), and 6:14 (1974). Source: A. C. Nielsen Co., *Nielson Television '75,* p. 8.

8. RAB (Radio Advertising Bureau) Radio Facts 1973 and TvB (Television Bureau of Advertising). Other research by the Nielsen Co. and by the Roper Organization put the average individual's daily viewing at slightly over 3 hours in 1974.

9. A clear description of the difference between ratings and shares is in Sydney W. Head, *Broadcasting in America* (Boston: Houghton Mifflin Co.), 1972, pp. 296–298. For application to national network audience statistics, see Les Brown, *Televi$ion: The Business Behind the Box* (N.Y.: Harcourt Brace Jovanovich, Inc., 1971), pp. 32–35.

10. *Broadcasting,* May 19, 1975, p. 72, based on FCC records as of March 31, 1975.

11. *Ibid.*

12. *Code of Federal Regulations,* Title 47, #73.242. No more than 50% duplication by commonly owned AM and FM stations in cities over 100,000 is allowed.

13. *Broadcasting,* May 19, 1975, p. 72, based on FCC records as of March 31, 1975. Although by December, 1967, there had been 823 commercial TV stations authorized, in the following half-decade a number of UHF authorizations were abandoned by licensees and deleted by the FCC.

14. *Ibid.*

15. *Broadcasting Yearbook 1974* reported 54 research companies for broadcasters. For a clera explanation of how ratings measurements are computed by various major companies, see Sydney W. Head, *Broadcasting in America,* pp. 296–304. He critically analyzes how ratings are used on pp. 304–315. See also: J. Leonard Reinsch and Elmo I. Ellis, *Radio Station Management,* 2nd rev. ed. (N.Y.: Harper and Row, 1960), pp. 278–293; this chapter on radio research describes various kinds of surveys and their values for management. See Yale Roe, *Television Station Management* (N.Y.: Hastings House, 1964), pp. 171–180, chapter by Julius Barnathan, "The Business of Research." Cf. Dr. Harrison Summers, "Qualitative Information Concerning Audiences of Network Television Programs," *Journal of Broadcasting* V:2 (Spring 1961), pp. 147–160.

16. The regular Nielsen service is subscribed to by each network for approximately $1,000,000 annually, with the new "instant" computation service costing each network an additional one-third million dollars. *TV Guide,* June 16, 1973. Cf. "Nielsen Newscast," XXII:3 (1973), pp. 1–3. The "NTI" ("Nielsen Television Index") reports national ratings; the "NSI" ("Nielsen Station Index") provides local ratings. See A. C. Nielsen Co., "NTI in Instantaneous Action," 1974 booklet.

17. For example, in 1972 at WPIX-TV in New York City, a news anchorman was offered in addition to his base salary of $75,000, additional salary per rating point (over 2 points) on the following scale: a rating of 3.0 would bring total compensation to $94,200; 4.0 would bring $113,400; 5.0, $132,600; 6.0, $151,800; 7.0, $171,000; plus almost $20,000 per each additional rating point after successive years with the local news on that independent station. *Variety,* August 9, 1972, p. 38.

18. Cited by Ernie Kreiling, "Hollywood Television Report," August 27, 1973, p. 3. At the national network level, an additional fractional rating point of 0.1 for a single half-hour represents approximately 65,000 homes; if the cost-per-thousand is only $4, a commercial minute is thus worth an additional $260. For a network that sustains a rating-point advantage over competitors throughout the 30-week season, the amount becomes significant. In 1972–73, CBS averaged 19.8 for the season, over NBC's 19.1. That total lead of less than a full point (0.7) reflected 81,900,000 additional homes for CBS from mid-September to the end of April over NBC's season-long total. Those homes thus reflected about $7,000,000 in time sales charges as the margin of CBS's billings over NBC's. Similarly, because ABC averaged a season-long primetime rating of only 17.5, CBS had a sales margin of $21,000,000 over ABC for its evening programming billings that year. Finally, if those raw numbers were translated into desirable demographics (thus not merely $4 CPM but as high as $9 CPM), then CBS's margin over NBC would be as much as $15–16,000,000. Millions of dollars ride on fractions of national rating points. *Variety,* May 30, 1973; pp. 31, 50. In 1975–76, the A. C. Nielsen Co., estimated a full rating point for network TV would represent 701,000 homes. *Broadcasting,* May 12, 1975, p. 10.

19. "Evaluation of Statistical Methods Used in Obtaining Broadcast Ratings," a Report of the Committee on Interstate and Foreign Commerce (Washington: U.S. Government Printing Office, 1961). "Martin Mayer, "How Good Are Television Ratings?" (N.Y.: Television Information Office, 1966). "How Good Are Television Ratings? (continued . . .)" (N.Y.: Television Information Office, 1969). "Television Ratings Revisited . . . A Further Look at Television Audiences," (N.Y.: Television Information Office, 1971). "Maintaining Rating Confidence and Credibility," (Broadcast Rating Council, 1972). The latter descriptive analyses are readable and brief. And, of course, the research companies making the rating surveys also offer booklets on their methodologies.

20. For a sampling of the kinds of qualitative research of cross-sections of potential audi-

ences, see *Journal of Broadcasting* XVI:1 (Winter 1971–1972), pp. 65–102; James H. Flynn III, "The Ideal Television Station: a 'Q' Study"; Joseph T. Plummer, "Life Style Patterns: A New Constraint for Mass Communications Research"; Ronald H. Johnstone, "Who Listens to Religious Radio Broadcasts Anymore?"

21. Radio Advertising Bureau, "The Listening Habits of Better-Educated Adults," August 1963, p. 4. The U.S. Census reported the average household income in inflationary 1972 to be $11,286; the median income was $9,698.

22. Sylvia Porter, "How Do You Rate on Family Income?" Lansing *State Journal,* May 14, 1963; and U.S. Bureau of the Census, *Statistical Abstract of the United States: 1974,* 95th ed. (Washington, D.C.: U.S. Government Printing Office, 1974).

23. Although there were twice as many families in each category a decade earlier, the 1972 figures reflected strong inflationary levels whose purchasing power could not be compared easily with 1963. Comparative figures are from the *Saturday Evening Post* (editorial), December 21, 1963, and from the U.S. Census Bureau for 1972:

	Percentage of U.S. homes:	
Gross Income	*1963*	*1972*
less than $5,000	50%	24.9%
less than 4,000	33	19.4
less than 3,000	22	13.7
less than 2,000	12	7.5
less than 1,000	5	2.2

24. Les Brown, *Televi$ion: The Business Behind the Box* (N.Y.: Harcourt Brace Jovanovich, Inc., 1971), p. 58.

25. *Variety* listings, June 13, 1973, p. 36. The 1973–74 and 1974–75 seasons reflected similar rankings for popular "light" shows and cultural or information programs.

26. A partial listing of broadcast programs through 10 or 15 months includes such content as: "Will Rogers' USA," "The Prado," the five-part life of Leonardi da Vinci, "Heifetz in Concert," the "Henry VIII" and "Elizabeth R" series, "El Greco," "Arthur Rubinstein," "Civilization," "Sol Hurok Presents," "America" with Alistair Cooke, Jacques Cousteau sea-life specials, various awards presentations, the National Geographic series, the Shenyang Aerobatic Troupe of the People's Republic of China, "Don Quixote," "Five Presidents on the Presidency," religious specials, "Peggy Fleming in the Soviet Union," the Olympics, Gilbert and Sullivan, "The People of 'People's China,' " Ibsen, F. Scott Fitzgerald, "The Autobiography of Miss Jane Pittman," "The Execution of Private Slovik," "That Certain Summer," "Pueblo," "Search for the Nile" series, and even the highly controversial "Sticks and Bones."

27. A study of allocation of space in six New York City daily newspapers in 1944 measured the following averages, as compared with similar data computed in 1968 for two New York daily newspapers:

	News	News pictures	Features	Advertising
6 newspapers average (1944)	25.9%	9.2 %	19.0%	45.9 %
2 newspapers average (1968)	14.1	5.63	13.8	66.23

Thus, almost one-half of all newspaper space was devoted to advertising in 1944, while two-thirds of all space was ads in 1968. But the National Association of Broadcasters' code (to which most TV stations subscribe) limited the percentage of airtime devoted to commercial ads and other non-program material (such as promotional announcements) at 9 minutes 30 seconds in any 60-minute period of prime time (12 minutes in those periods for independent stations), and at all other times 16 minutes in any 60-minute period; those figures equal percentages of 16, 20, and 26 per cents respectively—far from print media's 66 per cent! (Radio's code limitations are 18 minutes within a clock hour, or 30 per cent; one third of all AM and FM stations subscribe to the radio code.) Sources: Morris L. Ernst, *The First Freedom* (N.Y.: Macmillan, 1946), p. 290; Gary Pillon, "Newspaper Space Allocation" (unpublished term paper, University of Detroit, 1968), p. 7.

28. *Broadcasting*, March 21, 1966, p. 64.

29. *Variety*, May 23, 1973, p. 43.

30. Ira O. Glick and Sidney J. Levy, *Living with Television* (Chicago: Aldine Publishing Company, 1962).

31. Gary A. Steiner, *The People Look at Television* (N.Y.: Alfred A. Knopf, 1963).

32. Robert T. Bower, *Television and the Public* (N.Y.: Holt, Rinehart and Winston, Inc., 1973), p. 179.

33. *Broadcasting*, September 30, 1963, p. 72.

34. The Roper Organization, Inc., "Trends in Public Attitudes Toward Television and Other Mass Media: 1959–1974" (N.Y.: Television Information Office, 1975), p. 6.

35. Elmo W. Roper, text of speech delivered in New York City, December 7, 1965, distributed by the Television Information Office.

36. Cf. Robert T. Bower, *Television and the Public,* Chapter 5: "The News on Television," pp. 99–128; The Roper Organization, Inc., "Trends in Public Attitudes Toward Television and Other Mass Media: 1959–1974" (N.Y.: Television Information Office, 1975), pp. 2–5.

37. CBS Radio Network, "Affiliate Research/Promotion Reference Guide," 1972; p. 4. The average U.S. adult listens to radio 23 hours 48 minutes per week (based on 24-hour days or 168 hours a week).

38. Reported in CBS Radio Network "Affiliate Research/Promotion Reference Guide," 1972; p. 8.

39. Data cited by Television Bureau of Advertising, *TV Basics 16* [1973/74]. Household viewing by income for November 1974 reported in A. C. Nielsen Co., *Nielsen Television '75,* p. 9.

40. Bower, p. 14.

41. Dr. Robert T. Bower, quoted by Neil Hickey, "How America Sees Television," *TV Guide,* July 14, 1973, p. 5.

42. Bower, pp. 46–50. Cf. "Blacks Regard TV as Most Sympathetic," *Variety,* September 1, 1971, p. 1; Louis Harris poll found that 43% of U.S. blacks surveyed ranked TV highest among American institutions as "really caring about blacks achieving equality," compared with 39% so listing the U.S. Supreme Court, 27% newspapers, down to local real estate companies 14%.

43. Bower, p. 15.

44. Major selected works include: Hilde T. Himmelweit, A. N. Oppenheim, and Pamela Vince, *Television and the Child* (London: Oxford University Press, 1958); Joseph T. Klapper, *The Effects of Mass Communication* (Glencoe, Ill., The Free Press, 1960); Wilbur Schramm, Jack Lyle, and Edwin B. Parker, *Television in the Lives of Our Children* (Stanford: Stanford University Press, 1961); Robert K. Baker and Sandra J. Ball, *Violence and the Media* (Washington: U.S. Government Printing Office, 1969); Wilbur Schramm and Donald F. Roberts, eds., *The Process and Effects of Mass Communications,* rev. ed. (Urbana: University of Illinois Press, 1971); United States Public Health Service, *Television and Growing Up: The Impact of Televised Violence* (Washington: U.S. Government Printing Office, 1972); Seymour Feshback and Robert D. Singer, *Television and Aggression* (San Francisco: Jossey-Bass, 1971).

45. Dr. George A. Comstock, cited in *Broadcasting,* August 28, 1972, pp. 31–32.

For example, Dr. Stanley Milgram and Dr. R. Lance Shotland, sociopsychologists, reported a unique field study of viewers of a national network program with different endings in different cities; they noted that while depiction of violence on television may seem repugnant, it does not necessarily lead to antisocial behavior among the viewers: "We have not been able to find evidence for this; for if television is on trial, the judgment of this investigation must be the Scottish verdict: Not proven." But those investigators did note that their non-correlation between TV violence and real-life aggression in single-program exposure did not preclude possible cumulative, long-term effects of viewing many programs over a long period of time. *Television and Antisocial Behavior* (N.Y.: Academic Press, 1974). The substance of their findings had been presented verbally in 1972 to a section of the New York Academy of Sciences, and reported in *Broadcasting,* May 22, 1972, p. 47. Cf. *Broadcasting,* May 11, 1974.

46. Cited by Ernie Kreiling, "Hollywood Television Report," June 18, 1973, p. 1, quoting Dr. Cornelison from an article in the *National Enquirer* (mid-1973; no date given).

47. National Association of Broadcasters, *A Broadcast Research Primer* (Washington: NAB, 1966/71), pp. 2–4.

48. *Ibid.,* p. 6.

49. An excellent instance of detailed local research was WCVB's public-opinion research unit, taking community ascertainment a step further than usual. Survey questionnaires were mailed to more than 10,000 persons randomly selected within a 75-mile radius of the station; these were supplemented by 1,000 telephone interviews with members of the public. Before the station began its program service in March of 1972 (after replacing WHDH-TV, Boston), program planning was based on "a significant amount of data on the composition and concerns of its potential viewers." This local research was designed by the dean of Boston University's School of Public Communications who was a consultant to the station (and who held a doctorate in psychology). The public opinion research unit's director had a master's degree in education from the City University of New York and had studied broadcasting and communication research at Boston University. *Variety,* May 30, 1973, p. 39.

5

Programming

[I]t is our obligation to serve the people in such manner as to reflect credit upon our profession and to encourage aspiration toward a better estate for our audiences.

—NAB Radio Code [1]

Television is seen and heard in nearly every American home. . . . Television broadcasters must take this pluralistic audience into account in programming their stations. They are obligated to bring their positive responsibility for professionalism and reasoned judgment to bear upon all those involved in the development, production and selection of programs.

—NAB Television Code [2]

THE ROLE of the programming department and its manager has evolved over the decades of broadcasting: from the casual flexibility of the early innovative era of radio; through the tightly structured and creative golden age of radio networking (linking dominant stations in large and small markets); to the severely-patterned "formula" programming among proliferating competing stations and in reaction to the emergence of flexible, innovative television. These forms were followed by distinctive and specialized services in radio (especially with the advent of widescale FM programming) while television entrenched itself in nationally-serviced schedules and scattered efforts at local programming (usually in news, public affairs, and children's, often supplied by syndicated film and tape materials)—and itself meeting head-on yet new forms of local cable and even pay television. So the program manager's responsibilities have changed successively in radio and then in television, as the industry and art modified over the years.

This chapter will initially comment on areas generally common to both radio and television stations' local programming, then on key characteristics distinctive first to local radio and then to local television, and finally on major aspects of national network television.

A. Local Station Programming

THE PROGRAM DEPARTMENT

The program department is the "showcase" of a radio or television station. It normally employs more people than any other department of the station and produces the only *product* the station has to offer, whether it be entertainment or information. It, more than any other part of the operation, creates the station image or personality.

There are two broad areas of activity of the program department: (1) the planning of the overall program schedule and (2) the development and production of individual programs to fit that schedule. The station manager is involved in both of these activities, principally with the first.

It is the station manager's function to serve as the architect of the station's program framework. He provides the philosophy out of which program policy grows. He knows the expectations of the stockholders and of the public and he accepts the responsibility for the success of the overall program structure of the station.

The manager's programming blueprint needs to be clear and realistic and it should be flexible enough so that it may be adaptable to future change. It is finalized only after considerable appraisal of the resources and the objectives of the station.

Implementation of the blueprint is assigned to the program manager but the station manager must continue to evaluate the station's programming. He spot-checks concepts and performance. He notes places where improvements can be made. He confers with the program manager to suggest changes or corrections.

The ability to recognize where change is needed and to offer constructive advice is developed by experience in programming. Station managers whose earlier experiences in broadcasting were confined to sales or engineering need to make special efforts to approach programming. In radio, especially, leadership is necessary in this department where much of the station's success is dependent upon the inspiration of sensitive and creative people. Selection of an effective program manager is an important consideration.

THE PROGRAM MANAGER

In those early days of radio, when the title of the chief of station programming generally was program director, this was a key position. The assignment was challenging because of the numbers of programs that were planned, rehearsed and broadcast live from the station's studios. Even with heavy network schedules, there were many hours to be filled locally and the program director considered it a challenge to match the network quality of production. They created an aura of excitement in the radio stations.

With the advent of "formula" radio, which was radio's first major response to the competition of television, there was little need for live production. In a majority of stations, the program director served as a kind of chief office clerk. He arranged announcers' schedules, counted the number of times a particular record was played in a day, tried to maintain a measure of authority over the disc jockeys, and waited for direction from the station manager. He became a follower, overseeing mountains of paper. Today, with radio stations striving for identity, a premium is again placed on station creativity.

A similar scenario might be written for television stations: creativity was the hallmark of a program manager who could be inventive with meager materials in the dynamic chaos of early television. But the increasing segments of the broadcast day supplied by national networking and syndicated materials narrowed the field for local program innovation. Except for mounting news and public affairs programs, program management centers on the scheduling of ready-made product instead of building personalities and program forms in the local studios. The proliferation of independent channels, especially in the UHF spectrum, as well as the growth of cable television has brought the medium full-circle to the early exploratory days of imaginative production with small staff, limited space and facilities, and minuscule budgets.

The program manager or director is responsible, ultimately, for the sound of the radio station and the look-and-sound of the television station as broadcast through programs to the public.[3] His goal is to produce the best program service possible, given the available staff, facilities, budget, and time availabilities in the schedule. He must be conscious of the mutual dependence between his work and the sales department because "the programming effort is to provide a marketable product for the sales effort."[4] While program men must be idea men they must also be competent businessmen, combining creative judgment with practical judgment. The programmer must be conscientious in gathering and assessing relevant data; at the same time he must retain independence and creative sensitivity so that his decisions achieve the goal of attracting and pleasing audiences.

The good program manager is one who personifies show business. The world of entertainment in all its forms should be his number-one interest. In addition, he needs to be concerned about the communication of information. Company product is as strong as the man who supervises its growth and development. Projections into the future in station programming depend upon the vision and the wisdom of the manager of this department. Given a program manager with these and other qualifications, combined with the desire of station management to give him the right climate for growth in his department, there can be little limit to the constant progress which a station will make in program development and improvement.

BALANCED PROGRAMMING

Program balance, balanced programming—no one seems to know just what the terms mean. Perhaps this is as it should be. If there were a standardized definition universally accepted, then programming would tend to be similar on all stations.

Certain allocations of interest are obvious. It makes little sense, for example, for a station with a completely urban audience to devote part of its schedule to farm programs. On the other hand, farm programming is needed on the clear-channel stations, the regionals and the local stations in rural areas.

The alert program manager recognizes that the real key to program balance lies in a variety of offerings. A radio station format that provides a day-long diet of five minutes of news on the hour and fifty-five minutes of music all of the same type cannot be said to offer much variety.

In the early years of radio, the several stations in a market necessarily attempted to serve the diverse subgroups of the total audience by each scheduling different kinds of programming throughout the broadcast day. The Federal Communications Commission over the years required percentage tabulations of various categories of programs, as an index of diversified programming to the many interest-groups in the station's market. But as the number of AM, and then FM, transmitters proliferated in even middle-sized markets, the FCC eventually acknowledged that individual stations could provide specialized program service (all news, all music, even all classified ads) as a complement to the market's total service provided by all the varied station program services.

And yet, except for the relatively short-lived phenomenon of intense Top-40 tightly produced schedules, any single radio station does not attract the same individual persons all day long. Different people, with differing schedules of work and play and relaxation and travel, listen to the station purposely or by chance throughout the broadcast day. Thus every station must be alert to the "day-parts"—the demographics of a continuously changing population potentially served through the hours of each day. This calls for some range or variety of emphasis even within fairly homogeneous format content. By 1973 "the idea of programming a consistent sound all day has, for some programmers, lost many of its former applications"; instead there is need to appeal to different, though not vastly different, audiences at different times of the day.[5]

The question of balanced programming in television is partly like the early days of radio—a few channels serve each market (except for several massive metropolitan centers of the country)—and so each channel must attempt to provide a cross-section of program content throughout the broadcast day and week both to attract segments of the total local audience and also to justify its license to serve "all" the public's interest, convenience, and necessity in that signal area. Yet, there is the anomaly that most major stations are affiliated with national networks (only 95 out of 688 commercial stations are independents, two-thirds of them UHF), and so offer their local markets mostly national network service in early morning, daytime, prime-time, and fringe and late hours into the night. (Les Brown, TV-radio columnist of the *New York Times,* among others, notes that because network programs are virtually and even actually interchangeable among the networks—and even imitatively indistinguishable from one another in the few categories of program types— there is really only one national program service through three conduits, plus the alternate service of the Public Broadcasting Service.)

So any real balance of television programming at the local station level must be achieved by the programming department's efforts to produce (and sell, where possible) local news, public affairs, children's, or a rare local entertainment offering. The major opportunity to achieve some kind of balance in television thus, in fact, lies in *scheduling* programs rather than in creating variety of content and form.

Thus any discussion of program balance will emphasize the variety and diversity possible in programming formats for radio but mostly in scheduling for television.

It is worth noting that comments about a "philosophy" of programming for radio remained very similar over two decades, with only a few relatively short-term modifications or emphases as various "fad" forms appeared on the scene and then melted into the broader spectrum of fairly standard programming styles.[6] A 1956 appraisal could have been made with equal aptness in 1971:

> In general, as one analyzes programming, it is easily perceived that no one philosophy emerges as dominant. Radio is in a state of program flux, with operators trying all kinds and types of programming. Radio program planning is always in motion—and today it must move at a far greater speed than in the past. Research is beginning to play a major role and should serve as a stimulating guide in the future. [1956] [7]

> [T]he senior broadcast medium is now so alive, so flexible, in so constant a state of change, that the broadcaster who would stay ahead of the game has got to be running full tilt each day of his competitive life. . . . The truth is that, in 1971, it is radio which is outpacing its larger kid brother, television, in terms of innovation, excitement and—perhaps—communication itself. Radio is once again on the leading edge of broadcasting. [1971] [8]

In 1956, the owner of a group of radio stations (which programmed "formula" radio) concluded: "Eventually we feel that the listener realizes that the station is actually working in his own best interests to provide programs which are interesting and that the station is providing local creative effort." [9] That "formula" station's music and news was offered as programming that was not drab and dull and manifesting a certain sameness, by being done well and by incorporating new creative ideas to demonstrate to the audience that the station sought the public's listenership, good will and cooperation. Similarly in the early 1970s, two successful station programmers variously voiced their endorsement of the same philosophy of gaining and serving a public, and thereby making a profit: [10]

It's service to the public. Period. We do more for the audience than any-body else does.

I really believe this: you have to give honest service, you have to honestly do something, fulfill a need, then you go out and sell it. . . . How can so many stations survive? That's a problem, no question about it, but if you develop a distinct and strong personality, and serve that public need faithfully, you have an audience. A viable thing that is of great value, with great believability. That's the key.

The same fundamental philosophy of programming pertains to television as to radio: provide genuine service to the public audience.

TECHNICAL FACTORS

In attempting to provide adequate service to the public, broadcasters must take into account the total market in which they operate. For, as mentioned ear-lier, the number of competing stations and their respective program service can affect the kinds of audiences able to be attracted to a complementary or alter-nate (or even "counter") program service. Affecting both radio and television operations are such matters as frequency and channel allocation, innovations in broadcast technology, and the question of music licensing—all factors in deter-mining feasibility of various kinds of service to a community.

Radio Frequencies Reception

Periodically, the FCC has issued a "freeze" on all applications for various services (AM, FM, and TV) as well as for major facilities changes to allow time for considering revisions in allocations policy. Modifications of the FM service in the 1940s and the TV service in the early 1950s (with applica-tions "frozen" from 1948 to 1952) were classic instances of Federal regulatory efforts to determine engineering criteria and procedures which affected the licensing of broadcast stations.[11] From 1962 to 1964 and again from 1968 to 1973 the AM frequencies were subjected to such a freeze, so that government could set policies about future AM assignments that would be granted on the basis of rigid engineering standards. That effort partly encouraged new stations for markets with inadequate service, while it curtailed the entry of new stations into large markets.

Less directly affecting stations was the exploration in the 1970s to pass legislation requiring almost all radios manufactured or sold in the U.S. to have both FM and AM capability.[12] This "all-channel" radio bill—similar to pre-vious successful legislation for "all-channel" television receivers—was in-tended to put the FM broadcaster in a more equitable position in competing for potential audiences. Such legislation would strengthen the position of FM sta-tions while threatening the dominance of AM stations. It would result in more intense competition among all stations in a market. It could well result in a wider range of programming formats, including highly specialized services by individual stations, in efforts to attract highly fragmented radio audiences. This would suggest that the total public's many kinds of interests and needs would be well served—provided that the increased competition did not drive out smaller AM stations. Further, the combined manufacture of AM-FM radios would decrease consumer costs by eliminating separate purchase of FM sets— especially for automobiles. These increased sales of FM (combined with AM) radios would make possible a greater potential audience for the FM service. Probably the greatest gains from such proposed legislation would accrue to the smaller commercial FM stations as well as to those owned by special interest groups and educational institutions; their potential audiences would be greatly increased. Standing to lose ground might well be some AM stations whose programming might not serve selective audiences as well as some FM formats.

Television Channel Reception

Television reflects similar issues. The "all-channel" VHF-UHF receivers were mandated by law, making feasible the establishment of hundreds of UHF stations in intermixed markets, competing with strong VHF stations. While the legislation did make it physically possible for enormous numbers of people to tune in UHF signals, VHF channels sustained their dominance because of network programming and the established familiarity of their service, as well as because of the slightly difficult manual procedure necessary initially to dial UHF reception. Because it has been difficult for new UHF stations to compete with established and prosperous VHF stations in bargaining for feature and syndicated films, the UHF's claim to audience consisted of kinds of services that neither competing stations nor the networks can provide. Thus, without seriously threatening the established VHF service, the additional UHF channels provided educational and other diversified programs services to those in the public who so desired. The UHF program schedules have specialized in sports, ethnic, language, and even nationality programs.

In the early years of commercial television, homes in most markets could receive only one or two channels. By 1973, only 2 per cent of the population was limited to but one or two channels. Almost two-thirds (60%) of all homes in the U.S. could receive seven or more television signals—commercial and non-commercial. And 3 per cent of the population could receive as many as 13 or more television stations! [13] Increased numbers of stations, in television as in radio, have forced programming to cater to specialized subgroups of the markets' audiences in competing for attention and support. This has generated diversified program service to meet the publics' many kinds of interests and needs.

In 1973, the Office of Telecommunications Policy of the White House formally urged additional VHF television station channel assignments in the current spectrum (recommending almost 100 more than the then approximately 600 commercial stations).[14] It also suggested that a fourth national network would thus become feasible, linking many of those stations and some of the already-on-air independent stations. But studies by electronic firms and by the

Rand Corporation, supported by a grant from the Markle Foundation, discounted the financial feasibility of such "drop-in" stations or network.[15] Also, there was the threat of degradation of existing VHF service due to lowering of engineering standards.

Alternate Systems of Programming

There is little argument over the positive benefits that CATV produces for the public and for the television industry as long as it concentrates on bringing more choices, without duplication of programs, to markets with no service or with one or two stations. In the multi-station market, broadcasters found a different story. There, additional channel activation resulted in additional segmentation of the existing audiences. Any eventual settlement will either need to reaffirm or redefine the American right of free enterprise. Questions of prior rights and simple ethical business practices are involved. Certainly, CATV is a programming issue as far as the general public is concerned because its ultimate solution will determine the nature and cost of the offerings the people will get on their home television receivers. The initially sanguine prognosis for cable television became, by the mid-1970s, less optimistic as audiences found few specialized services offered successfully other than clearer reception of already existing channels. Program sources were not all that available. And costs for cable installation and service kept mounting. The prospects for cable seemed to lie in truly diverse service such as professional information retrieval, two-way purchasing and voting, etc. There is a clear parallel here with wired-music services which never supplanted commercial radio broadcasting.

Pay television, unsuccessfully experimented with in many North American locations, reappeared as one of the forms of cable television's services—providing first-run motion pictures and sports for specific charges to the viewer. There seemed to be no discernible adverse effect on commercial television viewing. Pay or subscription television's attractions appealed to selective interests; the amount of expenditure per home varied according to the quantity, diversity, and quality of programming that was able to be offered. Nevertheless, broadcasters feared future development of Pay-TV if it succeeded in "siphoning" off program features from free television.

Radio's growth in audience acceptance and satisfaction was enhanced by the introduction of not only FM but also stereophonic sound and later quadraphonic sound. These innovations led to purchases of new radio receivers and increased listening by the audience. Similarly, in television, the gradual introduction of color prompted millions of people to purchase new color receivers and heightened viewer enjoyment of programs. The kinds of programs, their formats and staging (as well as special effects utilizing color-code techniques) were all affected by the transition from black-&-white to color telecasting. While television programming was not so heavily modified and determined by color as radio programming was by stereo, it was still influenced by color's attracting ever greater audiences to their receivers.

COMMUNITY-CENTERED PROGRAMMING

Some of the greatest satisfactions in local radio and television can come from the development of the community-centered programming, particularly when the voices of the people who live in the area are featured. Such development can build a position of solid respect in the community.

As much care should go into the public service community program as goes into any other locally originated program on the station. Public service programming efforts should be regarded as station investments in the future growth and welfare of the area.

The station should be known as a champion for civic improvement and for the promotion of public safety, racial and religious understanding. Always it should take a strong stand in support of constructive projects and it should regularly expose any community "evils" which come to its attention. Mere notices, brief announcements, colorless paragraphs sandwiched in the day's schedule are not enough! Whenever the station reaches the stage where it is a true mirror for the community, then the man who has guided it to that accomplishment can take pride in this achievement. The station will enjoy acceptance and approval.

Local programming and news/public affairs (or informational) programming are perhaps the cornerstones of effective, responsible, and—hopefully—successful station service to communities which they are licensed to serve. Not only the FCC, but also audiences in that market, and local advertisers tend to be responsive to the presence or absence of a healthy community-oriented public service effort in announcements and in local programs.[16]

The FCC still looks to service in renewing licenses, especially when applying criteria in comparative hearings or where consumer or other special-interest groups have filed petitions to deny renewals. "Substantial" or even "superior" service is the keynote struck by the Commission in past decisions and by the appellate court (the U.S. Court of Appeals in Washington, D.C.). Congress, especially through its Senate Subcommittee on Communications, has expressed support about erosion of locally originated community programming among television stations particularly.[17] Dean Burch, before he resigned from chairmanship of the Commission, advocated strongly the adoption of gross percentages of broadcast time in several broad programming categories as a means for determining what constitutes substantially acceptable service to a community. Those categories included local programming and informational programming (news and public affairs)—not the traditional program type categories such as agricultural, religious, instructional, etc.[18] His remarks followed by two months the public release of outgoing Commissioner Nicholas Johnson's national listing, based on his staff's research and rankings, of the nation's major television stations according to their local programming and their news and public affairs service, among other categories.[19] In the single category of local programming, WLWT-TV (Cincinnati, Avco Broadcasting Corp.) scored first in the national rankings, although it scored 118th in news and public affairs programming. WPLG-TV (Miami, Washington Post-Newsweek) ranked first in news and public affairs but 10th nationally in local programming. The point here is that "localness," which implies community orientation in programming, is a matter seriously considered by the Federal Communications Commission.

Local coverage is a factor in media evaluation not only by the Federal government but by the public, which is increasingly concerned about local news, and by advertisers who need local target marketing.[20] Neighborhood newspapers, city magazines, radio stations reflecting metropolitan suburbs, and local television news services extending to one and even two full hours each early evening are able to provide citizens with information about local events such as neighborhood crime, deteriorating public services in their area (transportation, schools, garbage disposal, utilities), housing, narcotics, unemployment and strikes, racial problems and ecology. Alert programmers in some markets have bypassed close competitors by promoting such local activities as voter registration, free rock concerts, civic events including minority projects, basketball workshops, and drug addiction centers or phonelines. The local public's interest "in itself" is coupled with potential competition to local broadcast stations from cable operators whose appeal comes also from "localness," as well as from airtime potential derived from the FCC's prime-time access rule for television stations in the early 1970s.

WVOX-AM/FM in New Rochelle, N.Y., has capitalized on candid coverage of, and comment about, community affairs. The station uses "stringers" not only in the immediate area but throughout the state and even the country. The station's president, William O'Shaughnessy, has involved the station in community service activities, in strong editorial positions on controversial issues, and has made the station a vehicle for expression of widely divergent viewpoints on local as well as national issues—by invited guests, by discussion programs, and by wide-open telephone call-in shows. WVOX "is strongly in the black; it is one of the favored advertising outlets in the county. Billings are well above the $500,000 line, a profit area for a station of this size [500 watts AM-day, 3kw FM, day-night]. WVOX has, in fact, become the national prototype of the suburban station that succeeds by integrating with local 'gut' issues."[21]

Seven half-hours in prime-time were programmed by WVCB-TV, Needham (Boston), Massachusetts, with subjects of special interest to Greater Boston citizens, in the prime-time access period. Boston's only 24-hour television station, it programs a total of 51 hours of local production weekly, including a daily 90-minute live program, "Good Morning," with live remotes of features and entertainment as well as news. Its Public Opinion Research Unit (see previous chapter, note [49]) and management's regular meeting with community leaders and organization representatives assist the station in responding to community interests and concerns.[22]

Effective not only for meeting governmental guidelines but also for determining the continuing shifts in a community's needs and interests are processes of ascertainment (described in the previous chapter on Audiences and in the chapter on Regulation). Public affairs program planning can well be built on these surveys if they are properly conducted so that they truly reflect local citizen's concerns.[23] For example, WJBK-TV (Storer Broadcasting) surveyed the metropolitan Detroit community in successive years. Local conditions in the city and suburbs were reflected in the reports for 1968 and 1970 (see Table VIII).

TABLE VIII

COMMUNITY LEADERS AND CITIZENS RANK DETROIT
AREA PROBLEMS

PROBLEM AREA	1968		1970		
	RANKED BY			RANKED BY	
	LEADERS	CITIZENS	LEADERS	CITIZENS	
				Detroit Residents	Suburbanites
Race Relations	1	1	4 (18.3%)	3 (23.0%)	6 (10.3%)
Crime	2	2	2 (22.3)	1 (52.0)	1 (34.5)
Education	4	3	1 (24.1)	2 (27.0)	4 (16.0)
Teenage Problems	6	3	7 (3.1)	6 (13.5)	5 (11.7)
City Government	3	5	5 (6.7)	4 (19.0)	2 (25.0)
TV Programming	—	6	—	—	—
Civic Improvement *	5	7			
Inner City			3 (18.3)	5 (15.0)	7 (3.0)
Environment			6 (5.8)	7 (13.5)	3 (20.6)

* Including Pollution and Beautification.
Sources: "Detroit Area Community Needs," WJBK-TV2/Storer Broadcasting Co., Detroit, June 1968, Table XV [n.p.]; "Southeast Michigan Community Needs '70," WJBK-TV2/Storer Broadcasting Co., Detroit, January 1970; Tables III and IV [n.p.].

There are inherent values in conscientious public service, community-related programming which is at the same time entertaining or at least attractive to the audience. Therefore the broadcaster must be wary of granting free time merely because a topic or a cause is "worthy." Airtime is valuable! It must be used to attract and hold audiences if it is to sustain its value—whether measured in social impact of information and inspiring messages to the public tuned in, or in terms of dollars generated through advertising. Quality in production as well as in content is necessary to justify airtime in a medium of mass communication. Poor quality disserves the content and the "cause," the participants, the programmer, and the audience.[24]

NEWS

In some ways, the radio industry missed a golden opportunity in the news field. Radio could have become the number-one medium for news. Instead, it lost this distinction to, of all media, television! Not content with taking over radio's former dominance in many forms of entertainment, the television industry boldly moved to establish its leadership in the news area. Its network daily evening news coverage was expanded from 15 minutes to a half hour, it moved into the field of public affairs documentaries and, in spite of its more cumbersome equipment, it initiated more remote coverage than radio had ever done.

By 1975, 65 per cent of people surveyed nationally cited television as the source of most of their news, while 21 per cent so identified radio (down from 35% in 1959).[25] Over that same decade and a half, "credibility" rose from less than 30 per cent to 51 per cent of the audience who considered television the most believable news medium; radio in that time dropped from about 12 per cent to 8 per cent (newspapers as the most credible source dropped by one-third, from 32% to 20%, while magazines dropped to the 8% level). Certainly the expansion of national network news programming as well as of local news broadcasts at heavy-audience pre- and post-prime-time viewing hours—coupled with attractive visual effects and mobile technology for immediacy, vividness, and impact—contributed to television news' ascendancy. And two-thirds of all television news viewing is of local news programs.[26]

What was radio doing all this time? For the most part, it continued to be dependent upon the wire services for its news and it concentrated on five-minute summaries of news highlights or headlines. The radio industry showed little disposition to seek out local news on its own. At many radio stations with a program policy of music and news, the five-minute newscasts make the policy a misnomer. Music is given predominant attention and only token recognition is given to news. The news programming on those stations has been described "as something you sandwich in between music and disc jockey commentary, like a piece of processed ham between two stale pieces of bread." Furthermore, by the time the gimmicks that introduce the news (sounds of teletype, echo-chamber effects, filter mikes, sounds of fire engines, supersonic jets, etc.) and the commercials have been taken care of, there isn't a fair *five* minutes left for the news.

Yet, during the daytime hours radio remained the primary source of news for 46 per cent of all adult Americans, and for 54 per cent of adults living in cities larger than 500,000 population.[27] Still, 39 per cent of all adults reported television as their main source of daytime news, while 34 per cent said newspapers provided most of their daytime news.

Audience attention and credence generated by news service are important for a station as a sales medium. A responsible, competent news service benefits a station in audience numbers and revenue. Further, in the context of exacerbated local, national and world conditions, the American public wants news. So sponsorship of news programming has increased through recent decades. Many small- and medium-market radio and television station news operations must struggle to meet costs. But in larger markets, radio news operations produce revenue, while television news tends to "break even."

News long ago dropped its negative mantle of being an automatic dollar "write-off" by management. Serious, competitive, comprehensive news service can pay its own way and more, where management supports an adequately professional staff and news-gathering facilities.[28] Depending on cost accounting procedures, and whether in combined operations the radio and television staffs overlap, spots in news commercial time almost pay for the service; additional revenue is indirectly generated by news in prestige and audience for the station's total programming and commercials. (One station in 1973 reportedly earned 19 per cent of its total revenue from news spots.) [29] In 1974 local station managers affirmed that:

> . . . [n]ews is salable. It is not a profit-making operation. If you have listeners you can sell your spots for more.[30]

> We seem to be too worried about the ''cosmetics'' [of mounting the program production]; we should be more worried about the content of the program. We should worry about covering the news better and relating it to our audience. If you have better news, the numbers will follow.[31]

Thus broadcast managers claim that ''the most important program commodity we have is news''; and, while it is the most expensive programming, ''a good news operation makes a good station while a bad news operation makes a bad station.'' [32]

News and public affairs programming, of course, can create tensions among major forces in the industry and society itself. The duPont-Columbia study appraised the 1971–72 scene:

> The broadcasters were engaged in a desperate struggle to keep their wealth, their power and their self-respect—possibly in that order. The politicians, in the interest of their incumbencies, and perhaps their sense of propriety, seemed bent at one time or another of depriving them of all three. . . .
> Granted the primacy of electronic news among all the media, its practitioners still seemed to have the most precarious of platforms from which to launch their reports and commentaries. . . .
> It came from the very nature of U.S. broadcasting: a merchandising operation, managed by entrepreneurs, paid for by businessmen, licensed and regulated by politicians in ''the public interest, convenience and necessity.'' Uncertain budgets and time allotments for news and public affairs, growing in some cases from managerial nerves, or sponsor disapproval or public indifference, could also be blamed on the acts and threats of the adversary in Washington who often seemed more intent upon emasculating than reforming the broadcaster's vast enterprise.[33]

Management should be concerned first about the quality of the news service, whether a station be radio or television, and then about the audience and costs-*vs*-revenue of that service. The most obviously distinctive characteristic of competing television stations in a community is their local news service. Radio has come to depend on music and the overall ''sound'' of specialized services or format; but the quality of its news service should play a more dominant role if it wishes to stand out among competing signals and thus attract both audience and advertisers.

To build strong news capability, management must attract and support a capable news director, experienced in journalism and broadcasting.[34] Jay Hoffer quotes *Fortune* magazine's assessment of the integrity and independence needed in media:

> The quality of journalism depends primarily on journalists—not on government and not on the legal owners of media. Publishers and executives of networks and broadcasting stations now have only a small fraction of the influence on news that owners used to exercise. As commercial bias diminishes, what counts now, for better or worse, is the bias of reporters, cameramen and editors. Their ideological bent is far less important than their artistic bias, the way they select and present what they regard as significant.[35]

The news director, with support of top management, must be able to gather a staff—whether it be one other full-time person in the small radio station, or 100 in the large television station of a major market—who are competent and dedicated to the principles of good journalism. By late 1972, the Radio Television News Directors Association reported that three-fourths of responding radio news staffs had three or fewer full-time employees, while television or combined TV-radio news organizations had 10 or more full-time staff members; [36] the average TV news staff in the early 1970s was 13 employees.[37] Maintaining a qualified staff, according to the RTNDA survey, was the second-largest major problem at about one-third of all responding stations. The greatest problem (38% in radio, and 48% in television) was budget, according to news directors. Yet the duPont-Columbia survey at about the same time noted that 63 per cent of news and public affairs directors had larger budgets in 1971–72 than in the previous year, 47.5 per cent had larger staffs, and 39.7 per cent had more time available for news than in 1970–71.

Management's concern to support competence and integrity in news reporting might well emphasize (a) budgetary support for adequate staffing and (b) entrusting the news function to professional personnel free from interference or pressure.[38] Managers should support the hiring of personnel with adequate credentials—academic and professional; and they should encourage them to update and grow intellectually by reading journals, by attending occasional meetings of colleagues, and even by advanced formal studies if possible. A well-trained, conscientious staff can then work carefully and effectively with the news director who must assume responsibility for overseeing the news operation of a station.[39]

Management, including the news director, may choose to engage a research firm to appraise the local news operation and to make it more effective. A consultant should provide data for managers and the news staff, not replace their independent judgment. Outside consultants might lean toward recommending "packaging" news program formats that may work in other markets but which may not be the most appropriate form for the local market, station, and news team.

In the early 1970s, consulting firms for television news recreated the patterned, packaged formats that dominated radio in the "Top-40s" heyday of the 1950s. Efforts to sample local markets scientifically, then to apply to those data creative restyling of news presentations resulted in imitating staccato radio news—shortening TV "stories" to 90 seconds, and increasing the number of news items from the usual 10 to a new standard of 18 or 20 per half hour program. They emphasized personalities and magazine-style segments within the news broadcast, linking partners in news presentations by informal conversation among on-air presenters (nee newspersons). Marshall McLuhan supported what he called the "friendly teamness" [sic] format; he claimed it was truer to the nature of the medium of television—its immediacy and spontaneity constituting much of the ongoing *process* that is television, rather than the formalized package associated with more static print media. McLuhan posited approvingly that "in TV news . . . instead of reporters, you have only performers" and that "when the news team seeks to become the news source by means of direct dialogue rather than by remote report of the event, they are being true to the immediacy of the TV medium in which comment outranks the event itself." [40]

Although larger audiences were usually attracted to these faster-paced, less formalized news presentations (sometimes referred to as "Happy Talk" concepts), professional newsmen were often displeased with this emphasis on "performance" over journalistic reporting. But others noted that only transitions between news stories were lightened, not the news content; also, with increased audiences, more people were being exposed to news content—albeit briefer and more visual, deemphasizing abstract and complex issues in the news.[41] And, of course, higher ratings commanded higher rates; for Los Angeles local news programs in 1973, each additional rating point made every 30-second spot worth about $70 more.

Management should add to the local relevance of programming by preparing editorials. Slightly under two-thirds of the nation's television stations editorialized by the end of 1973 (a 2.5% drop from 1971).[42] Great care must be taken with the serious responsibility of commenting about events and issues of concern to a community. Management itself might best make statements of opinion and interpretation, especially when advocating community action on an issue. The practice of having news directors deliver editorials is questionable because viewers should be able to distinguish clearly the editorial comment from journalistic reporting and editing. In 1969, almost one-third of TV editorials were presented by news directors (that figure dropped by late 1972 to only one in ten); 41 per cent of those presenting editorials were "editorial writers," and only 11 per cent were station managers.[43]

Especially news departments at key stations in the largest markets (and network news staffs) must exercise continuing care about the objectivity and professionalism of their reporting. Management must support news directors' efforts to avoid sensationalism in news stories—their content and manner of presentation. Developing social circumstances in the past decade have occasioned new criteria.[44] While some guidelines have changed, basic rules remain the same. "Gang journalism" contributes to stereotypical interviews of available celebrities and politicians; rather than seeking out centrally significant persons, street reporters can become "walking mike stands" merely thrusting microphones before prominent persons at airports, outside government buildings, or at non-news-generating "press conferences." Nor should broadcast media artificially create personalities, becoming almost common carriers for sophisticated news makers and news manipulators—whether they represent status-quo establishment or anti-establishment "screamers and shouters." Media should not influence the course of events in any substantive way. Newspersons must be observers and reporters, not participants in the event either emotionally or physically—even though, as surrogates of the audience, newspersons conducting interviews quite properly are human beings interacting with other human beings. Presence of news crews should be muted, keeping a "low-profile" of neutrality. If at all possible, station policy should be opposed to newspersons' doing on-air commercials. In spite of advertiser and sales department (and even audience) interest, the news function should not become mingled with the sales function of broadcasting. The integrity of news coverage, and the believability and impartiality of radio and television newspeople, must be protected.

Most independent stations rely upon the radio wire services of Associated Press (AP) and/or United Press International (UPI) for their national and international news. Most small-market stations purchase the services of one or the other. The large-market stations use both and, in many cases, these are supplemented by their own correspondents. Network affiliates are aided by "hot lines" through which they are alerted whenever an important story is breaking. UPI maintains daily voiced news and actuality reports to some 300 radio stations. Spot news, commentary and features are supplied. A full-time staff of domestic and overseas correspondents is supplemented by special UPI newspersons on assignments around the world. Syndicated news companies provide similar services for independent television stations. Television News, Inc. (TVN) distributes filmclips by airmail or by AT&T video lines; it acquired the UPITN service (formerly the television news syndicate of United Press International). In recent years some network affiliates and even network-owned stations have subscribed to the services of Independent Television News of London. Network affiliates can pay a fee for additional closed-circuit feeds of a dozen or more hard news, features, and sports stories from their respective networks (ABC's Daily Electronic Feed, CBS's Late Afternoon News, and NBC's News Program Service).

Too much dependence upon the wire services and syndicated suppliers restricts the coverage of *local* news. The radio or television station that does not send a single member of its news staff into the community on a regular beat misses one of its best chances to increase its circulation. The use of direct lines to police and fire departments and to the city hall, as well as the use of "stringers," have their places in complete news coverage, but they are not substitutes for regular first-hand reports by a member of the station staff. The practice used by some stations of inviting listeners to telephone news tips to the station can create problems of inaccuracy or at least of redundance or even triviality. Local station news should emphasize just that: localness. Information that affects people's daily lives in the community—road conditions, closed schools, utility shut-downs, conditions and service in local hospitals—is what interests people.

Even the local coverage of community events is no guarantee that anything worthwhile will be reported. Stations need newsmen who can discover news stories overlooked by people who are not trained journalists. A special kind of writing and editing for the *ear* is needed. Often, the journalist who has no training in broadcasting may be too well trained in how to write for the *print* media. He may also be ineffective as an air personality. What is badly needed is a new breed of news personality who has training and experience in both journalism and broadcasting.

Mobile units, equipped with cameras, tape recorders and beeper phones have given news reportage a new dimension. In the larger metropolitan markets, cruisers and helicopters have provided continuing coverage of traffic conditions, informing commuters of highly congested areas and of street conditions during bad weather. Cruisers have been deterrents to crime in some instances as they have circulated on night beats through potential trouble areas of cities. To add immediacy to television reporting, stations in the 1970s introduced extremely light-weight portable television cameras (for live and videotape relay) comparable to compact transistorized microphones and audio recorders. This equipment made possible continuing, "instant" reports during the broadcast day during development of important events.[45] Similarly, greater use of super-8mm equipment and of still photography on 35mm slides made possible speed and graphic concreteness generally restricted to mobile radio in the past.

The radio as well as television station should produce documentaries dealing with community problems. The undertaking could be one of the most exciting production experiences on the station. Radio documentaries are relatively inexpensive in comparison with costs in live television or on film, although super-8mm color film can reduce costs (of 16mm newsfilm) by one-third.[46]

An understanding of the traditions of journalism and of journalistic integrity is needed. Proper recognition should be given to news programming and to the people who prepare and air it. A good newsman may rebel occasionally against some of the traditional rigidities of broadcasting, including formats and time segments. He may raise havoc with some established station practices. On the other hand, he will believe in the importance of news seven days a week. He also may supply a kind of enthusiasm that could be contagious throughout the station and that may hopefully infect other station employees.

1. Radio Station Programming

After the above comments about characteristics common to both radio and television programming, attention should be given to aspects of program content and scheduling which pertain specifically to the sound medium.

The program manager's role in radio has undergone radical change since the early days of broadcasting. There are signs that it may be on the verge of further alteration. To understand properly the background of the change as well as the evolution of programming, one needs to know some history of what has been broadcast.

Historical Trends

On Friday, November 25, 1960, a successful format of radio's "golden age" of programming died. On that day, the seven surviving radio network daytime serials broadcast their concluding installments. All seven were on CBS; NBC had dropped daytime serials on radio some months before. In their heyday, just prior to World War II, there had been twenty-five of them a day on CBS and twenty a day on NBC, filling an uninterrupted six to eight hours a day. They came to be known as "soap operas" because most of them had been sponsored by soap and detergent companies.

These hardy perennials of daytime radio had represented one of the truly original art forms the medium had created up to that time. Noted for their chronicles of human misery and misfortune, these serials had brought entertainment and even comfort to many women by dramatizing problems that were greater than those in the lives of the listeners. Following the daily episodes had become a regular habit and, as a result, the cumulative audience for the broadcasts was enormous. It was estimated that over half of the housewives in the country followed the serials. No other radio format had ever been so successful in captivating so large an audience for so long a period of time.

The serial with the all-time record as the longest-run "soap opera," *Ma Perkins,* was broadcast for twenty-seven years and closed after 7,065 consecutive installments. Three others, *The Right to Happiness, Young Dr. Malone* and *The Second Mrs. Burton,* each ran for almost twenty years and more than 5,000 broadcasts. Three relative newcomers perished with the veterans: *Whispering Streets, Best Seller* and *The Couple Next Door.*

It is characteristic of radio men to remember the period of network dominance in radio programming with nostalgia. There is good reason for them to do so. Once, the great bulk of radio programs featured the best live talent in show business. Those were the times when families came together night after night in their living rooms to share the comedy of such greats as Ed Wynn, Eddie Cantor, Fibber McGee and Molly, Fred Allen, Jack Benny, Bob Hope, Jimmy Durante and Burns and Allen. Those were the years of giant variety programs, *Maxwell House Show Boat,* Rudy Vallee and the Connecticut Yankees,

Edgar Bergen and Charlie McCarthy, and Kay Kyser and the *Kollege of Musical Knowledge*. Live drama was popular, too, in such programs as the *Lux Radio Theatre, First Nighter, Mr. District Attorney, The Easy Aces, The Goldbergs, Lights Out* and the productions of Norman Corwin and Arch Oboler. In an era of great dance bands, most of the late-night offerings were live, on-the-spot pick-ups of bands such as the Dorseys, Glen Gray, Benny Goodman, Fletcher Henderson, Jan Garber, Gene Krupa and Artie Shaw. Earlier in the evening, the orchestras of Paul Whiteman, Phil Spitalny, Guy Lombardo, Wayne King, Ben Bernie and others were standard listening. Vocalists drew their share of the audience, too, with popular singers such as Kate Smith, Bing Crosby, Morton Downey, Al Jolson and the Street Singer (Arthur Tracy) featured on daily or weekly programs. People arranged their Saturday-evening schedules so that they could listen regularly to *The Chicago Theatre of the Air*. They followed the speeches of Father Coughlin on Sunday afternoons even though many people disagreed with his remarks. Major Bowes and his original amateur hour encouraged local-talent contests. Nor was information neglected; people listened to the news through the voices of commentators Gabriel Heatter, William Shirer, H. V. Kaltenborn, Edward R. Murrow, Raymond Gram Swing, Elmer Davis and others. And every weekday evening around 7:00 P.M. local time, most other activities ceased while millions of people listened to the daily episode of those favorites of comedy and human affairs, the radio *Amos 'n' Andy*.

In the 1950s, the growth of television and the increase in the number of radio stations brought about radical changes in radio programming. Many of the network stars and the lavish productions moved to television. Throughout the country, radio stations began to shift from network affiliation. Within a few years, two-thirds of the radio stations in the U.S. were independents. Most of the independent radio stations were then faced with more hours than they knew how to fill. Many were not budgeted or staffed for live production and they could not have produced very much original programming even if they had been so inclined.

A kind of bandwagon effect began among the independents. Some successful formats were hastily duplicated. In the process, much of the quality of the originals was lost. In many cases, the second-hand versions were comparable to a small-town high-school stage production of a Broadway success. Sometimes the original was not worth imitating. Many programs consisted of hard-sell, high pressure materials tasteless in content and skimpy in production.

Into management positions in radio during this period of change came eager young men who had had little or no background in the great traditions of radio and apparently no interest in the future professional status of the industry. They were blessed with considerable energy, egotism and promotional ability and a consuming interest in the "fast buck." In another age, they could have been successful circus-sideshow or carnival operators.

In their search for successful formats, some of these young men began to scan the lists of the best sellers in recordings and then to feature those records on their stations. It was not long before the "Top-40" records of the day were played repeatedly. It was not long, either, before record manufacturers recognized a potential gold mine complete with free advertising for their product. Stations were soon using recordings as a vehicle to advertise the merchandise of local businessmen. The merchants paid for the service while the record companies received their advertising free. Station after station began to adopt the formula. Eventually most radio stations sounded alike.

Much of radio's programming became cheap and blatant. Music was largely rock 'n' roll, disc jockeys were arrogant and verbose, news was surrounded by the noise of teletypes or trains or rockets, and commercials were hard-sell. What appeal the format had was largely confined to teenagers and to adults who had the interests of teenagers. The formula seemed to be: do it cheap and without imagination for people whose desires are simple and undemanding.

Most broadcasters by the early 1960s were aware that the radio industry was operating far below its potential. Some managers changed their station formats. Others wanted to change but did not quite know what to do to replace them. A few managers had never accepted formula programming. Most stations continued to broadcast what came to be known as raucous radio.

Payola

The radio industry was hit hard by the "payola" investigations. Much of management's authority and initiative was forfeited to the "play for pay" people. Some managers claimed to have learned for the first time that their stations had been involved in the unethical practices of the disc jockeys. This seemed to amount to an admission that they had neglected the supervision of their programming. In 1958 and 1959, record distributors had their recordings artificially promoted in 23 cities for secret payments of a total of $263,244.[47]

In May of 1963, the FCC issued final rules on payola. Stations are now allowed to accept free records from manufacturers or distributors but not in excess of the amount needed for regular programming. No promises can be made to play any of the free records on the air. Any form of payment or service to a disc jockey or to management in return for a free air plug is prohibited. AM and FM, as well as television, stations that accept "money, services or other valuable consideration" in return for an agreement to broadcast any materials must make an announcement on the air that those program materials were sponsored and must inform the listeners "by whom or on whose behalf such consideration was supplied." Licensees and managers also must "exercise reasonable diligence" in discovering all cases where considerations are made. Both giver and receiver become equally liable for criminal prosecution under a law enacted by Congress following the investigations. All this was necessary enough. It is mortifying to admit it was necessary at all.

Clearly, the evils of payola need to be policed regularly by station managers. Disc Jockeys need to be given explicit rules and instructions. There should be no excuse for keeping on a station staff any employee who is unable to resist this sort of temptation. Payola is sellola! The things sold are station quality and integrity. Ultimately it is management's responsibility to know about and to correct any abuses or unethical activity by station staff members.[48]

REAPPRAISAL AND REASSESSMENT

Perhaps this is the time for a reassessment of radio's unique resources. Many broadcasters, caught up in the hectic day-to-day struggle for some kind of dominance, have not fully realized that a whole new generation of people has come along to whom radio is as novel as television. Radio's inherent strengths are still present in the medium even though they may have been discounted and overlooked.

No other medium of mass communication can utilize the factor of *imagination* as radio can. No other medium can isolate sounds, which by their very isolation are conducive to strong emotional impact. Copy can be written which can make a man hungry, or happy or excited. In some instances, pictures may be worth 1000 words. In others, words may be worth 1000 pictures. Speech, persuasion and eloquence are still prime movers of human response.

The intimacy of the illusion of person-to-person communication is another of the advantages of radio. The listener can select his own particular kind of program and listen to it my himself if he chooses. The ability of radio to reach the listener in his own selective environment should not be discounted.

There are other important factors unique to radio. Its *economy* of transmission and of personal reception is one. The cost-per-thousand for radio is less than for any of the other mass media. The *portability* of radio cannot as yet be matched by television. The radio listener can take his chosen programs with him wherever he goes. Radio is the most portable source of instantaneous news and entertainment. Radio is *flexible*. It can adapt to needed changes of program content faster than any other medium. It has the freedom to experiment with new program formats and to create new modes not common to other media. On radio a man, a voice and an idea can initiate a promising experiment. It need not be an elaborate or a costly innovation. Radio is everywhere. It has something for everybody.

All these advantages are inherent in the medium of radio. Their exploitation, however, requires careful study, original thinking and hard work.

Music and news formats seem to be admirably suited to the radio medium. They are the basic program elements which radio probably communicates best. The task ahead involves a search for new ideas and techniques for their presentation. It comes down to this: if you would presume to address the public ear, then you will do so successfully if you have something to share and something to say. If so, those stations which lead the way in programming should expect a high degree of audience loyalty in return. The route to leadership appears to be open to those who want to take it. Once again, radio must call for strong program managers.

THE STATION FORMAT

The determination of the overall format is the first step in the creation of a station image. The possibilities for unique identification of a radio station in any market seem to be considerably more numerous than for the special identity of a television station. Radio stations are, for the most part, independent of network affiliation and are in a more flexible position to change their formats completely at any time.[49] With some ten times as many radio as television stations and most of them in search of some kind of distinctive image, several standard formats have emerged with more undoubtedly ahead in the future.[50]

Jay Hoffer lists the following types of formats: Contemporary, in which he includes Top-40, "Chicken Rock," Underground, and Old Rock; Middle of the Road; Country Music; Rhythm and Blues, including Soul and Jazz; Classical; All Talk; All News; Religion; and Foreign Language.[51] The BF/Communication Services listed categories according to the percentage of the 955 AM and 643 FM stations in the top 100 markets which used those formats:[52]

AM Stations	*FM Stations*
258 (27%) progressive rock	249 (39%) album/standard/classical
201 (21%) middle-of-the-road	163 (25%) contemporary/ progressive rock
168 (18%) modern country OR country-&-western	116 (18%) popular middle-of-the-road
164 (17%) rhythm & blues/ethnic/ religion	63 (10%) modern country/country-&- western
164 (17%) standard/classical/album/	52 (8%) rhythm and blues/ethnic/religion

The *Top-40* station is fast-paced and loud. It has tight production. The sound of "rock" is the same throughout the broadcast day. News is minimal, consisting mainly of headlines. Many promotional techniques are used on the air including contests of various kinds.

The *middle-of-the-road* music station uses a popular approach. Its pace is conservative and its music is light. There is a predominance of instrumental popular and Broadway show music. Older tunes are favored. Newscasts are more complete. On-the-air promotion, when conducted, is presented in a dignified manner. Contests are seldom staged.

The *good music* station, usually FM, has as its basic commodity instrumental standards or "background" music. The music has few breaks for commercials. There is as little talk, including news, as possible. Consequently, the role of the disc jockey is diminished. The sound of the station resembles that of commercial-music services for offices and restaurants.

The *classical* music station has a calm, deliberate pace, in direct contrast to the Top-40 station. It may depart from lengthy programs of symphonies, operas and other music to present discussions of the fine arts and of contemporary affairs or education. News commentaries are broadcast in addition to news reports.

Specialized appeal stations concentrate on program fare that appeals to specific tastes and interests. Examples are: foreign-language, ethnic, jazz and sports stations. The *country-western* station merits special attention given later in this chapter.

The *all-talk* station offers a variety of non-musical fare with the exception of some commercial jingles. Conversation programs dominate the broadcast day with audience involvement in many of them. News is presented in quarter-hour or longer segments, augmented by specialized news programs dealing with sports, business, women's affairs, etc.

A variant of the all-talk station is the *all-news* station. This station format seems to appeal to the information-seeking public even more than the all-talk station does. There are no programs which are primarily entertainment on the all-news station.

The *small-market* station, located in areas of minimal direct competition, can offer a variety of program fare. At times during the broadcast day, several of the formats of other kinds of stations may be offered. The image of the station is achieved primarily through its coverage of local events. The smaller the market and the fewer its competitive stations, the greater is the tendency toward a variety of program offerings.

MUSICAL FORMATS

Some 80 per cent of all the programming of the radio stations in the U.S. consists of music. The introduction of long-playing and 45-rpm records in the late 1940s, with their extended playing times, better sound quality and non-breakable materials helped to insure the use of recordings as a staple of radio broadcasting. It also gave new impetus to the recording industry that earlier had been the target of predictions of collapse due to the availability of radio.

Top-40 and Contemporary Music

The contemporary "sound" depends on anticipating and responding to the swiftly shifting likes and fads of teenagers, reflected in the sales of phonograph records, audiotape cartridges and cassettes. Advertisers find the teenage market an important one to reach. The teenage group in the U.S. is expanding three times faster than the total population. Teenagers in 1970 constituted one-fifth of all the people in the country, and their annual spendable income was some $21 billion—10 per cent of all U.S. consumer expenditures. They own one-fifth of the automobiles and spend more than $1.5 billion a year on entertainment.[53] This group also has a major influence on many of the purchases that their parents make; the amount of family purchasing they are said to influence has been estimated at over $30 billion a year.

Although the teenage audience is an important consumer group, it would be a mistake for many stations in a market to adopt formats especially designed for this age group. Most teens listen to radio "stations" instead of to specific programs. Surveys of major radio markets indicated that only a few stations will reach the bulk of the teen listeners. For example, in St. Louis, two stations out of 15 accounted for 75 per cent of the teen audience.[54] Teenagers typically live actively with the omnipresent "sound" of one or two stations with dominant on-air personalities; teens study, drive, talk on the phone, and sunbathe with the companionable music and chatter of radio.

In the decade of the 1960s, companies were formed that syndicated program formats, identification musical jingles, and strict guidelines for performers. More music, less talk between songs, and fewer commercials (at higher rates, and in clusters) became the hallmark nationally of stations that subscribed to Bill Drake's trend-setting service. In broadcasting, competition often means imitation. The lower-keyed pace of the on-air disc jockeys and the less wide-ranging play-lists of current hit songs eventually gave way in the 1970s to renewed emphasis on the personalities who talked to and with their audiences. Whereas the 1960s emphasized production, the 1970s again emphasized personalities. Even syndicated radio packages began to emphasize personalities such as Wolfman Jack, Casey Kasem, and Dick Clark, plus "live-on-tape" rock concerts, and also comedy series.[55]

Tightly formated, stereotypical (not stereophonic) radio provided a natural matrix for introducing automation into programming. Transistorized electronics with computer-programmed schedules and on-air operation began to remove the announcer/disc jockey as the station's "living link" with the live audience. Initial capital investment solved long-term expensive staffing and scheduling problems in small- and medium-sized stations—especially stations owned by a single licensee, who could format all his stations in the country by punchcard and audiotape reels. However, the demands of competitive radio "on the move" with the localized, believably spontaneous sound of the human voice undercut excessively ambitious efforts to replace staffs with electronic robots. (Processing of marketing statistics, time availabilities, fiscal records, and programming logistics of bookkeeping were apt for the computer; the "living sound" of radio's on-air performance was quite another thing.) [56] Yet, automation did help FM radio achieve stability against its larger-audienced and better-budgeted competitive AM operations, especially for FM's more conservative formats and "background" music schedules.

Broadcasters who offer "rock" music have a further complication. Whether broadcasters enjoy or not a censorship role when dealing with lyrics, a decision to program "rock" music carries with it an obligation to audition songs for acceptability of lyrics for public broadcast.[57]

Middle-of-the-Road Music

While such formats as all-rock or all-country-western or all-jazz or all-classical music may result in a clearly identifiable image, managers of stations with a middle-of-the-road music policy have a more difficult task in impressing both listeners and advertisers with their individual images. Actually, the middle-of-the-road station has built-in variety right on the shelves of its music library. Imagination plus time devoted to planning can produce real rewards.

The big bands of Glenn Miller, Benny Goodman, Ray Anthony, Freddy Martin, Les Brown, Guy Lombardo, Harry James, Count Basie, Buddy Rich, Duke Ellington and others are still popular today and will be for quite some time; these are good sources of program material, along with present-day vocalists. Modern jazz that appeals to the "middle" group is provided by such artists as Oscar Peterson, Jonah Jones, George Shearing, Andre Previn, Dave Brubeck, Al Hirt, Pete Fountain and Ramsey Lewis Trio. Broadway original-cast albums are always good series possibilities; the "middle" audiences request them often.

Another type of middle-of-the-road program material is available from original motion-picture soundtracks. And the comedy or spoken albums of people like Jonathan Winters, Bob Newhart, Phyllis Diller, Bill Cosby, and George Carlin can be made into a series of popular features that can provide a balance to the musical offerings.

All major recording companies offer monthly releases of their new albums to radio stations for a nominal annual fee. Their best packages consist of a combination of pop and classical albums. The variety of music is outstanding. When supplemented by current single releases of the popular vocalists and instrumentalists of the day, any station can provide middle-of-the-road programming for all tastes.

Variety offers flexibility and also the opportunity to program to "dayparts"—by appealing to somewhat different audiences available to radio at different times of day. In surveying contemporary radio, *Broadcasting* magazine in 1973 noted that "the idea of programming a consistent sound all day has, for some programmers, lost many of its former applications." [58]

Country Music

In the last decade country-and-western music has evolved into an uptempo "modern country" sound with elaborate production and sophisticated orchestrations. It has partly merged with the sounds and musicians from rock music and from the "big bands" and orchestras with strings.

Stations with low popularity in their markets which switched to the early country format typically increased their ratings and their billings. Success bred success as well as imitation and competition. Small stations with low power and high frequencies which programmed the country sound were eventually joined by major stations that dominated local airwaves. In 1961 there had been 81 full-time country music stations; by 1970 there were over 650 stations. [59] The key to the early success of the country music format seemed to be exclusivity. As long as one station in a market offered this kind of music, it tended to do very well. When competition occurred, the share of audience left was often too thin for any station to prosper.

Country music listeners had never been restricted to the rural population or to people with little spending power. But in recent years the range of artists and styles of music within the "modern country" genre appealed to ever-widening audiences, including those in the largest metropolitan markets. Just as early "rock 'n' roll" grew into sophisticated rock with compositions performed by small groups, major bands, and even the Boston Pops Orchestra, so "modern country" emerged as a vital force within contemporary American music with increasingly broad appeal to large audiences. *Broadcasting Yearbook 1974* listed the following categories of country-related music, with the numbers of stations programming them full- or part-time: "the country and western" (1,080 stations), "countrypolitan" (5), "country rock" (2), "modern country" (44), "Nashville" (1), and "town and country" (3).

THE ALL-TALK FORMAT

The economic necessity for station specialization and the need for a different and an exclusive image probably spawned the all-talk format; otherwise, it might not have come into being. Most stations regularly schedule some talk programs in addition to news during the broadcast day. But by 1974, *Broadcasting Yearbook* listed 113 stations in large and small markets which programmed some form of talk as a major portion or as all of their daily schedule. Yet, in the 50 major markets, no more than 20 stations converted to exclusive talk formats, wholly abandoning music.[60] At least five of those stations were prestigious owned-and-operated stations of CBS and ABC.

"Talk" formats refer to all kinds and styles of content: hard news, telephone conversations, play-by-play sports, editorials, serious interviews with prominent persons, and informal interviews with passers-by. Many stations program talk during the daytime and shift to music through the night; other stations program just the opposite pattern.

Studies have shown that the listener to talk programs, once he is involved, gives closer attention to what comes over his receiver than does the listener to music. This is important to advertisers.

Some stations make considerable use of the telephone to involve the audience. Questions for people to answer (either pre-planned or suggested by members of the audience during the calls) or discussions of a wide variety of topics are often the themes of entire programs. Conversations are often broadcast live. The only insurance against profanities, obscenities and libelous comments is a sharp, intelligent and genuinely witty announcer who can think extremely fast. His only means for cutting what is said is a tape recorder that gives him a few seconds delay. In these few seconds, he must decide what needs cutting and delete it before the tape hits the air.

"Talk" radio that attracts attention and audience usually attracts increased advertising; but in other cases it loses revenue because of irritating or otherwise extreme statements on the air by listeners, guests, or air talent.[61] In 1973, the FCC commissioners and members of the Congress objected seriously to uninhibited conversations on the air about intimate details of sexual activity (so-called "topless radio" programs); the annual (1973) NAB convention in Washington, D.C., cautioned broadcasters about this as a major issue.[62]

If not overdone in a market, an all-talk station has advantages that can outweigh the disadvantages. Increased audience, higher ratings, and increased billings may be delivered.

A variant of the all-talk format is the all-news station. By 1974 a total of 68 stations reported that their total programming schedule or a major part of it consisted of news.

Whatever may be the future of all-talk and all-news stations, much credit is due the owners and managers of these properties for their innovation and foresight. They have refused to be imitators, with sounds similar to other stations in their markets. Radio as an institution could be more progressive if more managers sought more ways to be different.

SPECIALIZED PROGRAM SERVICE AND FORMATS

In an effort to attract and serve audiences competitively, many stations have reached out to large, specialized groups within the total market. The interests and needs, as well as the considerable purchasing power, of sub-groups in society have prompted formats designed to attract them to radio frequencies. Programming formats have been designed primarily for ethnic groups such as black or Spanish, for "underground" counter-culture people, and for those drawn to religion.

Ethnic Radio

Originally "black radio" had emphasized popular "soul" music and personalities. But it gradually reflected increasingly professional style with wide ranging diversity, to serve the diverse tastes of black Americans. Some such stations stress black music other than soul, such as gospel or jazz. Other parts of the black experience are reflected in programming of African music and talk. And as general-audience stations introduce music and discussion of interest to minority groups, the distinction between specifically "black" stations and others has become blurred.[63] This is so partly because white teen-agers have supported the upbeat tempo of black station programming. Still, one of the purposes of black radio is to link the black community by programming music and talk of black awareness.

The *Broadcasting Yearbook 1974* listed 431 stations that programmed some or a majority of their schedule to blacks, with 17 stations programming fulltime black-oriented content. Other categories listed included "black gold" (1 station), "black gospel" (1), "Jamaican rhythm" (1), "minority" (2), "rhythm and blues" (42), and "soul" (7).

The commercial viability of urban stations' focusing on the black population is clear. By 1972 nearly 75 per cent of all blacks lived in cities. More than

14 million blacks live in the 50 largest metropolitan areas; they constitute 63 per cent of the nation's total black population. National advertisers must reach this massive part of major-market population if their products are to succeed competitively, because black America's purchasing power lies somewhere between $30 and $40 billion.

Approximately 400 stations program for blacks sometime during their broadcast day; about 155 of them program exclusively for blacks.[64] But only 16 stations were owned by minority persons or companies, up from five black-owned stations in 1968. Management positions in those 400 stations have slowly increased, with most program directors being black. For economic reasons of attracting large audiences and advertising, as well as for total community service, many black stations reflect the sound and commercial outlook of any professional general-market station, seeking a wide range of audience both black and white.

Further, news services emphasizing information and issues particularly relevant to the large black population have been provided by the Black Audio Network—serving 80 per cent of all black-oriented stations, with 90 of the stations in major markets. In 1973, the Mutual Black Network was inaugurated by the Mutual Broadcasting System for stations that wanted news and feature service of interest primarily to the black population. In mid-1973, the National Black Network began as a radio network serving black communities with news and sports coverage; 42 stations, many in the nation's largest markets, initially subscribed to the network.

Another important group in the United States is the Latino population—persons of Mexican or South American heritage, especially the Spanish-speaking. By 1974, 270 stations programmed much of their schedules to this audience, including four stations whose schedules were wholly devoted to Spanish programming. Two stations programmed Chicano, one programmed Latin, and three stations "Ethnic" schedules. Groups of stations collaborated on regional networks to provide Latin programs: AAA California Spanish Network (11 stations), AAA Espanol Network (15 stations), All Spanish Network (12 stations—mostly border stations in Mexico), Amigo Spanish Group (14), Latin Network (10), National Spanish Language Network (26, some border stations), Radio Puerto Rico FM Network (3—all Puerto Rico), and Texas Spanish Language Network (14).

Programming for American Indians is featured on 21 U.S. stations, from one-half hour to 14 hours a week, with one station programming 80 per cent of its schedule for the Indian population.

Farm Radio

When the Communications Act was passed in 1934, it provided for clear-channel frequencies, to insure that rural areas would be served by programming, at least by ionosphere-reflected skywaves at night from distant cities. In the four decades since then, radio stations have proliferated throughout the land, providing local service to communities even in some of the most remote areas, although by 1972, an estimated 25 per cent of the nation still received at night only radio service provided by clear-channel stations.[65] By 1974, 49 stations programmed heavily or exclusively to the farming communities' special interests and needs.

In a 1973 survey of Wisconsin farmers, radio was cited as the most valuable single source of news—over television, newspapers, magazines, telephones, and state and Federal bulletins.[66] The business of farming depended upon radio for livestock and grain market information during all periods of the day. Livestock producers rated radio even above telephone as the most useful means for deciding when and where to sell and the price to pay for grain or other feed. Grain producers put only personal contacts with grain elevator operators ahead of radio as most useful for planning transactions.

Regional groups of stations collaborate to share information and other programming pertinent to farmers, including: California Farm Network (14 stations), Dakota Farm Network—North Dakota (12), Dakota Farm Network—South Dakota (11), New York Farm Network (18), Oklahoma Farm Network (12), Pennsylvania Farm Network (23), Voice of Southwest Agriculture Radio Network (8), Voice of Valley Agricultural Radio Network (2), Wisconsin Farm Broadcasting Network (9), and the Farm Directors Radio Network (more than 550 stations).

Religious

Radio has provided religious programming since the earliest days. The Federal regulatory agency institutionalized this part of a station's service by listing "religion" as one category of programs in the early composite-week categories. Because people have sustained their interest in religion and in religious broadcasts, not only has devotional and inspirational content been part of most stations' schedules through the decades, but by 1974 as many as 120 stations devoted significant portions of their schedules to religion throughout the week, five of them programming religion almost exclusively. They described their program service as "Gospel" (91 stations), as "Christian" (13), as "Inspirational" (9), and as "Sacred" (7).

In the early 1970s, 20 per cent of the U.S. adult population listened to religious radio "often"; 28 per cent "occasionally," 26 per cent "seldom," and 25 per cent "never." [67] Listeners tended to be those already committed to regular Sunday church services rather than those who did not attend or participate in institutional religion. Older persons were the heaviest religious radio listeners. Southern and midwestern residents, especially Protestants (particularly Baptists), supported religious radio more than did others.

Underground Radio

Demonstrating the diversity of radio has been the rise of "underground" or alternative radio. These stations—numbering 25 in 1974—programmed loosely as progressive-rock or as "free form" with few traditional structures in format or content. The formlessness, while encouraging creativity by performers and announcers, at times resulted in public criticism and FCC warnings—including the caution that free-wheeling radio "gives the announcer such control over the records to be played that it is inconsistent with the strict controls that the licensee must exercise to avoid questionable practices." That echoed the FCC's public notice of March 5, 1971, about licensee responsibility in playing drug-oriented music.[68] Some progressive-rock and contemporary format stations permit the on-air disc jockey latitude in selecting the sequence of recordings, yet "each record for air play is predetermined by station officials" including the program director.[69]

Drama

Radio program diversification included occasional efforts to revive the all-but-lost form of radio drama. By mid-1974 some appraisal could be made based upon experience. The nightly hour-long *CBS Radio Mystery Theater* was carried by 222 stations (all but 29 of them CBS affiliates), in 96 of the top 100 markets.[70] The five-a-week programs were fully sponsored by national advertisers. But the Mutual Radio Network's *Zero Hour* shifted format (initially Monday-through-Friday half-hours in continuity for a 2½ hour complete story, changed to daily individual 30-minute self-contained dramas) in an effort to gain audience for the 251 stations (82% MBS affiliates) in 40 of the top 50 markets. The series was not fully sold to advertisers, and Mutual in mid-1974 was still determining the future of the series. Soap operas—such as *Sounds of the City* (heard in 27 of the major "black" markets), *When a Girl Marries* (accepted by 40 stations for airing, with no sponsorship by target date of fall 1974), and other efforts still in planning stages by Bristol-Myers Co.—found uneven audience and advertiser interest. A total of 385 stations carried taped re-recordings of the original *The Shadow, The Lone Ranger, Fibber McGee and Molly, Gangbusters, The Green Hornet,* and *Tarzan.*

There is no sign of a revival of locally-produced drama on radio stations. Most stations built since dramatic creations were dropped by radio are not equipped with adequate space and facilities to produce such programming. Those that are so equipped might find some unusual gratifications in dramatic production, particularly if they are near a college theater, a civic company or a summer drama group. Much of the talent on local levels today is far superior to that which was available in those areas in the earlier, "great" days of radio drama.

Program diversification also made possible the syndication of other kinds of content, such as brief inspirational messages by Earl Nightingale (700 stations) and Nelson Boswell (150 stations). Horizon Communications serviced 200 stations with short commentaries by Arthur Godfrey and the late Chet Huntley. The rise of FM to independent status, along with AM, opened new opportunities for entrepreneurs in specialized syndication.

FM Radio

The future of FM programming remains ambivalent. FM stations independent of AM ownership tend to stress high-fidelity or stereo programming. In 1974, 74.6% of FM stations broadcast in stereo, and 14.1% featured "quad" at least some of the time.[70a] Some of these stations provide specialized music service; others broadcast a variety of music categories. Those FM stations that are a part of AM operations often duplicate varying amounts of programming primarily designed for the AM audiences. No consistent pattern of FM programming has emerged as yet. In the early 1970s, N. W. Ayer & Son advertising agency found that 124 FM stations in the nation's top-10 markets programmed the following formats:

Contemporary / Top-40	25.8%
Standard	19.4
Good music	17.7
Middle of the road	10.5
Classical / Semi-classical	10.5
Country and western	6.5
Other	9.6

By late 1974, the National Association of FM Broadcasters reported that for *all* FM stations in the country, "beautiful music / easy listening" had replaced "middle of the road" as the most popular FM format. The NAFMB surveys for 1972 and 1974 noted the following shifts in FM programming:

	1972	*1974*
Beautiful music / easy listening	19.3%	29.9%
Middle of the road	21.4	12.2
Country and western	10.6	11.5
"Double formats" (usually beautiful music plus one other form)	—	11.1

Unduplicated FM stations quite generally have provided vital and important additional radio services. Their program schedules show good balance between music and talk and there is much variety within each category. A few stations in metropolitan markets have successfully programmed a predominance of classical music but the majority have offered a wide range of programming, including rock and other AM-originated "sounds" and formats. Some professional broadcasters expect that AM radio will become primarily a medium of news and information while FM will increasingly become the carrier of broadcast music. Conversely, lengthy news programs are not suited to the FM form; comments range from "news is a tune-out on FM" to a prediction that the norm in FM will be two-minutes for news, with five-minute news becoming a rarity.[71]

There is much excellent production in the individual programs on most of the unduplicated FM stations. A low-key emphasis is consistent in the conversational approach of the announcers, in the soft-sell commercials and in the structure of the programs. Apparent efforts are made to avoid the strictly background or "wallpaper" kinds of offerings. Good balance is achieved through the avoidance of excesses of any single program type. The opportunity to broadcast in stereo undoubtedly has added much to the appeal of the stations.

Hopeful signs for the future of FM include: steady annual increases in FM set sales; a growing number of FM sets in automobiles; and a steadily expanding list of applicants for FM licenses. In the decade 1963–73, sales of AM-FM radios rose from 2 million to 24 million sets per year, contrasted with AM-only set decline from 23 million to 18 million per year.[72] In the early 1970s automobile manufacturers included FM with AM in one-fifth of all cars with radios; by 1976 half of all automobiles with radios are expected to be equipped for both FM and AM reception.[73] (The all-channel radio bill, if enacted into law, would swiftly accelerate this increase.) FM's penetration in major markets rose significantly in recent years: in New York, from 63.9 per cent (1968) to 71.1 per cent (1970); by 1972 penetration in Detroit was 89.2 per cent, in Los Angeles 83.4 per cent, and in Philadelphia 88 per cent. In 1974 New York's FM stations attracted 33.2 per cent share of the total listening audience and Detroit's FM stations drew 38.4 per cent of the radio audience; late in 1973, three of the top five New York stations in afternoon drive-time were FM stations.[74] The FCC reported that by March 31, 1975, there were 4,483 AM stations authorized and 2,819 commercial FM stations.[75]

FM appears to be headed for a healthy maturity, after having experienced a particularly hectic youth. Programming should be the least of its problems in the future. Its earning potential has become less critical a question in the last half-decade (although one-third of all AM stations and two-thirds of all FM stations lost money in the early 1970s). Within the decade of 1964–1974, FM's annual revenues rose from $19.7 million to $225 million—its share of total radio revenues jumped from 2.5 per cent to 14 per cent; the independent management consulting firm of Business Equities Corp. of Boston estimated total FM revenues of $732 million (30.8% of all radio revenues) by 1980. Moderate success, and even substantial profit, depends upon relatively small staffs to offset the lower revenue generated by the lesser commerical load than in AM programming. An important factor here in staffing, salaries, operations, and programming format is the introduction of automation. Initial high capital investment might make feasible a lean day-to-day operation if music is the primary programming staple. But to gain sophisticated audiences in competitive markets, the spontaneity of "live" announcing keyed in to local people and places and current events might eventually make the difference between just one more radio station and an FM station of distinction—with audience and advertisers.

Production Quality

There are identifiable characteristics of production that can make the difference between good and poor radio stations. The quality of production affects a station's popularity with its audience. In the achievement of professional production standards, there are few cut-rate bargains. There is no substitute for quality. The basic excellence of broadcasting reflects station pride and performance. Lacking one, apologetic management has neither.

This appraisal applies equally to radio and to television programming, whether a radio station's day-long live telephone-interview and music or a TV station's early-evening local news.

2. Television Station Programming

Aside from a network, a television station has two principal sources of programs: those purchased as film or videotape and those produced locally by the station. Of those two sources, most stations draw upon film for the larger share of their "locally originated" program schedule. While local public interest is one factor in selection, the dominant motive is economics: the product that will attract the largest audience for the most reasonable charge to advertisers.

Historical Trends

The compilations by *Broadcasting Yearbook* reflect trends in a decade of television station program scheduling. Between 1963 and 1973, while network programs accounted for a larger portion of affiliates' schedules (up from 57% to 61% of stations' programming), "local live" programming declined slightly (from 13% to 10%) and "local videotape programming increased (from 2.1% to 2.5%); total non-network film declined massively (from 25% in 1963 to 15% of all stations' weekly schedules in 1973). During the same decade, syndicated videotape programs increased five-fold in schedules (up from 2% to 9% of weekly programming). See Table IX for details.

Major changes during that decade affected non-network stations. Independent stations tripled their use of syndicated videotape programs (4.8% in 1963, up to 11% in 1973), while cutting by half their local live programs (22% to 10%) and cutting by a quarter their local videotape programs (4.5% to 3.2%). On the other hand, stations affiliated with networks increased origination of videotape programs (1.9% to 2.4%) and only slightly cut back on their local live originations (11.4% down to 9.3%), so that in 1973 all television stations in the U.S., whether independents or network affiliates, originated about one-tenth of their weekly schedules as live programs (primarily news, plus some special events—mostly sports).

TABLE IX

TELEVISION PROGRAMMING 1963–1973: LIVE, FILM, VIDEOTAPE, LOCAL, NETWORK STATION *

Survey dates (June)	NETWORK AFFILIATES		NON-NETWORK STATIONS		ALL STATIONS	
	Avg. Hrs. per Week	% of Total Schedule	Avg. Hrs. per Week	% of Total Schedule	Avg. Hrs. per Week	% of Total Schedule
Total non-network film						
1973	15:36	12.7	57:50	52.4	18:34	15.5
1963	24:32	21.6	64:28	69.1	28:33	25.4
Syndicated videotape programs						
1973	10:45	8.8	13:12	11.0	10:54	9.1
1963	2:03	1.8	4:21	4.8	2:17	2.1
Local live programs						
1973	11:29	9.3	12:05	10.1	11:45	9.8
1963	13:01	11.4	20:14	22.2	14:30	12.9
Local videotape programs						
1973	2:57	2.4	3:31	3.2	2:56	2.5
1963	2:09	1.9	4:10	4.5	2:22	2.1
Total network programs						
1973	78:17	63.8	12:25	11.3	73:29	61.3
1963	71:41	63.2	—	—	64:34	57.5
Avg. time on air for all programs						
1973	122:45	100	110:23	100	119:49	100
1963	113:26	100	93:13	100	112:16	100

* Source: *Broadcasting Yearbook 1974* (Washington, D.C.: Broadcasting Publications, Inc., 1974), p. 70.

Local Programming

The FCC tabulated reports from 514 stations in 1973 to determine program percentages in similar categories, further broken down into VHF and UHF as well as by market size (top 50 markets or below the top 50).[76] Those data showed that of 86 VHF affiliates in the top 50 markets, the median station programmed 15 per cent of its schedule as "local, including entertainment" (including commercials) if it billed more than $5 million annually, and 12 per cent if it billed less than $5 million. The FCC tabulated the minimum figure of 20 per cent in that category for the top fifth of those large-billing stations, and the maximum figure of 13 per cent for the bottom fifth of those stations. The median VHF affiliates in the smaller markets—below the top 50 markets—programmed only two-thirds as much local programming: 10.8 per cent if billings were over $1 million, and 9.1 per cent if billings were less than $1 million. UHF affiliates programmed about the same: 9.4 per cent (of those grossing over $1 million in billings) and 7.8 per cent (of UHF stations grossing under $1 million). The median independent station in all markets scheduled 17.6 per cent as "local, including entertainment" if they were VHF, and 13.8

per cent if they were UHF. The implication was that the larger the billings and the bigger the market, the more local programming was scheduled by stations. Nor did independent stations program much larger percentages of local originations than did network affiliated stations.

Those data were compiled by the FCC in an effort to suggest initial guidelines for what constituted "substantial service" to a community; the regulatory agency more than hinted that the top 20 per cent of station percentages clearly constituted superior programming in the public interest—which guide the other four-fifths of the nation's stations might attempt to emulate to assure license renewal.[77]

The Commission, concerned that the community in a station's signal area be specifically served by that licensee, has emphasized guidelines of "community identification" and "diversification of programming service and viewpoints." That diversity is affected by whether the licensee is a local individual or company, or instead is part of a group of stations owned commonly by a distant licensee. A study in the mid-1960s concluded that multi-station ownership favorably affected those stations' service to local communities, as measured by their schedules of local programming.[78] In the top 50 markets, group-owned stations scheduled 13.8 per cent of all their programs from non-network sources, while stations licensed to single owners scheduled 12.3 per cent non-network programming. In all markets across the country, group-owned stations scheduled 11.3 per cent nonnetwork programming, while single-station owned stations scheduled 10.8 per cent. The editors of that study noted that "because other sources of nonnetwork programming—independent producers, group corporations and other stations in the groups—were not included in the local 'live' programming data requested by the Commission's license renewal form [the source for compiling these data], the data . . . underestimate the full extent of nonnetwork programming." [79]

The FCC's data for 1973 reported that among VHF network affiliates in the top 50 markets, those with gross billings of more than $5 million annually scheduled from about 25 to 30 per cent of nonentertainment programming (news, public affairs, etc.) while stations billing less than $5 million scheduled approximately from 22 to 29 per cent of nonentertainment. The figures about group-owned stations in the late 1960s showed that single-owned stations in the top 50 markets averaged 27 per cent of nonentertainment, while group-owned stations scheduled about 25 per cent nonentertainment programming.

Critic Les Brown harshly appraised the status of local television programming by the 1970s:

> The typical station is not physically prepared to produce more than a few routine newscasts a day, a few unpretentious public affairs shows for the weekends, and perhaps a daily children's show interlaced with stock cartoons (*Captain Andy, Fireman Fred,* and the like), or an interview show for women. There is no such thing any more as a staff writer, except in the news department; the resident directors are usually involved with cuing up commercials within the local movies; the production staff busies itself with commercials for local automobile dealers or

department stores; and the director of programming is little more than a film buyer. Having toured numerous stations throughout the country in markets of all sizes, I have been impressed only with the size of their sales and clerical staffs. The outstanding exceptions are the television stations of Cincinnati, particularly WLWT and WCPO-TV, which still produce daily programs in the grand manner before studio audiences, utilizing local musicians and performing talent.[80]

When the FCC introduced its "prime-time access" rule, some stations attempted to program more locally originated shows; but most stations dipped into the reservoir of off-network reruns or into the increasingly wide-ranging assortment of syndicated programs that usually imitated previous network successes, especially quiz and game programs and formerly successful music and variety formats such as *Lawrence Welk* and *Hee Haw*.

Again, economics often reflected or dictated program strategies. In Los Angeles, for example, on a weekend in 1971, one network O&O station broadcast some children's programs, seven feature movies, and sports, while a competing network's O&O programmed at least twelve public affairs programs, a group of children's programs, football, and entertainment. Meanwhile one independent channel scheduled nine full-length feature films over Saturday and Sunday, plus programs of bowling, football, basketball, and two on boxing, in addition to some public affairs programs scheduled early Sunday and later in prime-time. A competing independent station that same weekend scheduled six successive feature films on Saturday, then football followed by three more movies; on Sunday that station presented six additional movies in succession, with a scattering of religion and non-movie entertainment programs. Film content constituted a substantive amount of local stations' schedules.

LOCAL STATION FILM PROGRAMMING

All stations—from healthy network-owned VHF operations in the largest markets to the tightly budgeted, small-staffed UHF network affiliates in the smallest markets and particularly the independent stations in all markets—build program schedules by purchasing film product.

> It will be recalled that the independent needs to produce or procure the 3,000 hours of programming per year which the affiliated station receives from the network. As a point of reference, let us stipulate that the programming of an independent station is 80% film. Therefore, the independent must buy sufficient film to fill 80% of 3,000 hours, or 2,400 hours of programming. Each month, then, will require 200 hours of film programming plus 50 hours of live studio, or remote, productions. And let's not forget that this is only the equivalent of the amount of programming that the network affiliate gets free. In view of the fact that the independent is operating 14 hours a day, or about 422 hours per month, an additional 172 hours of programming per month is needed to fill out the schedule—but this same 172 hours must also be produced or bought by the network affiliate. The independent station will probably program 80% of these hours with film, or 138 hours per month of additional film productions.

Some managers of independent stations assign to program directors, or film directors, the chore of buying film. Inasmuch as it represents so great an expense, film buying should be the business of the general manager. Remember, we are talking about an annual cost for film which could very well equal one-third of the total cost of operating the independent station.[81]

Local stations can purchase film (or videotape) of syndicated series and of theatrical feature movies.

Syndicated Film (and Videotape)

At one time, it was possible to operate a television station daily from sign-on to sign-off with nothing but film and not have to repeat anything that had been shown previously in the coverage area. The moment the major film companies began to concentrate on selling their products to the networks, first-run syndicated film for local station use became a scarce commodity. In place of first-run syndicated film, stations now buy re-run rights to series that have been shown on the networks. The sale and distribution of these "off-network" programs is provided by syndication companies. Through careful selection, a station can present outstandingly popular programs of former seasons from all networks.

Syndicated off-network material for a local station should not be selected on the basis of its appeal to station personnel. The program manager, film buyer or whoever is designated to pass final judgment must evaluate all purchases on the basis of his considered opinion of probable local audience response.

It makes little sense to buy a film package because it may be the cheapest available. The same value judgments used in the approval of local live-production efforts should be applied to the selection of the station's film offerings. Insofar as all local originations, whether live or on film, blend into a planned design, the station image becomes clearly recognizable. A hodgepodge of program offerings, some of which fit into no overall pattern, can blur that image.

Action-adventure, comedy, travel, game shows, variety musicals—the range is as broad as show business. Somewhere in all this availability is the most effective combination for each specific television station.

But within the several categories, a wide range of quality exists. The most expensive packages are not necessarily the best. No syndicated or re-run material was created for the specific public of any local television station. Much of what is available can become popular locally; but there are also many syndicated programs that do little, if anything, to enhance the station's favor in the community.

Off-network re-runs generally have found favor with many audiences, particularly series that have had extended runs of two or more seasons on a network. Those network programs which have been scheduled against popular competitive offerings on other networks can make good possibilities for local re-runs. Actually, there should be favorable chances for any off-network series with particular appeal for a specific local audience even if the series has been carried on the same station previously as a network feed. Only some 20 per cent of the viewers see the average original telecast of any program in a series. Any re-run that the other 80 per cent can see is a new show as far as they are concerned. But it would be difficult as well as unwise to attempt to select most of the local film schedule from off-network availabilities. Only some of these programs should be chosen. Even in a single-market situation, a station should avoid becoming a completely second-run house.

In addition to the long-established film syndicators, all of whom have materials that should be considered, several group-owned stations now produce a variety of film and videotaped offerings for syndication.

Can the local station look ahead to syndication of some of its own local production? With the growing need for program sources, it would seem that any series with good quality should be in demand. The sales organization necessary for the circulation of film or video tape packages might prohibit the small-market station from getting into syndication. Yet, the possibilities of fruitful program exchange with other similarly located stations or of participation in a group-station effort should be considered.

Feature Film

Feature film for television consists almost entirely of entertainment originally made for theater exhibition. It is desirable for station use because it fills large blocks of time and because of its popularity with the viewing audience. A feature film if properly promoted can often bring a higher rating to a station than any of the competing programs on other stations, whether network or local. After all, feature films are show pieces, many of them brilliantly conceived, splendidly cast and elaborately produced.

The value of feature films as a program product is amply demonstrated by their success on network schedules. No station's program offerings are well rounded and firmly entrenched for sales purposes without the benefit of feature film strength.

Most stations in large markets should purchase the rights for five to seven showings of feature films. Good-sized audiences can be attracted for each showing if there is an interim of six to eight months between each scheduling and if the feature is presented at different times of the day each time it is used. It is wise, also, to schedule the re-runs on different days of the week. In small markets, one re-run may be all that may be expected to pay returns to the station and the advertisers. One nighttime showing followed by a daytime re-run after a period of close to a year should be a profitable formula in the small-market situation.

STATION-PRODUCED PROGRAMS

If expert knowledge is needed in the selection of film offerings, it is even more necessary in the building and production of the station's locally produced programs. By and large, all networks stake equal claims on audience appeal. Therefore the local station must achieve dominance in its market through its local schedule, not by reliance on network affiliation. If the local station turns to syndicated film and feature movies, it may find market dominance equally hard to achieve. Available film for television cannot be monopolized by any one station, and the differences in appeal between any two stations' offerings can be only minimal. The only chance to acquire a clearly identifiable local image lies in local production.

Before the networks provided extensive program schedules, when film was scarce and generally inferior, local stations had to produce most of their own programs. Much ingenuity was shown by local program departments, even with only one camera and no remote facilities. Today, with more knowledgeable personnel and far better equipment available, the same degree of resourcefulness should result in outstanding local programming. Yet, far too many stations do not take advantage of this opportunity.

The production of local live (or videotaped) programs is not easy. It involves more personnel, more time and more expense than are needed to plug into the network or to transmit film. Sometimes, the return for all the extra investment seems hardly worth the effort, particularly if audiences are small and the ratings are low. Yet, anyone who manages a television station and who hires a program manager with a true dedication to the medium can never be satisfied unless he engages in the kind of activity that motivated him to enter this form of communication in the first place. The thrills of program creation, the discovery of new talent, the favorable comments from the audience, are gratifications that should feed his sense of fulfillment and personal contribution. He should never be satisfied in merely supplying facilities for carrying the creations of other people. If he is truly imbued with a sense of show-business, he will necessarily be involved with production because it is a part of his way of life and the product he displays will have to be of professional quality or he will not be satisfied.

It has been difficult for the writers of this book to accept the almost unbelievable naiveté of some owners of television stations. Those owners with upward of a million dollars invested in each enterprise have entrusted their capital, in too many instances, to management that either does not understand creative programming and production or is not interested in it. There have been cases where owners have been advised by management that it is impossible for the station to appeal to local audiences with station-produced programs other than news. It is our opinion that these managers have conveniently used this argument to cover their deficiencies in the program area.

At some stations, whatever local programming does get on the air is hardly ever distinguished or even distinguishable. An example to be deplored may be found in the news-weather-sports format on many local stations. Here, in too many cases, is a public exhibit of the station's professional disabilities.

Uusually, the news segment is presented first. An announcer reads the news from sheets of paper, making contact with the camera only intermittently.

Occasional still pictures are picked up by the cameramen. The director calls for some unmotivated switching in order to give some semblance of variety to the chief visual—the newscaster's face and shoulders. The weather segment departs from the use of script and, as a rule, the "weatherman" maintains a fair degree of contact with the camera. He is restricted to a stylized set that is shown in all seasons, featuring a map of the United States and a map of the local area, both with prepared weather markings. For some unidentifiable reason, most "weathermen" seem to feel an obligation to be clever and they try. Some stations have "weathergirls," who substitute pulchritude for humor. The sports announcer comes on strong and in a masculine manner provides the sports headlines of the day, followed by a reading of the scores of whatever sport is in season. Since the networks give little attention to this service, most of the scores and other sports information are national rather than local. Visuals on this segment consist of a scoreboard, an occasional still photo and, sometimes, some silent-film footage. The three segments are usually sponsored separately, necessitating an opening and a closing for each segment. The time needed to open and close together with the time for commercials within each segment leaves little opportunity to give much more than highlights of information. The programs give the impression of fast pacing, often to the point of confusion. Standard sets and substandard lighting are used.

It is true that there is a wide variation in the abilities of stations to create local programs. The metropolitan station obviously has far more resources available to it than does the small-market station. The comparative differences, however, should be in terms of quantity of output, not necessarily quality. In local production, resourcefulness is a far more important commodity than a huge budget.

It is advisable to develop one or two local program formats at a time and then concentrate on their improvement before attempting additional efforts. One outstanding daily local show with general audience appeal in addition to one well-produced daily news show would be preferable to a number of mediocre programs.

Many stations have not realized the potential for audience popularity in the locally produced daytime program. Robert Mortensen, when General Manager of Station WIIC-TV in Pittsburgh, stated:

> Many stations go to their film libraries during the daytime hours because they feel it may be more economical in the long run. We've found that local live programming, featuring staff talent, staff material, production and equipment is not only cheaper than running some of the dog-eared oldies that come in most of the film packages, but is one of the finest methods available for a station to interest new local advertisers in using the station as a selling medium.
>
> This is one area of local television that has so much to offer from an economic standpoint as well as from a public interest angle that I'm surprised more local stations haven't dumped their films for local personalities and live shows. It's done far more for us in prestige and profit than any network or syndicated offering could ever do.[82]

There is evidence of sufficient interest in good locally produced pro-gramming to warrant experimentation with new ideas and new techniques. Ex-amples of local programs with a great deal of originality and creativity may give some ideas concerning how new and different programs can be originated.

WBBM-TV in Chicago, handed out some 11,000 ballots to homebound commuters, telling them that a program on transportation problems in Chicago would be broadcast that evening and requesting them to watch it and mail their ballots to the station. More than 2500 ballots were returned. This was but one of the series of excellent programs on the station which used audience partici-pation.

Surveys, opinion polls, local responses to local questions may be the basic ingredients of good—and pertinent—program material. Telephone ques-tions and conversations can interest a community. As a variation, studio guests can speak on selected problems during the first ten minutes of each program, then the viewing audience may be invited to ask questions.

In Boston, WCVB-TV introduced an ambitious local schedule in 1973, programming 51 hours of local production a week including a live 90-minute daily morning series, six 30-minute locally produced programs for early eve-ning prime-time, a weekly on-location remote series, an additional two-hours-and-45-minutes of local news each week, children's and family programming during the daytime, plus 30 local specials on the subjects of entertainment, medicine, science, the arts, education, minorities, human behavior, religion, and industry.[83] Within a year the morning live show was linked by microwave to five New England stations. That program—featuring segments of live re-motes—earned a 43 share of the Boston metropolitan audience from 9:00 to 10:30 A.M.[84]

A study by ABC's owned-stations division reported in 1973 that the local or syndicated talkshow format in television had a high mortality rate over a half decade. The failure rate was 81 per cent of attempted television talkshow series. A total of 15 talkshows remained on the air, six of them network and nine of them non-network originated. Of those nine, two had been on two-and-one-half to three years, four had been aired three to three-and-one-half years, and only three had survived as many as five years or more.[85]

Children's Programs

Programs for children must be done *well*—not necessarily expensively—or else not at all! Children are loyal viewers but merciless observers. They are also sensitive and suggestible young human beings. Programming concepts, formats, vocabulary, actions, film segments, cartoons, personalities, and com-mercials must respect and even protect the youthful viewers whose perceptions and values are being reinforced and even formed by television. Locally pro-duced series range widely in costs for production, from $50 to several hundred dollars a program; commercial time varies from none to 16 minutes (as of 1976, the NAB Code limits "non-program" material in children's shows to 9½ minutes an hour on weekends and 12 minutes on weekdays).[86] Nationally,

TV stations spend about $175 million a year to produce an average of four-and-one-half hours of children's programming a week; less than 45 per cent of that total is recouped from advertising revenue.[87] Group owners and network station divisions explored how to improve the quality as well as quantity of creative programming for youngsters in the 1970s, supported and exhorted by citizens' group Action for Children's Television (ACT) and the FCC. ABC-owned stations invested $1 million in a weekly one-hour children's series in 1973–74, scheduled for valuable Sunday late-afternoon "fringe time," with the expectation that if the series was successful it would lose only about half of that investment.[88] Ironically, at a time when consumer groups and regulatory agencies were demanding increased efforts in children's programming, the high costs of producing local education-entertainment shows for youngsters caused some stations to curtail their ambitious studio efforts in favor of filmed material for children—threatening the status of on-air personalities conducting programs with puppets, animals, and live audiences of youngsters.[89]

Local News and Public Affairs Programs

More stations place local news programs in their top-rated local category than all other types combined. Few stations, however, give them top talent and production status. Every station should budget as high as it can afford for news because costs can usually be covered through sponsorship. Between 1973 and 1975 over half (56%) of TV stations surveyed had lengthened their newscasts (to two hours locally in many major markets); two-thirds (63%) had increased the size of news staffs; and three-quarters (75%) raised budgets for news.[89a] Mobile units are a "must" in any area where significant news is made daily. Helicopters have proved advantageous in large markets for reports of traffic conditions and for special spot news events.

Adequate equipment is nice to have, but adequate people are a necessity! The program man who greatly relies on stills and silent films, too frequently also relies on a still mind and a silent, not to say utterly secret, power of enterprise and invention.

In creating local programming, many stations have discovered that the greatest opportunity to be different lies in the public affairs field. The aims of the local public affairs programs should be to inform, to broaden understanding, and to stimulate community thinking.[90] In television, reality exists side by side with the illusions of show business. Whenever a public affairs program is presented, the public needs to have it made clear that they are witnessing truth rather than the fiction which may be seen at other times. The station has the responsibility to make the distinction clear by eliminating the elements of make-believe whenever it presents the factual. Every television station should have one individual (even on part-time assignment) designated to handle all public affairs programming. The function should not be assigned to a group of individuals nor should the duties be passed from one person to another over a period of time. Public affairs programming is too vital to be given casual treatment. Unfortunately, many stations have taken the easy way by giving lip

service and time allotment to a public affairs concept and failing to interest or
alert the public to a genuine community problem. A good public affairs program need not be divorced from entertainment. These programs should be
produced with all the skill, verve, and appeal of commercial programming. If
they are well done they can appeal to a long list of local advertisers. Qualities
necessary for sponsorship are: importance of subject, imaginative presentation,
good production-direction-writing, wide viewer appeal, timeliness and news
worthiness. In other words—*good television!*

TELEVISION PROGRAM SCHEDULING

As in radio so in television, scheduling must relate to the availability of
kinds of audience ("dayparts") and to the attraction of those audiences from
one program to the next ("audience flow"). Careful analysis of demographic
market data and of competing stations' ratings and program types must guide
the strategy of television programmers.[91] Basic options include (a) noting the
most successful competitive program at a given hour and attempting to "woo
away" that already-available audience with a similar show, or (b) counter-
programming by offering a type of presentation that no competing station
schedules at that hour in the hope of attracting the non-viewing audience to
their home receiver and to your channel.

Local Prime-Time Programming

In the 1970s, the FCC attempted to open the high-audience viewing hours
to local and other non-network-originated programming, in an effort to induce
stations to innovate program concepts and to reach their local communities at
prime-time hours when viewers could watch television in large numbers. The
concept had been promoted by Group W (Westinghouse) President and Chairman of the Board, Donald McGannon, because it made possible collaborative
production and syndication of programs to stations at peak-audience hours
which could generate adequate advertising revenue to pay for the programming.
Unfortunately the economics of local production vs. film and videotape purchase, and the mass tastes of the general audience vs. quality concepts in program creativity conspired against the success of the rulemaking. By the mid-
1970s most broadcasters and even many production companies (who initially
hoped to create product for syndication to individual stations for prime-time
local scheduling) regretted the ruling and sought to have it revoked.[92]

But many stations did make serious efforts to program for their large
local audiences during the early or late evening hours when network service
was precluded by the FCC ruling. And some syndicators such as Group W
produced handsomely mounted programs series and "specials" for local purchase. But the stereotypical game shows and off-network reruns of entertainment continued to attract the largest audiences and advertising; the marketplace
resisted the introduction of local or quality programming by Federal fiat.

Apart from the early-evening access ruling, responsible station management should make a continued effort to reach large evening audiences with programs of interest and value to them. When he was an FCC commissioner, Kenneth Cox urged local broadcasters to reach out to their respective communities at other than "ghetto" times in their schedules:

> Such [local public service] programs should be carefully coordinated with overall schedules. But to the extent that these efforts are realized, stations will indeed be serving the public interest. It will require money and the best talent which can be found. It will take time, and will occupy time on the air, the one commodity which stations have to sell. I have long argued, though my colleagues do not agree, that some part of this programming should be presented in prime broadcast time, when the largest potential audiences are available. If broadcasters are sincerely interested in seeing their efforts produce real results in their communities, this kind of programming should be presented when it can have the greatest impact. Money and effort will be needed to promote it in order to insure the best possible audiences. This is not only in the public interest, but in the long-range best interest of individual stations as well.[93]

COSTS OF LOCAL PROGRAMMING

The economics of local programming can be frightening when the need for live studio facilities, engineering, production and all other required elements are considered.[94] Some stations' program expenditures (total, including all programming, film and live) are less than 25 per cent of their total operating costs. This is *incredibly low* and it usually reflects a lack-luster programming effort or a weak competitive situation, or both. The average television station should expend at least 35 per cent of its total station-operating budget for programming. Stations that are not affiliated with an interconnected network may expect costs for programming to go as high as 55–60 per cent of the overall expense.

The most effective means of program cost control in a well operated television station is through long-range planning, especially of film programming. Any station involving itself in one crash film program after another in an attempt to find winners from the available syndicated half-hours and features will probably serve an unhappy audience and an unhappy auditor.

The overall cost of the film product depends upon the type of station and upon the competition for filmed shows in the market. Obviously, in a seven-VHF-station market such as Los Angeles there is a far greater competitive struggle for all film availabilities than is true in a three-VHF-station market such as Cincinnati or Atlanta. There is little uniformity of policy in film pricing. There are few guidelines.

Although there is no standard asking price for syndicated film, the average cost for each half hour for a station in a medium-sized market is doubled for the rights to three to four additional re-runs over a five-year period. A station in a small single-station market might be able to lease the same film for one showing for about one-seventh of what the competitive medium-market pays. And a station in the nation's largest markets, of course, pays premium prices for film or videotape properties. For example, in 1974 an independent station in Los Angeles might pay approximately $10,000 per half-hour episode of a popular off-network entertainment series, with rights to four runs over seven years; with 225 programs in a syndicated package, the total cost comes to over $2 million (to be paid within 36 to 48 months). Thus, the cost can be amortized over each of the four runs of a 30-minute episode at $4,000, $3,000, $2,000, and $1,000 (with advertising rates weighted to reflect the decreased audience interest as those runs are repeated over seven years). Those 225 episodes are scheduled as "strip" programming—the same hour each day Monday through Friday—in the hope of building audience support through the year.

The smaller the market, the greater is the chance that the cost of live production could exceed the cost of film rental. In a medium-sized market, both the costs and the drawing power of live production and film are somewhat comparable. Here, the rental of a syndicated half-hour film might be about equal to the investment in a local production of a half-hour studio square-dance or polka party, with, say, five musicians and four dancers.

The expenses of local production in proportion to film costs can be kept under better control in stations in major markets. Even here, a decision between local live shows and film programming is difficult because of the risk involved in popular acceptance of the local production when the popularity of film is to some degree predictable.

Les Brown aptly describes concrete considerations involved in local program production:

> The costs of local production vary from market to market, depending on whether unions are involved. In the largest cities, a fairly pretentious local show playing five days a week might cost $25,000 a week to produce, a more modest one $10,000 a week. The rule of thumb in cities the size of New York, Los Angeles, Chicago, and Philadelphia is that each rating point is worth approximately $200 a minute. In local programs, it is permissible to sell five minutes per half hour. It may take weeks, or even months, for a local program to build up a 10 rating; in that event, the program theoretically would gross $10,000 a day. Out of that amount, the station would pay commissions of 15 per cent to the advertising agency and 11 per cent to the station representative. Given discounts, in addition, and a certain number of unsold minutes, the net revenues would realistically average approximately $6,000 a day. For a program that cost $25,000 a week, the profit would be $5,000. Not bad—but what of the early months when the program played at ratings of 2 and 3 and was sold to local merchants at half price? And what if it never catches on and runs at a 5 rating for six months or a year?
>
> In the medium-sized markets, a single rating point is generally worth $50 to $60 a minute to national advertisers, and in the smaller ones perhaps $25 to $30. Since the small markets receive ratings only twice a year, there may be no proof of a local program's success for six months.
>
> The national advertiser, working through a New York or Chicago advertising agency, might buy minute participations in a movie or an off-network rerun

like *Gilligan's Island* in Wichita, Kansas, but he would eschew the locally produced program unless it had a satisfactory rating history.[95]

Purchase of a large off-network or other syndicated package commits the
station to a multi-million dollar investment over more than half a decade—during which time audience and advertiser interests may change, or competitive
program scheduling on other stations might upset the availability of audience.
On the other hand, a locally produced low-cost series can be mounted for a trial
13 weeks to determine audience acceptance. It can then be continued or cancelled, depending on its initial success; there is no long-term investment in
shelves of expensive film properties. For example, "Bowling for Dollars" was
a program concept franchised by its East Coast originators for $50 a program; it
was oriented to local citizen participation. The production was mounted in Los
Angeles in 1974 for $300 a program by taping a week's five shows succes-
sively on one evening a week. Another audience-interview format, making
public the personal fiscal needs of local persons, cost that Los Angeles station
about $600 a day to produce—compared with costs from $3,000 to $5,000 a
day for an off-network entertainment series programmed by the same station. In
both those cited instances, the ratings quickly rose to 5 to 6, then to 8 and 9
(enormously successful for early evening "fringe time"), and finally to 11 and
12—far outdistancing the high-investment syndicated re-run packages on competing stations.

A further risk, of course, is that an unsuccessful series destroys that time
period for the station. The audience shifts viewing to competitive channels.
Subsequent efforts at rescheduling the time period demand enormous promotion
for the replacement series, to win back the audience. Meanwhile there is the
audience-flow problem; subsequent programs following that time-period failure
suffer from a small inherited "lead-in" audience. Thus the risks are great in
programming strategy, whether locally produced or syndicated film or videotaped properties are being scheduled.

Feature film production, as noted earlier, has not kept pace with the use
of those features by television. Prices for their use have skyrocketed. Costs of
film features have increased greatly during the past decade in the large markets,
more moderately in the medium-sized markets and only slightly in the small
markets.

Financing a film program usually interests the manager, but such other
aspects of the film department as editing, shipping and receiving, keeping of
records, screening, cuing and filing far too often receive inadequate recognition. These are highly important parts of the job and they need to be done if the
film that the public sees on the air is up to the standard that the station wishes
to maintain. Competent personnel can become dissatisfied because of the routine details of the job and they can lose their pride in accomplishment if there is
no direction or sign of appreciation from management. Eventually, a great part
of film programming may be automated, but until that time arrives the people

who work in film deserve more recognition than they have received in the past.

There is a distinct advantage in involving the general manager, the program manager, the sales manager and the head of the film department in the decisions that determine the kind of film bought for the station. Each of these executives has a different interest in what is selected. An interaction of ideas at this point in a group-decision atmosphere can pay dividends to the station.

B. National TV Network Programming

In January, 1948, NBC bought full-page space in various newspapers to call the attention of the public to the "greatest medium of mass communications in the world—Network Television." At that time, the NBC television network consisted of four Eastern cities: New York, Washington, Philadelphia and Schenectady. Nine out of every ten people in the United States had never even seen a television program. Nearly half of the television receiving sets were located in the New York area and there were only 17 television stations in operation in the entire country. That advertisement may have seemed at the time a wild exaggeration or a mad prophecy. It turned out to be a rather sober projection of fact.

HISTORICAL TRENDS

In television's early years, the programming that caused people to be almost hypnotized by "the tube" was really televised radio. The program materials and the formats of popular radio shows were transposed to the new medium with little change. Later, programs were developed that utilized the unique properties of the medium. The production techniques painfully evolved were later to have their influence on the film and theater arts. The significant experimentation and the discoveries of new dimensions in television were basically network contributions.

Most of today's radio programming originates in local stations. In contrast, most of today's pace-making television programming originates from the networks. With few exceptions, American television has been network-dominated almost from the beginning. It still is, except for a few aggressive group-station owners dedicated to prestigious programming and a greater choice of program product.

Color Television

All around us in the world is a "sea of color." Yet, television, the medium which should be able to make the most effective use of this dimension, was exceedingly slow to adopt it.

Several factors accounted for the slow development of color television and all of them were interrelated. An early reluctance of set manufacturers to enter the field and consequent dealer passivity, an indifferent attitude of the public due to the cost of the television receiver, weak advertiser support and the relatively few programs which were transmitted in color, all held back development.

Without going into a complexity of legal and technical as well as psychological reasons, in 1965 a large part of the American public finally became excited over color television. Practically the entire NBC evening schedule, some 96 per cent, was offered in color during the 1965–66 season. CBS telecast half of its evening programming and ABC over a third in color. The following year, *all* prime time programs on all three networks were in color.

It was estimated that up to January 1, 1966, some $80 million had been spent on color by the networks, another $55 million by television stations and around $25 million by production companies, for a total of approximately $160 million.[96] The heaviest expenditures, however, were made by the general public, which by that time had invested around $2.8 billion. The number of color sets purchased increased from a total of 7 million by 1965 to 60 million by 1973.[97]

Audiences expect all stations to provide local programming in color. A station that carries network color and then shows its local programs in monochrome can lose sizeable numbers of viewers to its competitors who provide color all the time. Color adds to the emotional impact of entertainment programming as well as to commercials. With the approach of total color television saturation, the novelty factor has diminished. Color, alone, will not save a second-rate program; broadcasters must continually search for new program ideas and fresh approaches.

NETWORK ENTERTAINMENT PROGRAMS

Three television networks provide more than 10,000 hours of programming a year. Most of it is classifiable as entertainment. The entertainment program has consistently attracted the largest audiences.

To call the roll of television entertainers is to list a shining company of folk minstrels and folk heroes. Milton Berle was a champion of the pioneer day, when the variety stage moved into the American living room. The names in theatrical lights became the names on the family set. Sid Caesar and Imogene Coca, Phil Silvers, Ed Wynn, Ernie Kovacs, Bob Hope, Jack Benny, Jackie Gleason, Danny Kaye and Red Skelton were household comics. Straight and singing emcees, who presided over various acts, have captivated huge audiences week after week, including such people as Ed Sullivan, Arthur Godfrey, Perry Como, Ernie Ford, Garry Moore, Frank Sinatra, Dinah Shore, Jimmy Dean, Andy Williams, Sammy Davis and Dean Martin.

Drama of one form or another has been well received over the years. Crime and suspense stories hit their peak of popularity in the early 1960s, fell off sharply, then returned as medical and police dramas in the 1970s. Other "action-adventure" stories have maintained their audience ratings consistently well, especially among the prime demographic target for advertisers, men and women between the ages of 18 and 49. "Most situation comedies do not [deliver men and women 18–49], no Westerns do, no gameshows do, few variety shows do," according to Howard Eaton, Ogilvy & Mather advertising agency executive; motion pictures, especially ones of action-adventure, do attract this audience most desired by advertisers.[98] The Western series, surprisingly, was rather late in its appearance but has been popular ever since, although the ratings of this type of offering peaked in the 1959–60 season. Situation-comedy series have increased steadily in number and in popularity over the years, particularly the "character" and "topical" comedy of the 1970s, such as *All in the Family, M*A*S*H, Sanford and Son, Maude,* and *Good Times.*

Quiz and *audience participation* formats and game shows, borrowed largely from radio, were popular nighttime attractions in television's early years. After the quiz scandals in 1959–60 they re-emerged with great strength in the networks' daytime schedules. A decade later in the 1970s they also became staples of early-evening "prime-time access" periods, through syndication to local stations.

Feature theatrical film began to be used as a major network attraction in prime time during the 1961–62 season and it has become increasingly popular as a network offering ever since. By 1973, the ten network feature movies all seven nights of the week consistently rated among the top-35 shows and were sometimes seven of the top ten programs in given weeks.[99] To supplement the supply of theatrical motion pictures available for home viewing, production companies and networks themselves began to film feature dramas made especially for television.

Various *musical-variety* formats attracted large, regular audiences until the mid-1970s. In this category were such widely different kinds of programs as *Lawrence Welk, The King Family, Sing Along with Mitch, The Dean Martin Show, The Bell Telephone Hour,* and specials featuring Perry Como, Bing Crosby, Harry Belafonte, Liza Minnelli, and Tennessee Ernie Ford. By 1974, the musical-variety program had become an "endangered species" and appeared in network schedules as one-time-only specials instead of as weekly series.

Daytime and Late-night Programming

Daytime network television abounds in entertainment but of a somewhat different variety. Here the dramatic serials (introduced to TV when they had almost run their course on radio), game shows, various talk formats and network re-runs are the staples, with some morning programs for pre-schoolers and a late-afternoon set of offerings for the in-school crowd.

Late-night programming of interview-variety programs, special entertainment (contemporary music, drama, revues), and feature films have pushed network service back into the middle of the night, while daytime news, interview, and featurette programming has thrust network service forward into the early morning hours. NBC's long-time exclusive service with the *Today, To-*

night, Tomorrow and *Midnight Special* programs was finally joined by CBS and then ABC in the competition for the early-morning and late-night audiences.

There have been other forms of entertainment offered, but by and large these have been the mainstays of the types of network entertainment, year in and year out.

Program mortality rates have been high. But, then, show business was always "chancy." Casualties of new programs after one season on the air have averaged 20 or more each year since 1960. At the end of the 1973–74 season, no fewer than 30 prime-time network series were cancelled (predictably, the bottom 30 out of 80 series, with national Nielsen ratings ranging from 17.1 to 6.0).[100] After the 1974–75 season another 23 series were cancelled—9 by ABC, 8 by NBC, and 6 by CBS. Partly, this situation is due to insufficient audience interest plus an abundance of offerings of the same types. It is due also to the selection of some programs that are not strong enough in concept to last very long. Who remembers *Haggis Baggis?* And how long will *My Mother, The Car* or *Needles and Pins* be discussed with fond memories? An ancient, yet observant, show-biz maxim applies equally well to productions on the screen and stage. "It's always a bum season," some philosopher remarked, "for a bum show." Usually, it is a short season for a slight show.

Competitive Programming Strategy

But even programs of substance or at least of widespread national audience support also succumb to the realities and strategies of network television's competitive programming. Classic instances have been *The Firestone Hour* and *Lawrence Welk* musical programs. In both cases, advertisers sustained their interest and large audiences viewed the programs; but ABC noted that the shows attracted not only smaller audiences than other kinds of programs, but also the "wrong kinds" of audience—too old, rather than many of the high-product-purchasing group of 18- to 49-year-olds. CBS Television Network President Robert Wood graphically described the decision-making process that weighed factors affecting a major shift of programming emphasis by CBS for the 1970–71 season:

The Price of Success

It was obvious, of course, why our audience skewed toward the C and D counties [rural counties of less than 120,000 people, constituting only 31 per cent of the country's population] and attracted a greater share of the older generation than the young. We were the victims of our own success.

One of our programs had been a hit for 22 straight seasons—was actually as old as the Network. Another had been brought back, again and again, for 18 consecutive seasons. Still another for 17 years. Indeed, . . . close to one third of our entire nighttime entertainment schedule was back—by popular demand—for the sixth consecutive season. But as these shows returned year after year they had tended to maintain their popularity leadership through the deep-seated loyalty of those who had been following them from the very beginning. On the other hand, many of them were unable to pick up as large a portion of the younger viewers who had come of age in the more recent past.

Because we had so little program failure, we introduced relatively few new series. While such new programs might not draw as many viewers as some of the old standbys, they had the advantage of being new, novel, more "with it" in terms of the tastes of the moments, and thus more appealing to the young and the more sophisticated big-city audience.

In short, as a result of our success, we were inadvertently discriminating against urban viewers as well as our affiliates in the big cities. It was this situation that drove us to the conclusion that we must do more than simply hold the kind of audiences we already had. We had to take the bit in our teeth, change the program mix by dropping some of our old stalwarts in a move to broaden our base. This, then, was the philosophy on which we based our program judgments as we built a schedule for this fall [1970].

The Program Board

The actual schedule was put together in a series of meetings that ran from November 1969 into February 1970—meetings that involved long discussions, strongly expressed opinions, and many alternate suggestions by members of the Program Department and by people in Sales, Research, News, and Business Affairs, which handles our contractual negotiations. . . .

Making the Cut

The first big decision was which program series should be cut. We finally decided to drop six—or nearly one out of five of the 29 series which the Network had presented during the preceding season.

Cutting three of the six—a one-hour western and two half-hour situation comedies—was an easy decision. All three had poor track records during the previous season—not only overall, but in every age bracket and in every type of community. In each case it was clear that program fatigue had set in and that the possibilities of the particular formats had been exhausted.

But the decision to drop the other three was a far different story. Simply ticking off the titles will give you a rough idea of just how agonizing it was. The trio included Jackie Gleason, Red Skelton, and *Petticoat Junction*. Not only were the decisions difficult because all three had contributed so much to our past success, but also because each was still performing so well. Red Skelton was the seventh most popular show in all television. Gleason ranked 31, and *Petticoat Junction* was number 32 among all regularly scheduled series on the three networks. Yet we were driven to drop the shows in order to carry out our shift in programming strategy—that is to evaluate programs not only in relation to how many watch but also in terms of who watches.

You will recall that I pointed out earlier that among those watching network television CBS viewers tended to be concentrated among the older segments. . . . Skelton, Gleason's variety show, and *Petticoat Junction* had even greater appeal among older viewers than the CBS schedule as a whole, and more limited appeal among the young adults.

The same pattern emerges in terms of big-city versus rural appeal. . . .

[T]he audience shares in A and B counties and in C and D counties for Skelton, Gleason and *Petticoat Junction* [are] graphic evidence of an overwhelming small-town and rural appeal at the expense of big-city audiences.

Reasons for the Cut

When I take you through our final schedule, you may be puzzled about how we happened to drop these particular series rather than others. . . . What finally controlled the decision was a combination of many factors—not only the appeal of the programs among various audience segments but the mix and balance of our entire nighttime schedule—that is, program sequence, audience flow, competitive scheduling, innovation and experimentation, as well as program cost, advertiser interest and station acceptance.[101]

Those who criticize the networks for devoting the major emphasis of their programming to entertainment may do well to consider the intensely competitive nature of the medium. That kind of television programming has evolved which can attract audiences requisite to survival; executives select shows that appear to have the least chance of failing.[102] By the mid-1960s, there were few points of significant difference between each network's approach. All networks appeal to the public in similar terms for approximately equal shares of the viewing audience.

The instant "hit" is not entirely unusual in television entertainment. When it happens, even the program executives are at least mildly surprised. The "hit" series is, however, partly a stroke of luck which every producer hopes to achieve. In seeking to develop a successful series, it is not uncommon to appropriate a format that has already proved popular and to add a few new gimmicks. Fred Allen observed that "imitation is the sincerest form of television." Still, the new, "spin-off" venture often fails.

Occasionally, a special individual program will be so well received that the gears will start in motion for more of the same type. When *Death of a Salesman* received outstandingly favorable reactions, all three networks hastened to revive the experimental drama as a prime-time regular offering. Yet, few works of comparable artistry are available; probably, it is always a good season for authentic works of genius. The Christmas dramatic special "The Homecoming" attracted critical and popular acclaim, and quickly returned as a weekly series, *The Waltons,* which eventually became one of the top-five programs nationally for several seasons.

"Special" Programs and Audience

The "special" program has always been reserved for the most lavish production methods and budgetary support. Once labeled "the spectacular," it has been just that in comparison with many of the programs that are offered on a regular basis. Advertiser interest in the opportunities for enhancement of corporate image (among consumers and stockholders or investors) through the prestige value of the "specials" has brought about a continuing increase in the number offered and in their quality. *The Hallmark Hall of Fame* is one illustration of a prestige program that has appeared as a series of "specials" over a 20-year period.

In the 1971–72 season, the three national networks scheduled 272 prime-time "specials," including entertainment, news, and public affairs or special-events coverage. Of the top ten programs, five were Bob Hope comedy presentations, and two were musicals featuring Bing Crosby and Andy Williams. The second- and third-highest rated "specials" of the entire season were World Series baseball and the Miss America Pageant; the highest-rated special show of the year (with a 38.7 rating and an enormous 70 per cent share of the entire viewing audience that evening) was the Academy Awards.[103] On the other hand, the highest-ranked special drama that season ("The Homecoming") was 30th, with a 25.3 rating and 39 per cent share of that evening's audience. Other serious dramatic programs ranked 38th, 45th, 51st, 58th, and 65th (all *Hallmark Hall of Fame*); 78th; 87th; 91st; 93rd; 105th; 128th (*Playhouse 90*—with a 15.4 rating and 28 share); 137th (Hallmark); 170th, 176th (both parts of a "Life of Leonardo da Vinci"); 181st (Hallmark); 227th; and 239th. Predictably, such public affairs "specials" as *CBS Reports* achieved positions of 176th, 192nd, 215th, 256th, and 263rd. Specifically political-oriented programs had a firm hold on the year's bottom of the list; usually attracting less than one-tenth of a given evening's audience viewing television at the time of the airing.

Rank	Title	Network	Date	Rating	Share
256	CBS Reports: Night in Jail, Day in Court	CBS	1-27-72	7.1	12
256	Back from China	CBS	3- 9-72	7.1	14
258	Inquiry: American Indian	ABC	7-24-72	7.0	16
259	CBS News: To the Top of Everest	CBS	12-30-71	6.7	11
260	CBS News: India vs. Pakistan	CBS	12- 3-71	6.6	12
261	PGA Golf Preview	ABC	8- 4-72	6.5	15
261	Inquiry: Arms & Security	ABC	8- 7-72	6.5	13
263	CBS Reports: Picasso Is 90 & Chicano	CBS	10-21-71	6.2	10
264	Visit With the First Lady	ABC	9-12-71	6.0	13
264	Decision '72: Wisconsin	NBC	4- 4-72	6.0	11
266	Inquiry: An Echo of Anger	ABC	8-16-72	5.8	11
267	Can You Go Home Again?	ABC	4-24-72	5.7	9
268	CBS News: America & the World	CBS	12-30-71	5.6	9
269	Decision '72: Pennsylvania	NBC	4-25-72	5.1	11
270	Decision '72: New Hampshire	NBC	3- 7-72	5.0	9
271	The Nixon Team	ABC	8-17-72	4.9	11
272	Political: Sen. Jackson	NBC	11-19-71	3.5	7

Those ratings and shares reflect the sustained interest of American audiences in entertainment presentations, and the significantly lesser support for public affairs "specials" (including news, special events, and politics). The economics as well as the very nature of a mass medium's reaching a mass audience makes reasonable—if not desirable by critics, or more selective viewers—the kind of programming and scheduling associated with national networks.

Very similar patterns of success and less-than-success (measured by audience viewing) were repeated in the 1972–73 season, except that one of the lowest-ranked of the 197 prime-time "specials" that year was the three-hour "Long Day's Journey into Night" by Eugene O'Neill, featuring Lord Laurence Olivier, broadcast by ABC on March 10, 1973. That important dramatic event ranked 193rd and attracted only 11 per cent of the audience viewing television that evening, for a Nielsen national rating of 6.5. Even most of the *CBS Reports, NBC Reports,* and ABC News "specials" drew larger audiences! Bob Hope comedy "specials" were four of the 13 top-rated "specials" that year (ratings of 38.1 to 31.2; shares of 55 to 45). Highest-ranked shows included the perennial favorites of the mass public: Bob Hope, Jack Benny, Bing Crosby, Elvis Presley, and Perry Como, plus theatrical motion pictures ("Patton," "Goldfinger," and "The Ten Commandments"), two World Series games, and the Academy Awards.[104]

Mature Dramatic Programs

But by 1973–74 dramatic "specials" (filmed or videotaped) and "made-for-TV" movies began to grow in stature, attracting critical acclaim coupled with increased audience support. In fact, reviewers noted that drama in the medium of television was gradually surpassing motion pictures in sensitivity of content and delicacy of characterization and presentation. Awards as well as large audiences accrued to social-topic dramas such as "The Autobiography of Miss Jane Pittman."

Entertainment and drama critic of the *Los Angeles Times* Charles Champlin devoted a front-page feature article to commenting on the

> large and significant change in the relationship between movies for television and movies for theaters.
> What ['The Execution of] 'Private Slovik,' Tom Gries' recent superb handling of Tennessee Williams' 'The Migrants' and the very moving 'Autobiography of Miss Jane Pittman' all suggest is that there are controversial themes and unrelenting stories which television is now willing and able to accommodate but which could not by their nature find financial backing as theatrical releases.[105]

He noted that the "Pittman" story, with its "unsparing view of black life in America, . . . raised many a hackle, but it has been more widely praised as a triumphant affirmation of television's potential for dealing uncompromisingly with the social condition." Similarly, "That Certain Summer," sensitively treating homosexuality, "suggested that commercial network television could find and hold audiences with something more than diversionary formula entertainment." *TV Guide* offered similar supportive praise of television's emerging maturity in presenting serious dramatic themes in "made-for-TV" movies during the 1973–74 season, including treatment of topics such a alcoholism ("The Morning After,"), rape ("A Case of Rape"), dehumanizing aspects of sport ("Bloodsport"), and middle-age childbirth ("A Brand New Life").[106] Within two television seasons the medium offered other themes such as the crumbling of suburbanite marriages (Ingmar Bergman's original TV script "The Lie"), military honor codes ("Pueblo"), youngsters' life in a black ghetto ("If You Want to Give a Dance, You Have to Pay the Band"), stylized depiction of maladjusting war-veteran families ("Sticks and Bones"), rebellion within organized religion ("The Catholics"), abortion ("Maude"), hostilities within families in Northern Ireland ("A War of Children"), and full adaptations for television of classics by Tennessee Williams ("Glass Menagerie," "The Migrants"), Eugene O'Neill ("Long Day's Journey Into Night"), and Arthur Miller ("Death of a Salesman"). All were commercially sponsored except for CBS's highly controversial "Sticks and Bones." This is a partial listing; nor does it include the many dramatic works presented nationally by the Public Broadcasting Service (PBS) through non-commercial stations.

Whether caused by a growing necessity to use post-1960 theatrical feature films, by an increasing amount of audience sophistication, by a maturation in the industry, or by a demand for excellence, network programming grows steadily more "adult." Provocative themes and language that would have met mass resistance in television's early days are more frequently aired. There seems to be general audience acceptance of this change. Hopefully, a more adult audience is responsive to serious works of art.

NETWORK FILM PROGRAMS

Films were little used in early network programming. Television was a new medium that seemed to demand live production. Old feature movies and varied short subjects hardly seemed appropriate, especially when they were re-runs of materials produced by and for a competitive form of show business.

Policies about not using film were changed after Hollywood began to produce and syndicate programming especially for television. Actually, the local television stations were first to schedule the bulk of the new availabilities. Then the networks began to see possibilities in the Hollywood product. By 1959, they were the primary markets for West Coast film production and before long most of the network schedule consisted of filmed programming.

By the 1965–66 season, almost 85 per cent of the prime-time programming of the three networks was on film. The film shows included most of the dramatic programs, the action and adventure series and the situation comedies. Most of the prime-time variety and the quiz or panel programs were on tape. It became difficult for local stations to find syndicated film series which had not already been shown by the networks.

Almost twice as many off-network series were offered to stations in 1966 as were made available the previous year (since most of them were in black and white, the increase in offerings may be attributed to a race against obsolescence as color programming came more into demand).

The pace of film production changed considerably when the motion picture studios became major producers for television. Previously accustomed to as much as a year and a half for the completion of a feature film for theater exhibition, film makers quickly adjusted to turning out two half-hour films every week.

Program Suppliers

A total of 115 *new* program development projects for potential scheduling for 1973–74 were commissioned by the networks.[107] The projects represented series or made-for-TV movies, for which the networks made some financial commitment—whether for pilot, script, or merely treatment.

Supplier	(Series)	Total Projects	ABC	CBS	NBC
Universal TV	(7)	20	4	4	12
Twentieth Century-Fox TV	(17)	17	7	5	5
Metromedia Producers Corp.	(12)	16	6	5	5
Paramount TV	(9)	14	6	2	6
Viacom	(13)	13	2	6	5
Warner Bros. TV	(5)	13	3	3	7
MGM-TV	(8)	8	2	4	2
Tomorrow Entertainment	(7)	8	3	3	2
Screen Gems	(5)	5 *	1	1	2
Filmways	(1)	1	0	1	0
TOTAL		115	34	34	46

* (Network not known on one negotiation)

Among the many principal suppliers for the networks in the 1972–73 season had been many independent production companies, some in association with major studios (marked with asterisk):

Universal TV—Public Arts, Inc. (17)
Paramount TV (5)
Quinn-Martin Productions * (3)
Warner Brothers TV (6)
Associated Television-ITV [Britain]
MGM-TV (2)
Thomas-Spelling Productions
ABC Sports

George Schlatter Productions *
Jemmin Inc.*
Cave Creek Enterprises
Jeffersan-Sultan Productions
Blye-Beard Productions *
Humbug Co.*
Lorimar Productions
Mark VII Ltd.*

Goverton Productions *
Screen Gems (3)
Ashmont Productions * (2)
Spelling-Goldberg Productions
20th Century-Fox (3)
Gene Reynolds Productions *
Yorkin-Lear Tandem Productions (3)
MTM Enterprises (2)
Douglas S. Cramer Co.*
Thornhill Productions *
Punkin Productions
Arwin Productions
CBS-TV
Leonard Freeman Productions
Lucille Ball Productions
Alfra Productions

BBC/Time-Life Films
Harbour Productions *
NBC Productions
Claude Productions *
Greg Garrison Productions *
Clerow Productions *
Bob Henry Productions *
William Castle Productions *
NBC News
Talent Associates/Norton Simon Inc.*
Public Arts Inc.*
Universal International *
Oden Productions *
Romart Inc.
Leslie Stevens Productions *
Walt Disney Productions

For the 1975–76 season, 34 production companies prepared 84 pilot programs for potential sale to the networks (down from a total of 96 pilots the previous year). ABC ordered 28 pilots, CBS 25, and NBC 31. Companies developing pilot programs were the following (some in association with other entities such as MGM-TV, Don Kirshner Productions, UGO Productions, Mark VII), with the number of different programs developed in parentheses:[107a]

ABC Circle Films (2)
Acre Enterprises
Alpine Productions (2)
Abe Burroughs
Columbia Pictures TV (7)
Douglas S. Cramer Co.
D'Antoni-Weitz TV Productions
Filmways (2)
The Four's Company
Larry Gordon Productions
Jim Henson Associates
International TV Productions/
    Allied Artists (2)
Lorimar (4)
MGM Television (8)
MTM Enterprises (3)
Omnipresent Inc.
Paramount (5)

Patience Co.
Persky & Denoff (2)
Playboy Productions
Quinn Martin
John Rich Productions
Ruben/Rich Productions (2)
RSO Productions
Spelling/Goldberg (4)
Sweeney/Finnegan Films
Tandem Productions
T.A.T. Communications Co. (3)
Danny Thomas Productions
Thoroughbred Productions
20th Century-Fox (3)
Universal (12)
Warmth Productions
Warner Brothers (5)

Of those 84 pilots developed, 27 were sold to the networks for the fall season in 1975–76—nine to each of the three networks. Some of the other 57 unsuccessful pilots might be bought later as "second season" replacements for new or old series that did not attract sufficient audiences in the early weeks of the fall.

The film producer has certain advantages in selling his film to a network rather than to individual stations. He can recover his production costs sooner, he lowers his distribution costs, he needs far fewer prints of the film, and the networks usually absorb the costs of promoting the film.

Even with these advantages, the creation of a pilot film for a prospective series is a heavy risk. The cost of pilots, due largely to contract restrictions on talent and to overtime payments, runs considerably higher than the costs of subsequent programs in a series once it is sold. The investment in a half-hour pilot averages around a quarter of a million dollars. An hour pilot, usually involving on-location shooting, can cost well over half a million dollars.[108]

Some 20 pilots that are created each year are not accepted by the networks (although most are utilized on a one-time-only basis, often under some title as "Movie of the Week"). It should be understandable why many independent producers hesitate to invest such a sizeable amount of capital on a highly speculative risk. It should also be clear why so many producers who enter this competition tend to play it as safely as possible by developing programs similar to those that have already been successful.

On the positive side, once a pilot is accepted, there are the prospects of selling the rest of the programs in the series, and the possibilities of network renewals and of off-network syndication for United States television stations and for the foreign market.

The FCC's prime-time access rule opened the early portions of the lucrative, large-audience evening hours to local station programming; those stations promptly scheduled off-network re-runs and then began to purchase new syndicated properties. The Commission's purposes in instituting the ruling were partly realized, for they loosened the networks' almost exclusive dominance of evening television. Eighteen series previously seen on networks, plus 30 newly-syndicated series, filled those hours in the first year of the access rule; in the second year, another 31 series were sold by syndicators—distributed in from 172 markets (*Lawrence Welk*) to 11 markets.[109] Independent production companies, motion picture studios, network syndication divisions, and also advertisers (notably Chevrolet) and agencies were the sources of those filmed and videotaped programs.[110]

In the first season five series, in the second season another eight, and by 1974–75 54 series were sold by "barter" or "advertiser syndication." A national advertiser or production company pays all production costs, and the programs are distributed at no charge to stations in exchange for two of the commercial spots placed in the program; the stations may sell the remaining advertising positions for their own income. By 1970, according to Les Brown, "it appeared to be growing into a kind of secondary network" with advertisers controlling the content and form and distribution of the program series, and stations placing them in their local schedules. In 1973, 15 per cent of all syndicated programs were barter series, representing approximately $25 million in commercial time bartered for them, with more than 2,700 half-hours per week.[111] In 1974, a total of 28 program series were available by barter. But by 1975 (due partly to FCC revision and Court reversal of the access rule),

Chevrolet abandoned the two barter shows it had continued into 1973. And most of the barter negotiations concerned only several highly popular series, *Lawrence Welk, Hee Haw, Wild Kingdom, Police Surgeon* and either *Goldsboro, Untamed World,* or *Animal World.* Meanwhile, it was estimated that up to 15 per cent of all U.S. television stations refused to accept programs syndicated by barter agreement.

The dependence of the networks on the Hollywood production centers may lead to problems. Increasing costs of turning out pilots on speculation and the high mortality rate of these products after they are accepted could have the effect of drying up a major program source. There seemed a need for renewed emphasis on live and videotaped programming by the networks.

Videotape began to replace film as a key source of programming due to the increasing flexibility of electronic equipment, from portable light-weight color cameras to swift and precise editing. Producers, as well as talent, have come to rely on editing privileges before final approval of their product whether film or tape.

NETWORK SPORTS PROGRAMS

Even though sports programs are a form of entertainment for most fans, the category has such dimension in network offerings as to deserve separate treatment. In any case, expenditures for cultural, informational and dramatic programs are relatively insignificant when compared to networks' outlays for sports programs. Costs kept pace with mounting inflation generally, and with leagues and clubs that realized the enormous mass audience that viewed the games. A total of 13 million people paid to attend pro football in 1970; but 20 million regularly viewed those same games on television.[112] Production costs rose swiftly as more sophisticated coverage demanded elaborate technical facilities and engineers. Every Sunday during the 1974 football season, ABC employed nine color cameras, two videotape recorders, and two slow-motion machines—including a second unit of director and cameras for "isolated coverage" (repeat inserts of excerpted action). For the 1973 Super Bowl CBS employed 15 cameras, two video-tape and two slow-motion units.[113]

Football

Football has intrinsic appeal through its live action and its element of the unexpected. The isolated camera, stop-action, slow-motion and directional microphones have added to the interest in television coverage. In 1936 the CBS radio network *was paid* $500 by the Orange Bowl Committee for broadcasting the game. In 1972, NBC purchased the rights to telecast the Orange Bowl for $700,000.

When the first Super Bowl game was arranged between the champions of the National Football League and the American Football League, the question of television coverage rights was involved. CBS owned the contract for the televising of all NFL games and NBC held the television rights to the AFL games. The problem was resolved by permitting both of the networks to carry the game for a fee of $1 million from each network. CBS acquired sole rights to the game in 1968 and 1970 with NBC carrying the 1969 game exclusively. The rights to televise these three events cost $2.5 million for each game. This amount represented a new high for the rights to a one-day sports event. This is typical of the bidding for exclusivity in football telecasting. NBC paid approximately $3 million for the Super Bowl game on January 12, 1975, in New Orleans, and charged advertisers $214,000 for a commercial minute—the highest rate-card price for any once-only attraction on the air.[114]

The rights to the professional NFL regular schedule had cost CBS $9.3 million for the 1962 and 1963 seasons. In order to retain those rights for the 1964 and 1965 seasons, CBS paid the astronomical sum of $28 million. The rights to the 1966 and 1967 seasons, with an option to renew for 1968 and 1969, again became the property of CBS for the sum of $37.6 million. The NFL contract permits coverage of various regional games each week. CBS had the exclusive rights to all regular season games played in the conference over the two-year period. In addition, CBS paid another $6 million for the rights to two championship games, two Pro Bowls and two playoff Bowls. The network introduced an innovation in the scheduling of sports by instituting nighttime coverage of selected pre-season and regular-season games. ABC paid more than one half a million dollars for *each* of 13 Monday night games, for three seasons (1970–73), and in 1974 charged advertisers $100,000 a commercial minute.

ABC had paid $10 million for the rights for five years (1960–1964) to the AFL regular season and championship games. NBC, by bidding $36 million received the AFL regular season rights for the five years 1965–1969, with the league's championship and all-star games sold separately.

In 1970 the NFL and AFL merged into one league. In 1974, all three networks entered into four-year contracts with the NFL; the estimated prices for rights in the 1974–75 season were $56 million, divided among: ABC, $13.5 million (including $1.5 million for the post-season Pro Bowl); CBS, $22.5 million; and NBC, $17 million.

The National Collegiate Athletic Association (representing amateurs, be it noted) as well as the professional National Football League advertised for competitive bidding every two years. CBS carried the NCAA games through the 1962 and 1963 seasons. NBC had them during 1964 and 1965. Then, without announcing any open bidding, the contract for 1966 and 1967 was awarded to ABC for $15.5 million—an increase of almost $2.5 million over the preceding two years. An option for a two-year renewal on ABC was retained by the NCAA.

The total which the broadcasting networks invested in rights to professional and collegiate football games in one season (1972) was estimated at over $57 million. There was little difficulty finding sponsors who would pay as high as $75,000 per minute for game participations, $25,000 a minute for pre-game shows and $35,000 a minute for post-game shows.

Baseball

Football figures have been cited as illustrative of sports costs. The costs of baseball rights are on the increase, too.[115] NBC's contract for the All-Star games and the World Series in 1967 and 1968 cost $12.6 million, a 68 per cent increase over the same network's cost for those rights for 1965 and 1966. NBC also purchased the rights to the Game of the Week from the baseball clubs for an additional, $6 million each year for three years. In 1973 NBC paid $18 million for the entire package of regular season games, play-offs, World Series, and All-Star games.

Efforts to move major-league baseball into evening prime-time on the networks met with some success during the 1966 season, when night games were carried for the first time on selected holidays.

The Olympics

Every four years, the networks submit bids for the rights to cover the Winter and Summer Olympics. In 1960, CBS paid $660,000 for rights and production costs for the Olympic Games in Rome. Eight years later, rights to both the 1968 Winter Olympics in Grenoble, France, and the Summer Olympics in Mexico City were awarded to ABC. Total cost for televising the Winter event was estimated at around $6.5 million, including $2 million for rights. The Summer coverage on television was estimated to cost in excess of $12 million including $4.5 million for rights. It is estimated that in 1972 the network lost at least $1 million on its Olympics sports coverage of the Summer Olympics in Munich. But it gained prestige and audience attention by attracting almost half of all television viewers during the 17 prime-time evenings; excluding independent stations, ABC averaged 59 per cent of the three-network audience in New York City and 61 per cent in Los Angeles, with 26.0 and 29.9 ratings in each of those markets. (Beyond attracting massive audiences into a two-week viewing "habit" of tuning to ABC stations, the Olympic coverage was also used as a showcase for promoting ABC's new season of programming.) And that network received a Peabody Award for its spontaneous coverage of the tragic events that interrupted the Olympic games.

> Millions of television viewers had an uneasy armchair view of the drama in Munich last week after Arab terrorists seized Israeli athletes and turned the Olympic games into a 23-hour nightmare. Pictures and reports from the scene, via satellite, captured the tension and terror from a few hours after the guerrillas took the Israeli hostages in a predawn attack until it was confirmed that the violence had ended in a shoot-out that brought the toll to 17 dead.
>
> ABC-TV, in the midst of massive, exclusive U.S. television coverage of the summer games, was the prime beneficiary of the tragic news break. But CBS and NBC also were able to mount extensive coverage operations. . . .[116]

ABC noted that its coverage was "a unique cooperative journalistic effort" between its newsmen and sports commentators who jointly reported the unfolding tragedy.

For its record of more than 62 hours of prime-time coverage (scheduled, plus the added coverage of the tragic events), in addition to weekend coverage, ABC furnished almost one-third of the total of $30 million of television equipment—not including satellites—assembled by the German television networks, with NHK of Japan and the British Broadcasting Corporation. (Through those networks and networks of more than 100 other countries, approximately one billion people throughout the world viewed at least portions of the summer games—up from the 800 million who saw the Mexico City Olympics in 1968.) ABC alone added 16 color cameras (to the 100 provided by DOZ, the German coordinators), 18 of its own videotape machines, five mobile units, one portable mobile unit, three slow-motion machines, two separate control rooms, and eight film camera teams. The network also employed 300 production personnel, engineers, interpreters, and drivers.[117]

Other Sports

There are many golf series on television. In addition to coverage of all the major golf tournaments, special golfing events merit special reporting. At the 1969 U.S. Open Golf Tournament in Houston, ABC had 100 technicians, 24 cameras, 75 microphones and numbers of forklifts, scaffolds, and cable.

Network television covers the Triple Crown in horse-racing, including the Kentucky Derby, the Preakness and the Belmont Stakes. On occasion, it also carries other scheduled racing events.

An investment of more than $1 million is made for prize money alone in bowling series shown on television. The audience for these programs is estimated at some 7 million regular viewers.

Basketball coverage for the most part is provided by a "specialist" in the field of network television. Big Ten and pro basketball are available through special *ad hoc* line-ups of stations, by such companies as the Hughes Television Network. Such "occasional" networks also provide coverage of the National Collegiate events in indoor track, swimming, diving and skiing; the national indoor tennis championship; horse racing; various PGA golf tournaments; and road games of major league baseball. The sports fan has a permanent seat in the television grand stand.

NETWORK NEWS AND PUBLIC AFFAIRS

As the entertainment offerings of the three networks become more and more similar, each network increasingly depends for its distinctive image on its sports packages and on its news and public affairs programming.

In retrospect, the season of 1963–1964 may have been the breakthrough year for the networks in the field of news and public affairs. It was the year the Roper poll first disclosed the information that television was the public's major source for news; it was the year NBC and CBS doubled the length of their evening newscasts; it was the year the three television networks commited themselves to spend $70,000,000 for the production of news and documentary programs for the season, prompting *Broadcasting* magazine to editorialize: "Altogether the new surge of information programming is the healthiest trend to develop in broadcasting's recent history. It will do more than most others for broadcasting and for the country." Further, 1963–64 was the year the three networks averaged about six times as much "hard" news coverage as they had in 1950 and about 100 more hours of documentaries than they had carried as recently as 1959 (and over half of the documentaries were sponsored).

It was also the year, unfortunately, of the coverage of the events following the assassination of a President of the United States.

The Week-End of November 22nd, 1963

That awful week-end brought the heaviest possible challenge to electronic journalism. The cancellation of all regular programming and advertising, the thoroughness of the participation by the media, and the dignity of the coverage of all of the events were all indicative of the coming of age of radio and television as major news media.

The television audience on that week-end approached universality for the first time in history: 96.1 per cent of all homes with television sets, according to Nielsen, watched the week-end coverage on an average of 31.6 hours per home. The largest single audience of the week-end was assembled during the requiem mass, which was attended through television by more than 97,000,000 persons. Slightly fewer than those millions saw the burial service. At no time during the entire week-end was the audience less than 14 per cent of all homes, representing more than 7,000,000 people.

The reliance of the people on television in those hours of crisis is shown in the Nielsen report of the growth of the audience throughout the afternoon and evening of the assassination. At 1:30 P.M. eastern standard time, on Friday, November 22, the television sets were in use in approximately 23.4 per cent of American television homes. Fifteen minutes later, after the first reports of the assassination, more than a third of the television homes in the country were tuned in. By 2:00 P.M. the audience had increased to 42.2 per cent of the homes. Two and a half hours later, sets were in use in 75 per cent of all homes. By 11:00 P.M. the people in some 92.6 per cent of American homes had seen an average of almost six hours of television coverage. But these figures are all but irrelevant. The event surpassed statistics, surveys, and cost accounting.

The senseless tragedy in Dallas, the moving rituals of mourning, and the outpouring of the nation's love and grief were unparalleled in the American experience. Men and women whose hearts marched to the slow rhythm of muffled drums will long remember. That much of television can be trivial and tawdry—as much of quite ordinary life can be trivial and tawdry—is beyond question. But, let it stand also beyond question that in a tragic time ours was a common dignity and a common greatness. In shock and trial and bereavement, no people behaved more magnificently, no medium of communication served so selflessly and so well.

Other Special Events Coverage

Another sad event, the funeral of Winston Churchill, further enhanced the reputation of the networks for dignified coverage. Television further distinguished itself by its reporting of such events as the visit of Pope Paul VI to the United Nations and New York, the series of space projects and flights by the astronauts, and the historic trips to China and Russia by President Nixon. Those 25 manned space flights cost the networks an estimated $60 to $65 million, not counting millions more lost in advertising in pre-empted programs.[118] The first human landing on the moon, July 20, 1969, cost the networks approximately $11 million in expenditures and revenue loss, and took 1,000 network personnel; the U.S. audience for that historic telecast was 125 million persons—judged then to be "the biggest show in broadcasting history."

Perhaps as much as any other single influence, television helped to bring about public awareness of the civil rights movement and the efforts by minorities to be recognized and respected. Although networks and their news divisions in the early 1970s met with considerable criticism (especially from the Executive Branch of the Federal Government), the broadcasters were widely praised for their continued coverage of the series of revelations and hearings about the "Watergate" scandals and for their delicate presentation of the subsequent transition of power from the Nixon to Ford administrations in 1974.

Network television news departments have perhaps offered their finest service to the national public when the world events have swiftly triggered concrete manifestations of important issues. Networks responded with "instant specials"—consisting of partly news, partly documentary, and partly special events real-time coverage. An extreme example occurred on a single day, January 24, 1973 when special news coverage filled more than seven hours of NBC's television schedule, more than six hours of CBS's, and three and one-half hours of ABC's programming.[119] Major events that week included key steps to settlement of the Vietnam war, re-inauguration of President Richard Nixon, and the death of former President Lyndon Johnson (with attendant funeral services and state ceremonies). Estimates put that week's costs, apart from commercial losses in pre-empting commercial programs, at between $7 and $10 million for the three television networks. Swift compilation, editing, and mounting of historical footage on persons and former events, scripts, guest specialists, graphics, studio sets, crews, and newspersons—as well as AT&T long lines and other remote technical equipment, plus program schedule changes—have been marshalled by network staffs on short or no notice, often to critical acclaim. When the U.S. and Cuba broke off diplomatic relations in 1961, NBC prepared a special program on one-hour's notice; another, "Piracy in the Caribbean" was prepared in 12 hours; the networks received three-hour notice of President Nixon's announcement of a new Vice Presidential nominee; three and one-half hours elapsed between word of Nixon's significant firing of special prosecutor Archibald Cox in the Watergate inquiries and CBS's late-evening one-hour special report. A national magazine itemized some outstanding events that networks broadcast to national audiences within hours or as the events took place:

> Through the years, all three networks have done instant specials on a wide array of subjects: the deaths of world figures like De Gaulle, Churchill, Lyndon Johnson, Dag Hammarskjold, Patrice Lumumba; the inmates' revolt at Attica prison, the outbreak of the India-Pakistan war, the invasion of Cuba by anti-Castro forces, the detonation of a nuclear device in the People's Republic of China, the overthrow of Cambodia's Prince Norodom Sihanouk, the murder of Israeli athletes by Arab terrorists at the 1972 Olympic Games in Munich.[120]

And, as with the tragic death of President Kennedy a decade earlier, the national networks kept the nation informed day by day of the accelerating events in the "Watergate" exposures which suddenly climaxed in President Nixon's resignation and President Ford's assumption of executive responsibility for the nation in mid-1974.

Political Coverage

In 1952, television had its first opportunity to provide coverage of the Republican and Democratic Conventions for a mass audience. The 1948 conventions had been televised but the audience had been limited at that time and the production efforts had been minimal.

An estimated $25 million was invested by the three networks for the two weeks of coverage of the 1964 conventions. In addition, various network affiliated and independent stations covered the activities of state delegations for their home audiences. According to *Time* magazine, there were more people representing the three networks at the 1964 Republican convention (1825) than there were delegates (1308).

Pooled network coverage of the national political conventions seemed appropriate because of mounting costs of television coverage and the disappointing size of the audience. Some networks decided in recent years to continue to carry regular programming during the conventions, with "breakaway" coverage when events warranted, and with brief special programs towards the end of evening, summarizing the day's developments. Eventually, there may be a rotating system of coverage arranged by the networks themselves, as for the "Watergate" hearings in 1973 and 1974.

Starting with the Republican primaries of 1964, a new element of predicting was added to the coverage of election returns. CBS correctly predicted the winner of the New Hampshire primary just eighteen minutes after the polls were closed. NBC announced the winner of the Illinois primary fifty-five minutes sooner than either of the other networks and announced the winner of the Oregon contest twenty-two minutes ahead. CBS won by four minutes in the Maryland primary and then proceeded to name the winner of the California primary before the polls in some parts of the state had closed. Some question arose over whether such action represented responsible broadcasting. It was argued that in a close national election—the difference in time zones being a factor in the vote count—a prediction on a national broadcast could make the difference in the determination of the eventual winner. This objection seemed undercut by initial surveys about the media's effects on voters. But the issue was still under consideration, one partial solution being to keep Eastern polls open longer, with all polls closing nationally at the same "real-time" hour instead of the same clock hours.

More significant, the print media's buying of sampling and projecting services from television networks constituted a new departure in news reporting. Fred Friendly, then President of CBS News, called it "a milestone in American journalism." The sampling procedures developed by the networks became too expensive for even the largest single newspapers to duplicate, and the extrapolated figures proved highly accurate.[121] Presidential election-night coverage in 1972 cost the three television networks about $10 million; an estimated 120 million citizens viewed all or part of that single night's coverage.

Political advertising—purchased and donated—is an important factor in candidates' efforts and in broadcasters' business of serving the public. The Federal Election Campaign Act, implemented in 1972, lowered the charges that broadcasters could ask of political candidates for airtime; so figures did not rise much from the totals spent in 1968. Excluding time devoted to candidates in news programs, in 1972's primary and general elections, the political parties and candidates spent a total of $54,085,335 for broadcast announcements and program time on the nation's local commercial television and radio stations, plus $4,967,623 on commercial TV networks, plus $513,258 for commercial radio networks.[122] Additional airtime was granted at no charge to candidates that year: 18,483 hours of sustaining time or on sponsored programs were donated by local radio and TV stations; another 102 hours by TV networks, plus 53 hours by radio networks.

The Documentary

During network television's first decade, the documentary program format was considered too specialized in its appeal to be able to attract a mass audience, which may be only a way of saying assemblers of early documentaries didn't know how to do them well. The few documentaries attempted tended to prove both points. In those days, a documentary in competition with a program of pure entertainment almost always showed a discouraging rating. Sponsors, anxious to reach large audiences, considered the documentary a poor investment. The sponsors changed their opinions before the public did. By the end of 1960, there was considerable evidence of increased advertiser support for all informational programming.

Two important network decisions gave support to the growth of the documentary as an important format.[123] Both of those decisions required much courage and foresight in the light of the previous relatively undistinguished record in this kind of programming.

The first decision was to increase documentary budgets to permit more time, personnel and facilities to be devoted to their preparation. As a result, a type of program once dull and one-dimensional in its scope became exciting and as broad in treatment as it was possible to make it. Documentaries began to appear regularly in prime-time evening schedules. While their ratings still did not compare in size with the popular entertainment offerings, the size of their audiences showed as much relative growth as other kinds of programs.

The second network decision was to deal with certain controversial subjects previously judged too risky for presentation on national television. As a result, documentary units of the networks broke barriers of public sensitivity on various topics by bringing analyses into the open. Of course, Edward R. Murrow and Fred W. Friendly had pioneered this investigative reporting on substantive issues from the mid-1950s on, in the *See It Now* series on CBS-TV.[124] Some of the subjects examined on the air by network documentary units included: integration, poverty, urban development, campus morals, welfare inequities, unemployment, menopause, the population explosion, birth control, the bookies, the problems of adoption, the traffic in drugs, juvenile delinquency, abortion, cigarette smoking and cancer, and divorce. International issues were treated, including such problems as the Cuban crisis, the Berlin wall, the conflict between India and Red China, the Panama revolt, revolutions in South America and the Mid-East, the Kremlin, the Viet Nam and Laos situations, the common market and the emerging nations of Africa. Not all the documentaries dealt with serious subjects but even the lighter ones were used to inform, to broaden understanding, and to stimulate thought. Some representative subjects of this type were: the decline of royalty, the American woman, the festival frenzy, the circus, the decade of the twenties and American humor.

Documentary as well as news programs have been praised by no less a critic than then-Vice President of the United States, Spiro Agnew:

> . . . The networks . . . have often used their power constructively and creatively to awaken the public conscience. . . . The networks made "hunger" and "black lung disease" national issues . . . [and] have done what no other medium could have done in terms of dramatizing the horrors of war. . . . They focus the nation's attention on its environmental abuses. . . .[124a]

This reflects what *Broadcasting* magazine typified in local television journalism as a "quest for excellence: taking over as both voice and conscience of the community." [124b]

Sponsor and Affiliate Support

A key factor in the success story of the network news and documentary units has been their insistence on independence from sponsor control. No other network program group has been so divorced from the advertiser's advice and/or restraint in the selection and treatment of controversial subjects. In a few cases, there have been threats of cancellation. In most instances, the networks have backed their documentary producers and have announced that the programs would be shown over their facilities with or without sponsorship. They usually have had sponsorship.[125] George Norton, advertising vice president of General Telephone and Electronics, described demographic characteristics of the audience for this kind of program—attractive to sponsors of certain products, unattractive to others:

> Our research shows that news-documentary programs reach 27 per cent more professional and white-collar people than entertainment programs, 44 per cent more people with one or more years of college, 21 per cent more in the upper-income group.[126]

In spite of an increased emphasis on news and public affairs by the networks, the problem of securing the cooperation of affiliates has been most difficult. Two programs that became Peabody Award winners in 1965 were refused by many affiliated stations when they were broadcast by the networks. *Profiles in Courage* was not seen on 20 per cent of NBC's outlets; *CBS Reports* was refused by 45 per cent of the network's stations.[127] A study in the Spring of 1966, showed that substantial numbers of network-affiliated stations had not carried news programs on the war in Viet Nam.[128] Specials on February 12 of that year were broadcast by 42 per cent of the CBS stations and 30 per cent of the NBC stations. Fewer than half of the CBS stations carried a Vietnam special on February 18 while 65 per cent of the NBC stations carried a similar special the same evening. The study found that although sponsored evening newscasts may count upon affiliate acceptance, individual weekly public affairs programs are likely to be rejected or else carried on a delayed basis by a high proportion of stations.

It may be more profitable for the local station manager to schedule a local commercial showing of syndicated film in place of a network public affairs program; but it is a burdensome expense for the networks to develop these excellent offerings, and the cooperation of affiliates in carrying them should be little enough to ask. The refusal of sizeable numbers of affiliates to carry public affairs programs from the network may be a decisive factor in the reduction of the frequency of these offerings. It would seem proper for local station management to realize the valid demands made on their medium by a changing society.

THE COSTS OF NETWORK PROGRAMMING

The programs of the three networks in the prime nighttime hours alone cost millions of dollars every week. For the advertiser, the cost of the program's production and personnel is only a part of his total expense; the value of the airtime and the charges for network facilities must be added. Time and facilities charges vary with the time of day, the length of the contract, the number of stations on which the program is carried and other variables. The charges for prime time on a full network can readily exceed $150,000 an hour. Our concern in this section is not with those time and facilities charges but with the costs of various kinds of programs and the effect of these costs on program decisions. As a potential sponsor, the reader may ask himself whether he would rather buy an hour of *NBC Reports* for around $150,000 or an hour of ABC's *NFL Monday Night Football* at a figure of some $325,000 (half the game), or whether he would prefer to sponsor one of the top hour-long variety programs at a cost of $225,000 to $250,000. If the ratings were comparable, the less expensive series might at first appear to be the better purchase. However, there are other variables to consider, such as the demographic characteristics of the audiences reached, the type of program in relation to the type of advertising, the competition on the other networks at the same hour, and the prestige values of the program for the advertiser. The ideal program purchase for any advertiser is the series that comes in at the lowest budget, yet delivers the most people with the demographic characteristics the advertiser wishes to reach. This is no easy determination. Yet, this need to discover the ideal combinations is one of the reasons why commercial programming is such challenging work.

Network programming costs have risen steadily over a ten-year period averaging about 6 per cent higher each year. Color telecasting itself calls for increasing expenditures for film, photography, sets, lighting, locations and costumes. At least nine significant additional factors beyond the nation's general inflationary trend, which cause network program costs to increase are: "(1) TV's phenomenal success, which has enabled it to pay more and its suppliers to demand—and get—more; (2) the demand for increased production values; (3) unions; (4) the changing economics of programming, and especially the change in the syndication market; (5) talent agents; (6) residuals; (7) the increased reliance on film product, primarily Hollywood-produced; (8) a widespread acceptance of the inevitability of continuing price increases; and (9) show business." [129] All signs point toward further increases. The advertiser seems to expect the price to go up and the networks have yet to experience major difficulties in selling their programs.

The high costs of television programming have been a factor, however, in a shift away from program sponsorship to participation advertising whereby various commercial accounts appear within a program. Since 1960, the major amount of advertising in network television has been of the multiple-sponsor type. The trend away from single program or even alternate week sponsorship as much as anything else has made possible the use of feature film and 90- and 120-minute program forms. The costs of such programming would be prohibitive for single sponsors but by dividing the costs of the program among several participating advertisers, a feature or special of two hours or more can be sold. The A. C. Nielsen Co. tabulated the sponsorship pattern of evening specials from October 1970 to September 1974.[129a] While the number of specials has increased annually, the number having a single sponsor has remained about the same, so participating sponsorship significantly increased over the four seasons from 162 to 253:

	1970–71	*1971–72*	*1972–73*	*1973–74*
Single sponsor	94 (37%)	87 (32%)	92 (31%)	94 (27%)
Participation	162	181	208	253
TOTAL No. Specials	256	268	300	357

The enormous and continually spiraling costs for television programming—plus network stations' airtime and line charges—resulted in fewer new programs per season for a series, with re-runs occupying fully a third of the former fall-winter-spring broadcast season.[130] Traditionally, radio series had been scheduled for three sets of 13 weeks; television followed suit with 39-week seasons. Summertime was given over to re-runs and experimental programming. In the 1970s, series produced only 22 to 24 new programs, leaving more than six months of every 12 for re-runs.[131] Network cost accountants explain that the first showing of a national program does not generate enough revenue to pay all the costs (including production, payments to local stations for their airtime, to the telephone company for line charges, and to advertising agencies, plus the network's percentage for overhead). So re-runs are necessary to enable the program to produce profit. For example, a $200,000 program cannot recoup those and other costs except for the re-run, where the production cost is approximately only $30,000.[132] So great was the consternation of creative people (writers, production technicians) and unions in Hollywood, that the Federal government—through the White House Office of Telecommunications Policy—made public its criticism of the networks' oligopolistic competition that seemingly caused production costs to soar and occasioned the efficiency move to half a year of repeated programs.[133] Broadcast spokesmen countered that economics demanded such policies; and they noted that when the average network program is first broadcast, 131 million people or 86 per cent of the total potential audience do not see it, so they have another opportunity when it is rebroadcast later in the same year.[134]

Production costs of filmed and videotaped commercials have increased along with program costs. A one-minute film spot that could have been produced for $750–$1,500 in the early 1950s would cost a minimum of $4,000 today, and some budgets run higher than $25,000 per commercial.

If he who "pays the piper calls the tune," it would seem that he who "pays the piper" the higher fees will dominate the television "song-and-dance." As a matter of fact, he does!

As noted above, the networks created most of the television as we know it today and they still continue to dominate the programming of American commercial television. The public is most familiar with the various network programs because these are what most of the people see most of the time. But locally originated programs, especially in radio, and particularly local station time for spot commercials, are also critically important to total broadcast revenues. How these revenues are generated by local and national sale of time are discussed in the following chapter.

NOTES

Chapter 5

1. The Radio Code, the Code Authority, NAB, 19th ed., June 1975.

2. The Television Code, the Code Authority, NAB, 18th ed., June 1975.

3. Outlines and analyses of the program director's role in radio stations are detailed in Jay Hoffer, *Organization & Operation of Broadcast Stations* (Blue Ridge Summit, Pa., Tab Books, 1971), Chapters 2 and 3: "The Program Director" and "The PD's Staff & Public Relations," and also in Edd Routt, *The Business of Radio Broadcasting* (Blue Ridge Summit, Pa., Tab Books, 1972), pp. 169–171. See also; Sol Robinson, *Broadcast Station Operating Guide* (Blue Ridge Summit, Pa., Tab Books, 1969), pp. 125–130; and Jay Hoffer, *Managing Today's Radio Station* (Blue Ridge Summit, Pa., Tab Books, 1968), pp. 105–107.

A useful summary of the television program director's duties is provided by Edward A. Warren "Programming for the Commercial Station," in Yale Roe, *Television Station Management* (N.Y.: Hastings House, 1964), pp. 107–117; the PD must know his community, his audience, his own programming product and that of his competition, his budgets, his staff, his management, and himself (personal objectivity coupled with creativity and self-reliance).

4. Russell R. Barber, "Decisions Behind the Camera," *Journal of Broadcasting,* III:4 (Fall 1959), pp. 325; he offers a descriptive picture of the PD's work, drawn from a number of television stations.

5. "It's Back to the Tried and True for Top-40 Radio," *Broadcasting,* January 29, 1973, pp. 41–50.

6. E.g. See Richard M. Mall, "The Place of Programming Philosophy in Competitive Radio Today," *Journal of Broadcasting,* I:1 (Winter 1956–57), pp. 21–32.

7. *Ibid.,* p. 31.

8. Donald West, "On the Leading Edge of Broadcasting—Special Report: Radio '71," *Broadcasting,* June 21, 1971, pp. 41–80. This is an excellent synthesis of comments by broadcast programmers and of analysis by *Broadcasting*'s editor about trends in radio formats throughout America in the early 1970s.

9. Quoted by Mall, *Journal of Broadcasting,* p. 25.

10. Quotations are taken from West, *Broadcasting,* pp. 50, 80: Bob Smith, WOR (AM), New York City; and Hal Neal, ABC owned stations, New York.

11. See Chapter 9 on Regulation for details. Cf. "AM Thaw: Underserved Areas Get Top Priority," *Broadcasting,* Feb. 26, 1973, p. 47.

12. Barbara Salzman, "All-Channel Radio Bill: Static is Loud and Clear," *Los Angeles Times / Calendar,* Sunday, June 30, 1974, pp. 20, 81. The bill (narrowly passed by the House of Representatives, 44–42, on June 13, 1974) would require FM reception capability on all radios costing $15 or more.

13. Ernie Kreiling, "Hollywood Television Report," August 27, 1973. See also Nielsen "Newscast," 1973 (XXII:2), pp. 6–8.

14. "President's Adviser Urges More Stations," *Los Angeles Times,* September 2, 1973, Part I, p. 8; also "Whitehead Urges More TV Channels," *Los Angeles Times,* October 23, 1973, Part IV, p. 16.

15. Alexander Auerbach, "Among the Media: A 4th TV Network Wouldn't Pay Off," *Los Angeles Times,* Part VI: "Outlook: Business & Finance," January 6, 1974, pp. 6, 9.

16. Perhaps the best recently published description of these key relationships of broadcast stations to their communities can be found in Routt, *The Business of Radio Broadcasting:* Chapter 1, "The Station in the Community," pp. 15–49. He aptly distinguishes between the possibilities and realities of public service local programming in a major market as contrasted with small almost non-competitive markets.

Slightly dated only in publication date, but still intelligent and practical discussions of public service and community involvement programming are provided by: J. Leonard Reinsch and Elmo I. Ellis, *Radio Station Management,* 2nd rev. ed., (N.Y.: Harper & Row, 1960), Chapter 9: "Public Service," pp. 138–144. See also Hoffer, *Managing Today's Radio Station,* pp. 121–138. The latter emphasizes that public service must be popular and it must be mobile.

17. See: "Service Still Key to Renewal Policy," *Broadcasting,* August 23, 1971, p. 40. "Renewal Applicants: Fair Game Again?" *Broadcasting,* June 21, 1971; "Compensation to Challengers: Blackmail or Part of the Process?" *Broadcasting,* September 18, 1972; "A Spurt in the Price of Pacification: $1 Million Pledged by CapCities for Minority Programs to Scrub 'Citizen' Protests Against its Triangle Buy," *Broadcasting,* January 11, 1971.

18. Dean Burch, Address before the International Radio and Television Society Newsmakers Luncheon, New York City, September 14, 1973. (Copy from FCC, #06608) Prominent communications lawyer and former president of the Federal Communications Bar Association, Marcus Cohn, has argued strongly against any such establishment as restrictive and ultimately inhibiting; see Chapter 9 on Regulation. Acknowledging the complications in such rulemaking, FCC Chairman Burch recommended that within those limited categories percentage *ranges* should be established based on the market size and station strength (in revenue, audience, etc.); he would apply such criteria to television only, and only to VHF stations whether network affiliates or independents.

19. "The Performance of Network Affiliates in the Top-50 Markets," 264-page report, a table from which was reproduced in *Broadcasting,* July 16, 1973, pp. 46–47. Westinghouse Broadcasting's five television stations scored highest, with KPIX-TV, San Francisco (1st nationally), WJZ-TV, Baltimore, (2nd), KDKA-TV, Pittsburgh (4th), and KYW-TV, Philadelphia (5th) placing in the top five stations in the nation—according to the Johnson staff report; WBZ-TV, Boston, ranked 31st nationally. Another group's stations scored 42nd, 89th, and 125th; the owned-and-operated stations of each of the three networks ranked, respectively: ABC—13th, 76th, 102nd, 115th, and 117th; CBS—26th, 27th, 40th, 46th, and 74th; RCA[NBC]—12th, 14th, 39th, 43rd, and 116th.

20. The following points are cited by references to WPIX (TV), New York City; WIXY (AM), Cleveland; WVON (AM), Cicero/Chicago, Ill.; WNUS-AM Chicago; WCVB-TV, Needham/Boston, Mass.; WVOX-AM/FM, New Rochelle, N.Y. See "The Gallagher Report," issues of May, 1972; February 5, 1973, p. 2; and July 2, 1973, p. 3; also *BM/E* [Broadcast Management/Engineering], December 1973.

21. "Gutsy 'VOX' of New York's Westchester County Gets a Proper Home," *BM/E,* December 1973.

22. "Growing Public Interest in Community Affairs Sparks Local TV Shows," "The Gallagher Report," February 5, 1973, p. 2; "Boston's WCVB-TV Sets 51 Hours of Local Production a Week Including New Morning Strip, Six Access Series," *Variety,* August 22, 1973, p. 28; "The Happy Hookup," *Broadcasting,* June 24, 1974, p. 32.

23. Half-way measures, inadequate sampling, improper procedures, and careless handling or interpretation of data contribute nothing to the station's programming efforts nor to its responsible reporting to the FCC about its stewardship in a community; more serious than facetious is the caution to avoid half-ascertainment bungling or manipulating. Cf. Frederick W. Ford and Lee G. Lovett, "Interpreting the FCC Rules and Regulations: Ascertainment: Determining the Composition of the Community," *BM/E,* September 1973, pp. 16–18, 23.

24. Highly practical guidelines and "how-to" tips are outlined for users of public service airtime who are not fully familiar with demands, restrictions, or procedures in planning programs with little studio preparation or rehearsal time: A. William Bluem, John F. Cox, and Gene McPherson, *Television in the Public Interest: Planning, Production, Performance* (N.Y.: Hastings House, 1961).

25. TIO/Roper report 1975: 47% claimed newspapers (many of them noted both TV and newspapers) as the source of most news. The Roper Organization, Inc., "Trends in Public Attitudes Toward Television and Other Mass Media: 1959–1974," (N.Y.: Television Information Office, 1975), pp. 3–4.

26. *Broadcasting,* Nov. 29, 1971, p. 21.

27. A national survey interviewed 2,429 persons over the age of 18, between December 11 and 19, 1972, by R. H. Bruskin Associates for CBS Radio. Quoted in *Variety,* March 21, 1973, p. 60.

28. So noted by news directors and broadcast managers at a four-day seminar conducted by the International Radio and Television Society in Tarrytown, New York, February 11–15, 1974. The following comments were made at the same conference by experienced broadcasters from large and small markets.

29. The national network news operations lost money for decades, then in later years paid part of its way in television. But the network news "image" has always been an important identifying characteristic of the networks. In the duPont-Columbia School of Journalism survey for 1971–72, network news executives noted that "their product had never been harder to sell." Richard S. Salant, president of CBS News, reportedly expected his division's income to be $20 million less than the news expenditures for 1972. See the fourth annual Alfred I. duPont-Columbia University Survey of Broadcast Journalism, 1971–1972: Marvin Barrett (ed.), *The Politics of Broadcasting* (N.Y.: Thomas Y. Crowell Co., 1973; Apollo ed.), p. 90.

30. George Carpenter, Sales Manager, WHO, Des Moines, Iowa.

31. Richard Adams, News Director, Post-Newsweek stations, Washington, D.C.

32. Comments made respectively by Bob Rice, General Manager, WRAU-TV, Peoria, Ill., and George Lyons, Station Manager, WZZM-TV, Grand Rapids, Mich.

33. Quoted in "How the Vise Has Tightened on Broadcast Journalism," *Broadcasting,* February 19, 1973, p. 24.

34. Qualities of a competent news director are described in Hoffer, *Organization and Operation of Broadcast Stations,* Chapter 5, pp. 91–107.

35. *Fortune,* November 1969, p. 161, cited by Hoffer, *Ibid.,* p. 91. For some of the massive literature on bias and selectivity in broadcast media, see: Robert Cirino, *Don't Blame the People* (Los Angeles: Diversity Press, 1971); Cirino, *Power to Persuade: Mass Media and the News* (N.Y.: Bantam Books, Inc., 1974); Edith Efron, *The News Twisters* (Los Angeles: Nash Publishing, 1971).

36. RTNDA survey responses from 752 broadcast news organizations, cited in "Profile of a News Director," *Broadcasting,* December 4, 1972, p. 47.

37. VHF station average was 14, UHF stations 7; the largest news staff was 132, while seventeen TV stations reported only one fulltime news department employee, and three TV stations reported no fulltime newsmen. Irving E. Fang and Frank W. Gerval, "A Survey of Salaries and Hiring Preferences in Television News," *Journal of Broadcasting,* XV:4 (Fall 1971), pp. 426–7.

38. See Roger LeGrand (Vice President, General Manager, WITI-TV, Milwaukee), "Management—News, Public Affairs, Editorializing," *Broadcast Management* (Washington, D.C.: Association for Professional Broadcasting Education, 1973), pp. 111–118.

The debate continues whether cross-ownership among several media in the same market inhibits journalistic autonomy by undue concentration of economic and, by implication, news "power." Studies have noted that multi-media ownership tends to have a better record of locally originated programming, including news, than do separately-owned stations. See: James A. Anderson, "The Alliance of Broadcast Stations and Newspapers: the Problem of Information Control," *Journal of Broadcasting,* XVI:1 (Winter 1971–72), pp. 51–64; Paul W. Cherington, Leon V. Hirsch, and Robert Brandwein, (eds.), *Television Station Ownership: a Case Study of Federal Regulation* (N.Y.: Hastings House, 1971). Both the report and the book were prepared for and/or by broadcasters as background presentations to the FCC, with conclusions favoring the broadcast industry's status of multi-ownership by group owners and by multi-media, cross-channel owners. See: "Old Arguments, New Impetus for Action on Crossownership," *Broadcasting,* July 29, 1974, pp. 16–17. In 1975 the FCC concluded that 16 single-newspaper small markets with broadcast properties owned by those newspapers had to divest. Major markets with multiple print and broadcast companies were judged not to constitute a threat of monopoly control of media information or economics, so cross-ownership was permitted to continue; but no new acquisitions of cross-ownerships between newspapers and radio or television stations would be approved. "FCC At Last Defines Policy on Broadcast and Newspaper Ownership," *Broadcasting*, Feb. 3, 1975, pp. 23–26.

39. The enormous responsibilities coupled with exhausting detail of news gathering, editing, and reporting are reflected in many available publications, including: Reinsch and Ellis, *Radio Station Management;* Hoffer, *Managing Today's Radio Station;* Roe (ed.) *Television Station Management:* Jay Crouse, "The News Department" (Chapter 10); Irving E. Fang, *Television News*, rev. ed. (N.Y.: Hastings House, 1972); Maury Green, *Television News: Anatomy and Process* (Belmont, Cal.: Wadsworth Publishing Company, Inc., 1969).

See also analyses of specific topics such as: James K. Buckalew, "The Local Radio News Editor as a Gatekeeper," *Journal of Broadcasting*, XVIII:2 (Spring 1974), pp. 211–221; James K. Buckalew, "News Elements and Selection by Television News Editors," *Journal of Broadcasting*, XIV: 1 (Winter 1969–70), pp. 47–54; Donald S. Weinthan and Garrett J. O'Keefe, Jr., "Professionalism among Broadcast Newsmen in an Urban Area," *Journal of Broadcasting*, XVIII:2 (Spring 1974), pp. 193–209. Kaarle Nordenstreng, "A Policy of News Transmission," *Educational Broadcasting Review*, October 1971, pp. 20–30. "Special Report: Local TV Journalism's Quest for Excellence / Taking Over as Both Voice and Conscience of the Community, Station Newsmen Add a New Dimension to Traditional Reporting," *Broadcasting*, November 29, 1971, pp. 21–38.

40. So quoted in a full-page advertisement consisting entirely of McLuhan's analysis, by ABC Owned Television Stations, in *Variety*, August 25, 1971, p. 35. On July 21, 1975, the daily production log (not the official program log) for a major TV station in Detroit listed at five points during the half-hour line-up of news items the cryptic and symptomatic directive "bs," with corresponding multi-person camera shots of the on-air news team in spontaneous conversation.

41. For example, see "Broadcast News: Bending to the Times?" *Broadcasting*, October 12, 1970, pp. 56–59; "Happy News," *Time*, February 8, 1971, p. 65; Dick Adler, "The Happy Warriors of the Evening News," *TV Guide*, July 7, 1973, pp. 28–33; Richard Townley, ("How Show Biz Takes Over the News"—Two Parts), "The News Merchants," *TV Guide*, March 9, 1974, pp. 6–11, and "Who Decides What Is News?" *TV Guide*, March 16, 1974, pp. 13–17.

42. Ernie Kreiling, "Hollywood Television Report," December 31, 1973, p. 1.

43. James Johnson, "Local News and Editorials," in *Secondary Markets Television Session*, NAB Convention, March 27, 1973, (booklet of proceedings), p. 11.

44. Charles Harrison, News Manager, WGN-TV, Chicago, in panel discussion at the February 1974 Tarrytown conference conducted by the International Radio and Television Society.

45. "New(s) Deal for CBS-TV O&O's," *Variety*, January 31, 1973, pp. 39, 54. See: "Special Report-Big Changes in Local News-More Speed, More Depth, More Demands," *Broadcasting*, Aug. 19, 1974, pp. 41–78; "Electronic News Gathering-It Is Off the Launching Pad, With Full Flight Ahead," *BM/E*, Jan. 1975, pp. 34–50.

46. *Secondary Markets Television Session*, pp. 12–15.

47. That figure was cited by the House Legislative Oversight Subcommittee; quoted by Steve Millard, "Special Report: Radio at 50 An Endless Search for Infinite Variety," *Broadcasting*, October 16, 1972, p. 34.

48. See: "Interpreting the FCC Rules & Regulations: The Licensee's Programming Responsibility and Conflict of Interest," *BM/E*, December 1968, pp. 16–20. "The Gallagher Report," June 11, 1973, p. 1, noted that in business generally as well as in media, "Customers, stockholders, clients, advertisers no longer consider ignorance [by management] adequate defense. Too many top management executives deliberately shut eyes to criminal, unethical activities of second-echelon, line employees—particularly when end results 'benefit' company. . . . Entertainment industry rife with company-sponsored traffic in drugs, sex to keep performers happy."

49. In the early 1970s citizens groups in communities challenged the sale of stations or the programming policies when format changes were involved. The FCC's decision in some cases were appealed to the U.S. District Court in the District of Columbia and were judged by that court partly on the spectrum of program service available to each community's interests. Markets involved and the original and proposed formats included: Atlanta, fulltime classical music to middle of the road

(MOR); Sylvania (Toledo), Ohio, youth-oriented progressive rock to MOR; Denver, 24-hour all-news to country-and-western; Syracuse, N.Y., fulltime classical music to MOR; San Diego, classical-music to contemporary music; Phoenix, all-news to country-and-western; Cleveland, progressive rock to MOR; Chicago, classical music to contemporary music; Glendale, Calif., MOR to jazz, rhythm and blues; Jackson, Miss., MOR to black-oriented rhythm and blues (format change objected to by competing black-oriented station); Washington, D.C., all-classical to rock; Denver, all-news to country-and-western.

See *Broadcasting* magazine: "Court Asked for Basic Rule: Who Chooses the Format?" and "Another Format at Issue," August 7, 1972, pp. 18–20; "Unpredictable FCC Calls for Hearing on KFSD-FM Sale; Format Change the Key Issue," August 14, 1972, pp. 34–35; "How to Change Format and Survive Challenge," March 26, 1973, p. 94; "Format Changes: FCC Wins One, Loses One," May 7, 1973, p. 12; "FCC Gropes for Standards on Changes in Formats," May 21, 1973, pp. 45–46.

50. Useful descriptive summaries of the various kinds of formats may be found in the standard books: Reinsch and Ellis, *Radio Station Management,* pp. 51–58 and 72–90; Hoffer, *Organization and Operation* . . . , pp. 45–55; Hoffer, *Managing Today's Radio Station,* pp. 111–120 and 153–167; Robinson, *Broadcast Station Operating Guide,* pp. 73–84; Joseph S. Johnson and Kenneth K. Jones, *Modern Radio Station Practices* (Belmont, Calif.: Wadsworth, 1972), pp. 31–49; Robert L. Hilliard (ed.), *Radio Broadcasting,* 2nd ed. (N.Y.: Hastings House, 1974), pp. 108–123.

51. Hoffer, *Organization* . . . , p. 46; *Managing* . . . , p. 112.

52. "The Shape of Things in Station Formats," *Broadcasting,* June 21, 1971, pp. 76–77, citing data compiled in "Radio Programming Profile," by BF/Communication Services, Glen Head, New York. See same article for tabulated percentages of kinds of formats according to demographics, market sizes, and geographic areas, by The Pulse, Inc. in "1970 Pulse Annual Radio Review."

53. Major markets such as clothing and records depend heavily on the teenage dollar. Female teens buy 20% of women's apparel, 27% of all cosmetics, and 25% of greeting cards sold in the U.S. Male teens purchase 20–30% of all male clothing. Teens purchase 90% of all single records, 50% of all albums, 51% of all foutain drinks, 23% of all carbonated drinks, and they constitute one-half of the entire movie audience. Those figures were estimated by the Los Angeles Chamber of Commerce in 1967 in *The Dynamics of the Youth Explosion: A Look Ahead.*

54. Brand Rating Research, Inc., *Radio's All-Dimension Audience Research* [RADAR] (New York: The Company, 1968).

55. For an excellent summary history of the changing fortunes of Top-40 formats, see "It's Back to the Tried and True for Top-40 Radio," *Broadcasting,* January 29, 1973, pp. 41–54. See the earlier thorough analysis of the rebirth of radio in all its formats, by Donald West, "Special Report '71: On the Leading Edge of Broadcasting," *Broadcasting,* June 21, 1971, pp. 41–80. Cf. "Syndicated Programing's Renaissance in Radio," *Broadcasting,* Oct. 21, 1974, p. 48.

56. In the 1970s live music began to be broadcast again from clubs, recording studios, and particularly concert halls where popular rock groups performed. See "Live Music Wins Radio Fans," *Broadcasting,* January 10, 1972, pp. 62–63.

Even the national radio networks acknowledged the need for a more dynamic and current program service. The NBC Radio Network introduced two new program series—"Super Rock" (major disc jockeys interviewing rock stars and playing their records) and "Super Jam" (13 rock concerts under a single sponsor of casual clothing)—with 120 affiliated radio stations scheduling the first series and 190 affiliates the second show. "The Gallagher Report," July 22, 1974, p. 4.

A brief listing of the pros and cons of automation in radio programming may be found in Hoffer, *Managing Today's Radio Station,* pp. 101–102.

57. For example, see "Coast-to-coast Flap Over Drug Lyrics," *Broadcasting,* March 22, 1971, pp. 73–74.

58. *Broadcasting,* January 29, 1973, p. 50.

59. Figures from the Country Music Association, cited in "There's New Life in an Old Radio Art Form: Country Radio has Come to Town in a Big Way," *Broadcasting,* September 18,

1972, pp. 30–44. But the drift of traditional country music and country radio towards modern "pop," rock, and MOR sound began to concern musicians by 1975: "Is the Country Going Out of Country & Western?" *Broadcasting*, Mar. 24, 1975, pp. 47–48.

60. "Talk Radio in the Middle of America's Conversational Mainstream," *Broadcasting*, May 28, 1973, pp. 35–48.

61. "Talk Can Be as Touchy as Lyrics," *Broadcasting*, March 22, 1971, pp. 74–75.

62. "Summary—Index of Week's News," *Weekly Television Digest with Consumer Electronics*, March 26, 1973, pp. 1–2.

63. See "Growth Market in Black Radio," *Broadcasting*, January 24, 1972, pp. 16–21.

64. *Ibid.*; the *Broadcasting Yearbook 1974* listed 485 stations under its various categories of black-oriented programming; there is some overlap because stations reported portions of their schedule devoted to each of several kinds of formats.

65. Steve Millard, "Special Report: Radio at 50: An Endless Search for Infinite Variety," *Broadcasting*, October 18, 1972, p. 31.

66. "A Revealing Research Report . . . ," NAB "Highlights," August 23, 1973, pp. 1–2.

67. Ronald L. Johnstone, "Who Listens to Religious Radio Broadcasts Anymore?" *Journal of Broadcasting* XVI:1 (Winter 1971–72), pp. 91–102.

68. See "Another Scare Thrown into Underground Radio," *Broadcasting*, August 23, 1971, pp. 42–43.

69. *Ibid.*, quoting Allen B. Shaw, Jr., vice president, ABC-owned FM stations. See Johnson and Jones, pp. 57–58, for comments on systems of music selection in radio stations.

70. "Ups and Downs of Radio Drama," *Broadcasting*, June 24, 1974, pp. 26–28. See "The Gallagher Report," February 26, 1973, p. 2.

70a. These data, the tabulations below, and other data for FM in the 1970s—unless otherwise documented—are from: Rufus Crater, "Special Report: The Upbeat Tempo of FM 1974," *Broadcasting*, Oct. 7, 1974, pp. 41–43.

71. Comments respectively by Bill Drake of Drake-Chenault radio programming consultants and syndicators, and by Maurice Webster, vice president for division services of CBS Radio, in "On the Leading Edge of Broadcasting," *Broadcasting*, June 2, 1971, p. 62.

72. "The Gallagher Report," May 29, 1973, p. 2.

73. "On the Leading Edge of Broadcasting," *Broadcasting*, June 2, 1971, pp. 60–61.

74. Arbitron Radio survey, reported by *Broadcasting*, Oct. 7, 1974, p. 41; and "The Gallagher Report," June 18, 1973, p. 4.

75. "Summary of Broadcasting," *Broadcasting*, May 26, 1975, p. 55.

76. "The Real World of Program Percentages in Television Today," *Broadcasting*, December 3, 1973, pp. 26–27. The highly detailed listing offers figures for each category, with and without commercials included in the computations: news, public affairs, other non-entertainment, local including entertainment, local news, local public affairs, local other non-entertainment, and various combinations of those categories.

77. See "The Stuff of Which 'Substantial Service' is Made," *Broadcasting*, December 3, 1973, pp. 26–27.

78. Cherington, Hirsch, and Brandwein (eds.), *Television Station Ownership: A Case Study of Federal Agency Regulation*, p. 105. See also George H. Litwin, William H. Wroth, and Neil M. Moss, "The Effects of Common Ownership on Media Content and Influence," booklet published by National Association of Broadcasters, 1969.

79. See *ibid.*, p. 115.

80. Les Brown, *Televi$ion: The Business Behind the Box* (N.Y.: Harcourt, Brace, Jovanovich, Inc., 1971), p. 178.

81. Richard B. Rawls, "The Independent Station," in Roe (ed.), *Television Station Management*, p. 74.

82. Robert Mortensen, quoted in *Television*, August 1961, p. 110.

83. "Boston's WCVB-TV Sets 51 Hours of Local Production a Week Including New Morning Strip, Six Access Series," *Variety*, September 22, 1973, p. 28.

84. "The Happy Hookup," *Broadcasting,* June 24, 1974, p. 32. That figure translated to about 60,000 homes, or a rating of 4. In mid-1974 the 14 commercial minutes in the 90-minute program were sold as 28 half-minute spots for $100 each, thus generating $2,800 daily when all availabilities were sold.

85. "High Mortality of TV Talkshows," *Variety,* February 28, 1973, p. 48. Not included in the compilation were talk programs running longer than the five-year survey period (Jan. 1, 1967, to Jan. 1, 1973), or whose principal performer changed in those five years. Programs originated at WLWD-TV, Dayton; KDKA-TV, Pittsburgh; KTVH, Wichita; WNEW-TV, New York; WSBK, Boston; KHJ-TV, Los Angeles; WCAU-TV, Philadelphia; WJXT, Jacksonville; and WLS-TV, Chicago. It is noteworthy that six stations were group-owned—Avco, Group W (Westinghouse), Metromedia, Storer, RKO General and Post-Newsweek Stations; two were network-owned (ABC and CBS); and one was 100% owned by a newspaper (*Minneapolis Star and Tribune*).

86. "Television for Children: There's More than May Meet the Eye," *Broadcasting,* November 20, 1972, pp. 31–46; "NAB Caving Under Pressure to Restrict Children's Ads," *Broadcasting,* July 1, 1974, pp. 20–21; that "pressure" was reflected in public statements by commissioners of both the FCC and FTC. See "NAB's TV Board, by 8-to-4 Vote, Ratifies Code's Restrictions on Children's Ads," *Broadcasting,* July 8, 1974, p. 24.

87. "The Gallagher Report," August 21, 1972, pp. 2–3.

88. "ABC O&O's Peg Kidvid Anthology (Mag & Dramas) To Sun. Family Slot," *Variety,* August 15, 1973, p. 24.

89. Neil Hickey, "Skipper Chuck and Bucksin Bill Are Not Feeling Very Jolly: the Stars of Local Children's Shows Fear They Are Facing Extinction," *TV Guide,* June 2, 1973, pp. 4–9.

89a. "TV News: Still Growing," *Variety,* Mar. 5, 1975, p. 52; citing Marvin Barrett (ed.), *Moments of Truth?* (N.Y.: Thomas Y. Crowell Co., 1975), the fifth annual Alfred I. duPont-Columbia University survey of broadcast journalism.

90. On the need for creative, responsive and responsible local public affairs programming, see Kenneth A. Cox, "Broadcasters as Revolutionaries," *Television Quarterly,* VI (Winter 1967), pp. 13–20; reprinted by John H. Pennybacker and Waldo W. Braden (eds.), *Broadcasting and the Public Interest* (N.Y.: Random House, 1969), pp. 57–64.

91. For a descriptive analysis of the commercial stations' broadcast day, see Edward A. Warren, "Programming for the Commercial Station," in Roe (ed.), *Television Station Management,* pp. 112–116. Cf. also in the same volume Milton D. Friedland, "The Network-Affiliated Station," pp. 57–60, on programming.

92. Trade and other press headlines reflected the developing fortunes of the FCC's prime-time access rule: "Access Time & 'Network Quality'," *Variety,* October 27, 1971, p. 42. "The FCC's Glorious Dream Is Turning into a Nightmare," *TV Guide,* February 12, 1972, pp. 6–10. "CBS's Bob Wood Assails Anti-Rerun Campaign, Says Prime-Access Rule Abetted Job Crisis in Hollywood," *Variety,* September 13, 1972, p. 37. "F.C.C. Orders Rules Into Effect to Bar Syndication by Networks," *New York Times,* June 9, 1972, p. 15. "Key-Time Access: Ups & Downs," *Variety,* February 9, 1972, p. 39. "[FCC Chairman] Dean Burch Writes Off Access Rule as Failure," *Broadcasting,* January 15, 1973, pp. 19–20. "Major Producers Say FCC Plan Backfired," *Broadcasting,* January 15, 1973, p. 20. "A Dramatic About Face on FCC's Prime-time Access Rule," *Broadcasting,* February 19, 1973, pp. 20–22 (National Association of Television Program Executives informally voted 32.9% in favor of rule, 24.4% for revocation, and 42.7% for continuation of the rule but revised in one or more ways). "Demographic Breakdown of Poll on Access Rule Shows Variances," *Variety,* February 28, 1973, p. 48: reporting that in the top 50 markets, 75% of stations noted improved profits, 4% noted losses, and 21% said profits were the same; in stations in under-top-50 markets, 65% of stations profited more, 3% claimed losses; producers and distributors claimed that the access rule improved profit (49%) or no change (40%), while 10% attributed losses from the rule. "Viacom, MPC [Metromedia Producers Corp.] Urge FCC to Keep Prime-time Rule," *Broadcasting,* June 11, 1973, p. 29. "Group W Asserts Gut Issues Forgotten on Prime-time Access," *Broadcasting,* July 2, 1973, p. 41. "TV Rule: Point of No Return: Primetime Access Taken as Industry Norm," *Variety,* August 15, 1973, p. 1. "New

Access Rule [FCC's softening original rule] Costs Stations $40-Mil," *Variety*, May 22, 1974, p. 39. "Court Stays Access to Sept. '75, Remands Hot Case Back to FCC," *Variety*, June 19, 1974, p. 1. "Oh, What Tangled Webs Court Weave: Programs Shift, Sales Re-sold," *Variety*, June 26, 1974, p. 35.

   93. Cox, "Broadcasters as Revolutionaries," in Pennybacker and Braden (eds.), *Broadcasting and the Public Interest*, pp. 61–62.

   94. For practical details of local studio program production procedures, see Colby Lewis, "Production Management," in Roe (ed.), *Television Station Management*, pp. 123–142.

   95. Brown, *Televi$ion: The Business Behind the Box*, pp. 174–175.

   96. *Broadcasting*, January 3, 1966, p. 29.

   97. Electronics Industry Association figures, tabulated in *Broadcasting Yearbook 1974*, p. 73. These were cumulative totals, representing all U.S. *sales* of domestic and imported color receivers through two decades—not the number of color sets actually in service in the final year 1972.

   98. "Why Webs Love Cop Shows," *Variety*, July 4, 1973, p. 37.

   99. "By Anybody's Definition It's Every Night at the Movies," *Broadcasting*, January 15, 1973, p. 36.

   100. "Season Standings Reflect Strong CBS Position," *Broadcasting*, June 10, 1974, pp. 28–29.

   101. Robert D. Wood, "The Decision-Making Process in Television," address to Graduate School of Business, University of Southern California, November 23, 1970 (booklet published by CBS Television Network), pp. 7–9.

   102. See Brown, *Televi$ion: The Business Behind the Box*, pp. 125–128; also Alexander Kendrick, *Prime Time: The Life of Edward R. Murrow* (N.Y.: Little, Brown, 1969), p. 29.

   103. "Primetime Specials Ratings for 1971–72 Season," *Variety*, September 13, 1972; pp. 64–68.

   104. "1972–73 Primetime Special Ratings," *Variety*, June 13, 1973, p. 36.

   105. Charles Champlin, "A Topical Oasis in the TV Wasteland," *Los Angeles Times / Calendar*, February 17, 1974, pp. 1, 57.

   106. Dwight Whitney, "Cinema's Stepchild Grows Up," *TV Guide* July 20, 1974, pp. 21–26.

   107. "TV Development Plot for '73–'74," *Variety*, September 13, 1972, p. 37.

   107a. "Scorecard on Program Development for the 1975–76 Season," *Broadcasting*, Feb. 24, 1975, pp. 27–34.

   108. See Les Brown, pp. 131–137.

   109. "Tracking Syndication's Two-Year Olds" and "Last Fall's New Syndie Entries," *Variety*, February 28, 1973, p. 38.

   110. The 1970s saw a possible trend back to advertising agency impact on program production—as had been the pattern in radio's heyday. Some agencies oversee production of daytime soap operas such as *As the World Turns* on CBS. J. Walter Thompson advertising agency in the 1974–75 season was responsible for 30 one-hour specials, each supported by a single sponsor; several of those specials were in series of six. That agency was also in partnership with Survival Anglia Ltd. which prepared 16 projects for the 1975–76 season, including feature films for theatrical release. See "JWT: One Ad Agency That is Deeply Into TV Programming," *Variety*, August 7, 1974, p. 29. The William Morris agency—three-quarters of a century representing "talent" including actors, directors, and other negotiation—branched into packaging television programs. In the mid-1960s it prepared 22 package shows, many of which continue to run in syndication. For the 1974–75 season it negotiated 21 pilots for the networks, and it sold as series five new programs. See Peter Greenberg, "Good Things Come in Big Packages," *TV Guide*, July 27, 1974, pp. 4–7.

   111. "The Bounds of Barter Are Hard to Find," and "The Barter Business and Its Backers As They Stand in '74," *Broadcasting*, May 6, 1974, pp. 22–27.

   112. Melvin Durslag, "Harley Smydlapp Is on the Air," *TV Guide*, December 4, 1971, pp. 23–25.

113. Ross Drake, "Those Quarterbacks Downstairs," *TV Guide,* January 8, 1972, pp. 27–30.

114. "NFL's '74 Tab to Networks Up $9 Million," *Broadcasting,* May 6, 1974, pp. 38–39.

115. Major emphasis on baseball comes with day-to-day radio and television coverage of local teams by metropolitan stations, often linked to outlying towns' broadcast stations. In 1973 American League broadcasting rights for 12 baseball clubs went for $10,825,000; and National League rights for its 12 teams' coverage cost $13,560,000.

116. "From Triumph to Tragedy in TV Coverage of Munich Olympics," *Broadcasting,* September 11, 1972, pp. 22–23; see also "Fortuitous Fallout," *Broadcasting,* September 4, 1972, p. 5.

117. "Olympics May Draw Biggest Worldwide Audience Ever—and There'll Be Plenty to See," *Broadcasting,* August 21, 1972, p. 29. Despite its million-dollar deficit for the Munich Olympics, ABC signed a $25 million contract to telecast the 1976 Olympic Games.

118. "Apollo 17 Marks End of Space-age TV Series," *Broadcasting,* December 11, 1972, pp. 15–16.

119. "Great Events in Wild Week Test TV News," *Broadcasting,* January 29, 1973, pp. 17–18; "How Radio Journalists Handled Rush of Stories," p. 18.

120. Neil Hickey, "They're Off and Running," *TV Guide,* June 15, 1974, pp. 30–32.

121. During the decade after the 1962 elections, NBC News projected about 1,600 political "wins/losses" and was wrong only four times. Neil Hickey, "A Ripsnorting TV Evening for 120 Million Viewers," *TV Guide,* November 4, 1972, pp. 8–12.

122. "Political Advertising Leveled Off in 1972," *Broadcasting Yearbook 1974,* p. 78. Figures here do not include time on public broadcast stations and networks nor on cable television systems.

123. For a history and analysis of this format, see A. William Bluem, *Documentary in American Television: Form, Function, Method* (N.Y.: Hastings House, 1965).

124. For chronological description of the evolution of the Murrow-Friendly relationship and television documentaries, see Erik Barnouw, *The Image Empire* (N.Y.: Oxford University Press, 1970), pp. 45–56.

124a. Quoted by Frank Tippett, "Is the Truth Incredible?" *Look,* Sept. 7, 1971, pp. 46–49.

124b. "Special Report: Local TV Journalism's Quest for Excellence," *Broadcasting,* Nov. 29, 1971, p. 21.

125. An excellent summary description of documentaries in the context of networks and advertisers can be found in Brown, *Televi$ion: The Business Behind the Box,* pp. 196–203 and Barnouw, *The Image Empire,* pp. 157–160, 177–178, 181–185, 224–227. See also the classic analysis of the network documentarian's work in Fred W. Friendly, *Due to Circumstances Beyond Our Control . . .* (N.Y.: Random House, 1967); also Kendrick, *Prime Time: The Life of Edward R. Murrow.* Fred Friendly wrote a detailed analysis of one documentary that brought grief to CBS: "Television: the Unselling of *The Selling of the Pentagon,*" *Harper's Magazine,* June 1971, pp. 30–37. The efforts of a creative, investigative documentarian are recounted by David G. Yellin, *Special: Fred Freed and the Television Documentary* (N.Y.: Macmillan, 1972).

126. Quoted in *TV Guide,* February 26, 1966, p. 2.

127. *Time,* May 7, 1965, p. 61.

128. *Broadcasting,* June 20, 1966, p. 63.

129. *Television,* September 1961, p. 39.

129a. A. C. Nielsen Co., "Nielsen Newscast," No. 3, 1974, p. 14.

130. In 1973 the average half-hour entertainment program cost about $100,000. Where that $100,000 was distributed was itemized in "TV Costs: Dough-Re-Mi-Farther," *Variety,* September 12, 1973, p. 47. For a half-hour program costing $110,000 to produce, $56,000 typically went to "above the line" costs, including writer, producers, director, performers, and union benefits; another $41,500 went to "below the line" costs, including production staff, sets, equipment,

music, laboratory fees, etc.; and the final $19,500 went for technical facilities, plus promotion, administration, and testing.

131. See "The Realities of Reruns in Network TV," *Broadcasting*, October 2, 1972, pp. 15–16.

132. Bill Davidson, "Again and Again and Again . . . ," *TV Guide*, June 9, 1973, pp. 6–13. Although the networks had to abandon syndication of their product in the U.S., they still earn considerable return on their investments by foreign distribution of television programs, especially movie forms; see "Global Prices for Films on TV," *Variety*, January 5, 1972, p. 90. Distribution rates for half-hour episodes and for feature films are cited for 78 countries on all continents; 30-minute series earn from $20 each (El Salvador) to $3,500–$4,200 (United Kingdom).

133. "The President Takes Sides Against Network Reruns," *Broadcasting*, September 18, 1972, pp. 12–14; and "OTP Study Blames Network Rivalry for Excessive Reruns," *Broadcasting*, February 5, 1973, pp. 42–44.

134. Notably articulate in defense of the networks' policy on reruns was CBS Television Network president Robert D. Wood; see "The Wood Manifesto: Limiting Reruns Is a Cockeyed Idea, Runs Counter to Economic Realities and Viewer Needs," *Broadcasting*, September 18, 1972, p. 14.

6

Broadcast Sales

That has been one of the favorite subjects of radio's critics, ever since the medium's beginnings: that the entire mysterious process, the curious appeal of that sound, is placed in the service of commerce. American radio is a marketing tool; love it, live with it, analyze it, the whole bloody sound is there to move goods off the shelf. Broadcasters do not 'admit' this charge; that would be like admitting that Tuesday follows Monday. . . . 'And anyone in this business who isn't sales-oriented is in trouble.'

—STEVE MILLARD, *Broadcasting* [1]

SINCE 1922, when WEAF in New York broadcast the first advertising message as a source of revenue for operating the electromagnetic service, commercials have increasingly paid the way for radio and then for television. From that time, the broadcast industry has been supported, not by income from selling receivers (as originally conceived by the Radio Corporation of America), nor by subscription fees to listeners (as cable and pay television), nor by a governmental tax on receiver purchase or on annual use of a receiver (as in many countries today); instead, broadcast revenue has come from businesses that wanted to reach consumers for their products and services and so paid a "toll" to have their messages broadcast to the public. The public and the Federal government, as well as broadcasters themselves and the business community, have endorsed this system of advertising-supported broadcasting.[2] Despite criticism of this orientation toward the commercial marketplace, the general audience over the decades has continued to accept the basic structure of American commercial radio and television.[3]

In other chapters of this book are discussed management's important concerns for the programming and engineering departments. But neither of those departments could operate in a commercial station or network were it not for the contributions of the sales department. This branch of the broadcasting entity produces the revenue that pays for all of the station's and network's activities

242

and, through good management, makes a profit for the owners of the broadcast company.

A. THE SALES STAFF

The sales department is the station's principal contact with people in the world of business. Given a strong radio or television station in a community, the sales force can provide a needed service for merchants and institutional advertisers. Those businessmen depend upon mass communications media to reach people in order to inform as many as possible about products and services available. Few business enterprises question the values of advertising. Their corporate concerns are which media to use and which specific offerings of each of the media will most effectively reach present and potential customers.

All of the station's initial efforts, then, must be in the direction of building technical and programming assets to the point of promising excellent returns for the business community. It follows that it is vital that the sales representatives of the station be selected with care. A good station can become better with good salesmen! Good salesmen can become even better by working under good sales managers!

Sales as a Career

The number of salesmen per radio station is, on the average, less than the number employed by a television station; but the income for a salesman of local advertising, whether in radio or television, can be attractively high. The sales department offers higher individual incomes than any of the other departments of a station, except for top on-air performers. And sales experience in broadcasting is the most usual route to station management.

Certain definite advantages pertain to a choice of sales as a career: (1) In any industry, comparable grades of professional status are usually better paid in sales than in any other department; (2) the work of the salesman brings constantly changing challenges; (3) the opportunities to learn human nature are boundless; (4) the good salesman has little worry about a job since there are always more positions open in sales than in most lines of endeavor; and (5) the man who travels about meeting other people learns of opportunities that never come to the attention of the person who works with the same people day after day.

In spite of both immediate and long-range opportunities in sales, it is more difficult to find good salesmen than it is to find most other kinds of broadcasting personnel. Usually, there is a surplus of applicants for most other station positions, but almost always a scarcity of people who want to sell. With the opportunities in sales, the field should have greater appeal than it has.

All of this should suggest advantages in choosing a sales career by young persons with college experience. In radio-television, there are plenty of openings for the right people and there should be many opportunities for advancement. Stress is put on the "right people" because nothing can be worse than frustrations experienced in this field by those who are not naturally inclined toward a sales career. No one should ever go into sales work motivated exclusively by the monetary rewards. He must *like to sell* or he will be a failure before he starts.

QUALIFICATIONS AND FUNCTIONS OF THE SALES MANAGER

The ideal sales manager is one who has had experience not only as a salesman but in other phases of broadcasting as well. Since it is his function to market the station's product, the more he knows about the total station operation the better he is able to design the various commercial campaigns to achieve maximal results.[4]

He should be fully aware of the strengths and weaknesses of all communication media—newspapers, magazines, supplements, direct mail, billboards and other forms of advertising. With this knowledge he can study the competitive offerings of other media as well as those of other radio or television stations, and he can determine how his station can achieve leadership over that competition by providing better service.

The ability to analyze media includes a sensitivity for the values of research. A good sales manager should be able to raise significant questions for station research personnel to answer. His examination of data obtained from audience and marketing studies should suggest many sales approaches that he can recommend to his staff.

The sales manager needs to be experienced in marketing and retailing. With an understanding of each advertiser's particular problems and objectives, he should be able to make constructive suggestions toward building their business volume. Sometimes those recommendations may be unrelated to an advertising campaign. Confidence in his business acumen will cause merchandisers to place sizeable amounts of their advertising budgets with his station.

As manager of the station's prime income-producing department, he must be aware of station expenses. A good sales manager is as proficient in controlling cost items as he is in producing income. He knows how to keep expense accounts and general costs in line without diminishing the quantity and quality of sales.

He must be adept at sales analysis, able to use tools and procedures of budgeting, projecting, evaluating performance, pricing, inventory control, and research.[5]

The sales manager must be willing to join his salesmen on the street and to work with them in conceiving and making presentations to clients and their agencies. He must have the poise, together with the aggressiveness, to gain true respect from men who are successful salesmen themselves.

As an administrator, the sales manager needs to be a good organizer. He must have the ability and the inclination to delegate most of the routine paper work to capable assistants. The time he saves may then be devoted to the main functions of his position. These are (1) overseeing the sales staff; (2) directing the station's local sales, service, and sales development; (3) coordinating network and/or agency accounts carried on the station; and (4) maintaining contacts with the station's national and/or regional representative.

SELECTION OF A STATION SALES STAFF

In view of the perennial need for apt candidates for sales work, one of the most difficult tasks of the sales manager is to find and select people for new or replacement positions on his staff.[6] The responsibility is doubly important because wrong choices can be extremely costly. Beyond the time, effort and money needed to train new staff salesmen, the losses to the station caused by dissatisfied clients or by broken contracts are as large as they are difficult to estimate. Employing good salesmen can result in higher income for the station and excellent relationships with clients.

Since promising sales candidates are in short supply, the selection process should not be conducted haphazardly. Personnel people agree that the essentials in selection are: (1) a well defined job analysis in writing; (2) some valid testing procedures and (3) a good, intensive interview. The tendancy to employ on the basis of any single convincing physical, mental or personality trait should be avoided.

Before hiring any experienced salesman, his past record should be given prime consideration. If he has been successful in sales in the past, the chances are that he will be successful in the future; if he has been a consistent failure in the past, the odds against his success are usually too great for a canny gamble. A successful sales record in a field other than broadcasting may or may not be an indication of potential success in radio or television. If the man has been successful in selling intangibles, his chances of doing well in broadcasting may be better than one who has sold tangible merchandise. Any change to broadcasting from sales experience in a different field will require a considerable amount of time for indoctrination and adjustment.

The inexperienced person should not be ruled out as a possibility. This would be a foolish rejection of some people who have excellent long-range potentials. These people need to be given careful training and supervision. They should not be expected to produce significant results for some time after their initial employment. Given the patience, encouragement and understanding they should have, they can develop into some of the best salesmen the station can employ. Most of them will be highly appreciative of the time devoted to their development, and this will be shown in the amount of business they will later produce. It should be recalled that the most successful salesmen once had to be given that initial start by someone.

The interviewer should look for evidences of an extroverted personality, a high degree of intelligence, a gregarious nature, signs of perseverance, an ability to get along with people, a good appearance, correct manners, sincerity, a true interest in sales and, frankly, a strong desire to make money.

Two researchers, Charles F. Haner and Givens L. Thornton, were intrigued by the problem of trying to discover what behavior traits seemed to distinguish successful from unsuccessful salesmen with four medium-sized companies.[7] While their findings might or might not apply in the case of radio and television salesmen, there could be a strong possibility of an important carry-over. Haner and Thornton found that, of several hundred behavior traits analyzed, the most important in distinguishing between good and poor salesmen was the willingness of the salesman to study the needs of the customer on a careful and detailed basis. The next most important trait was the ability of the salesman to set goals and quotas for himself which he was willing to follow. Other factors, in order of their importance were: keeping the customers informed, persistence, analysis of the sales effort, knowledge of the competition, keeping the company informed, and coverage of the territory. Those factors *least* valuable in distinguishing between the good and the poor salesman were: social activities, drinking habits, personal traits, home life and group activities. In summary, job-oriented behavior traits were of highest importance; personal and social traits were of lesser importance.

The truly effective, truly successful salesman in broadcasting is the one who, after convincing his clients to use his station's facilities, follows through and makes sure that sales results happen which please the clients. Nothing is more desirable in sales than long-term relationships between salesman and client.

THE SALES MANAGER AND THE SALES STAFF

Bases for Assigning Salesman's Accounts

Several factors need to be considered before assigning a salesman to the local accounts on his list. His knowledge of certain retailer's stores, his understanding of the particular problems of a specific kind of business, and his previous experience in dealing with certain types of retailers are all important considerations. Most important, though, is the probability of compatible relationships between the salesman and the accounts. The sales manager needs to use his best judgment in the matching of salesman and client according to their temperaments, their interests and their probable general rapport. The compatibility of the salesman should be a major factor in determining how long he remains assigned to each accout.

Choice station accounts are usually assigned on a basis of either seniority or successful sales experience. A younger, less experienced member of the station sales staff should be prepared to build his initial list into lucrative accounts by providing excellent service to his clients after they are sold. Accounts, of course, should not be transferred once a good relationship has been established, unless there is no alternative.

It takes a good salesman, with plenty of patience and a thorough training in radio or television, to get on a conversational basis with many of the people who are assigned advertising and buying positions with retail establishments.

Some store buyers and advertising managers seem to favor the print media almost exclusively; unfortunately for the salesman of broadcasting, retail management listens to those buyers and advertising managers.

Radio-television salesmen assigned to such contacts should have backgrounds of experience or training in retailing as well as in broadcast media. They need to be able to talk the language of those who are engaged in every conceivable category of retail sales. Here a lack of merchandising know-how can be disastrous. It has been estimated that not one salesman in ten can qualify for selling the typical resistant retail establishment because the typical broadcast-media man cannot talk with the retailer intelligently about his particular business and suggest solutions for his more important problems. Nor do more than a few broadcasters understand any media except broadcasting.

Store managers, as well as buyers and advertising managers, feel comfortable with the printed ad. They can look at it, admire it and show it to their co-op people. It is tangible; broadcasting is not. The salesman will not make headway with these men by attacking their use of the print media. There is no profit in denunciation and derogation. Radio and television are so strong and have such an enviable success record in advertising for all categories of retailers that the "positive sell" is the only route to take. Broadcasters must acknowledge that newspapers will always be the basic buys for some retailers because of the nature of their fields. But these same retailers can gain much additional business through their intelligent supplementary use of radio and television.

It is the place of the broadcast salesman to make the client feel comfortable in the presence of *his* kind of advertising and to show how profits can be made from its use. It is his job to bring them to an open mind about radio and/or television.

Staff Sales Conferences and Reports

The sales manager should hold daily sales conferences with the members of his sales staff. Early each morning he should meet with them to check their contacts of the preceding day. In these meetings, strategies may be worked out for that day corresponding to time availabilities in the commercial schedule.

Each Monday morning, the sales manager should get individual reports from his salesmen that recapitulate their activities and reflect their work of the previous week. On the basis of these reports, the sales manager is able to spot troublesome cases where it may be advisable for him to assist a salesman with the client. Sometimes, in cases where on-air talent is involved in a potential sale, the sales manager may decide that a follow-up presentation involving the participation of that talent may help a salesman to conclude a sale.

At least four times each year, half-day or day-long meetings should be held, perhaps on week-ends, to engage in long-range planning. Representatives of the program department and the station "rep" should attend these sessions along with the sales staff. Outside consultants may also be included. Topics for major meetings (as well as for weekly, even daily general sessions) include, according to Jay Hoffer: sales policies, rate card, special events packages, client list (present, new, and potential), sales aids, oral sales presentations by staff members, internal station procedures that affect the sales operation, programming developments, a review of commercial copy style, and sales service and client cooperation.[8]

The sales manager should keep in his office records of each salesman's performance with his clients and with the agencies to which he is assigned. Regular reports of progress should be prepared for the station manager. These are not, it should be added, exercises in paperwork; they are supplements to and supports for brainwork.

Sales Quotas

It is the sales manager's responsibility to set sales quotas. By making realistic evaluations of each salesman's list of clients and/or agencies, he can establish proper quotas. He cannot, however, make them rigid expectations.

Many of the advertising budgets of the large retailers, particularly the department stores and the supermarkets, emphasize print media almost exclusively. These retail stores run page after page of newspaper advertisements every day, while they settle for a few spot commercials in radio and television. How can the local station increase its share of that retail advertising? What kind of work, determination, enterprise and imagination does it take?

It is imperative that a radio or television station's story be supplied to the station's "rep" in order to increase the chances of attracting the investments of national and regional advertisers. That same story, with chapters regularly updated, should be used as a selling tool for the local advertiser.

The station's master sales plan should consist of basic information about the station's circulation strength, its image in the community and within the industry, and its success stories. The sales plan should include descriptions of the facilities and special equipment which enable the station to perform its services efficiently. It should relate, in detail, the program and production repertory of the station, including whatever live talent is available and, in the case of television, the film library. It should mention whatever merchandising services are provided. Added to this general sales material, the sales plan should include special applications designed specifically for each individual advertiser.

In local sales, the data are used differently than for national sales. Locally, the contacts are more direct and personal. Very few negotiations are closed over the telephone. Local selling involves salesmen calling on men whom they have contacted many times before. Tailor-made presentations and specially constructed commercials or programs must be designed to meet special needs of specific merchants.

The local salesman in radio or television used to rely simply on his media's inherent effectiveness to make good on his promises to the retailer. Today's salesman knows that there is no magic in a broadcast campaign unless it is targeted to a particular client's needs and objectives. The modern salesman becomes as interested in helping the advertiser to grow and prosper as he is in gaining his commission from his sales efforts. In a way, the modern broadcast salesman works as much for his clients as he does for his station.

If he is truly informed about retailing, he should be able to make suggestions that will favorably surprise the merchant and make the salesman's counsel so valuable that the businessman will come to depend upon him for ideas. The retail-oriented salesman will know that the on-air advertising he can supply will be successful only if the store is modern in its services, its facilities, and its customer conveniences. The salesman should be able to show the retailer how to accomplish that modernization.

So the station's local sales representatives, its salesmen, must be experts in helping the retailer to grow. The advertising on radio or television is but one service which the salesman provides.

ANNOUNCER-SALESMAN COMBINATIONS

Announcer-salesman combinations can be effective in small markets. In fact, they are employed in some of the larger cities of the nation but the announcers (or other talent) do not usually bear the combination title. Even a neophyte as an announcer in a small town is somewhat of a celebrity within the coverage area of his station. He becomes a familiar name in homes throughout the trade area. Small-town merchants, especially those new to the use of radio and television, are frequently motivated more rapidly by sales visits from announcers than from other members of the selling staff because they are better known in the community.

Many small stations can offer a retailer only a modest amount of assistance in continuity and production. Once an announcer who doubles in sales gets to know a client very well, he can be entrusted with writing and producing that client's commercials and servicing the account.

Announcers who sell should visit their clients' stores often in order to become thoroughly acquainted with the merchandise and service. Then they can be true sales representatives of the stores when they present the commercials over the air. The announcer-salesman can be useful, too, in store promotions.

LEGITIMATE COMPLAINTS OF SALESMEN

A salesman has a legitimate complaint when availability schedules are not ready, when his client's copy is revised without his knowledge, when the rating reports are not delivered on time. Such procedures can be costly to him in sales commissions and reputation.

An efficient broadcasting organization must have complete cooperation between sales and continuity-acceptance units. The latter office should be instructed never to contact a client or an agency, local or national, without first clearing with the salesman on the account and with the sales manager. There is nothing more disturbing to a salesman than to discover that other people at the station have established relationships with one of his clients without his knowledge. Such action causes confusion, ill will, and eventually results in inept handling of the account.

Another legitimate complaint of salesmen is the implementation of new corporate sales policy without their prior knowledge. Policy changes affecting the sales department should be made only after each of the salesmen has been consulted.

Salesmen also have legitimate cause for complaint when people in other departments of the station show little if any interest in the work of the sales staff. The station manager must make sure that every employee understands how sales are made and how accounts are kept or lost.

Compensation Plans for Salesmen

Salesmen, unlike sales managers, are not usually paid on a straight salary basis. Most stations use a method of salary-plus-commission for their compensation.[9] The next most widely used method is the straight commission plan. Market size does not seem to be a factor in the choice of compensation systems for station salesmen. Most commissions are paid after billings. A few are paid after a logged account is aired. Some are not paid until after collections.

B. Time Selling

The sales manager must oversee his sales staff's efforts and evaluate their performance in selling the station's commercial time. By private conversation with salesmen, informal discussion with staff members, general sales department meetings, memoranda, and by forwarding printed materials (reports, statistical data, sales success stories, tips on selling techniques, etc.), he can motivate and support his salesmen's efforts to sell successfully.

The Salesman's Preparation for the Sale

Before a presentation is made to any local retailer, the salesman should make a study of that firm's past and current experiences in all forms of advertising and of its business successes in general. He should study carefully the field in which the retailer does business so that he will be able to discuss intelligently the prospective advertiser's interests and problems.

Such study will disclose, for example, that the problems of the owner of a shoe store are completely different from those of the owner of a jewelry store, say, in the month of April. The salesman will discover what the peak business months in the year are for such other enterprises as grocery stores, hardware stores and drugstores. He must know seasonal fluctuations that differ within various retail categories if he is to make the right sales calls at the right times.

In order to talk to the point in his presentation, the salesman needs to know the retailing methods of any specific client, including patterns of store traffic, uses of merchandise displays, the personalities of store clerks, the conveniences and services of the store and the kinds and quality of merchandise sold.

The basis of all effective selling to local retailers is complete information about each specific prospect or client and his business. No one, regardless of his background or experience, can be fully effective without pertinent knowledge. Studies of local retail establishments should include research into other local retail firms and those in other markets in the same category. For example, in the case of men's clothing stores, the salesman needs to know the problems of a particular store but he also needs to be thoroughly familiar with the men's clothing industry. A salesman calling on a men's-wear establishment should be well acquainted with the current ads in such publications as *Gentleman's Quarterly, Esquire, Playboy,* and the leading sports publications. Additionally, he should study the trade publications in the men's-wear field. Such sources of information exist for every kind of retail establishment and they are available in most large libraries.

Most radio and television salesmen have not taken the time to do their homework in the various trade publications of each retail category or they haven't known how to make that preparation. The more a salesman for radio or television knows about a retailer and his particular business category, the more successful he can be in helping to move his merchandise. This must be the first objective of any good radio or television salesman.

One of many reasons why radio and television stations have not garnered their fair share of department store advertising is that their salesmen have not understood the advanced planning of store buyers, merchandisers and advertising personnel. Time and time again, stations have spent vast sums of money for elaborate presentations to department stores six or eight weeks before the Christmas shopping season. The advertising budget for those particular stores probably were established in the first quarter of the year, if not early in the last quarter of the previous year. Advertising plans in most department stores and in many retail establishments are finalized six months or more in advance of their actual campaigns. This is especially true in the case of seasonal types of advertising where certain lines of merchandise have a consumer demand for a brief period of time. If the salesman from the station makes his calls after the advertising budget has been allocated for the year he simply wastes his time. Incidentally, some long-term business relationships between broadcasters and retailers have been formed by salesmen who anticipated store decisions on seasonal merchandise. The success of initial short-term contracts has resulted in year-round broadcast advertising by those stores.

Every retailer who is engaged in a bona-fide business and who practices ethically is a prospect for radio and television. The prospect potential is almost unlimited in any market, regardless of its size. In most markets, however, and especially the larger ones that include both radio and television stations, leading retailers can be persuaded to use the broadcast media only when specific campaigns are prepared especially for them.

In a small upper-Michigan community that has several radio stations, one broadcasting property boasts 101 local accounts out of 116 firms in the community. The business ranges all the way from an institutional-type show for an iron mining company to time signals for a shoe repair establishment. This is no accident!

The Sales Presentation

Few sales are made in one call. It is not unusual for a salesman to average five to six calls on a retailer, large or small, before an initial sale is consummated. Much of what follows below about *the* sales presentation really applies to a succession of visits by the salesman.

If the retailer has an agency, no matter how small and how inexperienced it may be in the use of broadcast media, the broadcast salesman should consult that agency before making a presentation. Many of the smaller agencies may resist the possible use of radio and television for their clients. Whenever this happens, it is both fitting and proper for the salesman to take his case directly to the client, explaining his intent in advance, of course, to the agency. Regardless of the agency's attitude toward broadcasting, whether cooperative or reluctant, the station should have direct contact with the client. The person who is contacted for the client should be the same individual who would have been consulted had there been no agency involved; he may be the advertising manager, the head buyer, or the owner-manager of a retail establishment.

In calls on retail establishments, the salesman must first sell the merits of his medium to the client. He must also convince the retailer that his advertising policy can be improved upon and that increased sales will result. After selling his medium and his concept, the radio or television salesman must then demonstrate how the station's programming, geared as it is to the community, can help the retailer reach his present and potential customers.

The station's coverage, its circulation and its audience composition should be shown in the sales presentation. The salesman must point out the availabilities which can do the most for the client and explain why.

The retailer needs every bit of service, advice and guidance that the salesman can give him, particularly if he is a neophyte in using broadcast media.

It is a good service to the retailer to furnish him with information on the tools used by similar business establishments which employ radio and television in other cities. The Radio Advertising Bureau (RAB) and the Television Bureau of Advertising (TvB) have large inventories of such success stories. Of course, evidences of local successes—especially by competitors—have motivated many a non-user of radio and television to enter broadcasting.

Any salesman will find that his initial presentation is made much more effective through the use of audio tapes, films or slides. These selling aids should first of all demonstrate the impact of his medium and then, with actual commercial samples produced specifically for the store, illustrate what can be done for the respective departments and for the store in general by broadcast advertising on his station.

Most large stations own broadcasting industry presentations on audio tape or on film or slides. These stations then add specific information about their own radio or television operations. Such presentations are effective; in fact, it is doubtful whether many major department stores would have given serious consideration to the use of radio or television without them.

In smaller stations without elaborate production facilities, TvB or RAB can be of major assistance in supplying films, slides and audio tapes. Any station, no matter how small, should prepare its own suplements for each prospective client. Salesmen with training or experience in radio or television production can be particularly valuable in this preparation.

A tour of the station's facilities, even if it is a small operation, can be very useful in explaining the station to the client. If conducted properly, it can make a strong impression on one who is not acquainted with the workings of a broadcasting station.

If locally prominent "name" talent is being considered in the retailer's campaign, there should be an opportunity for the merchant to meet that talent. Such a meeting can be arranged during one of the sales talks with the client or at a luncheon or dinner. In most cases, it is advisable to recommend air personalities to large retailers because sponsored talent can be made available for store events or sales meetings and can be an added promotion factor for the store.

It may be noted that nothing has been said about using ratings in the sales presentation. Unless a station is completely dominant in its market, its ratings will not be as important in making a sale as some broadcasters think they are. Most local retailers have a very modest amount of interest in a station's rating service. Their audience index is the cash register a day or two following the start of an advertising schedule.

Effective sales presentations include at least five characteristics, according to Jay Hoffer.[10] Organization of presentation material should be clear and logical. The presentation must be attractive and neat, supporting the "story." Creativity must be applied to ideas, but without superficial "gimmicks." The presentation must be brief, taking only the time actually necessary for key points and significant supporting data. And it must be direct, "asking for the order" at the conclusion.

FOLLOW-UP ACTIONS AFTER THE SALE

Some salesmen resent the job of servicing a sale after it is made. These men would rather close a sale, forget about it and get started on another prospect. Such an attitude runs counter to the purposes of selling. As noted earlier, the object of the sale in the first place is to perform a real service for the client. If the advertiser's air campaign is not successful, it will take more effort to get him back on the air than it did to sell him in the first place.

While it is true that in servicing accounts the salesman does not place immediate dollars in his pockets, in the long run he stands to gain by it. The salesman interested only in his immediate financial gain is not really interested in what advertising can do for the buyer. His selling methods can offset the very sales claims that the station makes. His quick gain can be a long-time station loss.

Traffic and Continuity

Two indispensable units in client service by any station are traffic and continuity.[11]

Traffic is the very heart of the operating organization. Its primary responsibility is preparation of the daily log showing all program and commercial placements minute by minute throughout each day. The people in traffic check for commercial separation of similar products, usually keeping two brand names for the same kind of product or service *at least* ten minutes (the better, quality-oriented stations allow fifteen minutes) apart in the schedule. At most stations, traffic also prepares the weekly shift of assignments for all announcers and, in some cases, the assignment of turntable operators and in unusual situations, even engineers. The rate of the traffic department varies, of course, depending upon the size of the operation and whether or not a network affiliation is involved.

Continuity, in addition to writing copy for the station, often is assigned the responsibility for rewriting agency or client copy for better air presentation. Those who work in continuity also check copy for compliance with the station's standards.

Before a salesman makes any call on a client, he needs to check with the traffic unit at the station to learn what availabilities exist in the schedule for the immediate and long-range future. This is his only assurance that what he may sell will be placed on the station at specific times of the day. If he makes a sale, he must inform the traffic unit immediately so that the blocks of time which have been sold may be removed from the availabilities list.

As soon as a sale is made, full information on all details of the contract must be supplied to the traffic department. Then requisition orders are made out and circulated to all units of the station affected by the filling of the order.

Once a sale has been made and reported, much work must be done before the campaign goes on the air. Format scripts may need to be written, preliminary production plans must be formulated, art work, slides and film arrangements need to be made.

In the case of copy supplied by client or agency, adequate time must be provided for filing that copy in order for it to be processed prior to air time. Most stations have found that a forty-eight hour deadline before air use of all copy, either audio or video, works best. In some cases, with certain retail establishments, this time has to be shortened in order to meet the competition from other media. Some daily general-circulation newspapers and some shoppers' guides have as little as an eighteen-hour deadline on copy in advance of publication. In general, however, after a retailer has used a broadcast facility for a period of time, it is not too difficult to get him to comply with a forty-eight hour deadline on all of his station copy.

Servicing the Sale

Between the closing of a sale and the beginning of its schedule on the station, the salesman needs to maintain his contact with the client. Normally, the nature of the contacts is left to the discretion of the salesman but he should be encouraged by the sales manager to use budgeted funds for this purpose. Luncheon dates or tickets to sports events or other entertainments favored by the client are two of many possible ways to let the new advertiser know that the station appreciates his business. Telephone calls from the salesman, the sales manager, and, in the case of large accounts, from the station manager help to keep a working relationship established during this interim period. Of course, regular contacts should continue to be maintained throughout the duration of the contract.

Once the advertising campaign begins on the station, the local client may begin to look for almost immediate results. There is no single conclusive yardstick for measuring the effectiveness of radio and television advertising. It is the duty of the salesman to use every method available to evaluate the success of the campaign. Such appraisal should begin as soon as the advertising starts and should be continuous thereafter.

The client will expect to measure the results of his advertising by noting an increase in sales. Even though there are other measures of success that could be equally important to his business in the long run, the salesman must be alert to actual sales results. If they should not develop as had been planned, adjustments may be necessary. The program or spots may need to be placed in different time periods. The commercial copy may need revision. In some cases, air personnel involved in the advertising may need to be replaced.

In any case, a regular relationship needs to be maintained between the salesman and the client. The advertiser should feel that the radio or television operation is his working ally in helping to build his business, his consumer strength, and his image in the area. Many stations and salesmen have done just that. There are cases where outstanding salesmen, dedicated to their clients' welfare, have won so much respect that they have been rewarded for their effectiveness in helping to make the enterprise successful. Some retail stores have even held bargain days in honor of a radio or a television salesman or a station sales manager or station manager. This practice, if carried too far, can discredit station personnel because of unfavorable reactions among competitors in the same field who also advertise on the station. On the other hand, it is a token of appreciation, affection and respect and it can hardly be ignored by the business community.

All billings and collections should be the duty of the station's accounting unit. Assigning salesmen to collect overdue accounts, a common practice at some stations, *should be avoided*. A salesman is employed to *sell,* and his time should be so valuable in that assignment that it should be an extreme waste for him to engage in bill collecting.

C. Local Sales

Sales can be distinguished as either (a) *local*—also called retail—which are accounts with local merchants and businesses, usually placed directly but sometimes through local agencies; or (b) *national*—also called general—which are accounts with national or regional businesses, placed through advertising agencies and often with the assistance of station representatives.[12] Total revenue in broadcasting is derived from local, spot and network advertising. Obviously, local and network advertising pertain to local and national sales respectively. But spot advertising (not merely spot announcements as contrasted with full-program sponsorship) can be placed either in stations' schedules on a local or regional basis or in networks' schedules nationally. In the present text, "local sales" refers to sale of station time to local retailers, while "national sales" refers to sale of station time (usually through advertising agencies and station "reps") to national businesses in the form of spot advertising. (Sale of network time is treated only indirectly in this section of the book.)

In radio, local sales constitute the largest source of income; in the early 1970s, 75 per cent of advertising was local, while the remaining one-fourth of all radio time sold was spot and network sales. In television, however, the revenue from local sales was only 22 per cent, while almost four-fifths of all TV time sold was network and spot advertising.[13] Yet, the total dollars generated in local sales by the average television station was considerably larger than the total dollars generated in local sales by the average radio station. Two factors in that differential are the competition of the greater number of radio stations and the far higher rates of television stations for airtime.

Local Sponsorship of Programs vs. Spot Announcements

Throughout the decades of radio's development, advertising in the aural medium was largely by sponsorship of entire programs. This was extremely effective for both local and national accounts because it permitted the closest possible tie between a sponsor and a program that served as an advertising vehicle. Whether it was Jack Benny for Jello or Pierre Andre on *Captain Midnight* for Ovaltine, the bridge of sponsorship made an indelible mark on the consumer. Television began with program sponsorship, but shifted to concentration on spot announcements as costs of television mounted and as smaller or specialized advertisers (national, regional and local) began to use the new medium.

A retailer gains much more in his home community through program sponsorship on radio and/or television than by using spot announcements. Beyond the sales effectiveness of announcements, sponsorship prompts audience identification, involvement, and reaction that will stimulate the community to express its response to a specific program. These reactions give store management an opportunity to correspond with those consumers who may write letters. It also gives the manager of the store, along with his buyers and other key personnel, further proof of the intimacy and effectiveness of radio and television. Stations do not receive many letters commenting on spot schedules or spot announcements.

An outstanding example of successful use of programming sponsorship is the experience of Oak Park Federal Savings and Loan, a one-office establishment in a large western suburb of Chicago. In 1957, it purchased Chicago Cubs' radio play-by-play over WGN, and has renewed annually for 17 consecutive years. As its major advertising vehicle in Chicago, baseball sponsorship helped multiply the growth pattern for the firm; total resources of the company grew from $70 million to $140 million in just five years, and resources by 1974 were approximately $270 million.

It would seem that in both radio and television, the purchase of some programming is essential, especially if the vehicle involved is one that, beyond its basic entertainment or service value, can reflect genuine credit on the sponsoring client. This applies generally to sports, news, and programs featuring good music. Listeners and viewers go out of their way to buy products and services of advertisers closely associated with such programs through sponsorship.

In some cases, it may be best to recommend institutional campaigns. Such is the case with the spot schedule of Carson, Pirie Scott & Co. on some Chicago stations. Other than for particular sale periods, such as end-of-month clearances, back-to-school campaigns and pre-Christmas sales, Carsons devotes a very considerable amount of money throughout the year to promote its quality of service, conveniences for its customers, news about the expansion of various departments, additional stores added to its chain, etc. Here, of course, the client is most interested in the type of audience the messages will reach. In the case of Carsons, or any major retailer, the people at the store and its agency obviously want to know the station's reputation and its impact on the community before purchasing advertising.

Spot announcements can often be more effective over a given period of time on radio than on television, assuming, of course, that the "right" stations are bought. This is because radio is still very much a *habit* medium. Listeners tune in their favorite radio *station* (with its program "sound") in the morning and often remain tuned all day, whether at home, in the car or on the beach. Television does not yet enjoy that kind of habitual audience. The television viewer is interested in *programs* and tunes to whatever station has the particular show he or she desires at a certain hour. Thus, changing audience composition is important. The station or the agency that fails to take change into account is not honest with itself or with its advertisers.

There are no hard and fast rules for commercial schedules. Spots can be very effective movers of some merchandise and services. They can be good reminder copy. On the other hand, for some kinds of high-priced items, spots alone without the strength of sponsored programming may prove ineffective.

Some advertisers have soundly combined spot and program buys. The astute advertising manager of the Kitchens of Sara Lee designed a dual buy of network specials *plus* spot announcements on local television (in 1973: $2,000,200 for national spots, and $173,000 for network television programs.) On the network, Sara Lee is thus able to focus attention on its quality line through its selection of quality programs. The company sustains this major impact with a well balanced local spot schedule. This is good advertising!

Maxwell House Coffee elected to make a similar move but chose to concentrate on local stations where prestige program vehicles were available. The series "Great Music" (with the Chicago Symphony) was bought originally on WGN-TV. The Maxwell House agency (then Ogilvy, Benson & Mather), wanted the client identified with the community through sponsorship of a distinguished musical offering. While the audience was small in size, it represented quality in every respect. As a result, the endorsement of Maxwell House Coffee by those viewers was prestigious. In Los Angeles, Maxwell House made similar moves to buy documentaries on a city's problems, and the sponsorship of those specials was supported with good spot buys.[14] (In 1973 Maxwell House split its national budget, spending $4,127,600 on spot TV, and $4,765,500 on network programming.)

RATES AND RATE INCREASES

A review of radio and television properties across the country will find few stations that are overpriced. Most of them are *underpriced*.

Veteran broadcasters recall the low radio rates in the late 1930s, when sponsors were "waiting in line" to buy time and programs. There were some great stations of that era with costs-per-thousand of less than ten cents. Yet the ownership and management of those stations were reluctant to increase their rates, and when they did, the increases were not very significant. This practice has persisted to the present. Throughout the broadcasting industry today, radio stations are much underpriced for the services they deliver and television stations are even more so.

While in small markets there is some very limited justification for a double ratecard with both a local and a national rate, the time will come when every station in radio and television, regardless of size and type of market, will have a single rate structure.[15] This change is essential if broadcasting is to reflect its true maturity as an industry.

These are unpleasant matters to discuss. Yet some expedient station operators have not only had a double rate structure but have had various departures from it to satisfy certain clients, distributors, jobbers and brokers. The *double billing* practice is perhaps as vicious as any development in the history of com-

mercial broadcasting and it has harmed the industry greatly. This practice—
billing the local co-op retailer according to higher national ratecard listings (to
pass on to the wholesaler or national advertiser) while actually charging the retailer only lower local ratecard prices so that some national money accrues to
the local advertiser—has been especially harmful to radio stations because national accounts have become prejudiced against the medium. And the FCC has
barred this fradulent billing procedure, levying sanctions of possible license
revocation and forfeitures of $10,000.[16]

Barter and Trade-out

Another station practice which the "reps" deplore is the trade-out of
goods and services, technically called "bartering." Although much of this
practice is a highly secretive transaction, the FCC estimated that in 1972 barter
and trade-out accounted for a probable $54.7 million in television and $38.7
million in radio. It is not confined to the lower-income stations but is a familiar
practice in most, if not all, markets. The classic trade-out transaction involves
the trading of station time for goods and services instead of money. The usual
commodities are merchandise for station contests, studio and office equipment,
automobiles, travel and hotel or motel accommodations. In recent years, syndicated radio and television programs have been bartered not for merchandise
but for station air time, whereby the program is made available to the station
with some commercial minutes given to the station for local sale; the syndicator
retains two of the other commercial minutes which he sells to national advertisers. Thus, in a sense, "free" program product is traded for "free" air time,
and both syndicator and station derive income from selling their respective
commercial minutes. (Many stations simply do not accept even this form of
barter.) [17]

So long as the arrangements are made on a straight trade-out deal between the station and the advertiser, the practice does not particularly offend
the station representative companies. They seem to deplore the kind of deal that
is made with a third party. The "reps" insist that such a transaction is the same
as the old practice of "brokerage" of station time.

The bartering practice has been criticized because broadcasters, in many
cases, get less in merchandise and/or services than the value of their station
time. The ratio of merchandise value to air time value often goes as high as
one-for-two, meaning one dollar's worth of merchandise for every two dollars'
worth of air time.

Whether called "bartering" or "brokerage," the real evil of the system
is that broadcasting unnecessarily sells itself short. Radio and television are legitimate business enterprises and they have tremendous power to get results for
advertisers. They do not need to maintain an inequitable system of charges!
Under the "barter" system, all advertisers are not treated equally. One advertiser pays the full card rate at the station; another gets the time in exchange for
a marked-up retail value of his merchandise or service. Given a few years of

this practice, all time would have to be sold by the "barter" system. Who would pay the full card rate after he discovered that the alternative was available? The Station Representatives Association said this about the practice:

> Bartering and/or brokerage of radio and television time is the most destructive practice that broadcast licensees have to contend with in their relationships with legitimate advertisers and their agencies who are willing to pay published rate cards for their facilities.

Stable Rate Card Structures and Practices

It would be unrealistic, within the confines of this book, to set up guidelines for rate structures for all the individual radio and television properties in the country. Certainly, in addition to the efforts of RAB and TvB along these lines, NAB might do more to stress the importance of proper rate levels and the need for strict adherence to them.

In a market in the Midwest, a broadcaster asked the president of a medium sized agency when he was going to stop chiseling on rates wherever he did business. The reply was: "As long as the industry is willing to make a deal, and almost every station is, why should I ever pay the full rate?" This agency president advised the broadcaster that it would take a miracle to get any business from him for this particular account unless a deal could be arranged. The agency president then proceeded to expound on his admiration and respect for the press, where the rate card is firm.

This is a tragic indictment of an entire industry! The area of ethics in sales should be one of the most important points of attack for the National Association of Broadcasters. No single station or group of stations can successfully oppose what the competition may practice. This is an industry-wide problem and it needs the kind of leadership that only the NAB can provide, together with upstanding broadcasters who give such a movement their complete support. Although neither the National Association of Broadcasters nor any other industry group can legally or practically implement any particular formula for rate adherence, yet integrity of station operation needs more emphatic notice from these important quarters.

Far greater stature would accrue to the broadcasting industry if more integrity were shown in radio and television rate management across the country. In some markets in this nation with four or more television stations and fifteen or more radio properties, all but two or three of those broadcast entities treat the rate card as a "rubber yardstick." A stable rate card openly sold to all advertisers on the same basis (including publicly announced and adhered-to discount sales for volume and frequency of commercials) reflects a stable station that knows the honest and true value of its airtime.[18]

Rate increases, when justified, seldom pose a problem to a good property. Prior to their implementation and as far in advance as possible, the station's own salesmen and its "rep" firm should explain in detail to the station's clients the reasons for and the merits of a proposed rate increase. When an explanation is given sufficiently in advance, problems ordinarily do not develop. Of course, it is recommended that whenever a rate increase is to take place, three to six months' protection should be given to advertisers of current record. The fundamental justification is that the rate increase is worth it.[19]

SALES DEVELOPMENT AND PROMOTION

The business of broadcasting has been particularly weak in sales development. Although broadcasting's share of the advertising dollar has been substantial, since the early days of radio it has been minor compared to what it should be relative to the potential impact of both radio and television. The successful efforts of the Radio Advertising Bureau and the Television Bureau of Advertising have achieved industry-wide progress in sales development nationally in both media; but not enough progress is evident on the local level. Too many broadcasters spend too much of their time attempting to conquer one crisis after another without taking adequate time to plan for the future and to broaden the base of advertiser participation in the station's schedule.

Every radio and television property, regardless of its size, should have one person under the sales manager who concentrates all of his time on sales development work. He or she should be young, aggressive, and able to chart a course of future business potential for the station. Certainly, if any property is to grow in revenue and in profit as it should, it has to extend its range of advertisers.

Some stations have established sales-promotion departments only to find that they became catch-alls for every department in the station except engineering. There have been cases where outstanding work by a station's sales force has been negated by inept handling of sales promotion either prior to consummating the sale or early in implementing the contract. A sales-promotion department, even if it consists of only one man or one woman, should involve only those persons who have had training under more experienced promotion leaders in the industry.

A good sales promotion department works with the client and/or his agency through the salesman assigned to the account throughout the course of a contract. It supplies regular reports on what has been done or is being done on behalf of a program series or a spot announcement campaign.

Promotion has been described as a sales tool for the broadcast sales department. Sales promotion pertains to what the station can do for the client, especially retail advertisers. (Thus it is distinguished from audience promotion, whose purpose is to build audiences for programming through print and press relations and advertising.) The station demonstrates to clients that, once they sign a contract for airtime, the station and its staff begin to go to work for that advertiser. The station offers to promote his time-buys and the programming associated with his product or service, through mailings to retailers, conducting conferences, and various other forms of "merchandising." In a word, sales promotion is a station's "advertising of a client's advertising."

What can a director of sales promotion and sales development be expected to accomplish? [20] He can gather the materials for and produce fact
sheets on the market and the station and its programming, write sales presentations, develop slide, film and flip card materials, take charge of all station exhibits and make trade show and convention arrangements, negotiate trade deals
for contests, prepare promos, design and produce marketing aids, write articles
for the trade publications, analyze and summarize ratings reports, handle public
appearances by talent, prepare trade advertising, prepare client brochures, keep
the station mailing lists up to date, prepare newsletters, assemble advertiser-
success stories, take charge of all station and personnel publicity, build audience promotion and prepare a salesman's handbook. If this isn't enough for one
or two people, then he can also be given the responsibility of keeping the atmosphere charged with new ideas for increased sales activity.

The sales promotion activity of a station will be strengthened considerably if its director is professionally trained in the field of research. Every year
broadcasters are being called upon by clients and agencies for more and more
research data. Here is a field that merits consideration by some of the young
men and women eager to enter the field of broadcasting. Good research people
are needed. Their work has never been more necessary for broadcasting's
growth and for its future development.

Trade Press Advertising

Too few stations take advantage of the audience that can be reached
through the trade press. The radio and television industry is served by a number
of fine publications, both vertical (broadcasting only) and horizontal (those
embracing all advertising or, as in the case of *Variety,* all show business).
Those stations that advertise in both types effectively—that is, properly and
frequently enough—have many success stories to tell about this area of corporate activity. And reprints of such ads can be used effectively in mailing to
clients and agencies.

Schedules of radio or television spots or programs are very rarely sold as
a result of trade press advertising. On the other hand, if the trade press is used
intelligently it can be extremely effective as an "image builder." While it may
take many months for a station to derive any tangible benefits from a trade
press schedule, the long-range results are well worth the time, effort and expense. Advertising among competitive peers demands original and creative
copy and layout. If no one on the staff can be both original and clever, then station management should either get someone or stay out of trade press advertising. [21]

Merchandising

The most confused, the most misunderstood, the most misinterpreted,
and the most ill-employed term in any form of advertising, but above all in
radio and television, is merchandising. Merchandising has many meanings, but
in general it refers to a station's assistance in an advertiser's selling efforts.

This cooperation is offered as a bonus by the station to attract and hold national and regional advertisers especially, but also local clients. Note that this service should be truly a *bonus* to clients who buy advertising time on the station; it is not a form of rate-cutting or hidden rebate of dollars.

The ineptness of broadcasters in handling merchandising is crystal clear to most agencies, large and small, whether they are national, regional or local in scope. Some stations, especially in the early days of television or during the first years of the great radio depression in the 1950s, all but ruined themselves by vending mistaken concepts of merchandising rather than their very real broadcast facilities. Even now some stations make brief mention in presentation to a client of their program strength, their ratings, facilities, and station personalities and then devote volumes of space or time to tell what they can do regarding merchandising and in-store merchandising at that.

In general, merchandising costs are at a proper level when considered as a supplementary service to the station's own broadcast facilities and programming. The great error in merchandising occurs when stations spend huge sums of money to put their specific merchandising services ahead of what they have to offer the public in the way of mass communication serving the community.

Merchandising, when well directed, can be an outstanding service of a radio or a television property for a client. There are some clients, especially in the food and drug field, who not only desire this service but demand it. There are others who have such in-depth merchandising plans of their own that they do not want the broadcast entity involved.

The man running local business correctly counts on much assistance from advertising media in publicity and promotion. This does not mean that a station should sell its side benefits and forget about its facilities and time; but there needs to be some assistance given to the merchant. Sometimes a store is willing to include the costs of such services in its advertising budget. Most stations endeavor to be helpful through their sales promotion departments in suggesting such selling aids to the store as window displays, point-of-purchase advertising and on-the-air promos, all of which call attention to the sponsorship or programs as well as assist the retailer.

The concept of in-store merchandising and similar forms of promotion involves station-client cooperation; it helps insure the client's success with the on-air advertising schedule, and it keeps the station's call letters before the public (and the client). Jay Hoffer describes in detail major forms of client cooperation by stations: in-store participation, air tag lines for local retailers of distributors' goods, newspaper ads, product sampling, direct mail pieces, playlist advertising, distributors' sales meetings participation by station personnel, retailers' sales prizes, air salutes of "best salesmen" of client's goods, public transportation ad cards, billboards, station newsletters and magazines, disc jockey appearances, station contests, technical facilities (such as spotlights) at client openings, and in-store checkups in collaboration with Media Survey, Inc.[22]

Many types of cooperation with advertisers may be termed merchandising ''at the point of purchase.'' It might take the form of promotion cards on behalf of an advertiser, such as a distributor for a beer or a wine, with signs appearing in restaurants and other public places; or pump islands with banners, flags and pennants at gas stations; or special shopping bags at a department store or a specialty shop for a particular week, with the printed material on each bag calling the attention of the public to the store's sponsorship of a radio or television series. Merchandising might also include direct-mail promotion to dealers carrying a product.

Merchandising can bring returns if done in good taste and if it represents, in the final analysis, a contributory rather than a major service of the station. Jay Hoffer cautions that ''only large stations doing considerable national and regional business can afford the services of a full-time merchandising director.'' [23] More often the promotion manager or, in smaller operations, the sales manager oversees the station's merchandising efforts on behalf of clients, especially for national sales business.

D. NATIONAL SALES

Broadcast stations both large and small, especially television stations, depend for a large percentage of their revenue from advertising airtime purchased by companies not in the local area. To negotiate this national and regional business most stations (except major ones with traveling sales forces or branch offices in metropolitan centers) must rely on two groups of middlemen. They are advertising agencies and station representatives who transact business on behalf of their respective clients, the non-local advertisers and local stations.

In 1972 more than 200 station representative firms negotiated the sale of local station time for non-network (or spot) advertising through the approximately 3,000 advertising agencies serving more than 14,000 national and regional advertising accounts—reflecting non-network billings that year of $1,167,400,000 in television and $384,000,000 in radio.

ADVERTISING AGENCIES AND BROADCASTING

After a company has determined its annual corporate budget for advertising, its advertising agency considers the relative values of each of the advertising media. Then, the agency must select specific properties within each medium. To some advertisers, the agency recommends that most of the budget be allocated to the print media. To others, the agency advises placing the largest share in broadcasting. Sometimes, the overall budget is fairly evenly distributed between media. The advertiser's own sales people, of course, may influence the decision by expressing media preferences.

When the amount to be spent in broadcasting is determined, further decisions must be made. What proportion of the amount will go to purchase radio and what proportion to buy television? What kind of vehicles (programs or participations) are desired and what kinds are available? How much of the budget should be used to purchase network services and how much should go into spot advertising on selected individual stations? Which markets should be selected and which stations employed in those markets?

Agency time buyers are ready with information concerning what is available in time, talent and facilities at the various networks and stations. They know, from "track" records, which availabilities are best suited to the needs of each of their clients. They make continuing studies of the audience composition of the various networks and stations at the various times of day. They know the "reach" of the station, its programming and its community image. They determine costs. Finally, they negotiate to buy time on the networks and stations offering the greatest return to the advertiser. Such selections have to be as productive as possible. A random or guess-work choice that does not bring results can be an open invitation to the client to take his business to a different agency.

Part of the effort to bring advertisers and broadcasters together in time sales is to note the target audiences sought by clients and then to match them to time availabilities in broadcast schedules. For example, in 1974, of a total of 8,067 television "avails" sought by advertisers, 2,271 (28%) of the requests were for audiences consisting wholly of women; and another 2,572 (32%) were for audiences of woman aged 18 to 49. Advertisers in only 745 instances (9%) wanted to buy audiences made up wholly of men.[23a]

The buyers of space and the buyers of time used to be separated into different departments in the agencies, and media decisions were made by account men. Today, the buying function is carried on wherever possible by people who are specialists in all media. Experienced advertising executives describe the new agency media people as "bright, aggressive, young and college trained—many of whom were, in addition, products of our fine graduate business schools. This is a change from the former image of the agency buyer as one who had little imagination but who relied heavily on his "horse-trading" ability and his belief in numbers. The modern successful buyer is a well trained professional with a wide range of knowledge and skills.

The 1970s were a decade of transition in advertising agencies as well as in many sectors of broadcasting and society generally. Added to media buying by numbers—by demographic statistics—was consideration of less tangible but often measurable characteristics of audience attitudes and reactions to programming and commercials, including their number, placement, content and style of presentation. Media researchers began to give attention to what they termed "psychographics"—definition of prospective consumers by psychological needs and life styles. (In print media special-interest magazines increasingly replaced general-audience publications, and they flourished.) In 1971 "the Gallagher Report" predicted that advertising media were entering a period of major readjustment, with innovative marketing essential to justify continually higher rates. Noting increasing numbers of "advertisers glad to pay premium for greater impact, larger number of prime prospects, more effective psychographics," Bernard Gallagher offered his analysis: [24]

Opportunity for reps, agencies, media services. To help advertisers break through cost-efficiency barrier. Top marketers unhappy with evaluation of media by size of audience delivered in specified demographic category. Want researched data to establish: 1) Audience's prospect-status. Each group to be divided into percentage of prospects, non-prospects. Prospects to be broken down into immediate, proximate, remote. 2) Psychological involvement created by medium. Weighted according to wants-to-buy attention, concentrated attention, general attention, no attention. 3) Impact exclusivity. Measured by distance from competitive advertising, all other advertising, media-generated distractions—combined with distinctiveness of position, format. Complex requirements to preclude buying of space, time units individually. Reps, agencies, media services to prepare media-tax packages priced against "evaluation grid" of new requirements.

In 1973 "The Gallagher Report" noted continued advertiser pressure mounting on media: "with increased media-buying sophistication, multi-level media-planning responsibility[,] cost-per-thousand becomes secondary to medium's environment, prestige, [and] implied endorsement." [25] Major advertisers looked to agencies' multi-level responsibility for implementing media strategies, with specialists responsible not only for the costs but also the effectiveness of advertising. Bernard Gallagher typified the need of agencies to develop in-depth specialization by concluding that "too many buyers [are] glorified clerks." Robert Innes, then a prominent New York-based sales executive, tended to corroborate that appraisal in his description of the structure of major agencies' media departments in 1974:

> The major agencies are now structured in the media department as follows[:] The media director, associate media directors, planners and buyers. The planners, using various sources of information (sales reports, individual market information, etc.), figure out what spot television weight they want in a given market for a product or products. This information is sent in written form to the person who will buy the schedules for given markets. The buyer frequently does not know the reason for a given rating point goal in a market. The buyer then tries to achieve the goal set. For example, in Chicago his goal may be to get 95 rating points in homes or rating points in demographics per week for a limit of $3,000.00 per week. He naturally tries to achieve his goal for fewer dollars. The buyers, in effect, are negotiators[,] which some agencies actually call them.
>
> The danger in this system is that the buyers will blindly try to achieve their rating goals without really knowing the aim and rationale of the client and planners. Frequently we run into situations where, say, for the given $3,000.00 the buyer may be able to achieve 125 points per week instead of his goal of 95. This confuses them. As they say, they don't need 125.
>
> The result of this structure is, naturally, that the planners must be pitched by the salesmen to okay any deviation from their "master plan." For exceptional media proposals—sponsorship of baseball, special events like parades, football games, etc.—the planners and the clients must be covered . . . with the agency's knowledge. This system instituted by large agencies frequently makes the buyers or negotiators merely spot buyers and not in the true sense media buyers. In ef-

fect, they turn into non-knowing human computers who eventually will probably be replaced by electronic computers for purely spot buys.[26]

The new role of the agency buyer has made new approaches necessary by the people from the stations and the networks who call on them to influence their buying decisions. For the small-market stations, this function is usually performed by the station representative organizations. Whenever direct presentations are made by the station, the station manager or sales manager usually makes them. Many larger market stations follow a procedure of assigning specific men from the station's sales staff to call on the list of agencies. This procedure guarantees that calls are made on a consistent and an organized basis.

Sales Manager's Relationship with Agencies

The sales manager has the important task of either calling on agencies himself or assigning his salesmen to make calls. An efficient sales manager soon learns the particular abilities of each of his men and what each, in turn, can accomplish at the various agencies. In both radio and television, contacts need to be maintained with large, medium and small agencies on national, regional and local levels. Some of these agencies place a high value on quality in advertising, often favoring an institutional approach. Others, largely local in nature, have little interest in the image created by their advertising. Their desires are confined to fast returns noted on the cash register. Knowing these variances at agencies the sales manager must consider the makeup of his sales staff as well as of the leading buyers and other personnel at the agencies. He needs to match his salesmen with specific agencies on the basis of the probable effective results those men may produce from the assignments.

The sales manager should never remove himself from selling. In addition to directing his salesmen to specific targets and working with them for improvement, he needs to call on at least some agencies regularly. Time and his station's circumstances and market conditions permitting, it is important for him to be active with at least one or two agencies so that he will not lose touch with the field. His calls also enable him to keep abreast of the problems his men confront.

After every agency call by a salesman, the sales manager should receive a report from that salesman early the following morning. Whether this is a verbal report or a briefly written statement, it is a necessary requirement so that the executive may be kept posted on progress or problems anticipated.

By maintaining month-to-month tabulation of all accounts with the various agencies, the sales manager can determine the gains or losses and strengths or weaknesses not only of each salesman but of the station in its relationship to agencies and clients.

The sales manager should also maintain relationships with those agencies that are called upon by the men of his staff. He should plan periodic trips to the major advertising centers of New York and Chicago and, whenever possible, Detroit, Los Angeles and San Francisco. These trips should be made at least once every three months. In many cases, the station's location may be such that it has within its State, or in a nearby State, a regional advertising center that generates considerable sales traffic. A personal visit by the sales manager every thirty days to all of the agencies in that market should be an all but absolute necessity. Some stations in close proximity to a major regional advertising center cover those agencies as frequently as once a week. Where this is done, rich dividends in added sales usually result.

It is perfectly in order for a salesman to call upon a national advertiser directly, but it is a cardinal sin for him to do so under any circumstance without first advising that advertiser's agency. There are times when a call on an advertiser by a station can be of great help to the agency, particularly when the sales presentation may involve a completely different approach from that which is normally pursued by the agency. In such a case, the call may enlighten the relationship between the advertiser and his agency personnel. One of the most successful selling organizations in broadcasting is that of the Avco (formerly Crosley) Broadcasting Corporation. It has not only given much consideration to discussing sales matters directly with advertisers; it has always instructed its sales personnel to advise agency executives of this intent. In no case has a strained relationship resulted therefrom; the effective results are known to the trade.

Importance of Station Image

The image of the station conveyed to advertising agencies has assumed increased importance in placing spot business. With so many stations trying to make impressions on the agencies, identifying outstanding features of any particular properties has become difficult. Station assets not found in ratings need to be communicated. Agency men generally agree that local station images are of greater importance in radio than in television due to the numbers of radio stations that make media selection more difficult. Some agencies consider station image of such importance that they employ personnel to collect as much information as possible about the various local radio and television operations in each market. They are interested in descriptions and verifications of qualities and services usually not reported. Cooperation from most stations in the gathering of such data is disappointing. If a station wants increased spot advertising, it needs to give the agencies proof of its prestige in the community and of those characteristics which make it different, desirable or unique in a market.

Agency Problems and Progress

Advertising agencies face constant challenges beyond that of competition. Rising costs for the advertiser, increased operating expenses, the switching of agency accounts, and greater emphasis on proof of performance are but a few of the problems the agencies have had to encounter in recent years.[27] In spite of these and other problems, and despite maintaining a traditional standard commission of 15 per cent, advertising agencies continue to grow and their billings continue to set new records each year. In 1952, BBDO (Batten, Barton, Durstine, & Osborne) billed $40 million in radio and television in what was then the largest business for a single agency. Today, some 25 agencies exceed that figure annually; and 14 of them bill over $100 million in broadcasting.[28] In 1972, the number-one agency for over a decade, J. Walter Thompson, billed $222.3 million in radio and television network and spot.[29] In 1973 BBDO was third-highest with $181.6 million in broadcast billings—$160.2 million in TV ($99.3 network and $60.9 spot) and $21.4 million in radio ($3.8 network and $17.6 spot).[30]

Agencies' service to their clients has been improved by using electronic computers. Analyses, media decisions, and billings that formerly took weeks or months of human labor can now be accomplished in a matter of hours. Differences between media and relative strengths of stations can be determined accurately without human guesswork. Already, the mountain of paperwork involved in the buying of spot advertising has been reduced significantly. Once the computer can be used to turn audience data into sales predictability figures, time buying will become a science or at least an activity capable of mathematical expression. By mid-1972, two-thirds of the large agencies (with $25 million or more billings) used computers, but of all-sized agencies (including several hundred small agencies with annual billings of less than $5 million) only one of four used computers.[31] Of the large agencies, 70 per cent used computers in billing operations, and 60 per cent used them for media evaluations. In 1974, broadcast and agency executives supported the efficiency of processing routine work through standardization of procedures, permitting sales staffs more time for the qualitative judgments and human negotiating needed for their primary job of selling. Among services supplied by computers are "speeding up billing and collections; helping to prepare budgets for campaigns; preparing hundreds and hundreds of different media plans and spotting discrepancies between the ordering and the delivery of broadcast advertising efforts." [32]

SPOT BUSINESS AND THE STATION REPRESENTATIVE

The system of station representatives, commonly called station "reps," began in 1932. Before that time, the process of representing individual stations to national and regional advertisers and agencies was true chaos. A brokerage system prevailed, organizations or individuals often represented competing stations in the same market, and general price-cutting was standard practice.

In 1932, Edward Petry started the first of the modern station-representative firms. Petry organized his company on sound business principles and ethical practices, thus establishing high standards for the firms that were to follow. Refusing to do business with time brokers, his company instead dealt directly with station managers. Petry insisted that the one station in any market

which the company selected to represent must be concerned with quality operation and fair business practices. Nationally, this made a select list of radio stations with great appeal as advertising media.

In the three years following the beginning of the Petry company, twenty-
seven additional station representative companies were organized. Since 1935,
there has been a steady increase in the number of national and regional "reps"
in broadcasting. The total of 231 firms listed by Standard Rate and Data Service (SRDS) in 1973 was divided approximately four to one between regional
and national companies. In order to qualify for designation as a *national* representative, a firm must maintain offices in New York, Chicago, and at least one
other major market. *Broadcasting Yearbook 1974* listed 234 "rep" firms.[33]

The role of the representative firm is to provide the national and regional
market with up-to-the-minute information about rates and time availabilities for
their client stations. Clusters of several stations up to fifty (or, rarely, even
more than a hundred small stations) are served by "rep" offices staffed proportionately with from five or ten people up to 250 persons at each of the three
largest organizations (Petry Television, John Blair & Co., and the Katz
Agency, Inc.). The representative firm is sometimes strictly a sales organization; but often it also provides other supporting services such as research, marketing, estimating, merchandising, traffic, sales service, promotion, press relations, and even programming (although no firms are involved with a station's
production or engineering).[34] By late 1974, several "rep" firms also offered
audiotape-served "networks" of radio stations to advertisers, for swift, widespread, and cost-efficient campaigns.[34a]

Commission rates to station "reps" for both radio and television vary
from company to company and from station to station. In earlier years, owners
of several station properties paid only 5 per cent commission to their "reps"
while stations since then have paid up to 15 per cent in order to be represented
in other markets. Although there is no standardization, some "rep" firms maintain standard rate policies. Usually, radio stations are charged more than television stations for representation; with few exceptions the usual rate for radio is
15 per cent. Almost all large television stations pay 8 to 9 per cent to their
"reps; medium-size TV stations pay from 10 to 12 per cent; and television stations in smaller markets pay 15 per cent to be represented.

The Sales Manager and the "Rep"

The station sales manager should work closely with his station's representative in every market where that company has an office.[35] The sales manager
must arrange for the "rep" to receive regularly all updated sales tools essential
to selling the station. These materials should include program schedules with
all changes noted, station brochures and routine sales presentations, and all
special campaigns that are prepared for specific clients. The sales representative
can be no more effective in selling the station than the data supplied by the
sales department permits him to be. Unfortunately, stations do not automatically receive spot business merely by signing with a "rep" firm.

The sales manager regularly must stimulate—even agitate—the representative organization, particularly in the case of those firms that are not aggressive. "Rep" organizations manifest widely varying levels of initiative. Some of them work around the clock to obtain business for the stations on their lists; the stations' sales managers contribute considerable energy to keep these sales companies supplied with data and give them maximum assistance. But there are other station representative organizations that hardly extend themselves beyond an occasional "strike"; indeed, all too many are found in this category. It is difficult to respect those "rep" firms and their salesmen who get their business by sitting at their desks or at a convenient bar awaiting agency calls for availabilities.

There is some cause for optimism in concern expressed by many of the station representative companies for more station integrity in the use of their rate cards and for less expediency in selling. It should be noted, however, that off-the-card deals are made regularly by some "reps" who care little if anything about the image or the reputation of the stations they represent.

The sales manager should insist upon a weekly call report from each of the offices of the station's representative. A sales manager who does not have this control over the station's "rep" does not truly manage station sales and is derelict in his obligation to top management. With these weekly reports, he can remain current on all national sales activity, he is able to compare the monthly and annual performance of the "rep" for the station, and he can analyze the station's overall ability to continue successful relationships with an agency and its clients.

Station representatives now provide services to television stations by recommending which syndicated films to purchase. The pairing of the right film purchases with the right advertiser can often result in added national spot business for a station. In these decisions, the "reps" can play an important role because of their knowledge of client desires and their accumulated data on the kinds of film packages available. Most of them maintain "track records" or ratings of the various off-network re-runs in several markets. This information is made available to the stations they represent.

Reliance of Stations on Sales Representative Companies

It is disconcerting to note substantial reliance by some station managers and sales managers on their station representatives for management advice having nothing to do with sales. In too many cases, the "reps" have, in effect, become station consultant without fees for extra services. It may seem absurd but it is today possible for a man to "manage" a radio or television station practically in name only. When problems arise, he has only to turn to his station"rep." There he may get answers to most of the problems that he is unable or unwilling to attempt to confront.

Such "authority" and responsibility given to sales representatives by some stations, results in informal transfer of considerable policy control from the station manager to the "rep's" president, board chairman or operations head. This sort of referral has led to some poor decisions damaging to individual stations and harmful to the total industry. Further, it can contradict Federal regulations about licensee control and management supervision of a station.

This is not to criticize a "rep" firm's involvement in occasional discussions pertaining to broad station policy, past, present or future. Nor does it advocate that the station representative should absent itself from all sales promotion and sales development plans of the station; this would be sheer folly! But the willful or witless transfer of a manager's basic responsibilities to an absentee station "rep" is inexcusable. It is one of the reasons for so many cases of lackluster performance by certain stations and by some sales representative organizations as well.

Having discussed the overall role of the station representative and criticizing some practices, it should be made clear that the good sales representative firms—and some are truly outstanding—have contributed significantly to the development of the radio and television arts. The inappropriate and improper involvement of "rep" firms in stations' affairs originate usually not from desires of the representative organization, but from the ineptness of ill-trained, ill-prepared station management. There are too many men and women in capacities of authority in radio and television management who lack the slightest idea of proper management of a broadcast property. Thus, the "rep" becomes a "crutch."

Self-Representation

At the opposite pole from those stations that have become over-reliant on the station "reps," are other stations that have terminated all relations with their national sales representative companies. Starting in 1959, a few stations began to represent themselves exclusively. Today, the stations securing national spot business without the use of station "reps," account for approximately one-third of the total national spot billings for the radio and television industry.[36]

The trend toward self-representation has an interesting background. In August, 1959, the FCC finalized an order requiring the networks to stop selling spot time for stations that they did not own. ABC had discontinued its spot representation division in 1952, but NBC and CBS were still in the business of representing stations. Under the FCC order, the networks could continue to represent their "O&O" (owned and operated) stations, but they had to drop all other stations from representation. The order affected thirteen stations.

Although self-representation has for the most part been confined to group-owned stations, there have been a few cases where other stations have joined the groups for purposes of representation rather than continue with their independent station "rep" organizations.

The regional representatives seem to be largely unaffected by the trend to self-representation. Their billings, of course, are considerably less but so are their overhead costs. Some regional representative companies bill as little as $250,000 a year; others bill one to two million dollars annually.

Spot Sales

How does a buyer in an agency determine the differences between stations in those markets where there are fifteen to twenty facilities? Does the small market station have a chance at influencing the agency buyer? Media buyers must negotiate for spot radio with 400 salesmen from fifteen "rep" firms representing 750 stations in the top fifty markets. "The Gallagher Report" attributed a 5 per cent drop (to $347 million) in spot radio sales partly to complexities in "antiquated sales methods . . . unchanged in 40 years." [37]

With so many stations, it is difficult to make reasoned differentiations among them. Undoubtedly, there have been cases in which more logical purchases might have been made. In partial explanation, agency time buyers and station "reps" have consistently complained about the lack of standard data from the local stations. Many sales data from stations are poorly organized and provide little of importance to aid buying decisions.

Competitive print, outdoor and direct-mail media supply useful demographic information. With computers now playing an increasingly important role in media and station selection, stations will have to supply their representatives and advertising agencies with information comparable to that submitted by the other media and on a regular basis. Otherwise, they will not only fail to gain but they may lose spot revenues as a source of income.

It has been said again and again, and correctly, that radio has been undersold and that its force in advertising has never truly been realized. Files can be filled with radio's success stories. Still the medium has never achieved its fair share of the advertising dollar. It has never really been properly sold. It will not sell itself!

Complete data on audience compositions at various hours of the day, broken down demographically, and opinions of audiences and advertisers regarding the station's service, contain basic information for those who have the authority to spend the national advertiser's budget. Apparently, gathering such material and preparing it in meaningful form has been too much work for some stations to undertake; or else their managers do not understand the very basics of station operation.

It is time for station managers to realize that exaggerated statements about station effectiveness impress very few people who count. Such distortions hurt the station in terms of its long-range income possibilities. There is no substitute for fact. But some managers persist in using half-truths, and, sometimes, downright untruths. This is bad for the industry. It is deplorable that those executives seem to believe that their claims are accepted.

Far too much internal warfare vexes the radio medium. Stations fight other stations in their markets. Although there is sufficient potential business for all stations, "infighting" too often results in losses of revenue for every station in the area. Radio management must somehow learn that the industry needs to improve its ability to attract advertising money from other media, not just from other (and rival) radio stations. With the increase in the number of television stations in most market areas, similar conditions prevail in the newer medium.

Consideration must be given to benefits to be derived from cooperative preparations of key data on a state-wide basis or, in the cases of the multi-station markets, a city-wide basis. Many small businessmen in broadcasting will benefit from this kind of federation. They *must* cooperate if they expect to compete in the spot market against the large corporations who are after the same dollars.

The crux of the matter is a realistic and honest appraisal of exactly what the individual station can do for specific advertisers. Once the station representatives and agencies can get this information regularly and know they can rely on it, the station will be in a good position to receive the spot accounts it deserves.

Factual data are a necessary supplement to, but no replacement for, effective personalized selling. Every station needs to campaign vigorously and steadily with the agencies and with the ''reps'' in order to achieve its goals.

Is there to be a crisis in national spot radio? Some agencies, admittedly the smaller ones so far, do not recommend spot radio to their clients. Salesmen from radio stations have not been given a very warm reception at some agencies for some time. Agency personnel have been critical of the presentations made by radio's salesmen, saying that they showed little understanding of the problems of specific advertisers, that they used valuable time to try to put other radio or television stations in a bad light, that they were so full of unproved claims that their sales arguments were meaningless.

Agencies complain about violations by some radio stations of the unwritten rule against calling on advertisers directly. Agency buyers have reported publicly that the salesmen from many radio stations are not as effective as those from television stations. Some of those agencies insist that radio salesmen appear to consider themselves in a training phase for later employment as television salesmen. The latter probably manifests itself in circumstances under which joint top management of a radio-and-television mutually-owned broadcast entity fails to operate its properties independently or favors television over radio. It is incredible to see the number of major broadcast companies whose executives in top management fail to give more than passive consideration to radio. These men create their own problems.

Unfortunately, the use of a double-rate system (for local and for national business) by many radio and television stations, is often confusing rather than constructive. In station presentations, frequent negative remarks about other radio or television facilities, plus inflated claims about the salesman's own station, have caused some agency buyers to reject the stations which those salesmen so poorly represent.

Is there already a crisis in national spot radio? Very clearly, there is for some stations. But there are many valuable advertising dollars in national radio spot schedules, and some stations are obviously getting it.

E. SALES AND ADVERTISING PRACTICES

Sale of airtime is affected by trends in broadcast practices. Among major developments in the early 1970s was the introduction of the 30-second spot announcements as the virtual standard for the television industry—replacing the minute-long commercial. This increase in individual time-units per hour meant a proliferation of announcements about different products and brands. Thus a two-minute break in daytime programming offered the viewer not two commercials but four commercials; although the total amount of time was the same during the "program interruption" for four "30's" as for two "60's," viewers often perceived the four commercials as a greater interruption than before. In a word, commercials became more salient than in past years. The use of station-break time for a series of 10-, and 30-second spots also added to the sense of "clutter" in the broadcast air.

In addition to viewers generally and critics, advertisers and their agencies at times voiced concern about the resulting effectiveness of their commercials upon the audience whose attention was diverted and diffused by multiple messages.[38] In 1970 Foote, Cone & Belding attempted to monitor station's degree of compliance with the NAB Code Authority's guidelines for commercials, although after a year it abandoned the effort. Early in 1971 Avco Broadcasting Corp. attempted to curb "clutter"; Avco's president John T. Murphy cautioned:

> Do we really expect anyone to recall eight different sales messages delivered in [a] 14-minute period? What about five messages in two minutes? . . . While I'm primarily addressing myself to my fellow broadcasters, I'm also speaking to you advertisers and agencies. All of us are affected . . . We capitulated and we accepted 30s, which added significantly to the clutter even though it did not increase the commercial time. And that move probably did more to stir up the current clamor than anything else.[39]

Avco unsuccessfully tried to cut back commercial time by 10 per cent, charging premium rates for airtime more free of commercials; but advertisers and agencies balked at higher prices for that kind of anti-clutter protection. Later that same year, Dancer-Fitzgerald-Sample (an agency that billed the largest volume of spots in 1971, $75 million), made public its intent to "treat favorably" in spot buying those stations abiding by the NAB Code, while penalizing stations that "deviated" from the Code criteria.[40] In 1973 Ogilvy and Mather's senior vice president and director of broadcasting recommended reducing clutter, partly by offering attractive rates for commercial lengths longer than 10- or 30-second spots.[41] In mid-1972, Bernard Gallagher surveyed more than 1,000 media and advertising executives about government regulation, industry initiative, and ways to improve the public's image of advertising. From the nine proposals listed, most respondents (from 61 to 71 per cent) placed first the proposal that "advertisers should reduce clutter by paying premium prices for 'editorial insulation' (e.g. substantially fewer commercials in half hour TV programs)." [42] Overcommercializing may generate increased revenue for a period of time, but it can undermine advertising's effectiveness with the public; it might even occasion governmental intrusion into business aspects of broadcasting.

Such involvement by the Federal regulatory agency in programming seemed threatened in 1974 by the FCC's initial proposals against children's programming being supported by advertising. Consumer groups such as Action for Children's Television (ACT) had lobbied throughout the early 1970s to eliminate all commercials from programs scheduled for children. The NAB precluded direct Federal action by amending its Code provisions restricting advertising time (as well as content) of children's programming. Typically, the Commission did not terminate its proceeding but instead exhorted broadcasters to continue to upgrade programming practices for youngsters through self-regulatory measures; and the FCC cautioned that rulemaking might yet be in order if broadcasters were not up to the challenge. [43]

Related to specifically children's programming is the matter of deceptive advertisements. The Federal Trade Commission has kept increasingly closer watch on false or misleading commercial presentations. ACT criticized deceptive ads that impressionable youngsters were exposed to in programs directed to them. The FCC refused to apply the "Fairness Doctrine" to products other than cigarettes (while they were still advertised in broadcast media)—termed counter-advertising—and that stand was supported by the courts. But the Commission did note that its public notice on November 7, 1961, advised broadcasters of their duty to protect the public from false advertising by taking all reasonable measures to eliminate such from their air. [44] The NAB Code Authority in 1973 established firmer guidelines for stations regarding commercials for non-prescription medication (drugs). Meanwhile, national advertising submitted for broadcast was screened not only by the NAB's staff but by the "standards and practices" staffs of the national networks. Obviously neither sets of offices could provide the scrutiny still necessary at individual radio and television stations for local and regional advertising messages. [45] Alert local staff members' efforts in continuity clearance will repay the investment of time with the station's reputation for highly reliable service to the community and a minimum of time and expense spent responding to criticism, threats, and even lawsuits.

A Caution

That there could be dangers of complacency due to progress and prosperity hardly needs to be mentioned. Competition on both the national and the local levels from other media does not stand still. In the national spot market and to a considerable extent in the local field, television and radio are competitive and must often sell against each other as well as against other advertising media. There are advantages in a rising curve of business in the broadcasting industry but there are also dangers, one of which is the rising cost spiral which accompanies the increased income. The next chapter of this book dicsusses the management of income and expenses in order to produce profit. For the moment, it is important to recall that the figures on revenue show only one aspect of the financial picture. It is a significant aspect, of course, for without a healthy income all else in commercial broadcasting could be written off as futile.

Still another danger is masked in a regularly ascending curve of income. Extra effort may not be expended to maintain and to increase rising revenues. But such increased effort is necessary in order to offset added costs. The condition calls for more energetic and more creative selling by the local-station salesmen, by the station representatives, by the agencies and the networks, and by the industry sales promotion organizations, the Radio Advertising Bureau and the Television Bureau of Advertising. The chief foe of progress is, indeed, not *competition,* but *complacency!*

NOTES

Chapter 6

1. Steve Millard, "Radio at 50: An Endless Search for Infinite Variety," *Broadcasting,* October 16, 1972, p. 31.

2. See Sydney W. Head, *Broadcasting in America: A Survey of Television and Radio,* 2nd ed. (Boston: Houghton Mifflin, 1972), pp. 144–146, and 254–261.

3. For example, the Roper studies regularly reported that most citizens not merely tolerate the commercial system, but prefer it to alternative forms of broadcast service supported by direct payment per program, by subscription, or by taxes. See Television Information Office, "Trends in Public Attitudes Toward Television and Other Mass Media, 1959–1974," based on report by Burns W. Roper, The Roper Organization, Inc. (N.Y.: TIO, 1975).

4. See Albert John Gillen, "Sales Management for the Network Affiliate," and Charles Young, "Sales Management for the Independent," chapters 13 and 14 in Yale Roe (ed.), *Television Station Management: the Business of Broadcasting* (New York: Hastings House, 1964), pp. 181–206. For sales management in radio, see Part III, "Sales," in Jay Hoffer, *Managing Today's Radio Station* (Blue Ridge Summit, Pa.: Tab Books, 1968), pp. 201–288; also Chapter 9, "The Sales Manager," in Jay Hoffer, *Organization and Operation of Broadcast Stations* (Blue Ridge Summit, Pa.: Tab Books, 1971), pp. 132–186.

5. See Albert John Gillen, in Yale Roe (ed.), *Television Station Management,* pp. 185–189.

6. See "The Sales Trainee" in Jay Hoffer, *Managing Today's Radio Station,* pp. 212–216.

7. Charles F. Haner and Givens L. Thornton, "How Successful Salesmen Behave: A Counseling Guide," *Personnel,* May–June, 1959, pp. 22–30.

8. Jay Hoffer, *Managing Today's Radio Station,* pp. 209–210.

9. For a sample employment contract for salesmen, recommended by the National Association of Broadcasters, see Jay Hoffer, *Managing Today's Radio Station,* pp. 206–207.

10. Jay Hoffer, *Managing Today's Radio Station,* pp. 254–255. He lists eight "basic ingredients" to be integrated into sales presentations: coverage map, population served, programming and personalities, community involvement, ratings, merchandising (or "client cooperation"), success stories, and rates; pp. 237–240, 254. He includes twelve pages that reproduce a local station sales presentation, including tables and statistical data; pp. 241–254.

11. Practical concrete descriptions of these two departments, including a ten-step procedure for routing commercial business from time of sale to program log, may be found in Jay Hoffer, *Managing Today's Radio Station,* pp. 181–186. See also Norman Ziegler, "Traffic Management

for Sales,'' Chapter 10 in Yale Roe (ed.), *Television Station Management*, pp. 217–224; and Chapter 7, "The Traffic Manager," in Jay Hoffer, *Organization and Operation of Broadcast Stations*, pp. 119–124.

12. See J. Leonard Reinsch and Elmo I. Ellis, *Radio Station Management*, 2nd rev. ed. (New York: Harper & Row, 1960), pp. 147–149, for their definitions of local and national business, and ratecard classifications. They note that the NAB Sales Managers Executive Committee recommended that when two rates are charged for the same local station time, those rates should be designated "retail" and "general."

13. Figures reported by Radio Advertising Bureau Research Dept., *Radio Facts: RAB Pocket Piece 1975* (N.Y.: RAB, 1975), p. 33; and by "The Gallagher Report," September 11, 1972, p. 2.

14. General Foods through its agency (Ogilvy & Mather, Inc.) buys from a special budget which, dependent upon the subject matter—e.g., hard drugs—will simply use billboard announcements; spin-off benefits result for the individual brand brokers or distributors as well as for the corporate company. In this way each brand is not charged ad dollars, the cost being a corporate one.

15. A concrete description of how rate cards are established, especially for stations in small markets, can be found in Robert H. Coddington, *Modern Radio Broadcasting: Management and Operation in Small-to-Medium Markets* (Blue Ridge Summit, Pa.: Tab Books, 1969), pp. 21–26. He notes that, although nationally or regionally sold products do gain from even the fringe-signal audience while local advertisers get little benefit beyond the immediate locale's audience, and although national advertising is placed through agencies and station reps so has at least 15% and more in commissions subtracted from the billing, still efficient and stable bookkeeping and sales derive from a single rate structure. However, Jay Hoffer, *Managing Today's Radio Station*, pp. 91–93, acknowledges that under some conditions "barter can be worthwhile—*provided* you have a genuine need for the goods and services that the *station* can effectively use" (italics in original).

16. Frederick W. Ford and Lee G. Lovett, "Interpreting the FCC Rules & Regulations: Fraudulent Billing Practices," *BM/E* [Broadcast Management/Engineering], November 1973, pp. 22–26. On this matter, the FCC issued public notices and memoranda opinion and order in 1962 (23 RR 175), 1965 (6 RR 2d 1540), 1970 (19 RR 2d 1506 and 1507), and 1973 (Seaboard Broadcasting Corp., Docket No. 18814 [1973]), and amended the "double billing" rule to include all forms of fraudulent billing, in section § 73.1205 of the Regulations.

17. See "Special Report" on broadcast barter, in *Broadcasting*, May 6, 1974, pp. 22 ff.

18. For a careful analysis of TV rate cards and practices, see William T. Kelley, "How Television Stations Price Their Service," *Journal of Broadcasting*, XI:4 (Fall 1967), pp. 313–323.

19. Jay Hoffer quotes approvingly two broadcasters' comments "that if properly handled, a rate increase can actually be a sales incentive. The fact you're raising rates creates an aura of success and everybody likes to be on a winning team" and "if a client buys from the station that sells cheap spots, he usually does so because they don't cost him much money anyway and not because he is sold on the station. On the other hand, advertisers have confidence in the station with a good rate." Hoffer, *Managing Today's Radio Station*, p. 220, citing *BM/E*, October 1965, p. 50.

20. For a highly detailed and practical descriptive listing of twenty-five areas of duties for a sales promotion manager, see Jay Hoffer, *Managing Today's Radio Station*, pp. 222–236; and for many examples of promotion, in text and photographs, see Jay Hoffer, *Organization and Operation of Broadcast Stations*, pp. 187–213. The description of promotion in this chapter, and much factual information, was provided by E. Boyd Seghers, Jr., vice president and manager, sales promotion and advertising research, WGN Continental Broadcasting Co., Chicago.

21. For some examples of trade advertising and its purposes, see Howard W. Coleman, "Advertising, Promotion, and Publicity," in Yale Roe (ed.), *Television Station Management*, pp. 151–167, especially pp. 157–160.

22. Jay Hoffer, *Managing Today's Radio Station*, pp. 277–283.

23. Jay Hoffer, *Organization and Operation of Broadcast Stations*, p. 214; brief chapter 12 is "The Merchandising Director," pp. 214–217.

23a. Roger Rice, president of Television Bureau of Advertising, "What's a 'Quality' Audience? It Depends On the Target," *Broadcast Daily* (NAB Convention issue), April 1975, p. 18.

Of 8,067 client requests for target audiences in 1974, these were the sex/age demographics requested in rank order:

Demographic	Total No. Requested	% of Total No. Avails	Demographic	Total No. Requested	% of Total No. Avails
Women 18–49	2,572	31.9	Total Teens	195	2.4
Total Women	2,271	28.2	Adults 50 +	177	2.2
Total Adults	1,031	12.8	Women 35 +	170	2.1
Men 18–49	916	11.4	Men 35–49	117	1.5
Women 25–49	891	11.0	Men 50 +	97	1.2
Total Men	745	9.2	Adults 25–49	82	1.0
Women 18–34	637	7.9	Women 50 +	66	.8
Adults 18–49	508	6.3	Adults 35 +	66	.8
Kids 6–11	274	3.4	Men 35 +	57	.7
Total Kids	264	3.3	Women 35–49	39	.5
Adults 18–34	225	2.8	Kids 6–17	35	.4
Men 18–34	218	2.7	Kids 2–11	28	.3
Men 25–49	215	2.7			

24. Bernard Gallagher (ed.), "The Gallagher Report," November 30, 1971, p. 1. See also issue of March 14, 1972, about psychographis vs. demographics as a key media tool in selling.

25. "The Gallagher Report," September 17, 1973, p. 1.

26. Robert A. Innes, vice president, Television Division, WGN Continental Sales Company, New York City, in correspondence to James A. Brown, dated February 26, 1974.

27. Lennen and Newell was an extreme example of the hardships; that agency billed $52 million in broadcasting in 1971 but declared bankruptcy in 1972; "Big Agencies in Broadcast Enjoy Solid Comeback Year," *Broadcasting*, November 27, 1972, p. 15.

28. *Broadcasting Yearbook 1974*, p. B-314.

29. *Broadcasting*, November 27, 1972, p. 15.

30. *Broadcasting Yearbook 1974*, p. B-314.

31. "The Gallagher Report," April 4, 1972, p. 1, reporting data from its questionnaire survey returned by 464 chief executives of advertising agencies (27 respondents from large agencies, 84 from medium-sized agencies—with billings between $5 million and $25 million—and 353 from small agencies).

32. "The Computer and the Buyers and Sellers of Broadcast Time," *Broadcasting*, April 22, 1974, pp. 44–46, reporting a seminar of 125 executives conducted by the International Radio and Television Society in New York City.

33. SRDS includes as "rep" firms the national sales offices of group-owned stations, which in addition to retaining a national "rep" also operate an office in New York or Los Angeles, staffed by station personnel to stimulate non-network spot sales (they are sometimes referred to as "rep pushers").

34. See Robert L. Hutton, Jr., vice president, Television Promotion, Edward Petry & Co., Inc., "The Role of the Station Representative—Backbone of a Station's Income" (booklet distributed by Edward Petry & Co., Inc., n.d.). Cf. "The Role of the Station Representative in the Marketing of Nationally Advertised Goods and Services" (booklet distributed by Peters, Griffin, Woodward, Inc., n.d.).

34a. More than six major "rep" firms—including Blair, Katz, and Eastman—in 1974 provided advertisers with any desired configuration of radio stations around the country (as few as 50 stations and as many as 1,962 in one instance). A one-minute spot distributed by dubbed tapes to such a "network" in Blair's top 100 markets cost $2,500—20% less than the cost for purchasing time available on the stations singly. Estimates were that between $15 million and $60 million (5% to 20%) of all spot radio business were generated by this new form of radio ad "package" distribution. "When Is Spot a Network? It's Getting Hard to Tell in '74 Radio," *Broadcasting*, Oct. 14, 1974, pp. 35–37.

35. Practical considerations of the mutual responsibilities of station management and the representative firm are described by Jay Hoffer, *Managing Today's Radio Station*, pp. 266–275. Cf. John B. Sias, "The National Sales Representative," in Yale Roe (ed.), *Television Station Management, pp.* 207–216; and in the same book, see Charles Young's discussion of the role of the station "rep" and self-representation for the independent station, pp. 203–206.

36. In 1967, this amount was estimated at $200 million. But because some major national advertisers split their ad budgets with retail outlets, spot billings are "local" or "national" depending on where the time was actually sold.

37. "The Gallagher Report," December 18, 1972, p. 2. In that same year, local radio sales rose 10 per cent (to $1 billion), and even network radio sales increased 12 per cent (to $59 million).

38. See "GF Unveils 'Clutter' Research Plan," *Broadcasting* December 21, 1970, pp. 20–21; "The Changes Facing Broadcast Advertising," *Broadcasting,* December 28, 1970–January 4, 1971 (combined issue), pp. 44–51. One agency president, Andrew Kershaw of Ogilvy & Mather, predicted that by the 1980s, the 10-second commercial would be the standard for television; that would result in six different product appeals per commercial minute! "The Gallagher Report," November 11, 1974, p. 3. Cf. "Less for More for Television Advertisers?" *Broadcasting,* November 4, 1974, pp. 28–29.

39. "Avco's Murphy Lashes Out at Com'l[sic] Clutter, Calls it 'Self-Immolation,' " *Variety,* January 26, 1972, p. 35.

40. "Biggest Buyer of Spot TV Says Violators of NAB Code Will Lose Out," *Broadcasting,* August 28, 1972, pp. 16–17.

41. *"Eaton's Rx for TV Clutter,"* Variety, July 4, 1973, p. 37.

42. "The Gallagher Report," supplement to June 5, 1972, pp. 3–4.

43. "ACT Won't Get What It Asked from FCC on Television for Children," *Broadcasting,* October 7, 1974, pp. 15–16; "FCC Muscling in on TV Programming?" *Variety,* October 16, 1974, pp. 33, 60.

44. See "Stations Cautioned on Deceptive Ads," *Broadcasting,* December 21, 1970, p. 30. Cf. "Court's 'Freedom Not to Air,' " *Variety,* May 30, 1973, pp. 1, 70—regarding the BEM case (Business Executives Move for Vietnam Peace) in which the U.S. Supreme Court supported the First Amendment press freedom of editorial judgment against unlimited access to the air by advertisers as proponents of views on issues, or in "counter advertising."

45. "NBC's Traviesas Says Commercials Pose Censors' Biggest Headache," *Variety,* May 17, 1972; "TV Code's Rx for Drug Ads," *Variety,* February 28, 1973, p. 33. "TB Pressure Point: Ad Acceptance," *Variety,* June 21, 1972, pp. 43, 54. Each network checks approximately 36,000 different commercials a year and rejects about 1 per cent of them.

7

Managing for Profit

Profits are a measure of effective, efficient operation and should be worn as a badge of accomplishment and of honor.
—PHILIP REED, General Electric Company [1]

Broadcasting in the U.S. is a business enterprise and economic motives are valid if they can be justified in terms of social ethics and technical excellence.
—ROBERT H. CODDINGTON, Broadcast executive and author [2]

THE COMPLEXITY of commercial broadcasting dictates the diversity of the manager's activities. He regularly confronts problems emanating from the programming, engineering and sales departments. His leadership of these three key departments occupies most of his attention and consumes most of his time.

There is, however, a primary responsibility which not only must affect his courses of action but also must condition his every decision. As the representative of station owners, his success as a manager is judged principally by the profit return he is able to produce.

Typically, the owners of a local broadcast entity are businessmen who have been successful in fields unrelated to broadcasting. To these men the ownership of a radio or television station is appealing for many reasons. It offers an opportunity to become engaged in a community service. It is an entrance to the exciting and colorful world of "show business." It supplies an element of prestige and potential power. Basically, though, it can earn a substantial profit on the initial investment.

To protect that investment and to provide satisfactory returns on a regular basis requires specific knowledge and skills pertaining to broadcasting which these owners do not usually possess. The owners employ a manager who is experienced in broadcasting and who, they hope, can produce the profits they desire. The degree to which he is able to fulfill that expectation, and also exercise his own professional standards, is the measure of his success and contribution to the broadcasting system.

Even though most of the manager's attention is focused upon the operational procedures of the three major departments of the station, his *modus vivendi*, then, must be governed by economic considerations.

In any business, the product, its distribution and its sale are judged of equal importance. In broadcasting, programming may be regarded as the product, and engineering as its distribution system. Sales results are highly dependent upon both.

As a catalyst for the programming, engineering and sales divisions, management should supply the vision and the leadership needed for a coordinated effort. As improvements occur in each aspect of the operation, station services should expand and the opportunity for profits should increase. The manager may delegate many tasks in programming, engineering and sales, but managing the station's finances is his direct responsibility. He cannot avoid the important decisions affecting profit or loss. Management must take complete charge of approving and administering the operating budget and controlling income and expenses.

In these areas are additional personnel who work directly under the manager's supervision. Their work crosses over the programming, engineering and sales departments, serving all three as part of the administrative function. Such are employees who perform the office duties—the secretaries, clerks, receptionists and telephone switchboard operators—but especially the "right arms" of managers in the area of financial administration, the accountants. The role of accounting is to furnish management with accurate data concerning income and expenses, thus helping to assure fruitful decisions in situations in which figures are either red or black and there are no gray shades.

ACCOUNTING

Proper accounting procedures are essential for management's accountability to the broadcast company's private owners, or to the stockholders if it is a public corporation. Ultimately every management decision will be reflected in dollars and cents, either on the company's income ("profit and loss") statement or on its balance sheet or both. It is imperative, therefore, that management attempt to quantify in financial terms the effects of its decisions before they are implemented.

Budgets, cash forecasts, cost justification surveys and income-and-expense analyses are financial tools available to assist management in the decision-making process. The manager should work closely with the station's financial officer—the controller, chief accountant, or whatever his title—who should develop his expertise and professionalism to meet the demands of modern business.

The Controller

Beyond recording financial facts accurately, the controller must analyze the effects of these historical data and, with management, attempt to forecast the financial impact of prospective actions.

He is responsible for realistically informing the station's management team of the financial result to be achieved in any programming, sales, promotion, publicity, engineering or other operation. To satisfy their own responsibility to the public, broadcasters must do many things which will not immediately enhance the profitability of a given television station. Nevertheless, it is essential that the financial yardstick be applied to all operations if intelligent financial planning is to accomplish an atmosphere of healthy growth.[3]

The controller supervises all accounting, including the staff which may consist of from three to 15 or 20 people. He maintains internal control procedures and regularly evaluates them, especially relative to individual department budgets. He is responsible for such industrial relations as providing accurate data for union negotiations on contracts, grievances, and arbitration. He oversees salary, hiring and firing of clerical persons and other personnel matters. The controller must determine policies for extending credit to the station's customers, to achieve maximum sales results while reducing the margin of risk in payment default. Usually he supervises office management of supplies, communication systems, furniture and equipment. He collaborates with the general manager on general financial management to achieve efficient *cost control* (not merely "cost reduction"). He works with the sales department to establish realistic rate cards for air time and production services which ensure maximum business and profit. He assists the research staff in analyzing ratings and providing factual data for various depeartment heads. The controller is intimately involved with every phase of station operation, each of whose responsibilities differ from that of the controller.

While it is true that every department head must be aware of the over-all profitability of a station, it is not necessarily inherent in the function of operating departments to provide for increased profitability in the general operation. In programming and production particularly, the need for creative work must not be subjugated entirely to the profit motive. The program manager must be responsible for the operation of his department so as to contribute to the over-all effectiveness of the station; but essentially, his department is concerned with creating product and exhibiting product in a manner destined to provide maximum audience for each segment of the broadcast day. In view of this, the controller should work closely with the members of the Program Department in evaluating and guiding their efforts to the end that their best creative work is produced at a level of cost which will allow the desired margin of profitability from a given project. There are many ways to produce a program and each different way entails a different element of cost.

. . . .

It is the controller's responsibility to work closely with the sales manager, too, to make certain that the time rates established provide sufficient margin of profitability and that sales policies in connection with rates are effectively followed. It is the controller, in the final analysis, who must make certain that an improvement in sales volume will be a *profitable* improvement. . . . . The controller should be an influential voice in maintaining the integrity of a rate position

that is equitable in providing advertising efficiency to the client at a figure that
will allow a reasonable profit to the station.

. . . .

> The experience and guidance of the controller, however, should be a strong
> force in persuading the Promotion and Publicity Department to obtain these im-
> portant elements of a station operation at a low cost or, in some instances, at no
> cost. . . .
> The rapid advances in technology in the television industry make it very
> difficult to maintain a proper balance between facility improvement and the con-
> tribution to profit that results . . . Obviously, the station must be equipped in a
> manner which will allow it to be competitive in its market place. The measure of
> this competition, however, must be judged by the result that is reflected on the
> television screen in the viewer's home and it does not require a one-for-one match
> with every item of equipment existing in the competitive station.[4]

Station accounting has progressed beyond the "green eye-shade" era.
The Institute of Broadcasting Financial Management (IBFM), organized in
1961, is an association of financial personnel in the broadcast industry who are
devoted to developing and maintaining progressive concepts of financial management. The IBFM has published an *Accounting Manual for Broadcasters* and
"operational guidelines" relating to specific problems germane to the broadcast industry, and position papers on various FCC dockets; it has also conducted
numerous industry surveys.[5] In 1972, IBFM established the Broadcast Credit
Association to act as a centralized source for agency credit information and
related problems such as collection of delinquent billings.

The theories and procedures of accounting are aptly discussed in other
published works, including some that emphasize accounting principles and
practices applied to broadcasting.[6] The business and accounting department is
responsible for bookkeeping and billing. (It may also be involved with personnel records including payroll, purchasing, storage of station logs and records,
supervision of office personnel, and network accounting.) A set of books properly kept records business transactions in a systematic way, objectively itemiz-
ing the expenses and income so that the status of business may be determined
and management can analyze the measurable reasons for profit and loss, properly attributing success or failure to the respective departments and sub-areas in
the station. Different stations will require various numbers of bookkeeping
records. Typical accounting operations include the following: *books of original
entry* (or journals) for detailed listing of debits and credits—cash receipts journal, cash disbursements journal, sales journal, voucher journal, and general
journal; and *ledgers* for regular summaries of the above according to specific
accounts—general ledger, accounts receivable ledger, accounts payable ledger,
and plant ledger.[7] These key reports thus provide the data for drawing up the
balance sheet and the operating statement.

The accounting department reports on unused facilities, idle time of personnel (technical and general administrative employees), economy of operation

of various departments, the use of supplies such as television tubes, actual and budgeted costs of programs (locally originated and purchased film or videotape properties), inventory of air-time hours available and commercial availabilities sold. The accountants must keep all records for preparing FCC reports, income tax returns, social security reports, fire and insurance claims, and legal actions. And, to provide management with data for planning profitable station operation, the accounting department draws up monthly balance sheets and the "profit-and-loss" (operating or income) statement.

Balance Sheet. The balance sheet represents at a given time how much a business has, how much it owes, and the investment of owners. A business has *assets,* which are the properties of value such as cash, equipment, buildings, and land. *Liabilities* are what that business owes—claims of outsiders on the business and its assets. The difference between the value of the assets and the amount of the liabilities is the *owner's equity* or net worth (also called ownership interest). Thus the basic balance sheet formula is ASSETS = LIABILITIES + OWNER'S EQUITY.[8] (A simplified balance sheet form, based on the IBFM model, appears below on page 286.[9])

"Profit and Loss" Statement. (The "P&L" is, of course, either profit *or* loss at a given point in time; the more accurate term is *operating statement* or *income statement.*) This financial record lists a company's activities through a period of time, insofar as they can be expressed in dollars. This statement reports the revenues of the business and the expenses incurred, showing the profit or loss that resulted from those activities during the reported time period. Whereas the balance sheet compares a company's position and any changes between similar accounting periods, the income statement indicates how those changes occurred. Management can thus determine the major areas within the station where expenses are exceeding the budgeted amounts, or where patterns of revenue *vs.* expense are shifting from month to month or between the current year and the past year. Bookkeeping records of the areas listed in the income statement can provide further details on the sources of expenses. (See the simplified sample of a typical P&L or income statement on page 287.[10])

STATION ASSETS

Assets, in the case of a radio or television station, are generally different from those of other businesses chiefly in respect to: (1) the kinds of property, plant and equipment; (2) the ownership of certain broadcasting rights; and (3) the possession of a unique kind of "good will."

Property. Amounts expended for land for the station structure and for its transmitter, tower and antenna system are considered station assets. The costs for voluntary improvements on that land, including sidewalks, parking lots, roads, landscaping, etc., are counted as assets, as are all assessments charged against the property and representing permanent improvements.

Plant. The cost of buildings constructed to house a station and/or its

BROADCASTING COMPANY
Balance Sheet
(Date)

	This Year	Last Year
ASSETS		
Current Assets:		
Cash	$ _____	$ _____
Temporary investments	_____	_____
Receivables, less reserves	_____	_____
Inventories	_____	_____
Broadcasting rights	_____	_____
Prepaid expenses	_____	_____
TOTAL CURRENT ASSETS	_____	_____
Fixed assets, less depreciation	_____	_____
Deferred charges	_____	_____
Broadcasting rights, noncurrent	_____	_____
Other assets	_____	_____
Intangibles	_____	_____
TOTAL ASSETS	$ _____	$ _____
LIABILITIES AND CAPITAL		
Current liabilities:		
Accounts and notes payable	$ _____	$ _____
Taxes and amounts withheld from employees	_____	_____
Accrued expenses	_____	_____
Federal income taxes payable	_____	_____
TOTAL CURRENT LIABILITIES	_____	_____
Deferred income taxes	_____	_____
Deferred credits	_____	_____
Long-term debt	_____	_____
Other liabilities	_____	_____
Capital stock	_____	_____
Additional paid-in capital	_____	_____
Retained earnings	_____	_____
Treasury stock:		
Common	(_____)	(_____)
Preferred	(_____)	(_____)
TOTAL CAPITAL	_____	_____
TOTAL LIABILITIES AND CAPITAL	$ _____	$ _____

BROADCASTING COMPANY
Statement of Income ["P & L"]
(Date)

	CURRENT MONTH			YEAR TO DATE		
	Actual		Budget	Actual		Budget
	This Year	Last Year		This Year	Last Year	
NET REVENUES	$	$	$	$	$	$
Cost and expenses:						
Program & production						
Transmitter						
Studio						
News and public affairs						
TOTAL OPERATING						
Sales Dept.						
Advertising						
TOTAL SELLING						
General and Administrative						
TOTAL COSTS AND EXPENSES						
Operating profit (loss)						
Other income and expenses (net)						
Income before federal income taxes						
Federal income taxes						
Net income	$	$	$	$	$	$

287

transmitting facilities is classified as an asset, as are the charges for permanent additions or alterations to those buildings. Stations renting or leasing buildings may count the costs of any improvements in either land or plant as assets.

Equipment. Radio or television equipment normally considered station assets includes the transmitter, tower and antenna systems, studio and mobile equipment, office furniture and fixtures and the vehicles used by the station.

Broadcasting Rights. All rights to broadcast program materials that have been purchased but not yet used (that is, they are unamortized) are station assets. Such rights may include public events where admission is charged, such as sports or concerts. They may also include such program staples as taped features, syndicated films and recorded libraries.

"Good Will." When an established station is sold, the asking price exceeds the total net assets of the station. The difference between the selling price and net assets represents the "good will" which the station merits by reason of operations. Factors contributing to a station's "good will" may include an affiliation with a network, the existing number of contracts for future network, spot and local advertising, and the station image in the community. Sometimes a seller will agree that he will not compete in the area of coverage for a specified length of time. Such an agreement can be advantageous to a new owner and may represent an asset. The possession of patents, copyrights or leases, likewise, may be included as a part of a station's "good will." And, of course, the FCC license (transfer of which is subject to the Commission's approval) represents an enormous asset, obviating the expensive, time-consuming, and uncertain procedures of filing for a new frequency, if one is available, against rival counter-applicants.

Other Assets. Other assets consist of items similar to the ordinary assets of standard business organizations. They may include: cash on hand or on deposit; all investments; accounts and notes receivable; those expenses that are prepaid (e.g. taxes, insurance, rents and expense-account advances); and unused inventories in the possession of the station.

The amount of gross investment in tangible radio properties in the United States increased from a total of $55 million in 1937 to over $500 million by 1965 and to more than $840 million by 1973. (The depreciated cost for those radio stations' and national networks' property investments in 1973 totaled $426,490,000.) [11] Television investment in tangible broadcast property totaled $1.7 billion by 1974, for the three national television networks, their fifteen owned-and-operated stations, and 474 VHF and 177 UHF stations. (Less depreciation, the net investment value as of 1974 totaled $749,104,000 for all television broadcast tangible property.) [12]

In 1960, the Collins Radio Company sponsored a study by the Industrial Marketing Studies of the University of Illinois to investigate radio technical facilities and equipment assets of all commercial and educational AM and FM stations in the United States.[13] Of the total assets of those stations, 43.9 per cent were in technical equipment, with an average investment per station of over $90,000. The average age of transmitters then in use was 7.7 years. Slightly over three-fourths of all the 50-kw radio stations had been on the air for 20 years or longer but over one-half of those stations were using transmitters less than 10 years old. A trend had begun for the retention of used AM transmitters for stand-by auxiliaries during possible power failures. The average station experienced more than five technical problems, in addition to power troubles, in an average year—all serious enough to force the station off the air. The average length of time that radio stations were off the air due to each technical difficulty was 3 hours and 48 minutes. The findings of the study showed that 30.2 per cent of all radio stations leased all or part of their land, 15.9 per cent leased buildings, 30.4 per cent leased office space and 8.3 per cent leased vehicles. No significant number of stations leased technical equipment.

Depreciation. The Collins study showed that the average life expectancy for studio equipment and office furniture and fixtures came to slightly under nine years. In only about one-fifth of the radio stations were there plans to replace studio equipment before its full depreciation. The average annual expenditure of AM radio stations for studio sound equipment was approximately $1690 per station. The average annual expenditure for office furniture and fixtures was $746 per station.

Depreciation write-offs have been a problem for the broadcaster due to the rapid increases in price of most broadcast equipment. Some managers prefer a fast depreciation rate that permits them to replace station equipment prior to its obsolescence. Other managers prefer to take a slower rate and retain their equipment for the full depreciation schedule or longer.

In 1962, the Internal Revenue Service adopted a schedule recommending a six-year depreciation period for broadcasting equipment. Other recommended depreciation schedules (Asset Depreciation Range) of interest to broadcasters were: land improvements, including tower and antenna systems, twenty years; buildings, forty-five years; office furniture, fixtures and equipment, ten years; automobiles, three years; light trucks, four years; and heavy trucks, six years.

STATION LIABILITIES

The ordinary liabilities of a station include: amounts due for prior purchases of goods and services; any collections made in advance for station services not yet delivered; unpaid balances on long-term notes, mortgages, bonds or other debts; dividends declared but not yet paid; tax monies due and all miscellaneous accrued expenses.

The category of miscellaneous accrued expenses includes various obligations of the station due at some future date. Normally, these liabilities encompass such items as: employee salaries, wages, commissions and other benefits; Federal and state income taxes; sales and use taxes; interest due on notes, mortgages, etc.; and materials received and used in trade or barter arrangements for which airtime "payments" have not yet been made.

Sources of Income

It has been noted that the predominant source of revenue for any station is the sale of time for network, national or regional spot, and local advertising. Secondary sources may include the sale of talent, the sale of recorded or transcribed materials, the rental of station facilities, merchandising activities, and interest and dividends from station investments.

Normal Station Expenses

Station expenses are usually categorized and budgeted under the four headings of programming, engineering, sales, and general and administrative.

Normally, the largest single operating cost of any station is for salaries and wages. This includes, in addition to the regular payroll, all overtime pay and the costs of paid vacations and holiday pay. Also included are the station contributions to various employee benefits. These include social security, unemployment insurance and workmen's compensation. Additionally, some stations provide such benefits as profit sharing plans, bonuses, group insurance, hospitalization and retirement pensions. For the convenience of employees, payroll deductions may be effected for such purposes as the purchase of U.S. Savings Bonds or for donations to organizations such as a united community fund. In such cases, the added cost of administration of the service must be regarded as a station expense.

Programming Expenses

The program department usually is the most expensive station unit in terms of salaries, wages and benefits. Other normal expenses of the program department include: the cost of rights to broadcast certain programs and events; music license fees; recordings and transcriptions; news wire services; film rental or purchase; shipping costs; sets and props; the costs of remote originations, including line charges; and any other miscellaneous expense for program production.

Film programming, when bought in "package" lots, can be amortized over the period when all the films in a "package" will be shown. Unfortunately, the Internal Revenue Service's Ruling 62-20 provides that broadcasters must charge their film contract expense equally over the contract life, although that is contrary to usual economic practices in a television station. The IRS has permitted sliding-scale amortization of charge-offs in some instances, provided the broadcaster can substantiate clearly the sliding-scale of revenues produced by the film package over several years' exhibition.[14] Stations typically write off a film with contract rights to four presentations by amortizing 50 per cent for the first airing, 25 per cent for the second, 15 per cent for the third, and 10 per cent for the fourth showing.

Music Licensing. One of the major operating cost items in broadcasting is the music license fee for performing rights. In 1972, the nation's 2,808 AM and 1,463 AM-FM stations paid music license fees of $32,765,000; and 865 FM stations paid fees of $2,851,000. In 1973, 666 television stations paid fees amounting to $41,557,000, and the three national television networks paid a total of $6,248,000.[15] More than an $80 million-a-year business, music licensing is controlled in the United States by three organizations.

The American Society of Composers, Authors and Publishers (ASCAP) is the largest and oldest. It was formed in 1914 and has a repertory of more than a million titles. ASCAP collects almost two-thirds of the annual payments made wherever music is played for profit. Initially, its revenues were collected from restaurants, hotels, dance halls, etc. Then motion pictures became a prime source. Today, broadcasters account for about four-fifths of the annual receipts.

Broadcast Music, Incorporated (BMI) was created in 1940, at a time when broadcasters were restricted from playing any music not in the public domain. An increase in fees by ASCAP was deemed too high by broadcasters. Hence, when their station contracts with ASCAP expired at the end of 1940 and were not renewed, stations had to program the old tunes. BMI was created and financed by the broadcast industry as a source for new compositions. The difficulties between broadcasters and ASCAP were resolved after some 10 months, but by then BMI had become a successful enterprise. It has some three-quarters of a million titles.

SESAC (originally the Society of European Stage Authors and Composers) is relatively small by comparison with the other two. Although originally representing European works, SESAC is now based in the U.S. and its repertory includes American creations. It is a privately owned organization, formed in 1931.

All three licensing organizations have found themselves in conflicts with broadcasters through the decades. ASCAP was yet to settle a dispute over a proposed rate increase which had been requested two years earlier. In 1967 BMI reached agreement with an All Industry Radio Station Music Licensing Committee on its first increase in station rates in its 26-year history. SESAC agreed to publish a catalogue of its compositions after the Federal Trade Commission had the company under investigation. ASCAP and BMI both received judgments by Federal courts in 1970 and 1971 against ABC-TV and CBS-TV, respectively.

Engineering Expenses

In addition to the payroll for supervisory and non-supervisory employees of the engineering department, other expenses usually include such items as: cost of tubes for transmitter, studio and remote units; cost of audio and/or video tape; rental charges for transmitter lines; and parts and supplies used in the station's technical equipment and in its maintenance.

Sales Expenses

Sales commissions and expense accounts are added to the usual costs of salaries, wages and benefits in this department. Other normal expenses may include: public relations, advertising and promotion that is directed to the audience; trade advertising and promotion directed to the industry; commissions for the station "rep"; and the cost of rating services.

General and Administrative Expenses

The salaries and wages of the station manager and all other employees of the station not assigned to programming, sales or engineering are included in the administrative budget. Additional expenses include some items associated directly with management and others used by all departments with their budgets controlled by the central administration of the station. These expenses ordinarily include: maintenance and repair of buildings and equipment; heat, air-conditioning, light and power; rents; telephone and telegraph; stationery and office supplies; postage; travel and entertainment; membership fees and dues; subscriptions; operating costs of station-owned automobiles and trucks; real and personal property taxes; state and local taxes; insurance; station contributions to charitable, educational, religious and welfare organizations; and legal, auditing and other consultant fees.

RADIO INDUSTRY PROFITS

In 1956 and 1957 the margin of radio revenues over expenses established a peak that was not reached for another six years. In 1958, the increase in revenues failed to keep pace with increased expenses, resulting in a sharp reduction in industry profit. Then, in 1961, total radio revenues took a real setback from their 1960 total, causing the margin of profit to reach the lowest point since 1939. More radio stations showed losses in 1961 than in any previous year since the FCC started publishing financial data about stations. Almost 40 per cent of all radio operations lost money. Yet, by the end of 1963, all preceding marks for profit were broken. Radio continued to set new records in revenues from sales and to set intermittent records in profits into the early 1970s (except for independent FM stations). But in 1973 the profit ratio for all stations dropped one-fifth (from 9.5% to 7.4%) in spite of largest annual revenues ever; while revenues had increased $103-million over the previous year, expenses mounted $126-million over 1972. (See Table X.)

Generally 65 per cent of radio's revenue is from local advertising. About 30 per cent is received from national spot and only 5 per cent from the networks. This follows a pattern whereby local sources of revenue have become increasingly the main support of radio stations and network income has declined steadily.

Over the years, the costs of radio station operation divide roughly into some 39 per cent of total expenses for general and administrative, 30 per cent for programming, 20 per cent for sales and 10 per cent for technical.

Wages and salaries are the highest expense item, slightly more than half of total costs. Other major expenses include royalties and license fees, depreciation, talent and news costs other than salaries.

TABLE X

AM & FM Broadcast Revenues, Expenses, and Income [16]
(in millions of dollars)

Year	Revenues	Expenses	Total	AM, AM-FM	Ind. FM	Profit Ratio (All Stations)
				INCOME		*Profit Ratio*
Year	*Revenues*	*Expenses*	*Total*	*AM, AM-FM*	*Ind. FM*	*(All Stations)*
1973	$1,510.4	$1,398.0	$112.4	$123.3	$(10.8)*	7.4%
1972	1,407.0	1,272.6	134.3	147.0	(12.7)	9.5
1971	1,258.0	1,155.2	102.8	117.8	(15.0)	8.2
1970	1,136.9	1,044.0	92.9	104.0	(11.1)	8.2
1969	1,085.8	985.0	100.9	106.4	(5.5)	9.3
1968	1,023.0	909.6	113.4	117.3	(3.9)	11.1
1967	907.3	826.5	80.8	85.0	(4.2)	8.9
1966	872.1	774.8	97.3	100.6	(3.3)	11.6
1965	792.5	714.7	77.8	81.1	(3.3)	9.8
1964	732.0	661.2	70.8	73.8	(3.0)	9.7
1963	681.1	626.2	54.9	58.1	(3.2)	8.1
1962	636.1	592.6	43.5	46.7	(3.2)	6.9

* (Parentheses denote loss.)

In 1972, the "typical" radio station showed revenues of $170,100 and expenses of $158,800. Profits for the "typical" station were $11,300 for a profit margin of 6.67 per cent before Federal taxes. The margin of profit in the industry in 1961, when the NAB survey did not include independent FM stations, was 4.8 per cent; comparable figures for AM and AM/FM stations in 1972 would show a profit margin of 7.65 per cent, with "typical" station's revenue of $188,200 and expenses $173,800, with pre-tax profit of $14,400.[17]

In 1973, 3,142 radio stations (2,907 AM and AM-FM, plus 235 FM) reported profits, while no fewer than 1,647 stations (1,306 AM and AM-FM, plus 341 FM) suffered losses. Nor was there consistency among the stations enjoying profitable operations. Seventy-two stations (including an independent FM) showed profits of over $500,000 for the year but 17 stations (including eight independent FMs) made profits of less than $25,000. There were 220 stations with revenues over $1 million; of these, 24 did not show profit.

The majority of radio stations in 1973 operated very close to the line between profit and loss. The margin of gain or loss for the year for 55 per cent of the stations was around $15,000 (991 stations ended the year's operations with a profit or loss of less than $5,000 on all their annual business, including two stations "breaking even" on revenues of over $1 million). This was hardly a desirable rate of return in consideration of the work involved in maintaining a broadcast service for a year. The investors in a majority of the nation's radio stations could have found a greater rate of return in some other forms of business enterprise.

The key factor in the determination of broadcast profit is management. Granted that there are radio stations in markets that are oversaturated or too small to support broadcasting, still, some stations do show fine profits even in these circumstances. Yet, when one station receives over a million dollars in revenue and loses money and when another station in a small market produces only about $200 a week for all its effort, it should be good sense and good business to re-assess the entities as management and business enterprises. The average profitable radio station may earn revenues almost twice those of the unprofitable stations, but their expenses may be only some 18 per cent higher. Again, the key factor is *management*.

Almost all of the AM and FM stations reporting annual losses reported depreciation expenses. Over half of this total reported that payments were made to station owners, partners and/or stockholders. Over half of the stations with losses took depreciation expenses and/or made payments to owners, etc., that exceeded the amount of their losses. Almost one-third of all the stations failing to show profit made payments to owners, etc. that alone exceeded their losses.

A question might logically be raised as to why so many radio stations continue in business when they operate at a loss. At least a partial answer may be ventured in the observation that station owners, partners and/or stockholders are given healthy payments before profit or loss or dividends are declared. Until 1962, this information was not requested by the FCC; station financial reports now show that about half of all licensed stations follow this practice. Another reason, of course—beyond mere prestige or personal satisfaction in owning a public broadcast property—is the possible tax advantage for a parent corporation that supports such a deficit operation.

TELEVISION INDUSTRY PROFITS

The general decline in profit in the radio industry in 1958 was experienced in the television industry a year earlier. Where some six years were needed for the radio industry to return to its former profit level, television came back much faster. Within two years, it exceeded its former profit record. There was a temporary slump in 1961, as there was in radio income, but it was not of any serious magnitude. After that year, television profits set new records until a "soft" 1967, set a new high again in 1968, slumped in 1970 and 1971, then rose to unparalleled heights in 1972 and 1973.[18] (See Table XI.)

Revenue. In all of television, almost half of all advertising revenue is generated at the network level (46%), one third through national and local spot (31%), and one fifth by local advertising (21%). The chief source of revenue for the three television networks is from time sales (in 1973, $1.8 billion, or 96%). Program and talent sales constitute the only other major revenue source (approximately $75 million, or 4%). The nation's television stations receive the largest share of their income from national and regional spot sales (in 1973, $1.2 billion), with local sales next in volume ($895.6 million), followed by income from the networks for their station time ($227.3 million).

Expenses. Network expenses for programs amount to approximately 50 per cent of total costs. The next highest cost is for payments to affiliates. Other expenditures, relatively less, are for agency commissions, administrative costs,

TABLE XI

TV BROADCAST NET REVENUES, EXPENSES, AND INCOME [19]
(in millions of dollars)
NETWORKS, OWNED-STATIONS, AFFILIATES & INDEPENDENTS
(Networks and Owned-stations in parentheses)

Year	Revenue *		Expenses		Income (before Fed. tax)		Profit Ratio	
1973	($1,758)		($1,470)		($288)		(16.4%)	
		$1,706		$1,341		$365		21.4%
1972	(1,598)		(1,385)		(213)		(13.3)	
		1,581		1,242		338		21.4
1971	(1,379)		(1,234)		(145)		(10.5)	
		1,371		1,127		244		17.8
1970	(1,457)		(1,290)		(167)		(11.5)	
		1,351		1,065		286		21.7
1969	(1,467)		(1,241)		(226)		(15.5)	
		1,329		1,001		328		24.9
1968	(1,308)		(1,129)		(179)		(13.7)	
		1,213		897		316		26.0
1967	(1,217)		(1,057)		(160)		(13.1)	
		1,059		804		255		24.1

* (Net revenues, after commissions and cash discounts)

payments to owned stations, technical costs and selling costs. Television station expenses usually consist of more than one-third for program costs, roughly one-fourth for administrative costs, and one-fifth for commissions to agencies and "reps." Technical and selling costs account for about 12 per cent each.

Profits. Pre-tax profits of the networks in the year 1973 amounted to a 13 per cent return (compared with 8% in 1965). The profits of the network-owned stations represented a 29 per cent return (down from 43% in 1965). All other television stations had an average profit return of 21.4 per cent (30% in 1965)—including 150 stations reporting losses out of 622 stations tabulated (deficit operations were 51 of the 425 VHF affiliates, 51 of the 112 UHF affiliates, 11 of the 32 VHF independents, and 37 of the 53 UHF independents).[20] Comparative figures for 1965 and 1973 provide a profile of station profitability through almost a decade. Stations with profits of $1 million or more for 1965 numbered 112 VHF (23%) and 20 UHF (20%); nine years later, million-dollar-plus stations totaled 137 VHF (30%) and 1 UHF (0.5%). Profits of $25,000 or less were reported in 1965 by 27 VHF (5.5%) and by 12 UHF (7%) stations; in 1973 such profits were reported by 20 VHF (4%) and by 13 UHF (8%) stations. Finally, losses were sustained in 1965 by 61 VHFs (13%) and by 29 UHFs (34.5%), compared with the 1973 deficits reported by 62 VHFs (13.6%) and by fully 88 UHFs (53%).[21]

As was the case in radio, almost all television stations claimed depreciation expenses (averaging from 7.5% for VHF to 9.5% for UHF stations); in most instances depreciation expenses were less than losses reported by stations. And many stations made payments to some station owners, partners and/or stockholders; but proportionately fewer television stations reported making such payments.

THE MANAGER AND PROFIT

With annual losses reported by more than 13 per cent of the commercial VHF television stations, over half of the commercial UHFs, almost a third of the commercial AM and two-thirds of the commercial FM radio stations, it should be obvious that the management of finances could be improved in many instances. One ultimate consequence of neglecting such improvement might be a reduction in the present number of radio and television stations. Much has been said about all the problems arising from an excess of radio stations, and it may be true that a larger number has been authorized than can be supported profitably. Any station, however, which has been authorized and has been in operation deserves a chance to survive. That survival, assuming that good programming, technical and economic practices are followed, will depend upon the effectiveness of the station's management.

Some managers, faced with continued financial loss, show a tendency to panic. They often decide to accept any types of commercial accounts, to cut their rates in order to get some semblance of business, to program as cheaply as possible without regard to quality standards, to cut personnel to a minimum and then hire the cheapest people who can be found, to get by with equipment that has passed its state of maximum utility, to oppose any improvements in their station facilities, to cancel their membership in state and national professional associations and in the industry Codes, and to cut all budgetary items to a point that will permit only minimal operating standards. Such action may produce an immediate financial improvement but it can also endanger the reserve potential of the station. Then, when further budgetary cuts may be necessary, there can be no effective retrenchment.

The manager needs to maintain a financial or operating reserve adequate to meet possible future emergencies. Such a reserve does not necessarily need to be in cash or securities. It may be created by prepayments of certain station obligations. It may be in the form of a manpower reserve. It may consist of certain station services that can be eliminated in a crisis. There are various other possibilities. Maintaining a financial reserve is important to any manager because increased competition can force him to draw upon it in the future.

By way of contrast, there have been managers who, when confronted with almost certain financial losses, have increased station expenses in order to become more competitive. Choosing not to make radical overall budgetary cuts, these managers have eliminated wastes and inefficiencies that have caused the stations to suffer financial losses. They have accepted the possibility of even greater losses over a short period of time so that their stations could become effective competitors in the future. These managers have had the courage to defend their strategies to their owners or stockholders. They have been fully prepared to find other employment should the station owners disagree with their policies. In every such case that has come to our attention, there has been no need for any change in employment. Instead, the vision, integrity and strength of these managers have been highly regarded by station owners. In almost every case, their stations rebounded to become solid competitors.

COST CONTROLS FOR GREATER PROFITS

A station can implement various economies without sacrificing either quality or standards. Constant and careful attention to cost controls can effectuate real savings. Many relatively minor budgetary items can turn into excessive costs due to wastes, inefficiencies or extravagances. To achieve economy, the administration of expenditures requires constant vigilance. Little is accomplished if the action is sporadic. The supervision of cost controls must be almost a daily process until it receives the cooperation and the enthusiastic support of the entire staff of a station. It has been said that the true test of real executive leadership comes when reduction of cost but not of quality becomes a major objective of the company. An effective manager can produce real savings without losing any cooperation or enthusiasm from his employees. He should, indeed, cause both to grow.

Mikita distinguishes appropriately between "cost reduction" and management's goal

> to establish an atmosphere of 'cost awareness.' Whereas cost reduction seems to carry with it the idea that reductions are to be made regardless of their impact on the over-all operation, the concept of *cost awareness* is entirely different as it connotes merely that at some stage of the development of a project, or a campaign, or in the consideration of new facilities equipment, the measure of profitability must be applied.[22]

The manager, as well as the controller, must possess enough ability and experience so that department heads respect their understanding of detailed station operations and their appreciation of specific problems in those departments. Familiarity with operational practice makes it possible for the manager to guide and even direct each functional department where personnel are absorbed by creative and technical activity.

Reinsch and Ellis [23] describe major ways in which a manager can strive for more efficient cost control, beyond exercising leadership in motivating all employees: utilize manpower wisely; work towards better union agreements; strive for good supervision; improve employee performance; encourage employee participation; improve working facilities; reduce costs of services; increase revenue from sales; and especially maintain budgetary controls as well as determine criteria for standards of cost operation and analysis.

Staff Economies

It seems to be fairly easy for employees to abuse such privileges as the "coffee break" or the use of the telephone for personal conversations, but of far greater importance is the development of a climate of work whereby the true potential of every member of the staff is realized. This subject is of such importance that Chapter 3 of this book was devoted to personnel practices and motivating people to accomplish those creative results of which they are capable.

Working Facilities

Investments in improved working facilities often produce returns far greater than the cost of the investments. Buildings originally designed for other purposes and then transformed to serve as radio or television stations often have space inefficiencies. In many cases, a simple rearrangement of the physical layout of the station facilities may result in more productive efforts by the station staff. The location of the office staff closer to the studios can improve the traffic flow and increase the work output of the station. A physical rearrangement of filing equipment or of desks may result in greater productivity. Some studio and control room arrangements require engineers to concentrate all of their attention on one activity when they should be able to oversee several. Offices can become so overcrowded that they hamper good work. Regular assessment of space considerations is recommended.

Mechanized Systems

The business machine and computer technology are not restricted to the accounting function. Most good-sized broadcasting operations have used one business-machine system or another for several years. There is no reason why a business-machine system cannot handle all of the routine traffic of a radio or television station from the time a spot is sold, including its placement in the schedule, to its eventual billing.[24]

Mechanization, in itself, is not a panacea. In cases of weak or inadequate control, mechanization only highlights the defects in an existing system. Inefficiencies cannot be eliminated by pushing a button that starts a machine. Under a properly organized and controlled operation, there are several possible advantages of a machine system to a medium- or large-market radio or television station. One advantage is the speed with which clear and neat logs and invoices can be prepared. Another is the ability to produce numerous reports and analyses from basic data. Station logs can be prepared from basic data cards and at high speeds. Commercial cards can be sorted: (1) by agency code to prepare invoices, (2) by salesman code to prepare commission reports and (3) by day and time codes to obtain daily or hourly breakdowns of revenue. Even breakdowns of revenue by products can be provided. Mechanization can be particularly valuable in the forecasting of revenues and expenses.

Sales Revenues

Astute planning and sales staff collaboration can generate increased sales volume, so that a radio or television station may achieve its fullest potential in a market. This revenue contributes to upgrading the entire operation. A small-market independent radio station in the Midwest more than doubled its billings by careful analysis of the "greater market" of its full signal area, by systematic scheduling of fully paid-for spots (no discounts, no rate cutting, and even no free air-time for public service announcements—content of which was covered in local newscasts and commentaries). Jerell A. Shepherd, owner and manager of KWIX, Moberly, Missouri, outlined a policy for trying to become "the finest small market radio station in the nation":

1. Do the most business.
2. Have the finest physical plant and equipment.
3. Have the best staff.
4. Render the finest and most service to our listeners and advertisers.[25]

While emphasizing service, news, and information programming with community and area involvement, Mr. Shepherd claimed that "we are more of a sales organization than we are a programming operation." And he doubled billings by determining concrete, specific, and demanding sales goals to be reached periodically. The initial goal was to make no changes whatever except in the total sales effort. He reversed the normal professional sequence: "We get the sales, and then we get better programming. . . . If you've got the money coming in, programming is all set. You can have the mobile news crews; you can have as many telephones as you want; you can have all the equipment, a capable staff—the works." He summarized his staff's sales success:

> It was built by no magic formula nor because the community was any more progressive than any others. It was built by hard work and a determined effort.
> It was built on the development of a fine sales staff and a fine programming staff.
> It was built by plowing back much of our earnings into programming after we achieved our earlier sales goals.

While particulars of his philosophy might be debated, the success in building sales revenues ultimately enhanced the quality of program service.

A particular concern of the manager is the problem of delinquent accounts—often a small but significant percentage of total business. Bankruptcy proceedings by a few advertising agencies in the early 1970s focused on poorly-managed procedures for extending credit and for resolving discrepancies and determining liability for default on payments. Three national organizations able to assist management in shaping policy and procedures in this matter are the Credit Association for Radio and Television, the Broadcast Credit Association, and Media Payment Corporation. For example, a survey by the latter group found that 89 per cent of responding radio-TV stations favored dual liability for advertisers and agencies in payment for broadcast advertising.[26]

Budgeting

The budgeting of annual expenditures is standard practice in any business. Problems of bugetary control usually can be solved by including the department heads in budget planning and by using administrative follow-up procedures at regular intervals during the budgeted year.

Budgets should not be prepared entirely by management if they are to be realistic in terms of the needs of the departments. The manager must, of course, give final approval to all budgets and he must be expected to exercise the right to veto or to cut any of the requests he deems unnecessary, but each department should be given full opportunity to propose. Each department head should be made well aware of the corporate budgetary goals and of the importance of departmental cost controls so that those goals may be achieved. Department heads and the station controller or accountant should meet at weekly or at least monthly intervals to review actual expenditures as well as each status of the budget balance for the department. Through such conferences, it should be possible not only to curb cases of overspending but even to effect some savings.

It is a wise policy for the station manager and the department heads to review at regular intervals the annual financial reports of the FCC as well as the various data from NAB on station revenues and expenses. From these reports, station executives can gain important insights into the financial practices of typical or similar stations in the various categories of transmission power, market and competition.

A manager and his staff must make decisions about plant and facilities, such as the advantage of leasing rather than purchasing some kinds of equipment. Careful estimates must be drawn up to determine when it might be profitable to expand studio or office or technical capacity; such capacity must be closely related to programming and engineering costs. The volume of programming or production services (commercials, promotional productions or packaged shows) should be related to the station's real capacity for output in terms of space, facilities, personnel, and overhead. Hoffer[27] suggests that management carefully analyze such questions as: Will cutting departmental operating expenses necessarily result in a higher net operating income? Will investing more money into programming and facilities be reflected in greater sales (more time sold, at higher rates)? How do current estimates compare with previous years? What rate of return is expected by station owners or company stockholders? Will predicted net operating incomes affect the station's tax status? Have reserves been provided to protect against economic recession? Are there any major projects in the future, such as building new studios or acquiring additional properties? Are competitors planning any major expansion?

Budgeting necessarily involves projecting estimates of future revenue and expense, sometimes even forecasting for five- and ten-year periods. This sets goals and parameters for business expressed in gross and net figures. These projections must reflect trends in the general economy, fluctuations in the local market's business and population, changes in costs for equipment and salaries and services, expansion of plant and facilities, increases or cutbacks in payroll reflecting cost-of-living scales and merit as well as increased efficiency (particularly if automated equipment is involved). Increases in air-time rate schedules and services must be anticipated to compete with other broadcasters and with non-electronic advertising media. Management must derive sound revenue data for these forecasts because business planning can be harmed as much by overestimating as by underestimating.

The Manager's Challenges

The broadcast manager is a man of at least two worlds. He is charged with properly operating a publicly licensed radio or television station to serve the local community. At the same time he is charged by his employers to oversee the entire station operation in a way that produces increasingly greater revenue.

Dr. Harry Skornia, a strong critic of American commercial broadcasting, recognized that the inherent organization of modern business as well as supportive legal precedent seem to militate against a full public-interest orientation by commercial broadcasting. He cited the Michigan Supreme Court which supported a Ford Motor Company stockholder who objected to Henry Ford's attempt to reduce the price of that company's automotive products. Dr. Skornia noted:

> The court held that the business corporation, created to operate for profit, must serve its stockholders first and the public only secondarily—the corporation interest, rather than the public, must be favored whenever profits may be affected. . . . A corporation's charitable or public-interest expenditures must advance the long-range prospects of profit making. . . . Therefore, a corporation created to operate for profit, regardless of any desire to serve 'public interest first' by its officials, must serve its *owners* and *stockholders* first, returning to them as large a profit as possible. Many corporations have been able to reconcile these two interests satisfactorily; how well broadcast corporations have done so will become clearer as the record is examined.[28]

But at this point the manager is confronted by several kinds of data which suggest that producing revenue and making profits might well contribute to a station's community precisely through its programming. A study of television station performance relative to revenues documented evidence from FCC files for several hundred television stations. The study quantified the fairly predictable conclusion that "stations with higher revenues broadcast more hours of local programming" than do stations with lower revenues, although those extra hours occur outside of large-audience prime-time. Also, more money is spent on local and non-entertainment programming in direct proportion to the additional revenue dollars of a station (a small network-affiliate spends 15 cents of

each additional revenue dollar on local programming, while a large network affiliate spends 17 cents).[29] Similarly, other studies have tended to support the
finding that multiple-station owners—with large revenues and capital—provide
diversity of views in non-entertainment programming, and provide more local
and public service programming for their various communities than does single-
station ownership.[30] A corollary research effort found that commonly-owned
media in a single market ("cross-ownership") also provided generally better
program service than did stations owned by companies not involved with other
media in the market.[31]

There are many theoretical and practical challenges to the broadcast manager. They involve economics, politics, sociology, law, psychology, and most
other human, artistic, and scientific disciplines. They relate to political candidates' use of air-waves, crime and violence on the screen, aesthetic and percep-
tual effects on the audience, "overcommercialism," and a host of other significant issues in society.[32] A scattered series of court decisions have given
precedent and support for state and local taxation of commercial broadcasting,
including local-oriented (intrastate) advertising, and net-income state taxes on
broadcast profits, gross receipts taxes, use taxes, and attempts at air-time sales
taxation.[33] The station's net income can be directly affected by the legislative
results of these patterns of inquiry.

What about more tangible trends for the economic future of broadcasting?

Although the national economy in the mid-1970s reflected inflationary
trends, with "tight money" and a sluggish market for stocks, price-earnings
ratios were never better for the broadcast industry.[34] Contrary to predictions
that, with corporate profits expected to go down, companies would not be advertising as much as in the past, advertisers generally sustained their budgets
for radio and television, and broadcast profits held their own and even increased. This somewhat reflected the growth of broadcast business during the Great
Depression in the 1930s, when broadcast entertainment was the least expensive
form for individuals and families with meager incomes, so advertisers sought
their attention through radio commercials.

An investment analyst noted late in 1974: "Essentially, I view the earnings of broadcasters as a step function. Profits go up, then they stabilize, then
they go up again. Stocks, on the other hand, are like a saw tooth. They go up
and down in response to the rest of the market." One aid to profit-making in
the slower economy of the mid-1970s was the cost-cutting efforts by networks
and especially stations. But one financial observer judged that most feasible
cuts had been made by 1975 and, unless revenue dollars increased, broadcast
companies could expect a lower profit-ratio in the latter 1970s. The Securities
Research Division of Merrill Lynch, Pierce, Fenner & Smith, Inc. compared
overall business and the broadcast media:

> Broadcasting is unlikely to be hurt as much as other entertainment business
> in the event of a general economic slowdown, because television and radio are the
> least expensive forms of entertainment; in fact, audience levels might even in-

crease. Gains in earnings are expected to exceed the growth of revenues, because broadcasters' costs are more or less fixed, and little overhead is added as income grows.[35]

The U.S. Commerce Department's annual *U.S. Industrial Outlook* for 1975 estimated broadcast revenue for that year to total $7.2 billion, a 9 per cent rise from 1974's estimated $6.6 billion.[36] *Television* would account for three-fourths of that total advertising revenue. Television revenues were projected to increase an average of 9 per cent each year through the decade of the 1970s, reaching a total of $6.25 billion by 1980. But television's pre-tax income (profit ratio) was predicted to drop to 17.1 per cent for 1974, then to 16.5 per cent in 1975—compared with roughly 20.6 per cent in the 1960s. By 1980 that profit ratio was expected to reach approximately 12.8 per cent ($800 million pre-tax income on revenues of $6.25 billion). Meanwhile, *radio* earnings in 1974 set a record of $153 million and were predicted to rise further to $177 million the following year. Profit-ratios were set at 9.5 per cent in 1974 (on revenues of $1,610 million) and at 9.9 per cent in 1975 (on revenues of $1,787). By 1980 radio was projected to produce revenues of $2.7 billion— based on radio's effectiveness as an advertising medium, increased productivity and efficiency through automation, and only a slight increase in the number of radio stations. The Federal agency estimated that in 1974 FM radio revenues (for stations reporting to the FCC separately from AM) should rise 20 per cent from the previous year to $236 million, with further increase of 30 per cent to $307 million in 1975. An independent management consulting firm projected total FM revenues in 1980 at $732 million, or almost one-third of all radio revenues; by 1975 FM was estimated as attracting a third of all radio listening in the country, and in many markets FM stations were contending with established AM stations for top rating positions.[37]

In summation, the Federal government projected for the latter 1970s continued increase in advertising revenue for all broadcast operations—AM, FM, TV, both networks and stations—but with decreased profit margins. The government report emphasized the continued growth of local advertising in broadcasting: in 1974, 34 per cent of all industry revenues was local business, and in 1975, 71 per cent of radio revenues and 23 per cent of television's gross were expected to come from local advertising.[38]

The station manager is faced with a challenging dilemma. He must provide programming and scheduling for a community with a Federally-regulated license at the same time that he strives for annually increasing profitability to the owners and investors in that station as a business. Les Brown, formerly of *Variety* and now the *New York Times,* noted realistically that "American television is a business before it is anything else, and within the broadcast companies the sales function is pre-eminent." [39] He added the sobering reflection:

> There is no other course but for broadcast managements to dedicate themselves to profit growth; their executive survival depends upon it. They must at the

same time convey the impression of being stable and sturdy in the face of the speculative and volatile nature of show business, and so to whatever extent possible they divorce themselves from the impressario risks and behave as companies engaged in the manufacture of goods. They deal, therefore, in programs that will be instantly accepted by the audience, rejecting new and experimental forms that might take weeks or months to catch on, if at all.

This chapter concludes with another statement of realism, but which avoids the perjorative judgment implied above. The comment is by "one who was there"—who had to meet payrolls and answer for profit and loss statements to owners. Joseph Mikita, vice president of finance for Group W, Westinghouse Broadcasting Company, New York, summarized the manager's multiple responsibilities:

> To satisfy their own responsibility to the public, broadcasters must do many things which will not immediately enhance the profitability of a given television station. Nevertheless, it is essential that the financial yardstick be applied to all operations if intelligent financial planning is to accomplish an atmosphere of healthy growth.
>
> Forecasting has become a necessity in television broadcasting because of the high cost of operation and because the profit margin is highly susceptible to unfavorable variations in an increasing sales pattern. There is a reasonably fixed level of operating costs which bears little or no relation to the amount of commercial business the station enjoys. Beyond this level of fixed costs, or 'break-even volume,' the television station can convert a substantial part of sales improvements to operating profit. Conversely, a drop-off in business is generally reflected in reduction in operating profit. It is essential, therefore, that for a healthy growth in profitability, the gross business improvement inherent in a young and dynamic industry contain within itself a satisfactory margin of profit. The measure of profitability must therefore be applied to new ventures in programming promotion, facilities improvement and, in fact, to any other area designed to increase the gross revenue of a station.[40]

NOTES

Chapter 7

1. *Time*, February 8, 1963, p. 75.

2. In "Meeting the Engineering Shortage," *BM/E* [Broadcast Management/Engineering], March 1971, pp. 44–45, 56, 75. Mr. Coddington is author of *Modern Radio Broadcasting* (Blue Ridge Summit, Pa.: Tab Books, 1969).

3. Joseph K. Mikita, "The Controller's Role in Management," in Yale Roe (ed.), *Television Station Management: The Business of Broadcasting* (N.Y.: Hastings House, 1964), p. 94; see his entire chapter 6, pp. 91–104, for amplification of the points here.

4. Mikita, in Roe, pp. 100–102.

5. Institute of Broadcasting Financial Management, Inc., *Accounting Manual for Broadcasters* (revised in association with Ernst & Ernst, 1972), 360 North Michigan Avenue, Chicago, Ill. This loose-leaf binder provides a 51-page single-spaced itemized listing and description of specific account entries together with sub-entries, and 16 pages of sample forms for financial statements.

6. For succinct, practical analyses see: Small Business Administration, "The Why and

What of Bookkeeping" (Washington, D.C.: U.S. Government Printing Office, 1965); Broadcast Management Department, "Accounting Manual for Radio Stations" and also "Accounting Manual for Television Stations" (Washington, D.C., National Assoc. of Broadcasters, 1961 & 1959); Dept. of Broadcast Management, "Internal Control in Broadcasting Stations" (Washington, D.C.: National Assoc. of Broadcasters, 1963); and Warde B. Ogden, *The Television Business: Accounting Problems of a Growth Industry* (N.Y.: Ronald Press, 1961).

Much of the NAB management material on accounting is reproduced by J. Leonard Reinsch and Elmo I. Ellis, *Radio Station Management,* 2nd rev. ed. (N.Y.: Harper & Row, 1960), pp. 193–207. Descriptive summaries of similar NAB material can be found in Edd Routt, *The Business of Radio Broadcasting* (Blue Ridge Summit, Pa.: Tab Books, 1972), pp. 250–261. Cf. Sol Robinson, *Broadcast Station Operating Guide* (Blue Ridge Summit, Pa.: Tab Books, 1969), pp. 197–204; and Jay Hoffer, *Managing Today's Radio Station* (Blue Ridge Summit, Pa.: Tab Books, 1969), pp. 50–55.

7. For details, see Reinsch and Ellis, pp. 191–193, and Routt, pp. 252–259.

8. See Small Business Administration, "The Why and What of Bookkeeping," pp. 11–17; National Assoc. of Broadcasters, "Accounting Manual for Television Stations," pp. 16–17.

9. Institute of Broadcasting Financial Management, *Accounting Manual for Broadcasters,* p. 11: "Financial Statement Forms."

10. Based on the form in IBFM, *Accounting Manual for Broadcasters,* p. 1: "Financial Statement Forms."

11. Federal Communications Commission, "Annual Report Fiscal 1973" (Washington, D.C.: U.S. Government Printing Office, 1974), data quoted by *Broadcasting,* December 31, 1973, p. 58. Investment in tangible broadcast property by CBS, MBS, NBC, and ABC's three AM networks and one FM network totaled $10,127,000. Property investment by 20 network owned-and-operated radio stations (14 AM and 6 AM-FM combinations—another 14 separate FM stations were tabulated elsewhere) totaled $20,252,000. And 4,229 AM and AM-FM stations represented gross property investment of $811,129,000 in 1973.

12. Federal Communications Commission, "Annual Report Fiscal 1973" (Washington, D.C.: U.S. Government Printing Office, 1974), tabulated data were cited in "TV Finances: '73 Goes Down as Record; Another in Works for '74," *Broadcasting,* Sept. 2, 1974, p. 21. Property investment of the three national television networks had an "original cost" of $245,798,000; less depreciation the value was $103,395,000. Property investment by 15 O&O TV stations was originally worth $93,954,000, and less depreciation amounted to $33,194,000. The 474 VHF stations' property value was originally $1,161,795,000 with a net worth of $491,153,000. And 177 UHF stations' tangible property investment was $299,110,000 before depreciation, and $121,362,000 after.

13. *Broadcasting,* June 13, 1960, pp. 98–99.

14. See the presentation by Harold Poole, a director of the Broadcast Credit Association and treasurer of the Institute of Broadcasting Financial Management, at an NAB panel discussion in Houston, Texas, March 20, 1974; published as part of a booklet by the NAB: "Beating the Profit Squeeze: A Financial Management Workshop," pp. 12–18. He noted at the time that the IBFM for several years had been advocating before the IRS a change of Ruling 62-20.

Cf. Ogden, *The Television Business: Accounting Problems of a Growth Industry,* especially pp. 119–137, "Station Accounting"—including amortizing syndicated film packages.

15. Coddington, pp. 165–167, describes the organizations and outlines their fee structures. Blanket ASCAP coverage for a local radio station costs approximately 2% of the gross income; a per-program contract charges a fee of 8% of the adjusted gross received for music and variety programs and 2% for program using music only as background. Similarly, BMI blanket contract fees range from 0.84% to 1.35%, based on the station's gross income; per-program licenses range from 2.81 to 4.50%. SESAC blanket rates extend from $90 a year for the smallest stations up to $6,000 for a 50-kilowatt station in a major market.

In 1970, NBC-TV paid $4,320,000 for annual music rights from ASCAP; CBS-TV paid $1,607,000 for BMI music used on the television network that year. See: "Must Buy All ASCAP Music, NBC Told," *Broadcasting,* Dec. 28, 1970–Jan. 4, 1971, pp. 74–75; "CBS Ordered to Pay BMI $1.6 Million," *Broadcasting,* Jan. 11, 1971, pp. 46–47.

16. FCC data cited in "Annual Report—1972: It Was a Very Good Year for Radio,"

Broadcasting, Dec. 31, 1973, pp. 57–58. The 1972 figures include 2,808 AM and 1,463 AM-FM combination stations, and 275 FM stations associated with AM stations but which report separately, plus 590 independent FM stations. In 1972, 224 independent FM stations reported profit (an average profit of $31,557), and 366 reported loss (averaging $43,333). Profit ratios are derived from total income and revenue figures reported here. FCC figures for 1973 cited in "Radio Record in 1973: Sales Up, Profits Down," *Broadcasting,* Jan. 20, 1975, p. 54.

17. Cf. NAB "Highlights," July 18, 1966, p. 3.

18. See "TV Sales: A Record in the Making After Two Bleak Years," *Broadcasting,* Aug. 2, 1972, pp. 14–26; "1972 a Whopper for TV Biz," *Variety,* Aug. 22, 1973, p. 23; "TV Finances: '73 Goes Down as Record; Another in Works for '74," *Broadcasting,* Sept. 2, 1974, pp. 14–22; "Television's 1973 'Operation Moneybag'," *Variety,* Sept. 4, 1974, p. 39.

19. Sources: U.S. Federal Communications Commission, *TV Broadcast Financial Data,* annual; cited in U.S. Bureau of the Census, U.S. Dept. of Commerce, *The Statistical Abstract of the United States* (94th ed.); published as *The American Almanac: 1974* (N.Y.: Grosset and Dunlap, 1974), p. 500: Table No. 815, "Television Broadcast Industry Finances: 1960 to 1971." Also, other FCC data reported in issues of *Broadcasting* and *Variety.*

Profit ratios are derived from income and revenue figures reported here in this table.

20. "TV Finances: '73 Goes Down as Record; Another in Works for '74," *Broadcasting,* Sept. 2, 1974, p. 18; based on FCC data for fiscal 1973.

21. Nevertheless, dollar amount of losses for UHFs were on the decline, in spite of the larger number of stations reporting losses in 1973 than in 1965. See: "UHF: Out of the Traffic and Heading for the Open Road," *Broadcasting,* June 10, 1974, pp. 35–45.

22. Mikita, in Roe (ed.), *Television Station Management,* p. 103. See: "It's the Little Things that Count in Money Management," *Broadcasting,* Apr. 14, 1975, p. 51.

23. Reinsch and Ellis, pp. 40–42.

24. See, for example: "Local Mini Plus Main Headquarters Computer—A Sales Oriented Team," *BM/E* [Broadcast Management/Engineering], July, 1974, pp. 38–41.

25. From a speech by Jerell A. Shepherd, at the 1968 NAB convention in Chicago, quoted in its entirety in "Profile 9, KWIX," by Joseph S. Johnson and Kenneth K. Jones, *Modern Radio Station Practices* (Belmont, Cal.: Wadsworth, 1972), pp. 174–82.

26. "Media Payment Starts to Modernize Standard Contract," *Broadcasting,* Nov. 4, 1974, p. 36. For detailed comments on credit collection options, see speech by Fred Cige at NAB convention in Houston, Texas, Mar. 20, 1974, reprinted in "Beating the Profit Squeeze: A Financial Management Workshop" (Washington, D.C.: NAB, 1974), pp. 2–5 and pp. 18–25. Cf. Milton D. Friedland, "The Network-affiliated Station," in Roe, *Television Station Management,* p. 64. Cf. Allen A. Dilworth, "Protect Against Slow-Pays: Insure Your Accounts Receivable," *BM/E* [Broadcast Management/Engineering], Dec. 1971, pp. 34a–34d.

27. Jay Hoffer, *Managing Today's Radio Station,* pp. 50–55; ample concrete details are provided for planning a new station and for budgeting one in operation.

See also Richard B. Rawls, "The Independent Station," in Roe (ed.), *Television Station Management,* pp. 70–80.

28. Harry J. Skornia, *Television and Society: An Inquest and Agenda for Improvement* (N.Y.: McGraw-Hill, 1965), p. 18. Predictably, Dr. Skornia proceeds to analyze what he claims to be the broadcasters' inability to serve the public interest properly.

29. Rolla Edward Park, "Television Station Performance and Revenues," (based on research funded by the Ford Foundation), *Educational Broadcasting Review,* V:3 (June 1971), pp. 43–49.

30. See Paul W. Cherington, Leon V. Hirsch, and Robert Brandwein (eds.), *Television Station Ownership: A Case Study of Federal Agency Regulation* (N.Y.: Hastings House, 1971). The study was sponsored by the Council for Television Development of 42 firms that owned 100 television stations and was headed by Ward Quaal, to respond to the FCC's June 1965 notice of proposed rule-making about limiting the number of stations under single ownership.

31. George H. Litwin and William H. Wroth, "The Effects of Common Ownership on

Media Content and Influence: A Research Evaluation of Media Ownership and the Public Interest,'' prepared for the NAB (Washington, D.C.: NAB, 1969).

Cf. continuing debate at the FCC: ''Old Arguments, New Impetus for Action on Crossownership,'' *Broadcasting*, July 29, 1974, pp. 16–17; ''Crossownership and the Evidence,'' *Broadcasting*, Oct. 7, 1974, p. 22. See also James A. Anderson, Robert L. Coe, and James G. Saunders, ''Economic Issues Relating to the FCC's Proposed 'One-to-a-Customer' Rule,'' *Journal of Broadcasting* XIII:3 (Summer 1969), pp. 241–252; these researchers reported that owners of more than one station in a given market (or owners of a station and a newspaper in the same market) generally did not find their stations more profitable than owners of only a single station in a market.

32. For example, in economics alone, a Stanford University report by a research fellow and two professors—under grant from The Brookings Institution in cooperation with the Departments of Economics and Communication at Stanford—offered a 30-page listing of ''A Selected Bibliography in the Economics of the Mass Media.'' It included the following:

J. R. Minasian, ''Television Pricing and the Theory of Public Goods,'' *Journal of Law and Economics*, v. 7 (October 1964).

J. H. Barnett, ''The Economics of Broadcasting and Advertising,'' *American Economic Review*, v. 56 (May, 1966).

H. M. Blake and J. A. Blum, ''Network Television Rate Practices: A Case Study in the Failure of Social Control of Price Discrimination,'' *Yale Law Journal*, v. 74 (July 1965).

R. H. Coase, ''The Economics of Broadcasting and Government Policy,'' *American Economic Review*, v. 56 (May 1966).

E. Greenberg, ''Television Station Profitability and FCC Regulatory Policy,'' *Journal of Industrial Economics*, v. 18 (July 1969).

33. The arguments are briefly outlined by William Joseph Kennedy, ''State and Local Taxation of Commercial Broadcasting,'' *Journal of Broadcasting* XVII:1 (Winter 1972–73), pp. 77–84.

34. ''Finance: High Profits, Tight Money, Sluggish Market for Stocks,'' *Broadcasting*, Sept. 16, 1974, pp. 39–41.

35. *A Special Report on the Broadcasting Industry*, Securities Research Division, Merrill Lynch, Pierce, Fenner & Smith, Inc.; quoted by Jay Hoffer, *Organization and Operation of Broadcast Stations* (Blue Ridge Summit, Pa.: Tab Books, 1971), p. 223.

36. These and following figures quoted from the Commerce Department, *U.S. Industrial Outlook* [1975], by *Broadcasting* magazine (''Government Report Plots Good Growth Through 1980 for Radio, TV, Cable,'' Nov. 11, 1974, p. 48) and by *Variety* (''Govt. Predicts 1975 will be $7-Billion Year for B'casters,'' Nov. 13, 1974, p. 42). See also ''Wall Street Expert Says Broadcasting is a Good Buy,'' *Broadcasting*, Dec. 16, 1974, p. 34; ''A Fair-weather Financial Forecast for Broadcasting,'' *Broadcasting*, Mar. 24, 1975, p. 45; ''A Good '75 Is Only Prelude to Excellent '76,'' *Broadcasting*, May 5, 1973, pp. 12–13; ''Looking to '85: a Bigger Pie, But More Slices,'' *Broadcasting*, Feb 24, 1975, p. 38.

37. Rufus Crater, ''Special Report: The Upbeat Tempo of FM 1974,'' *Broadcasting*, Oct. 7, 1974, pp. 41–48, citing in part a mid-1974 analysis by Business Equities Corporation of Boston.

38. The Commerce Department also attempted to project figures for the cable television industry, despite uncertain factors such as regulations and subscriber support. Cable revenues from subscribers (thus not including program fees or income from advertising or other services) were expected to reach $590 million by the end of 1974 (up 20% from 1973), $690 million the following year, and $1.5 billion by 1980.

39. Les Brown, *Televi$ion: the Business Behind the Box* (N.Y.: Harcourt Brace Jovanovich, Inc., 1971), p. 61.

40. Mikita, ''The Controller's Role in Management,'' in Roe (ed.), *Television Station Management*, pp. 94–95.

See Bruce M. Owen, Jack H. Beebe, and Willard G. Manning, Jr., *Television Economics* (Lexington, Mass.: Lexington Books, D. C. Heath & Co., 1974). Includes a 33-page bibliography listing 619 sources.

8

Broadcast Engineering

The world today listens to de Forest and pioneers of his class with an almost boundless faith. From what has been done no man would venture to place a limit upon what may be done in the domain of applied science.

—JERSEY CITY JOURNAL, February 20,1909

Some day the program director will attain the intelligent skill of the engineers who erected his towers and built the marvel. . . . The radio engineer has worked miracles in research, invention, and clever engineering. But a comparable knowledge of the basic factors of the social equations to be solved seldom is found in the executive offices of his employers.

—LEE DE FOREST, "Father of Radio" [1]

BOTH RADIO and television began as scientific and engineering phenomena. Those who work in broadcast engineering today have inherited the traditions established by the great inventors and innovators from Hertz to Marconi, from de Forest to Zworykin. Most of the marvels of broadcasting, which continue to amaze people even after they have acquired a fundamental knowledge of its process, were developed by members of the engineering fraternity. The image-orthicon camera, the Zoomar lens, audio and video tape, instant replay videodiscs, electronic color, stereo and quadraphonic sound transmission, and relay satellites are engineering accomplishments that might conceivably have been discovered and applied regardless of specific informational and commercial usage. But essential technical advances had to be made in the broadcasting process before the media could be fully utilized by performing talent and then by sales and business management. The evolution of broadcast technology brought together talent, programming, sales, and management people. They learned to respect mutual interests involved in the communications system that has grown into the vital medium as we know it.

THE STATION MANAGER'S RELATIONSHIP TO ENGINEERING

The engineering world is necessarily technical and apart. The engineer is not subject to the public criticism that is often directed at programming and advertising. In his unobtrusive way, he makes his contributions to the broadcasting process without fanfare. Few outside his own department, including the station manager, understand engineering work and motivations or are able to comprehend much beyond the simplest basic procedures. On the other hand, the engineer may be inclined to dismiss programming and sales considerations as having very little appeal for him. Even so, friction between the engineering and other departments is more often due to poor communication than to a lack of proper understanding and mutual good will.

Coddington has commented that a major distinction between engineering technicians and other staff members lies in a fundamental difference in their thinking patterns:

> The typical technician is prone to be *object*-oriented, while other staffers—salesmen in particular—are more likely to be *people*-oriented. This means that the engineer likes to apply his mind to the orderly world of the physical sciences, where a given mixture of causes consistently produces a predictable effect, while the salesman, say, prefers to engage in the more tenuous arena of social action and reaction. . . .
>
> [I]ndividiuals differ widely, and some technicians are as pragmatic as the most crassly commercial salesman. However, insofar as broadcast operations go, the engineer's prime responsibility is the anticipation, location, and correction of equipment faults; in other words, he is dedicated to the quest for perfection, in the sense that perfection represents the absence of defects.[2]

Once radio began to grow in maturity and sophistication in the early 1930s, the close ties between engineering and management that had prevailed in the formative years eroded in all too many cases. This division of technical and persuasional interests was not restricted to the local station level; it included networks as well. The breakdown of close collaboration between the work of the engineering department and administrative projects reflected gradual loss of a common language and lapse of a common concern.

It is hard to overstate the perils of estrangement. Most station managers are mere neophytes in engineering and rely heavily on chief engineers to supervise the technical affairs of their stations. They often run risks because of their paucity of technical knowledge in everything from the purchase of equipment and details of operations to the attitudes of the engineering personnel. Engineers, too often sketchily or arbitrarily informed (or ignored), sometimes miss opportunities to advance proposals that could significantly benefit the organization. With management playing superior and engineers playing canny, both may find themselves overspending on proposals of facilities or equipment and underachieving in broadcast potentials.

FUNCTIONS OF THE CHIEF ENGINEER

The chief of the engineering department has varied functions. He must maintain a balanced loyalty between management and the station engineers. He must sometimes assume the duties of an executive and, at other times, direct specialists in various phases of studio and station operation—studio control, short-wave remote relays, video-tape recording and broadcasts, transmitter work and equipment maintenance. He must take full responsibility for all regular maintenance checks and usually he is charged with building supervision and maintenance.

Management expects the chief engineer to maintain proper liaison and to provide all needed assistance to each of the departments of the station. More and more, his services have become vital to the manager on FCC technical requirements. He must be skilled in his relationships with the unions. He is expected to participate in community affairs. He must keep abreast of current trends and probable future developments in broadcast engineering and be able to make recommendations for the station so that it will keep pace with those advances. No small part of his many functions is the obligation to help the station manager acquire a greater understanding of the work of the engineering department and to keep the manager advised concerning its problems and its achievements.

In short, the chief engineer, no less than the station manager, usually finds himself in an assignment which is somewhat different from the sort of career he once anticipated when he started his work in the broadcast industry. Generally, he finds that many adjustments are necessary. When the man with rich engineering background discovers the gratifications in leadership and when the manager has the proper intellectual curiosity about the engineering department, the station has achieved one of the most important working relationships in broadcasting. The ideal is a station manager-chief engineer relationship so strong that the individuals operate with mutual understanding and mutual respect.

Balanced Loyalty

Historically, the engineer in broadcasting has not been inclined toward the business view. Yet, the chief engineer is expected to become a part of management's team. With the program manager and the sales manager, he becomes a member of a triumvirate indispensable to the station manager. At the same time, men who work in the engineering department expect their chief to represent their interests. The chief engineer is compelled to live a double existence, with his principal work in a field that is somewhat foreign to the manager and his duty to be loyal to corporate business and programming policy; this is confusing to one who would prefer to find his satisfactions in his own creative way and not be bothered with the details expected of an administrator.

In a sense, too, engineers form a closed fraternity. They can be jealous of their skills and prerogatives. Management may seem remote and indifferent to the men on the cameras or at the control panels. It is, therefore, doubly important that the engineering leader understand and communicate company policy to his department. Shared knowledge makes for mutual interest and cooperation. In a well run broadcasting establishment, the chief engineer is conversant with the what and why of the overall operation.

Even then, conflicts are likely to arise. The matter of control of overtime costs for the company at the expense of extra income for the men on the engineering staff is one problem. The question of priorities in cases where the engineers want more equipment or supplies than the manager judges the station can afford makes for friction between management and the chief engineer and the men on his staff. The need to sharpen engineers' awareness of a station's needs for cleanliness and good housekeeping when individuals seem to get more satisfaction from their own system of equipment care creates minor irritations. Perhaps the hardest task for the chief engineer—or for any administrator, for that matter—is to keep a flow of communication accurate and complete from management to the men in the department and from the men back to management. This is a function of a good administrator; and the chief engineer, often not disposed toward administration or communication to begin with, sometimes must be reminded that this is important.

It is no easy task to maintain the balance needed between the interests of technicians and the manager's office, especially when so much may be misunderstood or misapplied because of unclear or incomplete communication. It applies both ways: managerial directives and motivations may be misconstrued; and the technical language of the engineer often has to be translated simply for management.

Equipment Maintenance

One of the most important areas of administration for an engineering executive is *maintenance*. It has been proved in many operations, especially television, that the finest properties with the best engineering personnel cannot do justice to certain technical repairs and still perform their other assignments efficiently. In many cases, therefore, it is efficient and economical to send cameras and other equipment to their factory of origin for overall repair and updating.

A well-managed engineering department will get the maximum life out of all the major equipment in the station. It runs equipment checks oftener than is expected and takes special pride in the performance of all equipment. It uses various functional charts for troubleshooting studio, transmitter, or remote gear. It submits discrepancy reports for every malfunction, no matter how small. The efficient engineering department prepares an operations manual and keeps it up to date. All station equipment should be checked thoroughly at least four times a year in addition to the regular measurements for proof of performance.[3]

Some engineering staffs have increased efficiency by a system of rotating assignments among studio operations, transmitter duty, maintenance and remote work. Other stations prefer to assign members of the engineering staff to specific functions. The latter policy makes good sense when certain men prefer to work in studio production while others are better suited to assignments as far away from production personnel as possible. Assignments should be made by the chief engineer, and should be based on achieving maximum efficiency in terms of the special interests and skills of his men.

Building Supervision

It is advisable to make the chief engineer responsible for building supervision both in the studio building and at the transmitter. In a business based on electronics, almost every part of the building unit needs the chief engineer's guidance and supervision. Almost all physical aspects of a broadcast operation can benefit directly or indirectly from the professional supervision of the engineering department's chief executive.

In smaller operations—especially in small communities with both television and radio stations—there should be most careful planning by the chief engineer regarding the location of a combined transmitter and studio site. Except for stations located in very major cities, there is little reason why studio facilities should not be contiguous to the transmitter. While many stations in small- to medium-sized markets still maintain divided facilities, combined operations have become more and more feasible in most locations.

Relationship with Other Station Departments

The chief engineer must regard his role and that of his staff as a service arm of the radio or television station. While peak efficiency and specific cost control are demanded of engineering management, programming of the station must be done by the program department and not by engineering. In short, the engineering department is there to furnish the technical guidance and operational know-how to stage the station's programming.

A good chief engineer must work with the sales and program departments in sales and program development. He should demonstrate what can be done with videotape and with audio facilities in the studio and on remote locations. He should assist sales and programming on ideas which are on the drawing boards for future implementation. In most cases, the chief engineer of any radio or television station can be a willing colleague in this area, but he needs to be invited to participate. Once he realizes that his suggestions are wanted, he usually makes valuable contributions to the sales and program departments. Of course, the final command function must abide in the front office of station management.

FCC Liaison

Every broadcast operation relies upon its chief engineer for liaison with the FCC about technical operations. In fact, in many stations the only person who is truly qualified to handle many FCC matters is the chief engineer. In this regard, the chief engineer must be aware not only of his own abilities but of his shortcomings as well; he should call upon Washington engineering consultants whenever necessary to protect the company's interests in matters before the FCC. There are a few engineering executives at the station level who can handle all phases of their Washington activity without needing outside engineering-consultant aid. Today's engineering executive must be competent to deal with Federal agency requirements in Washington as well as at the station. For, it is not only difficult to add to or modify station holdings, it is difficult even to retain what one has, unless the chief engineer is able to keep management posted on regulatory and technical developments in engineering.[4]

Liaison with Unions

The chief engineer must carry the major responsibility for liaison with the union men who operate under him. This is true even of companies which are large enough to have their own directors of industrial relations. There must be the closest association with the union shop steward and with the president of the local, as well as with the national and the international offices of the union. Costly hours, days and weeks of negotiation and work tie-ups can be prevented if the proper rapport exists.

The chief engineer should not wait until just before union negotiations start or until they are well under way to explain to his men why certain steps must be taken or why particular approaches cannot be implemented. Those explanations should be an ongoing process, taking place every day as a part of the interpretation of corporate policy.

Automation. The increased cost of doing business in broadcasting is a constant concern to management, but this very economic fact could prove to be the catalyst bringing engineering and management closer together than they have been in the last five decades. Engineering needs to be made knowledgeable of the problems and the concerns of management. Management, in turn, should explain to all of the technically trained personnel what the requirements are for the immediate and the long range future. The road to management-labor relationships can be fraught with disaster unless all laborsaving possibilities and their effects on operations, personnel, and economics are investigated fully and honestly. This does not mean that the engineering payroll should be slashed out of hand. But the industry must continue to develop and plan for the future by taking automation into account—and this for every operation, regardless of size. The economic facts of life make this inevitable. Technical personnel should be apprised of the situation and the reasons for it.

With proper planning, automation not only may bring about sizeable savings, but it can gradually replace costly manpower without visiting undue hardships on individuals involved. Well operated stations with forward-looking management can, if sufficient advanced planning takes place, absorb into other phases of their radio and television operations all—or almost all—manpower affected by the introduction of automated devices. Technical personnel should be told exactly why automation gear—well conceived, well installed, and knowledgeably employed—can eliminate many of the human errors that constantly recur and which pose so many sizeable losses for each property over a period of time. Also, automated equipment can release highly qualified technical personnel from merely routine functions to pursue more productive (and even creative) duties, including careful preventive maintenance and supervision of complex, highly expensive equipment.[5]

In the 1960s, radio stations continually increased their automated technical and programming operation; larger stations also automated bookkeeping and paperwork. Television gradually followed suit. By the mid-1970s trade journal articles about automated equipment and procedures were commonplace.[6] *Broadcast Management/Engineering* magazine estimated the level of interest in automation at the time of the 1974 NAB annual convention as somewhat lower than the previous year; but the topic was the fourth-highest among 20 categories of new equipment in which radio broadcasters manifested interest (42% were interested in automated equipment in 1974, contrasted with 52% the previous year).[7] Television broadcasters' interest level was substantially lower, ranking automation last among 15 categories of new equipment (23% expressed interest in 1974, compared with 30% in 1973).

Recruitment

Engineering recruitment is of paramount importance to radio and television stations for they have never been able to recruit engineering personnel on a satisfactory basis. A source of supply for many stations is the large technical high school. Broadcasters need to make much more effort to recruit well educated engineering personnel, and the chief engineer should be qualified to perform this function after making contact with accredited schools and colleges.

Future Planning

A good engineering executive looks to the future and plans all technical requirements well in advance. He stays ahead of developments in the industry and plans steps that he can take in the future to provide better performance and, if at all possible, at less cost than in the past. A good engineering executive plans now for eventualities, even for revolutionary changes. His planning must be sufficiently in advance so that if a change is anticipated in five years, he can make arrangements to absorb either within his department, or in other phases of the station's operation, all of those personnel who would have to be relieved of their current duties due to the change.

So rapid has been the evolution of television that it is difficult to lay down firm rules for station housing, equipment, location and design. At best, the present day builder will inform himself about the basic functions, costs, probable needs and future expansion of his installations. Beyond that he will be well advised to hire the best architects he can find to consult with top programming, sales and engineering people. Once the basic requirements of a television installation are clearly visualized, details of design and construction can be worked out. In general, form will follow function.

Participation in Community Affairs

The chief engineer should be expected to take part in community affairs, but not necessarily in the same manner as other members of the staff. Not always will he be qualified to serve as a speaker before clubs and organizations nor will he usually be interested in this kind of assignment. But he can be highly effective as a member of organizations. Often, as a member of a church or as a counselor to various charity and educational organizations or as an advisor to the Boy Scouts or to various sports groups involving youngsters, he can be a better representative of the station than many others on the staff.

Engineers, as a group, are not much inclined to public speaking, but they should be encouraged to appear before technical groups to address themselves to developments of the art. Many engineers are capable speakers but have a reluctance to appear publicly. Certainly, with the growth in every area of responsibility of engineers and with the reliance that management places upon them, this reluctance should become a thing of the past.

Relationships with the Station Manager

Regardless of his engineering knowledge, the chief engineer cannot be truly effective unless his training in the broadcast industry has been broad enough to make him an important factor in the successful administration of the station. In addition to the intelligent scheduling of manpower with efficiency and cost control constantly in mind, the chief engineer's obligation to management is to seek every possible means of improving the technical performance of the radio or television station.

Never let anyone tell you that there is not a difference in the *sound* or in the *look* of well or poorly supervised broadcast properties. There *is* an engineering difference that is achieved sometimes by superior equipment and facilities. More often, it is due to well trained and interested personnel. For example, in the case of color television, on one station in a market, the quality of color broadcast can be a thrilling tribute to this dimension in television and, on another station in the same market, it can be an almost amateurish tint transmission. Even in the largest markets, some allegedly "major" stations repeatedly mismatch slides (IDs, PSAs, and even commercials) with voice-over announcements, display badly-timed or poorly-cued film leader strips, and lapse into extended moments of black during network and local program breaks; this reflects haphazard operations and inadequate technical supervision. Similarly, some radio stations publicly manifest inept or careless staff operations by repeated interruptions and failure of their transmission signal or by garbled audiotape from unattended malfunctioning automated equipment.

Every station manager and chief engineer should take the time to become familiar with electronics gear on the market or sometimes still on the drawing boards of the world's major suppliers. Serious investigation of equipment exhibits at the annual spring conventions of the National Association of Broadcasters is a must for any chief engineer and station manager who want to avoid getting caught in the quicksand of surging expenses. Management's knowledge of the field of engineering and of its equipment can make a difference in profit and loss for the future. There is no more useful pursuit for station managers than spending an hour or two each week over a period of six months or more acquiring at least a familiarity with the engineering field, its equipment and attendant problems.

Thus far, this chapter has stressed the interdependence of the chief engineer and his department with the general administrative routine of the station. While it may seem incongruous to find front office personnel delving into matters of engineering and certain engineering experts becoming interested in finance and general business activity, this mutuality of shared concerns and competence has long been needed in broadcasting.

Equipment Purchase

Managers of established stations must purchase new equipment. Replacement is necessary for equipment that is becoming outworn or outmoded. Sometimes, however, there is a tendency to postpone equipment purchases or the remodeling of plant or building in order to improve the condition of the annual financial report. This policy may have certain immediate gains, but it only postpones the day of reckoning. A manager who moves wisely and constantly in these matters strengthens his station's advantages over his competition and thereby improves his station's profit position. Many managers may not equate eventual increase of profit with the purchase of a new piece of equipment. They would change some of their buying practices if they did.

A *BM/E* survey of broadcast stations (reported late in 1972) discovered that many radio and some television stations lacked adequate test equipment.[8] Many radio operations did not have some kinds of basic equipment for testing their facilities; one station reported "no test equipment" because it relied on its chief engineer to provide necessary testing gear. And yet, proper maintenance—dependent on adequate electronic testing—is a major way to protect costly investments in sophisticated equipment. Seemingly, to save the relatively small expense of proper test and monitoring equipment, some stations run the risk of inadequate signal transmission and programming standards and of violating FCC technical regulations, as well as not protecting the longevity of capital facilities. The same magazine surveyed general interest in radio and television equipment at the time of the 1974 NAB convention; interest in TV test equipment had risen from 33 per cent in 1973 to 45 per cent (no figures were cited for radio test equipment).[9]

There are still some radio stations without mobile or remote equipment for covering community affairs. There are still a few television stations lacking adequate videotape facilities. What's more, some stations have not improved basic equipment in their studios, transmitters or offices for years and they give the appearance of poverty when seen by visitors. At the other extreme, many managers have acted on the recommendations of their chief engineers and have continued to show admirable profit margins while engaging in regular expansion of facilities and equipment. These men have proceeded on the sound management belief that one has to spend money to make money.

Parallels may be found in other businesses. The old-fashioned drugstore or restaurant, for example, which resists modernization, finds that a great part of its business goes to those other drugstores or restaurants that do spend the money to improve their plants. Some businessmen seem to believe they can be successful by keeping the costs down and operating on a narrow margin between income and outgo. But the margin soon becomes only enough for survival; and eventually, if the narrow view persists, even survival becomes questionable.

In broadcasting, the rate of technological change is rapid and constant. In order to maintain an improved profit position in radio or television and in order to achieve regularly improved standing among those with whom radio and television do business, facilities and equipment of many years' service are not assets if they are outmoded. The purchase of additional or replacement equipment and the improvement of building or plant should not be determined by mere physical obsolescence. Outlays should be weighed against contributions to profit which the expenditures can make. Decisions to spend are not easy decisions; only the manager with an alert and informed engineering department can make them wisely.

The most important cost-effective purchasing procedures reported by broadcasters are: automation (for programming and bookkeeping), if its use is carefully adjusted to the station's actual and anticipated needs; equipment surveys before buying, to analyze the range of alternative choices and to discover lesser-name equipment that costs less yet does the job as well or better than the "standard"; and checking reconditioned equipment that can serve as well as new but which costs far less.[10] The key for management is the twin concern of being both cost-conscious and quality-conscious. Excess can occur on the side on engineering or management:

> Driven by their idealism, many engineers manage to convince a technically ignorant management of the need for rapid equipment turnover when none exists. It also is true that many engineers are forced to nurse worn-out and obsolete equipment along for years after it has served its useful life simply because management is not cognizant of genuine new equipment needs.[11]

Because of the many factors that may influence the purchase of equipment, it is difficult to estimate the amount such expenditure should be at any particular station for any particular year. Annual equipment purchases for television stations may range from $10,000 to $500,000 and more. The total equipment bill for all of the nation's television stations may be conservatively estimated at $50,000,000 each year, exclusive of maintenance costs and engineering payrolls. Looked at in one way, that's a lot of money. Looked at in another way, it's a lot of progress.

FCC RULES VIOLATIONS

In early 1975, the FCC noted the most common violations of the rules by AM, FM, and TV stations; they are listed below in Table XII.[12] The proportionate violations by radio stations typically exceeded those of television stations, even when the greater number of radio allocations is taken into consideration. Logging failures accounted for the largest number of FCC citations of error by engineers at broadcast stations.

TABLE XII

MOST COMMON ENGINEERING VIOLATIONS OF FCC RULES [12]

SECTION	ITEM
	AM Violations
73.93	Operator Requirements
	No broadcast endorsement on operator permit
	Expired operator license
	Operator's position in non-compliance with requirement that the transmitter or its remote control and monitoring equipment must be readily accessible and clearly visible to the operator on duty
73.52(a)	Operating power, maintenance of
	Antenna input power in excess of that allowed
	Operation pre-sunrise and post-sunset at daylight power levels
73.47	Equipment Performance Measurements
	Failure to complete "proof of performance" measurements within the 14 months allotted between completion of proofs
	Failure to perform all measurements required for a "proof of performance"
73.932	Emergency Action Notification Procedures
	E.B.S. monitor not operating
73.39(d)(2)	Indicating Instruments
	Modulation monitor not calibrated or peak indication light inoperative, etc.
73.92	Station and Operator Licenses, Posting of
	Improperly posted
73.67	Remote Control Operation
	Power adjust control not operating
	Meters not calibrated properly or inoperative
73.55	Modulation
	Exceeding 100 per cent modulation level on negative peaks
73.111	General Requirements Relating to Logs
	Daily tower light check not recorded
	Maintenance log not maintained
	Failure to make quarterly tower light inspection
	FM Violations
73.265	Operator Requirements
	No broadcast endorsement on operator license
	Expired Operator license

SECTION   ITEM

Operator's position in non-compliance with requirement that the transmitter or its remote control and monitoring equipment be readily accessible and clearly visible to the operator on duty

73.268   Modulation
              Exceeding 100% modulation level on peaks

73.322   Stereophonic transmission standards
              Failure to maintain the 19 Khz pilot at the required injection level

73.932(a)   Emergency Action Notification System
              E.B.S. receiver inoperative

73.267   Operating Power: determination and maintenance of
              Antenna input power in excess of that allowed

73.254   Required Transmitter Performance
              Failure to complete "proof of performance" measurements within the 14 months allotted between completion of proofs
              Failure to perform all measurements required for a "proof of performance"

73.275   Remote Control Operation
              Power Adjust control not operating
              Meters not calibrated properly or inoperative

73.317   Transmitters and Associated Equipment
              AM and FM noise figures in excess of that allowed
              Frequency response deviation not within allowable tolerances
              Insulation of audio and control cables not meeting the standards of good engineering

73.281   General requirements relating to logs
              Daily tower light check not recorded
              Maintenance log not maintained
              Failure to make quarterly tower light inspection

TV Violations

73.682(a)   Transmission Standards
              Failure to maintain proper blanking level
              Failure to maintain proper reference white level
              Failure to maintain proper reference black level
              Failure to maintain peak modulation levels as illustrated in 73.699

73.699   Signal Standards
              Pulse durations not within limits illustrated

73.676   Remote Control
              Metering functions not within required tolerance
              V.I.T. signals not in compliance with regulations

73.687(b)   Aural Transmitter
              Excessive modulation levels

73.689   Operating Power
              Power levels not within tolerance
              Failure to calibrate power level metering systems within prescribed time limits

73.932(a)   Emergency Action Notification System
              E.B.S. receiver inoperative

73.691   Modulation monitors
              Aural modulation monitor not calibrated or inoperative

TABLE XII (*Continued*)

SECTION	ITEM

TV violations (cont'd.)

73.661   Operator requirements
          Operators position in non-compliance with requirement that the transmitter or its remote control and monitoring equipment be readily accessible and clearly visible to the operator on duty

73.671   Operating log
          Failure to make required entries

Logging Rules

In 1961, the NAB requested a rule-making procedure of the FCC on the subject of automatic logging devices to record information that was then entered manually in station operating logs. The FCC issued a rule-making procedure followed by a Report and Order and new rules became effective on July 19, 1963.

FCC rules now provide permission for AM, FM and TV stations to use automatic logging devices to keep operating (transmitter) and program logs. A third station log for maintenance is mandatory. Weekly inspections are required at AM, FM, and TV stations, whether or not automatic logging devices are used.

Under the rules, a decision on the use of automatic logging devices for operating logs is voluntary on the part of station management. If a decision is made to use the automatic devices, several conditions must be met. The Engineering Department of the NAB itemized the general conditions of use: [13]

1. The use of automatic recorders must not affect the accuracy of the basic indicating instruments.
2. The automatic logger must have an accuracy equivalent to that of the basic indicating instrument.
3. Calibration must be made at least once a week and appropriate results noted in the maintenance log.
4. Aural alarm circuits must be provided.
5. The automatic device must read each parameter at least once every 10 minutes.
6. For remotely controlled transmitters, the automatic logger must be located at the remote control point. For manually controlled stations, the logger must be located at the transmitter.

In addition, it is required "that all manual readings be taken prior to making any corrective adjustments and all readings, whether manual or automatic, must be taken during the absence of modulation. Arbitrary automatic logger scales may not be used. The logger need not be directly in the operator's view."

Operating logs, whether kept manually or automatically, must show final stage plate voltage and plate current, and antenna current. Antenna base current must also be logged once each day under any of three conditions: (1) when the remote ammeter is defective, (2) when specified as a part of the station license for directional antenna operation and (3) whenever a station operates a directional antenna by remote control. Momentary interruptions of the carrier wave do not have to be logged if there is automatic restoration; if restoration is not automatic an entry must be made describing the cause and length of the interruptions. If the operating log is kept manually, entries must be made at the start of each day's operation and at 3-hour intervals throughout the day.

In 1974 the Commission relaxed the rules that required measurement of the transmitter frequency at specified intervals by a frequency monitor located at the station. Since modern AM, FM, and TV transmission equipment demonstrates extremely reliable capability to maintain frequency control within limits specified by the Commission, it is no longer mandatory that a broadcaster have equipment to measure the frequency of emission. It is required, however, that the licensee take steps to insure that deviation of the frequency of emission beyond the tolerances specified by the Commission will be detected and corrected within a reasonable time period. The measurement of the transmitter frequency by an outside service will meet the minimum requirements specified by the Commission. Intervals of measurement are not to exceed forty days. It should be noted that the licensee will be held responsible in the event interference to adjacent channel assignments is experienced as a result of off-frequency operation.

The *maintenance* log requires information on meter calibration, inspections of tower lights, reports on inoperative equipment, reports on equipment tests and a weekly inspection report of transmitting facilities that must be made by a holder of a first class license. At the conclusion of each inspection, verification must be made by an entry in the maintenance log. Such entry must include the date and the actual time spent making the inspection, with starting and completion times noted. Travel time to and from the transmitter is not included. Notations must be made certifying that the inspections have been made and descriptions of any repair or maintenance work must be given. Any defective equipment must be described and reasons for failure to make repairs must be given.

All program, operating and maintenance logs must be available for inspection on request of any authorized representative of the FCC.

Radio Remote Control Transmitter Operation [14]

The FCC has authorized all AM, FM, and TV stations to operate their transmitter by remote control, provided proper application has been made to the Commission. The Commission adopted a rule, effective February 5, 1975, allowing all AM and FM stations to be remotely controlled without prior authorization from the Commission, provided that the transmitter can be reached by the operator on duty, by walking a distance from the control point to the transmitter, which does not exceed 100 feet in length.

The FCC has relaxed its operator requirements for some AM directional stations operating at power levels of 10 kw or less. The new requirements are based on how critical the designated pattern tolerances are. If a directional station is required to maintain a power level tolerance of 5 per cent or less and/or a pattern of 3 degrees or less, it is said to be "critical." A station designated as such must have an operator holding a first-class radio-telephone license on duty at all times. Other directional stations employing patterns of greater tolerance may employ operators with a third-class radio-telephone license, provided they have a designated first-class operator available. Provisions for the employ of lesser-grade operators for FM stations under 25 kw and AM non-directional stations under 10 kw remain the same as before. The designated first-class operator may be employed on a part-time, contract basis. Non-directional AM stations operating with power in excess of 10 kw and FM stations operating with power in excess of 25 kw may employ an operator on duty who holds a third-class operator's license, provided the station employs on a full-time basis at least one operator holding a first-class license. AM directional stations employing third-class licensed operators must have each day's operating logs checked and signed by the chief engineer in an effort to insure compliance with the Commission's regulations.

Most college graduates, who have majored in radio and television studies, should be able to take the examination and qualify for the third-class ticket. Testing normally covers three elements of FCC examination content: (1) basic law, (2) basic operating practice, and (3) basic broadcast, which is Section 9 of the FCC examination. Applicants who contact the nearest FCC field office are given a time and location for the test. They are requested to fill out an application (FCC forms No. 756 and 756-B) and to submit the license fees ($3.00) prior to taking the examination. Most radio and television stations, as well as most departments of radio and television in colleges and universities, have on file NAB study guides for the third-class license. These may be helpful in studying for the examination.

Due to complaints of broadcasters that they have found it difficult to secure operators with third-class radio-telephone certificates, the Commission had adopted a provisional radio-telephone certificate with broadcast endorsement. This is issued for a period of one year and is not renewable. Application must be made on FCC Form 756-C with a fee of $2.00. The form contains a section to be filled in by the holder of a first-class radio-telephone license, who certifies that he has instructed the applicant in the proper broadcast operating procedures and believes him competent to perform the operator's normal duties. It is expected that during the one-year tenure of this provisional certificate, the applicant will prepare himself or herself to pass the examination for a regular third-class certificate with broadcast endorsement.

A first-class engineer who is employed on a part-time contract basis should be regarded as an independent contractor and this designation should be so specified in writing. Other contractual items should include a statement of the engineer's specific duties, the rate of payment, a specification that he will supply his own tools and testing equipment, the policy in regard to the purchasing of supplies and equipment, a clause about non-disclosure of station information, and a statement of the length of the contract with termination and renewal conditions.

Again, it would be desirable if all differences in transmitter regulations based on amount of station power and nature of antennas might someday be removed. The NAB has worked on the development of equipment capable of taking samples of the electronic condition of any station's transmission system and of alerting station personnel to any deviations from allowable tolerances. As such equipment becomes available, there will then be no need for a continuance of the first-class operator requirement.

The Commission has adopted standards to allow the remote control of both VHF and UHF television transmitters. Inspection of the transmitter and associated equipment must be conducted once a week.

ALLOCATIONS TABLES

The FCC adopted a new FM allocations table in 1963. Supplemental action was taken a year later to permit ". . . existing stations which were licensed under the previous rules to increase their facilities and improve service in those cases where the previous rules would have permitted such increases and in some other cases where the public would benefit." The change in the rules enabled FM stations, in accordance with co-channel and adjacent channel separations considerations, to apply for increases in power and antenna heights. In some cases, the maximum permitted for the class of station could be allowed.

The maximum power allowable for Class A FM stations is 3 kw; antenna height is 300 feet. Maximums permitted for Class B stations are 50 kw in power and 500 feet in antenna height; for Class C stations, maximal power is 100 kw and maximal antenna height is 2000 feet.

A new UHF allocations assignment plan was issued by the FCC in 1966. A previous table, announced the previous year, was declared inoperable because of errors in the programming information that had been fed into a computer. This was the first time that the Commission's computer had been used in the drafting of an allocations table.

The 1966 allocations made more low-numbered UHF channels available, although they were not in areas of heavy population. The total number of UHF channel assignments was 1098, of which 590 were made available for commercial television. Since then, the FCC designated that channels 70 to 83 be set aside for a new class of 10-kw, low-power television stations to serve small communities.

Generally, the UHF table establishes six or more unreserved channels in each of the twenty-five largest markets, five or more in markets 26 through 75, four or more in the markets from 76 through 100, and three or more in the 101st to the 150th markets. In most cases, those markets under 150th in size were assigned two channels. No commercial channels were provided for markets under 25,000 in population. At least one ETV reservation was made for each state and most major population centers were given two ETV channels.

Pressures continue to mount for more frequency availabilities for land-mobile communications use. Such users of the spectrum as police, fire and other governmental services, as well as trucking firms, taxi companies and others who communicate with vehicles, have expanded significantly in recent years. With that expansion has come a need for more frequencies. UHF channels 14 and 15 were requested by the National Association of Manufacturers for land mobile use as early as 1963.

The Joint Technical Advisory Committee (JTAC), representing various landmobile interests, would like a part or all of the existing AM radio band and the existing VHF set of frequencies to accommodate the declared need for more land-mobile space.

The Commission has adopted a rule allowing the use of television channels 14, 15, 16, and 17 by the land mobile communications service in the major metropolitan areas where existing land mobile allocations are insufficient to meet current needs. Use of the allocated television channels is, of course, subject to existing or proposed assignment of these channels to the television service within a given area.

The television broadcasting services occupy three different bands in the spectrum. VHF channels 2 through 6 are assigned to the 54–72 megacycle range, VHF channels 7 through 13 are in the 174–216 megacycle area and the UHF channels 14 through 83 are in the portion from 470–890 megacycles. The JTAC argues that a single, more compact set of frequencies for all television stations would make for improved service and savings in the construction of equipment. The committee would like to have the existing band widths of television channels narrowed. It maintains that the present six megacycle band is not necessary because the average television receiver accepts only 3.5 to 4.5 megacycles of the band. It is noted by those who desire additional space that there have been few major changes in the utilization of spectrum space for over two decades.

The JTAC also recommended consideration of the possibility of moving all local AM radio stations to FM frequencies, and permission for regional and clear channel stations to increase their power so they might be able to cover greater areas. The committee contended, in a published report, that "work on the evaluation of the need and toward improving utilization efficiency should go on even though at the outset it would appear that existing investments in stations and receivers might dictate perpetual maintenance of the status quo." The FCC appointed a Land Mobile Advisory Committee to study the problem as well as the recommendations of the JTAC.

Power Increases

At sundown each evening, more than 25,000,000 people in the United States are uncertain whether they can get a radio signal that is listenable. This is the number of people who live in so-called "white areas," which have no primary nighttime service.

The FCC's solution for the problem is to duplicate thirteen of the remaining twenty-five clear channels and consider further the question of permitting Class 1-A stations to broadcast with power greater than the existing 50-kw limitation. The United States Court of Appeals has upheld the right of the Commission to revise the clear channels in this manner. By the mid-1970s, however, the Commission had gone on record as not favoring an increase in power for Class 1-A stations above the presently authorized 50 kw. With the so-called "freeze" on new AM assignments lifted, a number of construction permits have been granted for new facilities in this service, as well as the upgrading of existing facilities.

Opponents of higher power maintain that the Class 1-A stations would gain an unfair advantage in other metropolitan markets. The listener, however, does not respond to radio as he does to the high-budgeted television station, which "leap frogs" into his area. Radio is a local medium and whenever local broadcasts are available, they are preferred by the local residents.

WGN, for example, would be dominant in Milwaukee if power and the ability to deliver a signal were the only criteria, for it can be heard better in more parts of that city than most of the local stations. Those local stations, however, are consistently the favorites of the local citizenry. An increase in power from 50 to 750 kilowatts, as has been requested, would increase WGN's signal strength not 15 times on a linear basis but rather approximately a little less than four times. (The field strength increase is the square root of how many times the power is increased.) If the present signal is consistently better than most, if not all, of the stations in Milwaukee, yet does not attract those listeners, then an increase of four times or forty times the power is not going to interest them either. Milwaukee, of course, is used as an example of similar reaction in other metropolitan areas.

The situation in the "white areas" is an entirely different proposition. In the upper peninsula of Michigan, for example, there are two local stations in a town of 10,000 and another in a town only twelve miles away. These stations can be heard very well in the daytime but, at night, there isn't as much as a whisper only two or three miles away from the transmitters. The only nighttime radio service these people can get is the sporadic signal from some clear channel station in Minneapolis, Chicago, Detroit and, on a few rare occasions, Des Moines. Consideration ought be given to a sizeable American public that is underprivileged in the matter of radio reception.

In the late 1920s and early 1930s, stations were permitted increases in power from 100 and 250 watts to 1000 watts and, later, from 1000 to 5000. There was much hue and cry then about "super" power and, in those days, there were only a few hundred stations on the air. Since there have been 50,000-watt properties operating, the number of radio stations has increased to well over 6000. It would appear that the 50,000-watt stations did not stifle competition or manifest a monopoly. Rather, they helped greatly in the development of the broadcasting industry by their professional standards and by helping to make the public and advertisers conscious of the merits of this medium of communications. Higher amounts of power, even on a handful of stations, could benefit every station in the land, regardless of size or location. It could furnish proof to national advertisers that not only is radio "alive" but its operators are willing to continue to invest money in it and to experiment in the public interest. Many national advertisers could be won back to radio through such a sound development, and sizeable amounts of new business could be attracted. It could be further argued that all classes of radio stations should be allowed to increase their power in order to combat the vast increases in electrical interferences and in man-made noise levels.

Persons wishing to obtain a permit to construct a FM or TV station in a town which has not previously had a channel assigned by the Commission, may submit a request to the FCC that a channel for a specific class of service be assigned. The request should include the necessary documentation to show a need for such assignment—that is, that it would be in the public interest. In addition, a study must be conducted to show what channel or channels could feasibly be assigned that would comply with the Commission's regulations about spacing, etc. In the event that the Commission is being requested to make changes in the existing table of FM and TV channel assignments, such requests must be accompanied by a showing of channel availability, and in the case of FM, by the usual "preclusion" study. Copies of proposals must be sent to all licensees and permittees who would be affected by the change, and a draft of a Notice of Proposed Rule Making (to be issued by the FCC) must also be supplied.

In 1974 the Commission announced the ratification of a treaty between the United States and Mexico (The "United States-Mexico FM Broadcasting Agreement," effective August 9, 1973). It concerned the assignment of new allocations for FM broadcasting facilities within an area extending for 199 miles each side of the border. This treaty provided for a number of proposed future assignments by both parties, by the adoption of a new allocation table for cities within the designated border area. This agreement provided that existing and proposed future facilities would not be precluded from increasing their parameters to the maximum specified for the class of station concerned (Article 5, paragraph A(6)(b), of the treaty). Of significance was the adoption of new standards for the separation of the various classes of stations within the specified border area. Basically, the minimum acceptable mileage separation between stations has increased (Article 6, paragraph C). The Commission has further proposed that the new standards of separation under the Treaty be adopted for an area parallel to the designated border area and extending 199 miles therefrom. While proposed facilities within this secondary area are not concerned with the Mexican assignments, the Commission feels that United

States stations within the designated border area should be afforded the same protection with regard to spacing as new facilities outside the border area.

PERMANENT DEFENSE SYSTEM

The Emergency Broadcast System (EBS), designed specifically for use in case of a war emergency, went into effect in January, 1964. It replaced the former Conelrad system, which had been in use since 1951.

EBS uses AM stations basically, with FM and TV aural channels assigned to relay and network assistance when necessary. Under the alert system, a Federal government message would be issued to the Associated Press and to United Press International. They would flash the alert to stations via their teletype services. Immediately, on receipt of the alert, all regular programming must cease and pre-arranged announcements must be read. Stations not holding National Defense Emergency Authorizations (NDEA's) must advise listeners to tune to an authorized station. Then, these unauthorized stations must leave the air. Any station may apply for NDEA authorization. Stations have a right of appeal to the FCC in the event they are refused authorizations.

Priorities in the use of the Emergency Broadcast System are: (1) communications of the President and other officials of the Federal government to the public before, during and after an attack; (2) local messages; (3) state programs and (4) national programs and news.

Stations authorized to remain on the air may not broadcast any commercials. They may program music, when there is no information to be carried, and they also may broadcast information to specific individuals.

In the event of an emergency necessitating the use of EBS, daytime-only AM stations could operate beyond their normally licensed hours if no other service is available in the area. Unlimited-time AM stations could maintain their daytime facilities at night.

The United States Weather Bureau makes use of EBS for hurricane, tornado and other physical-catastrophe warnings.

These and the earlier topics of technical engineering are closely regulated by the Federal government on behalf of the public whom the airwaves are intended to serve. The following chapter explores in detail major regulatory matters that involve broader social, legal, and economic aspects of radio-television operations which are a primary responsibility of broadcast management.

NOTES

Chapter 8

1. Lee de Forest, *Father of Radio: the Autobiography of Lee de Forest* (Chicago: Wilcox & Follett Co., 1950), pp. 444, 446. Quotation above from *Jersey City Journal,* cited on p. 255.

2. Robert H. Coddington, *Modern Radio Broadcasting: Management and Operation in Small-to-Medium Markets* (Blue Ridge Summit, Pa: Tab Books, 1969), pp. 200–201. This book

offers extensively detailed descriptions and analysis of all engineering matters, including chapters on equipment tests, operating logs, plant, utilities, control room and studio facilities, microphones, antennas, and equipment maintenance and operation.

3. For detailed discussion of preventive maintenance of technical equipment, see Coddington, chapter 18: "Operation and Maintenance," pp. 268–286, especially pp. 272–276.

4. Cf. Coddington, chapter 5: "The FCC," pp. 60–70, especially regarding operating logs, Federal qualifications required of radio-telephone operators, official field inspection of technical operations; and also pp. 276–279 regarding proof of equipment performance and frequency checks.

5. See R. H. Coddington, "Meeting the Engineer Shortage," *BM/E*, March 1971, pp. 44–45, 56, 75. He urged radio station automation as supporting professional, skilled engineers with first-class radio-telephone permits, while eliminating "shift technicians" of only moderate competence who operate with restricted third-class broadcast-endorsed permits.

6. Using only one trade magazine as an example, *Broadcast Management/Engineering* published a major article in 1972 reporting various uses of automation in office and engineering operations: "TV Automation Systems—Now On Their Way," *BM/E*, Sept. 1972, pp. 30–37; the following year that magazine printed "An Automatic Television Monitoring System," *BM/E*, April 1973, pp. 23 ff. During 1974 the same publication offered the following articles: Virgil D. Duncan and Malcolm M. Burleson, "Understanding Automatic Digital Logging and Data Acquisition," *BM/E*, April 1974, pp. 30–32. "Radio Must Have a 'Personal' Voice—Automation is the Way For Many Stations," *BM/E*, July 1974, pp. 24–32. William A. Earman, "Automation—The Trend to Simplicity," *BM/E*, July 1974, pp. 34–37; this article offered practical advice on selecting appropriate equipment and procedures for automation, including automation in the small station. "Local Mini Plus Main Headquarters Computer—A Sales Oriented Team," *BM/E*, July 1974, pp. 38–41. Leo P. Demers, Jr., "Watch Out: Super VTR At Work," *BM/E*, July 1974, pp. 42–43. Joseph D. Coons, "How to Get a Data Processing System That Works," *BM/E*, August 1974, pp. 26–33. Maurie Webster, "Computer Inventory Control—A Dynamic Sales Tool," *BM/E*, August 1974, pp. 34–35, 55 ff. "Automation Helps a UHF to Survive," *BM/E*, August 1974, pp. 36–38. "Total Automation a Reality for Growing Number of Computerized Business Services," *BM/E*, August 1974, pp. 39–43. "Radio Automation Equipment—1974," *BM/E*, August 1974, pp. 44–45. "Another Step Towards 'Total TV Station Automation," *BM/E*, August 1974, pp. 46–47, 54 ff.

7. "The NAB Show: Riding the Wave," *BM/E*, March 1974, pp. 33 ff.; tables on p. 36.

8. "Too Many Stations Have Too Little Test Equipment," *BM/E*, Nov. 1972, pp. 34–35.

9. "The NAB Show: Riding the Wave," *BM/E*, March 1974, pp. 33–36, 38.

10. "Broadcasters Tell About Their Cost-Effective Buys," *BM/E*, October 1971, pp. 36, 45–49. Cf. Coddington, pp. 104–105, for tips on purchase of equipment, including used and reconditioned equipment.

11. Coddington, p. 201. He notes the advantage to the engineering staff and to the entire station operation of having access to trade publications, catalogues of manufacturers, and even books, as well as attending trade conventions. Coddington suggests that stations might make available to staffs a library of current journals and basic technical books to help them keep abreast of current modifications of equipment, so that they can assess equipment needs and accurately predict future needs for the station.

12. Listing was provided by a spokesman for the FCC by telephone from Washington, D.C. He explained that no detailed list of specific numbers of violations for each category was available for recent years. (See previous 1968 edition of this book for NAB mimeographed data, citing numbers of instances of each kind of violation for the mid-1960s.) Cf. "Interpreting the FCC Rules & Regulations: Commission Rules Frequently Violated by Broadcast Stations." *BM/E*, May 1975, pp. 26–28.

13. National Association of Broadcasters, "The FCC Decision on Automating Logging" (undated booklet, mid-1960s).

14. Many of the data cited in this section were provided by Hugh Paul, chief engineer of KUSC-FM, Los Angeles, who obtained current information from the FCC in Washington by telephone. Most of the data were not yet published by the Government prior to preparation of this manuscript for the publisher. For earlier modifications of these and similar rules, see "FCC Eases

Operator Rules for Small-station Radio Engineers," *Broadcasting,* June 5, 1972, pp. 51–52, and "Making Life a Bit Easier: Re-regulation Gets Under Way," *Broadcasting,* November 6, 1972, pp. 19–20; "Interpreting the FCC Rules & Regulations—Broadcast Re-regulation:Changes in Certain Station Reporting, Record-Keeping and Operating Requirements," *BM/E,* March 1973, pp. 25–26.

The Manager
and Regulation

Men are constantly called upon to learn over again how to live together. It is a hard task. When unprecedented disputes and difficulties confront them, they repeatedly turn for help to the government, as the recognized umpire.

—ZECHARIAH CHAFEE, JR.[1]

THROUGHOUT THIS BOOK, we have cited various aspects of station management where greater amounts of attention could result in increased efficiency. It is possible that managers could devote more time to these needs if they were not regularly preoccupied with government regulation. The continuous activity and threat of further action by the Federal Communications Commission and other government agencies seem to require an excessive amount of the broadcaster's time and attention.

Perhaps in no other activity of American life is the licensee so constantly reminded, and even threatened, that he must make modifications in his behavior in order to maintain his license over a period of years. Some reminders and threats are real; some are imagined. But the manager or owner is kept aware of possibilities of new government enrocachments by several sources. There are regular public statements by individual members of the FCC and by the Commission collectively. The trade press reports other governmental activities and recounts speculation. Whenever there are meetings among fellow managers or owners, the conversation seems to be dominated by discussions of government regulation, of interpretation and application of rules, and of legislative threats.

Why is so much of a manager's time occupied with thoughts pertaining to only one aspect of his responsibilities? Why aren't the guidelines clearer? Why must there be differences of opinion on the same basic issues that have existed in this country through all the years of broadcasting? What are the reasons for the differences of opinion and why have they not been resolved? A brief review of the origins of Federal regulation provides some context for these questions.

330

That will be followed by analysis of specific practices and issues in regulation. The final portion of the chapter will appraise the role of governmental regulation and industry self-regulation.

A. BACKGROUND OF FEDERAL REGULATION

In the formative years of commercial radio, between 1921 and 1926, there was much confusion in the standard broadcast band.[2] It was easy to obtain a license to broadcast. Merely filing an application with the Bureau of Standards of the Department of Commerce almost automatically put the applicant into broadcasting. A result of that loose licensing practice was mass confusion and cacophony on the various frequencies. An entrepreneur in South Bend, Indiana, for example, could be assigned to a particular spot on the dial; but if someone in Rockford, Illinois, or Green Bay, Wisconsin, had an affinity for that same frequency, he could use it to broadcast. As licenses increased in number, there were many cases where two or more stations in the same region used the same frequencies. This confusion prompted the broadcasters themselves to seek assistance from the Federal government.

By 1926, because of this confusion, a potentially great medium was on the verge of perishing in its infancy. Herbert Hoover, then Secretary of Commerce, concluded that a system of allocation of broadcast frequencies was the only solution to the traffic chaos. He envisioned the creation of an executive agency to implement and enforce an orderly allocation of frequencies. Mr. Hoover called upon Congress for enabling legislation and, after extended hearings in 1926 and early 1927, the Federal Radio Act of 1927 came into being. A five-member Federal Radio Commission was created; each man represented approximately one-fifth of the land area in the United States.

The five Commissioners, together with the first General Counsel, the late and great Louis Goldsborough Caldwell, and the first Chief Engineer, T. A. M. Craven (who retired from a period of eminent service as a member of the Federal Communications Commission in March, 1963), set out to establish a frequency pattern for all radio service in the country. As a result of their work, there came into being for the first time a designation of frequencies by class of service. The basic designations included local channels (serving cities only), regional channels (serving cities and metropolitan areas and contiguous regions nearby), Class I-B clear channels (whose frequencies were assigned to distant stations both day and night but protected over a wide area at night so as to reach outlying areas) and Class I-A clear channels (which did not have to share their frequencies at night with other radio stations in the United States and most of North America).

The Federal Radio Act of 1927 established clearly that (1) the radio channels were public property, (2) those who were awarded licenses to broadcast on specific channels or frequencies would be regarded as "tenants" of those frequencies, and (3) the licensees would be expected to serve the public interest

as part of the obligations of the "lease." The Act further established that
license applicants would have to qualify for the privilege of operating a radio
station through such tests as the Commission would devise. Freedom of speech,
as guaranteed by the First Amendment of the Constitution, was extended to
cover radio broadcasting.[3] It was this Act that applied to broadcasting the
phrase "public interest, convenience and necessity" (from an 1892 statute affecting railroads and from the Transportation Act of 1920). This was to become
the standard by which every station was expected to operate and by which the
regulatory powers of the FRC would be guided. A further major provision of
the Radio Act gave broadcasters the right of appeal to the courts on decisions of
the Commission.[4]

The increased strength and influence of the radio industry in the early
1930s was largely due to the resolution of the initial allocation problem. Secretary Herbert Hoover, a strong exponent of free enterprise, was reluctant at first
to support governmental regulations over broadcasting, but he was persuaded
by the broadcasters themselves that such technical controls were necessary.[5]
Mr. Hoover went on record expressing the opinion that he was disappointed by
the commerical exploitation of the medium in the late 1920s. Years later, Mr.
Hoover stated on several occasions that he felt he erred in the early opinion and
he later became a vigorous advocate of commercial broadcasting in the United
States.

In 1934, President Franklin Roosevelt recommended to Congress that the
FRC be expanded to include jurisdiction over all forms of interstate and foreign
wire, as well as wireless, communication. Acting on this recommendation,
Congress passed the Communications Act of 1934. The new law included the
major provisions of the Radio Act of 1927 and added provisions for the jurisdiction of the Commission. The name of the governing body was changed to
the Federal Communications Commission and it was enlarged to seven members.

The present Federal Communications Commission is still composed of
seven members and is still governed by the same basic legislative philosophy
that was developed for radio in 1927. Yet, intervening years have seen a phenomenal growth of AM broadcasting, the introduction and subsequent growth
of FM and television, all the advancements in radar, in microwave relays and
in space and satellite communication. The original documents that established
the FRC and later the FCC have proven applicable to forms of communication
the framers of the legislation could hardly have dreamed would become realities of the future. Still, it is possible that those two Acts of Congress in 1927
and 1934 may now have been stretched to the maximum of their applicability to
modern problems of communications. At least, there has been serious thought
in some quarters about the need for an entirely new Communications Act and
for a major reorganization of the FCC.

BACKGROUNDS OF COMMISSIONERS

Broadcasters have not been reluctant to criticize the backgrounds of many members of the Commission. Most of the appointees have had legal training and experience; a few have come from the field of engineering. Many broadcasters have contended that at least a few people with broadcasting experience should be appointed to the Commission, as were Robert Wells (1967–1971) and James Quello (1974–   ). Almost half of all the FRC and FCC commissioners had some prior experience in broadcasting.[6]

There have been few broadcasters who have evidenced a strong interest in or inclination toward such appointments, and "consumer" interest groups are critical of commissioners whom they perceive to be favorably disposed to the existing broadcast industry. It could be feasible for broadcasters to arrange for in-service "education" sessions for those new commissioners with legal or engineering backgrounds who lack first-hand experience in radio and television programming and operations.

In recent years members of the FCC have attended and participated in the annual conventions of the National Association of Broadcasters, making possible exchanges of opinions on policy matters. In general, there has been a disposition on the part of most of the recent commissioners to learn as much as possible about broadcasting. But when the combined backgrounds of the members of the Commission represent considerable experience in fields remote from broadcasting, the amount of understanding acquired in short and infrequent visits to stations or by participating in conventions is necessarily limited. Of course, their own reading and study, as well as briefings by career staff members of the Commission, contribute to their knowledge of the history, structure, and operation of broadcasting.[7]

Unless appointed to fill unexpired terms, commissioners serve for seven years. At the inception of their service, they must rely heavily on the Commission staff for detailed information and even recommendations about decisions. This middle staff includes not only the aides assigned to individual Commission members, but the heads and key personnel of the various bureaus which are a part of the FCC apparatus. These career staffers long outstay the appointed commissioners and thus contribute significantly to the continuity and pattern of the agency's deliberations. From 1927 to 1961, 44 persons served as commissioners of the FRC or FCC for an average period of only four-and-one-half years (ranging from six months to 19 years). In the following decade, Newton Minow served 27 months; his successor as chairman, E. William Henry, served less than four years. Up to 1973, others left the Commission after serving respectively five years, four-and-one-half years, four years, two years, and only nine months. Only two commissioners, Kenneth Cox and Nicholas Johnson, completed full seven-year terms of appointment.

THE FCC WORKLOAD

The overall workload of the FCC is enormous.

The licensing function of the former Federal Radio Commission and the FCC has been conducted with relative efficiency and equity. The welfare of the public has been the basic guide in establishing allocation tables, defining technical standards, deciding changes in power, structure, equipment and ownership, and in screening applications for licenses and renewals. These duties alone have been highly time-consuming. A staff of 1,772 employees (1973) in seven categories of offices and five bureaus assist on substantive matters as well as the more routine processing details. But the most important final decisions are the responsibility of the seven commissioners. The men who have accepted appointment to the Commission have been, for the most part, true public servants. They have generally discharged their assignments in a manner that has assisted the development in the U.S. of the finest broadcasting service in the world. In recent years, however, there has been needless harrassment of radio and television licensees, taking their time and energies from more constructive activities.

The establishment and supervision of technical standards in broadcasting and the approval of licensees and their facilities to broadcast should themselves constitute fulltime work assignments. Yet, this is only a part of the Commission's responsibilities. It is also charged with the administration of the entire broadcast spectrum. This includes the approval of all assignments and the supervision of their use by the telephone and telegraph services, all short-wave and amateur radios, remote pickup equipment, relay facilities, facsimile, international wireless activities, experimental research services, various industrial functions, marine, aeronautical, land transportation, disaster communications and citizens radio.

Authorizations for all uses of the electromagnetic radio spectrum totaled more than 5.5 million in 1972, an increase of more than 149,730 over the previous year.[8] In that same year, the FCC received more than 600,000 applications of all kinds relating to those spectrum services. Thus radio and television broadcast station authorizations represent but a small part of the FCC's paperwork; 8,618 AM, FM, and TV stations were on the air by 1975 (including 910 non-commercial educational stations). As if such a huge workload were not a sufficient assignment, the FCC has assumed the added responsibility of regulating more than 2,500 CATV (community antenna television or cable television) systems and has been given the authority to regulate this country's participation in satellite communications.

The mere maintenance of a balanced use of the various spectra brings pressures inconceivable to the average citizen. Requests for increased spectrum space come regularly from such agents of public safety as the nation's police or fire departments, from the military establishment, from industry and from the nation's space program. No private group could have been any more protective of the interests of the public in the administration of all these varied uses of the spectrum.

In regulating the nation's broadcasting stations, the FCC must make many difficult decisions. The scope of the Commission's work in a given year—in addition to the usual weekly actions on license applications, renewals, modifications and transfers—includes major issues such as rule-making and hearings about the "fairness doctrine" on controversial issues of public importance, political broadcasting, multiple ownership, policies about comparative hearings of competing applicants, limitations on the TV networks' control over programming, subscription television, UHF service, guidelines for automatic monitoring of TV programs and commercials, authorizations for lower-power classifications of FM stations, inquiries into children's television programming, educational broadcasting, warnings about fraudulent and "double" billing for commercial advertisements, station identification rules, re-regulation of technical requirements pertaining to radio stations, establishing directives about equal opportunity for minorities in employment and in programming, and modified allocations and use of frequencies.[9] There was other vital business before the Commission during the same time, including investigations and decisions. In fiscal 1971 alone, the Commission testified or commented on 25 matters of legislation pending before Congress, participated in 162 court proceedings, conducted (through its Office of Hearing Examiners) 113 formal hearings and another 203 hearing conferences; 253 FCC hearings involved broadcast facilities (81 AM, 110 FM and 62 TV). These broadcast-related activities were in addition to responsibilities exercised over cable TV, common carrier services, and the massive area of safety and special radio services, including the Field Engineering Bureau's 15,628 inspections of all classes of transmitting stations (2,062 of which involved broadcast stations and which occasioned 1,385 official violation notices to radio and TV station operators).

With such a volume of work, together with all the attendant pressures, the FCC does not have much opportunity to engage in unhurried philosophical thinking about its future relations with broadcasters. Former Chairman Newton Minow appraised the agency:

> [A]s we re-examine the status quo, I must confess that I have found the FCC, too, a prisoner of its own procedures. The Commission is a vast and sometime dark forest where we seven FCC hunters are often required to spend weeks of our time shooting down mosquitoes with elephant guns. In the interest of our governmental processes, and of American communications, that forest must be thinned out and wider, better marked roads have to be cut through the jungles of red tape. Though we have made substantial improvements in recent years, the administrative process is a never-never land which we call quasi-legislative and quasi-judicial. The results are often quasi-solutions.[10]

The FCC as Protector of Broadcast Interests

It would be easy to gain the impression after listening to disgruntled broadcasters that the FCC is nothing but a hindrance to the progress of professional and commercial interests in broadcasting. This is not totally true, in spite of the distress caused to broadcasters by some Commissioners (e.g. Newton Minow, Kenneth Cox and Nicholas Johnson).

The FCC has regularly acted to preclude practices within the industry which might constitute restraint of trade. It has regularly refused station licenses to those applicants with records of attempts to affect fair competition adversely or who have done harm to their competitors in other lines of commerce. It has conducted investigations of past antitrust actions against any applicants who might be suspect. It has refused to accept applicants who might restrain competition in any way.

The establishment and enforcement of the duopoly rule and the restrictions on the number of station licenses that any one person or corporation might hold have been consistent with the Commission's determination to foster the competitive climate within the industry. The chain broadcasting regulations, the elimination of network option time, and the limiting of networks' prime-time access to three hours of local stations' schedules, while not universally popular, were adopted in the interests of individual station ownership and of local management's autonomy in program selection. When hearings have been conducted on competitive applications or on significant policy changes, the FCC has demonstrated a high degree of objectivity and true concern for the best interests of the public.

Because of the Commission's concern with protecting the individual broadcaster against unfair competition and its refusal to compromise on qualifications for station licensees, radio and television stations of the nation have been assigned, with relatively few exceptions, to people of proper character. The occasional cases of unethical practices in business and in programming on the part of some licensees can hardly be blamed on the FCC. The record of the Commission in the application and transfer processes is both clear and consistent in its concern for the selection of people of character as licensees.

Nevertheless, the FCC was created to serve as a protector of all the publics' interests. These publics include not only the broadcaster and the advertiser, but the audience and even such special-interest groups as ethnic and cultural minorities. Nor is the FCC wholly autonomous and absolutely independent in its deliberations and decision-making. Krasnow and Longley aptly analyze the six major determiners of regulatory policy: the FCC itself, the broadcasting industry, citizen groups, the courts, the White House (including its Office of Telecommunications Policy), and the Congress with its various committees and subcommittees which oversee the FCC's stewardship.[11] Each of these forces mutually interact; they frequently occasion, and often significantly affect the outcome of, FCC actions.

The broadcast manager must be aware of the "political" structure in which he operates, alert to the changes that take place—changes in policies or in personnel which can affect what he is doing today as well as what he may be planning to do over a period of years.

The desirability of retaining a Washington law firm, usually one specializing in communications practice, is clear. Equally valuable is participation in the National Association of Broadcasters, headquartered in Washington, and closely attuned to governmental political affairs as they affect broadcasting.

While Congress has not made major changes in basic broadcast law with any significant frequency, its committee rooms often provide a sounding board for regulators as well as for others who have alleged grievances against broadcasters. This is because the FCC, like every other government agency, must appear for renewal of its funding each year, and is accountable to Congress annually for its stewardship. Members of the Congress, especially members of the Communications Subcommittees of the House and Senate Commerce Committees, are frequent recipients of complaints against broadcasters, with the latter Congressmen the most influential. Since members of Congress tend to be responsive to their constituents, their constituents who are broadcasters should take the opportunity to discuss broadcast problems with their elected Representatives and Senators, and to make their points to other fellow-constituents. Especially in recent years when organized citizen groups have formed a counter-influence among Congressmen and Commissioners and thus participate in this regulatory process, and with the increased activity of courts in broadcast-related decisions, the broadcasters (individually and through their professional associations) must present their case in this pluralistic political-social forum. [12]

Because of these contending forces, the FCC tries to compromise conflicting goals. FCC policy-making realistically seeks moderate change that will not generate debilitating opposition; thus the agency attempts to remain flexible and responsive to reactions by major parties and power groups, even to the point of deleting or changing proposed rule-making if opposition grows strong. The realities of policy-making also dictate that the FCC use its resources to resolve immediate problems without becoming immersed in massively complicated long-range issues. (This reflects as corollary a deficiency of philosophy and broad policy which can withstand future circumstances by offering consistency and predictability instead of a case-by-case approach to rule-making.)

Krasnow and Longley offer an assessment of the FCC that is reasonably sound as well as pragmatic, when they comment on "Why doesn't the Commission regulate the industry more vigorously?"

Such a question assumes that the public interest will be furthered by greater regulation. However, the history of regulated industries such as transportation and broadcasting has shown that stricter governmental controls may in fact disserve the public interest. Moreover, calls for the imposition of more restrictive regulations by the FCC usually do not take into account the highly complex, politically sensitive, and rapidly changing character of the communications industry. Under the system of regulation established by the Congress, the FCC has operated within a sequential, bargaining, policy-making process. America's stake in broadcasting is too fundamental and precious to be subjected to drastic or politically unpopular policies which do not allow the FCC to modify policies without excessive loss if new information indicates unexpected troubles.[13]

However, those authors perhaps underemphasize the serious demand for long-term principles and consistent, equitable guidelines by the regulatory agency on behalf of all parties affected, when they conclude their brief book on a practical note:

> The policies of the FCC are not abstract theories, but political decisions allocating material rewards and deprivations—decisions, in Laswellian terms, concerning who gets what, when, and how. The development of policy in this manner is not easy. Before any proposal can emerge as public policy, it must survive trial after trial, test after test of its vitality. The politics of broadcast regulation offers no escape from that imperative.[14]

Other appraisals of the FCC have been less sanguine. Some broadcasters, commissioners, Congressmen, researchers and academicians have lamented the agency's seeming lack of major policy and direction about large issues and problem areas, relying instead on *ad hoc* decisions on each case before it. A public assessment in 1949 noted that "The Commission has been found to have failed both to define its primary objective intelligently and to make many policy determinations required for efficient and expeditious administration." [15] And in 1960 a governmental report lamented that "the Commission has drifted, vacillated and stalled in almost every major area. It seems incapable of policy planning, of disposing within a reasonable period of time the business before it, of fashioning procedures that are effective to deal with its problems." But the courts of the land have supported precisely a flexible power of interpreting the Communications Act by the FCC.[16] More recent efforts by the Commission to make policy and to take initiative have often resulted in reversals of its actions by higher courts, especially in the late 1960s and early 1970s. And criticism of the agency continues.[17]

B. Regulatory Practices and Issues

License Renewals

The Commission has attempted to eliminate those grantees who have failed to show proper respect for the important public licenses which they have been assigned. It has a range of penalties that it can impose for violations of its rules by broadcast operators.

To enforce the Communications Act, the Commission can simply inquire by letter about alleged rule violations; it can also take the more serious step of sending investigators to inquire directly about the matter. In 1952 the FCC was empowered by Congress to issue Cease and Desist Orders for specific violations of Federal rules.[18] In 1960, as a result of the payola scandals, a further amendment to the Communications Act authorized the Commission to penalize by "forfeitures" (or fines) of up to $1,000 per day to a maximum of $10,000.[19] Additionally, the Commission may penalize licensees by short-term renewals (§307[d]), by denial of renewal at the time of expiration (§307[d]), and by revocation of license (§312[a]).

From 1950 to 1959, the Commission denied only three applications for licenses or for renewals of licenses, and in the same period it revoked five licenses. In the decade of the 1960s, the FCC denied 28 applications for licenses or for renewals of licenses, and it revoked 17 licenses. In 1970, 1971, and the first ten months of 1972, it denied 12 applications (seven of which were in litigation so remained on the air), but revoked no license.[20]

Since 1960, a much greater amount of time and attention has been devoted by the Commission to short-term license renewals. There has been an increasing hesitancy to renew licenses for the full three-year period in those cases where the evidence seems to show that stations have been lacking in efforts to ascertain and then meet the needs of the community. In the two-year period 1961–1963, the licenses of 14 stations were either revoked or not renewed, 15 licensees were in hearings to determine whether their licenses should be revoked or renewed, 21 stations were fined and 26 short-term licenses were issued. In 1964, there were four license revocations, five denials of renewal, 24 fines levied and nine short-term renewals granted. In 1965, two stations were placed in revocation proceedings, five were denied renewals of their licenses, 45 were fined and 23 were given short-term renewals.

In the fiscal year 1972, the FCC took final action to revoke or deny license renewals to four stations; it granted probationary short-term renewals to five applicants, and ordered 44 stations to pay forfeitures (fines), while issuing notices to 97 other stations of their apparent liability for fines for such practices as fraudulent billing, violating personal attack rules, unauthorized transfer or control of station, unauthorized rebroadcast of programs of another station, failure to give sponsorship identification, failure to file time-brokerage contracts, broadcasting lottery information, fictitious entries in station logs, use of greater power than authorized, and various technical violations.[21] In 1971 a record 20 renewal applications were designated for hearings because of alleged violations of law and character qualifications of licensees, permittees or applicants.[22] And a license renewal hearing of KMAC and KISS(FM) in San Antonio was concluded by fining the licensee $20,000 for repeated technical violations, while renewing the license for the remainder of the current license term.

The first television station to lose its license to operate, in a comparative hearing on renewal, was WHDH (Channel 5, Boston)—decided initially in January, 1969. Although some radio stations were denied license renewals over the years because of technical violations alone, the first television station to be

denied renewal solely because of repeated rule violations in technical operations was KRSD-TV (Channel 7, Rapid City, South Dakota) with its satellite
KDSJ-TV (Channel 5), late in 1971.[23]

While many kinds of violations occasion initial action by the FCC, *willful* and *repeated* violations—usually of technical regulations not related to programming service—are causes for license deletions. In 36 years (1934 to 1969),
the Commission revoked licenses of a total of 58 stations; among the multiple
reasons for revoking licenses, most were misrepresentation to the Commission
and technical violations. Program-related violations were cited against only one
station for false advertising, against another station for indecent program material, against another for overcommercialization, against a fourth for departure
from promised programming, and against two stations for fraudulent contests.[24]

Although citizen- and minority-groups have contested the renewals of
some station licenses (almost 50 challenges were filed in fiscal 1971), revocations have almost never occurred because of programming content. But the
Commission does demand an accounting of the three-years' on-air performance
as compared with the promises made in the last application which were the
basis for awarding or renewing the licenses, including program balance, commercial content and treatment of controversial issues. "Normally the prudent,
fair-minded, and successful operator has no trouble with this procedure." [25]

In mid-1972 the FCC began a series of actions to "re-regulate" radio by
easing operator rules for small-station engineers; late that same year the Commission deleted or modified seven more technical rules (affecting logging,
meter readings, station identifications, filing of some kinds of contracts, transmitting equipment inspections, and rebroadcast announcements). In 1973 and
1974 further rule changes were introduced affecting auxiliary transmitter testing, station reporting, and operating requirements and record-keeping.[26] While
lessening the burden of routine responsibilities and paperwork for station personnel, the changes might permit the FCC to concentrate more on total service.

All stations in a geographical area come up for renewal at the same time.
The table of expiration dates for three-year licenses is on page 341.

There have been proposals and legislative efforts (some supported or initiated by Congressmen and the White House) to lengthen the license period;
sometime in the near future, stations may be licensed to operate for five-year
periods. It could well be in the overall public interest and it will contribute
much to increased stability and maturity of the broadcasting art, if licenses are
granted for terms longer than the present three-year period. Critics of the media
often oppose this extension lest broadcasters become too independent of the
public and the regulatory agency. But by reducing by almost 40 per cent the
workload of the Commission in renewing broadcast licenses, five-year renewals
would permit more detailed qualitative study of licenses when they did come up
for review. Further, the five-year period, beyond greatly lessening costs for
licensees, would give added time to management to pursue its basic responsibility, serving the American public. Although legal procedures are less complex for the FCC in denials of renewal than with revocation, still at any time

1973, 1976, 1979, 1982, etc.

February 1 .... Florida, Puerto Rico, and Virgin Islands
April 1 .... Alabama, Georgia
June 1 .... Arkansas, Louisiana, Mississippi
August 1 .... Tennessee, Kentucky, Indiana
October 1 .... Ohio, Michigan
December 1 .... Illinois, Wisconsin

1974, 1977, 1980, 1983, etc.

February 1 .... Iowa and Missouri
April 1 .... Minnesota, North Dakota, South Dakota, Colorado, Montana
June 1 .... Kansas, Oklahoma, Nebraska
August 1 .... Texas
October 1 .... Wyoming, Nevada, Arizona, Utah, New Mexico, Idaho
December 1 .... California

1975, 1978, 1981, 1984, etc.

February 1 .... Washington, Oregon, Alaska, Hawaii, and Guam
April 1 .... Connecticut, Maine, Massachusetts, New Hampshire, Rhode Island, Vermont
June 1 .... New Jersey, New York
August 1 .... Delaware, Pennsylvania
October 1 .... Maryland, District of Columbia, Virginia, West Virginia
December 1 .... North Carolina, South Carolina

during a license period—whether three or five or more years—the Commission can call a station to account for failure to operate in the public interest.

Hearings in Local Communities

Section 403 of the Rules of the Commission permits the FCC to initiate hearings in a station's community at any time. One of the co-authors of this book is well acquainted with the implementation of this rule since he was directly involved with hearings conducted in Chicago in 1962. The announced intent of that investigation was described as "legislative" in nature, since the hearings were to be used to determine from public witnesses and from representatives of the licensees whether or not the five Chicago television stations, four commercial and one educational, were in fact attempting to ascertain the needs of the community and whether those needs were being served.

During the week of public investigation in Chicago, 99 witnesses from the general public were heard. Most of them represented special interest groups. While it was gratifying to hear over 60 of these witnesses, without any solicitation whatsoever from the station this co-author represented, speak in laudatory terms of its operation as a dedicated community-oriented entity in

television, he stands opposed to the hearing in principle. When he appeared
before the FCC inquiry, he supported the position taken by LeRoy Collins, then
President of the NAB, who had viewed the proceedings as unfair and unwarranted. This writer added the term "unfortunate" because it was felt that the
Commission should not have instituted hearings of this nature at a time when
the three network owned-and-operated Chicago television stations were awaiting their license renewals. The licenses of WGN Television and of WTTW, the
educational television station, had been renewed on November 22, 1961, for a
three-year period. This writer stated in his testimony that if one or all of the
Chicago television stations had erred as licensee(s), then one or all should have
been called to an accounting in Washington, under the normal quasi-judicial
procedures of the Federal Communications Commission, with all rights of due
process given to the stations involved. In the course of the testimony by public
witnesses, many of them made sweeping assertions without proper understanding of the facts involved. Yet, the licensees were not permitted, through
their counsels, to cross-examine any of the public witnesses.

After the Chicago hearings, the Commission conducted a similar public
hearing in the city of Omaha in January, 1963, with Commissioner Henry in
charge. Another parade of witnesses appeared to testify regarding the community service of the three television stations in that city. The testimony was predominantly favorable to the stations. Even the Nebraska state legislature came
to the defense of the stations and adopted a resolution calling the FCC Federal
intruders into both the freedom of broadcasting and the affairs of the State of
Nebraska. The NAB, which had been excluded from participation in the hearing, filed a memorandum with the FCC in which it took exception to the action
of the Commission in holding the local hearing and asked the FCC to call a halt
to any future hearings of a similar nature.

In the decade since then, the FCC has not repeated the procedure,
perhaps partly because of the increased public activity of citizen and special-
interest groups that challenged licensees after the pivotal WLBT (Jackson,
Mississippi) case in 1966.[27] In 1973, the FCC staff made itself available to individuals or groups wishing to discuss politics and cases affecting broadcast regulation. In mid-1973 the chief of the Broadcast Bureau announced that the
Commission would also hold a number of informal, regional conferences with
broadcasters as well, so that the regulatory agency staff and members of the industry could meet "locally" in a non-adversary context instead of in Washington.[28] This move to regional sessions with the broadcasters could prompt
requests for similar regional sessions with the non-broadcaster public, which
might be reminiscent of the public hearings in Chicago and Omaha.

Requirement of Public Notice

Since 1961, stations about to come up for license renewals have been
required to give public notice of that fact. In 1973 the rules were revised in an
attempt to close the gap between professional local broadcaster and members of
the listening-viewing audience. The hope was that mutual awareness and even

cooperation might preclude antagonistic formal pleadings in hearings before the Commission and in court proceedings. In effect, the rules were intended to inform members of the public audience of their right to appraise local broadcast station service, and to prompt comments to the broadcaster directly or to the Commission prior to the FCC's triennial review of the station's license. Starting six months prior to the expiration of the license the broadcaster must air (every 15th day until his renewal application is submitted to the FCC—thus for two months, because the application must be sent four months prior to date of expiration) an announcement similar to the following one, required twice-monthly during the latter four-month period:

> On (*date of last renewal grant*), (*station's call letters*) was granted a three-year license by the Federal Communications Commission to serve the public interest as a public trustee.
>
> Our license will expire on (*date of expiration*). We have filed an application for license renewal with the FCC.
>
> A copy of this application is available for public inspection during our regular business hours. It contains information concerning this station's performance during the last three years and projections of our programming during the next three years.
>
> Individuals who wish to advise the FCC of facts relating to our renewal application and to whether this station has operated in the public interest should file comments and petitions with the Commission by (*date first day of last full calendar month prior to the month of expiration*).
>
> Further information concerning the Commission's broadcast license renewal process is available at (*address of location of station's public inspection file*) or may be obtained from the FCC, Washington, D.C. 20554.[29]

The new rules also instituted procedures for making available to the local public documentation prepared by the stations as part of their application for renewal. These include data about policies and techniques for ascertaining community needs and interests, together with corresponding programming efforts during each year of operation. A newly required public notice of licensee obligations and of the public's opportunity for recommendations and appraisal was intended to facilitate this exchange of comments. The announcement is to be made twice a month in prime time throughout the three-year license period (except during the six months when the renewal notices are aired).

> (RADIO) On (*date of last renewal grant*), (*station's call letters*) was granted a three-year license by the Federal Communications Commission to serve the public interest as a public trustee. We are obligated to make a continuing, diligent effort to determine the significant problems and needs of our service area and to provide programming to help meet those problems and needs.
>
> We invite listeners to send specific suggestions or comments concerning our station operation and programming efforts to (*name and mailing address*). Unless otherwise requested, all letters received will be available for public inspection during regular business hours.

(TELEVISION) On (*date of last renewal grant*), (*station's call letters*) was granted a three-year license by the Federal Communications Commission to serve the public interest as a public trustee. Each (*anniversary date of deadline for filing renewal application*), we place in our public inspection file a list of what we consider to have been some of the significant problems and needs of our service area during the preceding 12 months and some of our programming to help meet those problems and needs.

We invite viewers to send specific suggestions or comments concerning our station operation and programming efforts to (*name and mailing address*). Unless otherwise requested, all letters received will be available for public inspection during regular business hours.

The Manager and Renewals

The role of the station manager in the renewal process begins the day he accepts his position. If he is truly in command of standards of quality for the operation, renewal should be no problem. He should insist that his program manager keep him supplied with a monthly performance report. This should provide a basis for determining whether proper balance and full community service are being provided. Such an insistence was instituted by one of the authors at WLW in Cincinnati in 1952 and has been employed since then by every Avco station and by all WGN Continental Broadcasting Company stations— WGN and WGN-TV (Chicago), KDAL and KDAL-TV (Duluth), and KWGN-TV (Denver). There has never been a problem on license renewal at any of these stations since this policy was instituted. In those cases where the top operating executive has failed to manifest his leadership in programming, renewal difficulties have almost invariably ensued.

If there is one function that a manager (with the owner who is licensee) should never delegate to another person, it is the preparation of all FCC reports including applications for renewal. True, the detail work can be done by others but the manager must exercise strict supervision over its preparation. He must also approve and bear full responsibility for everything that is finally submitted.

An FCC official has noted that major causes for delayed action on applications for renewal are incomplete detail on forms and neglecting to include documents or exhibits to which reference is made in the forms. Instead of substantive reasons for delay, mere clerical carelessness at the stations (almost always AM, rarely FM or TV) has contributed to repetitious refilings that can also be expensive.[30] So the manager should double-check the renewal filings before they leave the station for the FCC, to be sure that his staff and local counsel have included all information and materials intended.

In addition to the triennial license renewal, the manager must be sure that other periodic reports required by the Commission are properly completed and submitted on time. Major submissions include the following: [31]

Form 301: Application for Construction Permit or CP (also for any changes such as call letters, location of studios, operating hours, power or antenna system, or equipment)

Form 302: Application for license

Form 303: Renewal Application: every three years

Form 323: Ownership Report: annually, and initially within 30 days of grant of CP (Any changes must have prior approval of the Commission.)

    Form 314: Assignment of License (outright sale)

    Form 315: Transfer of Control

    Form 316: Technical changes in organizational structure

Form 324: Financial Report: annually

Form 395: Employment Report: annually

Proof of Performance: annually

Political Report: by Nov. 30 of primary and general election years

Copies of contracts: within 30 days of such agreements. These pertain to network services, ownership, sale of time to "brokers" for resale, sharing profit/loss of operations, mortgage and loan agreements, part-time engineer contracts, management consultants, and contracts with any sponsor of 4 or more hours of daily programming time. *Not* included are contracts with personnel, unions, or music licensing agencies.

Report on advertising to Federal Trade Commission: annually.

The Manager should consult paragraphs 1.611, 1.613, and 1.615 of the Commission's Rules for descriptions of materials that must be filed in the FCC's Washington offices. To guide him in conforming with Federal laws, regulations, and evolving policies as well as with any state and local statutes, the manager should have ready access to an attorney who can keep abreast of cases and criteria and who can interpret competently the legal labyrinth.

NEED FOR LEGAL COUNSEL

It often has been said in jest that broadcasters employ more legal counsel and at greater fees than any other American profession or industry. This may seem true to some station managers. However, there are numbers of radio and television stations, even some of substantial size, having no legal representation in Washington and little, if any, at home.

Unless a station has a manager who is trained in the laws of communications and of business, as well as additional legal areas affecting radio and television, that station needs to have local legal counsel available to assist it on various problems arising throughout the course of any year. Even if legal counsel cannot be employed on a regular retainer basis, there should be some arrangement whereby a station can get the benefit of local legal advice whenever it is needed. Even though legal services are expensive, the amount involved should be far less than the cost of errors resulting in refiling documents with the FCC or in complaint suits against the station, or the manifestation of other needless difficulties and attendant problems because of lack of legal guidelines. The risks of operation without at least stand-by legal counsel are too great and the chances are not worth taking.

In addition to being needed for interpreting FCC rules and regulations, legal advice is necessary for such matters as labor problems, taxes, depreciation schedules, and numbers of decisions associated with station promotions and contests. Among the recurring instances which are fraught with legal complexities that can raise havoc with a station's daily operations as well as with management at license renewal time are: equal time and political broadcasts; the fairness doctrine applied to controversial issues of public importance; editorializing; the right to access (Canon §35 of the American Bar Association), and the right of privacy; defamation by libel and slander (in news and documentary as well as entertainment programs); "payola" and "plugola" (sponsor identification), fraudulent and misleading advertising, overcommercialization; lottery laws; obscenity; censorship; and copyright laws.[32] These programming issues as they relate to the manager's responsibilities will be summarized briefly after the following comments about program report forms required by the Federal government.

Program Report Forms

In 1965, the FCC ordered the use of new AM-FM program forms for all applications for new stations, license renewals, requests for changes in facilities and assignments and transfers of control. New program-logging requirements were also issued.[33]

The Commission cautioned broadcasters about their responsibility to notify the FCC whenever "substantial changes occur" in programming and commercial practices, at variance with their promises made at license application or renewal time.

The resulting AM-FM report forms introduced new categories for analysis of programming by types: instructional programs (not "presented by or in cooperation with an educational institution"); station editorials; political programs; and educational-institution programs. These were added to the seven previous categories of agricultural; entertainment; news; public affairs; religious; sports; and "other" programs.

Instead of reporting the *numbers* of programs in a composite week, since 1965 broadcasters have computed total commercial *time* in hours and minutes.

And that report form of the mid-1960s introduced the significant new requirement that the broadcaster submit a statement of: (1) ". . . the methods used by the applicant to ascertain the needs and interests of the public served by the station"; (2) ". . . the significant needs and interests of the public which the applicant believes his station will serve during the coming license period, including those with respect to national and international matters"; and, (3) "typical and illustrative programs or program series (excluding entertainment and news) that applicant plans to broadcast during the coming license period to meet those needs and interests."

Unquestionably, this addition about audience needs and interests has been of greatest consequence to broadcasters. More than ever, it became imperative that the manager of a station establish regular two-way communication between his station and the public it serves. No longer can programming be designed by intuition and creativity alone. It must be keyed to the *actual* and stated needs and interests of the people.[34] The change also forces the manager to engage in long-range planning whether it has been past station policy or not. The requirement that "typical and illustrative programs or program series" be submitted makes such planning inescapable.

Many broadcasters resent being ordered by the FCC to submit these additional data. However, had there been sufficient evidence that most stations were conducting inquiries of this nature there would have been no need for the government order. If it is fair to say that station management has been irritated by program-data requirements, sometimes seemingly overdetailed and irrelevant, it is also fair to say that management has, in many cases, been enlightened by its own listing of the very details required for summarizing programs. Shortcomings have a way of showing up in station statistics. Vague and comforting impressions to the effect that a station is doing a fine demographic job may be subject to drastic reassessment once the actual programming output is factually examined. Management may, of course, dispute endlessly over categories. For the most part, such disputation is futile. Giving lofty classifications under public-service categories to make-do or lackadaisical programming is foolish as well as deceptive. What is worth transmitting is worth doing well. All excuses for feeble concepts and poor performances are poor excuses.

PROGRAM ISSUES

Radio and television managers are affected by four specific issues in programming which involve vital First Amendment freedoms pertaining to broadcasting: "equal time," the "fairness doctrine," editorializing, and equal access to courtrooms and governmental legislatures. The Constitutional guarantees of free speech and of the press were explicitly applied for the first time to radio and television media by opinions of the Supreme Court justices in mid-1973.[35] When applied to broadcasting, those rights occasion complex legal analysis and often difficult decisions for broadcast managers.

Equal Time

Section 315 of the Communications Act of 1934 regulates the use of broadcasting facilities by candidates for public office. Under its provisions, radio and television stations are not obligated to schedule political broadcasts; but if any "legally qualified" candidate does use the facilities of a station, all other candidates for the same office must be provided equal opportunities to use those facilities. But the 1971 addition of section 312(a) (7) to the Act demands that stations allow "reasonable access" to station time by candidates for Federal elective office (see below in text). Although popularly referred to as the "equal time" provision, the law's technical language refers to "equal opportunities" and thus demands only that *comparable* airtime (similar length and schedule placement of approximately equal commercial value), rates (including

any discounts), and treatment (facilities, services, style of presentation) be afforded to all opposing candidates. Spokesmen for candidates or his political
party, or for positions on public issues before the electorate, are not subject to
this provision of the law, but rather to applications of the related "fairness
doctrine," section 315 (a)(4).[36]

It is important for the broadcast manager to anticipate requests for airtime
during political campaigns by establishing prior guidelines and policies to be
applied to those requests.[37] All such requests by candidates or made in their
behalf should be carefully noted and filed, with specific information on the
disposition of each candidate's request, including time and length of broadcast
and charges paid; this record must be available for public inspection and retained for at least two years.

Who is a legally qualified candidate? The following is the definition of
the legal department of the NAB:

> In general, a candidate is legally qualified if he can be voted for in the elec-
> tion being held and, if elected, will be eligible to serve in the office in question.
> Thus, if the state law permits write-in candidates, an announcement that a
> person is a candidate for re-election would probably be sufficient to bring him
> within Section 315. In some states, however, a person is not a legally qualified
> candidate until he has complied with certain prescribed procedures—such as filing
> a form or paying a fee entitling him to have his name printed on the ballot.

Most station managers, if given the power of decision, would prefer to
have Section 315 repealed. They argue that its nuisance value whenever there
are multi-candidates for an office, each having the right to request "equal
time," creates problems greatly outweighing its benefits. The assumption at
law is that all candidates for the same office are equal. Realistically, however,
this is a false assumption.[38] Various fringe-party candidates reported by the
press on the back pages can and do claim broadcast time in radio and television
equal to the candidates of the major parties. Yet, in the elections that follow,
candidates of minor parties, or of no party at all, almost always receive an insignificant percentage of the vote. The legally qualified parties with candidates
most often on the ballots in the various states included: Republican, Democratic, American Independent, Prohibition, Socialist-Labor, Socialist, American Labor, Constitution, Christian Nationalist, Liberal, Independent, Socialist
Worker's American, America First, American Vegetarian, Greenback, Four
Freedoms and the Poor Man's Party.

The complexity of the problem of granting equal time to all candidates
for the same office becomes compounded when extended to all of the various
offices that appear on the ballot, including state legislators, mayors, council-
men, and all of the various other state, county, district and local offices. It can
become ludicrous, as in a case cited by Commissioner Robert E. Lee of the
FCC. In that instance, a legally qualified candidate of the Progressive Party
demanded equal time from a local station in behalf of his candidacy for the office of governor of a state. The station tried to comply with his request but had

difficulty in rigging a line to the candidate's place of residence—a Federal penitentiary!

In August, 1960, the equal opportunities requirements were temporarily suspended for the offices of President and Vice-President during the 1960 political campaign. This suspension led to the now historic "great debates" between John Kennedy and Richard Nixon. The networks offered time for as many as eight debates; four were held. The debates served the American public, which, for the first time, could see the two major candidates commenting on the same points at the same time and in the same place, although personalities and techniques of public speaking overshadowed the substance of issues.[39] Audiences never were less than 50 to 55 per cent of the adult population of the United States.

There has been no suspension of the equal-time rules during subsequent campaigns. There were controversial challenges, as might have been expected. The President's annual appeal for contributions to the United Community Fund was ruled by the FCC as a broadcast obligating broadcasters to supply equal time to all other Presidential candidates. Later, the Commission interpreted that the broadcast coverage of Presidential news conferences would entitle all of the candidates for the Presidency to similar claims. However, when President Lyndon Johnson delivered a speech dealing with the international situation in mid-October, 1964, carried by the major radio-TV networks, the Republican candidate asked for equal time and was refused by the FCC. The President's speech was labeled a bona-fide news event, bound up with the nature of his office.

An amendment to Section 315 grew out of a case in Chicago in 1959. In the spring of that year, several ex-officio public appearances of the mayor were filmed and shown as part of regularly scheduled newscasts. Since the mayor was a candidate for re-election the following November, Mr. Lar Daly, a declared candidate for the same office and a perennial candidate for some government post, asked the FCC to rule that he should be given equal time. This was the first instance of a request for equal time on news programs. The FCC ruled that equal time must be granted. Broadcasters vigorously protested the ruling, claiming that it would be next to impossible to administer and would interfere with proper coverage of news events. As a result of the complaints, Congress amended the Communications Act in 1959 to exempt from the "equal time" requirements of Section 315 certain kinds of programs where candidates may appear: (1) bona-fide newscasts, (2) bona-fide news interviews, (3) bona-fide news documentaries, and (4) on-the-spot coverage of bona-fide news events, including political conventions.

If a Congressman is a candidate for office, recorded radio or TV reports to his constituency are *not* exempt from the provisions of Section 315; a station is obliged to afford time to opposing candidates. If a candidate appears in a network-originated program or announcement which is broadcast by an affiliated station in the area in which the election campaign is being conducted, other candidates for the same office have a right to request equal time on that affiliate station. It is not necessary for a station to advise candidates of equal time availability; the opponents are responsible for initiating such requests. And a candidate must request the station for equal opportunities afforded an opponent within one week of the day on which the opponent appeared; after that deadline he may no longer seek equal time for that occasion.

On April 7, 1972, the Federal Election Campaign Act of 1971 went into effect. It amended Sections 312 and 315 of the Communications Act by imposing new requirements that broadcasters provide "reasonable access" to airtime and facilities, that they charge political candidates the lowest unit cost for airtime within a period of approximately two months before elections, and that they obtain certification that the candidates' expenditures are within campaign limits set by law.

The "reasonable access" provision was added to the Communications Act in 1971 as a new subsection 312(a) (7). It specified that a station's license could be revoked for "willful or repeated failure to allow reasonable access to or to permit purchase of reasonable amounts of time for the use of a broadcasting station by a legally qualified candidate for Federal elective office on behalf of his candidacy." For candidates to other than Federal offices, a station must continue to apply Communications Act guidelines existing prior to that 1971 amendment, such as "good-faith judgments" that the station was serving the public interest in determining which political campaigns were significant and of interest to its service area.

The "lowest unit charge" refers to the station's charge to opponents for the same class and amount of time for the same period; this rate pertains to a legally qualified candidate for a public office during the 45 days preceding a primary election and during the 60 days preceding a general or special election, including the election day itself. The rate is the absolutely lowest possible charge (thus local rate card, if national rates are higher) to the "most favored commercial advertiser" with the advantage of all frequency discounts, and other discounts or bonuses, regardless of the frequency of announcement by the candidate.[40] Outside those periods of 45 to 60 days, the "charges made for comparable use" by opposing candidates must be the same for all. In 1952 Congress had amended Section 315, making it illegal to charge more for political broadcasts than the normal cost of time for other commercial programs; a station with both national and local rates may not charge the higher national rate to a local candidate; no discrimination may be made in charges for time, so that if free time is provided to one candidate, the opponents have a right to the same treatment. Time segments of appearances must have similar commercial value for all candidates for an office; airtimes scheduled must be equally desirable. Political sponsorship must be identified by visual or aural announcements stating who or what organization paid for the broadcast (under Section 315 a station licensee does not fulfill his obligation by merely announcing that "this has been a paid political broadcast"); if the program exceeds five minutes in length, an announcement is required at both the beginning and the end of the program.[41]

The "certification" modification in Section 315(c) requires stations to have every Federal elective office candidate or his representative certify in writing that payment of broadcast charges will not violate the permissible limit to campaign spending according to the provisions of Section 104(a) of the Campaign Communications Reform Act of 1971. Section 315(d) makes the same provision for state and local elections if those states have adopted campaign spending limitations.

A particularly vexing provision of Section 315 is the "no censorship" clause. Under this provision, licensees of radio and television stations do not have the power to censor material that candidates broadcast. Even if the material is judged by station officials to be libelous, censorship of the political candidates' material is prohibited. But if the candidate makes defamatory remarks on the air, the station cannot be held liable provided it does not directly participate in that libel or slander. This position has been upheld by the United States Supreme Court.[42] The protection for the stations applies only to "legally qualified" candidates and does not apply to supporters of those candidates, or to proponents of ballot issues.

The Fairness Doctrine

Closely allied to the rules affecting broadcasting by candidates for public office is the FCC's "fairness doctrine" which is incorporated in Section 315(a)(4) of the Communications Act, and, since July, 1967, in FCC Rules and Regulations.[43] The fairness doctrine says that broadcasters must afford reasonable opportunities for presentation or discussion of contrasting points of view on controversial issues of public importance. If a single position on a controversial issue is presented on a radio or television station, then the station has the affirmative obligation to seek out responsible proponents of opposing or diverse viewpoints and to provide reasonable opportunity to use their facilities. (More stringent guidelines apply to rules on editorializing and personal attack.)

Unlike the regulations covering political broadcasts by legally qualified candidates, the station licensee may be held liable for defamation, libel or obscene material in the broadcasting of controversial issues. It is, therefore, necessary for station management to exercise supervisory control over the materials that are broadcast. Editing, or censorship, of those materials by the licensee is permitted.

One problem of applying the fairness doctrine is the wide range of interpreting the term "fairness." What may appear fair to one person may seem unfair or biased or slanted to others. As a consequence, treatment of almost any controversial issues can open up any number of requests by individuals and groups for opportunities to be heard.

The matter of propaganda is at the heart of many of the problems associated with the application of the fairness doctrine. Aware of the broadcaster's obligation to present more than one point of view, and confusing the various forms of "access" and "the right of access" as used in broadcast and First Amendment contexts, individuals and groups of many persuasions have become "regulars" in their requests for the opportunity to reply.[44] While some of these people and organizations are gaining some sophistication with regard to the fairness doctrine, there continues to be a general confusion between applying Section 315's "equal time" provisions to political candidates and applying the fairness doctrine to the presentation of varying views on issues of public importance. (Unfortunately, this same misunderstanding can be found among too many broadcast employees, as well.)

Another part of the problem is paying for production and airtime when the program of the first instance (the program where the discussion of a controversial subject occurred) was sponsored. A would-be proponent of another point of view may claim there are no funds available to pay for a like broadcast, but still claims the right to make known opposing views. The broadcaster may attempt to sell the time for a response on an issue but, not being able to find a sponsor, he still has the obligation to present major dissenting views about the argument.

It is important to note that, although the admittedly complex area has partly ambiguous guidelines and thus is often decided on an *ad hoc* basis by the FCC, the Commission's application of the amended Act of 1934 to "fairness" questions does provide some latitude to the broadcaster. For example, not every person or organization claiming to represent a viewpoint about a significant public controversy need be granted airtime. Managers are free to exercise their judgment "reasonably and in good faith" by selecting the "best representatives for various viewpoints on an issue." Nor does mere newsworthiness constitute a controversial issue of significant public concern; again, the broadcaster (often with his legal counsel) must make reasonable, astute judgments about what issues seem truly to constitute such "fairness" topics.[45] And the broadcaster is free to determine the format and other aspects of the program presentation. What the Commission looks for is the licensee's ability to justify his procedures and defend his judgment about providing service to his area, by identifying issues of major importance to his community and by affirmatively seeking out proponents of contrasting viewpoints (although the problems lie more with the number of advocates initiating requests for time on these topics or demanding time for response).

The question for decision in the future would seem to be whether society is better served by an insistence that all sides be presented, no matter how divergent, or whether station management should be depended upon to use good judgment in the presentation of significant facets of all important issues. The basic difficulty is that while printed media are capable of almost endless expansion, and live speeches to live audiences may take place from the soapbox to the largest assembly hall, radio and TV transmissions are limited to the number of minutes in the hour and the number of hours in the broadcast day. These physical limitations of broadcast communications would seem to require the adoption of new procedures. Most licensees, including corporate owners of network stations, have made great efforts to challenge the constitutionality of the "equal time" rule and the "fairness doctrine." Richard W. Jencks, a key administrative executive with the Columbia Broadcasting System, reflected the determined concern of his colleagues in radio and television when he cautioned the Federal Communications Bar Association about organizations that used the fairness doctrine as a vehicle to compel broadcasters to recognize their demands. The result, he warned, could be:

> . . . a broadcast press without purpose, without passion, which shuns tough issues and does not lead but merely presides . . . a common carrier of other people's views with no creative or vigorous voice of its own. . . . Life might be easier for broadcasters if they were made mere common carriers of controversy. There would be fewer problems with Congressional committees. It might even be profitable to sell time to partisans, and to reduce our investment in broadcast journalism. But I don't think either the commission, or most broadcasters want it that way.[46]

Although the U.S. Court of Appeals in the District of Columbia tended in the last dozen years to support claimants against broadcasters, even when the FCC had decided initially against those claimants, by 1972–1973, the U.S. Supreme Court justices and some of the appellate court judges in Washington began to revise those earlier judgments. Even Judge David Bazelon, long a liberal exponent of the public's right to access to the Federally franchised broadcast frequencies, publicly reflected on the wisdom of earlier patterns of decisions that limited broadcasters' prerogatives in determining program service.

> In the context of broadcasting today, our democratic reliance on a truly informed American public is threatened if the overall effect of the fairness doctrine is the very censorship of controversy which it was promulgated to overcome. . . . There is no doubt about the unique impact of radio and television. But this fact alone does not justify government regulation. In fact, quite the contrary. We should recall that the printed press was the *only* medium of mass communication in the early days of the Republic—and yet this did not deter our predecessors from passing the First Amendment to prohibit abridgement of its freedoms. . . . It is proper that this court urge the Commission to draw back and consider whether time and technology have so eroded the necessity for governmental imposition of fairness obligations that the doctrine has come to defeat its purposes in a variety of circumstances; that we ask whether an alternative does not suggest itself—whether, as with printed press, more freedom for the individual broadcaster would enhance, rather than retard, the public's right to a marketplace of ideas.[47]

His comments differed from comments and decisions of previous years by his own appellate court as well as by the Supreme Court, particularly in its 8-0 vote supporting the constitutionality of the fairness doctrine (the "Red Lion" decision of June, 1969). Judge Bazelon specifically questioned the highest court's argument about scarcity of frequencies as a reason for limiting stations and thus the public's right of access to station schedules; he noted that there were 7,458 broadcasting stations on the air compared with 1,749 daily newspapers being published in the U.S., plus cable company channels operating throughout the land. And the Supreme Court itself in May of 1973 by a vote of 7 to 2 decided against BEM's appeal which would have had the effect of requiring broadcast licensees to accept advertising on all issues without any editorial judgment about appropriateness or balance of the content.[48]

The whole issue of "fairness" in programming controversial issues arose out of the presentation of editorials by broadcast stations. The problem of editorializing, plus the difficulties of personal attack in broadcast statements are treated below.

Editorializing and Personal Attack

The issue of editorializing in radio and television began with the famous *Mayflower Case,* which resulted in a 1940 decision by the FCC. The decision read in part:

> . . . under the American system of broadcasting it is clear that responsibility for the conduct of a broadcast station must rest initially with the broadcaster. It is equally clear that with the limitations in frequencies inherent in the nature of radio, the public interest can never be served by a dedication of any broadcast facility to the support of partisan ends. Radio can serve as an instrument of democracy only when devoted to the communication of information and the exchange of ideas fairly and objectively presented. It cannot be used to support the candidacies of his friends. It cannot be devoted to the support of principles he happens to regard most favorably. In brief, the broadcaster cannot be an advocate.[49]

In June, 1949, the Commission issued a report saying that broadcasters might editorialize provided they allowed air time for opposing points of view:

> If, as we believe to be the case, the public interest is best served in a democracy through the ability of the people to hear expositions of the various positions taken by responsible groups and individuals on particular topics and to choose between them, it is evident that broadcast licensees have an affirmative duty generally to encourage and implement the broadcast of all sides of controversial issues over their facilities.[50]

In spite of the fact that some broadcasters had worked diligently through the 1940s to regain the right to editorialize, very few of them exercised their newly won right during the 1950s. The obligation to "seek out" opposing points of view may have seemed burdensome, injudicious or distasteful. In 1959, the Commission tempered its earlier interpretation and adopted a "fairness" obligation on the part of the licensee, replacing the obligation to "seek out." Then, in 1963 and 1964 came policy statements by the FCC which, although intended as clarification of the fairness doctrine, confused the broadcasters who were undecided about editorializing.[51]

The FCC, continuing to develop its policy, in 1967 adopted rulings that stations must give notice to any persons whose "honesty, character, integrity or like personal qualities" had been criticized and commented on in programs involving controversial issues of public importance—excepting newscasts or live coverage of news events, but including editorials, news commentaries, interviews, and documentaries.[52] The Supreme Court's "Red Lion" decision in 1969 affirmed the constitutionality and legality of the FCC's fairness policies and its regulations that broadcast personal attacks required a station to afford opportunity to reply by the persons or groups so attacked.[52a] In effect, the licensee whose station broadcasts such an "attack" must within one week of that broadcast notify the person or group attacked of the date, time and identification of the broadcast; must provide a script or tape (or summary if both are unavailable); and must offer "reasonable opportunity" to respond through that station's facilities. In the case of political candidates, notice of such attack and the offer for reply time must be given within 24 hours after broadcast (but if the program comes within 72 hours prior to the election, the station must provide such information and offer in advance of the broadcast).

These considerations apply to three often confusedly intertwined facets of the "fairness doctrine": the discussion of controversial subjects (regardless of format), the personal attack, and the editorial endorsement of a candidate for public office. And—while the fairness doctrine and Section 315 from which it came are most often cited when a person or organization feels "grieved"—one must remember that state laws concerning libel and slander often can be applied to the person making the allegedly offensive statements, *and* to the broadcast licensee. In addition, while a broadcaster may not censor the statements of a political candidate (in a prior effort to remove from them possibly libelous or slanderous material) and cannot be held liable under state laws, candidates might be well advised that the same protection does not apply to them.[53]

The right to editorialize, and even the obligation to do so, has been confirmed by the Federal Communications Commission and the Federal courts. And yet by 1974 almost half of all the broadcast stations in the U.S. never editorialized. Only 61 per cent of AM stations, 44 per cent of FM stations and 51 per cent of TV stations in the country presented editorials; the great majority editorialized only occasionally.[54] Thus, in the seven years since the NAB's own surveys in 1966–1967, the same proportion of radio stations aired editorials, but the proportion of TV stations that editorialized had decreased from 56 per cent to 48 per cent (possibly because of the addition of small-staffed, low-budgeted UHF stations to the total number of TV stations in that half-decade).[55] And that mid-1960 survey learned that one out of ten stations polled had editorialized in the past but were no longer doing so. As additional small-power stations proliferated, and as Federal guidelines on these matters became increasingly complex (by FCC interpretations, notices and responses, as well as by related cases in the courts), the percentage of broadcast stations carrying editorials decreased through the decade of the 1960s and into the 1970s. The NAB documented that smaller stations, with lesser budgets and staffs, avoided editorializing more than larger stations.

At the third annual convention of the National Broadcast Editorial Association in 1974, former CBS president and chairman Dr. Frank Stanton urged:

Any station manager worth his salt will learn the law, hire the people, sacrifice the time, explore the issues, risk corporate or governmental intervention and welcome adverse public opinion to have said on his station what he thinks needs to—or ought—be said. And if he does not care enough, perhaps because he is afraid of losing sponsors, offending public opinion, or creating problems with stockholders, then he does not deserve the job.[55a]

About 70 per cent of the radio stations reported to the NAB that either the owner or the general manager is the key person in determining the station's position on an issue, in writing the editorial, and in presenting it on the air. But among television stations, these responsibilities are delegated to editorial or news staffs or, preferably, an editorial board. Top management at 88 per cent of TV stations review and clear editorials before they are broadcast.

The editorial must be regarded as management's voice and it must represent station policy and point of view.[56] The choice for air spokesman should be someone who clearly represents management, embodies authority, is believable, and conveys the management "image." A full-time editorialist who researches and writes the editorials could be the logical person to broadcast them.

The responsibility is great, and if radio and television editorials are to command the same respect as do newspaper editorials, a basic investment in time, effort, research, production and talent is imperative. The point must be stressed that only those stations with qualified staff and resources should attempt to editorialize. Neither society nor broadcasting gains if the air becomes filled with uninformed, superficially biased or simply fatuous opinions. If a station manager truly wants to be an influence for good in his community through editorials of real social significance, it is his obligation to hire qualified personnel and allocate sufficient time for research. Then the station can be in a position to become one of the most significant forces in the community.

Half of the executives polled by the NAB aired editorials in order to exercise persuasion and leadership in the community. Yet fully another quarter of broadcasters limited their objective to simply informing the audience about station views on current issues. Among reasons for editorializing, the benefits to the community dominated executives' thinking: 87 per cent judged the practice as fulfilling the broadcasters' obligations as responsible members of their communities, 60 per cent noted that it provided additional editorial viewpoints for people to consider; increasing a station's prestige was put as another reason for editorializing by 57 per cent of executives. As a deterrent to airing editorials, radio executives—more than radio-TV or television executives—noted possible alienation of advertisers or creating bad feeling in the community. But more than half of the managers (51% in radio and 74% in TV or combined radio-TV operations) claimed selection of issues was not influenced by possible effect of editorial position on station revenue.[57]

Most broadcasters editorialized about issues of local interest (84%) and on topics where there were large differences of opinion (71%). Only half of the managers replied that they editorialized about statewide issues or about issues generating strong emotions in the community. Least likely as editorial topics were endorsements of candidates for public office and subjects involving one particular individual. Most executives preferred to avoid issues that were national or international in scope. In the late 1960s, editorials about community issues involved conditions or practices rather than people or groups.[58] Only two to three per cent used editorial time for "non-debatable issues" such as safe driving and caution about fire hazards ("Smokey the Bear").

In 1974, Dr. Stanton polled TV stations in the top 10 markets and reported that three-fourths of them express opinion in editorials but most focus exclusively on local issues.[58a] Only 14 stations (one-third of the total) had presented any editorials on the "Watergate" revelations in Washington; and five of those stations had referred only indirectly to the matter. Only one-tenth of the stations endorsed political candidates.

There do appear to be tangible benefits from station editorials. Stations that have broadcast editorials of meaning and significance have not found significant negative reactions from either state and city government sources or from advertisers. There is a growing tendency for those stations to grow bolder in their editorials as expected reprisals do not occur. The increased stature of these stations in their communities has become commercially beneficial. Some stations are even using their editorial success stories as evidence of the power of their broadcast operation to influence people.

The NAB's 1967 study of 1,243 men and women 21 years of age and older learned that half the people who had been exposed to broadcast editorials were satisfied with the number on the air, while 34 per cent of radio listeners and 42 per cent of TV viewers of editorials claimed they would like even more. Persons aware of editorials and actually exposed to them tended to be men, young adults, and college-educated. (Less than one in five persons in the national poll disapproved outright of all editorializing by mass media: 18% television, 17% radio and 15% newspapers; their major objections were that editorials give only one side of issues and that the media have too much influence on the public's thinking.) Contrary to the broadcasters' own practices, the national audience responded seven-to-one (86%) that issues of *any* scope—local, state, national, or international—are suitable for editorials. Equally revealing to the industry is that, when they were given a list of 15 specific issues ranging from relatively bland to highly controversial, nine out of ten respondents judged none of them to be unsuitable for broadcast editorializing and, significantly, the NAB reported that:

> Among the population as a whole, *two out of three people (65%) think more highly of a station which editorializes, while only 8% are more favorably disposed toward one that does not.* (The remaining 27%, many of whom have never seen or heard an editorial, made no choice either way.) [59]

Other Specific Program Issues

Among the many legal as well as ethical problems arising from programming are such issues for management watchfulness and judgment as obscenity, censorship, sponsor identification, sources of program material (including "payola"), double billing, lottery laws for contests, copyright, and the larger strictures on monopoly and restraint of trade. Obviously each of these areas demands competent legal counsel for individual cases. The NAB continually distributes informational reports and para-legal opinions and guidelines to assist station managers. And the management texts cited above briefly comment on these responsibilities of managment.

In the spring of 1973 the FCC explored recent developments in radio "telephone-talk" formats which emphasized intimate details of sex-related activities.[60] An effort to bring such matters to court for juridical determination failed when a penalized station paid the FCC-levied fine rather than contest the decision. But stations throughout the country understood the implied caution by the Commission and most of them modified or cancelled their sex-talk oriented radio programs.[61]

Earlier, station licenses had been jeopardized by disc jockeys whose spontaneous remarks and patterns of comments were not adequately overseen by local management. Compounding the problem was the incidence of allegedly obscene words or supportive references to drugs in the lyrics of contemporary songs. Again, the stewardship of management was called into question by the Commission when complaints were brought against stations for programming certain recorded songs.[62]

The FCC in March of 1971 issued a Public Notice regarding drug lyrics and broadcasters' responsibilities. It called attention to complaints made to the Commission alleging that the lyrics of certain songs promoted the use of drugs, and it warned licensees of their "responsibility" to know the content of lyrics they broadcast, just as they are responsible for all other material that they broadcast. The initial Notice raised more questions than it answered, leading the Commission to issue a second Public Notice a month later, which said that the Commission had no intention of banning the broadcast of any lyric, but merely wanted to remind licensees of their responsibility for program content. Concerned over future interpretation, two university-operated FM stations, WYBC-FM (Yale University, New Haven, Conn.) and KUOP-FM (University of the Pacific, Stockton, Cal.), asked the FCC to rule formally on the drug lyric policy adopted by WYBC-FM. When the Commission refused to rule, the matter was taken to the Court of Appeals (District of Columbia). The appellate court sustained the FCC's authority to issue the two Public Notices and its refusal to sanction or disapprove the WYBC-FM policy. In its decision, the Court of Appeals noted that the FCC had provided three options for broadcast licensees: (1) auditioning each selection before broadcast, (2) monitoring each selection as it is broadcast, (3) deciding about future broadcast after an initial broadcast—thus leaving broadcasters as much latitude as they enjoyed prior to issuance of the Public Notices. The matter was resolved in late 1973 when the U.S. Supreme Court refused to enter the case and let stand the FCC's two Public Notices. Since what is a minority decision today may become a majority decision tomorrow, it is appropriate to note the statement of Associate Supreme Court Justice William O. Douglas, who with Associate Justice William Brennan dissented from the Supreme Court's action: "For now the regulation is applied to song lyrics; next year it may apply to comedy programs, and the following year to news broadcasts."

Television, too, was under increasing scrutiny for alleged permissiveness in drama and comedy programs. The theme of "sex and violence" was sounded regularly in Congressional sessions in the 1970s. By 1975 House Communications Subcommittee chairman Torbert Macdonald looked cooly to the NAB's "family hour" effort at self-regulation which had been supported by FCC chairman Richard Wiley and Senate Communications Subcommittee chairman John Pastore. Congressman Macdonald even raised the perennial threat of licensing the source of national program service, the commercial networks. Meanwhile, the FCC sought to clarify the U.S. Code provision (Title 18, Section 1464) prohibiting obscene, indecent or profane *language,* to extend explicitly to *visual* depiction of such material.[62a]

The issue joined, of course, is the freedom of the broadcaster to program his Federally licensed station without censorship by the FCC's prior restraining action (or by *ex post facto* penalty that constitutes implied restraint against subsequent similar actions). The other side of the same coin, however, is the audience's right to freedom from what some consider offensive program content broadcast through a Federally-licensed airwave frequency. The manager must at all times know his personnel in programming and in the studios, as well as establish and uphold station policies for proper clearance of program content (scripted copy, ad lib commentary, and lyrics); he cannot delegate entirely to others the responsibility continually to monitor his station's daily broadcasts.

A continuing threat to proper licensee management of a broadcast station is the undisclosed payment of money or valuable goods to broadcast employees in return for on-air promotional comment or display or other consideration. The "payola" and "plugola" investigations of the late 1950s resulted in action by the Congress and the FCC, clarifying and strengthening Sections §317 and §508 of the Communications Act, and adding penalties of up to $10,000 and/or one year imprisonment for violations. Managers must exercise personal vigilance and must ensure that station procedures protect against programming content and personalities being used unlawfully.[63] In a word, whenever payment (in money or goods, as in a "trade-out") is made for commercial proposes, the audience is to be informed of the source of that payment. This sponsor identification is intended to inform the public, and at the same time protect management's control of personnel who might otherwise modify program content because of private advantage from outside the station. Further, the Federal regulations also protect the value of commercial time, which can be eroded if non-clients have access to broadcast promotion without paying commercial rates (while also contributing to "clutter" within programs).[64] The need for sponsor identification is even more apparent for individuals and groups who are not

commercial advertisers but who purchase air time for promotional announcements and for programming related to public affairs and politics. Again, the audience has a right to know the source of such "content with a viewpoint."

A form of conspiracy to defraud is the practice of "double billing,"
prohibited by Section 73.124 of the Commission Rules. Licensees must exercise diligence to prevent advertisers being charged for other than the exact service or program consideration contracted for. In effect, the advertiser pays
more than the actual rate for the commercial advertising, or at least his records
show a rate which is not paid to the station itself but to various middlemen such
as distributors or salesmen or station personnel.[65]

For more than three decades false and deceptive broadcast advertising has
been under the jurisdiction of the Federal Trade Commission rather than the
FCC. Section 14(c) of the FTC Act protects media that accept advertising from
outside sources, through ad agencies or directly from advertising clients. Nevertheless, stations (and networks on behalf of their affiliated and owned stations) have a responsibility to know the material that they are broadcasting.
And stations are still responsible on behalf of the public interest to protect that
public from false advertisements. But stations may be liable to FTC action if
they contract to write advertising copy or to produce radio or TV commercials
for clients; they then act as agents of those clients. Further, audience research
and market data can qualify as advertising material when the station misuses
them to promote the sale of station time or to elicit audience support, by making deceptive claims of audience coverage, market rank or competitive status
relative to other local stations.[66] Here, too, the NAB attempts to assist small-
staffed stations in appraising commercial advertising (at least for regional and
national campaigns) for acceptability on grounds other than outright deception or
fraud. In the context of heavy consumer criticism in the 1970s, however, it
serves a station well to check with NAB guidelines, with network continuity or
program practices and standards departments, as well as with their own local
policies to protect themselves against valid criticism.

Aggressive stations that mount contests and games to stimulate community awareness and audience participation in their programming activities must
be alert to avoid the element of "consideration" which constitutes a lottery and
is illegal. This caution is to be exercised with advertisements which announce
contests and games, because to broadcast such would be to air information
about a lottery which until 1975 was a Federal crime.[67] It is useful here to
recall that many Commission actions about license renewals and forfeitures
(fines) have resulted from misleading or illegal contest announcements. Three
key elements must be present to constitute a lottery: a prize, the element of
chance, and the more complex element of "consideration"—or what one must
pay or do to participate. And even though state laws may permit some kinds of
contests (e.g., bingo or state-sponsored lotteries), broadcasters are bound by
Federal laws affecting contests that are lotteries.[68]

Other legal issues that involve contracts and relatively large sums of
money for rights to broadcast include music licensing through the American

Society of Composers, Authors, and Publishers (ASCAP), Broadcast Music Incorporated (BMI), and SESAC (formerly Society of European Songwriters Authors and Composers). Stations and networks can hardly afford to do the bookkeeping on "per play" royalty payments for each song used in their daily schedules, so they must contract for blanket year-long fees to the respective licensing agencies. Expert legal counsel is required to assist in negotiating properly these important contracts.[69]

Similarly complex and important is the matter of copyright—for station-originated material that has been broadcast, and for material gathered from other sources (books, magazines, newspapers, stage plays, reports, research study monographs, etc.). Copyright laws have been in the process of revision and restructuring for a decade, but Congress by the mid-1970s had not yet drawn up a long overdue new copyright act. In the meantime, legal advice is essential to avoid law suits for infringement of property right in print and photographed materials.[70]

A major legal issue of significance to companies who are owners of several broadcast properties and/or newspapers is the question of monopoly control over communications media. In an age of conglomerates and corporate mergers the question becomes more prominent; and critics have challenged the FCC and Congress as well as the Department of Justice to ensure that there will not be concentrations of media that might restrain competition and trade within broadcasting, as well as limit the sources of information and communication to the public. Group owners of stations in regions of the U.S. or scattered across the land are particularly susceptible to such criticism. Yet, studies have indicated that the quality and amount of local-oriented community programming tends to be greater on stations owned by large interests as part of a group than on single stations owned locally.[71] Often, large size and diversity of resources gives economic stability as well as the opportunity for pooled experience and competence of personnel. Nevertheless, in the early 1970s there was continued emphasis by the FCC on diversity of ownership as a major consideration in license applications. Once again, legal counsel must be available to assist in preparing documentation to support multi-station entities as owners-licensees. The FCC has regulated against "duopoly" (owning two or more stations of the same type in the same service area) in Section 15.4, and has limited ownership of multiple stations in different areas to seven stations of each type (AM, FM, TV—of which only five may be VHF).[72]

Linked to the previously cited issue of defamation through libel and slander is the problem of broadcast news coverage of individual persons whose newsworthiness conflicts with their prior right to privacy. Discretion must be coupled with good sense and reasonable sensitivity to recognize a person's private activities and feelings where the public has no legitimate concern or where intrusion by media can cause unwarranted distress and problems for the parties involved and for members of their families. Dr. Fred Siebert points out that broadcasters meet complex problems in visually presenting news events which occur in "semiprivate" or quasi-public places (government buildings, sports arenas, controlled-admission halls), where permission must be obtained to report events. Cameramen must have legal access to a site and, unless the subjects are themselves in public notice, permission must be obtained from persons who will appear in televised reports.[73] This kind of issue is exacerbated in the case of broadcasters' access to trials and other judicial or legislative functions of governmental groups. For there is the correlative right of the public to know about persons and activities which influence society and affect his own life at least indirectly.

THE RIGHT TO EQUAL ACCESS

Different from the kinds of access that refer to the general public's limited right to use scarce broadcast frequencies or to air counter-comments under the fairness doctrine, is the issue of "equal access" for broadcasters.[73a] This kind of access has been described as the right to take microphones, cameras and auxiliary equipment—"the tools of the trade"—wherever the press takes its "tools" of paper and pencil. Thus broadcasters seek equality with print media in reporting events of public import, including the use of broadcast equipment in legislative and judicial chambers (most often banned in the latter, and becoming more and more common in the former but without universal rules or application). Broadcasters have argued that they are entitled to this privilege under the gurantees of the First Amendment.

Access to the Courts

In the case of broadcasting's access to the courts, Canon 35 of the Canons of Judicial Ethics of the American Bar Association has served as a restrictive force. Canon 35 was adopted in 1937 as a reaction to an inept and overly sensational treatment of the radio coverage of the Hauptmann trial in the Lindbergh kidnapping case in 1935. The Canon, later amended to include television, states in part:

> The taking of photographs in the courtroom during sessions of the court or recesses between sessions, and the broadcasting of court proceedings are calculated to detract from the essential dignity of the proceedings, degrade the court and create misconceptions with respect thereto in the mind of the public and should not be permitted.[74]

Although not a law, the ABA's Canon 35 has been adopted as a rule of court in many jurisdictions. The effect of Canon 35 in banning radio and television from the courts has made the problem of equal access a major issue of the broadcasting industry. While there has been considerable argument for a modification of the Canon, the original restriction has held over the years. The progress made in getting microphones and cameras into the courts has been almost negligible. For all intents and purposes, this remains one activity of modern society that is "off limits" for most of the electronic media.

Various arguments have been advanced against the admission of microphones and cameras to the courtroom. It has been held that broadcasting is basically an entertainment medium, hence not covered by the gurantees of freedom of speech in the First Amendment to the Constitution. Yet, the United States Supreme Court has ruled that broadcasting is entitled to the same guarantees as other media. It has been argued that broadcasters would use access to the courts not in a spirit of public service but in a spirit of entertainment. Still, in several cases where microphones and cameras have been admitted to trials, judges and attorneys have commented that the coverage was handled in the best interest of all concerned, including the general public.

It has been said that some attorneys and judges as well as witnesses might take advantage of broadcast coverage to engage in "show-off" performances in order to get publicity for themselves. However, where trials have been presented by the electronic media, judges have demonstrated that they were able to keep proper order in their courts. It has been claimed that the media would violate the rights of privacy of all the people in the courtroom. Legal opinion has held that there is no law guaranteeing personal privacy in public matters.

It has been alleged that permission for radio and television to cover the courts would result in such confusion of equipment and personnel as would prevent orderly legal procedures, thus jeopardizing the defendant's right to a fair trial under the Sixth Amendment. But with the development and miniaturization of cameras and accessory equipment, plus the demonstrated efficiency of pooled arrangements, facilities for court coverage without distraction are well known.[75]

In those few instances where exceptions have been made and where court proceedings have been broadcast, the reaction to the coverage has been largely favorable. In what was called "a majority of four and one-half," [76] due to the opinion of Justice John M. Harlan, Canon 35 was in effect written into a law by Supreme Court decision in June, 1965. Broadcasters may find encouragment in Justice Harlan's opinion. In urging the court to "proceed only step by step in this unplowed field," Justice Harlan forecast the possibility of the time "when television will have become so commonplace an affair in the daily life of the average person as to dissipate all reasonable likelihood that its use in courtrooms may disparage the judicial process." [77] Justice Harlan, while voting with the majority, implied that he might shift his vote in another case of this nature involving different facts.

Eventually, as Justice Harlan has indicated, the radio microphone and the television camera may come to be commonplace in the courtrooms. The right will not come without a considerable initiative on the part of the broadcaster. The burden will be on him to produce evidence that the electronic media will not disrupt the process of justice in any way. Douglas A. Anello, former general counsel for the NAB, summed up the sensible and only tenable view:

> It is up to us in the broadcasting profession to demonstrate that our conduct in courtroom proceedings can be as decorous as it has been on so many other equally important public occasions.

If and when the opportunity to broadcast any part of a judicial proceeding is presented, it is incumbent on all of us to do so with the utmost dignity. Ground rules should be agreed upon in advance by all concerned and should be strictly adhered to throughout the proceedings.[78]

In court trials especially, but also in other serious procedural activities in society, the presence of radio-television media must be planned and carried out discreetly by broadcasters; for the media do contribute in some way to the shape of events being reported, by their very presence and by the fact that they are relaying those sights and sounds to the public at large.[79]

Access to the Federal Government

The impression might be gained from daily Washington broadcasts that radio and television have equal reportorial access to affairs of the Federal government. While generally true of the Executive Branch, it is far from true in legislative and judicial areas.

Sessions of the U.S. Senate are closed to broadcasters. Committee hearings of the Senate can be covered by special permission of the chairmen and ranking minority members. Prior permission, however, is no guarantee of coverage. Access has been granted, refused, limited and arbitrarily expanded and restricted. The Senate hearings on the "Watergate" disclosures affecting multiple branches and agencies of government did demonstrate dramatically the impact that access to such sessions could have on the public whose representatives were conducting the meetings and whose elected or appointed officials were being interviewed. The flexibility of media in covering the sessions "live," by "gavel-to-gavel" re-runs the same evening, by abbreviated summaries at the end of a day or of a week, and by excerpts inserted into the evening newscasts suggested the important role for broadcast media access in a free, democratic, pluralistic society. But that same pluralism coupled with unavoidably selective perception caused many observers of the Watergate hearings to question the propriety of public disclosure of personalities and their partly private words, thoughts, and feelings, as well as overt activities in these complex political matters. At times it was difficult to distinguish between the objective value of live broadcast coverage of the hearings from the subjective interpretation and judgment of the social-political effects of the hearings themselves as well as of their coverage.

Usually, broadcasters have been better treated in Senate hearings than in the House of Representatives, where no radio or television coverage is permitted of full or committee sessions. The only exceptions in the House are in the cases of special joint sessions of the Congress. The House makes (and unmakes) its own rules; there is no appeal.

In July, 1966, President Johnson signed a Freedom of Information bill into law. A legal principle is now established that Americans have the right to examine nonclassified information and may go to court to force a governmental agency to make it available. However, it must be understood that the law applies to the Executive Branch of the Federal government only. Understandably, certain kinds of information may be withheld, including information bearing on matters of national security, FBI files, and private or confidential records such as tax returns and financial statistics.[80]

The attitudes of most U. S. Presidents during the last four decades have been reasonably cordial toward all of the mass media. President Roosevelt held an average of two non-broadcast press conferences a week and became famous for his "fireside chats" on radio. President Truman, while often brusque with the media, held an average of one non-broadcast press conference a week. President Eisenhower's press conferences were recorded for delayed broadcast, thus allowing editing of the material. President Kennedy inaugurated "live" press conferences on both radio and television; President Johnson continued the practice of permitting "live" broadcasts of his press conferences, as did President Nixon in his infrequent news conferences (although he, too, was often brusque with media representatives and expressed serious reservations about the media's level of objectivity). President Ford followed his predecessors' policies, including conducting hour-long, informal conversations with news correspondents on prime-time, "live" national television.

Access to State Legislatures

Regardless of argument, only 13 states officially permitted continued "live" broadcasts of legislatures in the 1970s. Those states were Alabama, Arizona, Georgia, Idaho, Illinois, Indiana, Missouri, New York, Oklahoma, Tennessee, Texas, Vermont, and West Virginia.

Access to City Councils

In attempts to cover city council meetings, broadcasters and other representatives of the mass media are sometimes the victims of a convenient maneuver known as the executive session. Many so-called executive sessions are in reality only "closed meetings." The business that may be conducted in an executive session has been defined:

> *Executive Sessions.* A body may exclude the public when it is considering or acting upon any of the following matters:
> (a) The dismissal, promotion, demotion, or compensation of any public employee, or the disciplining of such employee or investigation of charges against him, unless the employee affected shall have requested an open meeting.
> (b) The hiring of any person as a public employee.
> (c) Matters which, if discussed in public, would be likely to benefit a party whose interests are adverse to those of the general community. This provision shall include but not be limited to consideration of the acquisition of land.
> (d) Matters which, if discussed in public, would be likely to affect adversely the reputation of any person, other than a member of the body itself.
> (e) Welfare matters where federal grant-in-aid requirements prohibit publicity.[81]

City officials who use the "closed meeting" for other purposes may not realize a very real denial of "public interest, convenience and necessity." Here would seem to be a ready theme for radio and television editorializing.

The Challenge

In the fight for equal access, broadcasters do not ask for permission to cover all trials nor do they propose to cover all of the proceedings of legislative bodies. The commercial schedule would not permit such extensive coverage. What broadcasters do want is the opportunity to cover legislative and court-room proceedings at times when the event reported is of special interest to the public.

When and if broadcasters achieve equal access to the courts and to governmental sources, no aspect of their programming will call for greater integrity and professional competence. It will be no assignment for staff announcers who have little background in journalism. This coverage is too important for a reliance on microphones, tape recorders and cameras to transmit the whole message. The trained and experienced reporter's judgment will be an absolute necessity. To bring that judgment to bear in his own radio-television community is the duty and distinction of the responsible station manager.

Mass Coverage of Events

A Joint Media Committee on News Coverage Problems was formed by representatives from five professional news organizations: Sigma Delta Chi, The Associated Press Managing Editors Association, the National Press Photographers Association, the Radio Television News Directors Association, and the American Society of Newspaper Editors. This joint committee issued a statement concerning "Orderly Procedures for Mass Coverage of News Events." Noting that many public events are covered by the press with disruptions, the report cited a lack of preparation and organization as the reasons for turmoil at some crowded events. The committee recommended careful advance planning for public events so that orderly newsgathering may take place. Even unexpected happenings could be covered in a more orderly fashion if governmental, civic, police and other authorities would "arrange measures by which the media can do their job in an orderly fashion with a minimum of confusion." Local news executives are advised:

> On occasions where it is apparent that no adequate arrangements have been made and where a confused, disorderly situation could ensue, one or more of the senior news representatives in the area should take the initiative in proposing newsgathering procedures that will be fair and efficient. We believe that such an effort will not be taken as presumptuous or officious, but will be welcomed by all concerned.[82]

The committee recommended that where space is limited, a pooling arrangement is more satisfactory than no plan at all, or to grant privileges on a merely first-come basis.

C. APPRAISING THE ROLE OF REGULATION
THE LARGER ISSUES OF REGULATING
PROGRAMMING AND ADVERTISING

From the beginning, there has been all but continual disagreement between broadcasters and the FCC over program and advertising regulation. A basic point of contention is the phrase in the Communications Act which requires radio and television stations to be operated in the "public interest, convenience, and necessity." Since the establishment of the Act, it has been next to impossible to reach an agreement between broadcasters and regulators concerning just what those words mean. All broadcasters are not in agreement as to their meaning nor are all regulators. Because of this conflict over semantics, there have been misunderstandings on both sides.

Some members of the FCC have interpreted the phrase as a command to act as "watchdogs" over the content of programs and advertising. Broadcasters, who are notably over-sensitive to criticism, have considered inquiries from the Commission in these areas as threats of censorship. Over the years, the "cat-and-mouse" game has resulted in a sizeable waste of energy and time. Commercial broadcasters generally resent any intrusions of the FCC into these areas. The broadcasters are of the opinion that the particular province of the Commission lies in the licensing function and in the maintenance of proper technical standards of broadcast engineering. Broadcasters find nothing specific in the Communications Act giving the FCC the right to intrude into program or commercial issues.[83] But the courts have regularly interpreted the Act to give the Commission some degree of authority over the total program service provided the public by broadcast licensees.[84] The Commission in 1960, when outlining policy about programming, noted that it did not intend to substitute its judgment for that of the licensee in determining an apt program schedule for the audience in the local community. But the Commission did intend to make its determination about granting and renewing licenses on the licensee's efforts to determine the needs and interests of his community, and on the program service proposed to serve those needs and interests. Typically, the Commission depended on comparative appraisals between competing applicants for the same market, instead of attempting to establish any national "standard" or fixed formula which was to be applied to all licensees.[85]

Ever since the FCC issued *Public Service Responsibility of Broadcast Licensees* (or the "Blue Book") in 1946, a threat of government regulation of programs and commercial practices has hung over broadcasting. The tide has ebbed and flowed. It reached one of its high peaks of irritability to the nation's broadcasters shortly after Newton N. Minow became Chairman of the Commission in 1961. Mr. Minow provoked the broadcasters in his first appearance at their annual NAB convention with, among other castigations, his "vast wasteland" reference. He continued throughout his three-year term of office to admonish them to show improvement in their programming. An already overburdened Commission, made aware of possibly questionable practices in broadcasting by its new chairman, came to believe that it was obliged to oversee programming and advertising.

Regulation and Programming

In later years active efforts to establish Federal guidelines for programming were made by Commissioners Kenneth Cox and Nicholas Johnson. By the early 1970s the Commission partly followed Johnson's lead in exploring what minimum percentages of program schedules might be devoted to news and public affairs content. The FCC made public in 1971 tentative standards to determine whether stations were providing "substantial" service to their communities; stations in the top 50 markets would be required to provide at least 15% of their airtime to local programs and 15% to news and public affairs, while stations in smaller markets would have to meet minimum standards of 10% local programming, 5% to 8% for news, and 3% for public affairs.[86] Although the proposed rule-making was not implemented, Commissioner Johnson concluded his FCC term in 1973 by publishing his own recommended standards for program content and advertising.[87] Chairman Dean Burch continued to support through 1973 some percentage standards of "substandard service" in program categories.[87a]

Indicative of the complexities of rendering qualitative judgments about broadcast service was the FCC's effort in 1970 to support an existing station's license against competing applications at renewal time if that station provided "substantial service to the public." But the U.S. Court of Appeals for the District of Columbia reversed that policy statement in a unanimous decision, noting that a licensee should be expected at least to serve his public in a substantial way and so should receive no preferred consideration; they further asserted that a licensee who was challenged at time of renewal must instead prove that his past programming was "superior" as one of several attributes of his performance. The court's clearest comment on what constituted "superior" performance referred to the absence of "excessive and loud advertising," and it less clearly pointed to "quality programs," "creative and venturesome programming" and "other forms of public service." [88] The court suggested that another criterion might be the extent to which the licensee had reinvested proportions of his profit back into the service of the station's public. Although these efforts suggest concrete ways to introduce more qualitative evaluations into renewal appraisals, ambiguities remain about feasible implementation by a governmental agency as well as about the more fundamental issue of such evaluations of local broadcast service by a national regulatory body.[89]

The real center of the continuing controversy on the programming issue might be focused on two words that have been insufficiently explained to the broadcasters. Those words are "balanced programming." The FCC has insisted that there should be an overall "balance" in the program offerings of stations but the station operators have no clear indication as to what is really expected of them in this regard.

The earliest advice on the matter of ''balance'' in programming came from the Federal Radio Commission and it was confusing enough:

> . . . the tastes, needs, and desires of all substantial groups among the listening public should be met, in some fair proportion, by a well-rounded program, in which entertainment, consisting of music of both classical and lighter grades, religion, education and instruction, important public events, discussion of public questions, weather, market reports, and news, and matters of interest to all members of the family find a place.[90]

The categories that early stations were expected to include in their overall program offerings were later changed by the FCC. They became seven in number: entertainment, news, religion, agriculture, education, discussion and talks. These later became a part of the report forms, which reflected appropriate balanced programming serving the community's needs and interests, as described by the Commission's 1960 programming statement: [91] opportunity for local self-expression, development of local talent, editorializing, service to minority groups, and programs in the categories of children, religion, education, agriculture, sports, entertainment, news, public-affairs, weather and market reports, and political broadcasts.

For license application and renewal purposes, every station's overall schedule is checked to see how much time is allocated to each program category. Presumably, a great deal of weight of the decision on the granting of licenses and renewals is based upon the distribution of these program types. One of the evils of appraising programs by categories is that stations tend to conform in order to remain in the good graces of the Commission. Emphasis is not placed on broadcaster motivation for creativity but on the threat of punishment. Consequently, there have been untold cases where the dullest kinds of programming have been offered in order to qualify for overall quantitative approval by the FCC. So-called proper percentages of each category have been broadcast but little or no attention has been given to production, or to whether some of the categories really were of interest to the public. In order to attempt to satisfy the presumed requirements of the Commission, broadcasters have engaged in other scheduling practices not known to be good programming. Church services have been broadcast at the same time that competitive stations have provided the same kind of offering. Educational and other community institutions with little knowledge of sophisticated techniques of broadcasting have been permitted to prepare and produce their own programs, which have often turned out to be dull and sometimes only remotely related to the public interest. Superficial discussions of relatively unimportant issues have been broadcast. Rhythms of sequences in programming patterns have been illogically interrupted in order to broadcast the various ''category'' types. In many cases, programs in categories other than entertainment and news have been broadcast during ''light'' listening or viewing periods; yet, in overall quantity of time, they have counted with the FCC as much as if they were in prime periods.[92]

Possibly, there would be more general assent on the part of the broadcasters on the matter of program "balance" if there could be some measure of agreement on qualitative, as opposed to quantitative, standards. And yet such a procedure would involve regulatory guidelines that could be far more difficult to apply equitably or even consistently than merely quantitative standards. And it would involve a Federal regulatory agency in making judgments about complex and fragile criteria of qualitative content. Yet the Commission ought somehow to support efforts by broadcasters to program "quality" in all categories of content.[93] The responsibility for determining that quality seems to lie with the professional and (hopefully) dedicated broadcaster, rather than with a national regulatory body of political appointees and career civil servants.

There seems to be little question that a few broadcasters, if relieved of any need for concern with balanced programming as a condition for securing and maintaining licenses, would tend to concentrate almost totally on those program types that draw the largest audiences and would eliminate as many of the service types of programs as possible. It would seem unquestioned, however, that in spite of this possibility, freedom in programming *must* rest with the licensee, free of government dictates. Those stations that would not meet certain standards possibly might be disciplined by their own professional associations of colleagues and, more importantly, even ignored by the listening and viewing public. Of course, they might also affect the quality-conscious "good" station by wooing away the large numbers of less thoughtful members of the audience. Even so, it might be better to have a relatively few ill-run broadcast properties or even unfairly disadvantaged "quality stations" than to entrust to seven men and their staffs in Washington, D.C., the decision to tell all the communities in the nation what they should see and hear. There should be one "censor"—the listener-viewer who can freely turn the dial and channel selector.

When a broadcaster makes a statement under oath he should adhere to it. There should be no sympathy for the applicant who deliberately distorts his programming proposal with grandiose schemes of programs merely to get a license, then proceeds to violate those promises as a licensee. Lies or half-truths in either the application or the renewal forms are inexcusable and should be punished. There is a great difference, however, in that kind of applicant and the one who is sincere in what he proposes but who must make changes after he begins operation in order to meet a competitive situation. Throughout all the years of radio and in the relatively short life of commercial television, it has been the rule, not the exception, that program adjustments must be made throughout any broadcast season. Even the networks, in their highly competitive struggle, must make changes, sometimes drastic, within the first 13 weeks of a new entry in a fall-winter schedule. These network changes in some cases necessitate an adjustment by their affiliates in order to meet local competitive situations.

While the Commission has a legal and proper right to review performance versus promise, it should understand that there is no broadcaster who can predict with accuracy at the beginning of a three-year period what all of his programming will be for the next 36 months. Nor is there any broadcaster so lacking in competitive strength that he will be able to adhere "to the letter" regarding all the program proposals in his application. He just cannot do so and stay in a "solid" program and sales position in his market. In the final analysis, each station must perform for the ultimate individual censor, the viewer or the listener with the dial who regularly exercises his rights of selection and point-of-reception "censorship."

As noted earlier in this book, the FCC has given the stations greater responsibility for the determination of program balance and program quality. Each station must now make continuing comprehensive surveys of its listening and viewing audience to determine the needs and interests of the people and then make at least some regular changes in the program offerings, where feasible, to conform to the findings of the surveys. Even though some broadcasters have opposed this ruling because of the extra effort and expense it involves, we believe that it is a fair request and consistent with the station's obligation to the people under the terms of its license.[94] Certainly, this is *not* censorship. After all, a station programs for its audience's needs and interests or else it loses them and goes out of business.

Regulation and Advertising

Another point of disagreement between the FCC and the broadcasters involves a value judgment concerning commercial and sustaining programs. Sponsorship of a program—whether it be public service or entertainment—need not necessarily reduce its values for the general public. In fact, because of the increased financial support available through sponsorship, many programs enjoy wider and more creative research, resources and greater production effort, including higher-priced and better-skilled craftsmen, technicians, artists, and actors. And the fact that a program or series is supported by commercial sponsorship has often attracted greater audiences, partly through program promotion by the advertiser. Nevertheless, if no distinctions were made between commercial and sustaining programs, then certain qualitative definitions would have to be developed. Should a program of commercial revival religion receive as much credit as a program carried free from an established church in the community? Should a paid commercial for a trade school be equated as equal to a courtesy announcement for a state university?

The right of any meritorious community group to be heard even though it does not have the revenue to buy time should always be protected and encouraged. But because commercial broadcasting depends upon advertising for its source of income, it must serve its advertisers by attracting the largest potential audiences. So those program types and formats having the greatest appeal to the most people are offered most regularly. The FCC, as administrator of a public trust, suggests that exceptions must be made to this formula in order to accommodate minority audiences. Those smaller audiences normally are of less interest to most advertisers. Hence, programs broadcast to these special audiences are usually non-income-producing for the station. Even so, the great ma-

jority of broadcasters would include programming of this nature in their schedules whether the FCC encouraged it or not because stations must win the
support of the total public in their communities.

Unfortunately, there are a few broadcasters who disagree and who would
maintain a 100 per cent commercial schedule if they could. Although as citizens in a democracy free to determine their own course, broadcasters must determine their own programming and advertising policies, no licensee should be
permitted to continue in the broadcast profession if he fails his obligations to
his constituency—the people in his service area. This implies some power of
sanction by his professional colleagues through trade associations or, as a last
resort, by government.[95]

But the government itself is by no means monolithic, as evidenced by
many appellate court reversals of FCC actions, and by Supreme Court reversals of decisions by the courts of appeal. In the specific matter of "overcommercialization," members of government through the decades have expressed
concern about the salience of advertising in broadcast schedules. Under the successive leadership of Chairmen Newton Minow and E. William Henry, the
FCC in January, 1964, adopted a report and order proposing to establish standards for commercial advertising based on the limits set by the broadcasters'
own NAB Code.[96] Its purpose was not only to set maximum limits on behalf of
the public, but also to provide clear guidelines to broadcasters harrassed for decades by vague and vacillating "implied norms" that eventually depended on
"promise vs. performance" criteria in the Commission's appraisals.[97] The
commissioners had voted 4 to 3 in favor of adopting the NAB standards for
commercial time; but the full Commission voted unanimously to terminate the
rulemaking proceedings on January 15, 1964, because of strong opposition
from Congress to the agency's entering into the specifics of commercials as
well as program content and timing. (The House of Representatives by a vote
of 317 to 43 passed H.R.8316, previously unanimously endorsed by the House
Interstate and Foreign Commerce Committee; the bill prohibited the FCC from
adopting rules regulating the length or frequency of advertising messages in
broadcasting.) Subsequently the Commission reviewed licensees' records on a
case-by-case basis in an effort to discern any "advertising excesses" without
again attempting to draw up general standards as guidelines. Although this flexibility creates enormous ambiguity, it also preserves the principle of self-determination by professional broadcasters—including those who freely subscribe to
the norms of the NAB Code.

And yet many broadcasters inaccurately equate Federal "laws" with industry "codes," claiming that both are coercive in limiting the individual
broadcaster's autonomy of decision about standards. While it is true that the
Federal regulatory agency has continued to look to the criteria embodied in the
Radio and Television Codes of the NAB as implicit guides for reasonably acceptable programming and advertising practice, the broadcasters themselves
were the men to devise the Code limitations and those same broadcasters continually reappraise and modify the Code criteria. Perhaps active participation by

NAB members and Code subscribers is the best assurance that those Codes will indeed reflect the individual broadcasters' own self-determination as well as the consensus judgment of the Association.[98]

In 1972 a national survey of advertising and media executives reflected pessimism about the effectiveness of various kinds of self-regulation to preclude Federal regulation of advertising.[99] Table XIII itemizes proposals supported by the various groups of executives to meet criticism of advertising without government regulation. More than 90 per cent of the 1,046 executives expected more governmental restrictions on advertising within three years, mostly because of ads that were unethical and in poor taste. Slightly less than

TABLE XIII

ADVERTISING AND MEDIA EXECUTIVES' SUPPORT FOR PROPOSALS AS ABLE TO BE IMPLEMENTED WITHOUT GOVERNMENT REGULATION

	All	Advertiser	Agency	Media	Other
(a) Advertisers should reduce clutter by paying premium prices for "editorial insulation" (e.g., substantially fewer commercials in half-hour tv program)	61.0%	53.7%	67.8%	61.4%	61.5%
(b) Media should reduce clutter by restricting the number of ads/commercials they will accept	57.9	57.8	67.1	50.3	55.2
(c) Companies should research new product's effects on (1) public welfare, (2) environment; discard ideas without real value to public before going into production	45.9	38.1	50.1	45.5	52.1
(d) Advertisers should be more direct in advertising—avoid appeal to emotions	45.5	47.6	46.6	44.8	40.6
(e) Council of Better Business Bureaus should set up a committee to draw up & publicize a "black list" of products, advertising campaigns deemed harmful or unnecessary in terms of the public good	34.8	34.7	29.5	35.2	42.7
(f) Advertisers/agencies should appoint public representatives to pass on "fairness" of ads/commercials	32.2	36.7	26.0	30.3	37.5
(g) Media should voluntarily ban ads/commercials directed at children	24.3	27.9	18.5	22.8	30.2
(h) Media should separate all advertising from editorial content, i.e., be restricted to one section in newspapers, magazines; be presented all together at certain hours on tv, radio	19.9	18.4	17.1	17.2	19.8
(i) Advertisers should divert up to 40% of ad budget from research to determine advertising's (1) acceptability to the public, (2) effectiveness, before running it	19.1	17.0	17.1	20.7	22.9

Source: *The Gallagher Report*, XX:23, June 5, 1972, Supplement, p. 3.

half the 300 media respondents (and one-third of the 300 advertiser executives) judged that public agitation about regulation could be solved within the industry. Almost two-thirds of the respondents agreed that enforcement within the advertising field lacked sanctions to support its negative decisions about ads. One out of five media executives responded that they favored more government regulation of advertising, while three-fourths disfavored it. One-third of the media people fully expected "rigid enforcement of [the] fairness doctrine to permit challenges to ad claims" and two out of five expected "regulations restricting amount of commercial time on radio, tv." Two-thirds of all the respondents—executives from media, agencies, advertisers, and other research and public relations firms—anticipated the passage of "legislation to facilitate class action suits against deceptive advertising." One-fifth of media respondents expected "complete ban [of] TV commercials directed at children." Contrasted with their *expectations,* were their *desires.* More media people *wanted* (23.3%) than *expected* (20.7%) a complete ban of TV commercials directed at children; the desires of non-media executives were far less (13.3% of advertisers, 10.7% of agency personnel, and 16.3% of other executives). Far fewer media executives wanted than actually expected rigid enforcement of the fairness doctrine for ad claim challenges (22.0% to 35.3%) or regulatory restrictions on radio-TV commercial time (26.7% to 40.7%). It seemed noteworthy that one in three of the media executives recommended that the Federal Communications Commission become "more activist" in regulating advertising, while one in five recommended continuation of present levels of overseeing; less than half of the media respondents (46.7%) recommended that the FCC be "less activist." Slightly more media executives (35.5%) recommended more activism by the Federal Trade Commission; and more than one-half (52.6%) recommended the Food and Drug Administration to regulate advertising more actively. These data suggest that key media leaders are dissatisfied enough with the quality and amount of advertising that they support greater governmental regulation although it would affect their source of billings and income.

In an effort to penalize broadcasters who allow commercial advertising to clutter their schedules, some advertising agencies have attempted to "treat favorably" those offending stations' competitors when making time purchases for their clients.[100] In 1970 Foote, Cone & Belding (which placed $15.5 million in spot TV ads in one year) drew up "penalty lists" and met with "offending stations"; but after a year the agency "concluded regretfully" that this procedure did not solve the problem of overcommercialization because the "abuses were so great but very general." In 1972 Dancer-Fitzgerald-Sample, the leading TV spot-billing agency in the U.S. at the time ($75 million spot billings and $55 million in network billings), attempted to give greater consideration to purchase of time with stations that adhered to NAB TV Code for commercial standards. Criteria for evaluating stations included number of commercials in one hour, number of program interruptions, amount of "commercial stringing," and degree of product protection. Other agencies taking less formal and less public but similar actions included J. Walter Thompson Co. ($65 million in spot TV), Young & Rubicam ($46 million in spot TV in 1971), and BBDO ($52 million in spot TV). These initiatives by the ad agencies suggest that broadcast managers should keep alert to creeping over-commercializing, for their own best financial interests as well as for the public's benefit. The Gallagher Report survey in 1972 reported that more than two-thirds of the 1,046 responding ad and media executives (including advertiser clients and agencies) supported reduction of "clutter" by paying premium prices for "insulation" of fewer commercials per program unit. And more than one-half recommended that media managers reduce "clutter" by restricting the number of ads and commercials that they will accept. Noteworthy is that two out of three respondents judged these steps would improve advertising's effectiveness!

THE MANAGER'S RELATIONSHIPS WITH FEDERAL, STATE AND LOCAL GOVERNMENT

To understand the true meaning of service "in the public interest, convenience and necessity," and to apply this understanding to successful broadcast management, there must be an accurate understanding of the Federal Communications Commission, both structurally and in relation to the problems with which it deals. While the broadcast manager (and the owner-licensee) may deal with other agencies and levels of government, it is his relations with the FCC that will be paramount. It is important, therefore, that he acquire an understanding of his proper role and that of the Commission. In order for the broadcaster to insist on his rights, he first must have a clear understanding of just what those rights are. He also must learn to accept his responsibilities to the Commission, just as the Commission needs to balance its rights with its responsibilities to the broadcaster. Once the broadcaster and the regulator discern their proper relation to each other, they can proceed to work together for the general good of the people.

Beyond the FCC are other governmental agencies such as the Federal Trade Commission, the Justice Department and its Antitrust Division, the Food and Drug Administration, the Internal Revenue Service, the White House Office of Telecommunications Policy, and the two houses of Congress.[101] A manager (and the owner-licensee) might serve not only his own station's best interests but also the needs of fellow broadcasters by keeping abreast of and even participating in governmental activities, especially through Washington attorneys and the National Association of Broadcasters. Relationships with Federal officials can be mutually beneficial; but they can also possibly hamper proper administration and regulation. Each manager and company must exercise integrity in communicating and collaborating with Federal aagency personnel. Krasnow and Longley note the complex web that relates the industry and the Federal Communications Commission:

On a day-to-day basis, Commissioners are forced to immerse themselves in the field they propose to regulate; however, the line between gaining a familiarity with an industry's problems and becoming biased thereby in favor of that industry is perilously thin . . . .

The opinions and demands of the broadcast industry are expressed through consultative groups (such as joint industry-government committees), interchange of personnel, publication of views in the trade press, liaison committees of the Federal Communications Bar Association, social contacts and visits to offices of the Commissioners, informal discussions at state broadcaster and trade association meetings, and the formal submission of pleadings and oral argument . . . .

In the intricate and dynamic relationship between the FCC and the industry, the Washington Communications lawyer plays a special role—not only in interpreting FCC policies for broadcast licensees but also in shaping the policy direction of the Commission. In a recent study of Washington lawyers, Joseph Goulden has noted that, while the lawyer's historic role has been to advise clients on how to comply with the law, the Washington lawyer's present role is to advise clients on how to make laws and to make the most of them.[102]

During the past half-decade lawyers have attempted precisely those roles on behalf of citizen groups and critics of broadcasting as well as on behalf of clients in radio and television. This is the play of pluralistic forces that constitutes a democratic form of government. Therefore, the broadcast manager has as much a duty as a right to seek to affect favorable legislation and regulation through proper relationships with members of government.

Literally closer to home are other governmental relationships important to the station manager as well as to station owners. There is a need to maintain regular and effective contacts with representatives of state and local governments.

The station manager must be rightly judged a key citizen of the community by his mayor, his state legislators, his governor, and his area congressmen. He should have a close working relationship with members of his state legislature; here, exchanging information is vitally important to broadcaster and legislators alike.

Broadcasters will win the respect of all government officials if from week to week and from month to month the manager takes time from his schedule to work with them. Even though the manager cannot be present regularly with the people's elected representatives while they are in session, he can maintain regular communication with them through correspondence and telephone.

No one in communications has a greater responsibility or more impact upon the community he serves than the radio or television broadcaster. Sometimes broadcasters fail to realize their own power to influence. Unless they recognize and exercise this power with discretion, they can hardly expect political figures or civic leaders or even the general public to respect them or to regard them as community leaders.

Above all, the station manager must be a *man* before he is a manager.

And he must be a civilized, dedicated man with wide-ranging interests and sensibilities before he can properly define his duties in the "public interest, convenience and necessity."

THE STATUS OF THE COMMUNICATIONS ACT

From time to time through recent years, responsible specialists in law, government, and broadcasting have proposed a new Communications Act to reflect 40 years of changes in all services on the electromagnetic spectrum.

Although the Act of 1934 has served surprisingly well through the myriad developments of sight and sound broadcasting since it was passed by Congress and signed into law by President Roosevelt, yet an entirely new law dealing with electronic communications seems essential. Beyond specific consideration of recent and pending developments in electronic-related forms of communications services, it should also undergird the First Amendment by clarifying applications of the freedoms of speech and press to these media. A new law should reconcile the correlative rights of broadcasters and audience alike—the senders and the receivers who together make electronic communications happen, as well as making media socially significant and a revenue-producing business venture. It will be a formidable task to outline legislatively the essential rights to this public resource for all parties who send and receive electromagnetic signals.

But how does the broadcaster know that a new Communications Act would eliminate his present concerns? Might it not create even more restrictive situations? How many broadcasters, if called upon as consultants in the preparation of a new Act, could advise objectively concerning the content of such legislation? In too many cases station managers and owners have not yet thoroughly studied the present Act.

Actually, there has been far too great a reliance by station managers upon their legal counsels for most of the important actions that are inherent in the Act. We are not arguing that stations dismiss their attorneys (we have already underscored the absolute necessity for their employment). But they should be used for purposes which management cannot achieve independently. Managers *can* study and become "authorities" on the Communications Act. This is part of their obligation as licensees and should not be delegated exclusively to attorneys.

Any lack of knowledge on the part of station executives concerning the license for their operations is most deplorable. Each broadcaster should know the Communications Act in detail, key rules and regulations, and even major court cases. The owners of stations should insist that all station executives make a complete study of key documents and refer to them frequently. A similarly thorough knowledge should be required of every student who proposes to find a career in broadcasting, and it should be a part of every training program within radio and television stations. Close study of this material is essential to understand the many responsibilities of each station licensee and each employee.

The early pioneers in station administration did not rely upon Washington attorneys for explanations of the various provisions of the law. Those early station operators set a pattern for integrity and for a knowledge of every facet of the broadcasting industry which many of the current generation of managers could well emulate. We heartily recommend that managers of today study carefully the roles of such men as the late Harold Hough, Powell Crosley, Jimmy Shouse, Edwin W. Craig, Earle C. Anthony and Walter Damm, and others now semi-retired or retired, such as Mark Ethridge, Arthur Church, and Frank Stanton, to name but a few who have played key roles in the establishment of favorable working relations between broadcasters and government. They had a fundamental understanding of the mutual concerns of government and broadcaster. They read and digested the Radio Act and then the Communications Act. They knew their freedoms and their restrictions. They were able to serve their audiences and their colleagues better by being free of the kinds of conflicts that exist today between so many broadcasters and their governmental regulators.

Down through the years, many broadcasters have continued to maintain working relationships with members of the FCC and its staff and have found themselves in a position to aid the Commission in its task of regulating broadcasting. These broadcasters have known most of the commissioners who have served since the beginning of the Roosevelt administration and have found that most of them were willing to cooperate on all matters affecting broadcasting so long as the practices were honorable in intent and addressed to the principles embodied in the Communications Act. Those broadcasters who neither have a firm understanding of the Act nor have made any efforts to become acquainted with the commissioners except when they have been in trouble, have caused barriers to be erected between members of the agency and radio and television administrators; and the many have often had to suffer for the blunders of the few. It is most unfortunate that the indiscretions of some broadcasters, combined with a few notably poor appointees to the Commission, have resulted in a bureaucratic curtain that hinders the Commission's cooperative and constructive relationship with broadcasters. Those broadcasters contributing to this impasse could do much to raise that curtain, if they were so inclined. Since there has been little evidence of such inclination, other solutions must be sought for the problem. These include reorganization of the FCC and strengthening of professional standards for radio and television through self-regulation by the National Association of Broadcasters and other professional organizations. (In recent years citizen groups have called prominent attention to the complementary role to be played by consumers of mdia, whose actions can affect broadcasters' and advertisers' policies as well as deliberations of the Federal Communications and Trade Commissions.[103]

Reorganization of the FCC

A Committee of the Federal Communications Bar Association, headed by communications lawyer Leonard H. Marks (former Director of the U. S. Information Agency), was appointed in June, 1962, to study the FCC and to make recommendations, if it seemed advisable, for future changes in FCC structure and function. In its report, the committee called attention to a study which James M. Landis had made for President-elect Kennedy in 1960.[104] In that study, it was found that the FCC could not keep up with all the demands for policy-making under its existing organization. The committee also referred to a study of FCC structure made by the management consulting firm of Booz, Allen and Hamilton. One of the recommendations of that study was that further delegation of functions in the FCC was necessary. The Bar Association Committee found that the FCC did not have sufficient time either to develop a national communications policy or to carry out effective long-range planning. The pressures for adjudicatory decisions hindered both the policy-making and rule-making functions of the Commission. The committee recommended that the FCC be replaced by a new regulatory structure consisting of one administrator, a court of communications and a five-man policy-making commission. Such a change, it was felt, would give proper weight to the various Commission functions and would insure their greater effectiveness.

At the time of his resignation from the FCC, former Chairman Newton Minow strongly endorsed a reorganization of the FCC. He recommended that the seven-man Commission be replaced by a single administrator and a court of administration. The administrator's function would be the determination of policy and the supervision of its implementation. The administrative court would conduct competitive hearings and other judicial matters. Mr. Minow said: "The administrator would have . . . to articulate effective, logical policies or the administrative court would be at a loss in deciding the comparative case. And the court would have long ago established a coherent line of comparative decisions, rather than an unpredictable crazy-quilt pattern." Mr. Minow believed that such reorganization would minimize problems of off-the-record contacts with commissioners. "Those who make policy and regulate must necessarily have frequent contact with the industry in order to be well informed," he said. "Under the present system, the possibility of improper influence or at least of charges of such influence is always present. The administrative court, made up of jurists having *only* judicial functions, would not be a similar breeding ground for the *ex parte* contact." There could always be the danger that a one-man administrator might become a czar and assume control of the broadcasting industry. Mr. Minow anticipated this possibility. He stated: "His authority is prescribed by law. . . . If he attempted to [go beyond the law], Congress and the courts would quickly check the transgressions." Mr. Minow held the belief that such appointees would tend to remain in their positions longer than the average term of employment on the seven-man FCC (four and a half years, although Mr. Minow himself resigned after only 28 months as chairman).[105]

Author-scholar Sydney Head summarizes major reforms recommended by Newton Minow and by three government studies of the FCC as well as by other critics and commentators: appoint a single administrator of the agency, separate the judicial and administrative functions, insulate the agency from the Executive and Legislative branches of Federal government, select commissioners of special competence instead of merely for political reasons, replace routine with realistic standards and procedures in awarding and renewing licenses, ensure better representation of the public and its interest, and even sell to the highest bidders the right to use channels (which last proposal the present authors judge to be totally lacking in merit).[105a]

As of mid-1975 there had been no direct action to revise the Communications Act or to reorganize the FCC, although some reforms in regulatory procedures and guidelines had been introduced which reflected critics' recommendations about the Commission's procedures. For example, early in 1975 Marcus Cohn headed an American Bar Association committee that was formed to propose new policy on substantive matters in communications law; committee members included former commissioners Dean Burch, Kenneth Cox, and Lee Loevinger, and other lawyers with service on the FCC, the Office of Telecommunications Policy, and Washington law firms.[106]

One must respect the magnitude of the issue of government regulation, including the viewpoints of both broadcaster and regulator. The problem, however, is not impossible to solve, as it sometimes appears. It might take far less effort to find a satisfactory solution than it now takes to maintain what is at best an uneasy coexistence between the broadcaster and the regulator.

Is it not, perhaps, asking far too much of an already overburdened FCC to expect it to take the leadership in the framing and enforcement of qualitative standards? And is the regulatory climate conducive for the necessary subjective kinds of evaluations that need to be made in the areas of program and production quality? Aren't these the areas of the broadcaster's particular qualifications? Isn't he in a better position to know the wants and needs of the listeners and viewers in his particular community and to provide the sort of balance in programming that is tailored to meet those wants and needs?

INDUSTRY SELF-REGULATION

Many broadcasters have maintained consistently that industry self-regulation is preferable to government regulation in all areas except technical standards and the licensing function. These men have taken a point of view that most governmental actions would not be necessary once the industry removed all causes for those actions through a self-regulatory system. Such a development, they have argued, would be far more desirable than changes in either the Communications Act or the FCC's structure.

The majority of the owners and managers of radio and television properties are both capable and desirous of regulating themselves individually or in association with professional colleagues. The standards they would adopt and maintain would be in the interests of the listening and viewing public.

The real obstacle to a self-regulatory system has always been the deviant owner and/or manager. Having no real devotion to broadcasting as a profession, but rather interested only in his station as a source of income, he has shown little interest in even minimal standards. Although in a very small minority, he and his counterparts have successfully retarded the efforts of the majority to effect changes. Given a market of several stations, one operation that undercuts the rate card, accepts questionable advertising or approves sub-standard programming can force some other stations in that market to compete on the same terms. Before long, the general image of broadcasting in the area can be damaged.

It is true that other forms of business have their deviant operators, too, as do most of our social institutions. In most of those cases, however, the predominant weight of public opinion favors those who maintain high standards that are readily identifiable. In the case of broadcasting, relatively few people in the audience are able to recognize differences between marginal operators and those who do not really approve of loose operational procedures but feel forced to adopt them in order to stay in business. The public is, however, aware of those stations that consistently maintain the highest of standards. It may be time for those stations to inform the public of the reasons for their favorable images.

The nearest approximation to any sort of official "seal of approval" in radio and television is an NAB Code membership. The display of the code symbol, indicating station membership, unfortunately means little or nothing to the people in the audience. (The Association has attempted to make the symbol better known, and stations and networks have from time to time displayed it in prime time as well as at the ends of the broadcast day with a narrated explanation of the Code and the station's policies about program guidelines.) Station membership in the Code is fairly high, considering that the voluntary members must pay dues and abide by restrictions on kinds and times of programs and commercials. Slightly more than one-half of the nation's television stations and about one-third of the radio stations subscribe to the Code and pay membership fees.[107] Although much has been made of the fact that sizeable numbers of stations have shown no interest in an industry code, the fact that a large proportion of stations do subscribe indicates some desire for industry self-regulation. It might be assumed that most, if not all, of those stations are interested in industry self-regulation.[108]

The NAB was originated because of a need for industry representation before Congress. Thus, its first role was almost entirely that of a lobbying organization. As broadcasting has expanded, the range of functions of the NAB has grown. The scope of its services to members is shown in its organization structure. In addition to its Code Authority and a Department of Government Affairs, there are departments of Engineering, Legal, Public Relations, Research, Station Services, Broadcast Management and State Association Liaison.

Yet, in spite of a wide range of member services and an annual operating budget of several million dollars, it has not been an easy matter to keep harmony among the membership due to the wide divergence of interests in radio and television. Within the NAB membership are 500-watt daytime stations located in small towns, large 50,000-watt I-A clear-channel operations, independent FM stations and jointly operated AM and FM stations, group-owned television properties, satellite television stations without sufficient income to support local programming, and UHF facilities in VHF markets, plus four national radio networks and three national television networks. Issues that are vital to some kinds of operations mean little to other members. In recent years, however, there has been more cooperation among the numerous divergent groups—a tribute to the current NAB president, Vincent Wasilewski.

An added complication has been a general proliferation of industry trade associations. The manager may, if he chooses, belong to the National Association of FM Broadcasters, the Clear Channel Broadcasting Service, the Daytimer Broadcasting Association, the Association of Maximum Service Telecasters, the Association of Independent Television Stations, the Institute for Broadcast Financial Management, the National Association of Television Program Executives, the Radio Advertising Bureau, the Television Bureau of Advertising, the Television Information Office, the Radio and Television News Directors Association, the Broadcaster's Promotion Association, National Translator Association, All-Channel Television Society, CATV organizations, network affiliates groups, and his state broadcasters' association. There have been complaints about industry over-organization, with all the membership dues that have to be paid and the number of meetings to attend. Agitation occasionally arises to reorganize all or most of these organizations into a federation.

While serving as the first full-time Chairman of the NAB during 1964–1965, Willard Schroeder recommended organizational changes in the Association; and he cautioned that a more efficient operation would be possible only if stations were to become actively concerned:

> I submit you can have all this if you're interested enough to elect capable, intelligent Directors and then hold them responsible for delivering the goods. If you are indifferent and sit on your hands, you'll get just what you deserve— nothing. Expressions of opinion about NAB—good or bad—is constructive, providing it's well informed.[109]

The need to caution broadcasters about their indifferences is disturbing. At NAB national conventions, President Vincent Wasilewski has repeatedly stressed the critically important role of nation-wide support among the thousands of member stations. In the early 1970s, Mark Evans, chairing the NAB's committee on legislation for license renewal re-regulation, repeatedly warned that little progress would be achieved without the cooperation of managers from stations of all sizes in the country. Precious freedoms can be lost by a devotion to the status quo or through an unwillingness to engage in common efforts to advance the status of broadcasting. Whenever individual responsibility is not identified with leadership, chaos is pursued by collapse. This is true whether it involves the destiny of a nation, an institution, an industry or even individual endeavor. Broadcasters must recognize and combat the dangers of apathy, indifference, selfishness and complacency wherever they appear in the industry. This will be the only effective form of industry self-regulation and the only sure way to offset greater dangers which could lie ahead.

The manager must also realize that the powerful media of communication that he directs can perform against the best interests of the public. This can result whenever any station uses such devious procedures as bad taste in programming, slanted news or excessive advertising. Such practices can lead to more restrictions placed on the industry as a whole.

Certain elements of the public are sufficiently concerned about broadcasting and other media to take action that the broadcasters themselves should be taking. The chairman of the Association of National Advertisers has asked for a comprehensive study of television comparable to a study of government made by the Hoover Commission in the 1940s.

Representatives of 21 national organizations met in Washington late in 1966 to plan a "national congress on the rights and responsibilities of the public in commercial broadcasting." The organizations included groups from religion, education, business, labor and government. Since then there has been a proliferation of citizen groups and other public organizations critical of broadcast practices.[110]

R. Russell Porter, Associate Director of the School of Communication Arts at the University of Denver, believes that public dissatisfaction with broadcasting stems largely from too much reliance by broadcasters on a pursuit of numbers:

> Broadcasting, in this pursuit, has spread its sails to the winds of public taste and has drifted wherever those winds would seem to blow, and it is now reaping not the anger—but the unconscious distaste that inevitably arises in any person who has been over-wooed, over-fawned upon, over-complimented, over-seduced. The public, having been confronted so long and so often by its own image, is bored, annoyed, often shocked with that image—and its dissatisfaction is directed, not at itself, of course, but at its favorite mirror—radio and television.
> . . . In the struggle to discover public fancy, broadcasting may have kept its ear to the ground—but a man with his ear to the ground has a hard time scanning the distant horizon.[111]

Professor Porter urged broadcasters to conduct their own study of their media. He said:

> Broadcasting, while resisting current and continuing efforts toward regulation, must actively engage in thoughtful and scientific analysis of its structure, its processes, its capacities and its proper relationship to the social fabric and must substitute these understandings for those empirical judgments that up to now, and

understandably, have been its criteria for successful operation. . . . The demands
on these media and the expenditures involved in their use require that a higher
degree of sophistication replace our present hunches and imitative processes.

We agree that comprehensive research and analysis of this nature are
needed. Meanwhile, there is much that the individual station manager can do to
put his own house in order. One of the greatest needs of American broadcast
management is to get away from the operational aspects of radio and television
long enough and frequently enough to develop and practice a consistent philosophy of broadcasting. It becomes more and more apparent that such a philosophy is needed for the industry as a whole as well as for individual stations. For,
if the dangers of government control are to be minimized, there must be a well
defined set of principles in broadcasting, setting forth the various freedoms that
are sacred to the industry and also describing the responsibilities that accompany each of those freedoms. *If the industry is to call a halt to the trend toward
regulation of its programming, its business practices and its operational patterns, then it becomes vitally important that each station establish its own philosophy as well. The individual station should subscribe to the general philosophy of the industry, modifying it to that particular station's "personality" and
context.*
We have had a tendency to refer to "large" and "small" broadcasters
based on differences in market size, station power, capital investments, gross
sales, net profits or number of employees. But in one sense the only "small"
broadcasters are those who are either disinterested in or incapable of high standards of performance and who consequently need the sort of regulation that
they get.
The wisdom of Lord Beaverbrook, a giant in the field of journalism,
should be helpful to the broadcaster; on the occasion of his 85th birthday, he
said:

> I am not much impressed by all the talk about standards and codes. The
> code of a good journalist should be written on his heart. First, he must be true to
> himself. The man who is not true to himself is no journalist. He must show
> courage, independence and initiative. He must be no respecter of persons but able
> to deal with the highest and the lowest on the same basis, which is regard for the
> public interest and a determination to get at the facts.[112]

Most managers are in broadcasting presumably because they can derive a
greater sense of satisfaction than they could receive from other pursuits. They
could, with business acumen, make a living in those other lines of endeavor but
they could not find any greater opportunity to serve their communities. The
modern broadcaster knows that the character of his station as a community
force is the greatest asset he possesses. The more he does to make his station a
truly vital part of his community, the more he can rely on the people of his area
to defend the station against outside interference. He should not speak to the
community but rather as a part of it.

He knows, too, that he is in a dynamic industry, one that does not stand still for very long at a time. Movement and change, however, are not necessarily progress unless purposeful, and regular progress is necessary in order to maintain leadership.

NOTES

Chapter 9

1. Zechariah Chafee, Jr., *Government and Mass Communications,* V. I. (Chicago: Univ. of Chicago Press, 1947).

2. Cf. Sydney Head, *Broadcasting in America: A Survey of Television and Radio,* 2nd ed. (Boston: Houghton Mifflin, 1972), pp. 154–158; Erwin G. Krasnow and Lawrence C. Longley, *The Politics of Broadcast Regulation* (N.Y.: St. Martin's Press, 1973), pp. 9–16; Walter B. Emery, *Broadcasting and Government: Responsibilities and Regulations* (East Lansing, Mich.: Michigan State Univ. Press, 1961), pp. 10–26; Lawrence Lichty and Malachi Topping, *American Broadcasting: A Source Book on the History of Radio and Television* (N.Y.: Hastings House, 1975), pp. 527–643.

3. Through the decades there has been ambiguity about the correlative First Amendment rights of the broadcaster and of the audience or public. The Supreme Court's "Red Lion" decision in 1969 supported the public's right to limited access to media and thus seemed to abridge somewhat the editorial rights of the broadcasters whose facilities were to be made available to such claimants. In 1971 the U.S. Court of Appeals Judge J. Skelly Wright claimed that the broadcaster's freedom was circumscribed by the public's limited First Amendment right of access to radio and television. Yet his colleague of the same appellate court, Chief Judge David Bazelon, in November of 1972 modified his own previous stance by noting "no factual basis for continuing to distinguish the printed from the electronic press as the true news media." And in May 1973, when the Supreme Court of the United States decided 7–2 against demanding that broadcasters sell advertising time to whoever so requested, Wright's judgment was contradicted. For the first time Justices of the highest court in the land explicitly endorsed full protection of radio-TV freedoms under the Bill of Rights. Justice William O. Douglas' opinion was particularly outspoken: "My conclusion is that TV and radio stand in the same protected position under the First Amendment as do newspapers and magazines." Justice Potter Stewart concurred: "The First Amendment prohibits the government from imposing controls over the press. Private broadcasters are surely part of the press." Nevertheless, Chief Justice Warren Burger stated in his opinion that "a broadcast licensee has a large measure of journalistic opinion but not as large as that exercised by a newspaper."

For readily available excerpts of their opinions, see: "Broadcasters Win One at the High Court," *Broadcasting,* June 4, 1973, pp. 22–23, 80; "Editorials: the Conversions," *Broadcasting,* June 11, 1973, p. 58. Cf. Sydney Head, pp. 373, 378, 395, 427, 441–446; re First Amendment and broadcast media, see pp. 419–425. For discussion of these issues *passim,* cf. Donald M. Gillmore and Jerome A. Barron, *Mass Communication Law: Cases and Comment* (St. Paul: West Publishing Co., 1969), plus 1971 additional bound notes. *Red Lion Broadcasting Co., Inc.* v. *FCC,* 381 F. (2d) 908 (1967); and *U.S.* v. *Radio Television News Directors Association,* 395 V, 5, 367 (1969). See also 1974 decision by U.S. Supreme Court which did not distinguish between print and electronic journalism's rights: note 53 below.

4. Cf. Sydney Head, pp. 160–161, and 363–378.

5. In 1922 Hoover noted that "this is one of the few instances that I know of in this country where the public—all of the people interested—are unanimously for an extension of regulatory powers on the part of the Government" (quoted by Head, p. 159). In 1924 he repeated that "I think this is probably the only industry of the United States that is unanimously in favor of having itself regulated" (quoted by Krasnow and Longley, p. 10). There were some parallels in the broadcasters' efforts to gain governmental regulatory support against inroads by cable television in the 1970's. Cf. also Emery, *Broadcasting and Government,* pp. 16–20.

6. For descriptive backgrounds and appraisals of the commissioners see Walter B. Emery, *Broadcasting and Government: Responsibilities and Regulations,* rev. ed. (East Lansing, Mich.: Michigan State Univ. Press, 1971), "Appendix II: FCC Chronology and Leadership from 1934 to 1970", pp. 455–499. See also Lawrence W. Lichty, "Members of the Federal Radio Commission and Federal Communications Commission: 1927–1961," *Journal of Broadcasting,* VI:1 (Winter, 1961–62), pp. 23–24; and "The Impact of FRC and FCC Commissioners' Backgrounds on the Regulation of Broadcasting," *Journal of Broadcasting,* VI:2 (Spring, 1962), pp. 97–110. See also Les Brown, *Televi$ion: The Business Behind the Box* (N.Y.: Harcourt Brace Jovanovich, 1971), pp. 254–262. Cf. detailed interviews and analysis of each commissioner in 1972, in *Television/Radio Age,* April 3, 1972, pp. 48–67.

7. See Erwin G. Krasnow and Lawrence D. Longley, *The Politics of Broadcast Regulation,* (N.Y.: St. Martin's Press, 1973), pp. 23–31.

8. Federal Communications Commission, *38th Annual Report/Fiscal Year 1972* (Washington, D.C.: U.S. Government Printing Office, 1972), p. 27.

9. See FCC, *36th Annual Report/Fiscal Year 1970* and *37th Annual Report/Fiscal Year 1971* (Wash., D.C.: U.S. Gov't. Printing Office, 1970, 1971). In an address at the annual NAB convention in March of 1966, the then Chairman of the FCC, E. William Henry, summarized the accomplishments of the Commission in the preceding year. In addition to the usual weekly actions on license applications, renewals, modifications and transfers, Chairman Henry noted several major issues that were finalized. These included the assumption of regulatory powers over CATV, a proposal of new rules for over-the-air pay television, the outlawing of loud commercials, issuance of policy on overcommercialization, approval of new application forms for radio and television, a revision of the table of UHF allocations, limitations of AM-FM program duplication, action to prohibit double-billing practices and an investigation of the factors affecting network program cancellations.

10. Newton Minow. From text of speech delivered at annual convention of the NAB, Chicago; April, 1963.

11. See Krasnow and Longley, pp. 23–72, for a clear and convincing study of the anatomy of the regulatory process amid pluralistic influences. They outline key Congressional strategies for overseeing broadcast regulation (pp. 56–62): infrequent legislation by statutes and even by the fact of inaction on issues; power of appropriating funds for FCC budgets; investigations; advice and consent to the executive branch about FCC appointments; supervision of the FCC by the Senate Committee on Commerce and by the House Committee on Interstate and Foreign Commerce and their respective Subcommittees on Communications and on Communications and Power; and pressures exerted by individual Congressmen and their staff members. Depending on the issue under consideration, FCC commissioners on occasion have been answerable to Senate and House Government Operations Committees, the Science and Astronautics Committees, the Senate Judiciary Committee and its Subcommittee on Antitrust and Monopoly, the House Judiciary Committee and its Antitrust Subcommittee; the Senate Foreign Relations Committee, the Senate Select Committee on Small Business and its Subcommittee on Monopoly, and the Joint Economic Committee.

12. See Krasnow and Longley, *passim,* especially pp. 130–136.

13. *Ibid.,* p. 138.

14. *Ibid.,* p. 139.

15. This excerpt from the Hoover Task Force of 1949 and the following excerpt from Dean James M. Landis' 1960 Report on Regulatory Agencies to President-elect John F. Kennedy were cited by Nicholas Johnson, FCC commissioner, in his speech on May 13, 1967, to the Iowa Association of Broadcasters convention, Waterloo, Iowa. The speech was reprinted in John H. Pennybacker and Waldo W. Braden (eds.), *Broadcasting and the Public Interest* (N.Y.: Random House, 1969), pp. 23–41.

16. *Ibid.,* pp. 11–14, citing appellate courts, the Supreme Court, Congressional committees, and other governmental reports. Although broadcaster Gordon McLendon has publicly complained about the ambiguity of FCC rules and their applications, broadcast lawyer Marcus Cohn appraises favorably "the fact that the Commission has no specific and hard and fast rules. I happen

to think this is good. I was taught a long time ago that the entire administrative process depends upon a flexibility which is attuned to changing tides. Indeed, in one sense, the Commission ought to reflect the shifting standards, objectives and goals of society. If you ever get rules which are dogmatically specific, you will be assured of an unresponsive Commission." (Personal letter to James A. Brown, October 25, 1973, pp. 1–2.)

17. See Sydney Head, Chapter 21: "Regulation and the Public Interest: Facts and Fictions," *Broadcasting in America*, pp. 447–465.

18. *Communications Act of 1934*, §312(b).

19. See Title V of the Communications Act of 1934, §§501–509, particularly §503(b).

20. FCC, *38th Annual Report/Fiscal Year 1972*, pp. 172–173. See also John D. Abel, Charles Clift III, and Frederic A. Weiss, "Station License Revocations and Denials of Renewal, 1934–1969," *Journal of Broadcasting*, XIV:4 (Fall 1970), pp. 411–421.

21. FCC, *38th Annual Report/Fiscal Year 1972* (Wash., D.C.: U.S. Government Printing Office, 1971), pp. 73–76. In addition, the Commission conducted field investigations of 64 stations which were involved in major matters, such as censorship of political candidates, racial or religious discrimination in employment practices, payola, rigged contests, fraudulent business practices, deliberate distortion of news, filing of false ownership reports, unauthorized transfer of control of stations, false or misleading advertising, failure of licensees to maintain control over programming, and various allegations against two networks. Lesser matters were investigated through correspondence with other stations. Cf. FCC, *37th Annual Report/Fiscal Year 1971*, pp. 55–56.

22. Perhaps the most serious alleged violations were listed for the group-owned WIFE-AM/FM (Indianapolis, Ind.), KOIL-AM/FM (Omaha, Neb.), and KISN (Vancouver, Wash.): violation of the Fairness Doctrine; deliberate slanting or distortion of news by licensee; filing of incomplete or inaccurate political broadcast reports; evasion, misrepresentation, or lack of candor in responding to Commission inquiries; filing of fraudulent claims with an insurance company; failure to file a time brokerage contract; misleading announcements about awards of prizes in contests; concealment of revenue derived from "tradeout" agreements; attempts to coerce, harass, and intimidate former employees for the purpose of interfering with the Commission's processes.

Violations of laws other than the Communications Act are matter for investigation and appraisal by the Commission, to determine the licensee's (or applicant's) basic character qualifications to operate a station in the public interest. Such laws include monopoly, restraint of trade, unfair competition, Internal Revenue laws, false advertising and other deceptive practices, State and Federal laws relating to labor practices (unfair, discriminatory hiring and employment practices). Any violation of State or Federal law is subject to scrutiny by the FCC which, by Congressional act (§308[b] of the Communications Act) and by courts up to the Supreme Court of the United States, has a well-established positive duty to exercise such authority. Obviously the circumstances of the violation of law, the willfulness of the act, its repetition, its recency, and other factors are weighed on a case-by-case basis by the Commission. See "Interpreting the FCC Rules & Regulations: Non-Communications Act Violations by Applicants And/Or Licensees," *BM/E* [*Broadcast Management/Engineering*], May 1968, pp. 16–24.

23. Reported in *Broadcasting*, Nov. 8, 1971, p. 48.

24. See Abel, Clift, and Weiss, "Station Licensee Revocations and Denials of Renewal," *Journal of Broadcasting*, XIV:4 (Fall 1970), pp. 411–421; cf. Sydney W. Head, pp. 400–401.

25. Lawrence H. Rogers, in Yale Roe (ed.), *Television Station Management: the Business of Broadcasting* (N.Y.: Hastings House, 1964), p. 29. Similarly Joseph S. Johnson and Kenneth K. Jones, *Modern Radio Station Practices* (Belmont, Cal.: Wadsworth Publishing Co., 1972), p. 112, claim that "very few licenses ever have been revoked for bad programming, however, so the conscientious broadcaster has had little problem getting renewals. The aspect that worries the broadcasters is that the FCC requires numerous forms and filings to prove that they are worthy broadcasters."

At midnight, Thursday, June 5, 1973, WXUR-AM/FM, Media, Pennsylvania, ceased broadcasting; they were the first stations to be denied license renewals by the Commission because of violating the fairness doctrine. Fundamentalist preacher Dr. Carl McIntire and his attorneys had unsuccessfully fought the original FCC denial of renewal, but both the Commission and the U.S. Court of Appeals in Washington refused to reverse that action closing the seven-year-old stations. "Last Hopes Dashed by Court, McIntire Stations Go Silent," *Broadcasting,* July 9, 1973, p. 26.

26. See "FCC Eases Operator Rules for Small-station Radio Engineers," *Broadcasting,* June 5, 1972, p. 51; "Making Life a Bit Easier: Re-Regulation Gets Under Way, *Broadcasting,* Nov. 6, 1972, p. 19; "Interpreting the FCC Rules and Regulations: Broadcast Re-Regulation . . . ," *BM/E* [Broadcast Management/Engineering], March, 1973, pp. 25–26. Also Frederick W. Ford and Lee G. Lovett, "Interpreting the FCC Rules and Regulations; New Broadcast License Renewal Rules," *BM/E,* June, 1973, pp. 16, 18, 23–24. For details of such changes in 1974 and 1975, see the last part of the previous chapter on "Broadcast Engineering."

27. See below for details.

28. "FCC Plans to Rap with Broadcasters in Their Backyards," *Broadcasting,* May 7, 1973, p. 36.

29. This and following text quoted by Frederick W. Ford and Lee G. Lovett, "Interpreting the FCC Rules and Regulations: New Broadcast License Renewal Rules," *BM/E,* June, 1973, pp. 18, 23; for details and explanation see pp. 16–24. The commission adopted and released its rules in May 1973, which specified the text of the announcements and their frequency and daily time periods for broadcast by radio and television stations. Abolished was the former ruling that stations must publish newspaper notices of the impending renewal applications. (See note 58a below.)

30. Comment made by Robert Rawson, chief, Renewal and Transfer Division of the FCC's Broadcast Bureau, at NAB Seminar on Broadcast Regulation in Washington, D.C., November 7, 1969.

31. For brief treatment of key details of these forms and reports, see: Emery, pp. 257–277; Coddington, pp. 44–63; Sol Robinson, *Broadcast Station Operating Guide* (Blue Ridge Summit, Pa.: Tab Books, 1969), pp. 213–215; Edd Routt, *The Business of Radio Broadcasting* (Blue Ridge Summit, Pa.: Tab Books, 1972), pp. 385–386; and J. Leonard Reinsch and Elmo I. Ellis, *Radio Station Management,* 2nd ed. (N.Y.: Harper & Row, 1960), pp. 295–297. Because the license renewal process is critical to continued operation of a station, a concrete and graphic description of station procedures in preparing the renewal forms, partly dramatized by simulated personnel conversations, is provided by Routt, pp. 359–372; see also pp. 355–359 for similar treatment of considerations necessary in preparing an application for construction permit.

32. Analyses and commentaries about these issues can be found in several useful sources. Rather than repeated citations to them, a composite reference is here given: Sydney Head, *Broadcasting in America,* pp. 402–404, 413–414, 421–422, 429–446, and 463–565. Edd Routt, *The Business of Radio Broadcasting,* pp. 20–31, 36–39, 106–109, 274–282, 336–355, and 360–387. Walter B. Emery, *Broadcasting and Government,* pp. 53, 209, 290–306, 325–337, 366–367, 377–378, 450–452, and revised 2nd ed., pp. 91–102, 115–117, 211–212, and 271–277. Jay Hoffer, *Managing Today's Radio Station* (Blue Ridge Summit, Pa.: Tab Books, 1968), pp. 89–95, 121–125, and 154–157. Sol Robinson, *Broadcast Station Operating Guide,* pp. 63–71, 183–188. See also: Daniel W. Toohey, Richard D. Marks, and Arnold P. Lutzker, *Legal Problems in Broadcasting: Identification and Analysis of Selected Issues* (Lincoln, Neb.: Great Plains National Instructional Television Library, Univ. of Nebraska, 1974). Additional sources will be cited below in the text.

33. Program log analyses are reported in the form of a composite week of dates selected retroactively by the FCC for the years preceding license renewal. Stations filing for renewal in 1974, for example, were to draw up analyses based on their program and commercial log schedules for: Sunday, April 8, 1973; Monday, Dec. 11, 1972; Tuesday, March 27, 1973; Wednesday, Aug. 9, 1972; Thursday, May 31, 1973; Friday, Oct. 13, 1972; and Saturday, Jan. 6, 1973.

34. The NAB and FCC have published guidelines for broadcasters in conducting studies of their communities' needs and interests. In an effort to guide his interviewers conducting such a survey for a group of radio stations in Southern California, Robert M. Olsen (associate professor of marketing at California State College, Fullerton, Calif.) listed these interpretations of respondents' comments ("Open Mike," *Broadcasting,* Nov. 28, 1971, p. 13):

(1) A community problem, need, or interest is one which affects some or all of the segments of a license applicant's community.

(2) "Community" is a term having three levels of inclusiveness: (a) the immediate neighborhood in which a respondent lives, (b) the city or general locality in which a respondent resides, and (c) the entire area covered by the survey.

(3) A "problem" is an unfulfilled or unresolved need *as perceived by a respondent.* A "need" is an unsatisfied need as perceived by a respondent. An "interest" is a topic which stimulates a respondent to seek information and/or take action because of his involvement with the topic.

(4) A "problem" is a community problem for a respondent if he defines it to be a community problem. The respondent himself must be the arbiter of what is a community problem for him. The one exception is that a frivolous problem statement should not be regarded as a valid problem.

(5) A respondent need not have a personal stake in a problem, need, or interest. Once again, the respondent must be the judge of a topic's validity.

35. See note 3 above.

36. In 1970 the FCC ruled on "quasi-equal opportunities" during political campaigns, extending to political parties' supporters or spokesmen for a candidate the section §315 guidelines that a licensee must afford "equal opportunity" or comparable time to the opponents' supporters or spokesmen if they requested it. Thus, unlike the strict fairness or personal attack doctrines, *free* time need not be provided; instead, as in strict applications of section §315 to candidates themselves, stations need only provide comparable equality of access (same or similar time, rates, facilities) to spokesmen for both opponents; and the FCC allows the station to make judgments in good faith about which candidates and spokesmen concern the community's interests, thus avoiding the §315 strictures about equal opportunities for *all* candidates for the same public office. Of course, spokesmen's appearances in bona-fide newscasts, etc., are exempt from these quasi-equal opportunities provisions. Letter to *Nicholas Zapple,* 23 FCC 2d 707 (1970); *First Report,* Docket No. 19260, 24 RR 2d 1917 (1972). See NAB, *Political Broadcast Catechism,* 7th Edition, (Wash., D.C., NAB, 1972), pp. 35–36.

37. Helpful suggestions are provided in "Interpreting the FCC Rules & Regulations; Section 315 (Political Broadcast) Revisited," *BM/E,* September, 1967, pp. 18–24, and in the NAB's *Political Broadcast Catechism,* 7th Edition, (Wash., D.C., NAB, 1972). The Commission published a 100-question primer on Section 315 applications, titled "The Use of Facilities by Candidates for Public Office," (see 31 Fed Reg. 6660, 7 RR 2d 1901–1930).

38. Perhaps proportionate time relative to the previously measured "impact" of candidates could offer some guidelines. Cf. Branscomb, "Should Political Broadcasting Be Fair or Equal? A Reappraisal of Section 315," *George Washington Law Review,* XXX:63–65 (1961). For three differing views of this issue, see Pennybacker and Braden, pp. 129–147, including Nathan Karp's urging that divergent and "unpopular" positions and candidates precisely must be afforded widespread media exposure so that people have access to minority views, pp. 138–147. Thus the First Amendment freedom of speech might be seen to apply here, "guaranteeing that minority views . . . find their place in a free market place of ideas and communications," as Newton Minow noted, *Equal Time: the Private Broadcaster and the Public Interest,* ed. by Lawrence Laurent (N.Y.: Atheneum, 1964), p. 74.

39. See Sidney Kraus (ed.), *The Great Debates: Background, Perspective, Effects* (Bloomington, Ind.: Indiana Univ. Press, 1962) for texts of the broadcasts and a summary of 31 studies.

40. NAB, *Political Broadcast Catechism,* 7th Edition, 1972; p. 15.

41. It should not be forgotten that political broadcasting is big business for radio and television. A decade ago, the 1964 campaign established new highs for political expenditures in broadcasting, especially contrasted with the previous Kennedy-Nixon campaign when Section §315 had been suspended by Congress. In 1964 most of the total of $34,600,000 went to stations rather than to networks. Sustaining time on networks amounted to a total of only 4 hours and 28 minutes in 1964, compared to a total of 39 hours and 20 minutes in 1960 when the equal-time rule was suspended.

In the 1972 election, political candidates spent almost $60 million for radio and television on networks and stations; $52.6 was spent on announcements and $6.9 on program time. Candidates for offices of president and vice president spent in the primary and general elections a total of $14.3 million; candidates for U.S. Senator spent $6.4 million; for U.S. Representatives, $ 7.4 million; for state governors and lieutenant governors, $9.7 million; for all other state and local offices, $21.7 million. (F.C.C.: *39th Annual Report/Fiscal Year 1973* [Washington, D.C.: U.S. Government Printing Office, 1974], pp. 203–204.)

42. The Supreme Court decision in 1959 (*Farmer's Educational and Cooperative Union of America* v. *WDAY, Inc.*, 360 U.S. 252) ruled against previous State courts that State libel laws did not apply to broadcasters who were precluded by Federal law from censoring candidates' statements; nevertheless, legal counsel recommends protection from suits, by libel and slander insurance. Possibly the simple procedure of pointing out potential defamatory content to the candidate might prompt him to resolve the problem by personally modifying such portions of his prepared text.

43. Key sections of those Rules & Regulations are 3.119–120, 3.289–290, 3.654, and 3.657 (the latter for AM are duplicated for FM and TV).

For a readable and documented chronological account of the development of the fairness doctrine, see Sydney Head, pp. 439–444. For detailed citations of documents and for legal analysis, see Gillmore and Barron, pp. 671–710, plus their *1971 Supplement to Mass Communication Law* (softcover), pp. 178–249.

Successive Federal actions include: FCC, *Public Service Responsibility of Broadcast Licensees* (Washington, D.C., Gov't. Printing Office, 1946). *In re United Broadcasting Co. (WHKC)*, 10 FCC at 517–518 (1945). FCC, "Editorializing by Broadcast Licensees," 14 *Fed. Reg.* 3055 (1949). FCC, "Report and Statement of Policy re: Commission en banc Programming Inquiry," 25 *Fed. Reg.* 10416 (1964). FCC, "Letter to WCBS-TV," June 2, 1967; 67 FCC 641. *Banzhaf v. FCC*, 405 F. (2d) 1082–1103 (1968). *RTNDA v. FCC*, 400 F. (2d) 1002 (1968). *U.S. v. RTNDA*, 395 U.S. 367 (1969). *Red Lion Broadcasting Co., Inc. v. FCC*, 381 F. (2d) 908 (1967); 395 U.S. 367 (1969). *Business Executives' Move for Vietnam Peace v. FCC*, 450 F. (2d) 642 (C.A.D.C., 1971). *Friends of the Earth v. FCC*, 449 F. (2d) 1164 (C.A.D.C., 1971). The final judgment—reversing the D.C. appellate court and reconfirming the initial judgment by the FCC on the BEM claim to the right to purchase broadcast time to advertise a viewpoint on the controversy about the United States' involvement in the Vietnam War—came from the U.S. Supreme Court on May 29, 1973 (*Columbia Broadcasting System, Inc. v. Democratic National Committee*). Cf. note 3, above in this chapter.

44. Major examples include anti-cigarette announcements that were broadcast to counter cigarette commercials, as an application of the "fairness doctrine" principles; Congress eventually legislated against radio-TV advertising of cigarettes. Environmentalists sought under "fairness" provisions airtime to respond to commercials for oil products such as gasoline which contributed to pollution of the atmosphere. Similarly, businessmen opposed to the war in Vietnam tried to purchase air time to make counter-war announcements. Although the District of Columbia appellate court reversed the FCC and supported that last claim, the U.S. Supreme Court struck down the district court's ruling and reaffirmed the Commission's original decision by a 7–2 vote. (See note 3 of this chapter for chronology and excerpted opinions of the Justices.)

45. See the NAB analysis, "Political Broadcast Catechism," pp. 36–38. Cf. "Interpreting the FCC Rules & Regulations—'Fairness Doctrine: 1974' Part I," *BM/E*, October 1974; 'Interpreting the FCC Rules & Regulations—'Fairness Doctrine: 1974' Part II," *BM/E*, November 1974, pp. 20–21, 26–27, 61.

46. Speech before the FCBA in Washington, D.C., in June of 1971, when Mr. Jencks was president of CBS/Broadcast Group; he subsequently became CBS's major legal representative in Washington as vice president of the corporation. Excerpts quoted in "On the Unfairness of Fairness," *Broadcasting*, June 21, 1971, p. 88.

47. Judge David Bazelon, quoted in "Bazelon Says Fairness Is No Longer Fair," *Broadcasting*, Nov. 13, 1972, p. 32, from his dissenting opinion issued in November 1972, regarding a September 25 appellate court decision denying license renewal to WXUR-AM/FM, Media, Pa., partly because of fairness violations.

48. See note 3 of this chapter.

49. *In the matter of The Mayflower Broadcasting Corporation* and *The Yankee Network, Inc. (WAAB),* 8 FCC 333, 338 (1941).

50. *In the Matter of Editorializing by Broadcast Licensees,* Docket No. 8516; 13 FCC 1246; 14 Fed. Reg. 3055; 1 RR Section 91:21 (1941).

51. 2 RR 2d 1901; 29 Fed. Reg. 10416 (July 1, 1964). The U.S. Circuit Court of Appeals in the District of Columbia upheld the constitutionality of the fairness doctrine and these FCC interpretative rulings on June 13, 1967 (*Red Lion Broadcasting Co., Inc. et al., v. Federal Communications Commission and United States of America,* 381 F (2d) 908; 10 RR 2d 2001).

52. See 10 RR 2d 1911; 32 Fed. Reg. 11531. The FCC Rules resulting were Section 73.123 (AM), 73,300 (FM), 73.598 (Non-commercial Educational FM); and 73.679 (TV).

52a. Although CBS, NBC and the Radio Television News Directors' Association's (RTNDA) appeal to the Seventh Circuit Court of Appeals was supported on September 10, 1968, on the grounds of vagueness, unduly burdening licensees, and involving possible censorship and violations of the First Amendment, that Appellate decision was reversed and the validity of those rules was upheld unanimously by the U.S. Supreme Court, *United States v. Radio Television News Directors Assoc., et al.,* coupled with *Red Lion Broadcasting v. FCC,* 395 U.S. 367 (1969). For brief commentary and excerpts of major text from the Supreme Court's decision, see Emery, pp. 332–333, 518–529.

53. Broadcast media fall under libel (or written defamation) rather than slander (spoken defamation) because of broadcasting's wide dissemination and potential extent of injury. Libel refers to a false and malicious statement that subjects an individual to public hatred, contempt, or ridicule. But communications media have had the privilege of commenting and criticizing on matters pertaining to public controversy and general public interest. This "fair comment" privilege obtains as long as no actual malice is demonstrated, and its protection extends to matters of opinion but not to misrepresentations of fact; matter must be of public concern, not a merely private activity of a non-public person.

Court cases since 1964 have extended media protections further. "Actual malice" demands proof of knowledge that a statement was false or was made with reckless disregard of whether it was false or not, or even (Supreme Court, 1968) evidence supporting the conclusion that the party charged had serious doubts about the truth of his statement.

The Supreme Court has further expanded media's protection against defamation liability by including the "fair comment" constitutional protection not only to high public officials, but also to government employees of substantial responsibility, to public figures, and (in June of 1971, *Rosenbloom v. Metromedia*) even to coverage of "matters of public or general concern" regardless of whether the persons involved are famous or anonymous.

The NAB's legal department concluded in a memorandum to its member stations, February 1972, that: "It now appears that the broadcast licensee who presents program matter of a highly controversial or critical nature need not seriously consider the success of any libel action brought against him, provided there is no showing that the program matter contains a calculated falsehood or that in preparing the program the licensee exhibited a reckless disregard for the falsity of the material contained in the program. Moreover, it appears that any effort to circumvent the protection now afforded in the libel area by making use of State statutes which permit an action for invasion of privacy will also meet with constitutional obstacles. In 1967 the Supreme Court offered the media a qualified immunity from suit under invasion of privacy statutes where the media coverage involves a matter of public interest and no actual malice is shown on the part of the licensee (*Time, Inc. v. Hill*)."

Early in 1975 the U.S. Supreme Court, in an 8-to-1 decision, supported the appeal of Cox Broadcasting Corp. in an invasion-of-privacy suit. The Justices ruled that an individual's right to privacy must give way when the press—significantly including electronic as well as print news media—made public accurate information based on public court records. Justice Byron R. White noted that "great responsibility is accordingly placed upon the news media to report fully and accurately the proceedings of government, and official records and documents open to the public are the basic data of governmental operations." His conclusion was reasoned "in terms of the First and

14th Amendments and in light of the public interest in a vigorous press.'' Thus the highest court in the land passed judgment that reflected no distinction between newspaper and broadcast journalism. See "Supreme Court in WSB-TV Case Treats Print and Broadcast Press as One,'' *Broadcasting,* March 10, 1975, p. 44.

For a lucid and well-documented chronology of significant decisions and emergence of legal policy, see Milan D. Meeske, "Broadcasting and the Law of Defamation,'' *Journal of Broadcasting* XV:3 (Summer 1971), pp. 331–346.

54. About 10 per cent of all editorializing stations offered editorials daily (16.9% AM, 14.6% FM, and 26.2% TV), and even fewer editorialized weekly (15% AM, 13.9% FM, and 20% TV). "Extent of Broadcast Editorializing,'' *Broadcasting Yearbook 1974* (Washington, D.C.: Broadcasting Publications, Inc., 1974), p. 37.

55. Data here and in following paragraphs were reported in: "NAB Research Report/ Number 2, "Broadcasters and Editorializing: A Study of Management Attitudes and Station Practices,'' (Washington, D.C.: N.A.B., November 1967), p. 6; also, "Radio and Television Editorializing: Management Attitudes, Station Practices, and Public Reactions,'' (Washington, D.C.: N.A.B., 1967), p. 7. A total of 1,444 broadcast executives responded to the two-part survey; 1,276 radio stations (of which 400 were combined AM-FM operations) and 247 television stations were represented. (The NAB had not replicated the study by mid-1975.)

55a. Dr. Stanton was quoted by Mal Oettinger, "Broadcast Editorials: the Practitioners See Possible Overturning of the Fairness Doctrine,'' *Television/Radio Age,* July 22, 1974, pp. 24–25, 74.

56. Three-quarters (77%) of the executives responding to the NAB survey in the late 1960's judged editorials to be expressions of the *station's* view on public issues, whereas almost one-quarter (22%) preferred to editorialize about a *range* of views whether the stations' view was included or not.

57. Two areas of potential difficulty were reported by the NAB's national study. Only about one-third of editorializing stations reported adverse reactions from advertisers because of an editorial: 16 per cent of the stations reported instances of cancellation of advertising or threats to do so, 8 per cent said that sponsors tried to influence or change the station's editorial policy, and 4 per cent said that advertisers had increased spending in competing media (*ibid.,* p. 12). And more than half (55%) of radio stations and almost one-third (30%) of TV stations had received not a single request for rebuttal time to an editorial, in the year preceding the survey date; rebuttal requests were received on three or more separate occasions during the year by 42 per cent of the TV stations and only 19 per cent of the radio stations. (This suggests that people might not be listening/viewing editorials so much or so closely as to draw large response, or that the editorials are not that conducive to strong reactions. It certainly implies that editorializing does not necessarily bring in its wake endless demands for airtime to respond to expressed positions about controversial public matters.)

58. Stations whose recent editorials discussed community conditions, in nine out of ten instances discussed proposals for change; and three-quarters of the stations advocated those proposed changes. Three-quarters of station editorials concerning individuals or groups in the community were critical of them, one-quarter were favorable editorial appraisals.

58a. Cited by Mal Oettinger, "Broadcast Editorials . . . ,'' *Television/Radio Age,* July 22, 1974, pp. 24–25, 74. Oettinger described how one station in 1974 frankly editorialized about internal industry problems, criticizing the FCC:

"Herbert Hobler, licensee and spokesman for WHWH Princeton and WPST Trenton, both N.J., built an editorial around the announcement that the FCC requires of a station when its license is up for renewal, inviting public comments or criticism. Hobler said that the philosophy of the FCC in demanding such an announcement 'is an unconscionable incursion upon [broadcasters'] rights, which for every other media and industry in our free society, are inalienable rights.' Broadcasters have always welcomed the public's opinions, he said. 'Discriminatory and potentially troublesome public announcements beyond our control are unnecessary. . . . Certainly, there are no newspapers in the country that would buckle to any Federal edict forcing them to run a front page ad asking their readers to tell them how to run their business.' Hobler followed FCC right-of-reply regulations by sending copies to Chairman Richard Wiley and colleagues, but none availed himself of the 'opportunity to present contrasting views on a controversial issue of public importance'.''

59. NAB, "Radio and Television Editorializing: Management Attitudes, Station Practices, and Public Reactions," (Washington, D.C.: NAB, 1967), p. 20; italics in the original.

60. The extent of this kind of content, and the government's awareness and concern, was reflected in the range of Federal activities and obscenity-related topics that were discussed at the annual NAB convention in Washington in 1973. The FCC in that year fined WGLD(FM), Oak Park, Illinois, $1,000 for alleged violations of the obscenity clause in the Communications Act (and §1464 of the U.S. Criminal Code) for radio "sex-talk" shows. The Commission subsequently opened a general inquiry into broadcast of obscenity, indecency, and adult (so-called "X-rated") movies. Renewal legislation proceedings with Congressional committees in preceding weeks prompted repeated questions of witnesses about sex and obscenity in broadcasts. And three major speakers at the NAB convention commented on the matter: NAB President Vincent Wasilewski, Sen. Howard Baker, and FCC Chairman Dean Burch. Finally, the NAB TV and Radio Code Boards met to consider possible actions. Cf. "Sex Talk, News, & Renewals in NAB Spotlight," *Weekly Television Digest with Consumer Electronics*, March 26, 1973, pp. 1–2.

By 1974 the Congress demanded that the Commission take more specific action about the perennial issues of sex, crime, and violence in broadcast programming. Early in 1975 Chairman Richard E. Wiley reported to the State and House Communications Subcommittees and to the chairmen of the Senate and House Commerce Committees what steps had been taken in preceding months: discussions with heads of the television networks which resulted in a self-declared "family viewing" hour in the first hour of network evening prime-time; actions by the NAB television code review board to expand that "family hour" forward one hour into local station time, as well as program "viewer advisories" about content that might disturb members of the audience, especially younger people; and an effort by the FCC to define what it construed as "indecent" under the law, in a case involving Pacifica's WBAI(FM), New York—language in "terms patently offensive as measured by contemporary community standards for broadcast media, sexual or excretory activities and organs, at times of the day when there is a reasonable risk that children may be in the audience," adding that when young people are likely to be present, the factor of "redeeming social value" became irrelevant. See "FCC Puts a Chip On Its Shoulder in Declaratory Ruling on Indecency," *Broadcasting*, February 17, 1975, p. 6; "Wiley Plan to Clean Up Television Goes to Hill," *Broadcasting*, February 24, 1975, pp. 25–26.

61. Although there has been little court delineation of what constitutes "obscene, indecent, or profane language by means of radio communication" (18 U.S.C. 1464) because of the wide variance of community standards and criteria for decency, there have been efforts to make *ad hoc* determinations from the time of the Radio Act: *Duncan v. United States*, 48 F (2d) 128 (1931); WREC Broadcasting Service, 10 RR 1323 (1955); WDKD, Kingstree, South Carolina, 23 RR 483 (1962), and *E.G.Robinson, Jr. t/a Palmetto Broadcasting Company (WDKD) v. Federal Communications Commission*, 334 F (2d) 534, in which Judge Wilbur Miller of the D.C. Court of Appeals noted that "I do not think that denying renewal of a license because of the station's broadcast of obscene, indecent or profane language—a serious criminal offense—can properly be called program censorship. But if it can be so denominated, then I think censorship to that extent is not only permissable but required in the public interest. Freedom of speech does not legalize using the public airways to peddle filth." WDKD's license was refused renewal by the FCC for approximating such program content and for willful misrepresentation to the Commission; the appeals court avoided the censorship issues by affirming the FCC's decision on grounds of misrepresenting facts instead of for programming excesses; a petition for writ of certiorari to the Supreme Court was denied in 1964. *In Re Pacifica Foundation* 36 FCC 147, 1 RR (2d) 747 (1964) involved alleged indecency of program content, but the FCC judged the full circumstances of the broadcast and allowed the license to be renewed. A $100 fine was levied against WUHY-FM, educational noncommercial station in Philadelphia, for vulgar vocabulary, 18 RR (2d) 860 (1970).

62. "Coast-to-Coast Flap Over Drug Lyrics: One Firing, Innumerable Protests Arise in Wake of FCC's Notice Cautioning Broadcasters on Songs," *Broadcasting*, March 22, 1971, pp. 73–75. "Another Scare Thrown into Underground Radio: FCC's Hard View of Free-form Radio in KFMG Decision Unsettles Some Progressive Rockers," *Broadcasting*, August 23, 1971, pp. 42–43.

62a. "Wholesomeness to Be the Rule at 7–9 P.M.," *Broadcasting,* Feb. 10, 1975, p. 31; "Kids Brush TV Sex-Violence Alert," *Variety,* Feb. 19, 1975, pp. 1, 62; "FCC Wants Power to Move Vs. TV Smut," *Variety,* Feb. 26, 1975, pp. 37, 47; "Web Licensing Bill Eyed by Macdonald," *Variety,* Mar. 26, 1975, pp. 39, 60; and "Macdonald Slaps Family Viewing As P. R. Ploy, Suggests New Ideas," *Variety,* May 7, 1975, pp. 325, 334.

63. Routt provides sample affidavits for announcers to sign as station employees, testifying to their relations to other business enterprises and persons, and to be notarized: *The Business of Radio Broadcasting* (Blue Ridge Summit, Pa.: Tab Books, 1972), pp. 376–377.

64. For a chronological analysis of regulatory actions since the "quiz scandals" and "payola" revelations of the late 1950's and early 1960's, see Emery, pp. 291–295. The FCC adopted specific regulations on May 1, 1963 (22 RR 1575, 28 Fed. Reg. 4707) to implement Section §317 as revised and the newly added Section §508 of the Communications Act of 1934. Those FCC regulations are numbered 73.119, 73.289, 73.654, and 73.789. Excellent examples of proper and improper relation of station and suppliers are in Robinson, *Broadcast Station Operating Guide* (Blue Ridge Summit, Pa.: Tab Books, 1969), pp. 48–55.

65. Samples are provided by Routt, pp. 378–379, and by Jay Hoffer, *Managing Today's Radio Station* (Blue Ridge Summit, Pa.: Tab Books, 1969), pp. 93–95. See comments about "double billing" in Chapter 6 on "Broadcast Sales."

66. See Leon C. Smith, "Local Station Liability for Deceptive Advertising," *Journal of Broadcasting,* XV:1 (Winter 1970–71), pp. 107–112.

67. 18 U.S.C. 1304 prohibited broadcast of lotteries or information related thereto, subject to prosecution by the U.S. Department of Justice, and liable to penalties of up to $1,000 and/or up to one year imprisonment. Furthermore, the language of the statute specifically stated that "each day's broadcasting shall constitute a separate offense." The FCC Rules and Regulations banning lottery broadcasts for all AM, FM, and TV licensees were 3.122, 3.292, and 3.656 respectively; Commission penalties ranged from a "cease and desist" order to license revocation. Further guidance can be sought from parallel instances in Post Office Department rulings and from FTC cases.

But on December 20, 1974, the Congress sent to President Ford new legislation permitting broadcast stations to carry advertising and information about lotteries in their own state and in adjacent states. See "Open Sesame on Lottery Broadcasts," *Broadcasting,* December 23, 1974, p. 8; and "Lottery Broadcasts Effectively Dead as Issue in Courts," *Broadcasting,* March 10, 1975, p. 21.

68. For helpful guidelines, see NAB, "Broadcasting and the Federal Lottery Laws," (Washington, D.C.: NAB, 1962, Fourth Revised ed.); also "interpreting the FCC Rules and Regulations: The Lottery Statute: Contests and Promotions," *BM/E,* November, 1969, pp. 17–18. See also NAB Legal Dept. Memorandum "Interpretation of the Federal Lottery Laws Applicable to Broadcasting, 18 U.S.C. 1304," April 29, 1968, and " 'Consideration' Element of Lotteries Prompts Subscriber Inquiries in L.A.," NAB, *Code News,* April, 1972, pp. 2, 4.

69. See Sidney Shemel and M. William Krasilovsky, *This Business of Music* (N.Y.: Billboard Publishing Co., 1964), and *More About This Business of Music* (N.Y.: Billboard Publishing Co., 1967).

70. For major points of copyright see Walter Emery, "Chapter 22: Copyright and Other Legal Restrictions on Broadcast Use of Program Materials," *Broadcasting and Government: Responsibilities and Regulations,* rev. ed. (East Lansing, Mich.: Michigan State Univ. Press, 1971), pp. 370–379. For details see Harry P. Warner, "Chapter III: The Subject Matter of Copyright Protection," *Radio and Television Law* (Albany, New York: Matthew Bender & Co., 1948), pp. 40–91; also pp. 315, 403–404.

71. See Paul W. Cherington, Leon V. Hirsch, and Robert Brandwein, *Television Station Ownership: A Case Study of Federal Agency Regulation* (N.Y.: Hastings House, 1971), an analysis published by a grant from WGN Continental Broadcasting, Chicago. Cf. another study underwritten by the NAB: George W. Litwin and William H. Wroth, *The Effects of Common Ownership on Media Content and Influence: A Research Evaluation of Media Ownership and Public Interest* (Washington: NAB, 1969). On the other hand, multiple-ownership effects have been appraised as not good by Harvey J. Levin, *Broadcast Regulation and Joint Ownership of Media* (N.Y.: New

York Univ. Press, 1960); but Peter O. Steiner was not convinced by Levin's data, in his review in *American Economic Review*, LI (June 1961), p. 472; Steiner concluded that, whether or not there was joint ownership of stations or great effort at diversification, the difference to the broadcast service in the U.S. would not be appreciably altered.

72. Sydney Head nicely summarized the dimensions of concentration of media control in *Broadcasting in America* (Boston: Houghton Mifflin Co., 1972), p. 460: "In 44 single-newspaper towns the paper also owns the only television station. Over half the commercial television stations in 1968 belonged to multiple owners. An FCC Commissioner pointed out in 1969 that in the 11 largest cities in the United States, every network-affiliated VHF station belonged to a multistation owner or newspaper-broadcasting combine. A special FCC study of stations in Oklahoma revealed that though 73 different firms owned stations in the state, the four top companies took in 88 per cent of the broadcast income. The extraordinary profitability of the national network O&O (owned and operated)-station groups has already been noted." Dr. Head also states the case pro and con media diversification on pp. 429–434.

73. Frederick S. Siebert, "Clearance, Rights and Legal Problems of Educational Radio and Television Stations," National Assoc. of Educational Broadcasters, 1955; quoted by Emery, pp. 377–378. Cf. Paul P. Ashley, *Say It Safely* (Seattle: Univ. of Washington Press, 1958), p. 84.

73a. See above in this chapter, including notes 3 and 42; cf. Sydney Head on those kinds of access, pp. 375, 444–446, and 525. Yet another form of "access" is involved in the FCC's setting aside a portion of the television broadcast day to provide access to the broadcast medium to other-than-network material, whether provided by syndicators, local stations, or others; this Commission action is referred to as the "prime-time access" rule.

74. ABA "Canon of Judicial Ethics"; quoted by Sydney Head, p. 516. Texas and Colorado are the only States that have not adopted Canon 35.

75. For example, in the celebrated Billie Sol Estes case, in which Mr. Estes was convicted by a Texas court of embezzlement and other crimes, the conviction was negated by the Supreme Court because television during some of the trial violated the defendant's rights of due process (*Estes v. State of Texas*, 381 U.S. 532 [1965]); the TV equipment that originally distracted was later made physically inconspicuous (Head, p. 516). Similarly, in the case of Dr. Samuel J. Shepherd in Cleveland, Ohio, the Supreme Court reversed a murder conviction because of activity of newsmen and media during the trial in the courthouse. The American Bar Association's Reardon Report in 1968 sought to protect the judicial process in such contexts.

On the other hand, many courts have installed public address systems for the convenience of those participating as well as those in the courtroom as spectators. This was the case in the Federal District Court in Chicago in its old quarters and remains so in the Dirksen Court Building opened in 1966. In addition, recording equipment has long been a part of the normal courtroom scene there as a tool used by court stenographers. The new courthouse also contains a ceremonial courtroom with facilities for television equipment.

Because of the requests for media accreditation in the 1969 trial of Sirhan Sirhan (accused of the murder of Senator Robert F. Kennedy), a closed-circuit television system was installed in the Los Angeles County Courthouse. A single camera was concealed amid air conditioning equipment, and the picture and sound were fed to two other courtrooms in the building, converted for the use of the media.

In Ohio compact television cameras and videotape recorders were introduced in the 1970s to record pretrial deposition for later presentation to the jury and for review when desired by judge, attorneys or jurors.

For summary descriptions of major instances of broadcast media's intrusive effects on courtroom procedures and decorum, and for excellent history and analysis of the entire issue, see Donald M. Gillmor and Jerome A. Barron, *Mass Communications Law: Cases and Comment* (St. Paul: West Publishing Co. 1969), pp. 395–420.

76. *Broadcasting*, June 14, 1965, p. 50.

77. See *Estes v. State of Texas*, 381, U.S. 532 (1965); quoted by Gillmor and Barron, p. 410; cf. Herbert Brucker, "A Crack in Canon 35," *Saturday Review*, July 10, 1965, pp. 48–49.

78. National Assoc. of Broadcasters, *Highlights*, June 14, 1965, p. 2.

79. One need merely recall the tragic events in Dallas when Jack Ruby slew Harvey Lee Oswald, alleged assassin of President John F. Kennedy in November 1963; the scene included physical confusion and ambiguous policies affecting the media when police attempted to transfer Oswald to another police building.

80. However, revelations in Washington, D.C., in 1972 and 1973 demonstrated that many documents have been somewhat arbitrarily classified in order to prevent scrutiny of governmental activities that might not bear close study, for reasons other than domestic or national security. Thus the "classified" label can be used to circumvent the intent of the 1966 Freedom of Information Law.

81. Anon., "Open Meeting Statutes: The Press Fights for the Right to Know," *Harvard Law Review*, LXXV:1220 (1962). Copyright 1962 by The Harvard Law Review Association.

82. Joint Media Committee on News Coverage Problems, "Orderly Procedures for Mass Coverage of News Events," July 1, 1965. (Booklet)

83. For example, Lawrence H. Rogers II, chief executive of Taft Broadcasting Co. of Cincinnati, has noted: "The Commission is periodically concerned with both the economics and the content of broadcasting. In the former category, there is no direct legal authorization for this concern; and in the latter category it is specifically prohibited by law. Nevertheless, these are two of the favorite areas of activity by the FCC and the countless study groups, committees, and investigations that it conducts." (Chapter "The Business of Broadcasting" in Yale Roe (ed.), *Television Station Management* [N.Y.: Hastings House, 1964], p. 27.) Despite legitimate confusion arising from the vague guidelines of "public interest, convenience, and necessity," and the 1934 Act's section 326 prohibiting the FCC from censorship, that broadcaster seems to have discounted the confirmatory court decisions and other legal readings of the basic communications law. See note below.

84. For an efficient and authoritative survey, see Walter B. Emery, *Broadcasting and Government: Responsibilities and Regulations* (East Lansing, Mich.: Michigan State Univ. Press, 1971 ed.), pp. 46–50, 318–339. See also Sydney W. Head, *Broadcasting in America,* pp. 376–378, 420–425. Cf. Pennybacker and Braden, pp. 11–15; Krasnow and Longley, pp. 16–19, 137–139; Coddington, pp. 48–54 (citing FCC Form 301, Section IV-A, on p. 49); FCC's *Report and Statement of Policy Re: Commission en banc Programming Inquiry,* adopted July 27, 1960 (22 RR 1902 [1960]), which effectively superceded the "Blue Book" of 1946—*Public Service Responsibility of Broadcast Licensees.* For more recent application of the principle of FCC overview of programming, see Frederick W. Ford and Lee G. Lovett, "Interpreting the FCC Rules & Regulations: Children's Television Programming," *BM/E,* Jan. 1975, pp. 20–26.

85. See Robinson, pp. 34—48.

86. Christopher Lyndon, "F.C.C. Suggesting Guidelines for TV," *New York Times,* Feb. 22, 1971, p. 59.

87. According to Johnson, a station should schedule a minimum of 15% of its schedule with news and public affairs programs, the recommended level being 20% (127 stations studied met the minimum, of which 91 even met the recommended level); the standard for local programming was set at 10% minimum and 15% recommended (67 stations met that minimum level); as for commercialization, stations ought to have no more than 40 60-minute segments weekly which contain 12 minutes of commercials, while the recommended standard was half that or only 20 such segments a week (97 stations met the lower standard and 6 of those stations met the recommended level). The Commissioner's 264-page report analyzed 144 network-affiliated stations in the major 50 markets. "Johnson Bequeaths a Morning Line on Net Affiliates in Top-50 Markets," *Broadcasting,* July 9, 1973, pp. 25–26.

87a. Cf. address by Dean Burch to the International Radio and Television Society Newsmakers Luncheon, New York City, Sept. 14, 1973; also "The Stuff of Which 'Substantial Service' is Made," *Broadcasting,* Dec. 3, 1973, pp. 26–27.

88. *Citizens Communications Center v. F.C.C.,* 447 F (2d) 1201 (C.A.D.C. 1971).

89. On the other side of the coin, challenges to the program performance record of incumbent licensees have alleged major deficiencies. Thus other citizens have sought redress precisely through the rule-making and regulatory procedures of the Federal Communications Commission,

using the agency as a counter-lever to the entrenched commercial broadcast companies. The incidence of serious challenges or "strike applications" to licensees occasioned by the WLBT, Jackson, Mississippi, decision in 1966 and 1969, crested in the early 1970s, then seemed about to subside by 1973 after the WMAL decision, the Supreme Court's reversal of the U.S. District Court and support of the FCC in the BEA case, and the promulgation of the Commission's revised regulations for license renewal applications and exhibits of documentation (including ascertainment of community needs and problems, and programming service, as well as complaints by local groups criticizing the station's programming service). See *WHDH, Inc.* 16 FCC (2d) 1 (1969); 24 F.C.C. (2d) 383 (1970). Krasnow and Longley, "8: License Renewal Challenges: the Non-Independence of an Independent Regulatory Commission," *The Politics of Broadcast Regulation* (N.Y.: St. Martin's Press, 1973), pp. 112–126. "UCC Says FCC Fumbled Ball on License Renewal," *Broadcasting,* June 11, 1973, p. 26. "The Specialists in Intervention," *Broadcasting,* May 29, 1972, pp. 18–19. See Krasnow and Longley, "Citizens Groups," pp. 36–41. "Interpreting the FCC's Rules & Regulations: Broadcasters' Responsibility to Community Needs Reemphasized," *BM/E,* November 1968, pp. 16–18, 23. Leonard Zeidenberg, "Special Report: The Struggle Over Broadcast Access (II)," *Broadcasting,* Sept. 27, 1971, pp. 24–29. "Media: More Broadcasters Underscore Renewal-time Plight," *Broadcasting,* April 9, 1973, pp. 36–37. Martin Mayer, "The Challengers," Parts I, II, and III reprinted from *TV Guide,* Feb. 3, 10, 17, 1973. "Broadcasters Win One at the High Court," *Broadcasting,* June 4, 1973, pp. 22–23.

90. Federal Radio Commission. "Third Annual Report" (Washington: U.S. Government Printing Office, 1929).

91. *Report and Statement of Policy Re: Commission En Banc Programming Inquiry,* 20 RR 1902 (1960).

92. A technique of weighting programs according to their time of broadcast as related to available audience was proposed by Yale Roe, *The Television Dilemma,* (N.Y. Hastings House, 1962), pp. 65–67. But an analysis of all programming available in a major market according to weighted hours (based on audience availability as reflected in rate cards and in ratings reports by time periods) demonstrated that the net differences are minimal, with weighted and unweighted hours neutralizing each other in most categories; James A. Brown, "So You Can't Get Opera at 4 A.M," *Broadcasting,* Aug. 15, 1960, p. 60. A more recent analysis reemphasized the ambiguities and lack of substantive difference in these weightings: Paula Holt, unpub. research report, Univ. of Southern California, Dept. of Telecommunications, April, 1972.

93. Washington communications lawyer Marcus Cohn has advocated that the FCC reward those stations providing program service of high quality, by extending their license renewal periods from three to as many as six years. He suggested that perhaps 5 to 10 per cent of all stations would merit such extended renewal periods, thus rewarding them for excellence (by cutting down to half the paperwork and analysis needed for triennial renewal applications, and by citing them in this positive public way) and encouraging competing stations to "go and do likewise." He argued that if the Commission can make negative judgments about program service and assess fines ranging from $100 to $10,000, then it should be able as well to make major positive judgments and offer a scale awarding 4- 5- or 6-year renewal periods. Marcus Cohn, "Should the FCC Reward Stations That Do A Good Job?" *Saturday Review,* August 14, 1971, pp. 45–47.

94. Richard Stakes, executive vice president of WMAL-TV, Washington, D.C., estimated $400,000 as the cost to resist challenges in 1969; *Broadcasting,* March 26, 1973, p. 140. In New York between 1969 and 1973 the challenging Forum Communications law firm spent $300,000 and WPIX (TV)—with law firms retained in Washington and New York—about $1 million; Martin Mayer, "Can They Get a TV Channel Worth $50,000,000 for Just $400,000?" *TV Guide,* Feb. 10, 1973. Apart from challenges, the cost of preparing renewal applications can be enormous even for a radio station; the president of WMCA-AM in New York City assigns a fulltime person for three months to prepare the application, and pays a research company for 1,000 "man-in-the-street" interviews and for 350 interviews with community leaders. CBS Broadcast Group president John A. Schneider described a single license-renewal application for WCBS-TV, New York, filed in 1972, as weighing 13 pounds—a six-inch stack of documentation; it was completed in 7,920 man-hours by 19 executives, five secretaries and three temporary typists over three weeks who

assembled the material to send to the FCC, plus 204 hours of CBS lawyers' time and 228 hours of their secretaries'; "B'cast Regulation by the Pound," *Variety,* May 16, 1973.

95. Veteran broadcaster Robert H. Coddington acknowledges that "much of the federal regulation imposed on broadcasters has resulted from their own past abuses . . .": *Modern Radio Broadcasting* (Blue Ridge Summit, Pa., Tab Books, 1969), p. 60.

96. 1 RR 2d 1606.

97. See excellent summary of this history in "Interpreting the FCC Rules & Regulations: 'Overcommercialization' Revisited," *BM/E,* March 1967, pp. 18–25, 75. See also a detailed analysis of the mid-1960 actions by the FCC and Congress in Krasnow and Longley, "Chapter 7: Commercial Time Fiasco," *The Politics of Broadcast Regulations,* pp. 105–111. Cf. also Douglas A. Anello and Robert V. Cahill, "Legal Authority of the FCC to Place Limits on Broadcast Advertising Time," *Journal of Broadcasting,* VII:4 (Fall 1963), pp. 285–303.

98. See Bruce A. Linton, *Self-Regulation in Broadcasting* (Washington, D.C.: NAB, 1967), pp. 52–56.

99. "Ad Industry Opinion on Government Regulation of Advertising," "The Gallagher Report," June 5, 1972, p. 1; and Supplement, pp. 1–4.

100. "Biggest Buyer of Spot TV Says Violators of NAB Code Will Lose Out," *Broadcasting,* Aug. 28, 1972, pp. 16–17.

101. See Walter B. Emery, pp. 72–95.

102. Krasnow and Longley, pp. 32–33; reference is to Joseph C. Goulden, *The Superlawyers: The Small and Powerful World of the Great Washington Law Firms* (N.Y.: Weybright & Talley, 1972), p. 6. Less benign in appraising attorneys' impact on the system of American broadcasting that had "carelessly evolved" is Les Brown: "Confederate to the indolent FCC in keeping the original theory [of broadcasting] from realization was the specialist at law, the communications attorney. His first trick was to scare off the FCC from any attempt at considering the quality and effectiveness of a broadcaster's service to his public by charging government censorship. The lawyers have said over the years that the Commission is supposed to regulate, not evaluate, and any expression of dissatisfaction with the level of television programming by a commissioner was called an intrusion by the government into the content of the medium.

"Secondly, the attorneys succeeded in reducing to gibberish the key phrase in the Communications Act, 'the public interest, convenience, and necessity,' calling it too abstruse for the FCC to use as a criterion of performance and a station's right to a renewal of its license. The terms are not defined, they argued, and who is to say what the public interest is?" Les Brown, *Televi-$ion: The Business Behind the Box* (N.Y.: Harcourt Brace Jovanovich, 1971), p. 180.

103. See, for example, "Here, We Would Suggest, Is a Program for the FCC," *Consumers Reports,* February 1960, quoted by Harry J. Skornia and Jack William Kitson (eds.), *Problems and Controversies in Television and Radio* (Palo Alto, Calif.: Pacific Books, 1968), pp. 108–113. Cf. Nicholas Johnson, *How To Talk Back to Your Television Set* (N.Y.: Little, Brown, 1970), and also the many actions by the United Church of Christ's Office of Communication and the Citizen's Communications Center.

104. See brief summary by Lawrence H. Rogers II, "The Business of Broadcasting," in Yale Roe (ed.), *Television Station Management* (N.Y.: Hastings House, 1964), pp. 26–29. See also James M. Landis, *Report on Regulatory Agencies to the President-Elect,* committee print by the Subcommittee on Administrative Practice and Procedure of the Senate Committee on the Judiciary, 86th Congress, 2nd Session (Washington: U.S. Government Printing Office, 1960); cf. Krasnow & Longley, pp. 23–24 ff.; Sydney Head, pp. 449, 445; and Pennybacker & Braden, for Nicholas Johnson's "Reevaluating the Regulatory Role," pp. 23–42, esp. 34–36.

105. Letter to President John F. Kennedy, dated May 31, 1963, in Newton N. Minow, *Equal Time: The Private Broadcaster and the Public Interest,* ed. by Lawrence Laurent (N.Y.: Atheneum, 1964), pp. 279–289; cf. also pp. 258–259, and see Sydney Head, pp. 449, 454, 462–463.

105a. Sydney Head, pp. 462–463. Cf. Bernard Schwartz, *The Professor and the Commissions* (N.Y.: Alfred A. Knopf, 1959), cited by Head *passim,* pp. 447–463; see also Harry J. Skornia, *Television and Society: An Inquest and Agenda for Improvement* (N.Y.: McGraw-Hill, 1965).

106. "Closed Circuit," *Broadcasting*, February 3, 1975, p. 5.

107. By early 1975, a total of 414 of the 703 commercial TV stations (59%) subscribed to the NAB's Television Code, and 2,946 of the 7,005 commercial radio stations (42%) subscribed to the NAB's Radio Code. Those percentages represented a half-decade drop from 1970's figure of 65% for TV stations and a rise from 34% for radio stations. In addition to stations, Code members included three national television networks and four national radio networks. Code subscribers were not necessarily members of the Association; but almost half again as many stations were members of the NAB as were subscribers to the respective Codes.

Sources: FCC figures compiled January 31, 1975, cited in "Summary of Broadcasting," *Broadcasting*, March 10, 1975, p. 58. Code subscriber totals as of February 1, 1975, in "Subscriber Status," *Code News*, February 1975, p. 5. Comparative data from NAB letter of August 20, 1970, cited by Sydney Head, p. 469.

108. For a thorough analysis of the NAB's development of self-regulatory guidelines, see Bruce A. Linton, *Self-Regulation in Broadcasting* (Washington: N.A.B., 1967).

109. Willard Schroeder; from text of speech delivered at annual meeting of the Michigan Association of Broadcasters, September, 1964.

110. A partial list of citizen groups challenging station licenses includes: New Jersey Coalition for Fair Broadcasting; Black Citizens for Fair Media (New York); Paterson Coalition for Media Change (New Jersey); National Organization for Women (N.Y. City Chapter); Tri-City Coalition of Albany, Troy, and Schenectady; American Board of Missions to the Jews, Inc.; Mid-Hudson Valley Broadcasting Group; "Women for Socialized Medicine" (New York); Citizens Committee to Save WFMT (Chicago); Action for Children's Television; Black Efforts for Soul in Television; Colorado Committee on Mass Media and the Spanish Surnamed; Black Citizens for Fair Media (N.Y.); Center for Constitutional Rights (N.Y.); Action for Better Community Services (Rochester, N.Y.); Asian Americans for Fair Media (N.Y.); Boston Community Media Committee; Community Coalition for Media Change (Pittsburgh); Congress of African People (Philadelphia); Hartford Communications Committee; Urban League-National Media Action Team (N.Y.); Office of Communications of the United Church of Christ; First Delaware Valley Citizens Television (Philadelphia); Forum Communications (N.Y.); Chinese Media Committee (San Francisco); Friends of the Earth and Citizens for Clean Air (N.Y.).

Additionally, many legal firms and organizations serve as counsel and participants in the process of license challenging, including: Monroe County Legal Assistance Corp. (Rochester, N.Y.); Center for Law and Social Policy (Washington); Institute for Public Interest Representation (Georgetown Univ. Law Center); American Legal Defense and Educational Fund (San Francisco); Stern Community Law Firm (Washington); Communications Research Program, UCLA (L.A.); Welch & Morgan (Washington); Citizens Communications Center (Washington).

See: "The Specialists in Intervention," *Broadcasting*, May 29, 1972, pp. 18–19; "Citizen Challengers of Broadcast Practices Seek Nixon Audience," *Broadcasting*, Jan. 29, 1973, p. 30; Martin Mayer, "The Challengers" (Parts I, II, III), *TV Guide*, Feb. 3, 10, 17, 1973.

111. R. Russell Porter. From text of speech delivered to University of Denver Alumni Seminars in Los Angeles and San Francisco, January 27–28, 1962.

112. *Time*, June 5, 1964, p. 58.

Prospects
and Retrospects

What is past is prologue.
—National Archives Building, Washington, D.C.

THIS CONCLUDING CHAPTER of *Broadcast Management* first surveys the prospects for broadcasting's future, and then provides personal retrospects by the professor and by the professional broadcaster who were the authors of this volume.

A. PROSPECTS

SATELLITE COMMUNICATION

As a program, it was not outstanding. There were opening remarks by Jacques Marette, French minister of posts and telecommunications. Then Yves Montand and Michele Arnaud provided the entertainment. The show in its entirety lasted just eight minutes. Whatever was lacking in program and production quality was more than made up in technical achievement. This was the first instantaneous broadcast in history from the European continent to the viewers of the United States. It took place on July 11, 1962, and was made possible by Telstar, the first communications satellite capable of relaying intercontinental television signals.

Prior to Telstar, there had been the balloon satellite, Echo, which had been used to reflect radio signals that were beamed to it. Telstar, which had been placed in elliptical orbit deliberately, was cabable of reporting such space problems as radiation and micrometeorites from different altitudes. There were only from twelve to fifteen minutes each day when it came into line-of-sight vision between ground stations in Europe and Andover, Maine. An Associated Press dispatch described the technical feat of establishing contact with the satellite as being equivalent to hitting a basketball in Miami with a rifle fired in New York.

The significance of that first successful international telecast was almost entirely in its technological achievement. It was evidence of scientific progress already accomplished and of even more exciting developments to come. The event itself was one more example of the time-lag between technical advancement and the content of the communication message. Subsequent telecasts using satellite transmissions have exhibited technical brilliance; there has been a modest number of equivalent program achievements.

AT&T's Telstar and RCA's Relay, launched later in 1962, were low altitude systems that circled constantly, thus restricting their use to some twenty minutes each day. They were forerunners of the Early Bird, launched in April of 1965. This satellite was placed in orbit some 22,300 miles above the earth in synchronization with the earth's rotation, giving it a stationary relationship to ground stations, providing around-the-clock communication between Europe and the American continent.

Even though Early Bird, like its lower-altitude predecessors, was used mainly for telephonic messages, about 40 hours of television were transmitted during its first year of service. These included coverage of Pope Paul's visit to the United States, the splashdowns of Gemini VI and Gemini VII, a track meet in Russia and international versions of "Meet the Press" and "Town Meeting."

Lani Bird, a similiar high-altitude satellite to provide communication service between the United States, Hawaii and Japan, was launched in October, 1966. Troubles that developed after launching prevented Lani Bird from achieving a true synchronous orbit. Even so, the satellite could be used some eight hours each day, although the time changed from month to month. A second Pacific satellite, Lani Bird II, and a second Atlantic satellite, Early Bird II, were successfully launched early in 1967. The latter added Africa and South America to the existent links with Europe and Japan. Global interchange of live television via satellite brought the 1968 Olympics from Mexico City to more than 800 million people. Four years later, coverage of the athletic contests and the tragic unfolding of kidnapping and murder at the Munich Olympic Games was transmitted around the globe as the events took place. Unprecedented live television of astronauts walking the surface of the moon was relayed via satellites to the world's continents, in monochrome in 1969 and in color on subsequent lunar missions.

International sharing of entertainment, culture, and news and information became increasingly possible with the proliferation of relay transmitters in space. In 1967, satellites had carried a total of 225 hours of television communication for nations of the world; in 1968, 666 hours; by 1970 the load was 1,432 hours; and in 1971 TV transmission totaled 3,563 hours. The free world's television use of those active satellites was expected to more than double within five more years. By the end of 1972, 76 non-Communist nations (plus Yugoslavia) were served by 63 earth receiving and sending stations and by 13 communications satellites in the series launched by INTELSAT (International Telecommunications Satellite Corporation of 83 member nations). Meanwhile, the Soviet Union by then had launched 20 satellites, served by 35 earth stations, for relaying transmissions among its own bloc of nations.

Difficult questions of regulation and management have pursued the satellite communications program since its inception. When Telstar was launched in 1962, Congress enacted the Communications Satellite Act, creating the private stockholder-owned Communications Satellite Corporation (COMSAT), which manages and also owns 52 per cent of INTELSAT. Although the FCC was already submerged with work, the Satellite Act made the Commission responsible for regulating COMSAT. A major issue with far-reaching consequences involved licensing the various ground stations that receive signals from and transmit signals to the satellites. A decision had to be made favoring either the new Corporation or the various communications carriers. While wrestling with this problem, the FCC encountered an even greater question involving the use of satellites for domestic, in addition to international, service.

The ABC network filed a petition asking permission to control its own satellite for national network service to its affiliates, thus eliminating the conventional relays of AT&T. And the Ford Foundation submitted a plan for a domestic system to be operated by a non-profit corporation; service would be provided for the commercial networks and the profits would be used to support educational television.

Opposition to the Ford Foundation proposal formed quickly. COMSAT argued against authorizing such independent systems as proposed by ABC and the Ford Foundation. As the owner of the United States' part of INTELSAT, COMSAT claimed that it alone should be given the authority to own and operate any domestic system. AT&T and other common carriers wanted a multi-purpose system capable of handling various forms of communication in addition to television. The carriers asked for authorization to own such a system and AT&T submitted its own plan for an integrated operation. Finally, the commercial broadcast networks favored private ownership but questioned the power of the FCC to authorize the type of system proposed by the Ford Foundation.

There seemed to be two central issues. First, was it either legally or technically feasible to allow non-government entities to construct and operate domestic satellite systems? COMSAT said no; all others disagreed. The second issue was how to determine the entity that should be in charge of such a system. Should it be COMSAT, or one of the carriers, or one or more of the networks, or the Ford Foundation, or some as yet unidentified applicant? Both commercial and educational broadcasting in the United States hoped to benefit from any of the possible decisions (the savings in transmission costs alone for national networking would be considerable); but conventional common carriers could stand to lose considerable business and revenue. The evolution of Federal policy was reflected in subsequent disparate projects to harness satellite capability.

The United States' entry into domestic use of satellites came late in 1973 with RCA's leasing transmission time on Canada's Anik II to relay signals between the East and West coasts of the U.S. and between both those coasts and Alaska, using five earth stations. In November of 1974, ABC Radio began transmitting service to its four radio networks through the American Satellite Corporation's domestic satellite. Similarly, TVN (Television News, Inc.) demonstrated by Anik relay early in 1975 its proposed use of the Western Union domestic satellite to transmit television news to client-stations, potentially in 75 to 85 American markets; the $11 million for constructing earth stations in each market and for charges to feed news via "Westar" satellite one to ten hours daily were expected to total significantly less than the cost of communicating by conventional ground lines through AT&T. And American cable-TV interests formed in 1974–75 a Public Service Satellite Corporation to link institutions and organizations for education, health, and public television programming. This was prompted by the interim networking to Rocky Mountain, Appalacia, Pacific Northwest, and Alaska schools, with two-way transmission capability, via the Applied Technology Satellite (ATS-6) during 1974—the most powerful and sophisticated communications satellite in the sky by the mid-1970s. After a year of experimental transmission for the U.S., the ATS-6 satellite was to be repositioned to a new orbit over Kenya in Africa, to transmit to 3,000 villages on the Indian subcontinent, which were to be equipped with direct-reception receiving antennae costing $4,000 or less each. Eventually the ATS-6 was to be returned to the U.S. for transmitting programs overseas.

The Ford Foundation in 1975 investigated the feasibility of funding conversion of the Public Broadcasting Service to full satellite transmission—either by its own satellite, or by utilizing existing domestic systems such as Western Union's Westar I and II or RCA's space satellite scheduled for late 1975.

Thus, satellite relays in the sky competed with traditional ground networks supplied by AT&T. And direct-reception satellite transmission would compete with local stations and regional networks. (NHK in Japan planned for 1977 a domestic satellite to relay signals for regional re-distribution by stations; but it projected direct transmission to home receiving units whose initial cost of $5,000 could be reduced to $500–$1,000 by mass producing over 10,000 units.) Space technology in the 1970s was reshaping communications structures, processes, and content. Broadcast managers, at least in the large communications corporations, found their business affected by changing economic and legal factors introduced by satellites.

CATV

Of more direct concern to station managers has been the development of cable television (CATV). Originally a noncompetitive means of extending a television station's signal, "community antenna television" originated in 1948 in Pennsylvania and Oregon as a means of bringing reception to rural or other areas that were poorly served by inadequate signal strength of distant stations or because of poor reception due to topography. As the idea grew, it was generally confined to areas without adequate television service. Usually, a tall antenna was erected by the owners of a CATV system and subscribers' homes were connected with the antenna for a monthly fee.

CATV, in its original form, could hardly be called big business. Its revenues were small, from relatively few subscribers. Then the original concept of service to isolated communities with poor or marginal TV reception changed. The new function of CATV became directly competitive with regularly licensed stations. No longer were the small communities of very great interest. The larger metropolitan centers became attractive, especially when the programming of key stations in those cities could be extended to other places by microwave or cable. Loopholes in existing law made such an extension possible. CATV as the new service of "cable television" was no longer merely a local cooperative sharing of enhanced signals; it became a potentially lucrative business, akin to reselling another company's product (program service) with relatively little investment risked and no payment returned to the creators or suppliers of that product (artists, producers, networks, stations, or agencies).

Broadcasters, sensing that the problems had grown beyond their control, sent up a cry for Federal regulation of the CATV operations (parallel to the broadcasters' own request for help by the government in the 1920s, which resulted in the Radio Act of 1927 and creation of the Federal Radio Commission). Not all broadcasters, however, joined in that chorus. Some were already investors in CATV, having joined forces with this potential challenger to the established system of television. Thus broadcasters became divided over the issue of CATV.

Government Regulation

The FCC, already overburdened with its workload, responded to the broadcasters' cries for help. It proceeded to bring CATV under its jurisdiction even though the additional paperwork called for manpower not provided for in its budget. The first action was to issue a formal order in April, 1965, bringing under its control some 400 CATV systems using microwave relay. Then, in February of 1966, the Commission publicly announced that all 1,200 systems using cable were also to be regulated by the FCC.

Subsequent action by the FCC included a formal request to Congress that legislation be enacted to clarify and confirm the Commission's assumption of jurisdiction over CATV. The FCC asked that the legislation be prohibitive to the extent of denying any program origination rights to CATV. In June, 1966, the House Commerce Committee reported out a bill to confirm the authority as exercised by the FCC, granting in essence the provisions the Commission had requested. The bill contained a ban on all program originations except for limited types, interpreted to include news, weather and time services. Somewhat the same blackout provisions as adopted by professional sports were made to apply to CATV.

Indicative of the FCC's ambiguity in overseeing the development of cable television was its sequence of decisions about program origination by CATV systems. From initially prohibiting originations, the FCC in 1968 advocated such programming, and then a year later it *required* CATV systems with 3,500 or more subscribers to originate programs by April, 1971 (which ruling the U.S. Supreme Court upheld by a 5-to-4 decision).[1] The FCC's comprehensive 1972 report and rules affirmed that large-subscriber systems must operate "to a significant extent as a local outlet by origination cablecasting and . . . [must make] available facilities for local production and presentation of programs other than automated services." [2] By late-1974 the National Cable Television Association's national survey reported local programming was originated by systems in 1,533 communities, serving 4,684,785 subscribers in 50 States and Guam.[3] A total of 175 systems provided access channels to local individuals and groups as one of their origination services, but only 36 per cent reported that those channels were used more than one hour a week, and 22 per cent reported no use at all of the access capability. And yet, organizations such as the Ford and Sloan Foundations looked to cable television as a complement to commercial mass-audience broadcasting, because it could offer alternative programming and opportunities for local assess to channels—providing what it termed "television of abundance," rather than the spectrum-restricted television of scarcity.[4]

Compounding cable's complications have been the three tiers of governmental authority involved at the municipal, state, and Federal levels. For example, in 1973 when Sterling Manhattan Cable Television in New York proposed a transfer of its operations to Warner Communications for $20 million, approval was required from New York City (which authorized the franchise), New York State, the Federal Communications Commission, as well as a review by the Justice Department's antitrust division.[5] The appellate courts and the U.S. Supreme Court have been involved with such matters as program origination and copyright liability for programming "imported" from on-air broadcast sources. This multiplicity of governmental jurisdictions, coupled with the declining national economy in the 1970s, caused a sharp curtailment of expansion plans by new or already operating cable owners. Just to start a system, one to three years was often required to receive a local franchise; another one to two years was needed for state approvals in those ten states with cable statutes (and more states planning such); and "six months to infinity" were needed to get approval from the FCC.[6] Additional complications have been unresolved about copyright applications to retransmissions, which the NAB claimed were public performances for profit of works belonging to other parties. The U.S. Second Circuit Court of Appeals in New York reversed a lower court decision, and asserted that cable operators were subject to copyright provisions when signals were imported by microwave or wire from distant stations, but not when those signals were received by antennae for re-feeding through cable (the latter case causing the cable operator to be more a "viewer" than a "performer," in the Supreme Court's 1968 judgment.) [7] Meanwhile, the Senate Copyright Subcommittee had not yet completed its protracted hearings and reports on the role of cable in copyright provisions. (Senate and House Judiciary subcommittees on patents, trademarks, and copyrights had initially conducted hearings on cable implications for copyright in mid-1966.) Congress by 1975 had not yet passed its long-pending copyright bill.

One cable executive, Bruce Lovell of American Television and Communications and chairman of the National Cable Television Association's board of directors in 1974, lamented that "since 1966, all the commission has ever done is try to figure out ways to give us a little, little bit and still protect the broadcasters to the bitter end. That's been the entire regulatory philosophy of cable. . . ." [8] FCC chairman Richard Wiley noted in mid-1974 that the Commission was concerned about "the developing duplicative and burdensome overregulation of cable television";[9] but he also cautioned that "frankly, I am somewhat weary of hearing that our rules are irrational, that they were created simply to impede you and, most of all, that old bromide that they are simply the result of a commission sellout to the established interestes of the broadcast world. This is not the case and you know it or, at least you certainly should know it." [10]

Cable Programming

A major concern of broadcasters was the "siphoning off" of their program service by cable systems that relayed those programs to subscribers who paid for what the general audience was accustomed to receive free. That siphoning and relaying of shows on cable channels competes with the local broadcast stations in that cable market, who attempt to attract audiences with the same or other programs. Robert E. Button of TelePrompter (the largest cable operator in the country with a million subscribers to its several systems) looked to satellites to interconnect cable systems for "live" and specialized program service throughout the country. He emphasized complementary service to free on-air broadcasting, by offering "diversified programming . . . —special-interest programming, professional-interest programming, minority-interest programming stuff that the networks don't and can't afford to do" and by this means attracting new subscribers.[11] Further, cable importation of distant stations' signals caused some independent stations to become almost "regional" television stations, serving audiences far beyond their own signal-strength markets. The extra homes provided by cable's extended coverage were an extra bonus to advertisers and not sold on the rate card; but eventually the extended circulation of programming afforded by cable could well affect charges for air time (and for "cable time") at those independent television stations.[12]

Cable Advertising

In addition to the regular commercial programming brought into cable systems from distant television stations, advertising was accepted on local-origination channels by more than 300 of the 3,240 systems operating in the United States in 1975. The revenues from advertising on those cable channels in 1973 was $3.5 million.[13] By late 1974, about two-thirds of the over-600 systems originating programming accepted advertising, charging from $5 to $200 per minute. Ad revenues were up 40 per cent from the previous year, the median revenue being $7,500 (although one system reported advertising totaling $225,000). Sports was by far the most popular type of programming for advertisers, with news a distant second. The implied siphoning off of potential revenue from conventional over-the-air broadcasting was reflected in the top-ten advertisers on those cable systems (listed in order of billings placed): McDonald's, Pepsi Cola, Coca-Cola, Ford Motor Dealers, Kentucky Fried Chicken, Goodyear Tire Co., Woolco Department Stores, Grant's Department Stores, Hardee's Hamburgers, and Holiday Inns. Bernard Gallagher predicted that spot buying of on-air broadcast time in secondary markets would decline as advertisers penetrated those markets via signals imported by cable from major-market stations.[14]

Pay Cable

A more immediate and direct threat to conventional broadcast economics and programming came in the resurrection of pay television through cable systems. Early in 1974 some 50 systems offered their 50,000 subscribers an extra channel with specialized programming for which additional fees were charged, in addition to the regular monthly cable charges. Within a year the number of pay subscribers had doubled to 100,000.[15] Because different and superior programs ("software") seemed a key way to attract subscribers, cable systems made sports and recent theatrical motion pictures available on that extra "feature" channel, sometimes for approximately an additional $8 a month; other systems attempted to offer tickets to be exchanged for specific program offerings during the month. Twelve per cent of subscribers purchased the pay-TV service on systems that offered it.

Arrayed against these efforts of cable systems to provide specialized programming of popular interest at additional rates to subscribers were businesses whose services and income were threatened: on-air broadcasters, theater owners, the telephone company, and copyright owners. The Federal Communications Commission's task was to try to balance the conflicting interests of each of these major parties to the debate. At stake was not only financial investments and "empires," but also the quality and expense of program service to the people of the land.

At the same time, other media interests were not competing but instead held partial ownership in cable systems in three-fourths of all cable companies: broadcast-related ownership in one-third of the systems, program producers in one-quarter, newspapers in 15 per cent, publishing companies in 7 per cent, and theater owners in 4 per cent of the cable operations.[16]

While the initial promise of cable television was strong, especially in the early 1970s, the recession of the national economy by the mid-1970s and the regulatory quandary amid conflicting interests decelerated the rate of growth of CATV. As a partial solution, many cable companies began to consider merging—subject to close scrutiny by the Justice Department. The sanguine

"wired city" concept of urban centers interwoven with two-way service on 40-
or-more channel CATV systems gave way to more realistic concerns about economic viability of this new enterprise.[17]

Cable's Present and Future

The scope of cable in 1975 was statistically outlined by *Broadcasting*
magazine in a compact summary:

> There are 3,240 operating cable systems in the U.S., serving 6,980 com-
> munities. Another 2,718 systems are approved but not built. Pennsylvania has the
> most systems (300) and California the most subscribers (1.3 million). Operating
> systems currently reach about 10 million subscribers, perhaps over 30 million
> people—15% of the nation's TV households. The average cable system has 2,400
> subscribers. The largest (Cox Cable's, in San Diego) has almost 100,000. Some
> have fewer than 100. Teleprompter is the largest multiple system operator
> (MSO), with more than 1,083,000 subscribers. Industry revenues last year totaled
> approximately $800 million. Most systems offer between eight and 12 channels.
> By 1977, all systems will be required to have at least 20-channel capacity; those
> constructed after March 1972 must do so now. Monthly subscriber fees average
> $5.50, although many firms are now seeking rate increases. Installation fees range
> from nothing to $100, the average is $15. Costs of laying cable range from
> $3,500 per mile in rural areas to $80,000 in the largest cities. The average system
> has between 100 and 200 miles of cable. Nearly 629 systems now originate
> programing in their own studios, the average for 13.5 hours weekly. Equipment
> costs range from $25,000 for a small black-and-white operation to $200,000 for a
> color studio.[18]

To project what lies ahead, the prognosis for cable is not unlike that for
over-the-air broadcast. To the extent that cable television offers truly complementary service, with programming usually not available through commercial
on-air stations and networks—especially minority-interest content, including
public access channels and eventually two-way services—to that extent cable
will survive and gradually prosper. Television of abundance, of plurality of TV
signals and content, lies in the multi-channel capability of cable systems. But if
cable merely borrows and re-presents what free television already packages and
airs to the public, cable will struggle and compete weakly, if at all, with on-air
television. Unless, of course, television foregoes its heritage of spontaneity and
immediacy for pre-packaged stereotypical programming, leaning heavily on
storehouses of filmed product and abdicating its proper role of creative innova-
tor. Then cable can easily compete and woo away some of the public which
states it is bored with repetitious movies and other general fare in the home.

Cable must offer a wide variety of services not feasible for mass-audience
over-the-air broadcast. Part of this "software" programming must come from
videocassette and cartridge, and must utilize computer technologies (such as
receiver retrieval of specialized contents). And distribution can be to selected
sub-groups in the wired audience, such as hotels and professional offices and
organizations. For example, in 1974, more than 50,000 rooms in 80 hotels in

the United States were wired for specialized cable television service; almost 2 million persons a year used the service on a "pay-as-you-view" basis.[19] The Stanford Research Institute projected as many as 25 million pay-cable subscribers by 1984, up from the approximately 50,000 only a decade earlier.[20] Satellite relay, linking the nation's cable systems, might make feasible a fourth network in what otherwise is a three-network advertising-supported economy.[21]

The enormous financial potential in major events (such as outstanding theatrical movies, key sporting contests) when presented exclusively by cable threatens "free" television. Simple arithmetic indicates that one dollar per receiver from "merely" 2 million cable households equals $2 million. In conventional network television, (a) a national audience of 4 to 6 million persons is abject failure, and (b) advertisers often pay only several hundred thousand dollars for coverage of a single event. Thus sports and special-events entrepreneurs, and ultimately performing artists and writers and production personnel, can earn from cable ten- and twenty-fold income for program rights and talent payment over what they now receive from commercial television. Just as with radio at the turn into the 1950s, when television attracted both programming and audiences (and advertisers to support them), so network TV will find audiences, programming, and revenue attracted to the competing medium of cable. But in the process, "at what point will [entertainment and] other news become packageable for private audiences and barred from general airing? Or is pay-tv—meaning once again a special tariff on anything that evokes mass interest—becoming the irresistible alternative?" [22] (Pay-TV as such is discussed below.)

Perhaps the Canadian Radio and Television Commission's statements in May, 1969, and April, 1970, underscore guidelines appropriate to cable-TV's role among American communications services. Cable should offer:

> . . . community programming service of a complementary rather than a competitive nature to those already provided by other broadcasting services.
>
> [Cable should offer] the opportunity . . . to enrich community life by fostering communication among individual and community groups. In the development of programs of interest to communities, it is hoped that CATV programmers will be motivated by innovation rather than imitation. Local programs should be based on access and freedom from restraint of program schedules which are often less flexible in commercial broadcasting.[23]

Thus, from its inception a quarter-century ago as a form of a community master-receiving antenna, CATV gradually grew to loom as an economic threat to local commercial broadcasters. The FCC was designated referee to determine to what extent this expanding technology might interfere with the public's present system of advertising-supported "free" television service. The 1970s became a regulatory quagmire affecting the interests of commercial broadcasters, cable operators, and the public alike. Beyond being highly technical and legalistic, the issues involved have occasioned public statements and rule-making which in their complexity have inhibited vigorous growth or even stability. Ultimately, in the American system, FCC rulings must also be reviewed by court decisions. Whatever legislation is finally enacted must also be reviewed by the courts when challenged. The law will take its course. Meanwhile, all parties with financial interest and with concern for the eventual public service by communications media have attempted to make their views and needs known in the search for equitable resolution of cable television regulation.

The instances of vacillation and even bewilderment on the part of many broadcasters as well as of the Commission itself, point up the serious need for a basic philosophy for the electronic media. At few times since broadcasting began has that need been so obvious.

PAY-TV

Even before cable television came on the American scene, subscription television (or Pay-TV, among other names) had been proposed and initiated. Unlike the cable-TV subscriber whose monthly service includes enhanced signals of existing stations' programs plus some special programming on separate channels, the Pay-TV subscriber pays for individual programs that are available only to subscribers and which constitute the entire service.

Early attempts to establish over-the-air and wired pay-television systems met with little success. In 1951, pay-TV was tried in Chicago and, in 1953, it was begun in Palm Springs, California. Little progress was made in either of those cases.

The first experiment to receive much attention in the United States was one tried at Bartlesville, Oklahoma, in the late 1950s. The Bartlesville system confined its programming to current motion pictures. For that service during eleven hours a day, customers paid flat fees of $9.50 a month. Only some 500 families in the town of 30,000 population were attracted as customers and the experiment failed.

A pay-TV system was started in Etobicoke, a suburb of Toronto, in 1960. This system used three channels, giving the subscribers a choice of types of programming. In 1961, it came under the control of International Telemeter Corporation, a subsidiary of Paramount Pictures Corporation. The system was a pioneer in the use of leased cables. It closed its operation in May, 1965, after five years of programming. The reason given for its closing was that all of the information it needed had been obtained. Its subscriber list, initially numbering 5,500, had dropped to around 2,500. It was reported that revenue from subscribers, which had been expected to reach $10 per month, averaged only some $2. The experiment lost more than $2 million in the half-decade.[24] During its period of operation, current movies and sports had been the most popular offerings. There had been no discernible adverse effect on commercial television viewing. Its attractions had appealed to "selective tastes" and the amount of expenditure per home varied according to the "quantity, caliber and diversity of programming" that was offered.

Two pay-television systems operated in the United States in the 1960s. One was a broadcast system, WHCT, on UHF channel 18 in Hartford, Connecticut. The other was a wired system, Subscription Television, Inc. (STV), in Los Angeles and San Francisco. As a broadcast system, WHCT came under FCC jurisdiction; STV did not because, at that time, the FCC's authority over cable had not yet been established.

The Hartford Experiment

Pay-TV in Hartford began in June, 1962, as a three-year experiment, licensed by the FCC. The license was granted to RKO General for a system broadcasting coded or scrambled signals that are decoded by an attachment in the subscriber's receiving set. The system is called Phonevision, a technique developed and patented by the Zenith Radio Corporation. Subscribers pay for the installation of the decoder, a monthly rental fee and a fee for each program they choose to watch.

The Hartford license was renewed by the FCC in May, 1965, for another three-year period. There were several conclusions from its first period of operation. Its appeal had been chiefly to middle- and lower-income families. The average annual expenditure per family was slightly more than $60 in addition to the decoder rental fees. Motion pictures constituted the most popular regular program fare. Only championship boxing matches drew larger individual audiences. Subscription-TV viewing occupied only about five per cent of the hours the people devoted to television. Charges for programs varied from 25 cents for some of the educational features to $3 for a world-championship boxing match. The average amount charged for motion pictures was $1, for operas and ballets it was $1.50 and for sports events an average of $1.37.[25] Of the 500,000 homes in the area, fewer than 7,000 subscribed to the system at its height. In the typical week, the average subscriber spent only $1.20 and viewed one two-hour program.

The Zenith Radio Corporation assessed its six-and-one-half year project (including its patented "Phonevision" over-the-air coding-scrambling-decoding device limiting the signal's reception to subscribers only):

> The principal objectives of the trial operated by RKO General were achieved, and the successful Hartford project showed that STV [Subscription Television] can be a worthwhile supplement to television. These contributions by RKO General were invaluable in proving the feasibility of STV.
> In Zenith's view, FCC approval of nation-wide STV in effect terminated the experimental phase. There was no longer any real purpose to be served by a limited test operation utilizing 1961 black-and-white TV equipment not designed for today's color broadcasting. Therefore, on Jan. 31, 1969, RKO General, Inc., suspended the Hartford STV experiment it had launched on June 29, 1962.[26]

In 1971 the Zenith Radio Corporation moved to acquire broadcast properties in Los Angeles (KWHY-TV, channel 22) and Chicago (WCFL-TV, channel 38); it sought FCC authorization to operate the stations as subscription television transmitters.[27] But by 1974 Zenith owned neither operation.

Zenith and its subsidiary, Teco, Inc., had filed a petition with the FCC in March, 1965, for a rule to authorize pay-television on a national basis. The Commission's authority to receive applications for licensing nationwide pay-TV was upheld by a Court of Appeals in 1969, and the U.S. Supreme Court confirmed that action by refusing to review the case.[28]

In 1970 the Commission promulgated rules permitting pay-TV over the air or by cable. By mid-1973 two broadcast systems had received the FCC's approval for over-the-air pay-television on at least four stations: Zenith Radio Corporation and Blonder-Tongue Laboratories (Old Bridge, New Jersey).

West Coast Pay Television

Subscription Television, Inc. was the most ambitious pay system yet attempted in the physical coverage which it embraced, the program service that it supplied, and the $21 million stock offering it made. It contracted with two professional baseball clubs, the Dodgers and the Giants ($1.50 per game to subscribers) and offered movies ($1 or more) and plays or revues ($1.50). By 1964 it had 6,500 subscribers in Los Angeles and another 2,000 in San Francisco, who spent an average of $15 per month on programs. But it was forced to suspend operations in November, 1964, when the voters of California by a two-to-one margin passed Proposition 15, outlawing pay television. That proposition, however, was declared unconstitutional early in 1966 by the California Supreme Court. The majority opinion, in a 6-to-1 decision, stated that it abridged freedom of speech and was in violation of both the First and Fourteenth Amendments. But by then former-NBC-president Sylvester Weaver's Subscription Television, Inc., had gone into bankruptcy, having lost $20 million.

Other Pay Systems

By 1974 at least eight major pay-television entrepreneurs had begun hybrid pay operations by collaborating with several dozen already-existing cable systems in the United States and Canada.[29] Usually a basic fee of from $12 to $20 (annually or for installation of an unscrambling device) was augmented by per-program or per-unit-of-time fees, most often by some form of ticket decoder for reception of the fee-TV channels. Among the major companies linking pay-TV with cable operations were: Optical Systems Corporation (San Diego, Santa Barbara, Bakersfield, and Toledo); TheatreVisioN, Inc. (Sarasota, Florida); Home Theater Network (Redondo Beach, California, with plans to link cable companies by microwave); Trans-World Communication, subsidiary of Columbia Pictures ("Tele/Theatre" in Atlanta and Miami); Athena Communications, subsidiary of Gulf & Western Corporation which owns Paramount Pictures ("EnDe-Code" in Jefferson City, Missouri, and Daytona Beach, Florida); Television Communications Corporation, affiliated with Warner Brothers ("Gridtronics" in four cities); and Computer Television (two-way cable pay system in New York City), owned by Time, Inc. which also operates Sterling TV in lower Manhattan (plus links to Allentown and Wilkes-Barre, Pennsylvania).

Issues Involved in Cable and Pay-TV

The issues of CATV and pay-television can be solved in a fashion by government edict. The broadcasters of the country, however, should have anticipated these crises before they developed. Warnings were sounded in sufficient time about the consequences of delay by the industry.

The prospect of relief from government intervention into television programming may not be on the immediate horizon. Indeed, issues of the mid-1970s—"prime time access rules," children's programming, excessive crime and violence, and indecency or obscenity—have brought both FCC and Congress closer than ever to the area of programming judgment and decision-making traditionally reserved to the broadcasters by Section §326 of the Communications Act and the First Amendment to the Constitution of the United States. It is imperative that professional broadcasters prove they are capable of handling their own affairs—not only for their corporate and economic good, but also for the good of the public which their stations serve. True maturity in broadcasting will reflect professionalism and enlightened self-regulation which anticipate and respond to the needs of society and, by so doing, confirm license stability and enhance the prospects of long-term profits from operating a respected and successful broadcast property.

Although pay-TV experiments, whether over-the-air or by cable, have been limited, evidence up to the mid-1970s indicates that viewers prefer the same kinds of programming that they support on commercial television: sports and entertainment.[30] Thus there is understandable fear and caution about "fee-TV" siphoning from "free-TV" the most popular attractions. Two major effects will result: first, a "class" television service will provide a wide range of entertainment, culture, and information to those who can afford to pay monthly fees (estimated at more than $20 per month in 1974, or $240 per year per family). Those who cannot afford those additional fees will lose the service now provided by the support of advertising. Secondly, there is the danger that relatively low-audience news and public affairs documentaries and specials would not be programmed by box-office-oriented pay forms of television. Thus the current national news and information service provided by commercial networks would be removed from the American scene. And local pay- or cable-TV companies, competing for audience among several systems and within themselves with multiple channels, would be slow to mount expensive, small-revenue-producing local news service.

The economics suggest that promises of extraordinary programming fare might not easily be realized on pay-TV.

For example, a network may pay $600,000 for rights to air a major motion picture; it recoups its investment from advertisers whose messages reach the 25,000,000 people in 10 million homes tuned to that network's stations. But a major pay-TV system—linked by microwave, satellite, or merely by syndication—could offer $2 million or $3 million for that same film, because it could expect only 2- or 3-million homes to watch it and pay $1 each. Of course, if the fee is $2, and if the number of homes increases, then the ante rises to multi-millions which advertising-supported "free television" cannot match.

Thus, just as with radio when television became popular and then dominant in the early 1950s, so with television when pay-TV would become dominant in the early 1980s, the system as we know it—networks and commercial stations—would be reduced to occasional news service at best.

This is a serious question for policy-makers as well as industry economists. It affects not only the quality and cost of popular entertainment. It may well determine the national self-awareness and ability to communicate universally among American citizens. Future international crises, presidential addresses, space shots, local weather bulletins, and the like might no longer have access to the mass public's attention. The "television of abundance" can fragment the audience—offering a wide range of simultaneous content, but undercutting a swift and effective, truly national, system of communications.

THE ELECTRONIC FUTURE

As revolutionary as the space satellites were, they constitute but the threshold of a communications era that not even the most farsighted prophet of 50 years ago could have anticipated.

Dr. Joseph V. Charyk, president of COMSAT, visualized as only an interim phase the improved communications of conventional types such as more flexible television, telephone, teletype, and facsimile as well as aeronautical, meteorological, and educational services.

Home Television

One fairly immediate consequence of technical development, refinement, and mass precision manufacture has been a change in the patterns of home television viewing as families became multi-set owners. By its increased portability, television began to rival radio in its ability to attract the out-of-home audience. Small-screen sets in color made their appearance in time for the 1965 Christmas trade. (Stereophonic sound for television appeared to be enough of a possibility back in 1964 for the FCC to issue a Notice of Inquiry.)

Already on the market, the home color video recorder should come into more general use in the years ahead. Refinements of equipment, including standardization of color video cassette systems, and reduction of costs should result in a product of wide appeal. The viewer is able to tape programs off the air for later replay at his convenience; he may even adjust the recorder so that the television set will be turned on automatically and a program recorded while he is away from home. He may rent or buy programs much in the manner that he uses audio recordings. A major appeal of the home video recorder, however, may lie in the opportunity to produce homemade tapes. Adding a television camera to the recorder provides certain advantages over home movies: instantaneous playback, tape that can be erased and recorded repeatedly, and without need to have film developed or even to thread a projector.

Cartridges and Cassettes. In the early 1970s, major national and international manufacturers hurried to announce continuing developments in cassette and cartridge television "hardware" as fast as their competing systems could be turned out of the laboratories (sometimes even before experimental models were fully successful in those laboratories). In the initial excitement, sanguine predictions were multiplied about the scope of in-home (as well as educational, industrial, and professional) color-video playback systems. One optimistic study projected 3.4 million homes with "cartridge TV" systems by 1980, and annual sales of $1.8 billion for both equipment and videotape-recorded program content.[31] But an executive of the abortive CBS/EVR (Electronic Video Recorder) cautioned that those figures were "fairly unsophisticated conjecture based on the hopes and dreams of hardware manufacturers." At the same time, Cartridge Television, Inc., went public—the first major company solely in cassette videorecording—and sold 1.1 million shares in two days. That company's distribution was undertaken by two massive retail firms, Sears and Montgomery Ward. The company predicted that between May and December of 1973, as many as 100,000 people would purchase its sets, plus over 1 million cartridges of tape. *Fortune* magazine predicted up to $5.4 billion in annual sales by 1980 for the entire cartridge/cassette industry.[32] One national merchandise manager of a major retail chain estimated in mid-1972 that "in the next ten years 50 per cent of all dollars in home entertainment will come from cartridge TV," for both equipment and program content.[33] Yet, at the end of 1972, CBS, Inc. had announced that it would retire from the entire field of competitive cassette/cartridge television, turning over its EVR system to Motorola. As other entries into the crowded field increased, further predictions became more guarded. The blossoming industry of videocassettes slowed significantly by the mid-1970s.

Several major factors contributed to the slackening pace of the cassette industry. The proliferation of non-compatible systems of videotape, film, and disc recording made it risky for potential investors—corporate or individual consumers. A half-dozen competing forms of videotape devices were announced and marketed by 1974: two different one-half-inch cartridge/cassette systems, two other different three-quarter-inch systems, the Electronic Video Recording (EVR) on film stock, plus other non-tape systems of RCA (SelectaVision), Kodak (Supermatic 60), and Teldec (Video Disc).[34] Congress, the U.S. Office of Education, and other Federal agencies expressed concern about the lack of standardization and interchangeability among the competing systems.

Another factor was the perennial problem of any new communications technology: the chicken-and-egg dilemma of consumer purchase of equipment for which program content ("software") was not yet available. Cartridge Television, Inc. did announce early in 1972 that it held rights to more than 1,300 titles (including 300 feature films), and had entered into agreements with two Avco Corp. manufacturing divisions for production of 25,000 recorder/player units, with an option on an additional 175,000 units. But within a year of those enthusiastic surveys and predictions, Cartridge Television, Inc. (of which Avco Corp. owned 32 per cent of stock) filed for bankruptcy, announcing liabilities of almost $30 million, with assets of only $18 million. Avco Corp. stated that it lost $48 million in the venture (before tax credits). The risk of entrepreneuring new fields of communications technology was clear.[35]

Another factor lay in the sustained effort of commercial television to obtain rights to broadcast major "block-buster" theatrical motion pictures and outstanding sporting events. Consumers were slow to invest dollars in still-developing forms of communications (cassettes or cable TV) when they could receive "free" program service of highly attractive content by conventional advertising-supported broadcasting.

Beyond the obvious complications of standardizing equipment and the unavailability of outstanding content in videocassette form, there were the further issues of union jurisdiction, copyrights, and even of modes of distribution: outright sale of cassettes or rental of them (by tape libraries, sale or rental clubs, by mail, or retail point-of-purchase loan centers)—each involving problems of establishing low unit-cost-per-consumer while returning adequate revenue to investors.

Whereas in the early 1970s, many critics and even professional broadcasters predicted a major overhaul or outdating of commercial television, by the second half of the decade predictions of the demise of national networks and local commercial stations were muted. Audiences for "free" television continued to grow (as did the average viewing time per day—considerably over six hours per household and almost three hours per person in 1974). The broadcast industry's lobbying with Federal agencies countered the cable and cassette industries' lobbying with those same governmental agencies. The American consumers had grown accustomed to entertainment, news, special events, and other public service from the "free" TV receivers in their homes. They were slow to reach for the promised "television of abundance and selectivity" offered by alternative systems such as cable and cassette.

Media Systems

Future uses of television in the home may well embrace any number of purposes. In Tucson, Arizona, a 17-story, 411-apartment complex includes a basement grocery store that is part of a closed-circuit television system throughout the building. Women can contact the grocery by telephone, tune their television sets to Channel 2 and do their shopping by conversing with him while they inspect and select merchandise. Groceries are then delivered. The housewife may turn to a different channel that enables her to check her children at a swimming pool. A third channel permits her to inspect callers in the lobby of the building. Still another channel supplies news and classified ads.[36]

Through highly developed storage and retrieval centers of the near future, still or moving pictures, books, music, theatrical productions or other entertainments, or means of instruction may be brought into the home by television or by printout simply by dialing coded numbers. Then, the individual in the home may truly control his choices of entertainment and his means of recreation. Should he desire a newscast or a symphony or a book, he would be able to have it when he wanted it instead of at the time of a scheduled broadcast or other availability.

Some specialists believe that communications utilities in metropolitan centers will be inevitable developments. Such systems would

> . . . link homes, business offices, and stores in a community through wide-band high capacity transmission facilities to central switching and compuing centers to provide a wide variety of services. These would include color television and stereophonic FM radio, aural and visual telephone service, high speed facsimile data and newspapers, library reference, theatre and transportation booking services, access to computer facilities, shopping and banking services of all types, centralized charging and billing. Communications destined beyond this metropolitan area would be directed to a processing and transmission center which, in turn, would be linked through a suitable terminal station in the community to a worldwide satellite system.[37]

The late Brigadier General David Sarnoff, who predicted and entrepreneured both radio and television, visualized a society in which all of the mass media will merge into one system:

> With the introduction of microwave channels and the appearance of communications satellites and high-capacity cables, there is no longer any distinction among the various forms of communications. All of them—voice or picture, telegraph or data—pass simultaneously through the same relays in the form of identical electronic pulses. Henceforth—in marked contrast with the past—developments that extend the reach of one will extend the reach of all.
>
> This same process of unification will inevitably occur, I believe, in all media of communications. Not only television and telephone, but books, magazines and newspapers will be converted into identical bits of energy for transmission over any distance. At the receiving end, these electronic signals will be converted into any form we choose—either visual display or recorded sounds or printed pages.[38]

The Transistor and Microcircuitry

The discovery of the transistor caused a revolution in broadcasting. For the first time, a small piece of solid matter could be used to control electric currents. The days of the vacuum tube were numbered. Transistors are used universally in portable radios and television sets as well as in various other applications, including computers and space satellites. Today, research in semiconductor devices has progressed far beyond the transistor. Silicon solar cells have been used to convert sunlight to electricity, to power radio transmitters in space satellites, and to detect radioactive radiation.

The advances in electronics that were possible when the transistor replaced the vacuum tube have now been eclipsed by the microcircuit. By the 1970s, sales of this tiny development well exceeded a billion dollars a year. *Time* magazine described the capacity of the microcircuit:

> The transistor took the complicated network of wires in a vacuum tube and condensed it into a simple, solid piece of silicon or germanium; the microcircuit reduces an entire electronic circuit composed of dozens of transistors and other components to a tiny latticework of thin metal conductors mounted on a base of such material as glass or silicon. At Texas Instruments, which shares leadership in the microcircuitry field with Motorola and Fairchild Camera, engineers have developed a piece of silicon the size of a split pea into which they have fused the equivalent of thirty-eight transistors, five capacitors and twenty-six resistors—a complete circuit one-thousandth the size of a similar vacuum-tube circuit and one-hundredth that of a transistorized one. . . . [I]n the labs the entire circuitry of a TV set has been reduced to the size of a soda cracker; this may eventually lead to the long-heralded TV set that hangs on the wall like a picture. Scientists have also contained the workings of a hearing aid within the bows of an ordinary pair of eyeglasses, and now talk seriously of making Dick Tracy's two-way wrist radio a common reality.[39]

The Computer

The development of transistors made the amazing world of the computers available; microcircuitry now makes them more generally useful by their greater compactness, economy, and reliability. The computer has already revolutionized society with far-reaching consequences for the conduct of business and the style of living—affecting patterns of architecture, transportation, and communications (eventually people may *communicate* to work instead of *commuting* to work).

The phenomenal "memory" of the computer and its ability to perform calculations in a billionth of a second make it a formidable rival to the mind of man. If station managers exhibit some concern about the future role of computers in the broadcasting industry, such feelings should be understandable.

> One area made mercilessly vulnerable by the computer is that of U.S. business management. The computer has proved that many management decisions are routine and repetitive and can be handled by a machine. Result: many of the middle management jobs of today will go to computers that can do just about everything but make a pass at a secretary. As much as anything else, the computer is of great value to big business because it forces executives to take a hard, logical look at their own function and their company's way of doing business.[40]

Yet, for those who are more than managers of routine affairs, the computer should make the future even more productive. Some scientists maintain that, even without further advances in computer technology, the computer has provided enough work and opportunities for man for another thousand years.

The executive must learn to understand the computer's powers if he wishes to keep ahead of others in the organization as well as ahead of competing companies. He must challenge the computer regularly with the way he programs it.

> In a sense, the computer enhances the executive's powers by cutting through all the statistics and presenting several alternatives, which the executive can act upon. But in the growing dialogue between man and machine, the man who controls the computer has a huge amount of influence in the company.

General Sarnoff believed that by 1980, computers

> . . . will respond to handwriting, to images and to spoken commands. They will commune tirelessly with one another over any distance. They will recognize a voice, a face or a symbol among tens of thousands . . . and will have the power to learn through experience.[41]

The Laser

Theoretically, all radio and television broadcasts, as well as all telephone conversations in the United States, could be simulcast on one laser beam. The term "laser" is an acronym from the phrase "light amplification by simulated emission of radiation." An extremely intense and sharply defined beam of light, the laser can be so concentrated as to burn holes in metal.

Possible applications of the laser being studied include military, medical, biological and industrial uses, as well as for communications. The International Telecommunication Union described an early test:

> One of the most exciting laser experiments was performed on a moonlight night in May, 1962. When the beam from the laser was flashed into space for the first time in history, it lighted a small spot on the moon and then was reflected back to earth. The beam made the round trip in two and a half seconds. On three successive nights, United States scientists carrying out this project at the Massachusetts Institute of Technology sent 83 thin light beams pulsing through space, successfully lighting the moon each time.[42]

Scientists have discovered how to harness this small and powerful light beam so that information may be carried on it. Future broadcast transmissions by light waves instead of radio waves cannot be discounted as a possibility. A 1965 experiment by the U. S. Army was reported in which seven television signals from New York City were transmitted by laser beam, through the use of a low voltage modulator, across a ten-foot room to a television receiver. The picture quality was considered equivalent to the same programs as received through regular transmission on a home set. The Army electronic scientists who performed the experiment said that the programs could have been transmitted by laser "over many miles, instead of the width of the room."

In 1972, a demonstration of the first marketable laser-beam system was described by the *New York Times* in terms reminiscent of news accounts of first wireless experiments at the beginning of this century:

> A single light beam from a low-power laser mounted atop the CBS Broadcast Center on West 57th Street near 10th Avenue was carefully aligned to strike a 25th-floor window in the Gulf and Western Building. There a cylindrical receiver resembling a stovepipe picked it up and shot out another laser aimed at the roof of the New York Coliseum, where another receiver converted it to a conventional signal fed by cable along the roof, down a flight of stairs and into a portable color television set.
>
> The laser beam had carried a studio-quality television signal two city blocks east and three blocks north.[43]

Advantages of the laser beam over conventional signal transmission include its immunity to electrical jamming and interference, while it does not affect existing communications. The light beam can be sent indefinite distances (even to the moon and back). It is almost impossible to intercept the laser without detection. Most significant is the laser's capacity to transmit information. The one used in the New York demonstration operated at 500 trillion cycles per second; thus it could theoretically carry 100 million television signals simultaneously. Although the laser is expensive and unreliable in bad weather, that system was demonstrated in extreme pollution, haze, and light rain, and yet it transmitted a steady and clear television image.

To overcome atmospheric or meteorological conditions, laser beams can be projected through evacuated pipes and "fiber optics"—through which light can travel by continuous reflection off glass or liquid-filled hairlike tubes. A Bell Laboratories researcher estimated that a four-inch pipe with 100 separate laser light beams of different colors could carry approximately 2 million television channels or 4 billion telephone calls.

The firm of Perkin-Elmer, a Connecticut manufacturer of scientific instruments, announced in 1965 that laboratory experiments had shown that a laser television system could pick up pictures in total darkness. It was reported that the images, when they appeared on a television screen, were "exceptionally sharp and clear." It was stressed that before the system could have any use in television studios it would have to be "evaluated by industry experts." In 1972, the police in Cleveland's cultural center began the nation's first 24-hour day-and-night outdoor surveillance system utilizing television cameras and laser transmitters.[44]

Holography

The laser has been used in experiments to perfect the methods of holography, whereby three-dimensional pictures are produced without needing a lens.

The earliest discovery in 1947 was that both intensity and frequency of wave fronts could be recorded by imprinting interference patterns of light on a photosensitive surface to provide the information needed to reconstruct a three-dimensional image. The invention of the laser beam in 1960 provided the extremely cohesive light needed for holograms. The first completely successful three-dimensional image by this system was produced in 1965. And the world's first holographic motion picture was demonstrated privately in 1969 at the Hughes Research Laboratories.[45] In true holography, different areas of the picture are visible depending on the viewer's angle of approach. Further developments include a process of generating three-dimensional holographic images by digital computers, which control interference and scattering of laser light beams. This resulting image is called a kinoform. These and other systems offer a "stereo-scopic" system of television image production, providing all-encompassing video images, similar to the "wrap-around" sound of stereophonic earphones.

These creative applications of technology suggest issues that touch upon philosophy and ethics as well as management pragmatics. For instance, when viewers would increasingly experience visual and aural sensations integrated into three-dimensional phenomena at the point of reception, the distinction would become blurred between reality and artificial re-creation. What does or does not constitute reality might become a challenge at least remotely akin to hallucinogenic experiences. This suggests the need for perspective by media decision-makers, who must acknowledge the importance of presentational forms relative to content. "Through the hologram window we peer into a future world that defies the imagination, a world in which the real and the illusory are one, a world at once beautiful and terrifying." [46] These fascinating developments in the communication process offer exciting challenges to the inventors, entrepreneurs, creative artists, and eventually managers of media systems.

Gene Youngblood has likened the state of the art of holography in the early 1970s to the level of development of motion pictures in the early 1900s. He projects as certain that holographic forms of cinema and television will be common by the year 2000, "but more probably this will take place within fifteen years from now."

Other Technological Progress

As far back as the annual NAB convention in 1965, W. Walter Watts, an RCA group executive vice president, reported work under way to produce a miniaturized color television set that would be "about the size of a woman's compact"; it would be "cordless and operated by the heat from the human body." Solid-state technology has made possible a television camera that operates on sensors rather than a tube and is smaller than a pack of cigarettes.[47]

A group of chemicals called "liquid crystals" may be applied to production of flat television tubes, thin screens that can hang on a wall. The crystals provide a level of whiteness almost as bright as high-quality white bond paper, plus resolution approximately that of magazine photographs. The liquid crystal screen can be readily adapted to image projection, making it possible to vary the size of the image for large- or small-group viewing.[48]

The late Dr. Allen B. DuMont, a television pioneer, predicted that scientists would be able in another 25 years to provide electronic vision for the blind. Electrical waves would be fed directly to the human brain so that "a blind person will actually enjoy television pictures."

Already the physical barriers of outer space have been conquered. Soon the space barriers on earth will no longer exist. Someday, it will be possible to reach all of the people in the world simultaneously by television and radio.

General Sarnoff, one of the great prophets of electronic development of our time, has said:

> It should be relatively easy to design and produce low-cost, single-channel television receivers for use in primitive or underdeveloped areas of the globe. These sets could be built by assembly-line techniques, housed in simple metal or plastic cases, and equipped with transistorized circuits consuming very little energy. They could be made to run on batteries rechargeable by wind, hydraulic or even animal power.
>
> Such sets could be distributed throughout the developing regions in quantities suitable to local conditions. If they were programmed from regional stations transmitting through a few broadcasting satellites, the tragic effects of illiteracy could be virtually abolished in 10 years.[49]

All of these electronic developments—in various stages of research, laboratory experimentation, or demonstration—will affect the very experience of television viewing, modifying the contextual environment in which viewing takes place. Future improvements and new methods of presenting program viewing will necessarily change the impact of the video experience.

THE STATION MANAGER AND THE FUTURE

Most people are not fully aware of the impact scientific discoveries will have on their lives. Most broadcasters are more aware of the future effects of science on the communications industries than they are of the possible effects of those changes on the human society.

Largely due to technological achievements, the mass media are growing faster than the present apparent ability of their leaders to master them. The many changes are often accepted as phenomena of science rather than as challenges for equivalent achievement. Again, we quote the brilliant and dedicated David Sarnoff:

> Science begets humility. Its every discovery reveals more clearly the divine design in nature, the remarkable harmony in all things, from the infinitesimal to the infinite.

But the mortar of brotherhood is not a product of the laboratory. It must come from the human heart and mind, and therein lies the crux of man's dilemma. He has not yet learned, as a social and economic creature, to keep step with his science. He is technologically mature, and a spiritual adolescent. Having conquered nature, he must now learn to conquer himself.

The devices which science has given us are neither good nor evil in themselves. Their capacity for good or evil lies in the use we make of them. Thus, not in the laboratory, but in the human heart, in the realm of the spirit, lies the challenge of the future.[50]

It is more than a little frightening to realize that the world is being changed so much by scientific advancements while most people do not understand what is happening. Too many people do not care.

Station managers are being given technical breakthroughs with an amazing degree of regularity. Many of the discoveries offer these executives opportunities for outstanding achievement or for possible disaster. Yet, the top man in many broadcasting stations must still rely upon technical people for advice and, in many cases, he may not even understand the language. It now has become imperative that the station manager understand what is happening before he can make intelligent plans for using those discoveries. Robert W. Sarnoff, when he was chairman of the Board of the National Broadcasting Company, said:

> We are entering an era when the most progressive enterprises will possess built-in electronic systems to gather, digest, measure, correlate and analyze all information relevant to management decisions. They will link every corner of an enterprise, no matter how far-flung. And they will centralize management control by endowing the manager of the future with a vast new capacity for swift and efficient response to the most intricate and varied requirements of his own operations and to the most subtle trends of the marketplace. Thus, the new generation executive must not only have a basic understanding of these powerful aids but must also realize that they are, after all, only machines, and the answers they provide can only be as good as the questions that men ask them.
>
> More than ever before, success in business and industry will require of managers that they be both specialists and generalists. They must be knowledgeable in detail of their day-to-day operations, yet steeped sufficiently in science and technology to relate research and engineering developments to the specifics of their enterprises. And they must be equipped with knowledge of the economic, social, political and cultural forces that shape their environment.
>
> To the individual this signifies a longer period of schooling and broader preparation for his career—a trend already evident in the growing number of men and women who enter their careers with graduate degrees.[51]

B. RETROSPECTS

Having surveyed principles and practices involved in broadcast management—from the station physical plant and personnel, through audience research and programming, to sales and profitable administration, as well as engineering and regulation—it seems appropriate to look back over these areas in a final appraisal of the role of management in the industry and art of broadcasting. Whereas both authors of this volume collaborated at every step of the manuscript up to this point, the two final essays are individual syntheses by an educator and by a professional broadcaster who separately appraise the broadcasting scene in America in the mid-1970s.

THE PROFESSOR'S VIEW

by James A. Brown

This broadcast management book has stressed principles and practices of managing a business—usually the relatively small business of the local radio and television station, plus implications for larger contexts of network administration. The book has not attempted a sociological analysis of broadcast communications in contemporary society, although the authors on occasion have reflected on the larger responsibilities of the professional broadcast manager.

Therefore it seems appropriate at this point to comment on major patterns in American broadcasting from the viewpoint of a professor who is also consumer and critic—and often defender—of our present commercial system of radio and television. Commentary will emphasize broad issues rather than specific problems, because of the continually evolving circumstances in which broadcasting operates. (Detailed recommendations for concrete activities are more apt and timely for articles in journals and trade magazines.)[51a]

Central patterns selected for final comment include those that must undergird broadcasting and management: *professionalism* and *respect for human values*. Analysis of the structural factors of *economics* and *regulation* is then followed by comments about *programming* (especially news) and the *audience's* role in broadcasting.

Professionalism

The keynote of broadcast management must be professionalism. This implies qualitative values and goals, the exercise of personal responsibility, and the ability to serve others even when it may produce less income. The heart of professional service lies in *personal* integrity—when the manager lives by personal values, with service to others within and outside of broadcasting.[52]

Broadcast veteran Robert Coddington put it this way:

> The potential state of the broadcasting art today is extremely high, both technically and artistically. Whether in practice the medium advances at the rate of broadcasting's early evolution, or whether it settles for a stat[u]s of mediocrity will be entirely up to those who man the profession. We cannot look to the public for leadership in an area where they have no expertise; we cannot look to the FCC

for guidance when it is tied to political tradition and conflicting influences; we must exercise our own initiative with an unyielding dedication to increasing professionalism.[53]

A far-reaching and delicate proposal was suggested by Earl Warren when he was Chief Justice of the U.S. Supreme Court. He urged that corporations which are alert to the contributions made to their operations by specialists in finance, law, marketing, production, promotion, and personnel relations, should realize that the realm of ethics—what is "right"—ought also be represented by a counsellor who might advise regarding the social and personal human effects of given decisions. Might broadcasting, which more than other commercial enterprises deals with things of the human spirit (art, music, drama, humor, thought, human events, sport, and personal, family, and industry products for daily living), consider this suggestion: what is ethically right is ultimately good business.

There are now in broadcasting many professional persons who are often grieved by their company's decisions which they must personally carry out. Their own personal sense of "what is right" is often overlooked as an important source of guidelines within the industry and art of broadcasting. From his own experience with local and network broadcasters through the past 15 years, this writer is convinced of the personal integrity and good sense—that is, good artistic and ethical judgment—of many individuals in radio and television. There are countless individuals who exercise discretion and have a healthy sense of values when they are free to express them. But in corporate structures that have (in Donald McGannon's phrasing) a form, rigidity, and momentum of their own, most employees and even administrators are ruled by expediency. Although they subscribe to superior values operative in their personal lives, they are deterred from bringing those values into the marketplace of commerce and entertainment and public affairs. It is this author's conviction that there now do exist in broadcasting—among management, production staffs, and creative artists—countless disenchanted persons who are quietly dying inside because their deepest convictions and aspirations are being bartered away day by day across executive desks, cocktail tables, and directors' consoles. Their basically sound instincts for good art, good ethics, and good morals are imperceptibly being smothered. And they are not happy.

It is distressing that great numbers of creative, professional people in the media are increasingly disenchanted with the policies of their stations or networks. Discontent and even cynicism are voiced strongly and consistently enough by individual broadcasters in studios and offices to cause top management to take stock. Beyond serving the faceless public, beyond taking preventive measures against FCC inquiry, beyond precluding pressure visits by consumer groups, management should foster genuine productivity and should support quality and creative initiative among the people who make up the station and network. It is disconcerting that the most acerbic criticism of broadcasting is sometimes voiced from *within* the industry by thoughtful, trained, professional people. This is a strong caution-light, warning executive management to reassess very carefully their policies and practices. What they have been doing in the name of corporate profit or competitive solvency risks destroying employees' morale and the very spirit of creative communication which should be the hallmark of broadcasting. Apathy and discontent among staff is cancerous; it can infiltrate the on-air announcers, the office personnel, and the sales staff. This can only undermine ambitious efforts of management to achieve high profit-levels.

Thus the most serious threat to broadcasting comes not from external forces of critics, government, advertisers, or audience; rather it comes from within. Being people-oriented business, broadcast stations and networks depend absolutely on the creativity, energy, and dedicated commitment of the men and women who are broadcasters. If the structure stifles their initiative and smothers their opportunity for personal and professional fulfilment, the future is bleak indeed.

Human Values and Media of Social Communication

Man is a rational and therefore symbol-making animal. In order to organize and partly comprehend the complexity of his surrounding universe, man clusters similar and related concepts; he comes to grips with the richness of human experience by categorizing it. (This process can lead to oversimplification and stereotypes—reflecting personal expectations and subjective filtering as much as the data of reality.) Man combines diverse and complex sense perceptions by constructing concepts—rational symbols supported by sense symbols—through which he interprets, controls, and changes his environment, and indeed, by which he interacts with other persons and understands both himself and his community. These symbols—simplified, stylized, and sometime stereotypical conceptualizations—in turn modify his perceptions and so can affect what he perceives.

Television and radio are eminently symbol-making media. Thus they can aptly reflect man's own conceptualizing of the world of people and events around him. The visual image, the aural image, and the coupling of those images by juxtaposition through creative selectivity and editing can create new symbolic representations of our universe of thought and action. Those media images can also modify our symbol system, either enhancing or distorting our perceptions and understandings of our world-environment. This touches on the central issue of mass media in contemporary society. Holbrook Jackson underscored this "peculiarity of not being able to see things for yourself or to think for yourself. . . . [People] approach things and ideas through a haze of what has been learned or thought about them rather than by direct observation." [54] Similarly, R. A. MacKenzie emphasized

> . . . the affective aspects of symbols; they stir up appetites and emotions in a way that the conceptualized form of statement expressed in words can never do. They involve statements, or perhaps intuitions is the word, intuitions of value;

they present to us in a living way that which is desirable and hateful. Therefore, they appeal to us as wholes; they appeal to all our faculties, of course intellect and will, but also our affections, appetites, emotions, passions, etc.[55]

Broadcast media have about them an aura of reality and relevance. The millions of individuals who make up the mass population devote enormous time to radio and television. They increasingly have perceived the electronic media to be more credible than print media. Thus symbol-making man's consciousness and value-judgments stand to be enhanced or damaged by how broadcast media present and interpret reality to them in non-fiction forms (news, documentaries, public affairs, special events) and in fictional programming (serious drama, comedy, and entertainment, including interview and talk shows). Walter Cronkite, Johnny Carson, Captain Kangaroo, ABC News, *All in the Family,* and *As the World Turns* together provide the average viewer with his world of symbols. Those symbols largely stand for that larger world of reality not experienced first-hand by the viewer. Former FCC Commissioner Nicholas Johnson put it in strong language:

> Television not only distributes programs and sells products, but also preaches a general philosophy of life. Television tells us, hour after gruesome hour, that the primary measure of an individual's worth is his consumption of products. . . . Many products (and even programs), but especially the drug commercials, sell the gospel that there are instant solutions to life's most pressing personal problems.[56]

Edward R. Murrow lamented two decades ago that "television in the main is being used to distract, delude, and amuse and insulate us." [57] The head of the British Broadcasting Corporation's drama division noted that the unending stream of programming content juxtaposes news and comedy and commercials and drama, reducing all different kinds and categories to the same level in the viewer's mind—thus blurring the distinction between the real and the artificial, between reality and fiction. The entire range of symbols is appraised by the common criterion of "was this entertaining?"—did I enjoy it and did it please me? Politicians' performances, comedians' performances, and disaster victims' performances—in paid spot announcements, monologue routines, and interviews—are all reduced to similar fragments linked together by the omnipresent announcer and punctuated by multiple commercials, extolling mouthwash, sparkplugs, detergents, pharmaceuticals, and upcoming late-late movies. In the terminology of Eric Voegelin, only a small portion of mass media content is substantive, serving to build the human personality and the social community; much of it is purely pragmatic (commercial selling); and most of it is merely intoxicant, an unending divertissement to drown the anxiety of an empty life.[58]

Are we satisfied with the total performance of our mass media? Are broadcast managers adequately concerned about how their programming truly

serves their communities' pluralistic, diversified needs and interests? Jacques
Ellul has observed that myths and ideologies communicated by mass media
give individual persons a sense of coherence and worth, and relieve unbearable
psychological tensions amid people's anxious search for meaning, peace, and
fulfillment within themselves and with one another. We need myths. We need
symbols by which to understand and to communicate. But we need symbols
that reflect true reality, honest values.

Broadcasting, as it has developed since the late 1920s, has been a value-
orienting and value-forming medium of communication. It is an image- and
myth-making medium (with its models of dress, speech, actions, and aspirations of heroes in drama and entertainment and even news programs). It continues to become increasingly significant as an information medium—keeping
people in touch with the rush of complex events at home and around today's
world. Broadcasting, then, has an enormous influence on the symbol patterns
of society. Broadcasting's images and sounds become part of the structure and
content of people's imagining, understanding, and judgment. The responsibility
that comes with this power is enormous. How that responsibility is exercised is
in the hands of broadcast managers.

The major complicating factor in management's carrying out that responsibility is the fact that this medium of communication in America is also a sales
medium—for marketing and commerce. And, at times, that has made all the
difference. While advertising has made economically feasible much of today's
electronic technology, stable corporate structures, programming content, and
popular personalities, it has also affected and even dictated the formats, content, and personnel of the programming carried by radio and television signals.

Broadcast Economics

There is concern in the land that business interests emphasize profits for
owners and stockholders at the expense of quality of broadcast service. In
short, large numbers of audience are the prime requisite, to attract advertising
dollars and to increase profit margins. The "quality" of program service is
measured quantitatively by ratings and rate cards, by revenues and expenses.
This increasing preoccupation with non-content, non-effect aspects deserves to
be challenged.

True, broadcasting is a business; so it must not only break even but must
make a profit (to reward its investors, and to attract the capital necessary to sustain, compete, and expand in a reasonably healthy way). Therefore a station or
network must gain a large share of the available listening/viewing audience by
a successful strategy of program scheduling and content. Les Brown acknowledged the realities of mass media in his assessment:

> Commercial television does have its trials, and its failings, in abundance—
> but it works. It works as a business and apparently better than anything yet
> devised as a mass entertainment anesthetic that people will give their time to. It is
> so entrenched in the living pattern of the average American that he is bound to

resist strenuously anything that threatens to take it away from him. . . . The big thing commercial tv has going for it is the support of the advertising industry. The system works because there is someone to pick up the tab.[59]

Jack Gould long ago wrote in the *New York Times* that "no serious critic for a moment has questioned the need for an economically viable medium." But he underscored the impact of broadcasting on the public's consciousness and on the processes of society, and concluded that

> . . . television, in other words, cannot be equated with "almost any business." It isn't like any other business and to assume the contrary can only be a futile exercise in naivete.[60]

Yet, Les Brown characterized American broadcasting as considering the *advertiser* to be the customer—the one who is served by the broadcaster. The *viewer/listener* is merely the consumer; he is the product or merchandise which is offered to the client (the buyer or advertiser). The *program* is the bait that is used to attract the mass audience. That audience is sold to the advertiser in bulk (or mixed bulk, with demographic break-downs) in lots of 1,000—the "cost per thousand" (CPM) thrust that is the business of television and radio. Thus the broadcaster's first concern is not to serve the public interest, but rather to "serve up" the public audience to interested advertisers.[61] To the extent that this is so, we have overturned our initial priority: American broadcasting has become primarily a sales medium, and is only secondly a medium of communicating human values.

This reversed priority is reflected in *Television/Radio Age's* observation that leaders in broadcast station management, who for decades had guided the media, were nearing retirement age; second- and even third-generation broadcasters were replacing them.

> In a few instances, an orderly transition has been planned. In most cases, the commercial or sales manager is in line for succession.[62]

The implications for broadcast service are obvious from a respected industry leader's assessment that salesmen and managers are goal-oriented and concentrate on concrete problem-solving, as contrasted with newspersons (and programmers) whose concern centers on problems of humanity and problems of individual persons.[63] This writer seriously questions that pattern of management selection.

A central question is whether broadcasting—especially television, and particularly networks and O&O stations—can forsake as an absolute priority annually increasing profits. The broadcaster must honestly ask himself what level of continued growth in profit-making is compatible with a reasonably high quality of service to the public audience in his signal area. It seems that cutbacks in professional personnel, in level of quality of production and flexibility of scheduling, and in the amount of community-oriented local (and "live") programming have been major means to sustain the level of profits or even to increase that profit margin each year, no matter what the state of the economy or the competitive market. Creativity and the performance and morale of personnel (on-air and in-office) have suffered under this relentless demand for ever-increasing profitability.[64]

While television networks and VHF stations prospered during the past decade, UHF stations struggled to break even, and one out of three radio stations annually lost money. The inflationary spiral of costs could not account for all the losers' problems of balancing revenues and expenses. Possibly in some cases excessive salaries were paid to talent and chief administrators. Perhaps simply poor management of people and material contributed to inefficient use of resources and consequent losses.

As for radio stations, although it is exceedingly difficult to survive in highly competitive markets, a premium must still be set on professionalism which engenders flexibility and creativity to win audiences and advertisers, and thus revenue. One disenchanted broadcaster put it bluntly to a college audience: "Not only economics but a lack of ability conspire to smother creative radio." [65] He appraised the field as "so introspective and inbred that they can't distinguish between the diamond and the pile of crap." Nor did he see government regulation as a major cause of broadcasting's lack of creative initiative: "the industry is over-controlled out of *fear* more than out of *fact;* it is gutless." Radio's success in coming years will lie in emphasizing its unique qualities: imagination that creates through sounds and silences, flexibility that permits swift changes in content (including sales campaigns), relatively low cost of production, instantaneous and spontaneous "live" sound not limited by on-air automation. These characteristics are lost if radio becomes routinely mechanical—physically automated or spiritually imitative.

If broadcast management considers itself almost exclusively a business of dollars-and-cents and profits and inventories, instead of as an essential "software" communication service to communities of people, it will hardly compete with the still fragile and ambiguous, yet potentially creative and local-oriented, cable television. And the flexibility of consumer-oriented videocassettes may yet wrestle away from over-the-air broadcasters the large, affluent audiences that advertisers covet. A communications medium such as radio or television can be construed solely as a dollar-making business only until it collapses from its own dead weight. Creative personnel in exasperation will forsake mechanical, uncreative, uninspiring routine. And audiences will also forsake repetitious, imitative sounds and sights punctuated by endless strings of staccato commercials. Meanwhile, by default of on-air broadcasting, aggressive, audience-oriented alternative systems such as cable and cassettes will inherit commercial on-air TV and radio's creative challenge, along with its audience, and eventually its advertising base.

In this writer's judgment, American broadcasting must stress service as a medium of communicating human values; managers must see to it that the sales function serves a secondary role supporting that central purpose.

In our American system of commercial broadcasting, the dichotomy will undoubtedly persist: broadcasters and advertisers will continue to be confronted by critics and academics. Perhaps the mass audience is alternately drawn to or represented by both sides. And the Federal government oscillates between the two poles, acting as an ambivalent referee for "all" the people and all parties to the continuing debate.

Broadcasting and Government

To speak of braodcasting is necessarily to speak of government. The limited availability of frequencies occasioned, in 1927, the entry of Federal lawmakers into the realm of airwave utilization.[66] It must be remembered that in a nation with representative government, where the airwaves are considered to be a natural resource, the *people's* rights are paramount. Thus, for example, First Amendment rights pertain not only to the private broadcaster, but also to the public who theoretically own the airwaves (and who have invested a greater dollar total in the medium than have broadcast companies). Therefore, a broadcaster is expected to protect the First Amendment rights of that public, being in a real sense a keeper of the public trust. And so a professional broadcast manager should not worry exclusively about his *own* Constitutional right to broadcast what *he* wants; he should also be concerned with the *public's* right to be exposed to as wide a range of content as possible, because that is what the free marketplace of ideas is all about.

For the public to be exposed to as wide a range of ideas as possible is different from saying that most people (the majority) should simply get what they *want*. For sometimes the broadcaster will serve minority interests (cultural, ideological, as well as ethnic) by offering what those minorities want and what the majority may well *need*. Living in a democracy, we must be an informed public—sharing pluralistic views and judgments and tastes.

This raises the question: even if media do present wide-ranging, diverse, and alternative views, can we have enough faith in the public so to inform themselves? Typically, the mass public tends to use mass media in a "mass" way—not for forming substantive opinion or reaching decisions, but for entertainment and escapist relaxation. The public does, however, have a right to the *opportunity* to be informed. The pluralism of diverse views must at least be available in order for "the people" to make informed, valid decisions, if a democratic republic is to be sustained and even strengthened. This reflects the public's right to *know*—prior even to the right to speak ("access" to media), which itself is based on the public's right to *hear* ideas that are spoken. Public office-holders in government are elected by the people as their surrogates, so presumably "they know" what the people want and need. But broadcasters claim that they also are "elected" by the people by virtue of public support in audience responsiveness to kinds of programming available.[67]

Therefore, in a pluralistic, democratic society based on free enterprise, it seems appropriate for the respective needs and concerns to be continually advocated by the several interested parties: broadcasters, government, advertisers, and the public (including consumer and citizen groups, because the single individual cannot be pitted against sprawling corporations owning broadcast properties, nor can the individual effectively cope with massive government and its maze of agencies). If any one party to the continuing debate, by default or by excessive power, begins to referee for all the others then we are in trouble. This is part of what truly "free enterprise" is about. It seems that a "multiple adversary" process will keep all parties more responsible and responsive to the varied needs of society *vis-à-vis* mass media. And, after all, isn't an uneasy coexistence between the broadcaster and the regulator a reasonably valid relationship?

Even within government itself there exists an internal balancing function that protects against excess. (Unfortunately, these counter-forces also insulate against efficient overseeing of broadcasting's performance.)

Within the *Federal Communications Commission* there has been both successive and simultaneous diversity of opinion, particularly in the past decade.[68] Individual commissioners, as well as the Broadcast Bureau staff and the FCC's hearing examiners and judges, often differed in their recommendations and conclusions as they applied Commission policy.

Meanwhile, dozens of *Congressional* committees and subcommittees alternately queried the Commissioners and broadcast leaders about their respective responsibilities with the public trust of the airwaves.[69] Within those subcommittees, predictably, there was wide divergence of opinions about policies and practices affecting the broadcast industry.

Over against Congress and its regulatory agency was the *executive* branch, where presidential concerns were expressed with increasing frequency and intensity by Presidents Kennedy, Johnson, and Nixon—until the Watergate debacle of 1973–74 dramatically lessened the Ford administration's leverage, both directly and through its Office of Telecommunications Policy.

Finally, less influenced by political or economic or personal ties than the other branches of government, the *judiciary*—particularly the appellate court of the District of Columbia and the U.S. Supreme Court—sometimes supported, sometimes reversed the Commission's judgments on controverted issues. Opinions and votes by those justices often differed among themselves.[69a]

Thus Federal government has not been a monolithic harassment or obstacle to broadcasting's stability and growth. In areas related to First Amendment rights, in fact, the broadcasters can expect to find growing Federal support for wide-ranging discretion in their exercise of media freedom.

Licensing and Regulating. The central arena of FCC activity in broadcasting involves the licensing process. Although half a decade may seem a long period for licensing a station to operate, this author strongly recommends a five-year license. Beyond the broadcasters' own substantial considerations of long-term investment, stability of personnel, program development, and audience acceptance, the FCC can aptly appraise a half-decade of performance and make a reasonable judgment about a licensee's sustained service to the community. It is important to note that the Commission's present workload can make staff review of triennial renewals somewhat routine. But by cutting almost in half the load of broadcast license processing, Congress should demand that the Commission and its staff review very carefully every station whose record is criticized or questioned over that period of time. Again, five years gives potential complainants as well as broadcasters a significant length of time to prove their respective claims. This seems especially appropriate since the FCC now requires broadcasters to make available annually, even to the public, various kinds of reports. Stewardship can be looked into at any time during the half decade. Nothing in a longer licensing time precludes interim review or investigation of current and significant matters. The Commission may well issue warnings, cautionary requirements, and even monetary penalties—all short of and not directly involved with license renewal. A longer licensing period can help the Commission be a serious and effective regulatory agency, exploring controverted matters seriously, thoroughly, and expeditiously, for the benefit of both complainants and licensees.

In past decades, the threat of license revocation has tended to be mostly just that: a threat. The result has often been to stimulate broadcasters to more conscientious service of their communities. But rarely have threats resulted in denying licenses to incumbents. Of 37,000 license renewals over a 25-year period, only 72 licenses were revoked or denied renewal.[70] In 45 years of broadcast legislation, a total of only 78 licenses were lost by broadcasters.[71]

In recent years, major threats to renewals were generated by citizen groups who challenged licenses. Except for a few instances, the FCC rarely penalized broadcasters so challenged. Those expensive, time-consuming investigations and hearings did serve to prompt broadcasters to more careful stewardship of their service to the public. Typically, broadcasters do tend to be responsive to pressures; perhaps the status and momentum of their industry causes them to respond only to counter-forces matching their own. By the mid-1970s, the continuing warfare had subsided, with the FCC prodding procedures for reasonable and reasoned debate between licensee and challenger, to achieve some resolution without recourse to the Federal regulatory agency. Unfit or capricious or self-serving challengers found it increasingly difficult to use the license-renewal process as a forum for exacting special treatment from harrassed broadcasters. But at the same time broadcasters have been given notice that citizens can indeed mobilize to counter licensees' favored status as incumbents if appropriate program service is not provided for by management.

Some broadcasters have urged the FCC to determine guidelines so conscientious broadcasters can avoid ambiguity and caprice by the Commission's bureaus and staff. Multi-station owner Gordon McLendon pleaded eloquently for such standards, and Donald McGannon of Westinghouse's Group W also urged criteria defining substantial public service for "broad programming components (news, public affairs and locally originated programs) which make up a licensee's overall service to the public" in order to aid the broadcaster and the public, as well as the Commission, in evaluating that service.[72] The U.S. Court of Appeals for the District of Columbia in 1971 had recommended that the FCC establish both quantitative and qualitative criteria for "superior performance" as a guide and incentive to broadcasters. But the court reversed, as unduly favoring incumbents, the FCC's plan to renew without hearing licenses of stations that demonstrated they had "substantially" served their communities.[73] The question of what constitutes "substantial service" needs careful consideration by management as well as regulators.

The Commission had been burned before when it tried to adopt the NAB's own commercial time-limit standards. So in the 1970s the Commission employed the successful tactic of finessing the NAB into tightening its own Code provisions for children's programming and commercials, and for early evening "family viewing" content in programs scheduled between 7 and 9 P.M. The Commission meanwhile entered into a Constitutional and regulatory jungle of program-related decisions occasioned by several successive rule-makings about prime-time service by national networks to stations in the top 50 markets. The appellate court also edged the FCC into considering program content when it demanded that the agency consider the format change proposed by an applicant for transfer of radio license to new ownership. (The Supreme Court's "Red Lion" decision in June of 1969 had affirmed the constitutionality of the Commission's views regarding programming involvement; even the NAB's general counsel saw in that decision support for the FCC's authority to determine criteria for minimum percentages of program types.)

These and other issues, such as network re-runs of programs, brought the FCC increasingly into attempting to regulate matters possibly beyond its competence or its jurisdiction. The coming decade will force government and broadcasters to hammer out some resolution of this highly complex and enormously significant area.

This author's view is that the interplay of pluralistic counter-forces among broadcasters, audience, critics, advertisers, and creative artists and producers should shape the medium, emphasizing human values in the total broadcast service. The less government involvement, the better. Only when the public and the broadcaster cannot resolve their differences should minimal government involvement be sought. Because the basis for Federal regulation was originally spectrum scarcity of radio frequencies, the proliferation of all kinds of radio stations in recent decades—AM and FM, maximum power and low-power, commercial and non-commercial, broad program service and specialized formats—indicates that "scarcity" is hardly any longer a criterion for regulating radio.[74] Massive unburdening of radio station licensees seems wholly appropriate. The FCC must eliminate repetitious and non-significant, ineffectual paperwork processing, so that it can concentrate on the truly important cases and on patterns of policy appraisal. (Likewise, management must take greater care in preparing license renewal applications; carelessness or incomplete or unclear data in renewal forms and documentation accounted for one-third of all delays in FCC's processing of AM radio license renewals.)[75]

Countering this author's view, citizen groups and critics in recent years sought stricter control over broadcasting by the Federal government. Sometimes broadcasters brought this concern and criticism on themselves, such as when employing superficial and careless procedures and methodologies for ascertaining their communities' needs and wants. But serious broadcasters have usually endeavored to determine the true concerns of their audiences, compiling massive evidence at great expense as part of their program research instead of merely as an exercise to satisfy FCC requirements. Track records of stations and managers suggest that those with discretion and honest concern to serve their publics will have little trouble with consumers or citizen groups or with the Commission.

The "public interest, convenience, and necessity" will never be adequately described or defined. It is the broadcast manager's professional task to reflect on the impact of his medium and on his responsibility to contribute to the public through the program service of his station or network. Too often, that phrase has been interpreted to be simply "what the freight will bear"—in audiences' casual habits of viewing/listening, in audiences' and advertisers' tolerance for commercial clutter, in critics' forbearance of mediocre programming, in minorities' minimal demands or challenges. Instead of looking to external forces, including legal counsel and government, to determine technical applications of that phrase, the broadcast managers and their creative staffs should attempt to clarify for themselves what it means to serve the public's true interest and necessity as well as convenience. That effort must ultimately be manifest in the broadcasters' program service.

Programming

Over-the-air, advertising-supported broadcasting will have to respond to the challenge posed by cable and pay TV, cassette videoplayers, and even "guerrilla" underground TV, as they move forward onto the scene. Perhaps the best way for television not merely to survive but to flourish with new life is to meet head-on the challenges occasioned by new forms of communication media.

Thus, for example, the present system of television and radio must react to the fragmentation of audience necessitated by multi-channel cable. This means broadcast content must continue to be mass-oriented in both entertainment and news, including major events of broad public interest and concern. Broadcasting must compete aggressively with cable's low-budgeted, often nonprofessional characteristics of locally-originated programming; this calls for careful technical engineering and artfully conceived presentations, as well as increased emphasis on "live" and local as well as national content. Similarly, in order to counter the convenient availability of cassettes with their prerecorded material, on-air television must emphasize "live" and remote-location programming that brings into the home in real-time as it is happening the dynamic world of "now" in sight and sound.

Radio stations likewise ought to compete aggressively with the prepackaged recordings of tape and disc by emphasizing programming that is "live," community-oriented, audience-involving, and person-directed.

The aesthetic of a medium—as its ethic—is derived from the very nature of that medium. A *mass* medium, therefore, ought to attempt to reach enormous numbers of individuals. Further, the essence of speed-of-light broadcasting includes the characteristics of immediacy, spontaneity, and intimacy. But by the mid-1970s, tape and film reduced real-time *immediacy* to special-event "live" coverage such as sports, disasters, and presidential press conferences (the latter sometimes partaking of the first two categories). *Spontaneity* was all but lost by audio- and videotape's gradual dominance in studio procedure (except where editing was used only rarely, as in lengthy talk-interview entertainment programs). *Intimacy* is the one characteristic still perduring; individual viewer/listeners concentrate on the screen and loudspeaker because the host-MC or newsperson or singer is communicating as if one-to-one. As those three qualities of immediacy, spontaneity, and intimacy are restored and strengthened, over-the-air broadcasting will meet successfully the threat of new modes of sight-and-sound media.

A further characteristic of broadcasting must be *diversity*. While broadcasting is intended to be received by a mass public, it must still attempt to provide the many "publics" with a range of alternate choices in media experiences. This author strongly recommends that broadcast managers strive for authentic diversity in content and scheduling. Years ago Fred Allen sardonically lamented that "imitation is the sincerest form of television"; the medium must outgrow this dependence on sameness.

Serious attention must be given to creating programs that properly stimulate the minds and imaginations of young children—not only in the "kiddy ghetto" of Saturday and Sunday mornings, but also in the late-afternoon and early-evening hours. The "family viewing" concept of early prime-time, introduced in 1975, must not deteriorate into a merely mechanical response to pressure from critics. Programs for those hours should be created which will contribute to the growth of children and to supporting family values.

The wide-ranging studies about the effects on society of media violence and sex offer widely conflicting conclusions; that disparity of judgment makes this area—including the scheduling of programs with mature themes and treatment—a vexing challenge to the conscientious broadcaster.

As for commercials, enlightened self-interest hopefully will prompt broadcasters and advertisers to watch diligently over the commercial aspects of their operations so that a minimum of bird-dogging is required by the Federal Trade Commission and other governmental agencies. The cooperation of Better Business Bureaus and advertising associations can assist in policing advertising. And the NAB Code Authority must be supported strongly if broadcasters expect to demonstrate their mature response to the challenge of programming into the nation's homes.

Broadcast content and scheduling must also reflect responsible hiring and training of minority persons, to assist capable minority citizens to reach into their communities through local media—as on-air talent, as staff persons, and eventually as managers in decision-making positions at stations and networks.

News. Much has been researched and written about the enormous and complex area of broadcast journalism: news, documentaries, public affairs programming. It is difficult to assess adequately the impact of news in contemporary society. That there is impact seems evident; but the kinds and intensity of influence on the public is not always clear. In the meantime, broadcasters must be acutely aware of their responsibility to reflect the world of reality to people whose experience is limited and even replaced by the second-hand experience of "reality" as broadcast into their homes.

Marshall McLuhan sharply disagrees with those who condemn electronic media for creating apathy, indifference, and merely passive exposure to events through the surrogate of television cameras and radio microphones. On the contrary, McLuhan insists that mass media cause people to "know too much about each other. Our new environment compels commitment and participation. We have become irrevocably involved with, and responsible for, each other." [76] He asserts that "the living room has become a voting booth. Participation via television in Freedom Marches, in war, revolution, pollution, and other events is changing *everything.*" The entire community gradually becomes involved in the central acts of decision, as classically evidenced in the Vietnam struggle for American support, and in the Watergate revelations and counter-strategies through media by critics and executive branch and courts, until the final crisis and denouement of presidential resignation and eventual transfer of powers to two non-elected executives.

Former Vice President Spiro Agnew once cautioned against this power of national networks and their news presentations:

> Now, my friends, we'd never trust such power, as I've described, over public opinion in the hands of an elected government. It's time we questioned it in the hands of a small and unelected elite. The great networks have dominated America's airwaves for decades. The people are entitled to a full accounting of their stewardship.[77]

Perhaps television's "power" is often in the eye of the beholder; criticism of TV news can likewise be highly subjective. For example, networks were castigated for their coverage of the disorders and riots at the Democratic National Convention in Chicago in 1968. Critics claimed that the networks distorted reality by turning cameras and microphones away from convention proceedings to focus unduly on those "peripheral" chaotic events (despite their intrinsic significance as unprecedented public activity in such a context). Yet, one count reported that

> CBS allotted 32 minutes to demonstrations out of a total of 38 hours and 3 minutes. Out of 19 hours and 37 minutes of convention coverage, NBC devoted only 14 minutes to film or tape coverage of disorders involving demonstrations and police.[78]

Significantly, despite Mr. Agnew's reference to the government's lack of power through media, the Federal government has not altogether been outpaced in strategic use of mass media:

> By 1967 the federal government was spending more than $400 million a year on public relations and public information. The Executive branch, in fact, spends more on publicity, news, views, publications, and special pleadings than is spent to operate the entirety of the Legislative and Judicial branches. All together, federal expenditures on telling and showing the taxpayers are more than double the combined costs of news gathering by the two major U.S. wire services, the three major television networks, and the ten largest American newspapers.[79]

Perhaps a new form of political life has emerged in recent decades, whereby the government gains the assent of those governed by artfully conducted orchestration of the media. Certainly the Nixon administration was well aware of the power of television to capture the attention of the nation's viewers, who ascribe higher credibility to television than to other mass media.[80]

What about this credibility invested in broadcast media? The people's perception of television as most believable among media should alert broadcasters to their grave responsibility in presenting local and national news. Although Congressmen heavily favored newspapers over broadcasting as the most objective news medium, several independent national surveys over a span of recent years showed that the large majority of Americans looked to television as the most trustworthy and most influential mass medium.[81] By late 1974, the relative credibility of television news was two and one-half times as great as that of newspapers (51% to 20%, of almost 2,000 interviewees responding to which medium they would most likely believe if several media presented conflicting reports of the same news story).[82]

We may safely conclude that the popular mind is much influenced by television news. Robert Sarnoff noted more than a decade ago that "NBC News reaches more homes than the combined circulation of *Life, Look, Time, Newsweek* and *U.S. News and World Report* plus the total circulation of all major dailies in New York, Chicago, and Los Angeles." [83] And yet a major study discovered that slightly less than 50 per cent of the audience for network nightly news can recall even a single story that they viewed.[84] Perhaps John Chancellor's opinion may be closer to the truth: the reason why the public listens to their radios and watches TV news is primarily for *reassurance* that the "ultimate disaster" or even neighborhood catastrophe has not occurred. The audience is also partly mesmerized by the "glow and flow," whereby just having the radio or TV set on with its intermittent news outpourings makes them feel they are in touch with the rhythm of the world, without even having to give attention to the specific sights and sounds of the news. And those people who do seek information from broadcast news receive mostly a headline service with few details and almost no investigative or judgmental content.

This author would support the recommendations of Donald McGannon when he described broadcasting's goals for the 1980s. He noted that, as good as it may have been, there were shortcomings in broadcast coverage of the tumultuous events of the 1960s, and that television programming became "progressively tired and tiring entertainment irrelevant to the times." He called for "further expansion of news and information programs to background, clarify and make understandable news items and headlines." He further called "for the great instruments of broadcasting to do more than report and explain problems"; he urged that the time had come for radio and television to help solve those problems in society.[85]

The Audience

It is relatively easy to criticize mass media for lapses, excesses, all-pervading banality, or simply for being commerce-oriented in all that it does. But the complexity of modern broadcasting reflects the complexity of contemporary society; and they both reflect the inner complexity of the human person. It is difficult to make a simple assessment in final summation, without adding pages and pages of qualifying distinctions by way of more accurate commentary.

This author is generally impressed with the drama and news and public-event programs that appear on television, and by the around-the-clock service that radio offers the average person. Almost whatever we want or are interested in is already available to us in the media, although often not at the ideal times of day. But there is a range of worthwhile content in commercial broadcasting that is rarely acknowledged.

The vagaries of popular taste, and the inconsistency of public criticism, make the broadcast manager's honest effort to serve the public's true "interest, convenience, and necessity" an almost impossible task. The top-ten television programs, the radio stations most successful in attracting enormous audiences, all reflect light and even ephemeral content. Quality programming typically plummets towards the bottom of rating lists year after year. The public seeks simply light entertainment; often it will not tolerate substance. "The indulgence of the public only emboldens mediocrity; it causes genius to blush, and discourages it." That is no less true today than it was in 1792 when Friedrich von Schiller wrote it in his *On Tragic Art*. A five-volume study of the Elizabethan stage was praised by a reviewer because its author correctly "assumed . . . that London playhouses were producers of entertainment, rather than storehouses for playwrights"; [86] that can be aptly said as well of CBS Television City in Hollywood. In our own day, we have been glib to criticize broadcast media for being "tainted by commerce and trimmed by compromise"; yet those were exactly the words used by Robert Spaeight in appraising the theater of Shakespeare's time.

We should reflect on more than 2,000 years of staged drama, and consider how many theatrical plays of those centuries we even know, much less care about or read or stage in our own time. We can recall that of 8,000 plays copyrighted each year and recorded in the Library of Congress, only 80 plays are produced (for highly selective audiences) annually on or near Broadway, of which 15 to 20 may be moderately successful. We must therefore wonder at the enormity of the challenge to broadcast managers to program quality content to the total national audience of 210 million people 365 days a year. The fact that the medium produces several outstanding multi-hour presentations a month deserves more praise than the meager annual productivity of Broadway.

Books have been with us since moveable type for over 600 years. How many books of true significance and public acceptance are published annually? Daily newspapers have been around for more than a century. Movies have been on the scene three-quarters of a century. But radio was first heard clearly in the land in 1920. Television has elbowed its way through exuberant adolescence and is now just beyond its teens. As a mid-twenty-year-old, it continues to try to find itself, to achieve its proper identity in society. Hopefully, as it emerges into young adulthood, it will grow in stature and become the leader that our land longs for—in substantive drama, in perceptive and balanced news reporting and commentary, in refreshing and re-creating entertainment, and in more adroit and mature reserve in handling its commercial commitments.

While broadcasting must operate among forces that are interdependent in society, it must also accept the mandate to grow and mature. It must become independent with an identity of its own—not clinging in sustained adolescence to economic or regulatory or even popular-audience minimal demands. Aware of the audience's general tastes and its own immaturity as a medium, but committed to grow, broadcasting must provide the public with human values through quality program service. As they push beyond awkward adolescence, the maturing symbol-makers of radio and television must offer programming that gradually leads—responsive to the best, and not only the popular and common, in the mass audience. Franklin Dunham's optimistic challenge still echoes with relevance: "Give the public what it *wants* most of the time, and something of what it *would* want if it only knew about it!"

Frankly, this author is encouraged by what, on balance, the record shows about broadcasting. The arena of mass media is by no means hopeless. It is filled with challenge for the "guys and gals with guts" who can bring personal values and professional competence to the demanding role of broadcast management.

And so, instead of looking to the past years of broadcasting as the pattern of a wretched giant, I consider it the record of a magnificent adolescent. The coming decade will demonstrate, I trust, the maturing of a medium which can truly serve all the publics of this nation. Broadcast managers are needed who can guide broadcasting so that it becomes an active participant in the worldwide search for peace and unity among peoples.

THE PROFESSIONAL'S VIEW

by Ward L. Quaal

As we conclude these humble efforts in pleasant association with Dr. Brown, there are many thoughts that come before one as broadcasting in the mid-1970s is reviewed and appraised.

In preparing these final comments for this revised version of *Broadcast Management,* I can't help but reflect upon almost 41 years in broadcasting, a career that started while a freshman in high school in Michigan's Upper Peninsula.

In this span of four decades, I have experienced the good fortune of working in all areas of broadcasting from a small station of 100 watts in 1934, to the responsibilities of managing a major group owner with radio, television, CATV and additional subsidiary companies.

Broadcasting is where it is today because we are the greatest and the freest nation ever evolved in the history of mankind. We owe so much to our founding fathers, and we find ourselves in a situation today where actually it would be comforting to many of us if we could apologize to them for that which we now find lacking in our schools, our houses of worship and our homes. These great forefathers inspired all of us and they helped build this lovely land in which you and I have the good fortune to live, work, worship, and to educate our children.

Obviously, I am very much in love with our country, but also, with our great profession, the arts and the many fine people who constitute American broadcasting—free enterprise broadcasting that was born, nurtured and matured in these United States.

It is my great regret that some of the newer generations, both within and outside our profession, either never learned or have forgotten the basic tenets of *free enterprise* in our *free society.* They have lost touch with the spirit, the dedication, the zeal and the wisdom of the architects of what was then known as *broadcasting by the American plan* which since has been adopted in every free nation on earth *in toto* or in some modified fashion—adopted throughout the world because it is the most *solid!*

Let us *all* underscore *what is right in broadcasting!* There is *much* that is *right* about broadcasting! The present and the future offer that grand opportunity to all of us to plan the dynamic decades that lie ahead, decades that will see radio and television achievements that will dwarf even the magnificence of all the greatest feats performed since radio's first reporting of a political convention in the early 1920s to the glamour and the drama of the coverage of the moon shots and, one of the truly fine "hours" of television, in the reporting of the summer games of the Olympiad in Munich and countless other radio and television achievements, locally and nationally.

Over the years in this profession of ours, I have had many hesitations about many executive alignments in various companies. I believe I know the elements that make for success. I think I know how essential is *teamwork!*

It distresses me to find in government, in industry of all types, in sports, and certainly above all else, in our profession, the idea that the executive-head is *of all purposes* and all powerful. Let us face it, no executive is stronger than his team.

Most rewarding to me as a broadcaster who has devoted his entire adult life and much of his youth to broadcasting as a profession is to find so many individuals entering our colleges and univerisites determined to make a mark in this industry of ours. Certainly, it would appear that there will be no shortage of talented persons in all phases of broadcasting in the years to come.

Let us hope that these youngsters will realize the pioneering efforts of those who have come before us and those who are active today. Inexorably, we must look ahead as technology advances, styles change, and fundamental philosophies in government and business undergo transitions. Today's extraordinary advances—giving to this country the unquestioned world leadership in telecommunications—can be traced in direct lines to the wisdom of these men who envisioned the *dangers* of government versus private enterprise, of the free "radio press" versus government censorship! To our readers, let me say, our only "censor" should be that peerless combination of quality enriched with good taste!

In working with Dr. Brown on this book and looking to the past, analyzing the present and humbly attempting to preview the future, I would be very remiss if I did not select one man in the history of communications law who did the most to safeguard those inherent First Amendment freedoms that we cherish. I refer, of course, to the late Louis G. Caldwell, attorney of Washington and Chicago, and the first General Counsel (in 1927) of the Federal Radio Commission, the forerunner of today's FCC. A colorful, white-maned, brilliant man whose honesty and integrity were a legend, he wrote most of those provisions of the early radio law that were so sound in principle that they remain the keystone of the Communications Act of 1934, which otherwise has been so twisted and distorted by Congressional "patchwork," ridiculous FCC interpretations, and outlandish court actions as to make it punitive, as well as *contradictory!*

Mr. Caldwell was my mentor and my benefactor. I learned from him logic I shall never forget. Mr. Caldwell was aware of our awesome responsibilities as licensees and he never allowed his clients to forget them. But he never backed away from an encounter where fundamental free enterprise concepts were involved. Louis Caldwell was perhaps the most unforgettable person that it has been my good fortune to know! There are others, long departed, who were men of courage and integrity and who had great influence, not only upon my life, which is really unimportant, but upon the development of the broadcast media in the best interests of our nation and our people, and in the American tradition of being entitled to the rewards of their labors and of risking their

capital in pioneering radio, and latterly, television in which the losses were as-
tronomical during the first years of the industry.

It is only proper in these closing paragraphs of this book to mention a few
of these sincere and dedicated men: General David Sarnoff; Edwin W. Craig of
WSM, Nashville; Harold V. Hough of WBAP; James D. Shouse of CBS and
of Crosley-AVCO; and Earle C. Anthony of KFI, Los Angeles.

We owe an enormous debt to others of that first generation who are still
here—stalwart defenders of our system and men who are as young in zeal and
dedication as they were when it was fun to be a broadcaster with the rewards
indeed slim. Among these are such innovators and fine gentlemen as George
Storer, Sr., Rosel H. Hyde, Frank Stanton, J. Leonard Reinsch, Clair Mc-
Cullough, Stanley E. Hubbard, and John Fetzer, to name only a few.

I will not resort to an extreme effort to exhort all of our readers to defend
the freedom and the sanctity of American broadcasting. That is why you are in
our profession or you are studying to enter it, and indeed, it is the reason for
being for all of us. It is also the reason for the being of the National Association of Broadcasters which, in recent years, under the able leadership of Vincent T. Wasilewski, has made many more achievements than at any prior time
in its history. Let us face it, it is our *obligation* to defend that which you and
our predecessors fashioned by *popular demand*—the expressed wishes of a nation of 240 million Americans—including the 3% of self-anointed intellectuals
who preach, but seldom practice what they preach!

No one reading these remarks is going to say that everything is perfect in
our profession. Indeed, perfection has never obtained in more than 500 years of
print, 2,000 years of the theatre or in any other phase of our various ways of
life; but we in broadcasting have reached maturity far ahead of most businesses
and most professions and we should stand tall, and indeed, very proud. In the
words of that fine man of note, Johnny Mercer, let us strive to *eliminate* the
"negative" and *accentuate* the "positive"—let us all acclaim what is *right*
about broadcasting!

Now, finally, as we observe America's 200th anniversary, let us remember the accomplishments, not just of the American system of broadcasting,
but the accomplishments of all Americans! Let us think of those steps that we
can take to make American broadcasting better and more responsible; and that
certainly we can do, for we are far from the perfected state. Let us above all,
address ourselves to the importance of the re-writing of the Communications
Act of 1934, as amended. In this broadcaster's long career, it has been his hope
that some day, and hopefully soon, the Act will be re-written with the precious
First Amendment to the Constitution as the foundation of the new legislation.
Let us never forget that broadcasting cannot grow and prosper and better serve
the people of America unless it is just as free as the printed press!

Let us hope that those in the positions of authority will recognize that
broadcasting should have this total freedom! This would be the greatest gift of
all to all of the people of America involving the media that mean the most to
them 365 days of the year, every year of their lives.

NOTES

Chapter 10

1. David L. Jaffe, "CATV: History and Law," *Educational Broadcasting,* July/August 1974, pp. 15–17, 34–36; "High Court Upholds FCC's Ruling On Program Origination by Large CATV Systems; Tight, 'Nervous' Vote," *Variety,* June 14, 1972, p. 31.

2. FCC, *Cable Television Service; Cable Television Relay Service,* Section 76.201(a), p. 3287.

3. "More Local Programs with Better Quality Going Over Cable," *Broadcasting,* September 9, 1974, p. 62.

4. Sloan Commission on Cable Communications, [Report] *On the Cable: The Television of Abundance* (N.Y.: McGraw-Hill, 1971), pp. 167–168.

5. Bernard Gallagher, "The Gallagher Report," May 14, 1973, p. 1.

6. Frederick W. Ford and Lee G. Lovett, "A New Signal Heard," *BM/E–CM/E* [Broadcast Management/Engineering—Cable Management/Engineering], July 1974, pp. 16, 18.

7. "At Deadline: Court Ruling Sets Cable Liability on Distant Signals for First Time," *Broadcasting,* March 12, 1973, p. 12.

8. "Regulation Only Heads the List of Cable's Problems," *Broadcasting,* April 22, 1974, p. 26.

9. "FCC Issues First Sequel to 1972 Cable Rules," *Broadcasting,* April 22, 1974, pp. 22–23. See also text of the FCC's major report and order of 1972: "The FCC Delivers on Cable: After Years of Debate and Quarrel, CATV Gets Blueprint for Expansion; Question Now is Whether It Will Stick," *Broadcasting,* February 7, 1972, pp. 17–18, 21–36, 40, 44.

10. "NCTA Stunned by Tough Wiley Speech," *Variety,* April 24, 1974, pp. 37, 47.

11. "How Teleprompter Figures to Weave a Cable Network," *Broadcasting,* March 19, 1973, pp. 114–115.

12. "TV Indies' Joy Ride on Cable: Turning Into Regional Webs," *Variety,* November 29, 1972, pp. 43, 51.

13. "A Short Course in Cable, 1975," *Broadcasting,* April 14, 1974, p. 56.

14. "Cable TV Begins to Have Impact on Broadcast Advertising," The Gallagher Report, May 7, 1973, p. 3.

15. Vincent T. Wasilewski, "Pay-Cable Feared by NAB as a Siphon of TV Program Staples," *Variety,* January 8, 1975, pp. 97, 106.

16. "A Short Course in Cable, 1974" *Broadcasting,* April 22, 1974, p. 23; "A Short Course in Cable, 1975," *Broadcasting,* April 14, 1975, p. 56.

17. Even back in 1972, one cable executive cautioned about the fiscal challenge to cable's stability: "The total national savings-to-investment flow of new funds to corporate users is at a rate of only $25 to $30 billion a year. Of this the utilities, including the telephone company, take over half. *No other single industry—not the airlines, not the gas transmission lines, not the railroads—attract capital at a rate in excess of $1 billion a year, which is the rate at which cable must attract in order to reach a 40 per cent saturation in 10 years"* (italics in the original); Amos Hostetter, executive vice president of Continental Cablevision, at the 21st Annual Convention of the National Cable Television Association in Chicago, May, 1972; quoted in "The Videocassette & CATV Newsletter," May 1972, p. 13. Later that same year, Robert W. Sarnoff, chairman of RCA, looked to the linking of CATV systems into larger entities that would provide an electronics market of from $2 to $4 billion annually within ten years; "New, Competitive Marts Envisioned by RCA Head," United Press International article from London; Pomona, Calif. *Progress-Bulletin,* December 3, 1972, p. A-11. By late 1974, the three national television networks enjoyed unparalleled profits in spite of the nation's economic slump, so investors looked to them rather than to the slackened cable industry; Larry Michie, "Webs' Boom Dims Cable, Public TV," *Variety,* September 18, 1974, p. 1. See Herman W. Land Associates, Inc., *Television and the Wired City* (Washington, D.C.: National Assoc. of Broadcasters, 1968). Cf. Sydney W. Head, *Broadcasting*

in America (Boston: Houghton Mifflin, 1972), pp. 101, 242–243; also Ellen Cohn, "Wired-City Blues," *TV Guide,* August 24, 1974, pp. 6–8.

18. "A Short Course in Cable, 1975," *Broadcasting,* April 14, 1975, p. 56.

19. Paul Klein, "The Case for Pay Television," *Variety,* January 8, 1975, pp. 97, 106.

20. Vincent T. Wasilewski, "Pay Cable . . . ," *Variety,* January 8, 1975, pp. 97, 106. See also Walter S. Baer, *Cable Television: A Handbook for Decisionmaking* (Santa Monica, Calif.: The Rand Corporation, 1973).

21. Frank Beermann, "Still No Real Hope for 4th Network: Should It Come, It'll Be Cable," *Variety,* September 8, 1974, pp. 41, 68.

22. James Wechsler, *New York Post;* quoted by Wasilewski, "Pay Cable . . . ," *Variety,* January 8, 1975, pp. 97, 106.

23. John A. Niemi, "CATV in North America: Two Contrasting Patterns," *Educational Broadcasting,* July/August 1974, pp. 37–38.

24. David Lachenbruch, "Pay-TV Makes a Comeback," *TV Guide,* February 24, 1973, pp. 5–8; "Little Black Boxes and Self-Destructing Tickets," *TV Guide,* March 3, 1973, pp. 28–34.

25. Press release of Zenith Radio Corporation, March 10, 1965.

26. Public Relations Director, "Subscription Television: What It Is—Answers to Your Questions About Subscription Television," Zenith Radio Corporation, Chicago, Ill. [n.d.]; pp. 9–10.

27. "Zenith Now Eyeing Chicago for Pay TV," *Broadcasting,* August 23, 1971, p. 37. But cf. *Broadcasting Yearbook 1974* which does not list such ownership.

28. *National Association of Theatre Owners and Joint Committee Against Toll TV v. FCC,* 420 F. (2d) 194 (1969). See Sydney W. Head, *Broadcasting in America* (Boston: Houghton Mifflin, 1972), p. 241.

29. Described by David Lachenbruch, "Little Black Boxes . . . ," *TV Guide,* March 3, 1973, pp. 29–34.

30. Cf. Sydney W. Head, *Broadcasting in America,* p. 349 and note number 45.

31. Billboard "Cartridge Television News Digest," July 1971, p. 2.

32. Billboard "Cartridge Television News Digest," November 1971, p. 2.

33. "VidNews," May 15, 1972, p. 1; person quoted was not identified in article. A newsletter by Billboard Publications, Inc.

34. Members of the National Industrial TV Association were surveyed by Billboard publications about the audio/video systems most likely to meet their current and future needs; among the 79 responses (35% return), 87.3% preferred videotape cartridge/cassette with both record and playback capabilities; 54.4% looked to videotape reel-to-reel record & playback equipment as useful; 25.3% judged the videodisc to be effective for their needs; and 11.4% thought that cartridge film, playback only, would be useful to them. "VidNews," February 1972, p. 4.

35. Newspaper headlines chronicle the sequence of promotion and failure: "Cartridge Television Sees Minimum of 100,000 Set Owners By End of Year," *Variety,* April 4, 1973, p. 56; "Cassette Boom or Bust?" *Hollywood Television Report,* June 18, 1973, p. 3; "Cartridge TV's Debacle, $48-Mil Avco Loss," *Variety,* July 4, 1973, p. 1; "Cartridge Television Opts for Chapter XI," *Broadcasting,* July 9, 1973, p. 30; "How Much Red Ink for Cartridge Television," *Broadcasting,* July 23, 1973, p. 27. A year earlier, Richard K. Doan wrote "The Revolution Has Been Postponed: That Heralded Video-Cassette Era Has Run Into Delays," *TV Guide,* June 3, 1972, pp. 6–10. Cf. "VidNews," April 17, 1972, p. 5.

36. *Time* 20, 1964, p. 63.

37. Joseph V. Charyk; from text of speech delivered at the Broadcast Engineering Conference of the NAB, Chicago, March 30, 1966.

38. *Broadcasting,* December 20, 1965, p. 53.

39. *Time,* February 7, 1964, p. 89.

40. *Time,* April 2, 1965, p. 87.

41. *Broadcasting,* July 20, 1964, p. 65.

42. "From Semaphore to Satellite," International Telecommunications Union, Geneva, 1965, p. 333.

43. Roger Field, "Laser Video Is Intriguing, But Is It Useful?" *New York Times,* September 18, 1972, p. 37.

44. "Laser Detection Intrigues Visiting Policemen," *The Cleveland Press,* August 27, 1972 (n.p., reprint); and Raphael Schlesinger, "Electronic Vigil Guards U. Circle," *The* [Cleveland] *Plain Dealer* (n.d., n.p., reprint).

45. Gene Youngblood, *Expanded Cinema* (N.Y.: E. P. Dutton, 1970), pp. 399–403.

46. Youngblood, p. 399.

47. Noted by Robert W. Sarnoff, chairman of RCA, Inc.; 70 per cent of the $4-billion firm is in electronics and communication, and its research and development program annually totals about $130 million: "New, Competitive Marts Envisioned by RCA Head," United Press International article from London; Pomona, Calif. *Progress-Bulletin,* December 3, 1972, p. A-11.

48. Bruce Lane, "New Forms of Television Exhibition—the Electric Film-Maker," *Cinema* magazine, Spring 1972, pp. 8–11.

49. *Broadcasting,* December 20, 1965, p. 52.

50. Harold H. Martin, "David Sarnoff's Vision," *Saturday Evening Post,* February 16, 1963, pp. 56–59.

51. Robert W. Sarnoff; from text of speech delivered at Bryant College in Providence, R.I., July 25, 1964.

51a. See Robert H. Stanley (ed.), *The Broadcast Industry: An Examination of Major Issues* (N.Y.: Hastings House, 1975).

52. Advertising executive Clay W. Stephenson has lamented the widespread reluctance of the average individual to accept responsibility for the integrity of his company's product. He labeled this mediocrity and equated it with ethical and aesthetic conformity and with "senseless waste." And he concluded: "Judgments reflect the gutless 'compromise' thinking of committees rather than the imaginative thinking of dedicated individuals." ("Monday Memo," *Broadcasting,* March 26, 1962, p. 28.)

Ralph Nader noted that people tend to remove themselves from responsibility for a company's corporate action which, in terms of genuine public interest, is actually irresponsible. By "just doing their job, they've become complete amoral . . . they therefore become immoral." (In speech at Univ. of Southern California; reported in "Nader Hits Modes of TV Censorship," *Daily Trojan,* May 4, 1971, pp. 1–2).

53. Robert H. Coddington, *Modern Radio Broadcasting; Management and Operation in Small-to-Medium Markets* (Blue Ridge Summit, Pa.: Tab Books, 1969), p. 286. That broadcast executive's comments on pp. 3–4 of his book are worth quoting in full:

> Now, with over twenty years in the industry behind me—years spent in village and metropolis, in AM "peanut-whistle" and maximum-power VHF TV, I must admit that reality did not conform to the future I had envisioned. Recognizing even then the inevitability of television, I failed to foresee that radio would capitulate, rather than compete. I failed to anticipate the general attrition of those elements of talent and variety that had made radio exciting, just as I also did not envision the proliferation of radio stations to the point where competitive strangulation worked to the detriment of programming in general.
>
> In consequence, radio has not been as vital, as interesting a profession as I would have found it ten years earlier. Yet . . . I am encouraged to see the aural medium slowly emerging from its TV-induced doldrums. . . .
>
> This book is *not* intended to be objective. Underlying every page is a persistent idealism, an idealism scarred through the broadcasting years from the blows of imperfect reality; often submerged, perforce—but never subdued. It is this idealism that insists that radio serves a loftier purpose than a narrow profit motive admits; that a station's first objective is to be a constructive force in its community; and that this goal is best pursued by striving for the highest level of professionalism within our reach.

It is not my expectation to convert the experienced broadcaster whose concept of success is limited to financial profit. If anything, radio needs greater diversity, especially as measured by its air product, than it now enjoys. And the experienced broadcaster may find here some statement that provokes him to new accomplishments in justification of his views. The result is bound to enrich the medium.

54. Holbrook Jackson, *The Reading of Books* (Scribner's), quoted in *New York Times* book review section [ca. 1959–60].

55. Rev. R. A. MacKenzie, S.J., pp. 55–56.

56. Nicholas Johnson, "The Coming Victory of the New Television," *The Humanist,* July/August, 1972.

57. Edward R. Murrow, 1958; quoted by Frank Trippett (ed.), "Is the Truth Incredible?" *Look,* September 7, 1971, p. 46.

58. Eric Voegelin, professor of government at Louisiana State University, in a lecture presented to Marquette University conference on communication, March 20–23, 1956; published in *Problems of Communication in a Pluralistic Society* (Milwaukee: Marquette Univ. Press, 1956).

59. Les Brown, "Tomorrow's Technology: Thrusts and Threats," *Variety,* January 5, 1972, p. 75.

60. Jack Gould, *New York Times,* February 1, 1959.

61. Les Brown, speech presented at the annual International Radio and Television Society's Faculty-Industry Seminar, Spring, 1972; from tape cassette produced for IRTS by The Martin S. Sliesler Company: "The Business of Broadcasting."

62. Sol J. Paul, "Publisher's Letter," *Television/Radio Age,* September 3, 1973, p. 10.

63. That distinction was offered by Lawrence Rogers of Taft Broadcasting, speaking at the IRTS Faculty-Industry Seminar in 1973, in Tarrytown, New York. See Charles S. Steinberg (ed.), *Broadcasting: The Critical Challenges* (N.Y.: Hastings House, 1974).

64. Coupled with this critical issue is the matter of equitable sharing of dollar-flow between the networks and their affiliates and among the networks and the program suppliers (production companies). The fluctuating economy in the 1970s caused networks to panic at first (1971–72), then to prosper (1973–75), while production companies found it increasingly difficult to earn adequate income on their activities. More realistic contracts, reflecting the popular success and thus revenue-producing capability of series, seem in order to reward equitably the several entities who risk capital and careers in program product. Although experts in the field had predicted major overhaul or even dissolution of national television networks as we knew them in the 1960s, by mid-1970 the networks were turning more handsome profits than ever in their history; and their future prospects were equally bright. Former CBS-TV vice president for programming, Michael Dann, predicted a radical change in the national television networks by the mid-1970s. But the networks' pre-tax income in 1972 was up 106.5% from the previous year. The next year, those profits soared again more than 66% over the previous year's record. See "1972 A Whopper for TV Biz: Sales at $3-Bil; Profits Up 42%" *Variety,* August 22, 1973, p. 23; and Ernie Kreiling (ed.), "TV Industry Profits Rise," *Hollywood Television Report,* September 9, 1974, p. 5. Profits in 1972 were $110,900,000; in 1973 they were $185,000,000.

65. Ken Draper, executive of Programming db (radio program syndicators), in a lecture to students at the University of Southern California's Dept. of Telecommunications, December 7, 1972.

66. It is worth noting that, although broadcasters typically resent government intrusion into their private, capital-risk business, they invited the assistance of the Federal government in the 1920s; and in the last decade they have sought government help in fending off competitors such as pay TV and cable TV.

67. But critics have long noted that the audience may only "vote" or select from among those programs already provided in schedules. When broadcasters have on rare occasion introduced new formats or content in programming, the public has sometimes discovered that it now "wants" (needs?) the new kind of programming—such as documentaries, special dramas, sophisticated

musicals, creative children's programs. Once again Franklin Dunham's dictum is appropriate: Give the public what it wants most of the time, and also something of what it *would* want if it only knew about it.

68. Rarely has the denunciatory rhetoric of a Nicholas Johnson been heard in Federal agencies; his caustic, even bitter, condemnations of "Big-business broadcasters" won few supporters or even friends within the Commission. The urbane persuasion of Kenneth Cox probably encouraged more thinking along the lines of Johnson's views than did the latter's fulminations. But on the same Commission, Lee Loevinger regularly contested many of his colleagues' principles or applications. Further balance was afforded by chairmen Dean Burch and then Richard Wiley, who sought to hold broadcasters accountable for adequate service to the public but who also understood the realities of the free-enterprise system.

69. The 93rd Congress' second session in 1974 included at least 60 committees and subcommittees which held hearings and prepared reports on matters involving broadcasting. See Robert O. Blanchard (ed.) *Congress and the News Media* (N.Y.: Hastings House, 1974).

69a. See Kenneth S. Devol (ed.), *Mass Media and the Supreme Court: The Legacy of the Warren Years* (N.Y.: Hastings House, 1971).

70. Representative Lionel Van Deerlin (D-Calif.), member of the House Communications subcommittee, cited data in 1973; quoted by *Broadcasting,* January 22, 1973, p. 23.

71. Data cited by a group of professors from the University of Wisconsin, in letter to Representative Torbert S. Macdonald (D-Mass.), chairman of the House Subcommittee on Communications; quoted by *Variety,* May 23, 1973, p. 56.

72. Donald McGannon, quoted by *Variety,* April 18, 1973, p. 50.

73. See *Variety,* June 16, 1971, p. 27.

74. The scarcity argument loses weight when one considers the 1,750 daily newspaper in the United States, compared with 7,000 commercial radio stations and 700 commercial television stations. In some ways there is more "accessibility" for ideas and communication in broadcasting than in print media.

75. As for the paper-work in license renewal applications, the WCBS-TV application in 1972 weighed 12 pounds, 15 ounces, and was almost six inches thick. It took 7,920 man-hours of work to complete, with 19 executives, five secretaries, and three temporary typists working three weeks. An additional 204 hours of CBS lawyers' time, plus 228 hours by their secretaries, went into the single renewal application. "B'cast Regulation By the Pound," *Variety,* May 16, 1973.

76. Quoted by William Kuhns, *Exploring Television: An Inquiry/Discovery Program* (Chicago: Loyola Univ. Press, 1971).

77. Spiro T. Agnew, "Television News Coverage," *Vital Speeches of the Day,* December 1, 1969.

78. Robert Cirino, *Don't Blame the People* (N.Y.: Random House, 1971), p. 140; he was citing data presented in a staff report to the National Commission on the Causes and Prevention of Violence.

79. William L. Rivers and Wilbur Schramm, *Responsibility in Mass Communication,* revised ed. (N.Y.: Harper & Row, 1969), p. 97, citing as source an item by the Associated Press printed in the San Francisco *Chronicle,* March 19, 1971, p. 1.

80. The print media—principally the *Washington Post, New York Times,* and *Los Angeles Times*— investigated and reported the early findings of the Watergate tragedy. The broadcast media merely reported what those newpapers were printing in their daily editions. Yet the White House, through top staff members and the President himself, as well as through Clay T. Whitehead who headed its Office of Telecommunications Policy, regularly faulted television news with improperly emphasizing this otherwise "minor" incident and the subsequent cover-up through executive-level deception and perjury. And yet, television did not investigate nor did it announce new revelations other than what the print media had already uncovered and made public. But television did attract the attention of the mass public, who perceive television as most credible among the mass media. Thus the White House astutely assessed the popular impact of television over competing media.

81. Members of the U.S. House of Representatives who responded to the poll appraised the media's objectivity: 60% newspapers as most objective, 15% broadcast media and 15% "other"

media ("Print Media 4–1 Over Broadcast Fields in Objectivity: Congress," *Variety*, May 26, 1971, p. 54). A few months earlier, the Television Bureau of Advertising reported a nationwide study: 48% judged TV as "most authoritative" medium, 28% so appraised newspapers, 10% magazines, and 7% radio (TvB, Inc., "Counting the Vote" folder summarizing data by R. H. Bruskin & Associates, of 2,506 adults in June 1970; reported by *Broadcasting*, November 23, 1970, p. 41). That same study found TV outranking other media as "most believable" with 48%, while newspapers scored 25%, magazines 12%, and radio 10%. In that survey, American adults considered TV as the "most influential" medium (79%), with only 14% so appraising newspapers, and 2% for magazines and radio.

In 1971 the Opinion Research Corporation was commissioned to study news media; one question was "suppose there is some news you are very much interested in. Where would you be most likely to find out all there is about it?" TV scored with 46% of the 2,023 adults, newspapers higher with 50%, and radio only 12%, magazines 11%, and local libraries 9% ("Imporant News About the News Media for Advertisers and Agencies," *The Christian Science Monitor*, January 10, 1972, p. 5, reporting the study conducted in March 1971).

The first opinion poll ever commissioned by Congress (a subcommittee chaired by Sen. Edmund S. Muskie) was conducted by Louis Harris in 1973, comparing similar inquiries of 1966 and 1972. Among major institutions in American society—medicine, higher education, the military, organized religion, the U.S. Supreme Court, the U.S. Senate, the executive branch of Federal government, major companies, the press, and television news—only two enjoyed increased public support over the seven-year period between polls: television news was up from 25% to 41% of the public expressing confidence in it, and the press rose from 29% to 30%. In that same period, higher education dropped from 61% to about 43%, the military from 62% to 39%, the Supreme Court from 51% to 32%, major companies from 55% to 28%, and the executive branch from 41% to 18%!

82. Burns W. Roper, "Trends in Public Attitudes Toward Television and Other Mass Media, 1959–1974" (New York, Television Information Office, 1975); a report of the study conducted in late November and December, 1974.

83. Robert W. Sarnoff, "What's Right with Television," speech to NBC radio and television affiliates in New York City, December 2, 1962; reprinted as an NBC-published pamphlet, p. 12.

84. "Audience Finds TV Newscast Items Hard to Remember, Survey Reveals," *Variety*, October 6, 1971, p. 30.

85. Donald H. McGannon, quoted in "What Are TV Goals for 1980's?" *Broadcasting*, January 25, 1971, p. 36.

86. Eugene K. Bristow, Indiana Univ., in a review in the *Quarterly Journal of Speech*, October 1964, p. 328, reviewing Prof. George Winchester Stone, Jr.'s Part 4: 1747–1776, of the 5-volume study *The London Stage, 1660–1880*.

*   *   *

Index

451

American Federation of Musicians (AFM), 104
American Federation of Television and Radio Artists (AFTRA), 104
American Research Bureau (ARB), 92, 138-39
American Satellite Corporation, 403
American Society of Composers, Authors and Publishers (ASCAP), 291, 360-61
American Society of Newspaper Editors, 366
American Telephone and Telegraph Company (AT&T), 401, 402, 403
American Television and Communications, 406
AM/FM radio, 82 (table), 135, 168, 293, 293 (table)
Amos 'n' Andy, 180
Andre, Pierre, 256
Anello, Douglas A., quoted, 363-64
Animal World, 220
Announcer-salesman, 249
Anthony, Earle C., 378, 443
Anthony, Ray, 186
APBE-NAB study of broadcast managers (1962), 70, 71
Applied Technology Satellite (ATS-6), 403
Arbitron, 139, 140
Arnaud, Michele, 400
As the World Turns, 427
Asset Depreciation Range, 289
Assets, defined, 285
Assistant manager, 61
Associated Press (AP), 177, 327
Associated Press Managing Editors Association, 366
Association for Professional Broadcasting Education, 70, 94
Association of National Advertisers (ANA), 137, 138, 383
Audience(s), 132-57 *passim,* 273, 439-40; actual and potential, 136; and advisory council, 156-57; age categories of, 142, 148; attitudes and behavior of, studies of, 147-49; changing characteristics of, 142-44; composition of, importance of, 142; and cultural programs, 143-44, 145; dimensions of, 134-36; education categories of, 143, 148-49; income categories of, 143, 149; and local station research, 154-56; mail from, handling of, 156; Mediastat studies of, 148; and Nielsen data on TV viewers, 148-49; potential and actual, 136; profile of,

149-50; and ratings, 9, 134, 137-42 *passim,* 151, 211, 214, 215; and station responsibility, 150-54; teenage, 184-85; telephone calls from, handling of, 156; and working advisory council, 156-57; *see also* Broadcasting; Programming
Audience participation formats, 210
Audimeter, 138
Audit Bureau of Circulation, 138
Autobiography of Miss Jane Pittman, The, 215
Automation, 185, 193, 313-14
Avco Broadcasting Corporation, 118, 170, 268, 275, 344, 416
Ayer & Son, N. W., 192

Balance sheet: defined, 285; sample of, 286
Bands on radio, 180, 186
Bartering, as station practice, 259-60
Baseball programs, TV, 214, 215, 222, 223
Basie, Count, 186
Basketball programs, TV, 223
Batten, Barton, Durstine & Osborne (BBDO), 269, 375
Bazelon, David, 353; quoted, 353
Beautiful music, as FM format, 192
Beaverbrook, Lord, 384; quoted, 384
Belafonte, Harry, 210
Bell Telephone Hour, 145, 210
Benny, Jack, 145, 179, 209, 215, 256
Bergen, Edgar, 180
Bergman, Ingmar, 216
Berle, Milton, 209
Berliner, William M., 62; quoted, 33, 34
Bernie, Ben, 180
Bernstein, Leonard, 145
Better Business Bureaus, 436
Black Audio Network, 189
Black Communications Corporation, 92
Black radio, 188, 189
Blair & Co., John, 270
Blonder-Tongue Laboratories, 412
Blues and rhythm, 183
Bohn, Thomas W., 38, 70, 71
Booz, Allen & Hamilton, 379
Boston Pops Orchestra, 187
Boston Symphony, 145
Boswell, Nelson, 191
Bower, Robert, 147, 148, 149
Bowes, Major, 180
Bowling programs, TV, 223
Brain-storming, 109